W9-BCF-632

COLLECTIONS OF
THE NEW YORK HISTORICAL SOCIETY
FOR THE YEAR 1930

THE JOHN WATTS DePEYSTER
PUBLICATION FUND SERIES

LXIII

WILLIAM DUNLAP (1766-1839)
BY HIMSELF
(In the Theodore Salisbury Woolsey Collection)

DIARY OF WILLIAM DUNLAP

(1766–1839)

THE MEMOIRS OF A DRAMATIST, THEATRICAL MANAGER, PAINTER, CRITIC, NOVELIST, AND HISTORIAN

VOLUME I

NOVEMBER, 1786; OCTOBER, 1788
MAY 20, 1797 – DECEMBER 15, 1798

BENJAMIN BLOM New York/London

COLLECTIONS OF

THE NEW YORK HISTORICAL SOCIETY

FOR THE YEAR 1929

THE JOHN WATTS DePEYSTER
PUBLICATION FUND SERIES

LXII

First Published 1930
Reissued 1969 by
Benjamin Blom, Inc., Bronx, New York 10452
and 56 Doughty Street, London, W.C. 1

Library of Congress Catalog Card Number 78-84204

Printed in the United States of America

PREFACE

The volumes of the John Watts DePeyster Publication Fund of The New York Historical Society for 1929, 1930, and 1931, make available in print all the known manuscript memoirs of William Dunlap (1766-1839), who was, throughout his life, associated with literature, the stage, and the fine arts in New York, and who was the friend of many, and an acquaintance of most, of the actors, authors, and painters in the United States. His diary has been consulted in manuscript, to good purpose, by historians of drama and painting, and in this more convenient form, should be an invaluable source for many phases of American society and culture during the first half century of the Republic.

To the Trustees of Yale University Library, and to Dr. Andrew Keogh, the Librarian, The New York Historical Society is grateful for permission to publish the six manuscript volumes of the Diary presented to them by the late Professor Theodore S. Woolsey, and for their courtesy in facilitating the task of transcription and proofreading.

The Publication Committee appreciates the interest and assistance of members of Mrs. Dunlap's family, the Woolseys. Miss Katharine W. Carmalt's familiarity with her great-great-uncle's diary helped the editor decipher many almost illegible words, Miss Edith Woolsey, Mr. Theodore Salisbury Woolsey, Jr., and Mr. Heathcote Muirson Woolsey, graciously allowed the examination and photographing of a number of portraits and landscapes by William Dunlap, in the collection of the late Theodore S. Woolsey, and gave the editor access to Dr. Woolsey's notes and correspondence about Dunlap's paintings. Miss Geraldine W. Carmalt and Miss Ethel

Carmalt were equally kind in letting the Society reproduce their oil painting of Margaret Dunlap, family miniatures, and Dunlap's Anacreontic Society badge. The other descendants of the Woolsey family who generously permitted publication of portraits by Dunlap, are Mrs. Henry Ferriday, of New York City, Mrs. William Tidball, of Media, Pennsylvania, and Mr. William Samuel Johnson, of New York City.

The following collectors and institutions courteously consented to the reproduction of paintings by Dunlap in their possession: Miss Elisabeth Marbury, of New York, Miss Mary O. Marshall, of Charleston, S. C., Mr. Herbert L. Pratt, of New York, and Mr. Albert Rosenthal, of Philadelphia; the Museum of the Brooklyn Institute of Arts and Sciences, the Cleveland Museum of Art, the National Academy of Design, The Players, New York, the Rhode Island School of Design, Providence, the New York Society Library, the Society of the New York Hospital, and the Worcester Art Museum, Worcester, Massachusetts. The New York Historical Society thanks all these owners for their helpful co-operation.

The Diary has been transcribed, edited, and indexed by Miss Dorothy C. Barck.

ALEXANDER J. WALL,
Librarian.

INTRODUCTION

The diarist, William Dunlap (1766-1839), was a high-minded, conscientious gentleman, whose interests and friendships touched almost every phase of the intellectual, aesthetic, and cultural life of the early American republic. Like many of his contemporaries, he kept a detailed journal throughout his adult life. A small volume was always carried in his pocket, in which he not only noted his daily activities, but also made sketches of people and scenes, copied letters and legal agreements, entered his accounts, and drafted poems and a novel. This careful record was written in part with a view to publication, for as early as June 5, 1797, he was planning a history of the theatre, and many entries were made as source material for the *Rise and Progress of the Arts of Design.*

The thirty or more small volumes in which his diary was kept, have been scattered in the ninety years since his death; only eleven have been located for publication. Of these, six were collected by the late Theodore Salisbury Woolsey, and presented to the Library of Yale University in 1922. Four were bought from a second-hand bookstall in lower Manhattan Island by the late Daniel Parish, Jr., and given to The New York Historical Society on June 25, 1895. These ten manuscript volumes had been transcribed, set up in type, and partly indexed when another volume, *Memoirs 13,* was discovered and purchased by the Society in April, 1930; publication was delayed and pages re-numbered to include it in its chronological place.

Eight of the eleven manuscript volumes, including all six in the New York Historical Society, are uniform in appearance, six and one half inches high, four inches wide, bound in brown leather. On the shelf back of each is a gold number, and above it, an oval stained red, encircled by a leaf design in gold, with *Memoirs* stamped in gold in the centre. *Memoirs 16,* in the Yale Library, is stamped and lettered uniformly with these eight, but is a slimmer, taller volume. The other two volumes in the Yale collection are not numbered; one is bound in brown leather; the other has marbled paper covers, with leather back and corners, loops for a pencil, and a pocket inside one cover.

Dunlap's *Memoirs* have been printed *verbatim,* and in their entirety, only omitting from the last two volumes a few very personal references to the progress of his disease. Words crossed off in the manuscript are printed in italics enclosed in V-shaped brackets < >. Editorial interpolations are enclosed in square brackets [ ]. Correspondence, notes, portions of a novel, and other material not of a diary nature, are printed in smaller type than the other entries.

Although the eleven volumes of memoirs, here printed, are less than a third of the number which Dunlap undoubtedly wrote, they extend over a period of forty-eight years of his adult life, from 1786, when he was only twenty, to 1834, five years before his death, and furnish a representative picture of his many activities and interests. The three printed volumes into which the diary divides, represent three periods of Dunlap's life. The first includes two years of great importance to the history of the New York stage, when Dunlap was manager of the Old American Company of Comedians, and a lessee of the Park Theatre. The second volume is devoted more particularly to his life as an artist, when, after his bankruptcy, he painted portraits throughout the eastern states as a means of livelihood, returning to the theatre for only a short time as a salaried assistant manager for Thomas Abthorpe Cooper. The third volume, for the years 1832-1834, finds Dunlap, old, ill, and impoverished, summing up the knowledge and experience of a life time, in his histories of the American theatre and American arts.

Bibliography

William Dunlap used his memoirs as the basis of the autobiographical chapters in his *History of the American Theatre* (N. Y., 1832), and in his *History of the Rise and Progress of the Arts of Design in the United States* (N. Y., 1834, 2 vol.), which are the chief printed sources for the story of his life, and which bridge the gaps in this diary. In the former, he naturally treated principally of his connection with the stage; in the other, his work as an artist. A new edition of *The Arts of Design,* edited by Frank W. Bayley and Charles E. Goodspeed, with notes, additions, illustrations, and an index, was published by C. E. Goodspeed & Co., Boston, 1918, in three volumes. Citations in the present volumes, however, are to the New York edition of 1834.

A very excellent and complete biography of Dunlap has been written by Dr. Oral Sumner Coad, entitled *William Dunlap, a Study of his Life and Works and of his Place in Contemporary Culture* (N. Y., 1917, pp. 313). It was issued by the Dunlap Society, which was named in honor of our diarist. Dr. Coad's book contains, in addition to the biography, a scholarly study of Dunlap's original plays, dramatic translations, and non-dramatic works, and includes a bibliography of Dunlap's writings, and a partial list of Dunlap's extant paintings. Unfortunately Dr. Coad did not have access, when compiling his biography, to the six volumes of Dunlap's diary subsequently (in 1922) presented to Yale University. He later made a careful analysis of the Yale volumes, printed in *Studies in Philology,* for July, 1927 (University of North Carolina Press, XXIV, 403-412).

The history of the theatre in New York, and Dunlap's important part in it, have been delightfully and completely recorded by Dr. George C. D. Odell, in his *Annals of the New York Stage* (Columbia University Press, 1927, 1929, 4 vol.). Dr. Odell used Dunlap's manuscript in the New York Historical Society library, as one of his many contemporary sources.

Thomas J. McKee's introduction to Dunlap's comedy, *The Father of American Shandyism,* published by The Dunlap Society in 1887, lists Dunlap's plays, printed and unprinted, with the date of production, and gives a short account of Dunlap's relations with the theatre. *A Bibliographical Checklist of the Plays and Miscellaneous Writings of William Dunlap* was carefully compiled by Oscar Wegelin (Vol. I of *Bibliographical Americana,* edited by Charles F. Heartman, N. Y., 1916).

The best study of Dunlap as an artist is "William Dunlap Painter and Critic or The American Vasari", in the *Yale Review* for July, 1914, by the late Theodore Salisbury Woolsey, who had an especial family interest in his subject, as he was a grandson of Mrs. William Dunlap's brother. At the conclusion of his monograph, Dr. Woolsey compiled a list of paintings by Dunlap, including with pictures actually located, those known only through Dunlap's mention of them in his diary and the *Arts of Design.* Dr. Woolsey formerly owned the six manuscript volumes of Dunlap's diary which he presented to the Library of Yale University in 1922, and in his collection were several miniatures and small oils by Dunlap, reproduced in these volumes through the courtesy of his sister, Miss Edith Woolsey, and his sons, Theodore Salisbury Woolsey, Jr., and Heathcote Muirson Woolsey.

The earliest diary, 1786 and 1788

The earliest volume of Dunlap's diary which has been found is a small brown leather book, unnumbered, preserved in the Yale University Library. It was begun when Dunlap was only twenty years old, and may be the first diary that he kept.

The preface to this diary is found in Dunlap's own account of his childhood, in the *Arts of Design,* I, 244, ff., and in the *History of the American Theatre,* 232 *ff.* There he wrote about his parents, Samuel and Margaret (Sargent) Dunlap, his youth in Perth Amboy, and in New York City during the British occupation, of his ill health and his schooling, the early friendships which influenced his later life, and the accident which cost him the sight of his right eye. At the age of sixteen, he became a professional artist, sketching portraits in crayon. At the close of the Revolution, during the winter of 1783-84, General and Mrs. Washington sat to him for their portraits, at Rocky Hill, near Princeton. Besides a crayon sketch, Dunlap painted a full-length oil portrait of the General, which he took with him to England, when he sailed from New York in May, 1784, to study under Benjamin West.

The first volume of the diary narrates one of the events of his three-year sojourn in England, a walking trip from London to Oxford, in November, 1786, accompanied by Dr. Samuel Latham Mitchill. This little volume was mislaid in 1832, when Dunlap was writing his *History of the American Theatre,* and the incident of meeting the veteran of the wars in American is told in it (pages 244-246) from memory; it was re-told two years later in the *Arts of Design* (I, 263-265), copying directly from the diary, which had in the meantime been found.

The other sections of the first manuscript volume, while not in diary form, indicate something of his thought and activities during the first year in New York, after his return from England in October, 1787. There are fifty pages of notes and extracts, copied in October, 1788, from John Gillies' *History of Ancient Greece,* Charles Rollin on the study of sacred history, and the Rev. James Beattie's works. The only pages printed are Dunlap's original comments, inspired by statements in Gillies' *History.*

Following the notes on Greek history is a play, *Cuttgrisingwoldes,* dated October, 1788, based on the rivalry of two New York societies, the Philological Society, and a legal society. Of the Philological Society, of which Dunlap was a member, we learn most from the diary of his fellow-member, Noah Webster, published in *Notes on the Life of Noah Webster,* compiled by Mrs. Emily Ellsworth Fowler Ford, and edited by Mrs. Emily Ellsworth Ford Skeel (2 volumes, privately printed, N. Y., 1912). The Philological Society was organized in March, 1788, and the constitution and by-laws were drawn up in April. The Society's purpose was to promote a knowledge of the English language, and to ascertain and improve the American tongue. Meetings were held on Monday evenings, weekly or fortnightly, from March, through November 3, 1788, at least. Noah Webster wrote several papers for the Society, the first of which, on "the influence of language on opinions and of opinions on language", was read on April 28, and printed, at the Society's request, in his *American Magazine,* for May, 1788. On June 20, 1788, William Dunlap read to the members his new comedy, *The Modest Soldier; or, Love in New York.*

The most important event in the club's annals was its participation in the Federal Procession in New York City, July 23, 1788, celebrating the ratification of the Constitution. The Society marched as a body, uniformly dressed in black, with the President, Josiah Ogden Hoffman, at the head, and the arms of the Society carried by William Dunlap. There is a detailed description of the arms, with an explanation of their elaborate symbolism, in the New York *Packet* of August 5, 1788.

The ready identification of several characters in the play, *Cuttgrisingwoldes,* indicates that all the dramatic personages represented actual members of the Philological Society, or young New York lawyers. That the *President* meant Josiah Ogden Hoffman (1766-1815), who was really the head of the Society, is proved by the reference to *his brother, Martin,* who was Martin Hoffman (1763-1828). (See *Genealogy of the Hoffman Family,* 1899, pp. 200-205.) *Noah Cobweb,* who struggled "to teach the dunces grammar", was of course Noah Webster. *Neddy,* the *Chancellor's brother,* must have been Edward Livingston (1764-1836), younger brother of Chancellor Robert R. Livingston (1736-1813). The initial "L" beside *Neddy's* name in the list of *Dramatis Personae* corroborates this assumption, and also strengthens our surmise, based on the play on the name, that Lawyer *Sharping,* with a capital "C" before his name, was the young attorney, Leonard M. *Cutting.* The painter *Hot Head,* placed modestly at the foot of the list of characters, may refer to Dunlap himself. In the autobiographical sketch in his *Arts of Design* (I, p. 267) Dunlap names only two of his fellow-members, Noah Webster and Dr. S. L. Mitchill. Further study would undoubtedly identify stuttering *Demosthenes, Major Mars,* and his brother *Cypher, Dr. Pillar* (possibly Dr. Edward *Miller?*), *Witenough,* the Society's librarian, and the rest. Noah Webster's diary explains the references in the play to his (*i.e., Noah Cobweb's*) lectures, and to his intended departure from New York, which actually took place in December, 1788.

With the exception of the interest in philology and history shown by the first volume of his diary, and the autobiographical portions of the histories of the theatre and the arts of design, there is little material about Dunlap's first ten years in New York, after his return from England in October, 1787, until the second extant volume of personal memoirs begins in May 20, 1797. Dr. Oral Sumner Coad's life of Dunlap records all that has been learned about this important decade of his life, during which he was happily occupied with business, the theatre, writing, family affairs, and friendly intercourse with devoted companions. Dunlap became his father's partner in a china, looking glass and hardware store, about 1790. After Samuel Dunlap's death, at the end of 1791, William continued the business, at first with one of the Woolseys and Andrew Smyth; in 1796, Moses Judah became his partner. This business evidently served to support his family, and leave its head free to indulge his love for the theatre. He wrote several plays at this time, some of which were printed and produced at the John Street Theatre. He painted portraits of his family and friends, and designed the frontispiece of Royall Tyler's play, *The Contrast,* engraved by Maverick. The only painting of this early period that has been found, is the one in The New York Historical Society, of the artist showing a picture to his parents, which is reproduced in this volume.

William Dunlap married on February 10, 1789, Elizabeth Woolsey (1768-1848), daughter of Benjamin, Jr., and Anne (Muirson) Woolsey. They had two children, John Alexander Bredin Dunlap, born December 14, 1789, and Margaret Dunlap, born April 15, 1791. A third child, Hester Mary, was born August 26, 1792, but died in infancy. (Dunlap Family Bible, cited by O. S. Coad, in *William Dunlap,* p. 24). By his marriage, Dunlap became connected with a cultured Connecticut family with whom his friendship was ever most cordial and affectionate, and his intellectual intercourse very stimulating. He was particularly intimate with his wife's brothers, William Walton Woolsey (1766-1839), and George Muirson Woolsey (1772-1850), the "W W W" and "G M W" mentioned so frequently in his diary. Mrs. Dunlap's half-sister, Mary Woolsey, was the wife of President Timothy Dwight, of Yale, and William Walton Woolsey married President Dwight's sister, Elizabeth. (Benjamin W. Dwight, *History of the Descendants of John Dwight of Dedham, Mass.* 2 vol., N. Y., 1874).

During the 1790's Dunlap was a member of the Friendly Club, to which belonged his brothers-in-law, W. W. Woolsey and George M. Woolsey, Charles Brockden Brown, the novelist, Dr. Elihu Hubbard Smith, William Johnson, Dr. Samuel Latham Mitchill, the brothers Dr. Edward Miller and Rev. Dr. Samuel Miller, Anthony Bleecker, James Kent, and others, most of whom became illustrious citizens in their various professions of law, medicine, literature, and business. He was a member of the Manumission Society, the Standing Committee of which he attended frequently as secretary, according to the diary entries of 1797-1798. About the same time, he was a member of one of New York's sociable musical societies, the Columbian Anacreontic Society, which flourished from 1795 to 1803. Among the officers were John Hodgkinson, John C. Shaw, Joseph Tyler, Aquila Giles, John Bleecker, and Philip Ten Eyck. (O. G. Sonneck, *Early Concert-Life in America,* pp. 204-207). Dunlap's diary does not refer to his connection with the Anacreontics, but his name is engraved on a silver, lyre-shaped badge of the Society (pictured in this volume), owned by Miss Ethel Carmalt and Miss Geraldine W. Carmalt, of New Haven, and also on a small oval silver disk, perhaps an identification ticket for members, now in the possession of Miss Katharine W. Carmalt, of New Haven.

Dunlap began keeping a regular, detailed diary in the early 1790's. The ninth volume of his *Memoirs*, now lost, covered the summer of 1796 (see his entry for July 11, 1797, *post*). Extracts from his diary for May second through May ninth, 1797 (from what was probably *Memoirs 12*, now lost), are printed in his *History of the American Theatre*, pp. 168-171.

Dunlap's Memoirs, 1797-1798

The four extant volumes of Dunlap's *Memoirs*, numbered 13 through 16, afford a continuous narrative of his life from May 20, 1797, through December 15, 1798. They begin at the conclusion of his first season as one of the managers of the Old American Company of Comedians, at the John Street Theatre, in partnership with Lewis Hallam and John Hodgkinson, and record the break with Hallam, and the leasing and managing of the new Park Theatre by John Hodgkinson and Dunlap. In April, 1798, Dunlap became the sole manager. Dunlap's history of the theatre serves as a preface to these volumes, from his point of view; Hodgkinson's story is told in *A Narrative of his Connection with the Old American Company from the fifth September, 1792, to the thirty-first of March, 1797* (N. Y., 1797, pp. 28).

Manuscript volume *13* was purchased by The New York Historical Society in April, 1930. It contains several sketches of Francis Childs's house near Elizabeth, N. J., and a half dozen pen-and-ink drawings of birds. Volumes *14* and *15* were presented to the Society in 1895 by Daniel Parish, Jr. Volume *16* is in the Library of Yale University.

During the years 1797-1798, Dunlap was beset with the many tribulations of a theatrical manager, with little capital, and in a city terrified by an epidemic of yellow fever. In addition to his duties as manager, he wrote and produced an original tragedy, *André,* and translated and produced several plays by Kotzebue, whose popularity materially aided the box office receipts. He began, in his diary, a novel called *The Anti-Jacobin,* which is printed here for the first time. It was never completed.

During the six years following *Memoirs 16,* for which no diary is extant, Dunlap continued as manager of the Park Theatre, under increasing difficulties, until he was forced to declare himself a bankrupt in February, 1805. With his young family, he took refuge in his mother's home in Perth Amboy, and turned to miniature painting as a means of support.

Memoirs 23, 1806

The next extant volume of Dunlap's diary, *Memoirs 23,* is in the Library of Yale University. It begins January 1, 1806, with letters written by Dunlap to his wife, which, at his request, were copied into one of his small volumes, at first, by his daughter, Margaret, and later by another hand, possibly his son John's. The letters were written from Philadelphia, Baltimore, and Washington, whither Dunlap journeyed to paint miniatures. About the middle of the year 1806, he was invited by Thomas Abthorpe Cooper to become his manager, and so began his second (and final) business connection with the Park Theatre, which lasted until 1811, at first under Cooper, and after 1808, as Stephen Price's assistant. In September, 1806, he was concerned in publishing the first volume of *The Dramatic Works of William Dunlap,* containing four of his plays. The frontispiece was an engraving by David Edwin, of Mrs. Wignell (Mrs. Merry) from Dunlap's miniature of her, in the Woolsey Collection, reproduced in the present volume. The title page announced that Dunlap's dramatic works would be presented in ten volumes, but only two more were printed, and those not until 1816.

In *Memoirs 23* is a rather poor pencil sketch of a lady in a long gown, with a feather headdress and a veil, and in the middle of the volume is inserted a stencil silhouette, cut from paper, of a young girl, with a high headdress and long hair.

According to Dunlap's own statement (*post,* II, 335), he kept no record from 1806 through 1808, and utilized the pages at the end of *Memoirs 23* for his personal and household expenses, September 21, 1808 to June 28, 1811. There is evidently, then, no volume missing between this, and the one which follows chronologically, beginning March 17, 1811. Dunlap did not use his little books in numerical sequence, however. *Memoirs 31* follows *Memoirs 23;* and there were undoubtedly other volumes, now lost, covering the period between *Memoirs 31,* and *Memoirs 24,* which begins October, 1819.

George Frederick Cooke, in Memoirs 31

Memoirs 31, in the Library of Yale University, is devoted almost entirely, to George Frederick Cooke, the eminent English tragedian brought to the United States, under the management of Thomas Abthorpe Cooper, in November, 1810. Dunlap narrates Cooke's success in New York, and begins his daily entries in March, 1811, when he accompanied the tragedian to Philadelphia, for the purpose of restraining him from excessive indulgence in intoxicating liquor, such as had resulted in unpleasant performances on the New York stage. The diary contains a number of notes, made by Dunlap after Cooke's death, from his own reading and from the reminiscences of others, in preparation for the tragedian's biography, written in fulfillment of Dunlap's promise to Cooke, and printed at New York in 1813.

In the manuscript volume are several pencil, and pen-and-ink sketches: two landscapes; a reclining female figure after Wertmüller's *Danaë;* two female heads; two male heads; and a very carefully finished pen-and-ink drawing, with pencil shadings. The last is undoubtedly a portrait of George Frederick Cooke, and is reproduced in Volume II, *post.*

Late in 1811, Dunlap severed his association as assistant director of the Park Theatre, resumed miniature painting for a livelihood, and, at Gilbert Stuart's suggestion, began painting portraits in oils, also. In April, 1813, he tried to add to his income by establishing a magazine called *The Monthly Recorder,* but was able to publish only five issues. In 1814, he was appointed assistant paymaster-general of the New York State Militia, and during the next two years, he travelled over the entire state in pursuance of his duties.

Dunlap's pictorial diary, 1815-1816

There is no written diary extant for the years when Dunlap was travelling as paymaster. It is possible that he kept his daily record only in a pictorial medium. At any rate, fifty water color sketches which he made in those years give us at least his itinerary during 1815 and 1816. These sketches were sold at auction in Philadelphia, Pa., on March 10, 1905, and are listed and described in Stan. V. Henkels' Catalogue No. 927, of *Ivory Miniatures and Water Color Views in New York by William Dunlap.* Almost all of these views, thirty nine in number, are in the collection of the late Theodore Salisbury Woolsey, of New Haven, and have been examined and listed through the courtesy of Miss Edith Woolsey, and Messrs. Theodore Salisbury Woolsey and Heathcote Muirson Woolsey. The descriptive legends are written in Dunlap's hand, and some are signed or initialed "W D". One of the late Dr. Woolsey's views of Niagara falls is reproduced *post* in Volume II, as an example of Dunlap's landscape work, though it adds nothing to his artistic reputation. Descriptions of the eleven water color sketches not in the Woolsey collection are printed here from the Henkels Catalogue No. 927, with a note that the present owner is unknown. The catalogue numbers of all fifty sketches are added in parentheses, for identification.

Water Color Sketches by William Dunlap, 1815-1816

in the Collection of the late Theodore Salisbury Woolsey, of New Haven, Connecticut (unless otherwise stated)

Jan. 4, 1815. View taken as you approach Bellevue Hospital, New York, from the South. 4 x 6⅜. Present owner unknown. (no. 55)

May 20, 1815. Suburbs of New York. 6 x 8. Present owner unknown. (no. 48)

May 21, 1815. View taken from the Beach South of Brooklyn, distance Red Hook and Staten Island. 6½ x 12. Present owner unknown. (no. 43)

May 21, 1815. Piece of Fort Green from within. The distance near Sandy Hook. 6 x 5½. Present owner unknown. (no. 54)

May 21, 1815. Piece of Fort Greene. Distance, East River. 6 x 9½. Present owner unknown. (no. 38)

May 21, 1815, 11 O'clock A. M. Fort Swift from the north east. 6½ x 11¾. (no. 49)

June 17, 1815. June 16, after tea, ½ past seven, walked to Troy, Moonlight, Fire-fly, Sky Rockets, Village of Washington, Arsenal, Ferry, Doctor & conversation. Slept at Seymour's Hotel, in Elegant accomodations. Rose before 5 and walked to Mount Ida, drew this View of the Little Falls from 6 to 7 and then walked back to breakfast. 11¼ x 7. Present owner unknown. (no. 41)

June 17, 1815. Set off from Troy at ½ past 8 & attracted by the appearance of a bold rock near the road, I climb it & make this sketch of the beautiful plain between Troy & Lansinburg Lansinburgh & Waterford at a distance & the Hudson. 7¼ x 11½. (no. 40)

June 17, 1815, between 10 & 11. View of Waterford & the upper junction of the Mohawk with the Hudson with a piece of the cover'd bridge which connects L[ansingburgh] & W[aterford] 6 x 9½. (no. 44)

June 17th, 1815. Falls of the Mohawk or Cohoes from the South bank. After dining at Waterford at the Coffee House at 1 OClock in a style of elegant neatness, I walked to the rapids of the Mohawk & thence to the Cohoes crossing the bridge over the Mohawk which they have begun to cover. 9 x 12. (no. 64)

June 18, 1815 6 OClock morning. View from Mount Ida of the plain below, of the Hudson, of the Arsenal on the opposite shore. 6 x 9½. (no. 39)

June 18, 1815. Falls of Mount Ida on the poetsden [Poesten] Kill near Troy. Walk up the Creek passing 4 Mil[ls] all the Scenery truly picturesque. Arrive at the Mill where stopped yesterday we pass'd by it thro a narrow pass occasionally up some rustic stairs & proceed over the Mill race until I stopp[e]d to sketch a part of the rapid, then returning we pass throug[h] an Oil Mill & a grist Mill & ascend the Bank proceeding by the road to the plac[e] from which this view is taken, by the roadside, over the fence. 9 x 12. (no. 65)

June 22, 1815 6 o'clock. Bridge over the Mohawk at Schenectady—the spire is that of the old [Union] Colledge. 9 x 13½. (no. 46)

July 12, 1815 between 2 & 3 in the Afternoon. The Sketch is taken from the north side, nearly opposite the Entrance of Wood Creek into the Lake, the Mohawk boat is coming out of Wood Creek. A small stream joins the Lake at the place I struck it & from thence in a skiff I go on the Lake. The barrells are of Salt brought from Onandago, salt point. 8 x 12¾. (no. 45)

July 14, 1815. 5 OClock morn[g] A View of Wood Creek taken from the bridge over North Canada Creek at its junction with the first, having first the Bridge over Wood Creek at the place where formerly the portage ended which began on the Mohawk below Rome or at Lynches Fac[to]ries the scite of Fort Rickey. The house of Gilbert the first settler, & the lower lock of the present navigation. The boats were formerly carried from Lynch's Factory to Fort Newport, the loads brought here & then reloaded. Fort Rickey. Amherst's Expedition. Just above where the lower lock now is, was Fort Bull, which [was] taken by the French & the Garrison all Massacred, so says Gibbert. 9 x 12. (no. 52)

August 9, 1815. View on the Seneca River from the north end of Baldwin's Bridge, looking east or down the River. 6 x 9½. Present owner unknown. (no. 37)

August 9, 1815. 5 o'clock afternoon. View on the Seneca River from the South Side, above Baldwin's Village. 8½ x 12. (no. 42)

August 12, 1815. The north end or bottom of Cayuga Lake. Gypsum. Bridge. Entrance of the Seneca outlet. Bridge (in distance) over the outlet where it takes the name of the Seneca River. 7⅞ x 12¾. (no. 51)

[September, 1815] View of a part of the [Niagara] Falls, (those east of Goat Island) from the ravine which leads to the old Stone house distillery, past which is the path to the Ladder. 9 x 6½. (no. 47)

[September, 1815] [Niagara Falls from the American side] 9 x 12. (no. 66)

Sept. 6, 1815. My second view of the Falls, as approaching from the South, having ascended from the flatts where the Mill is (& several houses) this view is from the hill or bank by the road side. 8⅞ x 11. (no. 35)

Sept. 6, 1815. 2d View of Niagara. Before coming to Chippawa Creek. 9 x 11. (no. 22)

[Sept. 6, 1815] 3d View of Niagara [The Rapids] 8¾ x 11. (no. 56)

Sept. 6, 1815. 4th View of Niagara. The Rapids 8⅞ x 11. (no. 31)

Began Sept. 7th, 1815. Corrected & colour'd the 8th & 9th. View of the Falls of Niagara [Horseshoe or Canadian Falls] from the Bank above the table rock. 9¾ x 11 (no. 29)

Sept. 7, 8, 9, 1815. View from the Bank above Table Rock. 9 x 11. (no. 17)

Sept. 8, 1815. View from the Bank above the stone house (or old distillery [American Falls]. 9 x 11. (no. 24)

Sept. 11th, 1815. Forts George, Missi[iss]auga & Niagara. 9 x 12. (no. 67)

Sept. 1815. Barracks at Black Rock & redoubt, with a distant view of Fort Erie, as seen from the North. 5⅞ x 9⅝. (no. 36)

1816. View from Queenstown Heights to Lake Ontario. [Signed:] W D. 9¼ x 13½. (no. 53)

Aug. 28, 1816. View from the Hill East of Hudson. 8¼ x 10¼. Present owner unknown. (no. 58)

Aug. 31, 1816. Descending the hill to the Mohawk on the road to Ballston. 8¾ x 11. (no. 50)

August 31, 1816. Saratoga. [Signed:] W D. 8 x 10. (no. 61)

August 31st, 1816. Congress Spring, Saratoga. 8¾ x 11⅛. (no. 30)

Sept. 3, 1816. Baker's Falls, Sandy Hill. [Signed:] W D. 8⅝ x 11. (no. 27)

Sept. 4, 1816. Glens Falls from the bed of the River. [Signed:] W D. 8⅝ x 10¾. (no. 23)

Sept. 4, 1816. On the road to Lake George [Signed:] W D 8 x 10¼. (no. 62)

Sept. 5th [1816] View of Caldwell V. Lake George. [Signed:] W. D. 8½ x 10¾. (no. 19)

1816. View of the south end of Lake George. 8½ x 10⅞ (no. 34)

Sept. 6, 1816. Near Bakers Falls. 8½ x 11. (no. 32)

Sept. 7, 1816. View under the Bridge at Glenn's Falls. 8½ x 10¾. Present owner unknown. (no. 18)

Sept. 9, 1816. [Ships] Eagle, Linnet, Saratoga, Ticonderoga, Confiance as laid up at Whitehall. [Signed:] W D. 8⅜ x 10½. (no. 33)

Sept. 9, 1816. One of Commodore McDonough's Row Gallies, Head of Lake Champlain. 8½ x 11. Present owner unknown. (no. 26)

[1816?] [Ticonderoga] 9 x 11. (no. 69)

[1816?] Lake Champlain. 6 x 9½. (no. 68)

1816. View of Plattsburg from the bank of the Saranac near the Fort. [Signed:] W. D. 8½ x 11. (no. 28)

1816 Plattsburg. 8½ x 10⅜. (no. 21)

1816. View of the bridge over the Saranac, part of Plattsburg & the Fort. [Signed:] W. D. 8¾ x 11. (no. 25)

1816. Mouth of the Saranac. 8¼ x 10¼. (no. 20)

Dunlap's diary, 1819-1822

When his duties as assistant paymaster-general were concluded, in the late fall of 1817, Dunlap turned again to his palette, and at the age of fifty-one, as he himself recorded, he became permanently a painter (*Arts of Design,* I, 274). In 1817 and 1818, he painted a number of portraits in New York City, and acted as a salaried keeper in the rooms of the American Academy of Fine Arts. The next extant volumes of his diary record his efforts to earn a livelihood by portraiture outside of New York City.

Memoirs 24, in the New York Historical Society, and *Memoirs 26,* in the Yale University Library, include the entire period of two years and a half from October, 1819, to April, 1822, with the exception of four months in the summer of 1820. In his search for portrait commissions, Dunlap established a studio in Norfolk, Virginia, with some success, and visited Montreal and Quebec in the late summer of 1820.

In *Memoirs* 24, in the New York Historical Society, are about twelve unfinished pencil sketches of people, a crayon drawing of the State House at Annapolis, a rough map of the bays, around Norfolk, and a sketch of West's painting, *Christ Healing in the Temple,* which Dunlap saw in Philadelphia.

The manuscript volume, *Memoirs 26,* at Yale, contains a score of pencil, and pen-and-ink, sketches of women, which were probably made in Norfolk, where he painted portraits of a number of ladies. Several of the pencil sketches are reproduced *post* in Volume III, somewhat reduced in size and regrouped, as examples of his work, and as a possible means of identifying portraits painted by Dunlap in Virginia. There are also sixteen pen-and-ink sketches of scenes on Lake Champlain, the St. Lawrence River, Montreal and Quebec, drawn in August, September, and October, 1820. In the collection of the late Theodore Salisbury Woolsey, of New Haven, there are three water color sketches probably painted on the same northern trip: two of Montmorency Falls near Quebec, and one of the St. Lawrence River near the Falls.

The story of the next ten years of Dunlap's life, for which no diary has been found, may be read in his *Arts of Design,* I, 288-309, or in Dr. Coad's biography. Dunlap continued painting portraits, throughout the East, from Portland, Me., to Washington. In imitation of Benjamin West, he painted several large canvasses, *Christ Rejected, Bearing of the Cross, Death on the Pale Horse,* and *Calvary.* These were exhibited, with a charge for admission, in New York City, and many other parts of the United States, with some pecuniary advantage. Dunlap was one of the officers of the National Academy of Design, organized in 1826 from a Drawing Association, and four years later, he was appointed the Academy's lecturer on Historic Painting.

The last volumes of the diary, 1832-1834

The last two extant manuscript volumes of Dunlap's diary contain a continuous account of his activities from March 16, 1832 through December 26, 1834. These three years saw the publication of his two great contributions to American cultural history, the *History of the American Theatre,* printed in 1832, and the *Rise and Progress of the Arts of Design,* printed in 1834. The diary is filled with notes on actors and painters, which he used as a source for his histories. In spite of poverty, and increasing ill health, Dunlap continued painting portraits, reading contemporary English and American literature, and meeting his many friends in congenial intercourse, and he took an active part in the rivalry between the American Academy of Fine Arts and the National Academy of Design.

The diary for 1832-1833 is written in a small volume with marbled paper covers, a tan leather back and corners, a pocket in the inside front cover, and leather loops for a pencil. There are three water color sketches in the volume: two from the West Point Hotel, and one of a woman standing on a dock. This volume is in the Library of Yale University. The diary for 1833-1834, in the New York Historical Society, is lettered *Memoirs 30,* and is uniform with the majority of the other volumes of the diary; it contains no drawings.

Dunlap's last years

For the last five years of Dunlap's life, there is neither diary nor autobiographical account to guide the historian. Dr. Coad has gathered together what little can be found. Dunlap stopped painting about 1836, and in 1838 declined re-election as Vice-President of the National Academy of Design, on which occasion he sat to Charles C. Ingham for the portrait which is reproduced as the frontispiece of Volume III. At the age of seventy, Dunlap entered upon a new field, and began a history of the state which had been his home since boyhood. To obtain funds for preparing a more scholarly work, he published first, in 1837, a *History of New York for Schools,* in two small volumes, and continued studying and writing on the larger work. His financial status, always precarious, was helped by the gift, in January, 1839, of a check for $1000, the profits from an exhibition of over two hundred paintings by Dunlap's contemporaries, shown for his benefit at the Stuyvesant Institute, November 19, 1838 to January 5, 1839. After sending to press the manuscript of the first volume of his *History of the New Netherlands, Province of New York, and State of New York to the Adoption of the Federal Constitution,* Dunlap was stricken with paralysis, and though he labored on, correcting some of the proof, he was unable to finish the task, and the publication of both volumes of his history was carried through by friends. The second volume was not published until after the author's death.

William Dunlap died at his home in New York City on September 28, 1839, and two days later, was buried in his native Perth Amboy, in the churchyard of St. Peter's. His old age had been saddened by the death of his sweet daughter, Margaret, on June 9, 1837. His wife and son both survived him. Mrs. Dunlap died in New York, May 11, 1848; his son, John Alexander Dunlap, who had become a lawyer in New York, died unmarried, November 4, 1849. The tombstones of the family are pictured in the Rev. W. Northey Jones's *History of St. Peter's Church in Perth Amoby,* (1924), facing page 250.

Dr. Oral Sumner Coad's just and sympathetic conclusions about William Dunlap's life and service may well be re-printed here, from the biography issued by the Dunlap Society in 1917 (pages 127-28, 282):

"Dunlap's long life of seventy-three and a half years was one of continued devotion to cultural pursuits. He early swore allegiance to art and letters, and through privation and disappointment, in spite of obstacles that would have discouraged most men, he held his allegiance true until the day of his death. He had more than his share of afflictions, but his optimism bore him courageously through. In no sense a genius, he yet won for himself an honorable place in two spheres of cultural activity by dint of perseverance and determination. While deriving no little satisfaction from the distinctions and friendships which were his portion, he was always extremely modest concerning his ability. He carried through life a lofty ideal, and in all he did he strove to serve the highest moral and intellectual welfare of his city and nation.

* * * * * * * *

"In a survey of Dunlap's work, two facts stand out most clearly. In the first place, he was unusually prolific and surprisingly versatile. And in each department of his activity, while producing much that was decidedly bad, he also produced some results that were more than ordinarily good, considering his period. Second, whether his output was good or bad, his labor was prompted by motives which deserve complete respect. He lived at a time when American art and literature were compelled to struggle for existence, with no popular encouragement and support. Yet he was convinced that art and literature were of more value than dollars and cents. He allied himself with the exponents of these pursuits; and throughout a long life, marked often by severe poverty and distress, he remained faithful to the cause which he had espoused."

Other manuscript volumes of the diary, as they become known, will supply welcome additional details about Dunlap's life, but they cannot alter this estimate of the man, and of his contribution to the fine arts.

DOROTHY C. BARCK

CONTENTS

ILLUSTRATIONS

WILLIAM DUNLAP'S DIARY OF A WALKING TRIP FROM LONDON TO OXFORD

NOVEMBER, 1786

NOTES ON GREEK HISTORY

OCTOBER, 1788

CUTTGRISINGWOLDES

A TRAGEDY OF THE PHILOLOGICAL SOCIETY

OCTOBER, 1788

(Manuscript owned by YALE UNIVERSITY LIBRARY)

A WALKING TRIP FROM LONDON TO OXFORD, NOVEMBER, 1786

After securing a passage for our trunk in the coach for friday, Doctor [Samuel Latham] Mitchill & myself commenced our foot expedition to Oxford, on thursday Morning, Novr 16th 1786 at 11 O.Clock & proceeding on our way passed Kensington Gravelpits, Acton, Hanwell & stopped at Norcoat to refresh ourselves wth a draught of Ale. we asked ye name of the place & strange to tell! the people of the house could not agree in what their dwelling place was called, mine host calling it Southcoat & mine hostess northcoat. few couples in the matrimonial state could differ more widely even at St James's. passing on we observed a Youth following us, diverting himself with a dog, he overtook us & at the moment my friend dropping his stick, the lad flew from the middle of the way to save him the trouble of stooping for it, but Dr. M. having recovered the stick, thanked him & and we proceeded; I now observed him a lad, florid, handsome & well made tho' short, he seem'd lab'ring to utter something which his diffidence kept in, at last (after walking some time near us) he broke silence and remarked (in the welch dialect) the difficulty of a poor fellow travelling far from home, without mony, & destitute of friends. my companion entered into conversation with him & asking many questions concerning his situation & the circumstances which brought him into these difficulties received his narration in a tone, accent, & manner plainly indicating truth & simplicity. he had packed up his all & left his country (Carmarthenshire) to look for work or in other words to seek his fortune, he travelled to Bristol & from there to plymouth where his mony being expended he was obliged to sell his Cloaths in order to pursue his rout to London; when at the Capital no work was to be got & in endeavouring to procure it, his money was again reduced to threepence, with which capital he had sett off for Oxford, hearing as he expressed himself *"that a great many Welch boys came to school there"* hoping to meet some encouragement from his countrymen or at least to get home again; he informed us that having spent his last 3 pence he had arrived cold & hungry at the house we had just left at Norcoat, where the kind host & hostess had given him refreshment & two pence to pursue his journey. blessings on <*them*> Ye! thinks I, tho' <*they*> ye are ignorant almost of the small spot that ye dwell in & apparently poor, your hearts are not shut to the calls of humanity, nor your ears to the tale of sorrow!

Your dog is active & sprightly (says my friend) how can you support him, that are so very poor yourself? "Sir" says he (with a look which shewed the honesty of his heart) my dog <*has followed me faithfully*> has been the faithful companion of my travel & shares equally what little I receive be it ever so scanty. Noble spirited youth! how deserving of a better fate! had fortune bestow'd on thee riches, how nobly couldst thou have exerted that amiable disposition on the worthy of thy own species, which now thou hast hardly power to shew to a poor dog! we bestow'd on this brave Cambrian (for certainly such a mind must be brave) all the advice for his future conduct, which our inexperienced youth could give & with it what we could spare for the comfort of himself & faithfull dog. then did the tears of gratitude evince the truth of his tale & honesty of his heart, & he turned aside, to give vent for passions too big for utterance; As we Journeyed on but a little way, we met a Man whose garments declared him the son of misfortune, seeing we eyed him, he stopt & asked our charity, we then question'd him concerning his journey, he told us he was going to London to seek for work as a Currier still enquiring, he openly confess'd that he had been obliged to fly from his family (a Wife & four Children) for debt & enquiring the cause of his being so, he after some hesitation confessed the occasion was too great love of strong Liquors. he seem'd conscious of his fault; & commisserating his state we gave him our mite towards his success in the industrious line he must pursue to retreive his lost reputation & peace of mind.

Leaving behind this unfortunate, within a few miles two Men working in a gravel-pit attracted our notice, the Docter after examining the nature of the gravel enter'd into discourse with them, wishing to have a specimen of John Bull in all situations; he began by observing what happy people the English were, to which they agreed & seemed proud of the Idea of being happier than the people of any other country in their station, being perfectly content tho' hard at labour in a damp gravel pit for the sum of 13 pence per day, out of which they found themselves, cloathing provision &c. and kept there tools in repair. the youngest had the felicity of being in the matrimonial state & the prospect of a numerous offspring; his spouse he said, was at that time out of employ therefore what I call his scanty wages must be partly appropriated to her maintenance, most part of the year he said she had employment but at this time could do nothing but house work & even by cause of her *peculiar situation* was rendered almost incapable of that. having rec^d^ all the information we could expect from these industrious contented Britons, we rewarded them for their civillity & candour & left them. the first that now drew our attention was a boy drawing an Ass, whose load was two bags of what we afterwards found to be sand, we question'd him, but so extream was his bashfulness that hanging his head he seemed afraid of speaking to us. when he lifted his head we could see as fine a face as nature ever formed, but still characteristic of his station & the hardships he daily underwent; his occupation was to drive that Ass to a Village hard by where he sold one load of sand per day for which he rec^d^ one shilling, on which he & his Ass subsisted. as if for a contrast to this pretty boy, chance next threw in our way an Old Sinner, bending under the weight Age, its attendant infirmities

& a knapsack, after accosting him, Dr. Mitchill took occasion to admire his walking stick, upon which he offered it <*for*> as a Gift to him, and upon the offer being declined, he craved charity in *true stile.* we asked some questions, & soon found great part of his life had been spent in London, on which we gave him a trifle as recompence for detain^{g} him & pursued our rout, despairing of hearing anything but lies & evasions, from one who had been educated within the smoke of that seminary, where nature is so soon disguised or totally eradicated by art.

Night with redoubled darkness o'ertook us before we reach'd the place of our intended rest, and as we approached near a house (which we could distinguish but by the lights) we were roused by a strange hooping & hallow^{g} which we resolved to know the occasion of, coming near we percieved it was a Public house & the Men from whom the noise proceeded stand^{g} at the door, under a shed. they were Farmers who had been at Uxbridge selling their Grain it being market day & on their return had stoped at this place to enjoy themselves. as I attempted enterring the door one of these Jovial sons of Ceres, seized my hand & pressing it, invited me drink, which I instantly did & we entered into spirit of the scene by call^{g} for more Liquor. All then entered ye house & upon the arrival of our Bowl, the copious draughts were mixed, in token of Amity. then did we see John Bull in his humour! in his Glory! singing parts of hunting songs & cryings Tally ho! Hoix! particularly the old brown Wig who first accosted us, who answered the picture of squire Western to a tittle. we took a oppertunity of praising the happy state of English Farmers. A'nt we (they cryed unanimously) A'nt we the happiest fellows breathing, free & independent! Free & independant! for ever Huzza!. we joined in their joyfull notes & they call'd us hearty fellows! staunch cocks! Jolly dogs! one says, "Auy! Auy! ye be a brace of the roight sort I warrant ye"—"ye be Lununners tho' " says another the answer in the affirmative flattering his sagacity. "Ay Ay I thought so" says he "ha ha I could see that ha ha" Another then asked me if I knew the pastry Cooks shop Russell Street, Covent Garden, I answered yes, "Do you" says he "Why she's my own sister that keeps the House & I have been putting my boy prentice there" the Devil! says I "is't possible? I wish you joy give me your hand you damn'd hearty old cock you, here's to you. We then had some more scraps of hunting songs & one droned a ditty "consarning a Lady fair who died for love quite in despair" which done, I gave them a Hunting Song, to their apparent great satisfaction, they all joining in Harkaway! with a most glorious noise. time approaching for their departure, they offered to take us home behind them, assuring us of hearty Welcome & plenty of game the next day. we for several reasons declined this generous offer & part^{g} with them at the door set out again in the dark for Gerards Cross. we had proceeded about a Mile when we heard sounds, which the wise knight of la Mancha would perhaps have taken for the sturdy blows of some knights or Giants engaged in combat but which to our common sense of hearing, appeared only the blows of some neighbouring Blacksmith makeing horse shoes or hob nails. near the Forge of this son of Vulcan stood the Inn we look'd for, & enterr^{g} the Kitchen & Hall, we enquired of a huge tun of Flesh if we could have lodging there that night. this Falstaff in petticoats striking her fists in her Blubber sides & observing us top to toe, at last answered Yes, & desired us to be shewn into the parlour wher sitting round the fire were several Women & children who upon first entering gave me an Idea of Gipseys, but were as they informed us Travellers from different Waggons on their way to London. on leaving them my fellow traveller seem'd to think them going like lambs to smithfield especially two or three handsome lasses who were of the company.

[November] 17th Set off before breakfast but are obliged by stress of Weather to put into Beaconsfield, which we did not reach till <*well wett*> the Water had <*entered*> penetrated our sheathing & our sails were thoroughly wett. And here must I in justice make mention of the pretty daughters of Mine Host at the Black Bull Beaconsfield, & for their Beauty Neatness, engaging & obliging behaviour, *will I thus immortalize them & their Father's Black Bull, by a few strokes of my pen.* Oh Barren day! more Barren than ye Flints & chalk which we passed over & as heavy <*as*> to our spirits as the chalk mixed with the rain, to our heels, we finished ye days walk at Stoken Church.

I would advise the sellers of Silver or plated ware to settle along the road between Beaconsfield and Stoken Church, for the convenience of chalk to clean their wares with. I would likewise recommend to those worthy Citizens who wish to shew their taste by building country houses within the smother of London, by laying out an *Acre of Land* in circleses, crescents, squareses, gravel walkses, fountains, Rivers, & Canalses & by torturing gods trees, into every shape that he did not intend them to assume; who enjoy *Bon ton,* on a *Sunday,* & laugh at those who enjoy on a *Monday,* to notice the ingenuity, of a gentleman on the road between London & Oxford (if ever they travel *so far from home*) who has converted an Old Water Cask into two Summer Houses, and I can assure them that the half of a Water Cask when painted & a Chinese top put to it makes as pretty a *little House* (little Summer House I should have said) as any I have seen within many yards of the Metropolis, among ye Country Seats of London.

[November] 18th From Stoken Church we had not travelled many miles, when an Aged Man attracted our attention. he carryed nought but a staff in his hand, his garments were wretchedly tatered, & his shoes, worn out & falling from his feet, seem'd like their owner to have suffered much by the ravages of time, but *more* from rough roads and hard service. after the accustomed salutations, we began our inquiries & he told us that he was a Soldier returning from Shropshire to London for some papers he had lost which entitled him to Seven pounds a year; ye reward of his faithfull services. I then asked where he had served. "In America Sir" says he "Under Wolfe, I saw him fall. I rec^{d} this scar in my cheek that day. lay your finger in it Sir. I then felt interrested in the tale of this venerable veteran & with an <*unfeigned*> earnest tone demanded, what regiment <*did you*> he belonged to? "the 47th Sir" said he, still more earnestly I cried & what officers do you know of that corps? he then mentioned the names of <*his officers*> many of his old commanders till I asked if he <*knew*> remembered an Officer of the name of Dunlap. "Mr. Dunlap" says he "certainly I do, he was my Lieutenant to be sure I remember him!—and were you after the War before the late [war] in New Jersey, at Perth Amboy? I was not quartered at Amboy Sir" says he "but at Brunswick with that part of the reg^{t} <*there quatered*> we remov'd to N. Y. then to Boston. I was at Lexington & Bunkershill and was taken with Burgoyne at Saratoga. while he spoke his countenance was enlightened, & he seem'd to feel himself again a Soldier. "Suppose" says I looking him full in ye face "suppose I was son <*of that Lt D*> of one of your officers? "are you?" he cry'd who? Lt. D. <*upon my assuring him I was*> he seiz'd my hand with an honest ardour & could he have afforded a tear, I beleive it would then have started.

"After all these fortunate & unfortunate services" continued this son of Mars I am now in my native country without a halfpenny to buy food or procure me lodging on my weary journey. See" says he searching his rags.

"And how after all your hardships has your country provided for you? Why well says he £7 a year is enough for me in my native village but having lost my certificate I must return to London for another. tis hard" says he & to beg would grind me to the soul, but I am us'd to it [1] "See what I have lived on these two days" & he produced a half eaten uncooked Turnip. "I have eat nothing these

[1] This paragraph was written between the lines of the paragraph immediately preceding, but the original sentences were not crossed out.

two days but part of this turnip" we stood mute with astonishment which he construing into a doubt of his veracity cry'd out with indescribable emotion *"may I be damn'd if I lie"*. And may I be damn'd, poor old man if I doubt ye! We asked many questions, which he answered with frankness, & told us he should receive his papers immediately on his arrival at London, & go down again to his own country, (Shropshire) to pass in quiet the remainder of his days, he being now 66 years of Age. After receiving our contributions towards making his way lighter, he took us each by the hand lifted his watery eyes to heaven & blessed us. turning <*from*> to us at a few paces distance, he said looking earnestly at me, "if ever you see your Father, perhaps he may remember old Wainwright."

between the hours of one & two we gain'd sight of the University of Oxford, from Shotover Hill which view I sketch'd as may be seen in the second volume of my Works; descending the hill, we turn'd to the right & discovered a stone quarry, which we walk^{d} over, and then proceeded towards a Cluster of huts still farther from the road, the way to which was so interspersed with hills & dales, so strangely & confusedly jumbled together that one might imagine it the field of Battle after the victory obtained by Michael & his Angels, over Satan; allowing <*me to compare*> Greater things <*with less*> to be compared with less. we found these huts to be the habitations of the poor people who worked in the stone quarry, or rather we imagined so, for no living creature did we see but some hogs & a Girl who ran away on our attempting to speak to her. We then returning to the road arrived at Oxford.

Oxford dear Oxford the seat of my ease
Where I slumbered nine summers then lost my degrees
Where I pull'd off my boots and unbutton'd my knees
Where I fed upon ducks & attendant green peas,

Where I drank good port wine till I came to the lees
And wanted for <*nothing*> nought but <*comatable she's*> comfortable [word illegible].

When we arrived at the Angel Inn, we stopped & asked for lodgings & accommodations, which we received, after undergoing some reviews, which reminded me of the Greasy landlady of Gerards Cross. here however we took up our residence, and the 19th being Sunday, we had rainy Weather, but we managed to commence acquaintance with two honest Generous Cambrians Mr. Harries of Jesus Colledge & Mr. Bland [2] of BrazenNose with whom we dined in ye batchelors common Room of Jesus.

[November] 20th We paraded the Colledges & Chapels of the University with & under direction of Mr. Davies Fellow of Pembroke, who shewed us that attention which marks the Gentleman & Man of Knowledge, on such occasions; we broke off our researches at two, to Dine in Common Hall of Brazen Nose, with Mr. Bland. I pass over in silence the Curiositys & Beautys of Oxford. Are they not written in the book of directions called the Oxford Guide. but as I know of no writer Sacred or prophane, who has described the manner of dining in the Halls of Colledges, I shall note the manner of Brazen Nose. At the top of the Hall dine ye the Principal and Fellows, next, (at another Table) come the Masters, then the Batchelors, then the Gentlemen Commoners, then the Commoners & last the Serviteurs all at separate Tables. at the Fellows Table they have joints of Meat as in familys, but at the others, they dine on what they call commons, that is, the Bill of Fare is on the Table & every one orders what he likes, which is cut off by the Cook & sent in, on his plate, as in Eating houses at London. When diner is over the Principal rises & walks down the Hall followed by the Fellows, at the door he turns & bows to the Senior Fellow, who bows to him & turning

[2] Richard Harding Harries, Jesus College, B.A. 1787; Nathaniel Bland, Brasenose College, B.A., 1790. Joseph Foster, *Alumni Oxonienses, 1715-1886.*

bows to the next & so on; <*shaking their heads like Mandarin figures on a chimney piece;*> a more ridiculous scene Oxford does not afford, and that's saying a great deal.

[November] 21st We saw what remained worth seeing, & in the evening had a scene of fun, presented to us by chance, a Drunken Gownsman in the Kitchen, roaring ranting & swearing to the Chambermaid & the other Virgins of the House, in a stile that will not bear repeating, 'though from perhaps a future son of the Church & teacher of y^e^ *Gospell!* O temper of Mores as we say in Latin.

[November] 22nd [1786] We walked to Blenheim; (the House given by Queen Anne, to John Churchill first Duke of Marlborough for his great services &c &c) near Woodstock, and were highly Gratified with viewing the Park & the Palace, with its superb & elegant Furniture, altogether exceeding any place I ever beheld; the pictures were of course what most attracted my notice, many by Rubens, as for the other particulars of the House are they not written in the book of the Chronicles of the house furniture, commonly called a catalogue, & so we returned to Oxford, & the next day set off for London by the conveyance we came on, made Windsor in our route where we stop'd one day to see the beauties & curiositys of that Royal residence, we the next morning *went to Chapel with the King* & after breakfast set off again at 9 OClock & arrived in London (in Oxford Street) by 2 OClock, 22 Miles in five hours is good walking as Cicero says de oratori quintibus Mars et Apollo qualli

Jany 1834. The last few lines * appear to have [been] written after returning to London.

* Beginning "the pictures were of course what most attracted my notice," in the last paragraph, there is a perceptible difference in the ink and the pen used.

[The succeeding fifty pages of manuscript contain notes and extracts, copied by Dunlap in October, 1788, from John Gillies's *History of Ancient Greece* I, chapters 1-9; from Charles Rollin, and from the Rev. James Beattie. The following are the only original critical comments by Dunlap:]

In the Note on painting * great superiority is supposed to belong to poetical imitation over the Imitations of the pencil—I will endeavour to remove that distinction of quality and place the Sister Arts (both divine) upon a level; perhaps we shall find that if superior honours is due to Either, painting will claim the Crown. Let us examin[e] who they are, that place the Art of giving y[e] appearance of roundness, body & projection to a smooth surface of forming a Creation that shall strike the beholder with horror or move his Soul to gentle pity, in a degree inferior to that art, which by words sweetly arranged or intended to raise the same Images or Ideas in the readers Imagination which were originally formed in the Poets mind: Shall we not find them poets? Enamoured with the beauty of their divine powers? or those who tho' not inspired by the divine ray having their taste formed to admire the beauties of poetry & ignorant of or unattending to her Sister neglect her & exert their feebler powers to praise that which they know, and depress the unknown as any excuse for their blindness in not seeing her beauties or their indolence in not examining into her Merits. I believe none will deny the truth of this, and from this consideration we easily see why the Art which has not the oppertunity of boasting its own Merits is by the injudicious held inferior.

Let us suppose the Painter to be blest with the sweet powers of song, on what would his enraptured fancy dwell? What but the divine power of preserving to future ages even the features, the expressive Countenance of

* Gillies's note is as follows: "This is the chief superiority of poetical imitation above painting, that it can describe, in a few pages, what many galleries of pictures could not represent." *History of Ancient Greece* (Dublin, 1786), I, 76, (Chap. II, footnote 85).

some favorite Hero where we may see depicted, the Mind that could raise Empires or Humble in the dust the Haughty Tyrant; The power of presenting to the enraptured sight the glorious deeds of Men Immortaliz'd; So (says the beholder) so looked Brutus when at Pompey's feet great Julius bleed[g] lay, So looked Washington, when for the last time he addressd those troops who guided & led by him gained for their Country a glorious Freedom.

The rival sisters then would have fair Tryal, existing in the same breast, they would each exert their utmost power & display their brightest charms to gain unrivalled sway, then would the favoured Mortal place Painting on the throne & having power o'er poetry, Command her to sing the praises of her Sister.

> Such Fresnoy was thy happy envy'd state!
> On Tibers banks the poet-painter sate
> The heavn'ly Sisters in his Bosom dwelt
> Both he caress't & eithers influence felt;
> No longer Rivals, all their envy dead,
> Each helps to twine the Garland for his Head
> But still whene'er he sung his tunefull lays,
> The Theme was ever turn'd to Paintings praise.

Painting as the elder claims precedence of her Sister: ere Letters were invented men had no other way of communicating knowledge to each to each [*sic*] other at different periods of time, but by figures of Men & Animals representing the event the[y] wished to hand down to posterity, and this kind of Historic painting was in use among the Mexicans, when invaded by the Spaniards under Cortez. The Egyptian Hieroglyphics was but a species of Painting. Then, if any Man would pay Court to Poetry, He must first gain the favour of her Sister, without whose aid all his attempts must be vain: Then, every Poet was a painter <*& ev'ry painter was a poet*> Now, tis not necesary for the poet to be a painter, but tis absolutely necessary that ev'ry true painter, should be a Poet.

Let the sister Arts join & Mutually assist each other:

Let the painter illustrate the Poet & Historians page, let the Poet & Historian celebrate the Artist & his Art: When the Poet or Historian have related the causes of a great event, when they by their lively descriptions almost make their readers think they see a Chatham fainting in the House of Lords o'ercome with his exertions for his Country's service, Saint Paul surrounded by the admiring Islanders shaking unhurt the Serpent from his hand, then let them turn their eyes to the Canvass glowing with the tints of Copley & of West and own the Story's but for the Painters hand were lifeless & unfinished.

Gillies Hist: Greece II Chap:

Music much practised in the early ages—"it was not of the learned kind and therefore the better adapted to touch the heart." * Why Mr G: should suppose, what he calls learned Music to be less capable of touching the heart than Music in its rude state I cannot conceive—he says their music was not merely "an agreeable succession of melodious unmeaning sounds" are we from that to conclude that the music of the present day is such? If so, I must for the present think Mr. G: does not understand what he writes on: however in a note [footnote 86] he promises to treat the subject more fully hereafter, till then I defer my opinion.

Rollin, on the Lacedæmonian Government . . . When Demaratus told Xerxes that were the Lacedæmonians deserted by all Greece & reduced to a thous: or less men they would make head against his innumerable armies & never decline the battle; the king smiled & could not comprehend how men who were free and without masters to controul them, would expose themselves voluntarily to Dangers & to death: this reminds me of a circumstance which happened at this place; on the 24th of July 1788 when the inhabitants <*of this place*> walked in procession to shew their approbation of the Constitu-

* Cited from Gillies's *History of Ancient Greece* (Dublin, 1786), I, 76.

tion framed for them by a Convention of the States, after the procession, they all Dined together in a field without the City Congress the Foreign Ministers &c dining with them. The French Ambassador (Mr Moutier) [Le Compte de Moustier] turning to one of the directors, "Sir," says he "You have brought all these people together to eat & drink how do you think to make them return without riots intoxication & disorder?" he was answered that at the discharge of a signal gun they would quit their tables range themselves under their Standards & march home in the order they came. "Why where" says the Frenchman "are the Soldiers that are to make them do this?" "they need no force to make them behave with propriety, they act as Freemen and the sense of propriety would make the meanest American blush at disorderly behaviour on this public & joyfull occasion" It happened as it was said—they returned with the same decent but sincere marks of satisfaction with which they came out, and the Frenchman like Xerxes was convinced that Freemen need no force to compel them to do their duty.

Things blameable in the Laws of Lycurgus. 1st the exposing weak & deformed children: I agree with Monsr Rollin that this practice was contrary to Humanity & to the Religion of Nature (I say nothing of revealed religion as Lycurgus was not enlightened by revelation) but when we consider that the great view of all his institutions was to make a nation of Soldiers, I cannot set down this as altogether blameable: such a law now would be horridly detestable, but it then certainly had great influence in accomplishing the <*great*> purposes of this immortal Legislator. We must likewise remember that where the Men was handsome well made, kept healthy & strong by continual athletic exercise & the Women proportionably the same there would seldom be occasion to put this cruel Law into execution. I dont know that any such law or custom exists among the Savages of our Country, but we know that they are remarkably strong well made & handsome:

THE ARTIST SHOWING A PICTURE FROM *HAMLET* TO HIS PARENTS, 1788

BY WILLIAM DUNLAP

(Owned by The New York Historical Society)

Gillies Chap: 4th [Vol. I, 160 *ff.*]

685 [B. C.] the Messenians prepare to revolt, Aristomenes appears: Argos & Arcadia join; battle of Derae, doubtful victory: Aristomenes saluted king on the field of Battle, declines but accepts the title of Gen[l]: his Glorious exploits: Panormus & Gonippus: Eira:

Here would I fix the Scene of a poem: to open with Archidamia mourning the supposed death of the Hero, whom the Spartans had taken and thrown into the Ceada: he enters having escaped and enter'd the City by a secret way, time, night towards morn: recounts his adventure: retires to rest Spartans attack the Walls gain part: Panormus kill'd; the sight of Aristomenes changes the success, comes to the fight as the sun rises: Aanaxander endeavours to bring back the Spartan to the charge, kills Gonippus <*& is killed by*> Aristomenes pursues the Spartans into their Camp with slaughter: returns within the Walls: Spartans beg a truce to bury the dead: end of 1st day. 2d day preparation for funeral games in honour of Panormus & Gonippus: 2d 3d & 4th days till sunset of truce funeral games; Theocles in three parts sings the Exploits of Aristomenes, Panormus & Gonippus. Gorgus son of Aristomenes & Manticles son of the prophet, their friendship valour &c victors in the games: on the night of 4th day Arist: alone attacks the Corinthian Camp & 5th day offers the Hecatomphonia to Messenian Jove: the Corinthians join the Spartans with other reinforcements Gorgus & Manticles challenge the Spartan youth 6th day the single Combat brings on a general skirmish, in the night the Spartans gain admittance into Eira, confused fight valour Arist: Gro: [*sic for* Gorgus] & Man: Theocles fight continues till day: 7th day. death of Theocles: Aristomenes marches thro' the Spartans & leads his country towards Arcadia: End:

CUTTGRISINGWOLDES

Prologue

To the most Lamentable Comedy, and ever to be remembered Tragedy of Cuttgrisingwoldes: translated from the Greek by R: B: F:R:S:M:D:D:D:W:D: &c &c &c

Sit still good people for a while and hear,
The dolefull'st Story ever yet struck ear;
Of plots to which all other plots knock-under;
Of Lanthorns dark & other things of wonder;
Of little Men & tall Men linkt together,
(Tho long & short, yet all birds of a feather)
Resolv'd to dash thro' thick, thro' thin, thro' smother,
From dirt and Mire help out one-another
Nor stick at <*dirty*> nasty ways to please a brother
Of Milatary Men and Men of Larning,
Fine Gentlemen & Men of great dissarning,
Their plots frustrated & themselves confounded
Malicious pride & Self love sorely wounded
By Men whose good intentions, was their Shield,
Whose Honesty alone, gave them the Field;
By Men Who unacquainted with the Law,
Dare to expose the paltry deeds they saw;
Despise the folly of a shameless few
While *their own* deeds *bear light* whate'er They do.

(Cuttgrisingwoldes: None of the learned can find the meaning of this greek word, some think it may be translated brotherquills.)

Dramatis Personae

C. Sharping
G. Prim
Pocket-em
L. Neddy
Touchy
Cobweb
Mars
Demosthenes
Cypher
President
Pillar
Witenough
Firm
Steady
Hot-head [3]

Scene—Athens

Translated

Octr 1788

[3] For identification of some of these characters as members of the Philological Society, see the Introduction.

CUTTGRISINGWOLDES

Act 1.

Enter Sharping & Prim

Sh: Return my petition without e'en a trial?
I <*to*> used thus! give me a denyal!
I—I—I—I—a pleader at the bar?
For learning known t' excell them all by far!
A Man like me of settled reputation
Known thro' the Land, the first at an Oration.
Oh could my Father rise & could he speak
He'd cry was it for this I taught thee greek
Was it for this I had thee Lawyer dub'd
To be rejected by a petty club.

Pr: Oh Sharppy dear dont make this noise and clatter
Depend upon't you quite mistake ye matter
Our friend the President would have you try
To gain the End purposed, by & by
Your wit has gain'd you ennemies he says
And he said much dear sharppy in your praise
But thinks you'd better, put it off some days
In the mean time when ere you see them—bow
Duck down your head & cry how do—how do—

Sh: I will, I will, and I'll restrain my wit;
Once fixt they cant remove me from my seat;
My Wit is always standing in my way
Tis a Misfortune faith, hay? ant it? say!
The president has certainly been kind,
For now none of them knows I'd ere a mind
To be proposed; So we have time to sound

And ere we venture, we will try the ground;
To be oppos'd by such a set of boobies
Painters, clerks, Ironmongers, Doctors, loobies

PR: Hold you forget, to these tis you must bow
Pull off your Hat, and smile & cry how do,
When we have got you fixt then, then we'll let them know

SH: Here Cobweb comes

PR: he knows the whole affair
He joins with us and will our fortunes share.

Enter Cobweb.

COB: Good Morning gentlemen well how d'ye do
Always together. Are ye one or two?

SH: Two Sir, but if the simile is fair
We're like your shoes, tho' two, we're but one pair

PR: Good, good, I see by that you'll ne'er have done.

SH: He! He! I cant, I cannot stop a pun.

COB: I'm glad my friend that *that* was not presented
And you as well as me should be contented,
Now we have time disgrace will be prevented

SH: Neddy they all agree shall be admitted.

PR: Yes, and if you are not, they're neatly fitted
For he joins us, and then when e'er we please
We form a strong Majority with ease
Alter their constitution, change their law
If that wont drive them off—why we'll withdraw.

COB: I hope it will not come to this my friends
No violent measures use to gain your ends
Howe'er I think It will not be amiss
To give a trifling, distant hint of this

I'll try My influence, first, persuade, then threat,
If unsuccessfull I shall much regret.
My power is great among them well you know
What I point out, they will not fail to do,
By rhe'tric I could always yet persuade 'em
They know twas I and I alone that made 'em
When first I join'd them how oft did I hammer
Night after Night, to teach the dunces Grammer
My Rules, my lectures, ev'ry night repeated
Began to talk sometimes ere they were seated
To shew my zeal I ev'ry night held forth
And deep imprest th' Idea of my worth
Not soon forgot:—On me you may depend
Your suit cant fail, while Cobweb is your Friend.

SH: Thanks gen'rous Cobweb, thanks are still your due
To none am I so much in debt, as you.

Enter Mars

MA: What here my lads, why sharpy how do do
And Cobweb! what the De'il are you here too?
Well met my lads, I wanted much to know
Whether to that damn'd *bore* you mean to go
To that—society I mean—ye see
The greatest bore in natshure tis to me;

PR: Yes we must go to welcome Neddy in

MA: Oh ay! faith Ned will give a precious Grin:
To Night I'll motion to abolish reading
Why its a twaddle full as bad as pleading
Sure ev'ry gentleman at home can read
Of officers too, I cannot see the need
Why may'nt we meet & just do as we please
And ev'ry gentleman consult his ease
And not be call'd to order as we are
Bore'd and pig-major'd ever from the Chair.

Besides they've got such a dam'd vulgar way
Of <*still*> expressing what-so'e'er they say
That I am sure should I adopt the same
I into ridicule should turn my name
In genteel company could not show my face,
I could not faith: no, as I hope for grace.

COB: That notion's wrong you may depend upon't
We draw our language from the purest font
In my third Lecture I've discuss'd that point
And laid down rules not soon put out of joint
How'e'er good folks at present I cant stay
Or else upon the subject much I'd say

MA: (aside) I'm devilish glad he's forc'd to go away:

COB: Good day t'ye gentlemen, while in the mind
To Firms I'll go his sentiments to find

Exit Cobweb.

MA: What a curst boring fellow now that is
You may read Pedant in his very phiz
By Mars I swear and by my Major-ship
His very looks give gentlemen the Hip

PR: Say what you will Cobweb's a man of merit

SH: And Language too—and faith he does not spar' it

MA: Well then to night it seems we're all to meet
When Neddy's introduc'd & takes his seat
In the mean time I'm off—

PR: Stop Mars, stop, stay
Theres Firm & Hothead coming up this way
They'll stop here—let's hear what they have to say.

Enter Firm & Hothead

MA: How do ye gentlemen—good day—good day

H:H: Sharping how is't, I'm mighty glad to see ye
I just now heard the measles had been wi' ye

FIRM: We heard the Law Society were Ill
And that to cure them you had ta'en a pill

SH: Ha ha, not I, I'm very well I thank ye
Your at your wit, you dog—ha ha—now ant ye
Hot head & you could never yet be quiet
You're waggish Dogs, you know you can't deny it

H:H: You are pleas'd to compliment—we've no pretensions
And if we had we keep't in close dimensions
While in your presence:—For a wit you're noted
Your puns, your quibbles, ev'ry where are quoted.

FIRM: Ay and Mars too—I heard a Lady say
That you are quite extravagant that way
You put your Josephs Coat on ev'ry day

MA: Why Josephs Coat, more than all other Coats
Egad your Wit needs explanat'ry notes:

FIRM: Oh not at all, if you'll but recollect
Joseph, with Motley Coat his Father deckt:
From which some Wags have impudently said
That of the Motley tribe, Joseph may claim the head.

MA: Ahem—a-hem—(aside) curse his iron wit

PR: (aside to Mars) Faith Bully Mars that was a Clumsy hit
Pray Mister Firm (in scripture you're well read)
What do you think of what's of Balaam said?

FIRM: What the Ass said sir I suppose you mean?
I think that same a very moral scene.
Of Scripture I'm too negligent a Reader
But Sir, I think the Ass, a special pleader.

PR: A hem—A hem—Sir!

FIRM: Sir d'ye speak to me

PR: No sir not I—not I sir—he he he!

SH: Hot head there's some queer storys in that Book
But I suppose you never in it look
Unless to find out subjects for your pictures
But you ne'er think of making any strictures
Dont you conceiv't a most ridic'lous Joke
To make us believe that Balaams Ass e'er spoke.

H.H: Oh not [at] all sir I with ease believe it
I wonder Sir that you cannot conceive it
That one poor Ass should then a few words say
Now, Asses make orations every day
This ever since has stood as a precedent
They now study Law, this one had no need on't
And ever since poor Balaams Ass turn'd pleader
The asses of the bar, look to him as their leader.

SH: Ha ha—no no—now faith you are severe

H:H: No faith—I only sketch the things as they appear

PR: Come shall we go—gentlemen good day

FIRM: What all! I'm very sorry you can't stay
Of Scripture matters I have much to say

PR: We'll leave them if you please t' another day

Exit Sh: Pr: & Mars

FIRM: Was ever <*two such*> on the earth seen two such blockheads
Which would break first, suppose they were to knock heads

H:H: Mars would go first that you may with a glimpse see
Like paper lanthorn *his* is thin & flimsy.

Prim has good wit, he sometimes ought to lend it
To his friend Sharping

FIRM: No no he'd soon spend it
Prim knows, his own, he has expended long since
And now in stead he utters nought but nonsense

H.H: Prim is a Man of sense & Man of learning
In choice of Friend he's not shewn his discerning.
How'e'er the best of us at times may err
I beleive we've been in fault e'en now & here
We should not judge of others so severe.

Exeunt

Act 2d

Scene an Ironmonger's store

Enter Firm & Hothead

FIRM: I think that sharping must be mortify'd
To know that his admittance is deny'd

H.H: Yes full as much as if he'd been black-ball'd
And the whole tribe, depend upon't are gall'd.

Enter Cobweb

COB: Good day t'ye gentlemen I'm very glad
To meet ye here together, I have had
An application from a man of merit
Who seeing our design goes on with spirit
Wishes to join us—Firm there knows him
His name is Groves

FIRM: I'm sure I'll not oppose him
I know him for a Man of sense & spirit
Of gen'ral knowledge and acknowledg'd merit

COB: I do not wish at this time to propose him
While we're divided—some one may oppose him

H:H: Divided!

COB: Ay I mean about young sharping

H: Oh ho and is't on that string you are harping.

COB: I wish that matter fixt

FIRM: it soon would be
Bring forward his petition & you'll see.

COB: I'm told it will be the next night of meeting

FIRM: From me then it shall have a kindly greeting

COB: I cannot think why your're opposed to him
I rather think its 'cause you do not know him

FIRM: Better than me you sir can surely tell
But sir I think its cause I know 'm too well.

COB: He's certainly a Man of education
And bears to all, a spotless reputation
If he's rejected very much I fear
I cant say what—but it will cost us dear.

H.H: Fear what! What fear is there from his rejection
I should fear more, much more from his election
How'e'er sir uncontroul'd shall be my choice
Free is my mind & ever free my voice.

FIRM: From what you've said I think you must know more
Pray tell us what you've heard upon that score

COB: Why then—the gentlemen

H.H: Ay we know who

COB: Have partly said what they intend to do
If he's rejected—for they justly say
He'd make as good a Philo' full as they

They say too that if he is not admitted
The Philo's soon by many will be quitted.

H.H: Why let them go, their passage free as air
To stop them not one word can Hothead spare
Off may they go, and wing their flight together
All of a kind. All birds of one black feather
What! would they threaten us into compliance
Unfurl their flag & bid us all defiance?
No by my Soul it never shall be said
Hot head was drove the way he would not lead
Propose the greatest Man that e'er drew breath
I'd throw my black-ball full against his teeth
If threats were us'd to gain him his admission
No no—that would indeed be dastardly submission.

FIRM: I think so too—I'm not so to be shaken
And if you thought it Cobweb you're mistaken

COB: Not I indeed—I don't think thats their meaning—
Indeed such business I'd not be seen in
I only wish that all things may keep quiet

H.H: No no the Lawyers must kick up a Riot:—

COB: Well—well. I'm sorry, gentlemen content ye

Exit Cob:

H.H: Ay ay Sir—now go you to those that sent ye.
Well firm, why dont you speak ha! Whats the matter?

FIR: Why who can speak while you keep such a clatter.
The Lawyers now I think our minds will know
And if they chuse to leave us, let them go
Their Schemes as well as threats shall all prove vain
Without them we have stood and we can stand again.

Exeunt

Scene changes to Demosthenes Room

the Law Society meeting

First enter Touchy Prim & Mars

TOU: I just met Cobweb, he desires to see you
I told him that to night I should be wi' you
He then said firm & Hothead would say nay
So the petition must be kep't away

PR: We'll grind them for't be sure, ere long the day.

Enter Demosthenes & Pocket'um

POCK: So! gentlemen you're early here to night
I'm glad to see it well I think that's right
Well Prim you're president to night how do

PR: Why faith, I don't know well, I'm but so so.
I've got a strange confounded ugly cold
And deaf enough for husband to a scold.
You've heard my friend how sharping has been us'd
By such a motley set his suit refus'd?

POCK: Yes I have heard & sorry am to hear it
But we had ev'ry reason Sir to fear it:

PR: 'Tis an affront Sir e'en on the profession
That one of us should be refus'd admission.
But we can fit the lads, bring down their mettle
When we are done they'll look but monstrous little.

POCK: I'm sorry. I was pleas'd I must confess
Pleas'd with ye order of thier business

MAR: Ay, Ay, all that all that is well enough
But for my part I think t'was useless stuff.
Then their behaviour is so impolite.
Upon my word they bore me ev'ry night
Especially Hothead, all his actions shows it
What'e'er I move he's certain still t'oppose it

When'e'er I speak he straight begins to laugh
And answers me as if I was a calf.

Enter President

PRES: How do do gentlemen, Prim how do do
Ha! Pocket'um I'm glad to see you too

PR: Well now, let's see we are all Philo's here
Let's fix some plan before the rest appear.

TOUCH: Well Prim suppose you take the presidents chair
Then in due form we all may speak or hear:

Prim takes the chair: they seat themselves in order.

PR: Well gentlemen you (I presume) all know
How our request's been bandy'd to and fro,
How we've been slighted, how been illy us'd
And how our friends petition is refus'd
Now gentlemen I make this proposition
That we send in, instead of the petition,
Our resignations, this will much surprize them
Break all their schemes & shew how we despise them.
We then can form one by another name
The object & the business the same
We'll form it to th' exclusion of all others
Let none admitted be but learned brothers

(Demosthenes rises, and in rising knocks the powder from Mars's hair on his coat with his elbow)

DE: eh! hem! hem! Sir

MA: Oh Law! my coat's all powder

PR: I'll thank you sir to speak a little louder

DE: Yes sir—eh! hem! I think—eh! hem! hem! ee!
I—I—I—I—eh! hem! he—the—the—he—

PR: Oh Yes Sir—you exactly think with me

(Demosthenes sits down again)

POCK: For my part I agree in this affair,
Tho' Candidly before ye I declare
That I with sorrow shall the philo's leave
But to my brothers I must firmly cleave

Enter Neddy

PR: Oh, here comes Neddy—I have just been stating
Law 'gainst Philology & we're debating;
(If 'tis debates where all are of one mind
One flock, one feather, genus, stamp & kind)
But now let's hear, what says the Chanc'lor's brother
Shall we break up this club & form another.

NED: With all my heart, I never have been there
But for Initiation, so declare
I've nought against them, but I go with you
Like Wax, & parchment, to profession true.

PR: Well gentlemen since thus we all agree
In your proceeding guided be by me
Next monday night mars shall get up & speak
Tell the society that they grow weak
That Mr. Cobweb's going out of town
And without him no business can be done
That many members do propose to leave,
Then some one else some resignations give
This frights them—then the motion make
That we dissolve & ev'ry compact break
I second it—the question then is put
Crack goes the shell, & we divide the nut.

MARS: Agree

DEM: Eh! yes

POCK: Ay Ay.

TOUCH: agreed

NED: agreed

Law gainst philology must sure succeed.

PR: The president sits by & nothing says!

PRES: I do not speak because I cannot praise
In your attempt to break this knot of friends
I will not join, nor aid to gain your ends.
When you have left them I can never stay
I still must follow where ye lead the way
Or else be mark'd & shun'd like esops daw
By each assuming brother of the law
For keeping Peacocks company, rather
Than moving with the birds of my own feather
No farther Gentlemen I have to say
You may move on as Prim points out the way

Enter Sharpping & a multitude of Lawyers
Curtain drops

Act 3d

Scene: the Room

Philological Society's meeting.

Enter Mars & Pocketum

POCK: Who'll make the motion, Mars I wish you'd make it

MARS: No faith, I can't pon honor, no <*you make it*> deuce take it;
Here's Cobweb's letter here is Neddy's too
And Touchy's, there <*for the*> at first I think will do
Prim in reserve keeps Demosthenes letter
My brother Cypher joins for want of better:

Enter Witenough & Steady

POCK: How do do Witenough, how do do Steady
I'm very glad to see you here already
Witenough let me in ye lib'ry look
I wish to find & take from thence a book

(Pock: looks over the Manuscripts & pockets one)

Enter Firm, Hothead, Pillar & President
President takes the chair

PRES: Society's constituted, take your seats

MARS: please Sir to see on What this letter treats

PRES: (reads) To the president of the Phi: So:
With all respect I this my letter send
To let you know I can no more attend
Upon your Meetings as I soon leave town
Great obligations to you all I own,
I'm still a member tho' I am non-resident
Please so consider me good Mister President
At Compliments, you know is no great dab
Your ever gratefull friend Noah Cobweb.

Enter Cypher

FIRM: Mr. President, I beg leave to move
Some other Member shall our favour prove
And fill the place that Cobweb has resign'd
Pock'tem's the Man if I may have my mind

WIT: Second that motion, now be ye election
To Pocketum none here can have objection

POCK: Mr. President no further pray proceed
Of an examiner we have no need
Now Mr. Cobwebs going out of town
The loss is great we all of us must own.
There's Docter Deep you know has left us long since
To keep together longer would be nonsense.
There's several other Members will resign
The same intention Gentlemen is mine

I therefore move that we at once dissolve
And part by an unanimous resolve.

MARS: Second that motion

WIT: Mr. President
That sha'n't be put to vote by my Consent
Make such a motion sir & give no reason!
The motion in itself is downright treason
That Mr. Cobweb's going out of town
When Mr. Cobweb goes we tumble down
A good bar reason Sir, I think that may be
In common life t'wont satisfy a baby.

PRES: At present Sir I cannot put your motion

MARS to Pock.): We'd better wait a while I have a notion
Wait till Prim comes, wait till we are stronger
I think we'd better wait a little longer
In the meantime present him Neddy's letter
And Touchy's too, I rather think you'd better.

H.H: This is the strangest motion e'er was moved
And its necessity as strangely proved
I rather think the Gentlemen not serious
Or else they're surely both of them delirious
Mr President a motion now I make
That Docter Pillar order'd be to take
Mars by the wrist & if his pulse beats quick
We from that judge both blood and brain are thick.

MARS: You Sir in time may find that I am serious
These letters, too, will prove we're not delirious

H.H: You must not think sir that I mean to flout ye
You're right to bring Credentials about ye
For tho' I dont, yet, other Men might doubt ye.

PRES: Without more order gentlemen we stop
I therefore beg you will that subject drop.
And while I read, I beg you will attend

Or else to business I must put an end
(reads) "To the pres: Phi: Society
"My business prevents me from attending
"Upon your Meetings, therefore this I send in
"And beg you will accept the resignation
"Of your friend Touchy without indignation
This resignation do you chuse t' accept

PIL: Undoubtedly, no Man should here be kept
Not for a Moment 'gainst his inclination
Nor should his leaving create indignation

STEAD: Touchy may have much worth but we dont know it.
He has not come amongst us here to show it.

PRES: Gentlemen permit me to proceed
Another letter still I have to read
(reads) "To the Pres: &c.
"I'm sorry Sir th' apology to make
"But have nor time, nor pow'r to partake
"Th' advantages which doubtless would accrue
"From that attendance to your Meetings due
"And but for this, t' attend, I should be ready:
"With all respect, your humble servant Neddy.

H.H: There's no objection to the resignation
Let all move off that have an inclination

Enter Prim with a Dark Lanthorn.

PR: Tis monstrous dark, a dismal dirty Night

H.H: Suits dirty deeds

FIRM: You look enough to fright
A sober Citizen, If t'were my grief
T'ave met ye, I had ta'en ye for a thief.

PR: Had Thief met you, tho' no son of his Mother
He surely might have cry'd "I spy a brother"

PIL: Mr President here's a petition
This does not look like Need of a division

PRES: (reads) To the president phi: Soc:
"Fully convinc'd of what may be derived
"From a Society so well contriv'd
"For Study; humbly by this I offer
"Myself a Candidate, I nought can proffer
"But my good wishes, tho' not first at starting
"Perhaps you'll be outrun by brother Martin.
According to the laws sir this must lay
Upon the Table 'till a future day.

PR: Here sir's another letter please to read it
And then I've some proposals to succeed it.

PRES: (reads) To the pres: &c
"My avocations have so num'rous grown
"That not a moments time, I call my own
"My seat I therefore beg leave to resign
"Your Friend Demosthenes."

FIRM: Oh! most divine

MARS: The Gentlemen are falling off thats poz.

STEAD: We'll all agree that here we gain a loss.

H:H: Great Demosthenes too! Oh best of all!
If he deserts us we must surely fall
Since his admission he's been with us twice

PIL: What did he then?

H:H: Why lickt his sweet lips twice
Thrice scratch'd his arm & three times scratch'd his head
Got up, sat down again & nothing said.

MARS (to Pock:) I've told Prim all, he wishes you again
To make the Move you made before in vain

POCK: (aside) I will, they're frighten'd now I think that's plain.
I cannot, will not yet withdraw that motion
The Gentlemen now see (I have a notion)

It must be so, how can they longer meet
Sure 'tis unnecessary to repeat
The Names of those, who have to night re-
sign'd
I think we'd better break up by one mind.

PR: I think so too, of this I'm very sure
We shall make nothing of it any more
I therefore think we'd better now dissolve it
I wish the Members would at once resolve it.

H.H: Mr President, it can never be
And firmly still, shall be oppos'd by me
And many others, who with me disdain
To break an Oath or make a promise vain
How can a member reconcile t' his mind
The promise given, ratify'd & sign'd
At his admittance, with this plain attempt,
To break the bands which strongly still cement
Those who first founded, & who will support
This little structure for their own resort.
If members are displeas'd or should conceive it
Free is their choice to stay, or free to leave it.

PIL: So say I too, free let them bend their way
We need not go, because they will not stay:

CY: Good Mr. President we cannot leave it
So cleverly, I think as I conceive it.
For like a company in trade I'd make it
I think it may be so compar'd I take it
We've funds & books, if rightly I conceive it
And if we go away, why we must leave it
If we divide, why, then we will divide it
I think that right, none ever yet deny'd it
I'll preface this by saying I conceive it
Best to divide, unanimous & leave it.

H:H: Is it the property at which ye aim
To that I freely will give up my claim
Rather than parting you should make this rout
I Will subscribe a sum, to buy you out.

CY: I did not mean so

MARS: No my brother never—

PRES: To order Gentlemen, this is not clever

PR: It is of little consequence I think
So many members going, you must sink

H.H: That does not follow sir perhaps we'll rise
Dead weight remove'd, we mount unto the Skies.

PR: Well, well, I think we'll lay the matter by
For my part I resign,

MAR: And so do I

POCK: And I—

FIRM (to Prim): I beg to know Sir if you made
Use of the funds which were from me convey'd
This morning by your order, & if so
You'll please to let the president now know.

PR: Oh no Sir, no, we, sir, we did intend
To buy some books, & it was to that end
I drew upon you, but here 'tis again.
Good night—my lanthorn—I'll home thro' the rain.

Exeunt Mars, Prim, Pock: Cyph:.

PRES: Now Mister Hot-head as you are to read
We'll to our study's reg'larly proceed.
And tho' I beleive I shall be forc'd to leave you
I think this separation need not grieve you
You can pursue your study's as before
And with as much success, perhaps with more
Your institution I am sure will stand
While Virtuous pursuits unites your band
And at some future time, you'll bless our happy Land

(the End)

DIARY OF WILLIAM DUNLAP

MAY 20, 1797—JULY 26, 1797

NEW YORK CITY AND PERTH AMBOY

(Manuscript volume lettered *Memoirs 13* owned by THE NEW YORK HISTORICAL SOCIETY)

MEMOIRS 13

NEW YORK MAY 20th 1797. Rainy day and cold. Call on Johnson and Smith,[4] the latter informed me that his father had arrived in town: he is to stay at W W W's.[5] Pay Salaries &c. Went by appointment to Hodgkinson's[6] to meet Mr Whitlock; he has left his wife at Phil: having played the last season at Charleston at 30 Guineas a week. He has come on to see if our schemes admit of engaging her any way between this & next October, she being engaged for Charle[s]town again after that time. We told him that unless we should bring a Company to Philadelphia, we could offer nothing to Mrs Whitlock, & he seemed to think that there was little prospect of that. Hodgkinson informed me that he had by the wish of the commissioners sounded Jefferson as to his engaging with us in the New Theatre: Jeff: expressed unwillingness to do any thing in opposition to Mr Hallam but enquired the salary and Hodgkinson assured him as much as any other man in the Company. I blamed all this as premature; I told Hodgkinson that he ought [torn] these kinds of conversations committ

[4] William Johnson, a lawyer, and Elihu Hubbard Smith, a physician, Dunlap's most intimate friends. They were both Yale graduates, from Connecticut, beginning their professional careers in New York City. Elihu H. Smith was the eldest child of Dr. Reuben Smith, of Litchfield, Conn. Dexter, *Biographical Sketches of the Graduates of Yale College,* 2d s., 498; 4th s., 508-11, 607-8; Marcia E. Bailey, *A Lesser Hartford Wit, Dr. Elihu Hubbard Smith* (Univ. of Maine Studies, 2nd ser., no. 11).

[5] William Walton Woolsey (1766-1839) a prominent New York merchant, and brother of Mrs. William Dunlap (née Elizabeth Woolsey).

[6] For the theatrical situation at the time, Dunlap's relations with John Hodgkinson and Lewis Hallam, and the building of the "New" Park Theatre, see Dunlap's own *History of the American Theatre* (N. Y., 1832) Chap. XVII *ff.;* John Hodgkinson's *Narrative of his Connection with the Old American Company from the fifth September, 1792, to the thirty-first of March, 1797* (N. Y., 1797); G. C. D. Odell, *Annals of the New York Stage* (N. Y., 1927) I, 423 *ff.*

himself: that when we had finally settled with the Commissioners, he & I, ought to draw up some plan & then proceed upon it, to engage a Company for a stated time or number of seasons after entering the New House, at fixed salaries; and to keep such company together at certain smaller salaries untill the time of opening the New House. Read in Mitchill on contagion: Penant. After call at W W W's and find there Smith & his father a very respectable man of 60, somewhat like his son, but larger featured & taller. John Allen was likewise there. Drink tea at M: Rogers's,[7] and pass the evening at W W Woolsey's.

May 21st Sunday. Clear & warm. Read King [8] with the boy & look over the Atlas. Read Mr Erskines Pamphlet.[9] Walk out to [David] Williamson's nursery; this is the first day that I have heard any thing like a full churus of birds: the brown thrush has been for some days frequent, and the Catbird. I to-day saw several Boblinks. Call at Hodgkinson's he told me of quarrels he had had yesterday with Munto & Seymour: both complaining of ill-treatment: stupid dogs! Read Enc: Art's: Hypericum (St Johns wort): Botany: Sea-pie: Frutex: Malva: (Mallow). I believe that the bird I have called the *brown thrush* is, the Ground Mocking-bird of <*Catesby*> Lawson, the Fox-colour'd thrush of Catesby, y[e] Turdus rufus of Linnaeus & vulgarly called among us ground thresher (I suppose meaning ground thrush): it is Pennants ferruginous thrush. Pennant's Cat-Flycatcher is our Cat bird, he takes no notice of its song: it is the Muscicapa Carolinensis of Linnaeus. Enc: art:

[7] Mrs. Moses Rogers (Sarah Woolsey) was Mrs. William Dunlap's half-sister. B. W. Dwight, *Descendants of John Dwight of Dedham, Mass.*, II, 1099.

[8] The first two volumes of *A Voyage to the Pacific Ocean . . . in the years 1776-80,* (1784), were by Capt. James Cook, the third by Capt. James King.

[9] The publication of Thomas Erskine's *A View of the Causes and Consequences of the Present War with France,* from the 24th London edition, was announced in an advertisement, in the *Diary and Mercantile Advertiser,* for May 20, 1797.

Grosbeak, (Loxia). Evening violent rain & thunder. Allen & Smith pass the evening with us.

[*May*] *22d* Fine morning. Allen goes on, to take his place in Congress, this morning. Attend to a variety of business. Instruct both my children. Finish my drawing. Smith & his father dine with us. Read Fable of the Bees: preface: "his vilest and most hatefull qualities are the most necessary accomplishments to fit him for the largest, and, *according to the world,* the happiest and most flourishing societies." Does not this passage point out the author's meaning? This man clearly saw that what is termed nation[al] prosperity is, & can only be, the result of individual vice. He points out happiness as distinct from such prosperity. p: ix. Commerce, luxury & the fine arts incompatible with virtue p: 9. 1: 332, 354. I am delighted with the *fable.* Look in Enc: art: Mandeville. Dr. Smith & his son E H S came to tea: afterwards with my wife visit at And[w] Smyth's. Theatre "Mountaineers & Tom Thumb" for Miss Brett & Miss Harding: in the house 398 Ds: Hodgkinson says that [William] Henderson saw Lewis Hallam this morning & that he refuses any connexion with a Theatre where his wife cannot be employed, that he rail'd against Hodg. by the hour—said another Theatre would be built &c (all this Henderson told Hodg:) Henderson expressed his determination that Mrs Hallam should not be engaged, and said he looked upon it, that Hallam had declined any negociation & he was now ready to conclude with us.

May 23d Very fine weather. Read *King* with the boy. Read "Fable of the bees." Call on Hodgkinson to talk on business; he is gone to the Races. Call on Mr Henderson; he is out. Call at [Hugh] Gaine's, he says he saw Hallam yesterday: that there is no chance of accomodation with him, that his wife must play or he will have nothing to do with us, "and" says Gaine "if she was allowed to play she would be your destruction, this the Commissioners know." Gaine said, he asked Hallam what he intended to do; he said he did not know. Gaine supposes that he thinks to play in the old House against us. Return home; instruct the girl; read Fable &c. Mr [James] Sharpless the crayon painter called on me. Fable of the Bees. "Passions may do good by chance, but there can be no merit but in the conquest of them." p: 34. this is a great work. How forcibly does he depict the evils arising from dramshops & tippling houses & the misery of the deluded victims of vice who frequent or keep them; and surely we ought not to doubt, a moment, his meaning, when he excuses this evil as producing the great good of *adding to the national revennue.* Read *King* with my boy. Mrs Woolsey dined with us. After dinner walk, it was windy & dusty. Read Fable of the bees. May not Luxury be defined, that indulgence which is injurious to ones-self or others? if this is true, then, that definition which says "every thing is luxury that is not immediately necessary to make man subsist as he is a living creature," is false, because, much can be added not necessary to animal existance which shall encourage perfection & encrease happiness. Mandeville proves that even the excesses of luxury are no detriment to that national prosperity which the world admires. p: 65. As he makes trade the basis of national prosperity, so he makes the very existance of that trade, to depend upon vice. Drink tea at Mr Coit's the husband of Miss Howland's sister [10] & at whose house Miss Howland now stays; this was a visit from G M W's friends or relations, to the young lady as his acknowledged bride-elect. Call at M: Riley's and at Mr Sharpless's: at the latter place we saw some very curious needle work of the Lady's, a portrait of Mr Washington in black & white silk, very accurate & resembling etching.

May 24th There was again rain last night, but the morning is very fine. I called on Hodgkinson & we went

[10] Lydia Howland, daughter of Joseph Howland, of Connecticut, married Levi Coit; her younger sister, Abigail Howland, married September 27, 1797, George Muirson Woolsey, of New York, Mrs. William Dunlap's brother. B. W. Dwight, *Descendants of John Dwight,* II, 1095, 1100; F. W. Chapman, *The Coit Family* (1874), 126-127; Franklyn Howland, *Brief History of . . . Howland* (1885), 256.

to Henderson's but could not find him though we call'd several times. Hodgkinson afterwards met him and he appointed tomorrow morning to meet him at his lodgings. Read in Fable of y[e] Bees. Call on Sharpless who has hired a house on the North river side of y[e] Island about 2 & ½ miles from town where he intends to settle himself for the present. After dinner read with my boy in *King,* in Enc: art's Pomerania & Cossacks. Read Mandiville: this man is said by the Encyclopedists, to be a native of Holland, yet he writes altogether as an Englishman & certainly not as a Hollander at pages 110 & 111. Read Enc: Arts: Amsterdam & Holland & examine the map; Drink tea at M: Rogers's. Theatre "Hamlet & High life below Stairs" for Lee's benefit, in the house 303 Ds. Night rain.

May 25th Somewhat cloudy. Read King with the boy & examine the map of Russia as an accompanyment. Hodgkinson & self see Wm Henderson, and he has hired to us the New Theatre for 3 years and a half, or four playing Seasons to commence next Fall as soon as the house can be made ready for exhibitions, upon the following terms:

We are to pay on the gross receits of the house, nightly, thus,
If the receit amounts to 450 Ds: we are to pay 5 per cent, on that sum or any sum above it untill the amount of y[e] receit shall be 500 Ds when we commence a payment of 10 per cent, which continues on any sum under 600 Ds.

From 600 to 700....12½ [per cent.]
700 to 800 15
800 to 1200 17
1200 & upwards 20

We think to keep our nightly expences below 400 Ds: therefore calling the expence 400 Ds if we are confined in our receits to that sum or any thing under 450 we pay no house rent.

On 450 we are to pay	22.50
499	24.95
500	50
599	59.90
600	75
699	87.37
700	105
799	119.85
800	136
900	153
1000	170
1100	187
1199	203.83
1200	240
1300	260
1400	280
1500	300
1600	320

On a house of 400 Ds we gain nothing

449	we gain	49
450		27.50
499		74.05
500		50
599		139.10
600		125
699		211.63
700		195
799		279.15
800		264
900		347
1000		430
1100		513
1199		595.17
1200		580
1300		640
1400		720
1500		800
1600		880

I asked Henderson if he thought it would be advantageous to the property to engage Mrs Hallam, he said, "just the reverse." He recommended to us, still to hold out the idea to Mr Hallam, "that as long as he did not play in New York or join in any Theatrical scheme in N: Y: we were ready to give him a certain part of the profits of our business" to this we assented. We told him we should now proceed to forming a Company, and he said every exertion should be made to finish that part of the Theatre which is necessary for beginning the performances, and such scenery & machinery as will set us a-going in which case we offer'd to lend our part of the profits, or part of it, towards the finishing, if the Commissioners should want the mony.

After leaving Henderson I had a meeting with Hodgkinson to settle on such salaries for himself & family as should satisfy him for the term of the lease: I insisted on his own nomination of each sum and complied without hesitatation with all. The result was the following, which I copy from the paper written at the time in his front room in Fair Street

"From the time of opening the New Theatre, John Hodgkinson & Wm Dunlap undertake the Direction & management of the business, John Hodgkinson taking on himself the direction of the stage, rehearsals &c, and performing the first line of playing for the weekly salary

first for playing	20 Ds per week
for his wardrobe	5 Ds
for services as Manager	30 Ds
	55

Wm Dunlap, having a voice in the selection of pieces, acting as Treasurer & accomptant, examining, correcting, & revising, such new pieces as shall be got up, attending in conjunction with John Hodgkinson to all engagements with performers & other arrangements for the Theatre and their Mutual benefit, shall receive weekly 24.

John Hodgkinson engages for his wife Frances Hodgkinson that she shall continue her services as a performer, for the term of these agreements, *viz* during the term of the lease by which we have possession of the New Theatre, at the weekly salaries,

for play[g] & ward[be]	25
for extra wardrobe	5
	30

John Hodgkinson engages, as guardian, for Mary Harding, for her services during the above named period, at the weekly salary, for play[g] & wardrobe of 15."

I call'd on Mrs Lovegrove & paid the remaining 200 Ds on the note in her hands which I took into my possession. Sharpless & his wife with other company drank tea with us. Evening met the Standing Committee [of the New York Manumission Society].

May 26th Very fine morning. Call on Hodgkinson, he says he yesterday saw Jefferson for the purpose of forming an engagement with him, but Jefferson held himself bound to speak to Mr Hallam as last year when a seperation between H & H was in agitation he had promised Hallam not to quit him, and he promised to speak to Mr Hallam immediately. I call'd on E H S & his father. Home read in Mandeville. Wrote to Nathan Smith of New Windsor in behalf of a black woman. Read King with the boy. Call on Mrs Levy & Miss Morton, but could not see them, the first was Sick, the second, out. Hodgkinson inform'd me, that on Jeffersons asking Hallam for his determination, by which he (Jeff.) might be guided, Hallam told him that he could come to no decision untill the Commissioners of the New Theatre had *answered his proposals.* We (H & self) immediately called on Henderson to know if any proposals had been made by Mr Hallam, & he said, "no." Paid Hugh Gaine 234 Ds, on Hodgkinson's account. Pass a little time in Gahn's counting house with Roulet & Smith, & then go with the latter to see Mrs Levy & Miss Morton, but they were not to be seen. Smith & his father with Roulet drank tea with us & afterwards the Smith's & my Wife visited the Theatre. Crosby's night "Chapter of Accidents &

Tom Thumb" in the house 301 Ds:. I went to Jefferson's room and in presence of his wife, he having confirmed Hodg:s report, I told him what had passed between Mr Henderson & us; I told him that we had hired the house and that Mr Hallam had nothing to do with it; that, we must immediately make up a company, he was in possession of our terms and Mr Hallam could have no pretence for giving him an evasive answer. He promised to speak to Mr Hallam immediately. In the course of conversation, Jefferson called Mrs Hallam "The worst woman that ever lived." He said he was considered by them & their friends as one of their party.

May 27th Hodgkinson pointed out to me Mirvan Hallam's advertisement in which Mrs Hallam is announced for two characters & to speak *an occasional address.* Pay accounts & Salaries. Johnson told me that Hodgkinson had spoke to him & mentioned terms of agreement for the New Theatre, but he seems not satisfied & hints at a something to be secured to Mrs Johnson as a benefit. The terms we offer them is for him 17, her 25, total 42 Ds weekly. Home, read King with the boy & attend to Geography & spelling. My Wife is endeavouring to lead the girl to Geography. Read in Mandeville. Enc: art: Ortolan (Emberiza). Whilst reading Mandeville, W W W called & took me home with him where I dined with E H S & his Father, who leaves town this afternoon. Call on Hodgkinson, who is agitated about the necessity he supposes himself under, of playing with Mrs Hallam, on Mirvan Hallam's night, as Charles Surface is known to be his character, & Mirvan Hallam has put him in the bill. At Dinner, Smith told me, that he saw Miss Morton in the Street this morning & made an appointment for me & himself to drink tea with her & Mrs Levy, this we accordingly did, in company with Miss Susan Morton [11]

[11] Miss Eliza Susannah Morton married Josiah Quincy, of Boston, June 6, 1797. (*The Weekly Museum,* June 10, 1797). Her autobiography, *Memoir of the Life of Eliza S. M. Quincy,* which was privately printed in Boston, 1861, alludes to her friendship with William Johnson and Dr. Elihu H. Smith (page 58), but does not mention Dunlap.

and her intended husband Mr Quinsey of Boston. Home, read Mandeville. Rain, wind & thunder.

May 28th Sunday. Fine morning, instruct my children. Margaret reads in a school Geography. John as usual in King's continuation of Cook's voyage. Call on Hodgkinson, and after some conversation we agreed to meet Tyler immediately & I went to his house: he promised to meet me at Hodgkinson's in ¼ of an hour: we accordingly met & proposed to him to engage with us in the same situation for the New Theatre which he occupied in the Old. He said it was his wish & asked our terms. We answered 20 Ds per week. He said he should expect some rise on Mrs Tyler's salary which is 12 Ds, on account of her wardrobe. We did not object & he named 2 or 3 Dols in addition. He asked if Mr Hallam had any concern in the business & we answered that he had not, but mentioned our wish to have him satisfied: he said it was much to be wished: that Mrs Hallam ought to be content with enjoying a sinecure & retireing: that as to any opposition Theatre it could not be, he had no idea of any thing of the kind. Hodgkinson mentioned a wish that Tyler should make his engagement for 3 years. He parted from us saying he would think on the terms & determine.

My boy in addition to the reading he does with me has begun to day to read Sandford & Merton. Read Mandeville. Afternoon walk with my Wife & Children: Drink tea with them at W W W's.

May 29th Walk about 5 Miles with my boy. Attend to accounts. paid D Williamson 10 Ds: for trees for my orchard, which with 20 Ds p^{d} last December is 30 Ds. Read King with the boy. I drew up at Hodgkinson's wish, proposals to Hallam which, I have left with Hodgkinson for consideration: he tells me he has seen Jefferson who says Mr Hallam wishes him to defer answering us untill *after Mrs Hallam's appearance.* Read Mandeville. Smith call'd on me. Evening, Theatre: Falconer's night: "Fops fortune" changed to "Fontainbleau" on account of the indisposition of Mrs Melmoth who was to play "Louisa" in the house [blank] W W Woolsey & his wife, and Wm Johnson were at my house when I came from the Theatre about 9 O Clock.

May 30th "The Morning lowrs" An expression of Tyler's yesterday morning respecting Mr Hallam was "He is certainly a sensible man but he is very weak." Read Mandeville. Write on y[e] minutes of the standing Committee. Read Mandeville:—reflections—How disgusting would be to me now that company & that conversation which in an earlier period of my life gave me pleasure & in which I strove to shine. How preferable is solitude, to the presence of vice, unless your exertions can amend it. "O what to Man so pleasant is, as fellowship of man." but then it must be the fellowship of like to like. I remember, while in London, that having learned a new song & sung it with the applauses of my companions, I, after singing it at a club in the Strand near Charing-cross, went, tho' pretty late, to the Bucks-lodge at the pewter platter near Holborn in the hopes of being asked to sing. And many a time have I sate & listen'd to stupidity & ribaldry in the shape of song or story in the impatient hope that my turn would soon come, or that the person now exhibiting would call upon me to perform next. Read Kings continuation with my boy. Call on Hodgkinson and in his library look over Paul Sandby's views, and a work by an Italian entitled "Picturesque Tour:" We determine on the following proposals to Hallam to be sent in form of letter—thus—

"Sir

It is from a sincere wish to avoid contention that we now address you. We have engaged the New Theatre for 4 performing seasons from the time of our entering into possession. We offer—To purchase from you, your part of the Wardrobe, Music, Scenery & other properties, belonging to the Theatres now owned by yourself and us, at such valuation as shall be agreed upon by ourselves or our mutual friends: and, moreover, we offer to pay, or cause to be paid, into your hands, or any Agent's empower'd by you, one fourth of all profits that may arise to us from performance in this, or any other, City, by any Company under our Management, during the time of our lease of the New Theatre, & if renewed to us, by the proprietors, we will continue said payment during the term of our possession of said Theatre to the end of your natural life. And that you may be assured that this allowance shall be liable to as few casualties as possible, no deduction shall be made for the extra & casual expence which all Theatres are subject to, but, your ratio of profit shall be calculated, immediately after the nightly expences & rent to the proprietors, or equivalent for rent, shall be paid: the nightly expence being estimated at the same as the performers shall pay for their benefit charges; and this proportion of profits shall be paid, during the time of performing in New York at such stated period as you shall require. In return, we expect, to be left in possession of the old Theatre untill it shall be sold & a division of the proceeds take place, and also that you or your family shall not be concerned in any other Theatre or exhibition in this City, or otherwise oppose, or injure, that business the profits of which you share.

We shall expect a written answer from you, untill Thursday evening 6 OClock after which time, if we receive no answer, we shall conclude all negociation to be at an end between you & the subscribers."

To this was subjoined a statement of the terms on which we have engaged the House.

In a note we say "we mean by extra and Casual expences, all expences incurred by purchases of Wardrobe, by Scenery, repairs of houses &ca, but all travelling expences must be deducted before any division of profits can take place."

Rain. G M Woolsey had to dine with him Messrs Coit, J Aspinwall, B W Rogers & W W W. Teach the children. Evening read Mandeville.

May 31st Cold & wet. Read King with ye boy. Read Mandeville. Call at Hodgkinson's he says, he showed our letter address'd to Lewis Hallam, unto Gaine, Ten Eyck & John Shaw, who all approv'd of it: he likewise showed it to Wm Henderson, who *read it,* and much approved of it. I wrote to John Faxon of New Port respecting our leased Theatre there, desiring it to be kept unoccupied for the reception of Mr Williamson who is, by agreement with Hodgkinson, to go there with his company or part of them, and to support part of ours there, at his risque, he paying the rent of the present year. I observe that P Freneau has published, in his paper,[12] a very bad translation of the religion of *Ibrasha* from *Reuf*. Paying Accounts. The weather has become fair. After dinner I walk out to Mrs Clark's house, where Sharpless has taken up his abode. He had just returned from town and was sitting down, reading, near a closet full of books; his wife was cleaning ye house. They shewed me their pictures & her needle work. I much admired the latter but could not help thinking of the great consumption of time they must have caused; they have all the effect of fine etchings. Finding, about ½ past 4 that they had not dined I took my leave & turned my steps homeward. I had an oppertunity for the first time this spring to observe the song of the Cat bird, which tho not so sweet or so varied as that of the ground thrush (turdus rufus) is yet charmingly melodious. I have seen the Cat bird repeatedly this spring but it has been always mute. I stop'd at Williamsons nursery & found in blow a tree whose flower I sketch'd. Evening: Theatre: Mirvan Hallam's night "School for Scandal & Pannell" To see Mrs Hallams re-appearance on the stage the house was crowded with her supporters & others, whom curiosity drew thither. Her address was in rhime & written by [William] Milns. I did not arrive in time to hear it, but was told, that it was a confession of error & promise of amendment to the Audience, who received her with three cheers. Hodgkinson's appearance in Charles was marked with applause and towards the conclusion of the play Mrs Hallam seemed to be forgotten while the attention of the Audience was attracted to H & H: in the scene preparatory to the screen scene when Charles drags Sir Peter "into court" the characters were forgotten by the Auditors who applied every speech to Hallam and Hodgkinson instead of Sir Peter and Charles.

"*Sir P:* Give me your hand. I have suspected you

[12] Philip Freneau was editor and publisher of *The Time-Piece and Literary Companion,* 1797-1798.

wrongfully. I shall think the better of you as long as I live." *Charles.* "I have not seen Sir Peter a great while & I want to have a little chat with him"—and some others—were received with shouts of applause & fixed upon the men. Hodgkinson triumphed in this as the advances & acknowledgements came from Hallam. Mrs Hallam appeared pretty, but powerless in every respect, & very bad in the screen scene.

June 1st 1797. Fine weather but cool. Read with my boy in King. Write on Accounts. Call on Hodgkinson, and on E H S, look into Smith's Thucydides, and the monthly review for Jany 1797. Home teach^{g} & read^{g} in Encyc: vol: 16. Go with my boy to W W W's and bring home "Coxes Russian Discoveries:" read in it. Go to Hodgkinson's at 6 O'Clock to know if any answer had come from Hallam. Hodgkinson was gone out to ride, his wife told me that Mirvan Hallam had been from his father with a message, to know whether those proposals meant to exclude him from an engagement as a performer. I told Mrs Hodgkinson that they did not: she said her husband had replied that he did not conceive that they excluded Mr Hallam but that an engagement was open to him if he did not expect more than others as a salary, or something to this purpose; and that Mirvan H was to come back. I left a message for Hodgkinson, that I was engaged for the evening, & that to any message from Hallam he should require untill tomorrow to give an answer. In going to Mr Coit's I again call'd at Hodgk's, he had not return'd home nor had Mr Hallam sent any answer or message. From Mr Coit's G M Woolsey & my wife, Miss Howland and myself proceeded to Ricket's Circus where I pass'd some hours pleasant from my Company, not the performances. Chambers sung to please me but acted in the pantomime most rantingly execrable.

June 2d 1797. Read with the boy as usual. Go to Hodgkinson's (if any stranger was to read this might he not say are you thus constant attendant on Hodgkinson & does he never come to you? the truth is, I wish to keep my house free from visits which partake of the Theatre & particularly Hodgkinson's) he had received no further message from Hallam: I told him that as the time stipulated for an answer was pass'd we must proceed as tho' our proposals were rejected: I therefore went to Wm Johnson's to consult with him about keeping possession of the property for the support of the Company during the summer, he advised me to proceed to shipping the goods for Hartford or elsewhere without noticing Mr Hallam, taking an inventory of what we used & being ready to account for it & the use of it. I returned to Hodgkinson's, he shew'd me a letter from Boston in answer to one from him to the proprietors of the Haymarket Theatre, in which they appear willing to let him have the House for a summer Theatre & press him to come thither as soon as possible to settle terms. On an idea mention'd that the performers we wished to engage were averse to our terms as it respects benefits, very truly stating that on a house of 800 Ds, after paying the proprietors, the profit would not be so much as on 600 Ds in the present house, we went in search of Henderson to endeavour some amendment, but not finding him we went to the Theatre to see Tyler & Jefferson; the last said that Mr Hallam had last evening given him to understand that every thing would be settled & that he had received proposals which he might accept; the business of the benefits seemed to be Jefferson's only objection as it was with Tyler whom we conversed with immediately after, except that he seemed inclined to demand more salary for his wife than at our last meeting. We again went in pursuit of Henderson and met him, at length, at Gaine's, we stated the objection and he promised to consult with Polluck & Morton about it immediately. Gaine told us that Hallam had been with him yesterday & intimated that he would not accept our terms and that nothing would do but an opposition Theatre, at the same time both Gaine & Ten Eyk told us that, Brazier [13] the principal counsellor of Hallam had been there this morning, as they thought, to sound them, and intimated that Mr Hallam would be satisfied with being concerned with us in the business as a partner. Mr Hallam sent a message to us by his son. "My father's compliments to you both gentlemen, and he will to day consider on your proposal, and put his thoughts on paper, which you shall have tomorrow befor 12 OClock." "Very good, Sir," was the answer.

Call at Smith's & read in the reviews of Jan^y^ & Feby. Afternoon rain, pass an hour with Mrs Hodgkinson. Home, teach the children. Rain again. Munto call'd on me with a wish to put off his night untill tomorrow, he said Martin whose night (2d trial) is on Monday has no objection. I told him as an individual I would not object if he thought tomorrow night would do better. He went away seemingly undetermined, about 7 OClock, Hodgkinson, Martin & Miller came to my door thro' the rain: Hodgkinson with his usual peremptory tone questioned me if I had given Munto permission to postpone his play: I repeated what had past: Martin said that he did object to it, but complied for fear of being thought hard. Hodgkinson did not chuse to come in but requested me to go with him. I put on my cloak & did so. He said Munto had changed his farce to "Three weeks after marriage" and on his saying he could not play "Sir Charles Racket" for [him] had insisted on it & swore he would advertize it with Hodgkinson's name, & Mrs Hallam's for "Lady Racket." He in the walk to his house, told me that he had seen Mr Henderson who said there would be no difficulty in accomodating matters in respect to the benefits & Hodgk: having mentioned 10 percent on the gross receits, great or small, during the benefits, he intimated that that mode would be adopted: He told me that in a conversation between Henderson & Carlisle Polluck which took place before the above mention'd assurance from Henderson, Carlisle Polluck had proposed advertising the Theatre to be let to the highest bidder

[13] Philip Brasher, an attorney at law.

as if it was now disengaged: this was told Hodgkinson by Hyde [14] the keeper of the Coffee house where the words passed. When arrived at Hodgkinson's house after much railing at Munto for changing the Farce to make him play with Mrs Hallam, he proposed to me to send to the printers & order them not to change the farce in their advertisements. This I declined, saying that I had had nothing to do with Mr Munto's bills, that he had of himself advertised the Pannell with Mrs Hallam and that I should take no notice of any thing he did. He (Hodg:) now chose to rail & wish all the Theatres on the Continent on fire with oaths & imprecations. I asked him if he had not positively refused playing Sir Charles Racket? He said he had. I then advised him to forbid the printers advertising him. He said that as by my authority Mr Munto had postponed his play that I ought to interfere. I denied both premises & conclusion: but offer'd to walk with him to the printers. He said he did not choose to go out in the rain. I replied with some acrimony (and if any, certainly, too much) that he would have me "run round to the printers in the rain" (his own phrase) instead of him. He replied, with truth, that he had not proposed my going but sending. I said that I had nobody to send, that I did such things myself when I saw any necessity, which in the present instance I did not. I walked off; & thus ended this foolish conversation. Evening read Mandeville.

June 3d 1797. Cloudy morning. I am feeble & feverish. Walk with the children. Pay salaries. Munto does not change his farce: I told him in the Box office that I consider him as *now* indebted to us 300 Ds his night having passed; he answered "very well." Hodgkinson informed me, at the Theatre, that Mr Hallam had sent to him, his son, to know whether Mrs Hallam was to be engaged at the New Theatre or not & on what terms, that, he answered by saying, the proposals made Mr Hallam were

[14] John Hyde, keeper of the Tontine Coffee House, corner Wall and Water Streets. N. Y. City directories, 1797, 1798.

distinct from any negociation for engagements & that the only way to discuss such a subject would be to have a meeting. that in return Mr Hallam appointed 10 OClock tomorrow morning to meet us in the Green room each party bringing a friend. Clears up rather warmer than it has been of late. Read with my boy. Read Mandeville; in the dialogues he explains his meaning fully "No virtue without self denial." Virtue, he says, is a victory over untaught nature. This is right, it is the same as our maxim of "ignorance is vice, wisdom is virtue." He professes to set up pure christianity as the standard of virtue & to shew that National happiness or prosperity, according to common acceptation, is incompatible with such virtue, as we show by the same process of reasoning that it is incompatible with justice. (See 335, 336 &c) It appears to me, now, that when religionists & Philosophers quarrel about the qualities of human nature they misapprehend each other. The Philosopher speaks well of human nature because he speaks of what *he* contemplates in it, a capability of improvement. The religionist has been accustomed to view as man's nature what was only the effects of his ignorance. The Nature of man is evil, says one; Ignorance is evil, says the other. The Philosopher is as ready to allow that the ignorant & vicious man is odious, as the religionist can be. But the religionist says that this odious creature is only to be amended by punishment or the fear of it & that it is his nature to cling to this odious state & prefer it to virtue; whereas the Philosopher says that if ignorance is removed & the being in question, convinced, as he asserts may be done, that virtue is itself happiness, the nature of this being, is, to prefer virtue or in other words to prefer happiness.

Evening Theatre "Bank note & Pannell" for Mr & Mrs Munto. In the house Ds: 193: I had an oppertunity of looking at Mrs Hallam thro' my glass; she appeared bloated in the face, & stupid eyed & if my apprehensions do not very much wrong her, she was partly intoxicated: if she was not her playing is worse than, even, I before deemed it. Hodgkinson having engaged no friend to go with us tomorrow to meet Hallam I promised to ask Smith in the morning.

June 4th Sunday Cloudy morning: Read Mandeville. Call on Smith & Johnson, the first is to go with us. I talked over the business of engaging Mrs Hallam again by way of satisfying the party, and as Hugh Gaine says, letting her convince the public of her worthlessness. I do not like it; but Hodgkinson's fears urge him to do it. Mr and Mrs Johnson wish it, and that strenthens Hodgkinson in his wish. They all expect that her habitual intemperance will disgust the public & Mrs Johnson thinks that her popularity will be encreased by being contrasted with Mrs Hallam. Teach my Children. Read Enc: Art: Cayenne. Call on Smith before 10 but he being obliged to visit a patient, I waited for him, looking over a map with Wm Johnson & tracing Buonaparte's march. At 10 OClock S & I go to Hodgkinson's & with him to the Green room, we waited not long before Mr Hallam came in with Mr Phillip Brazier. Mr Hallam saluted us with good morning gentlemen & after seating himself and Brasier took out our proposals. He said he wished to know, whether we would engage him and his wife as performers in the New Theatre & on what terms. I observed to him that as we had made him certain proposals, if he was not willing to give an answer to them or if he rejected them, it would facilitate business if he in turn would make his proposals and leave us to give an answer. He said must look to his labour for his support, and supposed he was now to make his terms as a performer with us, the same as with Mr Wignell or any other person. I answer'd "precisely so." He looked over the proposals and observed "You say you have engaged the New Theatre for four seasons from the time of your entering into possession, but the time of your taking possession is uncertain and it appears at present to be distant, in the mean time you require possession of this old Theatre, thus you may play here again in case of the other's not being ready & instead of one half of the profits I shall only receive a fourth. I stated that it was within the verge of possibility that we might play in this Theatre but that it had never enter'd my head & certainly was not our intention. Hodgkinson stated, that the time mention'd by the Commissioners for being ready was October next, that it might be, perhaps Novr or even December, but that in the mean time we contemplated supporting the Company in Boston & Hartford. The probability of profit from the Boston plan was then discuss'd. Mr Hallam now mention'd the offer to purchase his part of the Wardrobe &c and said that it was his determination not to "fritter" away his property in that way but that all must be sold together. he then dwelt lengthily on the value of the Theatre in Philadelphia. I replied that it was not our object to buy, but to sell, that we did not look towards Philadelphia, as a place to play in. Hodgkinson now at some length would willingly have persuaded Hallam that it would be wonderfully to his interest to form a company & play at Baltimore in the Winter when Wignel was at Philadelphia & at Philadelphia when Wignel was at Baltimore. this scheme was talked over for some time but the old man, said he had no wish to take charge of a Company; that New York agreed with him better than any other place; that he must be hard driven before he left it &c and I was obliged to bring back the conversation to the present proposals. Mr Hallam reminded me that in the first proposals sent him by me, the offer was to buy all his Theatrical property & to allow him one fourth of the profits of our business. I replied that those proposals were then made, as a ground on which to negociate, that no negociation took place in consequence of them, that affairs had undergone a material change since then & that I did not consider them as any way connected with the present business. He then addressed me upon a supposition that other matters were adjusted, and pointedly asked me, whether he & his wife would be engaged. Hodgkinson was silent, & I answer'd, that "there could be no objection to engageing Mr Hallam, but as to Mrs Hallam"—I hesitated. He said, that, her engagement was a "sine qua non." Hodgkinson said that he had sent word to Mr Hallam by Mirvan Hallam, that, the engagement of Mr & Mrs Hallam depended upon the demands being compatible with the engagements already made with others. Mr Hallam said something about his salary and I immediately said it should be equal to the first salary given. Hodgkinson added that it should be the same he received. Mr Hallam said *"that,* Mr Hodgkinson, is more than I expected; as to parts I shall think nothing of such things, tho' at my time of life there may be a few I should wish to retain, but I will do any thing in my line. I will give up Hamlet and play the Ghost, I will give up Ranger and play Mr Strictland, Dogberry I will retain." Hodgkinson interrupted him to express his satisfaction. Mr Hallam proposed to me, to give in, in writing, the terms on which Mrs Hallam could be engaged & the parts she could have &c. I told him I had no objection, but Hodgkinson took it up, saying, that as to future business Mrs Hallam would have such as her standing in the Company and the line she play'd, pointed out, that he could go so far as to say that she could have, mostly, the characters she *had* play'd, but that new plays must be left to the Managers. This seemed unexpected and satisfying to Hallam. To an objection he made, that his one fourth of profits was to be shared to him after deducting an unnamed sum as benefit charges, it was answered that the sum must be fixed, & 400 Ds named as the probable amount to which he made no objection. I now address'd him concerning the purchase of the property, and told him, that if other matters could be adjusted, I would have him consider, whether he could not agree to the sale of Wardrobe &c as asked by us: that we wanted to purchase only what we could use & that if we purchased the houses &c it could only be to sell them again, and consequently we should expect only to pay what they will sell for: I told him that buying all this property was what I could not turn my mind to & pressed him seriously to consider, whether he could not reconcile it to his interest to sell what we wanted, if the other arrangements could be fixed, and let the other property remain as it was untill the favourable moment offer'd to sell for our mutual advantage. He said he *would* consider of it, and seemed to wish to determine the business in that way but to be afraid. I asked him for the time when we should receive his answer; he said tomorrow or tomorrow night. We press'd for an answer as soon as possible, that Hodgkinson might go on to Boston. We parted with civility & I suppose it pretty well understood that if he agrees to the sale of the property as demanded by us, the matter is fixed. Home: read King wth the boy. Write on the above conversation. After dinner, read with ye boy: Lie down. I am much afflicted with ill feelings and head achs. 5 OClock afternoon finish the above writing. John comes to tell me that tomorrow he is determined to begin to learn french if I will teach him. After tea read in Gibbon with my Wife & consult the Ancient Geography: Smith & Johnson came in & staid untill ½ past 9. Having been invited in the morning by Hodgkinson to sup with him on Woodcocks, I went up & spent half an hour with him at table; Martin was there with some others & I asked him if Mrs. Hallam was any ways disorder'd by liquor last night, telling him that I saw the beginning of the farce. He said she *was* intoxicated & that if I had staid the farce thro' I should have had no doubts; that it was apparent immediately to those who played with her and so much so to the Audience that many turned with disgust from the exhibition before it was concluded. Hard rain.

June 5th 1797 Fine morning. A few days McKesson's Nephew [15] accosted me in the street & said his Uncle had desired him, to endeavour some settlement with me. I told him I wished it & that it was necessary I should first know his Uncles demands, which he promised to obtain.

[15] Probably John McKesson 2nd (1772-1829), nephew of John McKesson (1734-1798). They were both lawyers in New York. See manuscript genealogical notes by William Kelby, and by William M. MacBean, in the library of The New York Historical Society.

As the following Lines are written by Mr Milns and were spoken by Mrs Hallam on what is considered as her return to the Stage they are of consequence to my Theatrical history.

"These flattering plaudits cannot fail to raise
A *wish* to merit such transcendant praise;
It can but be a *wish* for ah!—my heart
Knows *merit* could not claim its thousandth part:
But, like the lavish hand of heaven, you
Give largely, e'en tho' nothing should be due
O'ercome with joy, my anxious, throbbing heart,
Disdaining all the little tricks of art,
Conceals those feelings in a gratefull breast
Which *may* be *felt*, but *cannot* be *express'd*.
Time has now swept ten rolling years away,
Since flattering plaudits grac'd my *first* essay;
Young, giddy, rash, ambitious and untaught,
You still caress'd, excusing many a fault;
With friendly hand, safe led me thro' the way
Where lurking error watches to betray:
And shall I such advantages forego
With my consent? I frankly answer No:
I may thro' inadvertency have stray'd
But who, by folly *never* was betray'd?
If e'er my judgement play'd the foolish part
It acted not in concert with my heart.
I boldly can defy the world to say,
From my first entree to the present day,
What 'er my errors, numerous or few,
I never wanted gratitude to you.
On your indulgence still I'll rest my cause
Will you support me with your kind applause?
You verify the truth of Pope's fine line
"To err is human; to forgive, divine."

Thus was this extraordinary performance printed in Freneau's paper "the Time Piece." the marked words in italics. Read King wth ye boy; who afterwards came to me to learn the french Alphabet. Make out a list of the plays & farces performed by our Company, for the purpose of ascertaining the business of Mr & Mrs Hallam in case we engage them. Call on Hodgkinson & talk over business. Evening, Martin's second trial for a Benefit in the house 475 Ds to the "Spanish Barber" & "Two Strings to your bow." Mr Hallam took me from y[e] box lobby & conducted me to his dressing room: He there told me that he had concluded to sell the part of the property we wished if we could agree upon the terms. I remark'd that if we could not agree, there was a mode pointed out by the proposals *viz* abiding by the decision of other men; "very well," he said. He talked about salaries, & I gave him to understand that his & his wife would be of the highest. He talked about having the plan of the salaries for the company laid before him. I replied that we would agree with him as to the sum fixed for charges, & his division of profit must be on receits over that sum. "Very well, very well," he said. He now proposed that instead of his taking the last night of playing this season, for his benefit, which would be friday next, we would make up a ticket night for friday & play another week for him, letting him have the monday, there certainly could be something done for the two other nights, if I had no objections, he should be glad,—as Mrs Hallam *must have a benefit somewhere*—if not at the Theatre, at the Circus —and as the 300 Ds charges would be secured by him— he thought Mrs Hallam might have a benefit in the Theatre & take the Wednesday. I told him as to playing another week I had no objections provided it did not interfere with Hodgkinson's going to Boston for that he must go; that was agreed to. As to Mrs Hallam's having a night at the Theatre I would mention it to Hodgkinson & give him an answer. He again mentioned the possibility of playing another season in the old house. I told him that *if we did* I had no objection to engaging that he should, as now, receive half the profits. All was mighty smooth & we parted. The Spanish Barber pleased much. I mention'd the above conversation to Hodgkinson & we agreed that he might take a night for his wife & we would arrange ticket nights, one for each week.

June 6th 1797. Having for a day or two talked of a jaunt to the Falls of Pesaick, we this morning determined upon starting immediately & as soon as some little business could be fixed & the Carriages got ready we proceeded. The party is W W W's & his wife in their chaise; Benj W: Rogers,[16] and his sister Elizabeth in their Father's Coachee with my wife & me. We arrived at New Ark about one OClock and dined there, and after a very pleasant ride got to Patterson about 5. We immediately walked to the Falls, climbing the rock near the Canal, by means of a broken ladder. Our ladies had never been at the place: I revived the ideas I experienced when here with Smith & Johnson. We returned to tea to the Hotel, a large house built since I was here, where we lodge. The borders of the pesaick are colour'd by the Iris now in bloom. On the rocks near the Falls was the Kalmia, the wild Colu[m]bine & the wood pink. The settlements along the river are dutch, it is the holiday they call pinkster & every public house is crowded with merry makers & waggon's full of rustic beaux & belles met us at every mile. The blacks as well as their masters were frolicking and the women & children look'd peculiarly neat and well dressed.

June 7th I arose early & walked about the foot of the mountain; returning I fell in with Rogers, who having brought a fowling piece with him, had just killed a black bird, I presume a female from the fullness of the feathers; he soon after shot a high-hole or *Clype,* "whose plumage shone like gold," and then a King bird "Tyrant fly-catcher," this last bird has the point of the upper mandible of its bill hooked or turned downward thus  somewhat like the ashcolour'd shrike or Butcher bird. I went to the Hotel & from thence before breakfast the party crossing the river at the bridge visited the falls on the opposite side. Between 9 & 10 OClock we began our ride homeward on the opposite side of the river from that on which we came & stopped to dine at a homely Inn adjoining the Causeway between New Ark and Paules hook. We arrived safe at home about 5 O Clock.

[16] Benjamin Woolsey Rogers and Sarah Elizabeth Rogers (who in 1800 married Samuel Miles Hopkins) were children of Mrs. Moses Rogers (Sarah Woolsey), Mrs. William Dunlap's half sister. B. W. Dwight, *Descendants of John Dwight,* II, 1095-97.

Smith drank tea with us, & went with me to the Theatre to see Hodgkinson's "Knights Adventure or Man of Fortitude:" it with [*sic*] received with great apparent pleasure by the Audience & much applause. In the house 349 Ds:

June 8th Fine day. Call on Hodgkinson but he is too much engaged in preparing for an Anacreontic dinner to attend to much business. Call at M: Rogers, Benjn is sick to day. Write on Minutes of the Standing Committee. Read Mandeville. Very sleepy. Read in Wilkes view of ye Stage: Enc: Partridge. Parus or Titmouse. Pasquin. Beaumont & Fletcher's "Little french Lawyer." Enc: Negropont. The sickness of B. W. Rogers was only for 2 or 3 hours. Evening: Standing Committee.

June 9th. Cloudy & sultry. Call at Hodgkinson's. By a letter from Williamson we understand y^{t} his company is dissolved and part of them engaged with Harpur in the Providence & *New Port Theatres*. There seems to be an uncertainty of Williamson's playing in ye Fall at Boston, therefore we think that it will be best, for Hodgkinson to go to New Port on his way to Boston & either insist on the occupants taking in a part of our people, or giving up the Theatre, in the last case, Williamson & his wife will head such Company as we detach there. Our Company must play in Hartford 2 months or more & then, all united, go to Boston & play untill the house here is ready for us. We went in pursuit of Wm Henderson & at length, taking seperate routs, I found him & appointed 12 O Clock to see him at his lodgings: he was much pleased y^{t} we had settled with Hallam as we have. Mrs Hallam has advertised her benefit and says "The Managers having politely offered Mrs Hallam a benefit"!!! We appointed with Hallam 9 OClock tomorrow morning to see him & settle characters &c for him & Mrs Hallam.

At 12 OClock we met Henderson, he said that the Committee agreed to take 10. per cent on the benefits. We press'd him for some written memorandum of our agreement; he promised to speak to Polluck & Morton & have one made; tho' he said the principles of the agreement

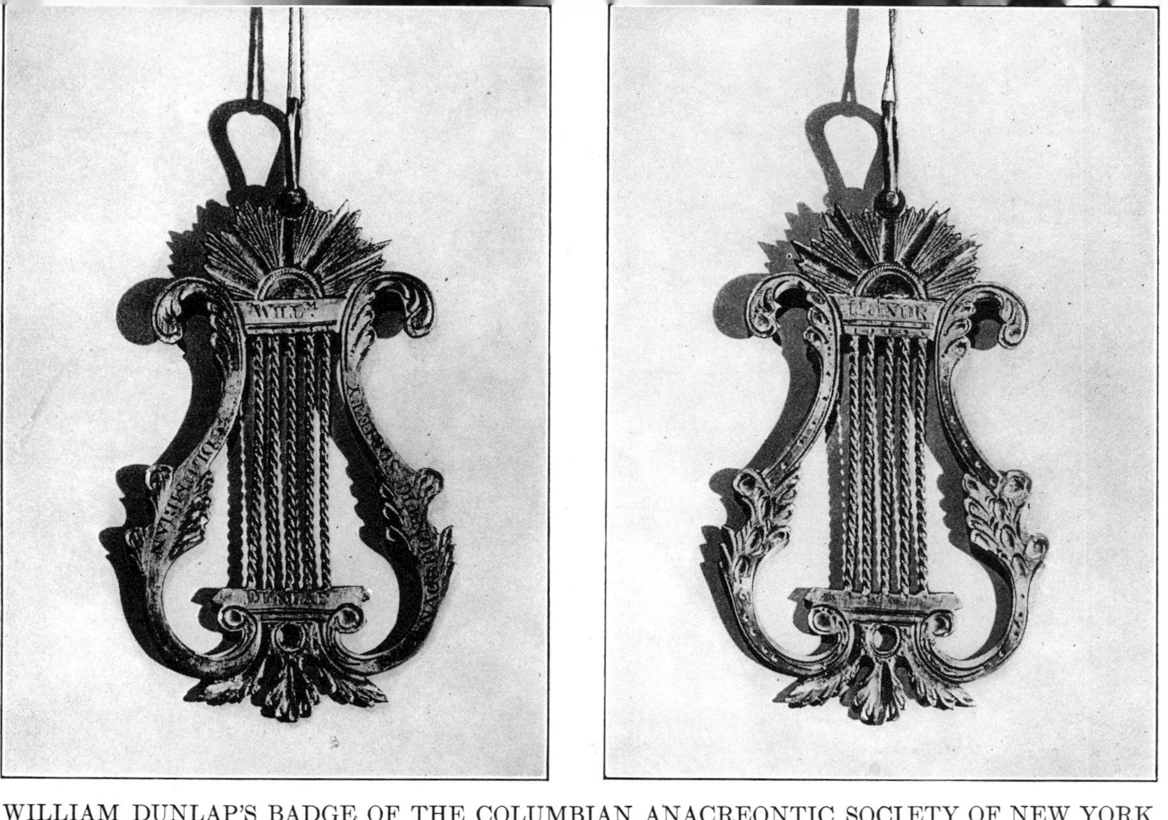

WILLIAM DUNLAP'S BADGE OF THE COLUMBIAN ANACREONTIC SOCIETY OF NEW YORK

(Courtesy of Miss Ethel Carmalt and Miss Geraldine W. Carmalt)

were very well known & agreed to by all parties. He said the Committee would expect that such monies as we could spare after opening the Theatre should be lent to them, to pay their loan from the Bank, they paying us interest. We made no objections. Henderson press'd the necessity of adding to the Company another good man singer instead of Munto & an Irishman, saying that Collins could not be tolerated. Teach my children before & after dinner; the Girl, Geography of New York, the boy attending; The boy, King, Geography & spelling. We had a pine apple at Dinner, the boy asked for the seeds, after dinner we examine the Enc: art Ananas, Bromelia & the culture. Write on Minutes of ye Stand^g Comm:. At the request of my boy I take the children to a bookstore and purchase a small abridgement of the history of England for them. Read in *Morse*. Evening Theatre "Way to get Married & Tom Thumb" a ticket night at which times certain persons are permitted to sell tickets & half the amount of each ones sales is his profit; In the house Ds 324 by which we lose upwards of Ds 90. part of ye evening at W W W's.

June 10th Attending to business. Hodgkinson is preparing for his departure for Boston this Afternoon & I with my Wife & Children to Amboy for a day or two.

AMBOY. We arrived here about half past 8 OClock. We left N: Y: a quarter before 4, found Mr Van Duzer's Waggon in waiting for us, and proceeded very pleasantly over Staten Island, in the coolest part of ye day on a good road lately mended. The blackberry bushes are loaded with blossoms: the farmers complain that their maize has been taken up by the birds before it had time to sprout. My expences are 5/ ferryage to Staten Island. 16/ stage hire to Amboy ferry. 3/ ferryage to Amboy: and 2/ porterage. *total* Ds: 3.25. Call to see Mrs Terrill & Mrs Brown.[17]

[17] Mrs. John Terrill (Sophia Watson-Waterhouse) and her daughter, by her first husband, Dr. John Waterhouse, Mrs. John Brown (Sophia Waterhouse). See Whitehead, *Early History of Perth Amboy*, 128; W. N. Jones, *History of St. Peter's Church in Perth Amboy*, 214, 486, 496.

June 11th 1797 Sunday. Still fine weather. After breakfast walk with my Wife & children up to the hill, over my little farm and to Aaron Bloodgood's & return home about 12 OClock. John has brought his history of England with him to which he pays great attention. My Wife has brought with her "Leonidas." W W W carried Ossian with him to Pesaick & on our return I read one of the poems to the company at his request while at ye house by ye Causeway. Read in Leonidas. Afternoon at Mrs Terrill's. Evening walking & at Mr [James] Parker's, part the family are at one of his farms called Tulip hill, the old Lady, Betsey & Gertrude are at home.

June 12th Go out with my Gun. Stop'd at Corrington's, cross over to my Orchard; but three trees have fail'd of 120. Kill 5 snipe, 3 red wing'd black birds, 2 Larks and a Bittern. I chas'd & caught, without injuring, a young *Killdeer,* tho' unfledged it ran very fast: there were two in Company: Do they breed but 2 at a time? Young birds of many kinds are beginning to take flight. The wild rose, Iris and blackberry blossom are the most conspicuous flowers in the fields. Afternoon read in Glover's Leonidas. Evening walk.

[June] *13th* Walk with my boy. Visit Mrs Parker and Major Skinner. After dinner very warm, read Leonidas. Gust of wind with a little rain. Drink tea with the Parker's. Call at Mr Ravaud Kearny's: he wishes me to buy his land on the hill, adjoining mine & the place on which I wish to build when I can: he says there is 10 & a half acres and asks £150 for it. My feelings have been delightfully better since my coming hither.

June 14th 1797. Up by half after 4 & picking Currants & Gooseberrys in the Garden, to bring with us to New York for pies. About 7 OClock we left Amboy, were detain'd untill past 8 by *Butler* at the opposite ferry: after a pleasant ride arrive at Van Duzer's & get home at half past 1 OClock. Call at M: Rogers's & W W W's. Evening

Theatre Mrs Hallam's benefit "Young Quaker & Three Weeks after Marriage" In the house 300 Ds: Mr Hallam last monday night had in ye house 230 Ds:

June 15th Walk out to Williamson's with my boy. Read with both the Children aided by Maps. Call at Hodgkinson's; his wife says he did not get off for Boston untill Sunday Morning 8 O'Clock. She says Mrs Hallam was so far intoxicated last night that she was drenched with quarts of tea before they ventured her on & when she did appear her situation was plainly discernible & noticed by the Audience. I call in at the Theatre a few Minutes. Call at Smith's he was reading "Political Justice for the first time tho' so well acquainted with the doctrines; he is much disatisfied with the fifth book. Read in King with the boy. Smith dines with me & we read in Mandeville. It is very warm. Mr J Heard from Woodbridge has come to town & puts up with us. Thunder shower, the first rain, sufficient to lay the dust, since the 4th Instant. Evening, pleasant; Call at Mr Hobson's & Mr Coits, not at home: pass an hour with Miss Alsop, Mrs Riley, Wm Johnson & Smith. Read in Enc: Art: Bittern —genus Ardea, order Grallæ. Pennant Arctic Zool: Bittern.

June 16th Finding it necessary to borrow some mony untill next Fall or winter I with considerable difficulty brought myself to request the assistance of Mr Rogers, he says he has in his hands Ds 1000, belonging to Mrs Smith of Stamford which he thinks I may have but he must first write to Major Davenport. Read with John. Call at the Theatre & order preparations for packing the Scenery & wardrobe. Go with Saml Bowne to collect subscriptions for the use of the African free school, an irksome business, we got near a hundred Dols. Hear Margaret read. Read Mandeville. More rain & thunder. Evening Theatre: Ticket night: Inkle & Yarico & Miss in her teens, closing a long season. Gamage conversed long with me respecting the sale of the Land on which the

Theatre stands, he says a person has been with him who wishes to purchase: I should judge that he wants to speculate on it, but that he gives me what I think a high valuation of it Ds 10000. We lose upwards of a hundred Dols: to night. Read in Morse.

June 17th paying Salaries. Read with the boy in King. Read in Morse. Mr Saltonstal a young man of good sense & an improv'd mind call'd on me & is to dine with me tomorrow. Mr Hallam appointed Monday to call on me & look over the books. The people are packing up at the Theatre. Noon; a shower, slight & succeeded by a hot sun. After dinner read Mandeville. Read with the boy in King which leads us to examine the Enc: art Balæga [*sic*], the battle of the sword fish with the Whale: with the Girl, Geography of ye United States. I am giving the boy some Idea of Arithmetic. Read in Morse. 5 OClock hard shower in the beginning accompanied with hail, wind about north, continuing 10 minutes. Mandeville says that he wishes to expose the vileness of Man's nature because "the more we are persuaded y^t^ the greatest excellencies that ye best of men have to boast of are acquired, the greater stress it will teach us to lay upon education." there is great good sense in this, as in the greater part of this excellent work. Drink tea at M Rogers, W W W, G M W, Smith & others there. Go to Hodgkinson's to see his wife, the Johnsons there.

To Virtue

Fairest amongst the fair thou art,
Queen, Mistress, Empress of my heart,
Elected Sovereign, from whose sway
Folly oft leads my mind astray.
Tis thou, & thou alone hast powr,
To give what every mortal craves,
Yet from thy arms I fly each hour,
And shun the certain bliss——

What a whim is this!—for me to be rhyming at 11 OClock—Yet sure some verses of this kind (not quality) in praise of virtue might do some good.

June 18th Sunday. Attending to the outline of the history of England with John in his abridgement & ye Encyclop:. Acc^{ts}. Rain last night & to day untill 9 OClock; still cloudy. Read King with the boy & examine the Maps corresponding; his mind is attracted to a great variety of objects during these lessons & by answering his questions my mind is exercised & my knowledge encreased. Collins call'd to inform me that in a vessel arriv'd from Providence R: I: has come three of the proprietors of the Boston Haymarket Theatre, Osborne, Gardner & Blake, that they miss'd Hodgkinson, who pass'd them on the way. I call'd at Mrs [Ann] Anthony's boarding house to see the above gentlemen & being shewn into a room where several were, I enquired for Mr Blake, a gentleman answered to the name and I asked him if he had had any correspondence with Mr Hodgkinson concerning the Theatre? He said, no, but probably a relation of his Mr Geo: Blake had. He politely added "but I can introduce you to one of the proprietors," turning to him "Mr Gardner" Mr Gardner rose & I introduced myself to him: Mr Blake then introduced me to Mr Osborne. I told them of Hodgkinson's journey, they knew of the negociation begun by Blake; Osborne said there was no doubt of Hodgkinson's obtaining the Theatre "and on his own terms"; said that they wished him to play there as long as he could in the Fall, that, he would have full houses, the people were tired with the mismanagement of the Companies there; that Hodgkinson alone is worth them all, tho' there were some pretty good Actors if they had minded their business; Barret, but he had behaved very ill. I mention'd our Company's staying awhile at Hartford, but they both wished it to go immediately to Boston. I invited them to dine with me tomorrow & they accepted the invitation. Saltonstall dined with us & John Aspinwall came in afterwards & the conversation turned on religion—this is to be [illegible].
Call on Mrs Hodgkinson to communicate the news respecting Boston. Rain in violent showers & some thunder. Read Mandeville. He says p: 488. "if men were swayed

in their actions by the principles they side with, and the opinion they profess to be of, all atheists would be devils & superstitious men saints" Atheist & Deist is much the same with him, he says he means one who denies a providence & future State: there is great ignorance shewn in this passage. He asserts that it is very extraordinary, if not a proof of the truth of revelation, that Moses should conceive an idea of *one god* among a people of gross idolators: but the Chinese are idolators, e i the vulgar, but the learned are said to be Deists and even Atheists, and it is to be believed that the Egyptians had the notion of a first cause, either in common with, or derived from the Indians, long before Moses. I had yesterday some agreeable conversation on man, & society, with Saltenstall: Has not the human race so far progressed towards wisdom, as to have become ashamed of ignorance? Does not this cause those varied diguises which seem to be the basis of polished society? Will not Man throw off these disguises, and, content with nothing short of real wisdom, advance rapidly to the attainment of it?—Finish the Fable of the Bees. Read in "The rights of Woman." Henry Mitchill & his amiable wife call to see us.

June 19 Messrs. Gardner & Osborn, going on to Philadelphia at 1 O'Clock, excuse themselves from dining with me. Read Geography with my little girl and King with the boy. Attending to the business of the Theatre. Smith dined with me: we are to walk out to Sharpless's this afternoon, my wife, with M: Rogers's family, rides. Reading Mrs Woolstencroft: she has much strength of mind, tho' her piety & philosophy appear a little, or perhaps not a little, incongruous. Smith mention'd a newspaper paragraph mentioning the Marriage of Wm Godwin to Mary Wollstoncroft. Walk out to Sharpless's & pass some time very pleasantly. After walking home, I went with my wife to Mr Coit's to see Miss Howland.

June 20th Writing on accounts. Read with my boy & Girl. Call at Theatre & Hodgkinson's. Call at E H S, to crave his assistance in obtaining subscribers for the School: he read to me his review of Barton's memoir on y[e] Rattlesnake, to be publish'd in the medical repository of Mitchill, Miller, & himself: he likewise read to me several verses, lately composed; Kent came in: he has promised me to come down to Amboy with his wife to see us this summer. Bo[t] of Smith, Bartrams travels p[d] 12/. Call on one De Grove in behalf of a Black woman & children but could not see him. Hodgkinson has returned but has gone to bed for rest. Call at Mr Coits to see Miss Howland. Walk some distance in the street with Miss Morton & appoint tomorrow afternoon to drink tea with her. See Hodgkinson. He has secured the New Theatre Boston for 4 Seasons The following is the agreement

"Memorandum of an agreement enter'd into at Boston this 16th day of June 1797, by & between John Winthrop, Caleb Stimson, Joseph Blake jun[r] & George Blake all of said Boston being a major part of the Trustees of the Haymarket Theatre in said Boston, on the first part & John Hodgkinson of the City of New York for himself & William Dunlap of said New York of the second past witnesseth

The parties of the first part for themselves and the proprietors of said T do hereby contract & agree, to & with the parties of the second part that they shall use occupy & improve all that Building called y[e] H: T: being all the parts thereof which have been used as a T: meaning to except the cellar under the same for & during the period of 4 Seasons including this present season each season to consist of sixty playing nights, commencing in June or July & terminating in October or November & also during the period aforesaid to use occupy & improve all the Wardrobe scenery & machinery which at present belong to said T: & all the other utensils in the same, and the said parties of the first part do further contract & agree to & with the said parties of the second part that said T: during said period shall not be employed as a Theatre or plays pantomimes or rope dancing or any other kind of public exhibition be performed therein by any other company unless by the consent in writing of said parties of the second part. And said parties of the second part on their part for themselves their heirs *ex a admin* do covenant and agree to & with said parties of the first part that will take and improve said T: the period aforesaid on the terms aforesaid & in consideration of the premises will well & truly pay, or cause to be paid to the parties of the first part or any other agents of said Proprietors as rent therefor ten per cent upon the gross receipts of said Theatre subject to no deduction for any expence or any other thing whatever which said sum shall be paid to them at the expiration of each and every week, & that after the present season in case said parties of the first part shall so elect they will well & truly pay or cause to be paid to them in lieu of said *ute* of ten per cent the sum of Fifty Dollars for each & every night of performance each season to consist as aforesaid, & s[d] parties of y[e] second part do further covenant & agree as *fasaid* to & with said parties of the first part, that at the expiration of said 4 seasons they will peaceably & quietly surrender the possession of said T: as well as all the wardrobe scenery & machinery & other utensils to said parties of the first part or any other agent of said proprietors in as good order & repair as the nature of the business will admit, meaning further to except from said Theatre stands in the Lobby for one or more persons to sell fruit & other kinds of refreshment which have heretofore during the last season been occupied as such "it being further understood that a few admission tickets as the last season is also to be *issued* for each & every share held by s[d] proprietors"

The penalty mentioned is 10000Ds: & it is signed by the persons mentioned in the beginning: witness'd by *Em*[l] Jones & William *Howll.* The words under which I have made lines I can not be certain of owing to illegible or bad writing. Agree with Capt[n] Hempsted to carry the Theatrical goods to Hartford. Drink tea at M: Rogers, Mrs Coit, Miss Howland, Miss Huntington whom we had seen at Stamford last winter were there as was W W W & wife who came home with us & pass'd the evening.

June 21st 1797. Part of the morning with Smith: then with Hodgkinson we agreed upon some business & I receiving a message from Mr Hallam went to the Theatre, he wanted his account I told him I had not had time yet to close the books and must have some days, he enquired concerning Boston, I told him that we had obtained the Theatre at 10 per cent on the receits, he said, it was "a Damn'd deal of money." He asked the time we intended the company to stay there this season, I said, untill the New Theatre was ready, then he'd be damn'd if we play'd here this winter" I told him I might be mistaken but I expected we should have possession by December. He said we had better have carried the company to Philadelphia. I asked him to go with me & meet Hodgkinson to settle respecting Mrs Hallam's characters: we met in the green room, some characters that Hodgkinson insisted on her keeping if she played, she (after his going to her) consented to play & other matters were explained. Hodgkinson asked him how he intended spending the summer giving him to understand that Mrs Hallam could not play at Boston: he intimated a design to come to Boston & play, but promised his determination. I told him I should give him an inventory of the Wardrobe &c. He intimated that he had thoughts of purchasing the old Theatre & ground. On returning to Hodgkinson's we had an interview with Tyler & finally agreed to give him 22 Ds for himself & wardrobe & 15 for his Wife & her wardrobe, weekly. I agreed that Hodgkinson should receive 50 Ds as performer & manager during this season at Hartford & Boston, & he agreed that I might bring forward a play each season & receive the whole profit of a third night. Hodgkinson brought me a letter from Mr Munto in which he tells us that he is willing, in consideration of the debt he owes us, to continue his services, provided he is no longer to be *insulted* by the business which is given him, that he must not be expected to play such parts as Woodville, "Wheel of Fortune" Captn Dudley, Col^{l} Dormont, &c &c &c that he must have the *whole* second line of Opera: that Mrs Munto expects *some regularity of business* & that they must have more than 22 Ds per week, finally if this meets our approbation *he shall want* 30 or 40 Ds!!!! Take Pelisiers Music for "Sterne's Maria" in my hand to carry to Miss Morton & call on Smith, after passing an half hour with him, he went with me to Mr Morton's where we agreeable pass'd the first part of ye evening; we then went to W W W's & staid there, my wife having preceded me, untill near 10 OClock, on returning home S sup'd with us. I am anxiously awaiting ye loan of 1000 Ds from M: Rogers.

June 22d Walk on ye Battery where I found Mrs Hobson & one of pretty little folks. M: Rogers has let me have Ds 600 for which I have given my note payable in 90 days with lawfull interest. Read in King with my boy. Go to Hodgkinson's for the expediting of business. Agree that Falconer shall go on with Hodgkinson as Box Office keeper, treasurer, & Book-keeper at a salary of 18 Ds per week. We go in search of Wm Henderson to get from him a memorandum of our agreement with ye Trustees but can not find him. I let Munto know that as he is in no want of an engagement by what he says in his letter (his words are "I am not Distrest for a Situation") and as we conceive by the whole tenor of his letter that he does not think of remaining with us, I would take his note for his debt & not trouble him any farther. Miller who join'd the Comp: at Hartford last year seems disatisfied with his situation & talks somewhat of quitting & trying his own profession Bookselling & Binding: I rather advised him to it. Hodgkinson received a letter from Mr Winthrop, Boston, requesting our permission for Powell, late manager, to take a benefit night in the Theatre we have hired. We wrote in answer our assent. Williamson writes to Hodgk: that the proprietors of the Federal Street Theatre are much chagrin'd at his having taken of their opponents, the Theatre which has so much hurt them: He wishes to have authority to point out a plan to avoid opposition, that he may be enabled to secure the Fed: St: Th: for himself. Hodgkinson has written to satisfy him and the gentlemen of the old Theatre assuring them that if they allow us 5 months in the years, summer & fall, the winter months & spring, e i, the remaining 7 will be secured to them without opposition. Advises Williamson to make a cheap establishment for Hartford & hints at letting him have the Philadelphia Theatre for the Fall; as we understand Wignell will be in Baltimore. Afternoon Mr Hallam call'd on me, asked about what plays would be done in Hartford, I told him I did not know. he said he supposed principally new & that he should not be wanted there—that, he understood

Wignell would remain at Baltimore untill winter & having mentioned Williamson, I started the Idea of some use being made of our property in Philadelphia by putting Williamson in there, with a good company: He seemed much to approve the idea, & he having in one or two instances talked as if he considered Mrs Hallam now a member of the company, I wished an immediate conference in Hodg:s presence & proposed his walking with me up to Hodgkinson's to talk over the arrangements for Phil:. He excused himself, and I then made an appointment with him for the morning in the Green Room. We call to day at Henderson's after 3 OClock, but the great man being at table, sent us out word, that he would see us at 9 tomorrow morning.

June 23d We waited on Wm Henderson & presented for his signature a memorandum of our agreement with himself Jacob Morton, & Carlisle Pollock as heretofore stated; he read it more than once, said it was right, but declined signing it untill he had consulted the above mentioned Gentlemen. At half past one tomorrow we are again to see him. Henderson wished it left undetermined, but I told him that I did not choose to proceed any farther upon uncertainty and stated that altho' they, the proprietors, were proceeding only in the manner they would have proceeded without any bargain with us, yet we were entering into risques & expences in consequence of the agreement that were very serious. He allow'd the propriety of the argument. We met Mr Hallam & he enter'd into a scheme by which he & his wife are to be employ'd at Phil: with Williamson &c &c during the Fall & untill we open here. He agreed to go to Hartford to meet Williamson & settle the arrangements. I asked him if he had the paper with him which contained our proposals. He said he had not. I told him I wished to refer to it, as we were all together, that there might be no misunderstandings. He said it was all very plain, that we all understood the division of profits which was to take place—adding you never intend to play in this house again. Hodgk: answer that we should not & went on to state the probabilities of ye New house being finished in good time. In speaking of the Philadelphia scheme, I mentioned to Mr Hallam, that as our agreement with him only went to his giving us the possession of the old house in New York, any business done in the house at Philadelphia would be at the risque of the proprietors according to their interest in the property & the profits divided in such proportion. He said he understood it so of course. About two hours after the preceeding conversation I met Mr Hallam at the door of the Theatre, he said he was seeking me; that on examining into the intelligence concerning Wignels stay at Baltimore he found it amounted only to his having permission to play there 10 Weeks, and upon the probability that he would come to Phil: after the expiration it would be wild to think of the scheme: I parted from him to communicate this to Hodgkinson who did not seem much pleased with Hallam's conduct, but said if Mr Hallam did not join in the scheme he might be idle this summer. Munto gave me his note for the sum due from him & I sent him to Hodg: to talk about a farther engagement. I had just dress'd myself for dining a[t] W W W's, when I received a message from Hodgk: requesting me to step up to his house immediately: It rain'd but I went. What was it for? He had received a message from Munto that he would wait on him & had appointed this hour (3) for him & me to meet him. I told him that he could arrange matters as he thought fit with Mr Munto & pleading my engagement left him. Dine at Woolsey's with Miss Alsop & Miss Howland, Betsey Rogers & B Woolsey Rogers, G M W, my wife & Doctor Wells. Evening clear. The weather has been of late remarkably cool. Old Doctor [John] Bard drank tea at W W W's, he is upwards of 82 years of age, and a very pleasant companion; full of anecdote and remarkable for politeness.

June 24th Munto call'd on me & says he has settled every thing with Hodgkinson & goes on with him.

Mitchill breakfasted with us. I call'd on Hallam & paid him 120 Ds. Settled a variety of business. Call with Hodgkinson on Henderson, Carlisle Pollock was with him: he produced the following as a memorandum of our agreement & promised that on Jacob Mortons return to town the signatures should be placed to it: we being in the mean time to have it copied, and Hodgkinson's signature affixed & left with me.

"Memorandum of an Agreement between Carlile Pollock, Jacob Morton, Edward Livingston & Wm Henderson on behalf of the Proprietors of the New Theatre in this City for the first part and John Hodgkinson & Wm Dunlap Managers of the Old American Company of Comedians of the second part.

The parties of the first part agree to rent to the parties of the second part, the said Theatre and the property belonging to it for the term of three years and six months to be computed from the time the same shall be ready for Theatrical exhibition, on the following terms and conditions viz

That there shall be at least one hundred nights of performance (unless some public calamity prevents it) in each season between the 1st of October and 10th of June.

That the parties of the second part shall pay to the parties of the first part weekly upon the gross receipts of each night of performance, except Benefit nights, at the following rate

On any sum from 450 to 500 Ds, 5 per centum

do	500	600	10	do
do	600	700	12½	do
do	700	800	15	do
do	800	1200	17½	do
do	1200 to any higher sum 20 do.			

And on Benefit nights (which are never to exceed 27 in any one season) there shall be paid 10 per centum on whatever sum the gross receipt of each night may be

The parties of the first part reserve the right of making such disposition of the rooms in the front of the Theatre (one for a Box office excepted) as they may judge proper

Previous to the parties of the second part, taking possession of the premises this agreement shall be drawn up & executed in legal form and such other provisions inserted as may be judged necessary to fulfill the intentions of the parties respectively

The parties of the second part engage that during the time they occupy the New Theatre the Old house in John Str[t] shall not be opened for any Theatrical exhibition whatever with their consent

or concurrence and they stipulate that they will not dispose of their interest in that property upon any terms in which a condition to that effect shall not be included.
New York June 24th 1797

The paper from which I have copied the above is drawn up by & in the hand writing of Wm Henderson and assented to by Carlile Pollock in whose presence it was delivered to us. Our goods sail for Hartford. Read "Rights of Women."

June 25th Sunday. See Hodgkinson & wife off about 7 OClock. Ride to *Belevue* with G M Woolsey & my boy: this is the place Kemper used to keep. Gill is with me copying the inventory of our Wardrobe. Read *King* with my boy. "Rights of Women." Visit at Mr Coits & Riley's to see the females of the families, with G M Woolsey. Call on Miss Morton: she is much pleased with Maria's song in my opera (the music). Read Enc: art: Magnolia. The Magnolia Glauca is now in bloom. Ex[a]mine Gill's inventory. Smith & Johnson pass the afternoon with us. Evening my Wife & self pass an hour with Mr & Mrs Hobson.

June 26 1797. Write on minutes of ye Standing Committee. Accounts. Borrow money for the first time of a Broker and gave my note at 60 days from this date for 500 Ds & received 475 Ds being 2 & ½ per ct. per month. A very warm day. Read a little in Gibbon & Mrs Wolstencraft. Smith a little while with me. Evening Miss Howland & G M W call'd on us & we went with them to M: Rogers's & W W W's.

June 27 Clear weather & warm. Rec^d from Saml Coates of Phil: a Copy of the last Convention's proceedings with an account of the manner in which the French Consul proceeding respecting a black held in slavery by a French man in Phil: Summoning the parties, he enquired of the pretended master "Are you a french citizen?" "Yes." "No French Citizen can hold a slave." To the black "You are free" and gave him a certificate of the same. Write on Acc[ts]. Mrs Hallam play'd last night at Rickets's Circus & I find the people think she disgraced herself by it. Very warm; noon a shower; but after still very warm. While busily employ'd with my account books Hallam came in. I told him I should by tomorrow morning be able to make out the accounts—he said that he was going sooner than he at first intended—that he should start on thursday morning and should like to have a rough draft by which he could estimate what was due to him. I told him that I believed there was cash due to him Ds: 623. He seemed very well satisfied. I told him that Hodgkinson had overdrawn me very much & tho' I held myself accountable to him, I should be glad if he would only draw on me for enough to bear his expences or as little as possible & leave the balance untill the opening of the Boston Theatre, for that *then* we should be in cash whatever the result of the season might be. He said "certainly" and even then he should not want more money than his salary. I asked what money he should want? He said Ds 300. I said he should have it. He said he did not fully understand the Boston arrangement. "Are things to *remain* as they *now are* untill the opening of the New Theatre here?" I thinking he meant the company's salaries answered "*yes.*" "Ah very well" says he "very well *that's* what I wanted to know." It immediately occurred to me that I was not understood & I added "I beg your pardon, dont let me be misunderstood; We, Mr H & self, consider our connection with you as at an end; our partnership is dissolved & the books & accounts closed. We now have made up & are supporting a Company at our own risque altogether." "Ah very well" says he "then from this time I am to share one fourth of the profits." "No, Sir," I replied "I certainly do not understand it so, you have no share in the profits untill the opening of the New Theatre according to the meaning and I believe the words of our proposals, to which you agreed." "I certainly did not understand it in that light," said Mr Hallam "*that* makes a very material difference with me, I do not know whether it will be worth my while to go so long a journey as to Boston merely for my Salary." "Sir" I answered "as to profits from Summer business much, if any, is not to be expected, but you will recollect, at the time we sent in our proposals to you, we had not the Boston Theatre: Our intention was to support at our own risque a Company during the summer fit for entering the New Theatre next winter & we offer'd you one fourth of the profits of all our business after that time. I have a copy of ye proposals in my pocket" & I took out this book "O" says he "I have the letter, tho' I had it not in my pocket when you ask'd me for it before" alluding to the conversation at the Theatre on ye 23d Instant. I read over the necessary part of the proposals. "You are right, those are the words, you are right" he repeated "tho' I did not understand it so." "As to profits" I remarked "from a summer expedition I imagine they will not be worth disputing about; if we can clear ourselves I shall be well satisfied." He said, "being upon mere salary was but poor business" I replied "that we ought not to expect much between play^g season's, that he would be better off this than last, year, as he risqued no loss; whereas last year we lost considerably." He ask'd how long the company would play in Hartford, I told him 2 weeks, playing 10 nights. He asked if the company were to have double salary. I said certainly not: that it had been customary for us to play occasionally 4 nights in a week here & if we played only 2 we payed the same. He said he knew it, "but" says he "some of the people expect it & if it is not done there will be a scism in the Company." I replied that I could not conceive that any of performers would be so unreasonable or so unjust; that they must know that we kept up the comp: at Hartford without chance of emolument and at great risque of loss, that if they were paid the same at Hartford as at N: Y: they were greatly paid, for as to playing 5 times in a week when there was no study or any trouble but to go on & speak what had been prepared at N: Y: it was not more if so much as play^g in the usual mode with the usual attention to getting up new pieces, and, that if the demand was made in the manner he seemed to fear, I would not consent to it, but rather give up any part of the Company. I now enter'd on the subject of the property in John Street & press'd the necessity of a sale: he talked of buying & said, if he did so he should improve the property for building on, remarking that at any rate, he understood, the terms of the sale would prohibit any kind of public exhibition on the spot. I mention'd Gamage's plan of selling off the old house, dividing the ground into lots &c he said he thought it was likely to answer best & agreed that Gamage is a good judge of such affairs: I asserted that the property would sell better now than hereafter, which he thought probable, & I press'd ye appointing some person as an agent to transact the business; to this he gave no direct answer, but having complained of the account sent him by Hodgkinson which remained without explaining & of his being left responsible for the property by Hodgkinson's not taking up the Bonds, I told him that a sale of the property in John Street would enable Hodgkinson to fulfill his agreements in that respect. When he was going I told him I would see him tomorrow about 10 OClock & we would consult Gamage further on the business. "Very well" he replied "but what has passed this afternoon has altered my determination, I shall not go so soon as I intended, I shall not leave town before monday at any rate.

Drink tea with my wife & children at Mr Coit's; evening call at W W W's. Hallam mentioned this afternoon certain information that Wignel returns to Phil: to play in Septr. He suggested an idea that as he was not to share profits at Boston perhaps he would stay at Hartford with Williamson.

June 28th W W W and wife leave town for Northampton. Write to Hodgkinson the above conversation with Hallam. G M W goes on to day with Miss Howland to Norwich & from thence *he* goes to Boston: I have given him a letter to Saml Cooper whose attention to me when there I remember with pleasure. Endeavouring to settle

Crosbie's business: I have offered to pay 50 Ds more for him rather than surrender the wretch to a jail. Bo^{t} of Hugh Gaine, Hume's hist: of Eng: with Smollet's continuation making in the whole 21 vols: Duod: at 7/ ye Vol: Read with the boy Humes life & Kings continuation. Afternoon at Johnson & Smith's. Buy at [John] Fellows's Paine's Agrarian Justice & read in it. Drink tea with Mrs Woolsey our mother. Walk with Johnson & Smith; see the Magnolia Glauca in bloom: a tree more than 20 feet in height & spreading. Evening: a fire destroys a Brewery, near the *Colleck*.

June 29th Walk with my boy out to Williamson's. Call on Gamage. He says that he had a talk with Hallam by appointment yesterday & advised him to purchase the John Street property; & intimated that Hallam would do it. I asked him if he knew any person who would transact the business of negociating the sale and he offered himself. He mention'd as his valuation of the property £3400. I reminded him of the valuation he had before made of 10000Ds or £4000. He said he should better be enabled to judge in the course of to day, as some lots equal to ours were sold yesterday. Call on Johnson & Smith & bring home with me T Dwights letter on Religion & Smiths answer both of which I read aloud to my wife. Read King with my boy. Read in Rights of Woman. Creech's Lucretius. Enc: Art: Java. Smith's manuscript Memoirs, the vol. which contains his letter to Dwight. Very warm to day. Read "Rights of Woman." Read Adam Smith's letter which is published in ye octavo edition of Humes England, immediately after Hume's little history of his own life, and which is from stupidity or superstition omitted in the Duod: edit. which I have just purchased. Evening walk on the Battery. *Young* [18] formerly a bassoon player in our orchestra has this evening shot a constable thro' the heart who had arrested him for debt: he is lodged in jail.

[18] John Young, an English musician, shot and killed Robert Berwick, a deputy sheriff. *Greenleaf's New York Journal,* July 1, August 8, 19, 1797; *The New York Gazette,* July 1, August 17, 18, 1797.

June 30th Very warm. Read Rights of Woman. Call on Hallam & appoint to meet him at Gamage's at 1 OClock. Call on Smith & Johnson; read in Monthly review 1796: Schiller & Co's "Hours." At one o'clock, met Hallam in Gamage's presence. We talked over the necessity & propriety of selling the property, but Hallam soon began to scold about Hodgkinson, that he had not fulfill'd his engagements by making the payments he was to have done on the bonds, that he had left him responsible, that he had gone off without saying anything to him & was speculating upon his (Hall^{s}) property. We agreed with Mr Hallam that Mr Hodgkinson ought to fulfill his engagements but told him that the payment on the bond had not been paid in consequence of the Executors of J. Henry rather wishing it to remain as it was & to receive interest than to receive the money & vest it in Bank stock. I told Mr. Hallam that we knew the money would not be demanded of him. He said it had not been, Mr. Gaine had not asked him for any money. Gamage afterwards observed that all this had been explained by him to Mr Hallam's satisfaction long before & that he was only endeavouring to raise difficulties. I told him that Mr. Hodg: was obliged by his contracts with me to have all his payments made on that property by the ensuing May & that the property if now sold should be applied to making the payments. I led him to agree that Gamage & Staunton the builder should give us their valuation of the property, to be a guide to us in receiving proposals from purchasers &c. Gamage accepted the task of negociating a sale. This conversation was interrupted by Mr Hallam beginning to talk of having misunderstood us, as to the time his one fourth of profit from our business was to commence. He said he certainly understood that he was to receive one fourth of the profits from the Boston season. I went over the same arguments to convince him that we could have had no intention of any division taking place untill we began to play in the New Theatre, as I had done on ye 27th instant; and added that I had no notion of misconception & misunderstandings after having well considered the paper to which he had agreed, & after having discussed the contents in presence of witnesses with the paper in his hand, which I asserted was so plain as not to admit of misconstruction or misunderstanding. He walked about the room, I sate still. He said he should never have thought of engageing himself as an hired actor to go down to Boston & spoke of it being a degradation to him so to do. I replied, that, he had himself proposed an engagement in our Company, that, it was not a matter of our seeking. As a proof that he was to be considered a sharer in the Boston scheme he mentioned his property being used in the scheme, his part of the scenery & wardrobe. "Sir" I replied "was it not a part of our proposals and agreed to by you that you should sell that property to us" he assented—"how then is your property used? An inventory is taken & when a valuation is made we shall pay you; we take the property at our risque & are accountable to you for your part according to the terms of the sale. I hope that objection is fully answer'd." He made no reply. He enquired upon what terms that man meaning Williamson was to have the Hartford Theatre? I told him I did not know: but I supposed it would be for him (W^n) to pay the sum required as annual rent for the place. "If so" I continued "the place is very well disposed of for it is a place where nothing but loss is to be expected, with our Company. "So" says he "I am only to be concern'd where there is loss to be incurred?" I asked him what he meant? "Am I not" he replied "under engagements to those people?" I told him I conceived not and after a pause of a minute I address'd him thus "Hallam, Hodgkinson & Dunlap did enter into engagements to play a certain time each year at Hartford & pay a certain rent for a Theatre there under certain penalties e i to have theatrical performances exhibited by a part of *their company* & as good a part as they had the command of: but H H & D have no longer a Company—there is no longer such a firm in existence, the connection between J Hodgkinson & myself and you, ceased to exist some time back and there is no partnership connection remaining—such is my conception of the matter & upon such principles I have acted & shall continue to act: we have now taken the Company upon our own risque altogether & whatever losses may happen you have nothing to do with them." He said "*that* alter'd the matter materially, if he ran no risque—that alter'd the matter." As he still murmured at not being allow'd a share in the profits of the Boston season and I asserted that the proposals to which he had acceded were so worded that he could not understand it otherwise than that the division there stated was to take place from & after the opening of the New Theatre in N. Y., I regretted that I had left my copy of the proposals at home, having put this book out of my pocket its accustomed place because of the great heat of the day, he said he would go home for the letter & did so, going out with some indignant expressions at the idea of going down to Boston as an hired actor, to which I replied (tho' I believe he was out of hearing) that, he was not wanted there. During ye short absence of Hallam, in going next door,[1] Gamage employed himself in persuading me to give way to him that the business of a sale of property might be effected: I told him that I doubted of the policy of giving way to Mr Hallam, that he was a man, not to be relied upon & that if he persisted thus in raising difficulties I should adopt measures that would make him (using a vulgar expression) "hawl in his horns." Mr H returned with the paper, he sate down between me & Gamage, took out his spectacles, which he holds always in his hand, and read the proposals aloud: when he had finished he was silent & I declared them to be so explicit as not to admit of misconception. He folded up the paper & put it away without remark. I took the oppertunity of this pause to give him his account & Ds 300, observing that I had not enter'd into particulars which the books would explain, he said it was sufficient "every way in the world" his accustomed manner of speaking. I now resumed the subject

[1] The New York City Directory of 1797 lists Lewis Hallam, comedian, at 18 John Street, and John Gamage, physician, at 20 John Street.

of the sale of property, and he agreed to have it immediately valued, himself to ask Staunton to assist Gamage. I asked him if he went to Hartford? He said he did not know, he did not see what he should do there. I asked him if he had heard any thing further respecting Wignel or the Phil: business? He did not answer the question but began to tell me of a letter from Prigmore to Chambers offering him an engagement in a Sadlers Wells scheme which he was setting up at Baltimore: this exhibition Hallam concluded was to be in our Theatre there, which we had heard was in good repair & had been let out repeatedly to different showmen, by whose authority he said he did not know or who had been left in possession of the keys. Gamage asserted that the Baltimore property was guarenteed to Hallam by J Henry (and consequently by Hallam to Hodgkinson & so to me) and that Hallam ought to insist on the heirs of J Henry giving him possession of it. Hallam said he would get Prigmores letter & let me see it & requested me "as I am more a man of business than him" to write to P & get a statement of the situation of the Property. Gamage mention'd the propriety of selling the Phil: Theatre, to which H made no reply. Hallam asserted that in a message sent him by Hodgkinson & bro[t] by Mirvan Hallam, Hodg: had given him to understand that he was to receive ¼ of the profits at Boston: I only remarked that I knew nothing of such message & was not bound by Mr Hodgkinson's messages sent without my concurrence. I remark'd, repeatedly, that no profit ought to be expected from the summer scheme taken altogether & that if I escaped without loss I should esteem myself very fortunate: these last remarks concerning y[e] profits were made before Mr Hallam read the proposals. Returned home very unwell & so continued till evening when I was, apparently, relieved from head ach by the warm bath. Read in "Rights of Woman." Botanic Garden note concerning y[e] Upas examine the Map of Asia. Read Enc: Art: Camphor, Laurus Camphoria, Japan.

July 1st Warm but not so much so as yesterday. Free from head ach but feeble. John having yesterday landed Captn King safe at Stromness, has begun Hume's England with my comments & the modern & ancient Maps. At Smith & Johnson's: we purpose an expedition to the west banks of ye Hudson. Afternoon call on Gamage he says Hallam & himself call'd on Staunton & Hallam engaged him to give in a valuation, which is to be done to night. Gamage is willing to undertake the agency for all our property and will himself go to Phil: which property he thinks he will sell as a Theatre for 8 or 10,000 Dols:. He says, Hallam's wife rails at the thought of his selling the property & swears she will never sign another deed. Rec^{d} a letter from Hodgkinson. The Goods arrived the 28th instant, he thinks the proprietors are much disatisfied & that he will have no success. "I wish we had gone to Boston at once. On beginning to unload I observ'd several of Hallams Trunks directed with his own hand: I really fear trouble in that quarter: dont neglect to forward me your loan as *early as possible,* for if the Theatre cannot the *first week* pay something like expenses, I shall close immediately: if you can send 500 instead of 450 it will make the matter more certain." "June 29th Hartford".

After drinking tea at my house, Smith, Johnson & myself embarked in ye Hobuck ferry boat & crossed to a very pleasantly situated place. The district called Hobuck is about 1 Mile square and is joined to the main land by salt Meadow, having every appearance of being once an Island. We walked untill 9 OClock, & then returned to the Ferryhouse to lodge. The Chesnut trees are now in bloom, one in particular attracted our attention from its extraordinary size & beauty. The Liriodendron Tulipfera had thrown off most of its blossoms.

Hobuck July 2d I was up by 4 OClock & about 5 Smith & self leaving Wm in bed walked to Mr John Stevens's place on the highest ground of the district. This gentleman owns all the land in the Neighbourhood & is improving the place on which he has built in the Style of English nobility: he displays taste and has, undoubtedly, the finest situation I ever saw. He has planted out a hedge of Lombardy Poplars this spring consisting of 4 or 5000 trees, I think the gardener said 5000: they are planted about 10 Inches asunder & cut to the height of 6 feet. The chequered hedge of Poplars they think will not do & indeed it appears slender. As we were about returning Wm met us & agreeing to return to Steven's after breakfast we went back to the ferryhouse. On returning to Stevens's, the sun had burst out and added lustre & beauty to the scene which lies subject to that commanding situation. The City of N: Y: so unseemly in itself, gives pleasure at this distance from it, while the low hills of Nassau seen over it & stretching southward to the narrows form a pleasing line of horizon to the prospect in that direction. To the south by west we first see the point from whence we had just come, & beyond it, Paulus hook a peninsula streching into the bay & connec[ted] to the main by low meadows in the manner of the place on which we stood. Beyond Paulus hook is the bay & its small Islands untill Staten Island nearly meeting Nassau at the Narrows terminates the view. Between Nassau or Long Island & Staten, we see the most distant land of the prospect, the highlands of Navesinck at least 30 Miles from the spot. Westward the view is immediately bounded by the aspiring rocks beyond the salt meadow which form the genuine bank of the Hudson. To the North we view the Majestic Hudson. From this enchanting spot we proceeded thro groves filled with sweet music, till we came to the meadow, over which is a causeway, which pass'd we ascended the rocks or bank of the river & looked down on Hobuck & its lordly Mansion. We returned about 3 to the ferry & tho' the sun had very great power the southerly breeze kept us from suffering; but on entering the City in the evening the air appeared suffocating.

New York July 3d Very warm morning. Write to Hodgkinson, tell him of my intention to employ Gamage, of the leading circumstances respecting Hallam &c. Call on Gamage; he says the valuation is to be ready at 12 O'Clock: he shewed me a plan by which to sell it, it is something in this way.

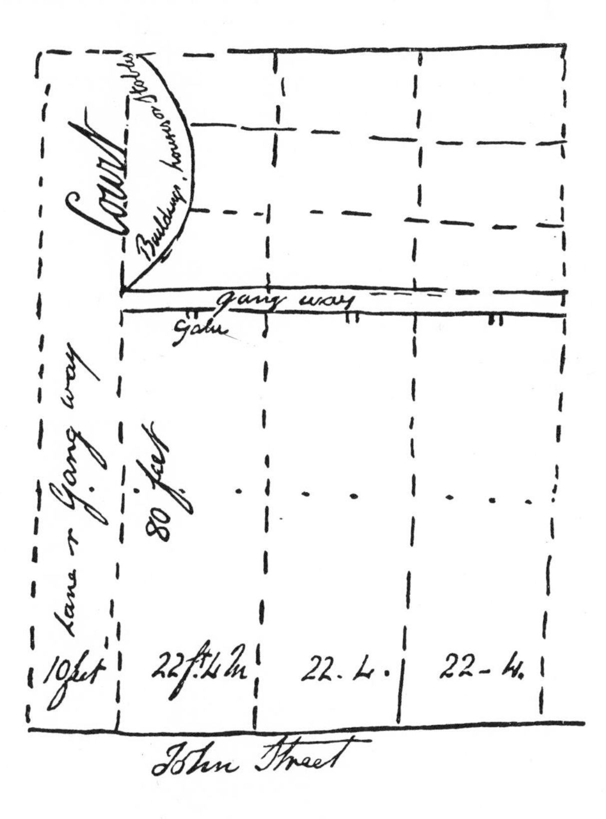

Gamage says that he was offered last night for one Lot in John Street & an attendant Stable lot £1000, and that Staunton tho' he will not value the land thus divided, approves of the plan & confess'd that a front & rear lot was worth £ 1200. Gamage now places the value at £ 3600 for ye land & ye old house, to be remov'd £ 200 more. He advises to advertise it for private sale & ask £ 4000. The property at Phil: Hallam told him, he (Hallam) has the lease of. Of the Baltimore property we seem to know nothing. At Smith & Johnson's: Roulet, who call'd in there says the thermometer was at his house out of the town, in a northern exposure, at 90, yesterday. Call at Gamages he gave me as his valuation the following

"Doctor Gamage thinks the property of the Old play House as it stands is worth, without the buildings £ 3200

the Buildings 200

£ 3400

He said he meant this valuation as of the property lumped, and not as divided into lots according to the plan. Read Hume with the boy. Between 5 & 6 OClock Mr Hallam call'd on me. He shewed me Staunton's valuation which is for land & Buildings £ 2950. He talked of his intention to purchase, but said or rather intimated, for he never speaks out unless thrown off his habitual guard, that he must see Hodgkinson and come to some settlement of accounts with him before he would any thing and out of a conversation of some length this was all I got from him on the subject. As to the Philadelphia property, he talked of the necessity of purchasing certain rights or shares which he says Wignel & Morris have in it as contributing to the Building. Now Gamage says that those people cannot claim, & at any rate, if they do, Hallam must answer as he gave a warrantee deed to Hodgkinson. When Hallam spoke of his settlement with Hodgkinson as necessary to his determination respecting the sale of property, he expressed himself in every other respect perfectly satisfied & talked much of his exertions in the line of playing marked out for him, for the good of the Company: "No hired actor that you have shall do more than I am willing to do." He told me that he had, some time back, received a letter from Prigmore wishing to treat for the Baltimore Theatre, belonging to us, this he never answered. He says that Henry made a bargain "over a bottle" with the proprietor of the ground on which they built the Baltimore Theatre, for the ground on lease, he knows not for how long a time, to pay 15 Box tickets a year as rent & he believes there never was any writings. For the ground on which they built the Annapolis Theatre they were to pay £ 10 a year & for Phil £ 17.

Evening at Riley's & Coits.

July 4th 1797. A day of Noise & parade. I call'd on Gamage. He thinks I ought to let Mr Hallam know that unless he takes measures or consents to a sale, I will apply to the Court for a division. Read Hume with John. Read Rights of Women. Evening make some calls with my Wife.

July 5th Cool & pleasant morning. Make preparations for going to Elizabeth town & Amboy. Borrow "Kalm" from Drummond. Call on Smith and Johnson. Call on Kent but he was not in. Call on Hallam he says he goes tomorrow: I am to see him this afternoon at 4 OClock. Write to Hodgk: "I am enabled to send by Mr. Hallam 450 Dols: I hope this will suffice, indeed I have strong reasons to hope it, nothing gives a more fatal slap to a mans credit than paying for money as I am now doing." Call at Cozines to enquire after his son Augustus who by some accident is wounded very badly in the arm by the discharge of a pistol. Call at Mr [John] Murray's, it is here feasting-time for the marriage of Susan to Mr. [William] Ogden. Purchase some water colours & pencils at F Barrow's. I have to day a second time borrow'd money of [John A.] Hardenbrook the Broker, giving my note or rather D[unlap] & J[udah]'s note endorsed by me payable in 60 days for 600 Dols: & receiving in return 567 Ds thus paying 33 Ds. Call on Mr. Hallam & give him a letter for Hodgkinson, likewise counted out to him 450 Ds: He on my questioning him *intimated* that if he could agree with Mr. Hodgkinson he would immediately come to a bargain for the John Street property which he intends he says to purchase. He mentioned that the valuations given in were by no means conclusive, and I told him I had good reason to believe that we could have £ 3600 for the property immediately: he agreed that the more it was worth the better for both parties. He mentioned that Mrs Hallam is to go with him tomorrow. He promised to let me know whether he & Mr Hodgkinson came to any conclusion immediately & I told him it was a matter of moment with me, if it was only in consideration of the interest I must pay on the property. We parted with civility. Going out I passed *her* she stood in the door way talking with a person whom I believe to be Osborne one of her partizans: I did not put on my hat untill out of the door but I did not look at her. Hallam had partly descended the Stairs but hung back on seeing her at the door. Afternoon writing on accounts. Sharpless & wife call'd on us. Smith & Johnson drank tea with us & we all went to see Mrs Woolsey. Go with my wife to Mr Murrays & M: Rogers's.

July 6th preparing for Amboy & Elizabeth town. About 9 O'Clock left New York and reached the Kills about 12 when we landed on the Staten Island side at one Buskirk's, here we all sate down under an Apple tree & John read in Hume, the 1st Vol: of which I had brought in my pocket: about 2 we left Staten Island & arrived at E point past 4 suffering from the heat: a stage man was waiting & we soon arrived at Elizabeth Town at Mr Croel's where we feasted on the meal commonly called *Tea* and on fine Gooseberries. Our night was not quite pleasant owing to the closeness of the room, tho' as usual we slept with open windows.

July 7th Eliz: town. Up early, walk with John. After breakfast ride with my Wife & children to various parts of the Town. Call on Mr Williamson who has not yet rec^{d} the money from y^{e} Morris County Sheriff but is to have it next week & expects to be in Amboy. Walk to

MRS. BENJAMIN WOOLSEY, JR. (ANN MUIRSON) (1737-1807)
By William Dunlap
(Courtesy of William Samuel Johnson, Esq.)

Frances Childs's new House: Mrs Childs was just riding off to N: Y: but introduced me to Miss Blanch and her sister who showed me the house, a plan of which see p: 147.[2] I walked thro' the Shrubbery, which has been neglected since Child's absence in Europe, but on which there appears to have been considerable attention bestowed. I drew sketch p: 144, from the shrubbery on the town side; sk: p: 142 from the New Ark side & sk: p: 140 from the Amboy or south side. Return to Mr Croels read in Hume with John. This is the Hay harvest. Where the Mowers have passed we see the Boblink, blackbird, Robin, Meadow Lark & other birds very busy among the grass stubble. I see no Cat birds, tho' they sung sweetly last Sunday at Hobuck. The Robin has not ceased his song, but the ground Thrush is totally mute. The wild rose yet blooms in the fields & along the fences where it in some places almost forms a hedge. The Catalpa is in full bloom & the number of trees about this place not only add to the beauty but the fragrance of the town; it is deservedly a favorite here. The Weather is cloudy & therefore pleasant. Ride with Mr Croel to his farm near the point. He shewed me his improvements: the farm is almost all taken up in timothy grass for mowing, it is in excellent order and well manur'd by means of salt hay which is made manure of by throwing it in great quantities into the Cow yard & Hog pen: the latter the best. He shewed me some spots where a quantity of human ordure had been thrown from a sink; it caused the Timothy to grow very luxuriantly & to ripen long before the other parts of the field: at this time it was of a different colour from that around it & very large & far past the time it should have been mowed. The land which is

[2] The sketches of Francis Childs's house at Elizabeth, to which Dunlap refers, are drawn in the manuscript volume, on the following pages: p. 147, a simple ground plan of the house; p. 144, a water color drawing, carefully executed, showing the house as seen from the east; p. 142, a rough pen-and-ink sketch of the house from the north; p. 140, a careful, unfinished pencil sketch of the most imposing aspect of the house "seen from south by east." On page 138, is a faint pencil drawing of the south side.

mowed here yields a profit of upward of £ 6 an acre. Night: showers.

July 8th Eliz: Town After breakfast ride w[t] my Wife & Children. Walk. The Cat bird I saw but it was silent. I made sketch. Call'd at a Saw mill & enquire the price of posts for a garden fence 2/: Miller or Sawer Jacob Crane. After dinner walk with John: we went into a field where there was several Bobolinks: I observ'd the manners of the bird & sketch'd its setting on the reed grass: It is much in motion & its actions are gracefull; it sings on the wing almost, if not entirely, without ceasing; open mouthed; see the rude sketches p: 148. Light Showers.

July 9th 1797 Sunday. Sitting in the entry Mr Crowel asked what church I went to: I replied that I did not go to any: He appear'd astonish'd and asked me whether I conceiv'd it to be my duty to stay away from public worship? I said I was fully convinced of it. "Well" said he "how differently people see things, now I think it as much my duty to go to public worship as to provide for my family." When going to Methodist meeting at 9 OClock I voluntarily offerred to accompany him & his family: One Morrell [3] preached & prayed, a man, as Crowel says "plucked as a brand from the burning:" he was before his "conversion" an officer in the American Army, a very vicious man and confirmed sot, so that the Methodists think his conversion little less than miraculous. He appeared to be a pretty sensible man, with a sufficient degree of priestly pride. His sermon was from a text which describes a Devils having left a man and then wandering about among "dry places" but finding no rest he returns to the man, whom he finds purified & "garnished" on which he departs & again returns bringing with him 7 other Devils more powerfull than himself who with him enter into the man & the last condition of this man is worse than the first. The preacher told

[3] Probably the Rev. Thomas Morrell (1747-1838). Edwin F. Hatfield's *History of Elizabeth, N. J.*, 622-625.

his ignorant Audience (for ignorance was written on every countenance of the small number of people there, and stupidity on most, except some youth) that in those days God suffer'd the Devils to take possession of the bodies of men, that he might manifest his power through Christ in the casting them out. At the present time, he said such instances were less frequent, tho' there were many people at this time sorely afflicted by disorders for which physicians could find no names, which disorders were occasioned by some devil having enter'd into the bodies of such people & thus afflicting them. "But now" says he "the devils enter the souls of men" *There* he represented the devil as being quite at home, the soul of man being his proper habitation e i unregenerate man: there he found every congenial disposition. He expatiated on the great number of Devils which he proved by a text which asserts that the devil tempted all the children of men at one time now, says he, as the Devil or prince of Devils, is not omnipresent he could only do it by his agents & those agents must be equal in number to the inhabitants of the earth, all of whom they tempted, so he asserted they were in greater numbers; & their power he proved by the text which asserts their opposition to Michael & the Angels. These beings he represented as roving about seeking whom they should devour & having possession of all the unconverted. *"When the unclean spirit is gone out of a Man"* this he represented as taking place at y[e] time of conversion "for no devil goes out of a man unless forced" *"he walketh through dry places"* this passage he remarked, is, of acknowledged difficulty, he supposed it to mean that the dissapointed Devil retired into the Wilderness to hide his chagrin at being discomfited: *"seeking rest: and finding none he saith, I will return unto my house whence I came out."* "My house" exclaimed the preacher "how confident he speaks, as if the soul of man was made for the Devil." *"And when he cometh he findeth it swept & garnished."* here he expatiated on the joy & fearlessness of the newly converted, cleansed & decorated by

Angels, who still more numerous than the devils are always hovering near to assist those who resist the devil. How powerfull must be such representations on ignorant minds, coming from a man whom they consider as infinitely wiser than themselves, if not immediately inspired, and confirmed by all their early prejudices & by a book which they believe came from Heaven! But the happiness of the new converted as well as all human happiness he represented as being purposely interrupted by God for fear man would not think sufficiently of future joy in heaven: the devil who was driven out returns to attempt coming in again: here the poor sinner is warned to watch & pray. The Devil, as the preacher interprets it, not being able to get in, *"goeth & taketh to him 7 other spirits more wicked than himself"* for devils he remarked are of different capacities, tho' all as wicked as they can be, as men are of different capacities and the angels in heaven, and the elect who tho' all as happy as they can be, yet being of different capacities there is among them different degrees as thrones, principalities &ca. *"and they enter in & dwell there."* Here according to the preacher the first devil gets in by the aid of his 7 helpmates "and the last state of that man is worse than the first." Here the different degrees of sinfulness were enumerated, the last & greatest (all vices & crimes being mention'd before) being Deism—crime of horror! mention'd in a thundering voice accompanied by blow of vengeance on the Cushion. The discourse ended in exhortations to vigilance & encouragement from the certainty that unless the man consents the devil cant get in him tho' he should be attacked by "thousands & thousands & thousands & millions of thousands" of these mischievous spirits at once. At 10 OClock Mr Crowel went to another meeting but I staid at home, taught my boy & read in Hume. The day was very warm. Evening secured places for myself & family in the Stage to Woodbridge.

July 10th 1797 Amboy. At four OClock this morning we left Eliz: town; the morning fine &, with summer clothes on, cold. About 6 we arrived at Woodbridge & after breakfasting with Mr & Mrs Heard, we accompanied by them, came to this place. The morning becomes warm. Mr & Mrs H return. Open my box of books & arrange them. Read with John. Receive a letter from Hodgkinson, viz

"I commenced last night to 67 Dols:! my present opinion is, we shall *close* at the end of the Week. Warner, last friday fell from the Wing grooves above & receiv'd a serious hurt, which in the fixing of our scenery threw us considerably aback; however by additional hands & hard work I believe we shall have all ready for the different pieces. I enclose you my arrangement for the week, which, strong & novel as it is, I fear will not produce near 100 Dols nightly: Mrs Melmoth & every body here, except Hallam, nor is Williamson yet ariv'd. I beg you to send on to me, as soon as possible."
Hartf[r] July 4th"

The enclosed arrangement was cut from the news paper & is as follows Monday "Comet & Miss in her teens" tuesday "Way to get married & New York Balloon" Wednesday "Siege of Belgrade & two strings to your bow." thursday "Next door Neighbours & Children in y[e] Wood" Friday "Man of Ten Thousand & Tom thumb" and for Monday y[e] 10th (to night) "The Man of Fortitude & Lock & key." All advertised in a sufficiently flourishing manner & with some judgment. Write to M: Judah. Read wth John & Margaret. Hot, because calm & clear from noon untill 2 OClock but afterwards the fresh south came sweeping over our wide bay, cooled by its passage on the Atlantic and render'd the remaining day & evening truly health-inspiring. Read "Rights of Women" Walk with my Wife & Children & receive calls from our neighbours.

July 11th Up about day light: a thunder shower: after which, I work in the Garden untill 7 OClock, the children with me, John howing up weeds, Margaret picking Currants for breakfast. Write to Hodgkinson as follows

"I have received your second—miserable prospect to be sure, but I hope the 4th of July did something for you. You have before this, the mony & Hallam & his wife with you. If he will take the

John Street property it should be at £ 3800, the property deliverable next June or July; if you can come to a settlement of this kind wth him let it be done legally. Any measures you may think best to adopt with him to accomplish this desirable purpose and to obtain his consent for the sale of the Phil: property, I do hereby concur in. We can perhaps force a sale by legal measures but the disadvantages would be great and are if possible to be avoided. I have order'd the Candles on to Boston & with them some of my pamphlets which I hope you will not think a trouble to place in any booksellers hands you may think fit, for sale, Archers 50 Cents, Tell truth 25 Cents."

Calling at the post office to forward y[e] letters to M[oses] J[udah] & J[ohn] H[odgkinson] I rec[d] a few lines from M: enclosing the following from Hodgk:

"By the Hand of M Le Massue who is going to France to see his Family, I can take the oppertunity of letting you know our situation; I clos'd the Theatre last Night—the business bore a dreadful Face; but the 4th of July, & advertising that on account of the great expence I must make *Friday*, the *last Night*, gave a spring that has answer'd better than expectation:—Monday 67 Ds: T: 195, W: 97, Th: 94, F: 237, total 690 Ds:. There are *several* of the Company that *want money*, previous to going to Boston which I have not as yet to give them. I purpose opening, Monday 18th if possible. Mr Nicolai stands indebted to M Le Massue *16 Ds:* which was of consequence to him previous to sailing: I fear'd the money myself, & therefore have requested Le Massue, to *ask you for it* & I will stop the money from Nicolai at Boston. On Monday a meeting of the proprietors proposing to liberate me from further engagements: if you have not sent on: do *immediately* for I cannot stir till them ——" Saturday Morn: July 8th 1797."

I opened my letters again & acknowledged the receit of them, ordering y[e] money p[d] to Le Massue. Walk out to my little farm with John, on the way James Kearney overtook me riding in a chair, he stopt & entering into conversation introduced the contiguity of his father's lot to mine, told me that his father he believed would sell it for £ 100. I told him that I might be tempted to give near that for it. Wm Taylor & his wife overtook me, in their chair, he entered into conversation about my land and advised me to sow the orchard with grass seed. I found Corrington in my orchard preparing to sow Buckwheat, his negro ploughing; I directed Timothy seed to be sown in a low spot where I believe it will be necessary to take up some trees; Corrington advises to plough & manure the orchard & says the trees will thrive doubly to what they will if it is laid down in meadow: I believe he is right. I found Bloodgood & 2 sons in the young Bloodgood's field, the sons reaping, the father ploughing. I had some friendly conversation with them & then return'd home. A stake cut from a Button wood tree & stuck in the earth, in a low spot, to support a young apple tree is growing, having put forth leaves. Our journey hither this time, for me, my wife & children, in 19/. Read Hume with John. Read in 9th vol of my Memoirs (last summers transactions) Drink tea with Miss Thorp & after a little walk with the Children call at Mr Parker's, he is out of town, pass an agreeable hour with the Ladies. Take John into ye sea water.

July 12th. Work in ye Garden. Buy fish which are brought hither regularly from the sea-bass banks. Clean my Gun which somewhat out of order & gives me some labour. Hear John & Margaret read. Robins, Cat birds & Ground thrushes in the Garden some of them feed on the green peas. Mr. J Taylor says he will put up the division fence between my land & his according to the survey made by Halstead last year for Lovegrove & desired me to speak to Halstead; I accordingly did so, he says he marked the line on paper & put up stakes at the north & south corners of mine, a line drawn from which gives me my 10 Acres, which were formerly sold by Elias Marsh to Wm Alexander titular Earl of Sterling. A young Marten not yet vers'd in flying has attracted the Children's attention. This is a warm day tho' pleasant here. Read in Rights of Women—it appears to me that this woman had no clear Idea of the basis of morality—there is much good sense in her volume, but much error, a bad style & strong indications of vanity. She assumes the character of a philosopher and teacher, as such she is not great. Drink tea at Mrs Terrils, Mr & Mrs Kid from Fredericksburg about 20 miles from Esopus, were there: the old man is respectable & converses with good sense. He says that Wolves & Bears are so numerous with them as to destroy their flocks or prevent the keeping any: Deer are in great abundance. A Mountain lies between them & Esopus. I was this morning up before the sun.

July 13th Up at ½ past 4 & work in the Garden till breakfast. From 8 to 1 I rambled with my gun. Shot some Larks, Killdeers, & small snipe. Quail are in great abundance. The Black birds are not so plenty as when last here: Robins exceedingly thick but not yet in flocks, indeed, I believe there are not any birds in flocks here at present. I saw some Herons or Bitterns but they were shy: Started one rabbit. The day is hot; the earth dry. Read Hume with John: read Rights of Woman and Kalms travels. John is unwell which causes us much uneasiness. A virtuous man would not be dependent for happiness on the health or sickness of a puny boy.

July 14th Up before 4 OClock. Work in the Garden untill 9 OClock with the interval of breakfasting time. I took my gun into the Garden to dispute the peas & Currants with the Robins. John is better, read Hume with him. Read Kalm & Pennant. Write to Prigmore as follows

"Sir

I address you in consequence of a letter rec^{d} by Mr Hallam from you on the subject of our Baltimore Theatre: had I known of your letter at the time of Mr H's receiving it I should not have been so tardy in writing to you. If your scheme is still, as then, I should thank you for a line, explanatory of your wishes & as minute a detail of the present situation of our Theatre, as your engagements will permit, with any information relative thereto, or to the situation & uses it has been put to for some years back. Any information of this kind will oblige all the proprietors & particularly

Your friend

W D"

"Please to direct to me at Amboy"

Read in "Rights of Women" & my own memoirs Vol: 9th. A very light shower. Walk with my wife & Children. Water the Garden. Call at Mr Kearney's.

July 15th Up at 10 minutes past 4. Work in the Garden untill 7. Read Hume with John & Geography with Margaret, both attending to ye Maps. Read in Rights of Woman. Paint on sketch p: 144 Read wth John in Hume. Read Kalm: cat bird (Muscicapa Carolinensis) swallow'd by a black snake p: 48 Vol 1st. Button wood (Virginian Maple, Waterbeech, Plantanus occidentalis) Persimon (Diospyros Virginiana)

Mr Kalms catalogue of Forest trees that grow spontaneously in the woods near Phil: it is to be noticed that he passed through woods altogether in going to Bartram's.

Quercus Alba, ye White oak, in good ground.
Quercus rubra (I presume nigra) black oak
Quercus Hispanica, Spanish oak, a variety of ye above
Juglans Alba, hiccory, three or four varieties
Rubus occidentalis, American blackberry shrub
Acer rubrum, maple tree wth red flowers, in swamps
Rhus Glabra, smooth leav'd sumach
Vitis labrusca and Vulpina, vines of several kinds.
Sambucus Canadensis, American Elder tree
Quercus phellos, swamp oak
Azalea lutea, ye American upright honey-suckle
Cratægus Crus galli, Virginian Azarole (Hawthorn)
Vaccinium ——, a species of Whortleberry shrub
Quercus prinus, Chestnut Oak
Cornus florida, Cornelian Cherry (Dog wood)
Liriodendron Tulipifera, Tulip tree
Prunus Virginiana
Vaccinium ——, a frutex whortleberry
Prinos verticillatus, winterbery tree
Platanus occidentalis, Water beech
Nyssa aquatica, tupelo tree, fields & mountains
Liquidamber Styraciflua, sweet gum tree, near springs
Betula Alnus, Alder
Fagus castanea, Chesnut tree
Juglans nigra, Black walnut
Rhus radicans, ye twining sumach
Acer Negundo, ye Ash leav'd maple
Prunus domestica, wild plumb tree.

Ulmus Americana, white elm
Prunus spinosa, sloe shrub
Laurus sassafras, sassafras tree
Ribes nigrum, Currant tree
Fraxinus excelsior, Ash tree
Smilax laurifolia, rough bind weed wth bay leaves
Kalmia latifolia, American dwarf laurel
Morus rubra, Mulberry tree
Rhus vernix, poisonous sumach, wet places
Quercus rubra, red oak, but a peculiar variety
Hamamelis Virginica; Witch Hazel
Diospyros virginiana; Persimon
Pyrus coronaria; Anchor tree
Juniperus virginiana; red Juniper
Laurus æstivalis; spice wood (a species of bay)
Carpinus ostrya; a species of horn beam
Carpinus Betulus; a horn beam
Fagus sylvatica; Beech
Juglans ———; Butternut tree: the translator queries is this ye Juglans baccata of Lin.?
Pinus Ameracana; Pensylvania fir-tree
Betula lenta; a species of Birch, on the banks of rivers
Cephalantus occidentalis; Button wood
Pinus tæda. New Jersey fir-tree
Cercis Canadensis, sallad tree.
Robinia Pseudacacia; Locust tree
Magnolia Glauca; Laurel leav'd tulip tree
Tilia Americana; Lime tree.
Gleditsia triacanthos; honey locust tree, or three thorn'd acacia
Celtis occidentalis; nettle tree
Anonna muricata; Custard apple

Receive letters from M: Judah & Joseph Falconi the latter wishes to hire our Theatre: Write to Hodgkinson on the subject: Write to Moses Judah; & thro' him send a message to Falconi. After excessive heat we have a gust, first of wind and then rain with some thunder, during which the wind seemed to go nearly round the Compass but the north prevailed and we are cool enough. Evening another shower from the South East, sharp lightning & distant thunder. Read Newspapers. Kalm. Verbascum Thapsus (great Mullein). Hibiscus esculentus (okra) Miller calls it "Ketmia Indica folio ficus, fructu pentagono, recurvo, esculento, grociliori, et longiori." Capsicum annuum; Guinea pepper. American Nightshade (Phytolacca decandra). Juniperis Virginiana (Red Ceder) Plantago Major (broad plantain) Chenopodium Album (Goosefoot). Tansey (Tanacetum vulgare) common vervain (verbene officinalis) Cassia Chamæchristax, "its leaves are like those of ye sensitive plant or mimosa" & contract when touched. Is not this the plant I have in these vols formerly called mimosa? Bartram told me that there was no mimosa a native of the northern or middle States, indeed he told me their boundary river but I have forgotten.

July 16th 1797 Sunday. Up about 5 OClock: pick peas and Currants; the latter are of great use to us and contribute much to our pleasure; I eat them, when picked & washed & strewed with sugar, for or rather with my breakfast & with the juice we make a very pleasant drink, by mixing it with water, sweetening it & adding to 2 quarts, 3 table spoonfulls of brandy. After breakfast walk out to Aaron Bloodgoods with my Wife & Children, where, leaving them, I went with him to see my salt meadow on the sound near the brick kilns: observed a large bird which made considerable noise, he call'd it a Killwillet, a large snipe & said it was "good eating." We all got home about 12 OClock. The Cornus Florida is on my farm, its berry is not yet ripe, it is monospermous: the Liquidamber (sweet gum) is very frequent & grows in every situation, tallest where surrounded by other forest trees. Read Hume with John. Read Kalm: Virginian wake robin (Arum Virginicum). Sarothra Gentianoides, like to a Whortleberry bush. Gnaphalium margaritaceum (life everlasting) Dogs bane (Apocynum cannabinum) used as flax.

Plants shewn by Bartram to Kalm which are likewise common to ye northern parts of Europe viz

Betula alba, common Beech tree
Betula nana
Comarum palustre, meadows of N Jersey

Gentiana lutea, great Gentian
Linnæa borealis, Canada, creeps on ye ground
Myrica Gale, from Susquehana
Potentilla fruticosa, between Delaware & N York
Trientalis Europæa.
Triglochin maritimum

Indian corn, Maize (Tea Mays) Ivy (Hedera Helix) The sassafras is bad fire wood, the birds eat ye berries before they are ripe, the bark is used in dying. Black woodpecker wth red head (Picus pileatus) Chenopodium Anthelminticum (worm seed or Jerusalem oak) of the common privet or Ligustrum vulgare, hedges are made in Pensyl: but not approv'd by Kalm. Of the Acer Rubrum (red Maple) he says they make sugar in Canada; Is this the sugar Maple. Bidens bipinnata, (Spanish needles) I believe cockles. Convolvulus Batatas, (Bermuda potatoes) *sweet potatoes*. Ground hog (Badger; Ursus Meles) A kind of Mole perhaps Sorex cristatus, the American mole only makes cover'd walks, the European, hills. Myrica cerifera (Tallow shrub, Candleberry tree, Bayberry bush) Peny royal (Cunila pulegioides) Phytolacca decandra (Poke).

Paint a little on y[e] sketch p: 144 but want a ruler & compasses for y[e] Architecture. Read with John in Hume. Read Kalm again: Impatiens Noli Tangere (Balsamine) Colinsonia Canadensis (Horseweed) our Author seems very credulous & by his account the elder Bartram was full of wonderfull cures performed by means of plants.

Plants in blossom Octr 18th in Pensyl: viz "a Gentiana; 2 species of Aster; common golden rod, or solidago Virga aurea; a species of Hieracium; the yellow wood sorrel or Oxalis corniculata, Fox glove or Digitalis purpurea; the Hamamelis Virginiana or Witch Hazel, common millefoil or Achillæa Millefolium; & dandelion or Leontodon Taraxacum." in some trees the flower buds were already form'd for ye next year, as in Acer Rubrum

& Laurus æstivalis a species of bay. Visit at Mrs Terrils: walk with my wife.

July 17 Up at 5: work in the Garden untill half past 7; breakfast: work a little more in ye garden & attend to my fruit trees. Read with John in Hume. Walk down to Mrs Parkers & pass an hour with ye old Lady & her daughters Betsey & Gertrude: talk of making a drawing of Staten Island point &c from one of their windows. After dinner: read with John, my wife as usual attends to Margaret: Walk out with my Gun attended by John, saw several Bittern but they were too shy for me to shoot; the red wing'd blackbird is still here tho' not very numerous; I shot two turtle Doves (Carolina pigeons) on my return I examine them with Penant's description which I think accurate. Receive letters from Hodgk: & M: Judah: the first writes thus

"Williamson & Solee, the manager of Charleston, are here & will treat for this Theatre when we are gone, with the proprietors:" "Your last mentioning Mr Hallams affairs, only strengthens my opinion that there will be more hot water, if that woman can kindle fuel to boil it. I approve *Gamage* being a negociator, but not Stanton: I suppose him prejudiced & partial. As to Mr H's mentioning so repeatedly my non payment of ye Bond: there was an unsettled account; a breach of contract & other things, but more particularly large sums of money lost by his public controversy, that untill a final adjustment can take place, would prevent my paying him one pound had I millions! I wish all the property sold & speedily. Mr H will not then be long without my balance due to him. the meeting on Monday wth the proprietors is for the purpose of endeavouring to gain a liberation of our contracts entirely: I hope it will succeed to our wishes."
"Saturday July 8th 1797."

He adds "8 P. M. Hallam is just arriv'd and has given me 450 Dols:." This letter is of the same date with that p: 108

Read News papers rec^d from N. Y.

July 18th Up a quarter before 5: Work in the Garden. Read Hume with John; & teach Margaret. Weather continues very warm. Rec^d a letter from M Judah informing that John Kent had left our employ. Write in return &

to Kent to induce him to return. Read "Rights of Women." Plato the black man who tills the field back of my Garden, shewed me an insect whose food is the leaves of the potatoe plant & by their numbers do considerable mischief: it is about ¾ of an inch in length or more, the head like a large pixmire with antenae, shells which cover the wings striped length wise & shorter than the body, which is encircled with with narrower stripes (potatoe bug). "Rights of Woman" 8th 9th 10th 11th &c. these chapters have much excellent sense in them. Read in Kalm. Walk out after tea with my Gun, see some small snipe, Black birds, Cat birds, ground thrushes, robins, King birds, Bitterns, Doves, Larks, & Quails but shot only 1 Blackbird.

July 19th Up at ½ past 4. Set out with my Wife in a chair (hired) for Richard Hartshorne's, to enquire concerning Adam's daughter. Our ride was pleasant but longer than I expected, Mr Hartshorn living 3 miles beyond Rahway; he received us with polite hospitality & his daughter gave us a breakfast of Coffee: he told me he had spoken to John Parker on the business and is to go to Bru[n]swick to ye Circuit Court ye day after tomorrow to prosecute the business. We returned home about 10 O'Clock. On our ride we started from under a bridge, a beautiful large bird of the Heron kind, colour appeared to be an uniform silver grey, legs yellow. Quails walking in the road & sitting on the rails by the way side. Read Hume with John. Read Rights of Woman. Mr John Heard, his wife & son John, Dined & passed the afternoon with us. By a paragraph in a News paper I see that Collins having challenged Crosbie the duel was prevented by the magistracy & Collins fined 3000 dols & sentenced to a years imprisonment. Betsey, Gertrude & Caty Parker drink tea with us.

July 20th Still, hot, & dry. Up a little before 6, work an hour in the Garden. After breakfast walked an hour & half with my Gun. There is a spot a little way from the town, near the sound where among Cedars & Button wood trees the turtle doves take refuge. I started several but could not get a shot. I started an old Muskito hawk or Whip poor will & two young ones, as the old one flew near me I shot it: On returning home I examine ye bird with Penant: it proves to be the long wing'd, or lesser Goatsucker (Caprimulgus minor Americanus) Penants description of the bird is accurate with these exceptions, primaries rather dark brown than black, the bar on the primaries passes over only 3 feathers & is white but on 2, Crescent under the throat, rather a dirty yellow than white, tail dark brown, motled with light brown, no black or white. Doctor Garden & Mr Clayton have led Penant into a great error in representing this as a scarce bird near the sea, on the contrary they are very numerous in every part between this place & Paulus hook. Their note of *Whipoorwill* I have not heard lately & should conjecture that it is their song & like the song of some other birds, only emitted at a certain season of the year, perhaps the season of incubation. I dont remember hearing the note later than June. The noise they *now* make, in the evening, is very peculiar & difficult to describe, I should suppose it might be produced on a bagpipe <*or by the bursting*> it is hollow, sonorous & flat, & is heard when the bird is considerably high, sounding as if close by the ear. The bird I shot was not dead when I came up to it & shewed much rage & many signs of resentment, opening its hideous large mouth with a low & hissing sound. I have often started them in the day time from the ground. The tail is forked or divided, excepting which, the representation in ye Arctic Zoology is pretty accurate, altho' the prominent nostril is omitted (see my sketch p: 134, 135.) and the eye too small & too near the bill: a naked skinny part under the eyes is likewise omitted. I shot two small birds, one larger than the other, they were in company & I supposed they were male & female of the same species, they go under the general denomination of Blackbirds, their colours are black or deep brown & rust, with yellow throats mixed with brown: I have been searching Penant & examining the birds: I suppose them to be Buntings but cannot determine the species (see sketch p: 132.) I saw for the first time at Amboy the Bob-link, a few of them mixed in with a number of birds about the same size of it, they were all feeding on grass seed. Were they not the male & female birds, (a few of the first) & are they not the rice Bunting? Read Hume wth John. Read in Kalm. Finish reading Mrs Woolstencroft. After tea walk with my Wife & children on the beach. Water the Garden.

July 21st 1797. Up about 5 O'Clock. Weather hot & dry. Work in the Garden. Read Kalm. Read Hume with John: read Kalm: read Hume with John: Dine. Read Hume with John. Read Condorcet on the Human mind to my Wife. Read Kalm. Rec[d] a letter from M: Judah: write to him in return. Call on M: Halsted, surveyor; & by his permission, copy roughly the situation of the salt meadow on the Rariton belonging to me. Water the Garden.

July 22d 1797. Up a quarter before 4 and with my gun proceeded towards Aaron Bloodgood's who, by appointment, was to go with me to see my meadow on the Raritan. I shot a killdeer on the highest part of Mr Kearneys lot & the noise of my gun started a Bittern from a neighbouring pond who sluggishly flew, shrieking hoarsely, away; while a quail whirring swiftly & silently escaped in an opposite direction. After breakfasting with the farmer & his wife, he joined my walk which proved a pretty long one. On coming near Crow's landing on a creek which winds thro' a part of the Raritan meadows, I saw some killdeers & small snipe, I fired, shot a killdeer & before I could reload 2 large snipe or *kill willets,* came, & with loud cries flew circling around me, but before I was ready they flew off. We crossed the creek in a boat & proceeded about a mile & half over the meadows: here were Killwillets (one of which I killed) Bittern & Blackbirds, with smaller birds like sparrows & the meadow wren. I shot some more killdeer on our return, some small snipe, & a mudhen, a pretty large bird about the size of the killwillet. We got some Buttermilk at Col[l] Crow's. Returning home I shot some Larks. The *Kill-willet* on the approach of any person to the meadows or to the place they occupy, get up, & with shrill cries fly towards him untill coming near they wheel off & forming a circle again return; this they sometimes repeat 4 or 5 times before they retire & shooting at them only en-creases the apparent resentment with which they menace the sportsman. A skillfull sportsman can not fail killing this bird while it thus bays him! Tho the morning was cooler than any of late & clouds hang around, yet the day is very hot. I returned home about 12. Read Hume with John. Read Penant. Read Kalm. Rec[d] a letter from M: Judah: extracts: "Mr Falconi was here yesterday, I informed what you wrote, he said he had been fearfull of not getting the Theatre & had applied to Ricketts for his Circus, & received great encouragement, but Mr Wignell has come forward & engaged it of R by giving a larger sum, untill the 1st of January next: he commences playing the 2d week in August." "I have paid Mrs Love-grove 14 9/100 Ds: but did not take a receit as I did not recollect your mentioning it." With this letter I received the 17th Vol: of Enc: my indian rubber: a bag of flints; papers from Mrs L accounting for y[e] charge of 14 9/100 Ds: & some News papers. Evening, Bathe.

July 23d Sunday. Up at 6 OClock. Clouds still floating about. Collect vegetables from y[e] Garden. Read Hume with John: read News papers. Read Hume wth John. John writes daily. Look over the Enc:. Walk & pick Blackberries. Read H with y[e] boy. Read in Enc: art: Scotland, Sector, Scriptures, Serpents. Read Hume with the boy. Walk with my Wife & Children. With my Wife call at Wm Taylor's to see Mrs Ogden (Susan Murray). Read in Enc: Arts: Slavery & Sleepwalking. This day showers have fallen around us in every direction & have cooled our air, but vegetation is almost destroy'd around y[e] town by the scorching heat & lack of rain.

July 24th Up by 5 OClock & with John walk out to Aaron Bloodgood's 2 miles, to get some Butter. We pass'd thro a thick fog which on clearing leaves us exposed to a hot sun. Rec[d] a letter from W Johnson

"With reluctance my dear friend I inform you that I cannot have the pleasure of seeing you at Amboy, at least, for 3 weeks to come. To day I am respited from the Court of Justices and on Tuesday the Supreme Court will sit & it is necessary for me to be here.

Elihu has some patients who require his attendance, so that you must not expect to see him soon. I envy you the tranquility and health you enjoy in the Country, that is, I wish to enjoy them *with you.*

Mr & Mrs Woolsey had not return'd yesterday, they are expected to day. My affectionate regards to Mrs Dunlap. Adieu

Yours sincerely
W Johnson

N. Y. Saturday July 22.

Read Hume with John. Begin a letter to T Holcroft in the 14th Vol: of these memoirs. Read with my little girl. Read Enc: Afternoon read H with John twice, & read again wth Margaret. Read in Kalm. Penant; art: Partridge (what I commonly call quail) This bird not only breeds in the latter end of Ap[l] or beginning of May as Pennant remarks but again in June & July, & certainly does not collect in flocks untill August. Bloodgood tells me that the Cock takes charge of the first brood while the hen lays for y[e] second. K: Bluebird, (Motacilla sialis). Red bird (Loxia Cardinalis) Purple Daw (Gracula Quiscula). Red wing'd Stare (black bird: Maize thief: Oriolus Phœniceus) The weather has become cool. Walk with my wife & Children. Night rain.

July 25th The pleasant & much wished for showers still continue with intervals. Up at ½ past 5; work in the garden. After breakfast loosen the earth around my young trees in y[e] field beyond y[e] Garden. Write to W Johnson. Begin a letter to J Hodgkinson informing of Wignels plan: finish it. Rec[d] a letter from John Kent in which he excuses himself for leav[g] my employ & charges Moses Judah with assuming an intolerably proud behaviour & with not being a man of truth. This letter gave me uneasiness when I considered how much of my property I entrust to this young man. Read Hume with John. Read Kalm, Penants artic & British Zool: Penant seems to think the opinion of swallows remaining torpid under water altogether absurd, yet the testimony of their so doing seems very good. Hunter's opinion against it, is much. The noise made by the Goatsucker in England is (Pen: Brit: Zool:) likened to a large spinning wheel: this bird is put among the swallows: I do not think the reasons good: Kalm says, one caught by his servant made no resistance "never attempted to bite when held in the hand." For a few days past I have heard the song of the Locust, but there are very few of them.

July 26th Up by 5, work in the garden. After breakfast take up some potatoes & put down the roots again for further growth. Ellis Baron's (called Barnes) came for us with his waggon or Coachee & we went with him to his farm at Woodbridge about 6 Miles. I could not prevail upon John to go. Return in the evening. This afternoon the Robin sung as cheerfully as in June, their song had ceased about Amboy. The Whipperwills three or four sometimes together were flying about at noon day making their common cry which is not unlike the martin's, an additional reason for placing the Bird among the swallows. Mr Barons says that the red gum, which he at first supposed to be a different tree from the white, but afterwards thought it to be only the heart of a large gum tree (Liguid Amber Styraciflua), is as durable even as red Cedar when exposed to the air & rain & that to have good red Cedar you must have the heart or red part, the other (and small trees have little or no red) drays very soon.

I tonight for the first time this summer heard the chirping of the *Catydid.*

May 25th 1797.	I have now paid for my Land at Amboy to C L. Ds:	1577.18
	To Aaron Bloodgood	10.
	To Williamson for Trees..	30.
August	To Aaron Bloodgood.....	1.
October	For trees & labour........	20.
	To Corrington for rails....	24.
1798 Feby 22	To Ravaud Kearney, in part payment for his lot.	100.
		$1762.18

(see p: 111 vol: 15)
[*Post,* page 266.]

DIARY OF WILLIAM DUNLAP

JULY 27, 1797—DECEMBER 13, 1797

PERTH AMBOY, NEW YORK CITY, AND BOSTON

(Manuscript volume lettered *Memoirs 14* owned by
THE NEW YORK HISTORICAL SOCIETY)

MEMOIRS 14

Perth Amboy July 27th 1797. I arose at half past 4 OClock and worked in the garden untill breakfast. Went with the children to Mr. Parkers where I left Margaret. Read Hume with John. Read in the 15th Vol: of Enc: which I borrowed on the 25th from Mr. Parker's family: on which evening I read several arts: in it to my Wife: particularly potatoes. Read this morning to my wife art: Platonism, finding the opinions of Plato in respect to a first cause of the Universe & co existing matter, very similar to ideas of my own expressed in *Ufrasia*. I took up y[e] Vol of my memoirs & read to my wife one of the dialogues between Joseph & Abbas. Rec[d] a letter from W. H. Prigmore, informing me that a Mr Yeates or Yeater (for I cannot well ascertain the letters) appeared as the owner of the old Baltimore Theatre and offered to sell it to him & that they had nearly closed the bargain for 200 Ds:, but Mr. Yeates wished to consult his partner Mr Bowley: he (P) wishes to hire it, and to hire our Philadelphia Theatre. Read Hume with y[e] boy. Read in Enc: art[s] Platonism, Plotinus, Plover &ca: r[d] Kalm. Hume with John. Walk out to my Farm: the buckwheat is well up. Evening at Mrs. Terrills & Mr. Parkers, the story of the All-seeing boy has reached this place & meets of course, with believers.

July 28th. Before day we had a violent gust of wind rain & lightning. I was up before 5 & worked in the garden some hours: Read Hume with John & teach Margaret. Write to Holcroft. I had an oppertunity of observing that the young blue bird is considerably like the young Robin. I saw yesterday, in a boys hands, a young flying squirrel. I took him & examined his peculiarty.

Afternoon walk a little way with my gun: shot a rabbit. The male Boblink has disappear'd. Return to tea at Mrs. Terrills. Read Condorcet. We have a fine rain.

July 29th 1797. Up by ½ past four and walk wth my gun untill ½ past 8. Read Hume with John. Rec[d] a letter from Hodgkinson. Andrew Bell having seperated a child from its mother, his slave, the Mother by her cries has made the town re-echo & has continued her exclamations for 2 hours incessantly & still continues them. I am sick, at oppression. Read again wth John. Read Condorcet. Are the words "instinct" & "intuitive" in the original as applied p: 90, 91, American edit.? Read Condorcet, & Hume (wth y[e] boy) alternately. Read Enc: Art: promises. Write to Holcroft.

To Thos. Holcroft.

In April last I received your letter of December. Placed in a country where men, altogether devoted to literature are so rare, that, I yet, have never known one, the idea of a man whose time is so unremittingly employ'd in literary pursuits as that the reading a Tragedy, or attending to a request for a pamphlet, should be serious interruptions was never forcibly impressed on my mind; I must therefore hope to be excused for the intrusions I have been guilty of. My expectations in regard to my Manuscripts, were, that you would look them over, & inform me in few words whether you thought them worthy of the stage or of publication, & whether, there was discoverable in them, that strength which would enable their author, when possessed of more knowledge and juster views of mans duties in society & prospects of happiness, to be of service to his fellow men. Your reasons for not attending to them are satisfactory, especially after having read the Drama you call Wm Tell: Your opinion in respect to that publication I think just & the knowledge of that opinion is, to me, salutary. I believe either of the tragedies is preferable to the Opera of the Archers or Wm. Tell, tho' all of them were written before my mind receiv'd that impulse which is communicated by a clear & undoubting tho' every enquiring philosophy, based on immutable Justice.

I ought to have commissioned a bookseller to send for your narrative; I feel the impropriety of the request to you, & <*which*> at the same time that I return you thanks for sending it to me, I <*must*> am obliged to <*take*> adopt the mode of procuring it which I ought at first to have <*done*> thought of, for I have not yet received it. Your opinion of America is just, your definition of independence true, but at your last paragraph I must pause, for it appears to me, either, that you have not clearly expressed yourself, or, that the sentiment is false.

You say "that which is in itself essentially good will, as I suppose, be good at all times and in all places." Now I querie whether there is any thing in itself *essentially good* except it be virtue, justice, benevolence, or the exercise of them towards beings capable of happiness. But is there any peculiar mode of communicating that knowledge which <*is or*> leads to virtue, of exercising Justice or benevolence, and bestowing happiness, which *is in itself essentially good?* A Theatre (the institution to which you had direct reference) is only good as it is a mode of communicating knowledge; and I believe a state of society may be imagined, in which a Theatre, meaning such an establishment as we now know by that name, would not be productive of that end: if so, a Theatre would not "be good at all times and all places" neither is it "essentially good." If I err in these reasonings, you will look upon my errors with the complacency of a wise man &, if you thing it usefull, point out the cause of my wandering.

To hold a fellow man in slavery appears to be essentially wrong because it is obviously unjust, debasing the holder and brutalizing the slave, to deprive man of liberty when such privation is not necessary for the safety of his fellow men, is undoubtedly wrong. In this country, owing to the vices of the English Colonial system, we have slaves; and, altho' within 20 years the opinion of the injustice of slave holding has become almost universal (an additional proof of the general prevalance of truth) still there are in our southern states thousands of men deprived of <*their natural rights*> even a shadow of liberty and in some <*instances*> districts exceeding in number the depraved beings who live on the produce of their labour. To restore a man to his liberty appears to be an act in itself essentially good: yet is it so? Are there not circumstances in which such an act would be productive of evil? It appears to me at this moment that nothing is in itself good; but, that that which is good, is only so, because it produces happiness. Justice requires that we should do that which will produce the greatest portion of happiness, and in exerting ourselves for this purpose we must be guided by the knowledge we have acquired. Now, we see a number of savages who have been torn from their native country and forcibly fixed in another, as servants to ignorant & selfish masters. The masters, seldom thinking for themselves, have been <*guided*> induced by the laws of their country to adopt the manner of living which has now become habitual to them. The question here may be asked would these savage Africans be made happier by a decree of our national Legislature similar to the decree of the French Convention by which their

Colonial slaves were liberated or by any other measure which should suddenly leave them at liberty, without altering those peculiar circumstances with which they are now surrounded: which should give them liberty without knowledge suiting the society into which they have been forced, without property, & with sentiments hostile to their former masters, the possessors of ye property of every denomination & consequently of ye means of subsistence? Before we answer this question we must take into consideration that The masters, such as I have described them, must be highly irritated at that which they would consider as an act of eminent injustice; their pride wounded by seeing those whom they had considered as a herd of brutes, elevated to the rank of man, & becoming formidable or dangerous from their numbers, their ignorance, habits & necessities; Every sordid passion of their souls set in action by having that which they considered as their most valuable property, <*these herds of slaves,*> (because making <*their herds*> remainder productive) wrested from them; We must remember y^t thus circumstanced, they would become enraged or desperate, and reason, as well as experience, points out as the consequence, devastation, misery & murder. If such would be the <*consequences*> result, surely, the act here stated, would not be an act of justice for the effect of justice is <*benevolence*> happiness. To do justice to the oppressed is right, "in itself essentially right"; but to do him justice I must add to his happiness, and the means of adding to mans happiness depend for their fitness upon circumstances, & therefore, as it appears to me, cannot be "essentially right."

The investigation of this subject is serviceable as an exercise to my own mind; if my errors are very glaring and consume your time unprofitably, you will, perhaps, before coming to this paragraph throw my letter aside: but the sentiment stated by you, seems to me, in its application, or misapplication, to lead to such extensive evil, that I should not think I discharged my duty to you or to the world, over whose opinions you have undoubtedly some influence, if I dismissed the question without as serious an examination as my energies and knowledge will admit.

In May last, I met in convention [4] at Philadelphia, certain other delegates from different States representing the Abolition Societies or friends of the blacks; <*when*> at which time Robert Patterson, a man in my apprehension of much strength of mind & many excellencies, advocated the above mentioned French decree, arguing, thus "it is morally right that all men should be free and what is morally right cannot be politically wrong." Dr. Benjamin Rush, another delegate, likewise advocated the decree and approved of the above reasoning; repeating with enthusiastic admiration a sentiment

[4] Dunlap gives an account of this convention in *History of the American Theatre,* 168 *ff*.

attributed to Condorcet "Perish the colonies rather than we should depart from principle." These Gentlemen, as it appears to me, confounding abstract principles with actions and things, have thrown circumstances quite out of consideration; & concluded, that, as there are abstract principles which are in themselves essentially right, so, there are actions and things which are in themselves essentially right, a conclusion mischievous as it is false. "Let us do our duty," the 2 delegates above mentioned proceeded, "and trust the event to providence." This may satisfy the religionist, but the unshackled enquirer, must do nothing but with a view to consequences. "What is morally right cannot be politically wrong" so say I with Mr. Patterson. But what is morally right? I answer To do justice unto all, that is, to produce the greatest possible quantity of <*happiness*> felicity; not this or that mode of acting for the purpose. Man must make use of his knowledge to enable him to determine what will produce happiness: & of this knowledge, existing circumstances, must make a very important part. Man is the creature of circumstance and by circumstance must his every action be modified. "Perish the Colonies rather than we should depart from principle" What principle but that of universal benevolence is worthy of being adhered to? yet, "Perish the Colonies!" Let misery & death be inflicted upon thousands! Why? Perhaps, that great future good may be produced. Assuredly we may inflict a *greater* temporary pain, to remove a permanent <*or mortal*> disease; but we must be <*well assured*> fully convinced that there is no other remedy.

A certain English writer, induced by the same view of the subject which, as I suppose, misled Messrs. Patterson & Rush, violently assaults the character of George Washington, because, as he states, Mr. Washington is a slaveholder. The Author does not chuse to suppose that Mr Washington is gradually preparing the minds of his slaves for emancipation & giving liberty to them as he finds them fitted to receive it, that is capable of using it for their own advantage & the benefit of those around them. He does not seem to reflect that Mr. Washington gives justice to his fellow citizens as well as to his slaves; or, blinded by a maxim, considered as in itself essentially right, he cannot see, that liberty, may, under certain circumstances, injure the possessor & those around him, or, in other words, that <*freedom from restrain*> there are individuals in certain situations requiring restraint by coercion.

Let it not be supposed that I am an apologist for the conduct of George Washington; he may for aught I know, be a slaveholder from the most selfish and sordid motives; tho' I by no means think myself authorized to draw such a conclusion. I mention the circumstance only as an additional proof of the errors into which men may be led, by supposing any thing right or wrong, but as productive of happiness or misery.

July 30th 1797. Sunday. Last evening Moses Judah [5] arrived here. Dug potatoes in the Garden & pick'd Currants, having got up at 6 OClock. Read Hume with John. Finish writing the above to Holcroft. Hodgkinson in the letter I rec[d] yesterday, dated from Boston July 24th tells me that Collins having ill treated his wife & seduced or attempted to seduce Mrs King, was discharged the Company & finding that [Richard] Crosbie had mentioned some part of his conduct he challenged him: the Duel was prevented by [Joseph] Tyler's informing the magistrates & the heroes after lieing in jail from <*Saturday*> Sunday evening to Monday were examined, Crosbie dismissed & Collins recommitted for trial, but afterwards liberated on condition of quitting the state.

[FROM JOHN HODGKINSON]

"I engaged Crosby for Boston & *relied* upon his services the first night here in Melanthon [6] & so *we* parted. Monday evening I met the proprietors & some warm & I think rude language on their part took place: in conclusion they would not liberate us from our Engagements but permitted us to send another Company: in consequence, *Solée* goes with a very good Company next week. I left Hartf[d] tuesday morning by 2 OClock, saw a play in Providence Wednesday evening & arrived in Boston thursday: my firm intention was to have open'd Monday last, (17th) for tho' we play'd Friday night, I had a Vessel ready, who took the goods & sixteen passengers for 80 Ds: & sail'd by 4 OClock Sunday morning (11th)—to my great dissappointment Mr & Mrs [John] Johnson, Mr [John] Martin & Mr Crosby, all staid behind, & depriv'd the Co. of a weeks salary; for the goods arrived safe time enough to have opened: In consequence I do not open 'till tonight the 24th & am very fearfull of my success 'till September the people have been so harrass'd & drain'd. my expences also by the engagement of the Powells are considerably heightened & God send me a safe deliverance, for I tremble for one month to come. After that I shall pull them in thick & threefold. the weather is dreadfully hot, to lend a helping hand. I will in my next send you a list of the Company & salaries annex'd. My advances & payments have been large. I will subjoin you a list partly.

[5] Moses Judah was Dunlap's business partner, in a looking-glass and hardware store. See New York City Directories.

[6] In *The Grecian Daughter,* by Arthur Murphy.

Mr Henry	12
Mrs Collins	20
Adet	10
Bellanger	10
Munto	35
Tyler	45
	132

Freight	100
D^{o} to Boston	80
Carting	20
Jones	20
Carpenters, property men, house cleaners, Letters	60
	412 Ds

I spoke to Hallam on his arrival & he appointed a meeting with me on Sunday last when he got to Boston: he did not *arrive* at the time appointed, nor have I scarce seen him since!!"

I observe by the papers that Hodgk: did open the Haymarket Theatre Boston on Monday 24th with ye Grecian Daughter & Romp. Read Condorcet. After tea walk out to Woodbridge with Moses to enquire of the Stages & then walking up the post road returned to Amboy by the Brunswick road.

July 31st 1797. Up by 5 OClock. Foggy. Work in the garden from 5 to 7 & from 8 to 9. Moses departs for New York. Write to Hodgkinson.

"I have received yours of the 24th. In my last I informed you that Wignel has taken ye Circus; I since learn, that Rickets intending to go <*Boston*> Canada has *let* his Circus untill Jany if he goes thither & only for 3 months on a certainty. May it not be necessary to look towards P: if W: stays until Jan^{y} & the New T: should be unfit? I have rec^{d} a letter from Prigmore (*here I mention its contents.*) I am sorry for the disagreable events which took place at Hartford. *Let nothing ever induce you to receive Collins into the Company again.* But be careful that you do not do injustice to Mrs K, or prevent her, by severity, from retrieving her errors whether intended or committed: excuse my freedom on so delicate a subject. You do not inform me, upon what terms *Solée* has the Theatre. I admire your dispatch & hope success. Remember me."

Read Hume with John. Look over the Atlus with Mrs Brown our neighbour. Rec^{d} a letter from E[lihu] H[ubbard] Smith enclosing Dr [Benjamin Smith] Bartons list or Catalogue of trees and plants for me.

EXTRACT

"Mitchill thinks the Rice Bunting and Boblincon are the same. I know nothing of the Rice Bunt^{g} by that name, but what I find in [John] Galton's History of Birds. If his account is just they are not the same. He says the R: B^{g} did not appear in Carolina till rice was introduced; and that they only dwell where there is rice. Now, I have been familiar with the Boblincon from my infancy; & no rice grows in N England. Beside, neither the definition nor the figure of Galton are those of the Boblincon.

"Since you have been absent, this very week indeed, we have had a visit from Dr Barton of Phil: He stayed with us one day & part of another: & we, [Samuel Latham] Mitchill, [Edward] Miller & myself were constantly wth him. His apology for not sending you the promised Gatalogue is the occupation of business & of printing his new work, which is now published. He is going to Niagara; and possibly may return this way in about 7 weeks. While here he made out the inclosed Catalogue of Trees & Plants, natives of America, of which there are no correct plates or drawings. It is not as ample as one he had formed, but which, being packed away among his things he could not readily get at. Yet I think there is enough work for you in it.

"I had a short letter from Charles [Brockden Brown], a few days ago. As usual, it is difficult to learn from it, what he is about. He, however, relishes the proposal of writing for the New Hampshire paper.[7] I have written to Dennie on the subject.

"The first N° of the Medical Repository will be published next week—Shall it be sent you?"

The rice Bunting according to [Thomas] Pen[n]ant appears in Carolina in September & then *only the female* which is properly the rice-bird. In the spring both sexes transiently visit Carolina. Now we see the male Boblink *only* in May & June, they disappear and the female appears *alone;* before september it is probably <*both*> they disappear. Penant says that stragglers remain in the country all ye year (Carolina). We see them in flocks

[7] *The Farmer's Weekly Museum,* of Walpole, N. H., edited by Joseph Dennie.

but not so generally spread over the country as other birds neither do they appear like natives, of New Jersey at least; I know nothing of their nests, eggs or young. Walk to ye long ferry to enquire for a carriage to go to Spotswood. Read Hume with John. Read Condorcet, Enc: art: Pyrola. it is Decandria monogynia (Bicornes) Calyx quinquepartite, 5 petals, capsule quinquetocular, opening at the angles. Platanus. this is monœcia polyandria: the occidentalis will grow from cuttings (see Vol: 13 p: 109) Poison & Poison tree: here after giving N. P. Foersch's account as in [Erasmus] Darwin, but abridged, they mention a memoir, which controverts it in all its parts, of Mathew a Rhyn, published by Lambert Nolst. We drink tea at Mr Parkers. I took the oppertunity of looking over the Encyclopedia for certain articles of Barton's Catalogue: Gaultheria, it is Decandria monogynia (Bicornes): exterior Calyx diphyllus, interior quinquefid: corolla ovate: the nectarium consists of 10 subulated points. Lythrum (purple loosestrife) decandria monogynia. Lobelia (Cardinal flower) syngenesia monogamia. Gerardia, this is didynamia angiospermia (Personatæ) Gaura, Octandria monogynia (Calycanthemæ) Ceanothus americanus (New Jersey tea) pentandria monogynia. Cephalanthus occidentalis (see Vol: 4th of these memoirs, date July 19th)

Barton's Catalogue

1. Gaultheria procumbens, called mountain tea, is a small evergreen, at this time in berry.
2. Kalmia latifolia & Rhododendron maximum.
3. Andromeda mariana, grows by ye sides of roads &ca, bears a white blossom: now out of flower.
3. Lythrum Verticillatum, now in blossom, grows along the causeway, near ye Hackensack.
4. Lobelia siphilitica.
5. Dirca palustris, or Leather wood, called also Moose wood. Flowers early in the spring.
6. Magnolia glauca, or Beaver tree.
7. Magnolia acuminata or Cucumber Tree.
8. Cornus Canadensis, grows near the falls of Pasaeg. a very small shrub.

9. Verbena hastata; a beautifull plant growing in the meadows near Elizabeth town, and along the causeway, now in flower.
10. Rhus radicans or Poison Vine, called also Mercury.
11. Gerardia flava, now in flower.
12. Laurus Benzoin, called spice Wood, grows in a rich soil and flowers early in the Spring.
13. Pyrola maculata, or spotted wintergreen, now in flower. A very common plant.
14. Pyrola umbellata, called in Pensylvania, Pynsisensa which is the Indian name: an evergreen—now in flower.
15. Guara biennis, of which there is no plate.
16. All the different species of Vaccinium or Hurtleberry.
17. Our common Hickory, and our common Butternut (y[e] Juglans cineria of Wangenheim).
18. Plantanus occidentalis, or common Button wood.
19. Ceanothus Americanus, or New Jersey tea. very common—now in flower.
20. Cephalanthus occidentalis, now in blossom. This is also called Button wood—grows by the sides of creeks, runs, &c.
21. Mitchella repens, a beautiful evergreen with white blossoms.

I brought home from Mr P's y[e] 3d Vol: of Enc:

August 1st 1797. Up by 5 OClock, cool as has been the weather lately, cloudy: work in the Garden until 9 with y[e] interval of breakfast. Read Hume with John. Call on Mr Kearny he now asks £130, for his land on y[e] hill. R[d] again wth John. Read Condorcet. Walk up to the hill. Neighbours visit us. r[d] Enc: art's: Bradypus Sloth. Botany.

August 2d. Up at 5. Still no rain tho' the cold east wind continues with clouds. Work in the Garden both before & after breakfast. Read Hume with John: read news papers. Talyrands memoir & Palmers [8] oration; this oration gives me a higher idea of the man Than I had; indeed, it is energetic, philosophic & benevolent. Talyrand has the same idea with many others *viz that Americans are less passionate than other peoples.* Their actions as a nation certainly accord with this character. Is it not,

[8] Elihu Palmer, *An enquiry relative to the moral & political improvement of the human species . . . Oration . . . in . . . New York on the Fourth of July.* N. Y., 1797.

if so, because they have been less shackled with civil & religious prejudices than any other people? To suppose that there is any physical cause for Americans being less passionate or less under the dominion of passion, than other people, appears absurd: we can therefore only suppose the cause moral. And shall we not find a sufficient cause in their liberty & its immediate consequences, a habit of thinking and its attendant tranquillity. Thinking gives strength to reason, and before Reason the Passions fade away. Desirable state! from which at present we are very far removed; tho', perhaps, nearer than any other Nation. Read Condorcet: Enc: art: Pyrrho. A little rain. Walk. Read wth the boy. read Condorcet. Think on my romance of Charles Tomson: In the journal of the Heroine we find a letter from her friend who had been by her parents to France, in which that friend expresses her pleasure in finding those schemes of virtue which had been the topics of their conversation, developed in the writings of the French philosophers & promises to send her the books. Finish reading Condorcet.

August 3d. Wind still East with very slight showers. Up at ½ past 5 work in the Garden. Read Hume with John. Walk with my Wife & Margaret. Receive a letter from Hodgkinson written the day after his last (25 July). "You will be sorry to hear of our commencement last night to 220 Dollars! it was very hot to be sure: every thing off with the loudest approbation & if I can but fight over 5 weeks I have no doubt of doing every thing we wish. Mr. Solee the manager of Charlestown has leas'd the old [John Street] Theatre for 5 years & after several meetings for mutual good understanding, we have at last signed Articles not to interfere with each others Seasons during the term of our holding under penalty of 10,000 Ds: nor to engage the performers of each other with[ou]t mutual consultation & consent. "*our* seasons are for 5 mo: from June to October, the others 6 from Nov: to April." he advises me to see Wignel & threaten that if he plays in N: Y: in the summer seasons we will assist in establishing a Baltimore winter theatre & have a summer comp: in Philadelphia: he wishes me to supply him with sperm: Candles & hard & complains of the expence. "My additions to the Company are Mr & Mrs C. Powell 32 Ds: Mr & Mrs S Powell & miss Harrison, 42 Ds: Mr & Mrs Simpson & 2 Miss Westrays 50 Ds: Mrs Pick, 12 Ds: the latter on acc[t] of y[e] approaching illness of Mrs Hodgkinson & the present one of Mrs Seymour (who has been confined to her bed ever since before we left Hartford & is pronounced in a Consumption) became absolutely necessary."

In our walk I plucked a branch of the Cephalanthus Occidentalis: some of the blossoms had fallen & the fruit was swelling the balls, some had not yet burst out & some were in vigour & very oderiferous: there are many of these small trees in this neighbourhood. Receive news papers from N: Y: read them. Read Kalm: Enc: arts: Sierra Leona, Senegal, Scripture. Rain all the afternoon.

August 4th. Wind at N: E: with rain. Up at ½ past 5, work a little in the Garden. Read H with the boy. Clean my Gun. Read Enc: art: Portugal, Pleasure. What reason have we to suppose that the person who declared himself to be Sebastian at Venice, was not that unfortunate prince? This work (y[e] Enc:) is very generally diffused over America: it is a great misfortune, perhaps, that this edition was not compiled by philosophers instead of religionists. R[d] with John. Read Kalm. Enc: arts: Burgundy, Quercus &c. Penant Art: White partridge. A great deal of rain. John as he often does sails round the world on the map & visits the places Cook introduced him to. Call at Mrs Terrills.

Aug[t] 5th. The weather is changed & seems clearing off with showers. A humming bird flew into the room & my wife shutting down the windows I caught it. Tho' I have often seen them in motion, & preserved, I never had a living one in my hand before, it is, to be sure, very beautifull: this was a female & answers to penants description except some streaks of spots down the throat and a very brilliant spot of crimson & gold where the throat unites with the breast about the size of a pea. Rec^{d} two letters from Hodgkinson. Read Hume wth John. John reads for me penants Art: of the Honeysucker. Finish reading Kalm. Write to Hodgkinson. Showers continue wth some thunder. Evening, walk with my wife & Children. Read in penant. Night rain.

August 6th Sunday. Cloudy; wind at west. Walk out to Bloodgoods to get Turnip seed & butter: the old man walked with me to my nearest lot or orchard; he is to plough up a swamp of about an acre, carry the swamp earth & spread upon ye adjoining ground, cart in sand & clay in its stead & sow it with Timothy: I think by this means to improve some acres into meadow, between the orchard and the south east Wood. Pick mushrooms. Bloodgood & I had some farther talk on the subject of my becoming proprietor of the lot now his son's & he (the son) farming the whole for me—he has consulted his son about it & I believe it will take place when I can purchase. Home: read Hume with John. Call at Mr Parker's. Read *Rousseau*. L'amour de soi, is here defined. (1st Dialogue) that sentiment which induces the individual to seek happiness; Amour propre, is that sentiment which derives satisfaction from the unhappiness of others. The man who best knows how to love himself will be the most virtuous man. Read in ye 9th vol: of these memoirs. R^{d} Hume with John. It rain'd again during the mid day.

August 7th. Preparing to visit New York. After breakfast I walked off for Woodbridge, the two Children by agreement go with me as far as the Barracks to carry my little bundle; I took them nearly to the parting roads, kiss'd them, sent them back hand in hand, after walking some way I looked back thro' my glass and saw that Margaret had submitted that John should drive her as his horse with a rush whip & they both were galloping into town. I got a place in a Stage & left Woodb: about 9 OCl: Mr John Heard with me, in the stage was Mr Van Allen of N: Y: one of ye Editors of ye Diary a young man. At Eliz: town I call'd at Crowells: here Dr [Nicholas] Romayne joyned us. There was likewise in ye carriage a pensylvania Farmer, he spoke highly of the effects of ye Gypsum—Ashes for Turnips—Lime on some soils —Indian Corn should have but 3 grains to the hill & should be depriv'd as it grows of the young shoots. I talked yesterday with Bloodgood about the Gum. (see Vol: 13 p: 130) he knew that the old trees gave red gum timber and knew the durable qualities of it, but said, people generable [*sic*] cut them young for house timber as they were so straight & tall. The meadow & marshes near the causeway from New Ark to N. Y. are now rich with flowers, as we walked partly over I plucked a flower of the Decandria class the pistillum of which was passed horizontally thro' the erect stamina in a singular manner: knowing that Romayne formerly lectured here on Botany I asked him what it was but he did not know it, nor any other of the plants in bloom, even the Azalia Viscosa. About 3 OClock we arrive at *New York*. Mr. James Davenport of Stamford is dead. I call'd on Smith & he on me but we afterwards met at W W W's. To enable him to open the Circus [9] as a Theatre, [Thomas] Wignell has now a note for [blank] Ds: for discount in the Bank endorsed by Hugh Gaine. I call'd at Mrs Fortunes [10] to see Mrs [Joseph] Jefferson, in his last letter to her he said they were preparing the Siege of Belgrade for Wednesday & had hopes from it. I call'd at the New Theatre & learned that Henderson is out of town: they have proceeded very well: Robertson thinks things are rather more forward than he calculated for. At Woolsey's I was introduced to Mr. [Hezekiah L.] Hosmer M[ember

[9] Ricketts' Circus or Amphitheatre, Greenwich Street, south of Rector Street, New York City. Stokes, *Iconography of Manhattan Island,* III, 986.

[10] Euphemia Fortune, boarding house, 13 John Street. N. Y. City Directory, 1797.

of] C[ongress], Johnson was there likewise Miss Alsop. Call at M: Rogers the family are out of town.

Aug[t] 8th. Rec[d] another letter from Hodgkinson. In his 3d letter from Boston he tells me that, his 2d night, Mrs Johnson's appearance brought 144 Ds: that his expences will be weekly upwards 1000 Ds: & is much distress'd: this is dated July 27th. In his 4th he says that he for the purpose of opposing Wignel, has let *Solee* have the Phil: Theatre who goes off there immediately. "Mr and Mrs Barret, Mr & Mrs Williamson, Mr & Mrs Jones, Mr and Mrs. Cleveland, Mr & Mrs Barnard (*he* is a capital Comedian just arriv'd) Mr & Mrs Hughes, Mr & Mrs Whitlock, Miss Broadhurst, Mr Bates & two Darleys are ready on the spot, these with many others subordinate form a most capital Company & will by comparison with *his* stand very pre eminent." he talks of forwarding opposition to him at Baltimore &c. "Hallam has never yet spoken to me, but seems studiously to avoid it; & you know I detest his conduct & principles so much, that if he never enter'd into any treaty or bargain with *me* personally, it would be a cause of considerable happiness: On Saturday I paid him no Salary & wish you to inform me if the *interest* upon his property is to be included as usual?" He say the weeks receipts are 628 Ds: "disbursements full 1100." that Hallam would not go with a division to Newport, he then states this plan "Solee going to P: leaves Hartford vacant; I shall propose a division of the Company to go on small salaries till the latter end of September & if their *benefits* do not make up their balance of Salary, receiv'd by those that stay & Journey I will on their return pay the deficiency: this will for the present lighten my expence from 60 to 70 Ds: nightly. If they object, I will propose an acceptance of two thirds salary for 6 weeks & if neither of these can be accepted I *will shut* up the doors: this will want money to put the scheme in execution, & I have none, nor hope of present relief from my embarrassment but from you: but let what will be the consequence I will trouble you for no more after: Williamson setts of Wednesday & I shall be obliged to give a draft on you for 150 & what you can borrow I dare say you will send me immediately &c" In the 5th letter (rec[d] to day) dated last friday Aug[t] 4th he says that on Monday 2d Week he took 380 Ds & on Wednesday to Seige of Belgrade 299 Ds: "I have accomplished the Hartford Scheme tho not so much to my own ease in point of numbers as might be wish'd: the Hallams would not stir, but I have engaged *Chalmers &* Williamson the singer for that and N. Y. next Winter. Wignell would have had them there if I had not, & the Hartford scheme could not have been carried on. Chalmers has accepted of 25 Ds weekly for the Winter, and Williamson 18—these engagements will both be of consequence to us & prevent their opposing us—the Hartford party are

Chalmers
Cleveland
Williamson (singer)
S Powell
Dickenson
Kenny
Seymour
McKnight
Simpson

Mrs S Powell
Mrs Cleveland
Mrs Simpson
Mrs Seymour
Miss Westray
Miss E Westray

Music: Nicolai, Adet, Joli, Falconer.

I have contracted with Solee the Manager of Charlestown to play one night in Hartford as he passes thro' sharing with us after the receipt of 100 Ds:. Three nights at N: Y: (if the Theatre can possibly be prepared which I will thank you to look to) *sharing* with us after 200 Ds: & in Phil: we are to share all receipts after the expences are paid. it will be necessary for you to give letters of Authority to Mr. Solee at Phil: & also to acquaint him that the property is bound to Mr. Bradford as a Printer: this last circumstance Hallam recently acquainted me with." He then presses me for money—says I must pay Williamson 100 Ds: &c &c.

I got up to day at 6, it rained in the night & rains untill late in the afternoon. Write a little on yesterdays events. Call on Smith: he shewed me last night a letter from Brown in which he make many charges against himself as to his conduct towards me last winter in terms mysterious & unintelligible; now S shews me 2 dialogues called Alcouin sent on by him to be forwarded to Dennies paper: there is much truth philosophical accuracy and handsome writing in the essay. S. read me some of his own productions since my absence. I recd from him No. 1 Vol: 1 of ye Medical Repository & paid as the proposals require. Miller came in & we had some pleasant conversation. I call'd at Gaines and learned that Wignell has gone to Boston, & that his Co: expect to play about the 25th Inst. I was again at Smith's, he pointed out to me the review of the memoirs of Emma Courtney: there is strength in it. I dine at W W W's.[11] Home & write. At the store & again at Smith's where Mitchill came in & joined us: we resumed the subject of the Rice Bunting & Boblincon but we could not come to a conclusion—it was questioned if the Whippoorwill was the same with the night Hawk, I doubt it not: we had much pleasant conversation. Drank tea at Home wth G M W [12] & Jos: Sterlitz. Look for Staten Island boats & call on Miss Alsop, there I found Smith & Johnson. Home to meet John Kent, who agrees to resume his situation in my employ. Call at W W W's & pass an agreeable half hour. Captn Heard sups with me & I go to bed past eleven.

Augt 9th. Up at 5 & prepare to return to Amboy. Borrow 200 Ds which M: Judah is to inclose in a letter which I leave open with him for Hodgkinson. In the letter I tell Hodgkinson: that Mr Hallam is entitled to no interest as formerly, because we do not employ any of his

[11] William Walton Woolsey, brother of Mrs. William Dunlap. See Introduction.

[12] George Muirson Woolsey, youngest brother of Mrs. William Dunlap.

property, hav^{s} purchased his part of what we use, but that of any thing we may receive from the N: Y: or Phil: Theatres, Mr H has as formerly half. After an early breakfast I sate off for Amboy in company with Mrs Woolsey my wifes mother & Mr John Heard, we dined at Mr Heard's and he & his Wife went down to Amboy to tea wth us. Call at Mr Stevens's with my wife.

Amboy August 10th 1797. Up at half past 5, walk with ye Children & pick Mushrooms. Work in the Garden. Read Hume with John. After diner walk out with my Gun; the singing birds are fast disappearing. Mrs Parker & her daughters were with us in the Evening.

[Aug.] 11th Up early & work in the Garden; read E H S's dissertation on the plague at Athens with very great pleasure. R^{d} Hume with John. Mr & Mrs Crowell from Eliz:town came to see us & staid till after tea. R^{d} H wth John. Read Mitchill on Manures: M[edical] R[epository]

[Aug.] 12th Rain. Read Morton on ye continued Fever &c. M: R: Read Hume with John who was much struck by the story & affected by the fate of Gourdon the Archer who killed the ruffian Rich^{d} 1st. read in Med: repository. Mr Heard sending his Coachee for us, we all went to Woodbridge to dinner & returned in the evening. Showers. Read in Enc: Arts: Siam, Siberia: examine ye maps. Night hard rain.

August 13th Sunday. Showers. John reads Alexanders feast for me. Read Fourcroy speech on Nitre, M: R: this gives a very clear conception of the formation of Mitchill's Oxyd of Azote. R^{d} wth John, Hume. Read over again M: on Manures & finish the pamphlet. Day proves fine. Walk. R^{d} again with John in Hume & 2 Articles in ye Enc: viz Blois & Becket.

[Aug.] 14th Up early. Quite cool. Work in ye Garden. After breakfast go with Dr Wright the physician of the place over to Staten Island to shoot Snipe: return about 4 OC: Drink tea at Mrs. Terrils. Read in [Erasmus Darwin's] Botanic Garden. Rec^{d} a letter from M: Judah informing me that Solee had arrived in N: Y:

New York Augt 15th Arrived here after a pleasant passage by water about 3 OClock. Rec^{d} letters from Hodgkinson filled with ill fortune—write to him.

"I have just received yours of the 9th Aug^{t} & one written since, without date. In my last but one to you I advised either to proportion the Salaries to the receits or close. I now repeat it. In my last I sent you 200 Ds: the receit of which by you must be since your last. I can send no more; we may as well stop at once. How I shall pay what I owe *here* I know not. As to the loan of 500 Ds: at Boston it must be paid but more time must be given—for any other loan made there I will not be responsible"

I will not finish this letter untill tomorrow—I feel distrust of myself. Falconi has call'd on me & I have promised him the Theatre after Solee's departure. Smith drank tea with G M W & self and went with me to M: Rogers[13] & W W W's, the families were out Betsey R excepted: we went to [James] Kents & pass'd the evening there, Boyd & W W W joining us. Kent read us the Gov^{rs} request to him (as Recorder) with the other Magistrates to attend the execution of Young on thursday next: the Sheriff being apprehensive of a risque, the Govr has order'd out a large detachment of the Militia with arms & ammunition to attend the Sheriff: these orders Kent read to us. G M W has been to see a learned Pig to night. Weather still cool.

Augt 16th Up a little after 5: my night was restless and unhappy, my present feelings are those of debility and sickness. Write in continuation [to John Hodgkinson:]

"unless made for, and applied to the purpose, of closing the business & discharging such part of the enormous company we are now

[13] Moses Rogers, husband of Mrs. William Dunlap's half-sister, Sarah (Woolsey) Rogers.

burthen'd with as will give some hopes of supporting the remainder during the Autumn. The proprietors of the Theatre, knowing your situation will undoubtedly give time for the payment of their dividend and you must seize this opportunity of gaining an alteration in the terms on which we hold it, paying a certain sum *only* after the receit of a certain sum; I am convinced that we cannot pay 10 per cent on the *receits* of a summer scheme; ye number of nights which you have contracted to play in Boston must be lessen'd, so as to give an oppertunity of passing by some of the hottest weather without playing; unless these matters can be alleviated, we had better give up the Boston Theatre, and for the future, *lay by* 6 or 7 weeks in July & August, play on reduced salaries or as we can, a losing game, at Hartford, and make our N: Y: seasons as long *as possible.*"

The morning is very fine, I walked up to the old Theatre, they are making preparations. Saw Gamage for a few minutes. Went to the New Theatre, there has been a good deal done since I was there & much is doing: To H in continuation

"by playing in the Fall in N: Y: we shall prevent a summer establishment there, a matter of vast consequence; & it will be better to play thro' a long season at moderate profit, and thereby prevent such an establishment, than thro' a short one at the greatest possible advantage with such an encumbrance. That there would be some disadvantage in giving up the Boston scheme I grant, but there can be none to equal what *you* have suffered, and the loss and distress occasioned by attempting to keep up a large establishment thro' the summer, in short, by acting upon great uncertainties and promising too much. I feel for you Hodgkinson. I began this letter last night but was too much distress'd to go on. I have bent the whole force of my mind to the subject & the result is as above. If we cannot obtain the Boston Theatre on better terms I hope we shall never exhibit in it after this Fall—indeed—at any rate—after we shall be fixed in our new Th: I believe we shall be better without it. I will write tomorrow in continuation—read this more than once & take no offence at it, our interest is one."

After breakfast I again went to the old Theatre to look for Solee & repeated the visit in vain. I saw Cooper, he behaves like a boy. I saw Barnard, apparently a smart Man, he is engaged with Wignel. I went down to Williamson's lodgings & saw him & his Wife. I came up with him to rehearsal & saw Barret—a fool—a coxcomb—an old Coxcomb. I call'd at M: Rogers's but saw nobody, call'd at W W W's & saw his wife & children; call'd at J[ohn] Cozines. he was out, his sons arm is cut off & he is getting better—call'd at A[ndrew] Smyth's. Solee call'd on me & proves to be a very genteel, acute, frenchman, who lodged at Mrs Amy's New Port when I was there with my Wife, 4 years ago I believe it is. Began another letter to Hodgkinson. Smith drank tea with me & we walked together. I call'd Gaine's, he is out of Town. Evening at W W W's & M: Rogers's.

To Hodgkinson

"Solee play'd twice at Hartford, the 2 nights together 170 Ds: He understands your agreement with him as intending that, at the close of his performing at N: Y: whatever shall remain after deducting 200 Ds: per night from the gross receits shall be divided between him & us; and at Phil: the same calculation to be made at the close of his season, deducting the nightly expences & sharing the remainder; & moreover, that as we are to share equally with him in profits at Phil: so we are to be at half the risque. Whether this is the intention of your agreement with him you can best judge. He supposes his expences at Phil will be 250 Ds: per night. Wignell has gone to Phil: which has determined Solee to go thither immediately, leaving the Company to play here 3 nights & then follow, if his letter to me shall authorize them. I mentioned to him Wignell's journey to Providence with Hallam, and he apprehends some attempt to prevent his getting possession of the House. I have engaged the Theatre after Solee's departure, to Falconi, he to pay me ¼ of the receits after deducting the expence, which can be but trifling. I now again read over your two last letters—the reduction of Salaries is indeed a great point gain'd—you should write on to Hartford and have matters explained there. I do not see the necessity of my coming to Boston, as you do; if you can go on with the business, you can employ an accountant which will be less expensive than my journey & support. I have seen Hyde who undertakes to send the Beds &c for you. Think again & again of what I said in my last respecting the Boston scheme—if we are away henceforward in the Fall we shall have Wignell or somebody here, & even independent of that, I think our interest requires us to quit Boston after this season."

Aug[t] 17th This day I left N: Y: again and got home to my family in the evening, leaving this little volume behind me, consequently I have not written on it from the 17th untill now the 24th having yesterday return'd to New York: in the interval my employment at Amboy has been pretty much as heretofore, my reading principally in Darwin's Botanic Garden. On my arrival yesterday I call'd on E H S who show'd me Godwins late work "The Inquirer" which he has purchased for me. I found a letter from Hodg: dated Aug[t] 18th in w[h] he says "I rec[d] last Saturday your letter wth 200 Ds: & hope now not to want more than the payment of the Bill borrow'd from Mr. Stimson, but for Heaven's sake take care of that." He tells me that on Monday he had 297 Ds: & on Wednesday to his own piece 517 Ds: & he still wishes me to come.

Aug[t] 24th 1797

"To J Hodg:

I yesterday rec[d] yours of the 18th; it gives me breath. Solee opened here last friday (18th) to 374 Ds: and play'd again on Monday to 315. I hear much praise of Mrs Williamson little Pickle. Last night (Wednesday 23d) Wignel opened with "Venice Preserv'd" & "Who's y[e] dupe" to (I presume from appearances) very considerably more than 1000 Ds:; the performance was highly approved & I believe Mrs Merry has made a lasting impression. With the money I receive from Solee I hope to pay Mr Williamson the 100 Ds he lent you. The New Theatre goes on & Robertson thinks may be ready in December. My notes, given to set you off are now falling due. I have again to borrow for their payment; if I can raise more for you I will; but as to coming on to you at present it is next to impossible."

Running about to see & borrow money & to settle the unfortunate debt contracted for Crosbie. Settle Crosbie's affair. Call on Wignel, not up. Call again on Wignel but did not see him. I saw Reinagle & Morris. Having inoculated or buded some trees on the 20th at Amboy I now read the article "Grafting" in y[e] Enc:. Dine with W W W. Smith, Mitchill & self go to see some Elks which are in town, 2 males, a female & a fawn. Surely if *Penants* figure & discription of y[e] Moose, (which he says is the same species as y[e] Elk,) are accurate, the Elk is a very different species of the Cervus. Smith took y[e] dimension & I sketch'd the Animal. Read Enc: they follow Penant. Smith drank tea with me & we went to the John St. Th: where to a very thin Audience 130 Ds: was performed "The Gamester & Romp." Mrs Barrets performance was very respectable & her appearance Majestic, there was not much else to praise but Mrs. Williamson's Romp. Barret is not equal to the first place in a Company *now* & *here*. Wignel was there & most of his performers, he was mighty friendly. Harwood unexpectedly address'd me & I exchanged a few words with him. Wignel's folks were tittering at the performers & Williamson declares *Cooper's Pierre,* execrable, Morton's Jaffier very so so, & Mrs Merry's last nights performance "below par." Barret says he saw "nothing to be frightened at." Got to bed near 1 OClock.

Aug[t] 25th 1797. Up after 6 a little. Solee arrives & informs me that Mr & Mrs Whitlock will be here to-morrow, as he must stand his ground owing to y[e] Fever gaining footing in Phil: He proposes playing here one Month. He rec[d] possession of y[e] Phil: Th: from North, to whom he return'd the keys: he is pleased with y[e] Theatre.

MEMORANDUM FOR M JUDAH

On Monday morning at 10 OClock, call on Mr Hardenbrook with the note enclosd for 500 Ds: endors'd by G M Woolsey & receive his check for the amount paying his demand for discount & charging y[e] same to my acct. & take up y[e] note due that day. At the same time, give Mr Hardenbrook D[unlap] & J[udah]'s note for 400 Ds or 500, if he pleases at 60 days endorsed by me, for his check to the amount, settling the discount & immediately procure post-notes for the sum & remit it enclose to Mr Hodgkinson, Boston. The Note for 600 Ds: for Bank disc[t] you will not neglect."

Mr. Solee & I had a long conversation he seems to consider himself as engaged in a scheme with Hodgk: & me which he is to conduct, we incurring equal risque with him & sharing the Profits. I differ'd in opinion with him & length agreed to leave the matter as the following letter will set forth.

Augt 26th

To Hodgk:

I am sorry to inform you that Mr Solee's intended opening in Phil: is, for ye present, impeded by the appearance of a contagious fever there, which has very much alarm'd the inhabitants & must prohibit Theatrical exhibitions for some weeks to come, perhaps untill winter: this circumstance renders it necessary for you immediately to answer my question, whether it was the intention of your agreement with Mr Solee, that, *as we were to share profits so we were to share risques,* put to you in mine of the 16th instant, for, Mr Solee, having play'd the 3 nights agreed for & finding it necessary to continue here at least 3 or 4 weeks, has brought on from Phil: Mr & Mrs Whitlock (at least they are to be here tomorrow) is making preparations to stand in opposition to Wignel, and supposes that by his agreement with you, *we,* are bound, to stand at half his risque.

I have differ'd in opinion with Mr Solee concerning the meaning of your agreement with him, not supposing that you would involve me in so extensive a scheme without my consent; but, at the same time agreeing to abide by your decision or explanation, e i, if you, in answer to this (which Mr S & self shall anxiously expect) say that your agreement wth Mr S involves *us* in all the expences of his scheme and all its risques I shall acquiesce. In the mean time, I have agreed, that Mr S goes on with his exhibitions and if it appears that it was not your intention to enter on these risques, Mr S will determine on some other arrangement & shall not be charged with any rent for ye use of ye Th: during ye time he awaits your answer; if your agreement is, as he explains it, then, the intermediate time, shall be included in the scheme, as tho' no difference of opinion between him & me had arisen."

I then require of him to know Hallams opinions &c.

The last evening I was again at the Circus where the "Road to ruin" & "Prize" was perform to 500 Ds or more.

As soon as I had finished the above letter to H & eat a hasty breakfast I departed for Amboy in the Stage. Van Allen was again my companion to Woodbridge, he seems fixed in unbelief but by no means in a perfect system of morality, tho' I should judge well dispos'd: we had much conversation. I dined at Mr Heard's and he & Jack went down to Amboy with me, where I found the family well. Thunder & rain in ye night.

Amboy, Augt 27th 1797. Sunday. Ride out to Woodbridge with my wife & breakfast at Mr Heard's: a lovely morning. We talked of a trip to Bethlehem. Return home. Read Hume with John. My wife reads in the Inquirer. Read in Darwin. Walk out to the Hill with my Wife & Children.

Augt 31st. Nothing material has happened during this interval: I have read in the Inquirer, read with John & walked out with my gun, particularly on Monday ye 28th when I went down on the Amboy salt meadow with Mr Patten of Woodbridge to determine some fencing. Wednesday Afternoon I walked out & drank tea with ye Heards, my wife going out with Mrs. Truxon. Thursday (to day) I went with my Wife to Brunswick, from thence to Spotswood, where we dined & I engaged a hundred apple trees at 15 Ds: & then returned home by the way of South Amboy. The Philadelphians are flying from the contagious fever we see many on their road to N: Y:

Septr 1st 1797. Very warm. August has been a cool month. Receive a letter from H in which he says his intention was by no means to share risques with Solee, this is in answer to mine of 16th Aug^{t}: I write to Solee sending an extract from Hodk's letter & telling him I will answer any proposals he may make me for the Theatre.

[Sept.] 2d. Hot sun, but considerable wind. Receive another letter from Hodgkinson. Take my gun & my boy & walk out to Bloodgood's. Attend the funeral of James Goelets little boy. Read in *enquirer,* and read with John in Humes England. M: Judah informs me that Solee play'd on Saturday last, to 70 or 80 Ds: he then repaired & clean'd the house & brought out Mrs Whitlock in Isabella to 280 Ds: & was last night to play in opposition to Wignel, "School for Scandal" at both houses!! Our peaches are now ripe, 3 Trees of my setting out now bearing in the Garden, 1 of them bore last year.

[Sept.] 3d Sunday. Walk out with my wife & children to the hill, we met the Bloodgoods, the old man tells me that a Man of y[e] name of Kenzie has taken possession of a part of my meadow on the Raritan, & has mow'd & stack'd it & I have appointed to meet the Bloodgood's on y[e] Meadow tomorrow, & to see Kenzie & let him know whose property it is. Read H[ume] wth John. Writing *releases* between Bloodgood and myself for an exchange of Salt Meadow. Read in *y[e]* Inquirer, essay on professions, this reminds me of Mandiville. I have been myself a shopkeeper but I never was a thorough bred one. I never forgot the dignity of man, the tone of my voice, my gesture and my attitude were regulated by those of the person who addressed me; to the polite, I was polite, not from an insidious motive, but from genuine sympathy; with the haughty, I was reserved, and to the insolent I was—I fear sometimes insolent—always repelling. This Essay on trades & professions has no novelty, to me, yet its congeniality to my own sentiments makes it delightfull.

Aug[t] [*sic* for September] 4th I went in search of Kenzie but did not find him. Wild pigeons now begin to appear tho' not in great numbers. Read H[ume] with John. Go with my Wife & her mother to Mrs Truxon's. Call at Mr Parkers. Read to my Wife in the Inquirer.

[Sept.] 5th Work in the Garden. Read with John. Write on y[e] releases. Read in Inquirer.

[Sept.] 6th Walk out early with my Gun in search of pigeons but got none. After breakfast I walked down to Corringtons gave some directions respecting my Buckwheat & purchased 400 rails for fencing. I then went up to young Bloodgoods, John with me. After dinner John & I walk to Aaron Bloodgoods we signed the releases.

[Sept.] 7th Preparing to return to New York wth my family. Afternoon walk with my Wife & Children, meet Mr and Mrs Heard coming to see us & return.

[Sept.] 8th All day in the Boat coming to N: Y: where we arrived at ½ past 10 much fatigued.

New York [Sept.] 9th Not well, and my mind much disturb by the difficulty of borrowing money, more by the necessity.

[Sept.] 10th Sunday. Morning with Smith & Johnson. Afternoon, Johnson at my house. Evening at W W Woolseys. M: Judah goes to his Father's.

[Sept.] 11th Attend at the store. Write to Mr Chalmers. "Before the receipt of this you will be in possession of 2 Boxes of Sperm: Candles, one of 30 lbs. the other of 29¼ lbs. Ship'd on board the Sloop Geneva Captn Josiah Hempstead.

Mr Wignel's answer respecting the note is, that if you will get it out of the hands of Mr. Sergeant, he will pay it. If I can serve you in this business let me have your directions."

Write to Hodgkinson

"Since my last I have received several letters from you, the last of which is dated the 5th Inst. I will acknowledge & answer them regularly in my next, by this post I must be brief. The first money you can spare send it to me, if it is only 50—nay 20 Ds: at a time. Falconer was in town 3 days, I was at Amboy and did not see him. Wignel has not accepted Chalmers's draft, but says if he will get the note from Mr Sergeant, it shall be paid, of this I to day inform Mr Chalmers to whom, by request, I have sent 2 Boxes of Sperm Candles. There are no favourable accounts from Phil: I am not well. Adieu."

Continued "Fennell made his first appearance here in Zanga [14] on Friday night, I did not get to town untill ½ past 10, therefore did not see him; the people here with whom I am conversant speak of him as the best Tragedian they ever saw. Mr Gaine's words to me on the subject of the comparative merits of our Company & Wignel's, were "The people thing *they* have some good Actors, but no actor so generrally good as Hodgkinson."

This morning has passed away as Saturday did, in anxious attempts to borrow money. Finish reading the

[14] In the tragedy, *The Revenge,* by Edward Young.

Enquirer. Begin to Copy the letter to Holcroft. Hear John read: but every thing is done with distracted attention

To Hodgkinson

"On Friday evening Solee play'd Bunkers Hill by right from Mr Barret & for his benefit after expences, there was about 500 Ds in y[e] house as I learn and Saturday night the piece was repeated to something above 200. The week before last his (Solee's) *weeks* receipts were something above 200 Ds:. Mrs Williamson, Mrs Whitlock & Mrs Barret have <*many*> admirers, the first, many; but the men of that House do not go down & throw the Company quite out of estimation. I sent on "Bunker Hill & some News papers by the Young Eagle: Mr Burke is here and has had some wprds with Solee & Barret on pretence of not having authorized Barret to play the piece except in the environs of Boston, tho' y[e] written authority contains no such limitation: He says he had agreed with you to have it play'd here *he* having every 3d night—this he told Mr. Judah —however he has bargained with Solee to let him play it & take a share in the profits and to night is advertised as the Author's night with a few words in the *Authors own* style on the Bill. The piece is—as it ought to be execrated."

Sept[r] 12th 1797. To Hodgkinson in continuation—

"I now proceed to inform you of last nights Theatricals—first conjuring you, if you have any money to spare, not to lend it to any stranger as in the case of Taylor, but however small the sum, send it to me in U S notes: for besides the trouble of having Taylors note accepted & collected and the risque of disapointment, I must at any rate wait 30 days whilst I am paying 3 p Ct per month for the money—more—while I am running about town to borrow, subject to mortifications which almost weary me of life. I last night saw Mrs Merry's Juliet with much delight, there were a great many people present, the first and most respectable of our people; whilst at John Street, Bunkers Hill was performing to a mere rabble, amount[g] to a house of about 200 Ds—and even they execrated it."

As you say you "shall be exceedingly anxious" till you have my sentiments on your scheme of buying up the Circus's, I will proceed to give you such ideas as my limited information & other circumstances suggest. You say "Ricketts's lease expires next year" now I am informed that it runs 4 or 5 years yet to come: of this I shall be informed to certainty. Lailsons Circus is roof'd & I beleive nearly finish'd in a style of much elegance. If *these* were ours, cannot others be built? And if Circus's can be built which will answer as Theatres, cannot Theatres be built on similar plans? If Lailson can build shall I not believe that Wignel can build? And I do believe that if he built out of the town he would have business in Sept^{r} & Oct^{r}, we away. Far be it from me to contemn your schemes for our mutual advantage, tho' I believe the present to be founded on a mistake. <*If Wignel had*> You, I believe, suppose the law prohibiting Wooden buildings includes the whole City, whereas, without infringing that law, Wooden buildings may be erected any where to the northward of Cherry Street Beekman St^{t} or of a line running across the Park from Beekman Street to Partition Street and thence to ye Hudson, thus leaving without the verge of prohibition many lots nearly as well situated as the New Th: I have consulted the law & good Counsel."

The time, which, by our engagement We must stay at Boston, makes me look on that scheme with some thing more than dissaprobation. Think not that I mean by this to cast any censure on your negociation or that I have forgot that it once met with my approbation."

The greater part of this day has been pass'd in fruitless attempts to raise money. Gamage gave me hopes that he could procure 900 or 1000 Ds on my land at Amboy but he has not yet accomplished it. I saw & had some conversation with Wignel this morning. He says that he came on from Philadelphia with an intention of hiring our J St Theatre for 12 nights, and then returning to Philadelphia. That Rickets offer'd him his Circus. That the Yellow fever alter'd his plan. That he mentioned to Hodgkinson a wish to put the 2 Companies on friendly terms, joining so far as to put down those people who on wild schemes were giving or rather offerring enormous salaries & injuring the business—that he mention'd a scheme of exchange of Theatres after we should obtain possession of the New Th: but that Hodgkinson did not relish it & *he* said little on the subject. He mention'd something respecting *Henri.* I must speak to him further on that subject. In the evening I call'd on Miss Morton. She gave me a flattering picture of Pellesier's music to *Maria* and play'd 2 of ye airs for me. Night quite unwell.

Septr 13th prevented from sending my letter to Hodgkinson by calls for money. I went through the various parts of the New Th: to day with Ciceri. Afternoon at

[David] Williamson's nursery, his gardenner was budding peach trees.

[Sept.] 14th Write in continuation to Hodgkinson

"Last evening I attended the representation of the *Iron Chest*. There was not, I think, 200 Ds in the house, this must in part be attributed to announcing Columbus for Friday. In John St[t] "Jealous Wife & Barnaby Brittle" 30 or 40 Ds: I believe the general sentiment respecting our Company & Wignels is, that we have the best, tho' Mrs Merry, Fennel, & Cooper are in high estimation, and Moreton, Bernard & Harwood, all favourites to a certain degree. Mrs Oldmixon is not much admired. The Marshall's have joined Wignel. Hallams Mercutio is preferred to Bernard's and Harwood has suffered by comparison with Jefferson & you. I rec[d] much pleasure from the Iron Chest, notwithstanding the disgusting circumstance of Mrs Morris playing *Lady Hellen*. Fennel's Rawbold was exquisite and Cooper's Mortimer, in general, good. Morton's Wilford was, some few passages excepted, very wrong. Wignel's Fitzharding was very respectable and I need not say that Harwoods Sampson was good. Old Morris was despicable, Mrs Francis bad & Mrs Oldmixon unimpressive.

I hope the cool weather has strengthen'd your Coffers, in the which hope I live."

Still endeavouring to borrow money.

Friday [Sept.] 15th Rainy. Looking for money: Attending to John.

[Sept.] 16th Still disappointed in borrowing. Walk with Smith. I visit the New Th: Daily. Collect seed of the Magnolia Glauca, and Cytisus Laburnum. Evening with my Wife at y[e] Circus to see a piece of Columbus.

[Sept.] 17th Sunday. Attend to John. Write to Hodgkinson.

"I suppose my not hearing from you is the consequence of my not writing to you when I was last at Amboy. I hope there exists no cause of greater consequence. I feel, now, no doubt of our having possession of the New Theatre early in December: I attend there daily and yesterday *treated* the workmen on our joint account; I doubt not your approbation. On friday night Wignel play'd Columbus, to something above 600 Ds: the John St[t] Co: put off untill Saturday. On Saturday Wignell repeated Columbus to, I think, less than 200 Ds: There was not a place taken in John Street & they put off until *further notice*. Solee has again been to Phil:; I have not seen him since his return. I hear Prigmore is in town. *The Yellow fever is at Baltimore*. I begin less to fear Wignells making any permanent establishment here; he can never have the same Novelty again, & if we do but determine to begin our seasons here in October we are safe. Columbus is sincerely despised, & if its being represented now will operate to prevent our getting it up, I shall congratulate myself. Mrs Jefferson has Bourville Castle for you & some more News papers. I am yet in total embarassment & cannot raise a Dollar on my land because it is not in this City. Gamage has endeavoured to assist me & I have reason to think I shall be reliev'd for the present thro' him in about a week; in the mean time my credit & my peace suffer. Is there no sum due to you from Hyde's estate, which you can help me to by an order?"

Read in Memoirs of 2500. Read with John. Read in my manuscript plays. Enc: Wm. Johnson calls on me: we walk round Corlaers Hook & return to tea. Smith joins us & we pass y[e] evening together.

[Sept.] 18th. Copy the above letter to Hodgk: Call at the New Theatre. Endeavouring to procure money. Read with John. See by a Boston paper that Hodgkinson has been writing a farce for the day of launching the Constitution Frigate at Boston, called "The Launch."

To Mr James Chalmers

"I have seen Mr Henry Nicols & delivered your letter. I again waited on Mr Wignell respecting the note; he says the reason he does not pay the money, on the offer of Mr N to exonerate him, is, that the note is in an Attorney's hands who has already sued for the amount and obtained special Bail. Mr Nicols has written on to P for y[e] note, but owing to the distress & confusion there I fear still further delay

I remain &c

To Hodgkinson

"Has prosperity made you proud that you write not to me? O! that it may be so! I give you credit for your design upon the Launch-gazers. Solee is almost aground—there must be trouble &

distress there soon—tomorrow Bunkerhill again! Tonight, In G St^t Columbus. I took the liberty of enquiring of J[ohn] C. Shaw, whether you would have any thing to receive on Hydes dividend, he has promised to let me know, what balance there is in your favor after deducting your purchases at the sale. If you can, empower me to receive whatever may be due to you; and send me any thing in the shape of Bank notes however small their value. Francis has paid me ye 10 Ds:."

Rainy afternoon, pass some time at the New Theatre. Evening read in the Enquirer. Go to Greenwich Street Theatre Columbus. Am^t of house between 3 & 400 Ds. Audience seemed pleased.

Septr 19th Copy the above letter to Hodg: mention last nights transactions at Greenwich St^t. Endeavouring to borrow money. Call on Mitchill; Hammersley was there, the subject Mr Hammilton's pamphlet. After Hamm: went out we conversed on chemistry & Agriculture. Street Manure & one third leech'd ashes, is, he says, the best manure & lasting. Call at New Theatre. Afternoon walk out of town. Evening Manumission society & a little while at John St^t Th: with my Wife. Receiv'd a letter from Hodgk:

[Sept.] 20th Copy ye letter to Chalmers which is on ye opposite page. Write to Hodgk:

"I rec^d yours without date giving me an acct. of your business up to ye 13th. Respecting Fennell, he was certainly much approv'd in Zanga & the representation of ye Tragdy highly spoken of. I was much pleas'd with his Rawbold: I have heard no one else mention it. He has play'd once since, in the infamous part of Roldon in Columbus without making any impression, except of dissatisfaction: —He play'd it in consequence of Mr Fox's illness. Solee has again gone to Ph: I fear——

At John St^t last night B[unker] H[ill] in ye house ab^t 200 Ds:. The people here expect much from our N Th: and the additional strength of our Company, & I doubt not of success, if we can but rub on untill we are fixed.

You will perceive by my letter of yesterday that I had knowledge of your "Launch". May it enable you to give me some relief. Williamson has rec^d 20 Ds from me. I shall do ye best I can wth Hallam."

Even^{g} at ye Th: Green: St.

[Sept.] 21st I sailed up to Flushing L: I: in company with my wife's mother. Visited Wm Prince's Nursery. Dined at Mrs Aspinwall's. Afternoon walked to Jamaica, 4 & 1/4 miles.

[Sept.] 22d Walked from Jamaica home. Visit the New Th:. Evening at ye Th: Gr: St^{t}.

[Sept.] 23d Still disappointed in all my expectations of borrowing money. Call on Kent. Read in Mandeville. Read as usual with John in Hume. Evening Club met with me, the first this Season. Kent, W W Woolsey, Smith & Johnson: G M Woolsey went to day towards Norwich to be married.[15] Club interrupted by an alarm of fire.

[Sept.] 24th Sunday. Read with John

To Hodgkinson

"On Wednesday night last was performed in Greenw: St^{t} "The Rivals & Critic" Fennell was to have play'd the lover of Julia, but an apology was made & Wignel performed in his stead. Mrs Malaprop Mrs Oldmixon; Julia Mrs Merry; Lydia Mrs Francis; Acres Harwood; Captn Absolute Morton; Irishman Warren. The scene wth the Italians in ye Critic was well managed, a Duett was sung & "Ting Tang ta". Mrs Oldmixon as first singer & Morton in Sneer supported the scene. Harwoods Sir Fretfull was in part very well, Barnards Puff, totally abortive. Thursday John St^{t} Douglas & Sultan, I was not there. Friday night Greenw: St^{t} "Country Girl & Rosina," to bring out Mr & Mrs Marshal. Moody Warren; very poor: Sparkish Bernard, very fine, in the manner of Dodd with a song introduced, humorous & well executed: Harcourt Marshall; execrable: Nephew Morton very pleasing: Peggy Mrs Marshall; some merit in the acting, but without power and very very inferior to Mrs Hodgkinsons. I did not stay to see Rosina but understand that nothing gave the least pleasure but Mrs Oldmixon's Phoebe. The relief I expected from Gamage has failed, my disappointments have no end: my note of 600 Ds not yet paid off & about the first of Novr I have taken up 2 of 500 each, beside paying the draft

[15] To Abigail Howland (1776-1833), daughter of Joseph Howland, of Norwich, Conn. *See* Mrs. Howland's *Family Records,* and Dwight's *Descendants of John Dwight.*

I accepted for you drawn by Mr Mechler. Solee is yet away. Hallam has not arrived. To morrow night in Gr: St[t] "Merchant of Venice" & on Wednesday "Othello" Shylock Cooper; The Moor Fennell."

Write to Chalmers

"I have heard nothing farther from Mr Nicols since my last. In the Public stores is a Box marked James Chalmers from on board the brig Pallas Capt[n] White from Leith deposited Dec[r] 10th 1795. This is all I can learn respecting it; any directions you may give shall be attended to."

25th Sept[r] I cross'd Staten Island on foot to Amboy with my gun, shot one Quail & one Snipe.

Amboy [Sept.] 26th paid Moor for cutting salt hay 9 Ds 50 Cts. Bloodgood undertakes to purchase posts for fencing & put up y[e] fence for me. Shoot a Quail & a Kill deer. call at Mr Parkers he is very low having been sick ever since we were here.

[Sept.] 27th Walk to Rawway on my way to N: Y: I came this way, to see R Hartshorne about Adam's daughter.

[Sept.] 28th Walk out to Hartshorne's from Rawway & back again to breakfast—he has gone to Philadelphia. Walk to Eliz: Town. Embark for New York & arrive in the Even[g]. Receive letters from Hodgkinson giving an Account of the success of his "Launch."

[Sept.] 29th Hearing that Raineigle had called on me, I went to the Circus & saw Wignel, he wishes to hire our John Street Th:. Was introduced to Mr & Mrs Merry. Evening at Gr: St[t] Th: "Othello & Romp"

[Sept.] 30th Write to Hodgkinson

"On Monday last in Greenwich St[t] Merch[t] of Venice, on Wednesday, English Merchant, last night Othello & Romp. I saw Othello throughout & was pleased with the greater part of Fennell's playing: Mrs Merry was enchanting. Wignell has applied to me to let the John St[t] Theatre to him untill the New Theatre is ready

MRS. ROBERT MERRY (ANN BRUNTON)
By William Dunlap
(In the Theodore Salisbury Woolsey Collection)

or circumstances will allow him to open in Phil: He says he cannot go to Baltimore or Philadelphia at present; If we will let him have the old house, he will take it on liberal terms, (to be fix'd between him & me after your answer) if not he must prepare for the cold weather where he is. Our friends here think he will do us no more harm in John St[t] than in Greenwich St[t], perhaps less, & we may receive something from the property. I wait your opinion."

Afternoon write to Hodgkinson.

"Solee promises me to pay the 160 Ds next thursday, the statement concerning Hartford he disputes, saying he had permission to play twice at that place, that the 2 nights were only 180 Ds: people were disapointed in Fennell's Othello—there was a great house to it. They think that the play is better done by our company & as to the "Romp" it could not bear the least comparison in any of its parts. I have seen Mr Jones, who says he cannot pay the money at present but hopes to do it in a few days."

Walk out to Williamson's nursery and engage 10 Cherry trees, 10 pears and 10 plums. Wm Johnson drinks tea with us & I attend club wth him it being his night. Kent, Smith, Johnson & me made the little party but it was very pleasant. Kent remark'd that men of information were now nearly as free from vulgar superstition or the Christian religion as they were in y[e] time of Cicero from the pagan superstition—all, says he, except the literary men among the Clergy. Godwin's Enquirer lay on the table: I read his remarks on the profession of the priesthood. Kent was highly pleased with it, & with such other parts of the book as he looked into. After club broke up, I pass'd half an hour at y[e] Greenw: St[t] Th: seeing "Capt[n] Cook" a pantomime.

October 1st 1797 Sunday. Read Morton's Comedy of "A cure for the heart ach." I was somewhat pleased with the first part—I believe it will play well. John, undertakes to read Shakespere's Richard 2d to himself. Write to H[odgkinson] in continuation

"Wignel last night play'd the "Jew & Capt[n] Cook" to about 100 Ds: Sheva Bernard; Eliza Ratcliff Mrs Marshall. Your conversation with Hallam I highly approve, & believe your statement perfectly just. Is Mrs S Powell engaged for this place? I hear there has been another Launch in Boston—how does Mrs Hodgk: ?"

Read in Belloy's works. A plan of a Novel has struck me to be called the "Anti Jacobin." Why do I plan so much & execute so little?

[ANTI JACOBIN]

"TO THE REVEREND NATHANIEL BEARDSLEY

Reverend Sir and my dear friend

We now await, but your presence, to give the finishing, or rather as I should say the compleating, blow, to our happiness, by the exercise of your blessed and sacred function in rivetting together the young couple; for Harry Colbert has arrived from Europe, more manly but not less handsome than when you saw him here. The fortune so unexpectedly left him by his uncle has made him an unexceptionable match for Eliza, and we want nothing now to clinch the bargain but your blessing and the holy ceremony.

I remain with every sentiment of esteem & respect, Rev[d] Sir

Your most obed[t] & very humble Servant,

BARNABY BURTON.

Mr Beardsley read this letter, which he found wedged between the frame & glass & covering the corner of the picture which hangs over his Chimney piece, within 5 minutes after alighting from the Federal Stage waggon in which he had returned to his parish from a meeting of the presbyterian Clergy held in Philadelphia March the 7th 179-. The evening was cold and Pompey brought in a replenishing armful of hickery. Mr Beardsley sate down in his elbow chair precisely in front of the fire place; ordered pompey to cease from his illjudged labour and leave the room; then deliberately taking down the wood from the smoking pile & laying it on the hearth, he altered the position of the handirons, replaced the sticks in systematic order, raked the coals under the fore-stick saw the cheerful blaze aspire, swept the hearth, rung the bell & stretch'd his legs in token of returning enjoyment.

The momentary twilight of the Season was gone, Pompey had put to the window shutters before he heard the summons of the Bell which he now obey'd by enterring & placing on the table near his master's elbow, a candle, a pipe, & paper of tobacco & on the hearth a tankard of Newark Cider.

"Boy" said Mr Beardsley looking at pompey and stretching his arm towards the letter of Barnaby Burton "Boy, when was this epistle left here?"

"He was a bwought hee day befoh yessuday Suh"

"At what hour?"

"Bout a haf pass a seben in a ebening Suh."

The minister of the Gospel took out his silver watch from the <*pocket*> fob of his black plush breeches saying "Retire" then looking at the dial plate "Nearly two days ago" he ejaculated "and not yet married——" but his countenance assumed a doubting appearance, not by any means usual <*&*> when he <*proceeded*> added "I hope—for there is no orthodox clergyman near & Mr Burton could not employ an episcopalian." He again paus'd then seized the Tankard, and forgot the doubt. The scenes of hymeneal festivity pass'd before his closing eye & he soon nodded, forgetfull of the past, content with the present, and fill'd with the <*pleasant*> blessed prospect of happy futurity—at the wedding of Colbert & Eliza.

The fore stick was burned in twain & Mr Beardsley yet slept. The pile of <*burning*> blazing hickory fell with a crash—the Man of God started, his yet-booted leg displaced the shovel which clattered & clanged in its fall. Mr Beardsley awoke. On the second ringing of the Bell, pompey enter'd with the Bootjack. "Call the rest of the family to prayer" pompey went out and return'd with an old female black his mother. The priest turned his face to the wall & leaned on a chair, pompey and his mother knelt down behind him at two other chairs. Mr Beardsley returned thanks to the unseen hand which had warded from *him* all danger thro' the day, he pray'd for protection thro' the night, no blessing did Mr Beardsley omit praying for, no evil but what he prayed might be turned from *him* & and from the land in which *he* lived, but above all Infidellity—Mr Beardsley became thoroughly arouzed—pompey & Dinah fell *asleep*.

In the morning Mr Beardsley arose betimes, for he had resolved to dine with his good friend Barnaby Burton, which to do he must ride full 15 miles and the parsons horse, like his master was not easily moved—forwards.

For Buckwheat cakes Dinah was noted, the Coffee to day was remarkably good and a relish of fricassee'd chicken had given the pious man as much satisfaction as a spiritualist who had seen fifty four years of earthly probation can well take in objects of sense.

Pompey who was as much afflicted with rheumatic pains was more lame than common this morning: yet nothing was defective in his service to his awful master.

"Boy" said Mr Beardsley"——

Writing on the above & the train of thoughts produced by it, has given me, again, a taste of the "Heaven of invention" almost forgotten. Read in Enc: Evening at W W W's, Mrs Woolsey y[e] younger made some indirect attacks on my *infidelity* we had much pleasant conversation, Beattie on Truth gave rise to it. Read in Enc: Metaphysics.

Octr 2d Write in continuation to Hodgk:

"When does Chalmers join you with ye Hartf^d party. Can Falconi be put into that Theatre by you? When do your benefits commence & how long do they continue? Can the Archers be play'd for the benefit of the Author? It is the only chance I can have to put in balance against trouble, risk & loss."

[ANTI JACOBIN]

"I remember I did once promise you, in consideration of your faithful services, and forasmuch as I hold in abhorrence every species of slavery as well bodily as mental, that, notwithstanding the great charge of your bringing-up, I would manumit you or set you free, in a short time.

Yes, Suh, you was so good as pwomis me so, five yees ago last Janua.

No, no, not so long. How old are you boy?

Fauty five yee old las settembah Suh.

You must be mistaken.

I dunno suh, my muddah he say so.

I hope the lessons you have received from me have fully impressed upon you the great duties of Christianity, among which one of the greatest is duty to parents. I will give you an oppertunity of practising this <*duty*> virtue, by liberating your mother at the same time with yourself and you may thus have the felicity of supporting her by your labour during the remainder of her days."

The priest soon after mounted his horse & rode slowly towards Burton farm. He appeared self satisfied: but whether his satisfaction arose from the consciousness of having done justice or from the reflection that he should be relieved from two personages who would soon become little better than burthens on him & at ye same time gain the credit of having proved himself the friend of manumission, it would be presumptuous in us to say.

Seven miles and an half had Mr Beardsley proceeded on his destined way, when a servant of Mr Burton's met him and delivered a second letter.

"I conclude then" said Mr Beardsley "that the young people are not yet married."

"No Sir" was the answer.

"Very well ride back and tell them all, that *I* am coming, & shall *dine* with them."

So saying he was putting the letter in his pocket to read at his leisure, when the servant made the unlucky observation that he believed the letter was intended to save him the trouble of riding so far. Mr Beardsley <*rode*> turn'd up to the half-way house, alighted, called for a room, and read as follows.

Reverend Sir & my good friend

It is now two days since, in the fullness of my hearts content I indited a letter to you inviting you to come over to Burton farm & complete my happiness by the Union of my only daughter to a man who I then thought a man of honour, religion, and fortune. Happily you did not come & I write this to let you know that you need not come, for I have discover'd that the fair promise of this mans godliness and our happiness has been mildew'd, blasted, destroy'd, damn'd, by that which threatens, and will infallibly, without some special interposition of providence in our favour, overwhelm us with "clouds & thick darkness" debauchery irreligion & poverty, I mean my friend, that last invention of the serpent, the old Dragon, *Jacobinism*. Yes my friend, Harry Colbert on whom I had fixed my hopes is a rank Jacobin, the match is broken off, I have forbidden him my <*house*> roof & instead of being the house of joy mine is the house of mourning."

Barnaby tho' hurried by his feelings into an unusual strain of eloquence, concluded in his accustomed style of formality. The parson folded up the letter & strided twice across the room. "A Jacobin" he exclaim'd. The word Jacobin is a kind of pandora's box shutting up within its compass the seeds of every evil if not the evil itself: the seven letters J, a, c, o, b, i, n, comprise all the signs necessary to indicate, innovator, disorganizer, anarchist, antifederalist, heretic, sceptic, materialist, infidel, deist and Atheist. "Jacobin" again ejaculated Mr Beardsley. He <*thought of*> reflected on the dreary change in his friend's house & he turned his thoughts to his own: he recollected that no dinner had been provided for him at home. "I will go & support my friend" he cried "I will see this Jacobin, I will know if the Lord will enable me to put down this enemy of faith and Godliness." The servant was still at the door; "Ride on young man & tell your master that *I* will, notwithstanding, *dine* with him." Mr Burton's servant rode off on a quick trot & Mr Beardsley with all due dignity follow'd on a slow jog.

The divine had passed the locust trees & was <*opposite*> between the two black walnut trees which with a Button wood, almost coved'd the house of Mr Burton, altho' now devoid of foliage, when casting his eyes upwards, no uncommon thing we presume in a man of his cloth when alone, he saw Eliza sitting at the great window which enlightens the Stairs and entry. She had a book in her hand but was looking out, at the window, their eyes met, & the parsons were immediately cast down, we do not say that bashfullness was the cause. The lovely apparition of Eliza flitted from the window and vanish'd like the shade of Dido at the appearance of *her* pious acquaintance under the Walnut trees of Hell.

Read in Belloy. Visit ye New Theatre. Afternoon walk out to Sharpless's, he has finish'd a portrait of Mitchill, unlike, begun one of E H Smith and wishes to paint one of me: Smith's is very like. Call at Robson's with my wife. Call in at Gr: St^{t} Th:

Octr 3d Very fine weather. Read Hume wth John as usual, he is very intent on Shakespere's historic plays. Visit the New T: Write to T Cleveland.

"I with pleasure enclose 65 Ds U. S. notes, I must be your debtor for I Dollar untill I see you as the notes will not allow me to send the whole."

Write to J Hodgkinson:

"I wish to know the fate of your 3d representation of the Launch. Monday Wignell play'd the 1st part of Henry 4th & Captn Cook to 340 Ds: Falstaff Mr Warren, Hotspur Cooper, prince of Wales Moreton; Shall I never see Falstaff again, will you never play him? Phillip Ten Eyk asked me something about a note due from a person near providence, do you understand? if you do, write me the state of the business. Solee has again been to Phil: & has again return'd; he promises to see me to day for a settlement. He is in debt to every body. Whitlock & wife are off; there was no playing last week in John St^{t}."

Octr 4th Write to Hodgkinson in continuation.

"Last night at John St^{t} a ticket night, "Jane Shore & Poor Soldier" Jane Shore, An American Lady; Alica, an English Lady; both first appearances. The American has figure and voice and tho' in the main abominably bad, prov'd that she had capabilities. The Englishwoman prov'd Irish, and her *first* appearance, her *fourth* or *fifth* according to her statement to me previously; for she had offer'd herself to be the Mrs Merry of our company some time back. Collins requests that his note may be sent on & wishes to settle his account, pray indulge him. He says you are to give him credit for a certain manuscript & parts, you will know what it is & let me know. I have paid Mr Tyler's landlord 50 Ds: for him & have rec^{d} the money advanced Mr Taylor."

Read in Belloy, Hume & Adams.

ANTI JACOBIN

Silence quietly awaited on the Dinner table of Mr Burton to day, undisturbed but by the occasional calls for Bread & Cider, Kayan & Mustard made by the <*Spiritual*> Ghostly man, who shewed himself as usual not only a champion of the spirit but an unsparing destroyer of the flesh. The grace before meat was short, the thanksgiving long mingled with prayers for a continuation of that bounty which renders supportable the painfull watch which the pious keep and represses the anxious aspirations after the relief they expect by a removal from this sinfull world.

Smith spent the evening with us. G. M. Woolsey return'd to town bringing his bride.

Oct[r] 5th Fine morning after yesterday's storm.

ANTI JACOBIN

The prayer at Infidels <*being over*> a component part of every public address to Heaven, being over, Eliza withdrew, and pipes and tobacco having been furnished for the gentlemen Mr Burton began the tale of his disapointments somewhat as follows:

"You must remember five years ago seeing Harry Colbert at this house, he had then finish'd a collegiate education, which was intended, by his deceased Father, to fit him for the study of the Law and which had exhausted all that the Rev[d] Mr Colbert had left to this his only child: this last circumstance made Young Colbert's Guardian so perfectly easy as to his future destiny that having paid him a few dollars as a ballance of the acc[t] the youth found himself perfectly uncontrouled with a wide world before him in which he saw nothing but flowers and sunshine. I endeavoured to persuade him to pursue the path his father had pointed out for him & an imminent Lawyer, pleas'd with his promising talents offer'd to take him into his office and give him his board, but I know not why Harry could never be persuaded."

Mr Beardsley exhaled a curling volume of smoke, and thro' that side of his mouth, which was unoccupied by the pipe squeezed out the little word "Idle."

"Why I do not think" replied the historian "that he was in love with work, and yet he never held back his hand when his assistance was required by any of the neighbours & the farmers all around delighted in him: and I'm sure he was not afraid of the Lawyers Office because of the books, for he was reading night and day; & besides a great many books which he had collected when at College, he was continually borrowing from the gentlemen in the neighbourhood particularly from Mr Gillmore the minister. I am no judge of these things myself, but *they* used to say that he thought deeply and I remember he sometimes used to ask you serious questions."

Mr Beardsley took his pipe from his mouth.

"Sometimes impertinent ones. I found it needless to answer him for he was never satisfied with my replies or explanations. He was too much of an enquirer; it boded no good. Enquiry is an enemy to faith, & without faith there is no salvation."

Mr Beardsley returned the pipe to his mouth & look'd satisfied.

"I do not think that his character was idleness" said Mr Burton "but some how or another he saw every thing in a different point of light from other people, and yet every body lov'd him. He was constant in his attendance at divine service—but to return to my story. He seemed very fond of my Eliza who had then just return'd from Boarding school where she had been since y[e] death of her mother and taken the charge of my house."

Afternoon, walk with Smith out to Sharplesses. Evening at W W W's and Gr: St[t] Th:. Visited to day G. M W's Bride. Saw Lailson's Circus.

Oct[r] 6th Write to Hodgkinson

"Last night at Gr: St[t] "The way to get married & for y[e] last time Capt[n] Cook" in the house I judge from 350 to 400 Ds:. They were obliged to put off on Wednesday on acc[t] of the rain. Tonight "Hamlet." I have concluded that Wignell must not have the John St[t] Th: I am impatient to hear from you. Solee has paid me the 10 Ds you lent him, the 30 Ds paid for him, and 20 Ds on the note of 130 Ds: which you had not yet paid when you wrote. He does not seem to have determined in what manner he shall dispose of his forces for the present. He wants Munto & wife for Charlestown. I told him I thought you would not object & that I would mention it. They are going on briskly at the New Theatre and I feel confident of opening early in Dec[r]. Messrs Juymond & Langlais[16] open the new Circus on tuesday next. Wignell has in rehearsal " Wives as the were & Maids &c"

Call at Gaine's, Mrs Fortune's, New Theatre, Mr Coits, Mr M: Rogers's.

[16] *Sic* for Monsieur Jaymond and Mr. Langley, "the American Equestrian." The circus was advertised to open on Tuesday, Oct. 17, 1797. *N. Y. Com. Adv.*, Oct. 14, 1797. Lailson's new Circus and Ricketts' Circus (or Theatre) were both on Greenwich Street. Dunlap's *American Theatre,* 214; I. J. Greenwood, *The Circus* (N. Y., 1909), 92; N. Y. *Daily Advertiser,* Nov. 4, 1797.

ANTI JACOBIN

"this made me more pressing that he should determine on some profession or mode of obtaining the favour of Fortune, and at the same time he was made to understand, that otherwise I did not wish to see him at my house. Harry soon after quitted the country, leaving with me a very affectionate letter, and with Eliza all his Books."

Read New York Magazine & London monthly review, write for ye N Y Mag: [17] remarks on St Pierre's praise of Innocence & Generosity.

Octr 7th Call at N Th:. Read as usual with John. He is learning ye Multiplication table. Read in reviews. G M W & his bride dine with us. I hear that Hallam is in town. E H S pass'd the evening with us. Received a letter from Hodgkinson, his business is bad & he in very low spirits.

Octr 8th Sunday. Write to Hodgkinson.

"They played Hamlet in Greenwich St on friday with the Irishman [in] London, am^{t} about 300 Ds:. I rec^{d} yours of Octr 4th yesterday. I cannot possibly be more exact as to the time the New Theatre will be ready than I have been, I still say early in December. By all means begin your benefits as soon as possible after receiving this, they may pay expenses and rent for 5 or 6 weeks and by that time, you must turn your face this way. Sell your phaeton & horses even for credit if you can get such security in notes as will help pay our debt to the proprietors: mention any thing to me that I can do the same by & I will do it. My resources from my store are again stopt by an alarm spread in the Country of Yellow fever here: this hurts us, for I had devoted the receipts there to support our theatrical establishment: however our being acknowledged lessees of the New Theatre an object of great expectation will give us credit to push thro'. It appears to me at present necessary for me to come on to Boston in November, to settle out accts. there & I hope break the ties which connect us <*there*> with it; for I still

[17] "On innocence and generosity," signed "D," appeared in the October, 1797, issue of *The New-York Magazine, or Literary Repository,* pp. 518-19, commenting on two extracts from Bernardin de Saint Pierre's *Vindication of Divine Providence,* which had been printed in the same magazine the preceding month, from the translation by Henry Hunter, D.D.

believe that if we begin our seasons in N Y early in October & finish early in June, no competitor can hurt us. You are, like myself, too much elated with prosperity, too much depressed with the reverse; the time has arrived wherein we must more than ever distrust the dictates of mere feeling, we must act in concert, deliberately but <*slowly*> firmly, the New Theatre is our present sheet anchor and must bring us up. Hallam arrived yesterday, I shall soon come to an explanation with him. I shall endeavour to convince Henderson that it is the interest of the proprietors to assist us in the support of the company by a loan to be repaid out of the first receits. If you indulge yourself in the ideas of selling out & retiring to England, we are lost; those ideas if now entertain'd will palsy your exertions—dismiss them <*that*> I pray you for the present. I believe three years of your spirited<*management*> direction, with strict attention to your interest as a manager and less solicitude for your reputation as an Actor, will put you above the necessity of being either manager or Actor after & leave you at liberty to retire where you please. The public expect much from Chalmers & Williamson let them not slip from you. I have seen Solee to day. I have more confidence in him than for some time past; he has appointed tuesday morning to pay the balance on the note. He has engaged Cooper, for Charlestown, whose difference with Wignell is now declared hostility. Wignell, deceived by the name Fennell gained <*by*> in Zanga has treated Cooper *en Cavalier,* and will find himself injured by it. I have promised Solee the Hartford <*division*> Theatre for his Boston division, untill you leave that place, leaving it to you, to put him in possession; he is to pay 100 Ds for 5 weeks this will help pay our loss there."

Walk with Smith & Johnson who pass the evening with us.

Oct[r] 9th Walk with y[e] Children. Copy the above for Hodgkinson. Call at the N Th: Look for Henderson but cannot find him. Ten Eyck tells me that Cooper & Wignell had a formal meeting yesterday, that Cooper made known his intention of leaving him & Wignell promised to arrest him.

To Lewis Hallam

It is now more than three months since certain conversation took place between us in presence of Dr Gamage, concerning the disposal of the John Street property, and Dr Gamage accepted of the agency in selling it. You talked of buying yourself: if so, you undoubtedly expect to buy on the terms others offer and it is all one to me who buys; but I cannot consent to hold the property any longer than the time necessary for adjusting a sale. Dr Gamage informs me that purchasers are ready and no doubt if they offer more than you are willing to give you will think the property well sold. For your determination on this subject I will wait upon you tomorrow at ½ past twelve OClock if the hour suits you, otherwise at your own hour."

Before the above was sent I met Mr. Hallam & appointed a meeting tomorrow. Evening had G M W & his wife with other friends to sup.

[Oct.] 10th Disapointed in not meeting Solee. Cooper & Wignell have settled differences. Read wth John & in Reviews.

[Oct.] 11th Dine at W W W's with G M W & friends.

[Oct.] 12th Dine at M: Rogers with G M W & friends. Read in review. rec^{d} a letter from Hodgkinson in which he informs me of bad business—he had play'd the Archers once with success and had advertised it again.

[Oct.] 13th Write to Hodgk:

"I yesterday rec^{d} yours of ye 8th, I could gain no assistance from Henderson, he says he has borrow'd from the Banks untill he is ashamed of asking. Hallam is very friendly but I have not yet been able to get his consent to the sale of property, tho' I argued the matter strenuously—he made some attempts at complaint in the Boston business but I silenced them—he wanted money, but soon acquiesced in the impossibility of my letting him have any. He mentioned an allowance for his part of the property employed, I told him I considered it as purchased by us—he said *not 'till it was paid for*. I then told him that I had no objection to considering it still his. I then told him that I always had considered Mrs Hallam as engaged only for the New Theatre. We talk'd of Wignells proposals for the John St^{t} Theatre I told him that it appeared to me Mr Wignell was not in earnest & further that I thought it not impossible but our own Company might be driven in there by the ill success at Boston. He mentioned reports of Wignells getting into Lailson's Circus for a permanent establishment. I told him it would never <*be worth*> answer Mr Wignells <*while*> purpose to come here for the months of July August & September or pretend to play in opposition to the New Theatre in October, which I presumed would be the month we should open in for the future. Do that, says he, and you are safe. He seemed very full of a scheme of sending off a company to the West India Islands as soon as it could be done with safety where he can command the Theatres which are already built & plans building one at Barbadoes. Mirvan [Hallam] to be the leader. I returned again & again to the business of sale of property, and must yet return again. What do you mean about *letting the Boston Th:?* Solee has paid me 30 Ds: more. Hyde has lent me 100 Ds: to be repaid 1st Nov. Wignell play'd on Monday to less than 300 Ds: Next door neighbors & Robin Hood" on Wednesday, "Iron chest & Animal Magnetism" to less than 200 Ds: to night he brings out "Wives as they were &c" Cooper has made up wth Wignell & dissapointed Solee.

Sunday Octr 15th Write to Hodgk:

With my mind occupied, and somewhat depressed, by the circumstance of having in my house as almost hopeless case of <*the prevailing*> fever, I yet cannot pass the post day without giving you a line.

You have been imprudent, I fear, in writing to Chalmers concerning Solee; Jones has been to Hartford & was informed by Cleveland that Chalmers read your letter publicly at the Theatre; and Solee says much to his disadvantage. Solee further says that Chalmers & Williamson to his knowledge have not considered themselves as engaged to us. Solee will be in Boston next week. Wignel play'd "Wives &c" to about 450 Ds: It was badly played.

The person sick in my family is an apprentice, Mr Judah's only assistant in the store, the incident, whether he recovers or not will render my absence from N: Y: improper."

Read in reviews.

Monday [Oct.] 16th Last night Abel Beers died between 12 & 1. About 10 OClock we put him in the earth without tolling of Bell or preaching of priest. This good lad was left fatherless & motherless when 2 years old to the protection of an uncle, who childless himself placed his paternal affections on the boy, who became the sole object of his love within the last year, by the death of his wife: the good old man, goes home to day, desolate.

[Oct.] 17th ANTI JACOBIN

He went to England, from thence to France thence through the Netherlands, Holland, Germany, Switzerland Italy and had been but a short time at Madrid when he heard from me that his uncle (who had been long at enmity with his only brother, Harry's father, because he preached resistance to Britain at the time of our Revolution,) was dead and had made him heir to a fortune which it was supposed would prove £8000 Sterl^{g}. Of this event the Executors had informed me, as a mean of conveying the news to Harry."

With a degree of celerity somewhat uncommon Mr Beardsley interrupted the speaker with "How could you know which way to send intelligence to the Vagabond?"

"Harry" replied Mr Burton "<*ceased not to*> took every oppertunity of writing to Eliza, from the time of his arrival in England, and as she always showed me his letters, which were not only free from Love but appeared to be dictated by an experienced brother rather than by a raw & unguided youth, I was far from being displeased with the circumstance. He likewise sent her books.

"Novels & plays" puffed out the priest with a cloud of tobacco smoke.

"Sometimes, but I believe <*not*> in general books of philosophy.

"Philosophy!!"

"And as she occasionally wrote to him we always had information of the time he intended to arrive at, or stay in, any of the cities he visited: for my part I <*never*> seldom trouble books you know, but his letters were very edifying I can as——

Thus far had Mr Burton proceeded without noticing the agitation which the word *philosophy* had produced <*in Mr Beardsley*>, when he was startled at the loud repetition of the hated word accompanied by the crash of a pipe which the disciple of the meek Jesus had broke into innumerable pieces over the brazen head of the handiron.

"Philosophy," repeated Mr Beardsley "And so you have been encouraging your daughter's correspondence with a philosopher!" he strided twice across the room then approaching his friend "Do you know what a philosopher is? he <*in*> asked in a thundering tone.

"What? I cannot say——" hesitated the astonished Mr Burton.

"Then I will tell you. Some Bawdry, a large portion of Atheism and a full measure of Jacobinism, make a philosopher." The parson sate down & began to fill a *second* pipe saying with a sneer "And you was surprized to find him a Jacobin."

Mr Burton began to excuse himself.

"How could I tell? before he left home the young man went to church, he never said any thing against the constitution, he wrote me a very pretty letter on receiving my communication concerning the £8000—how could I suspect that he was not sound at heart—

and £8000 you know Sir is a pretty fortune for a young man to begin the world with:—to be sure if I had known—but you shall see, my friend, the very beautiful letter which he wrote to my daughter & judge for yourself whether I could have any reason to suspect the treatment I have experienced."

Here the good old Barnaby quitted the room <*&*> but soon returned with two letters. The parson composed himself & Mr. Burton read.

"My excellent friend

The fifth year of my exile is passing away, and <*by*> <*owing to*> in consequence of an event which your good Father has communicated to me, it will probably be the last. My wanderings so pregnant with instruction are at an end, new prospects open on me, new schemes of usefulness & happiness arise & are approv'd of by a mind, which feels itself not yet divested of all prejudices whenever the recollection <*America*> of my country is revived. When I <*arrived in*> left America, driven by poverty and an insuperable aversion to engage in any profession, which I considered but as engaging in those scenes of hypocrisy chicanery and misery which <*I imagined that*> I saw around me, youthfull hope buoyed me up, curiosity pushed me on, and conscious rectitude of intention prevented my sinking under any pressure of circumstance however unexpected or severe."

Evening at W W W's.

Oct[r] 18th Write Hodgkinson in answer to a letter I rec[d] yesterday in which he informs me that he rec[d] a severe wound on the cheek with a sword in playing Wm Tell the 2d time.

ANTI JACOBIN

"When memory recalled that congeniality of sentiment which had attached me to your company, I felt the glow of self approbation at the consciousness of never having attempted to gain your affections by professions of love, or fetter your will by promises of future connexion. I have written to you, as to my most esteemed friend: I have addressed myself to your mind, alone, to the reasoning or combining faculties, to that part of the individual which knows no sex: and if ever I <*indulged*> detected the flattering hope that those powers which I perceived by your letters were daily expanding and perfecting might hereafter be <*united*> leagued <*by*> thro' the social customs of our country in united efforts of benevolence with mine I instantly checked the fascinating illusion, and, wishing, perhaps with a sigh, that you might not at least be linked with a common worldling, I have rouzed my faculties to their usual task, of meeting present <*events*> circumstances with the cheerfulness of virtue, and casting aside all prospects of future events whose causes were not apparent. But with new & unexpected powers "new schemes of happiness and usefullness arise" and I now look forward to a fixed place of abode in my native country, a life devoted to literary pursuits, and made additionally happy and additionally usefull by an union in views and interests—with thee Eliza. I cherish these hopes undoubtingly for I know the virtues of Eliza and I know *myself*. I shall return to Madrid before the time I may expect your answer to this; if there is a coincidence in our views & wishes I shall, then, immediately return home, if not, some change will be made in my plans & my return may be delay'd. If I was to say that thy rejection would make me unhappy, thou wouldst know that, either now I speak falsely or in former statements of my principles, deceived myself or wished to deceive thee—no my friend I know no unhappiness nor will I know it: united or <*seperate*> asunder we will both be happy for we will both be virtuous."

October 20th During this interval I have rec'd 2 letters from Hodgkinson informing me of continued ill-success. I have written to him. Moses Judah has been & still is sick: we were at first much alarm'd but now feel as if the attack was not from the dread fever, or, as if the timely remedies had fully warded it off. This day I rode out to Harlaem with Dr Gamage to see Hallam who is out there at Mariner's Tavern [18] with his Dog & gun: our purpose was to obtain his consent to the sale of the John St^t property, which he gave, promising to be in town tomorrow "and fix the business." Evening, Smith Johnson & W W W pass'd with me, we were as usual when together.

[Oct.] 21st Attending to business. Evening club at E H S's with whom was G M W, Dr Miller, Mitchill, Johnson & self.

[Oct.] 22d Sunday. Read in reviews. Dr Adams's defence &c. teach ye children as usual. Evening at G M Woolsey's.

[18] Capt. William Marriner's Tavern, First Avenue and 126th Street, New York City. *See* I. N. P. Stokes, *Iconography of Manhattan Island,* III, 979.

[Oct.] 23d Write to Hodgkinson.

"It is impossible for me to come to Boston untill after ye time fixed for your closing, my notes must be settled here, which I now think I can accomplish & have some money in hand.

For the purpose of paying, at least in part, our Boston debt, I have given Solee my endorsement at 90 Days, and taken his obligation in return payable within 2 weeks of opening in Boston, the greater part in the first week, I must therefore be in Boston at the time of Solee's opening. I know that there must be some risque in such an agreement but I doubt not your concurrence under the present circumstances. You will no doubt discharge as far as you can all tradesmens demands against us; to the proprietors you may pledge yourself and me, that I will be in Boston and discharge the debt or give sufficient security that it shall be discharged soon after opening in New York. Solee wishes to engage Munto & Wife, I suppose you have no objection. I fear, Simpson & family are no acquisitions to us, but I doubt not you will look well, to not bringing on with you too heavy a company. Mr Judah is still sick tho' out of danger. I last week followed Hallam out to Mariner's at Haerlaem. Gamage with me, and he consented to the sale of the property, I agreeing, to suffer my part, to be applied to discharge your debt, e i leaving it in the hands of the Agent, as a loan to you."

I put into Hallam's hands a paper for his signature empowering Gamage to offer the property in John St^{t} for sale: this I did at Gaines where I met him, he said he should see Gamage & was return^{g} me the paper, but I told him to keep it & if he approved of it, sign it & give it to Gamage, if not return it to me.

Evening Gr: St: Th: Mountaineers. I was pleas'd with what I saw of Morton's Octavian, otherwise we play ye piece better.

Octr 24th preparing to go down to Amboy. I met Hallam at Gamage's this morning and he gave orders for advertising the property. We were very friendly as has been the case since his return. A Storm prevents my going to Amboy. Read "Adams."

[Oct.] 25th prepare to go to Amboy by the way of Paulus Hook. Arrive at Woodbridge to dine & walk to Amboy.

Wednesday, Nov[r] 1st 1797. I returned home from Amboy having lodged the preceding evening at Mr J Heard's Woodbridge. During this stay at Amboy, I rec[d] from Throgmorton's Nursery Spotswood 100 Apple trees & from Williamson's N: Y: 10 plums, 10 cherries & 10 pears, making 30 trees which I assisted in planting on the home-lot Amboy with 15 of the Apple trees viz: 5 Bow apples at the upper end & 10 summer pippins, five on each side y[e] lot proceeding downwards: the remainder of the Apples, viz: 30 Newton pippins marked No. 1, 30 Spitzenbergs, 10 Summer pippins, 5 redstreaks & 10 of what kind I do not recollect, making 85, Bloodgood planted for me as an addition to me Orchard on y[e] hill, compleating it to 200 trees. I had 12 Common cherries taken up from Corrington's & planted out on the hill, likewise, 12 slips or suckers from the root of a Quince tree from the Garden. I agreed to give Mr Ravaud Kearney £140 for his lot on the hill adjoining mine & had it survey'd by Mr M: Halsted.

Nov[r] 6th Monday I again went down to Amboy, put out some young shrubs of the Althea Cannebina & slips of the Cytisus Labernum & Lombardy poplar. I likewise had a number of common cherry trees brought from Woodbridge & planted on y[e] hill and some Locust trees. Finish'd reading the Italian which I began when last here.

[Nov.] 8th Return to N: Y: Smith & Johnson pass the evening with me (the early part) I afterwards called in at y[e] Greenwich St[t] Th: & saw Mrs Harding murdering Jane Shore. Cooper did the last scene of Hastings very well. I can not admire Fennells Shore. Sup with G M W & wife.

[Nov.] 9th Read in [William] Milns' Columbian library to which I have subscribed. Before my last visit to Amboy, I visited Milns & saw his preparations for publishing, he has his own press & Copperplate press &

[Cornelius] Tiebout was engraving likewise all under the roof. I bought of him an Octavo close printed French edition of Buffon. I have bought of G & T,[19] Mickles Camoens and of [John] Fellows The System of Nature a translation. I have read the Monthly review for July. This morning at Smith's room I saw Perkins the point-man. While at Amboy October 26th I wrote for the *Anti Jacobin* ye following

"The good old Barnaby unfolded the second letter without attending to the agitation of the zealous priest, who strode thrice around the room & was only aroused from his indignant meditation by curiosity to know how female delicacy would reply to this accursed letter, when he heard the sonorous drone with which Barnaby had commenced reading the answer of Eliza.

"If the letters of Harry Colbert display his mind, let him return undoubting to his country. His pupil, less exalted than himself, feels her happiness but too much interested in the event. An amiable and indulgent parent, who reads without disguise the heart of his child, joins in recalling thee, Harry, from thy long exile."

"That was all she wrote," remarked Mr Burton.

"All!" ironically exclaimed the parson. "And this is a specimen of the correspondence you have been encouraging and of the man you had chosen as the husband of your daughter! You have been in the habit of reading the letters of a raw, self-opinionated boy who has adopted the opinions and the *cant* of the modern deistical, atheistical diabolical philosophers, and you have perceived no harm in them. O my friend, my friend! you have needed advice since I left the parish!"

"I always lamented your going away."

"It is now" continued Mr Beardsley, 4 years since I removed to ——— at the call of my duty."

"Nobody could blame you, it was a hundred a year more than we gave you."

"I will be bold to say Mr Burton, had I remained here, and favour'd as heretofore with your confidence, this disapointment should never have happened. But go on. What opened your eyes?"

Read in N Y Mag: and "The System of Nature" drink tea at G M W's.

[19] (Hugh) Gaine and (Philip) Ten Eyck's book store, 148 Pearl Street, New York City. *See* city directories.

Nov[r] 10th Compleat my set of [Erasmus] Darwin's Zoonomia: read Mitchills preface thereto. Read in the System of Nature. Afternoon call on Milns & talk of his teaching my boy English grammer. Bring home Buffon. Evening Gr: St[t] Th: An opera [*Abroad and at Home*] written by Holman of Covent Garden Th: wretched stuff. Talk with Mr Merry concerning a Tragedy which he has lately written, "The Tuscan Tournament" he says the story was related to him by Fennell. Morton says it is full of incident & the last act almost all pantomime.

Nov[r] 11th Teach my boy. Read in Buffon, in the System of Nature, in y[e] Enc: arts Motion and Grammer. Write or copy my letter to Holcroft. Call on Cleveland & wife who are on their way to Charlestown.

Nov[r] 12th Last night Club met with me, Dr Miller with us. Write remarks on the Love of Country for the N Y Mag: [20] Stormy day.

[Nov.] 13th Send off my letter to Holcroft. Receive 2d No: Medical repository. Read in it and in Zoonomia. Prepare to go to Boston.

[Nov.] 14th Yesterday my mother return'd from Amboy. Evening, seeing Falconi's exhibition.

[Nov.] 15th Visiting. Evening at Gr: St Th: Much ado about nothing very badly play'd. Cooper did not appear to understand Benedick at all. Mrs Merry was not herself in Beatrice.

[Nov.] 16th Set off in the stage, after leaving a letter for Hodgkinson, in case I should pass him on the road. Very cold. Arrive at Rye at 4 O'Clock, & from the ill-concerted or rather interestedly concerted manner of con-

[20] Dunlap's "Remarks on the love of country" were printed anonymously in *The New-York Magazine, or Literary Repository* for November, 1797, pp. 582-84; his comments were occasioned by an extract from Bernardin de Saint Pierre's *Studies of Nature,* printed in the same magazine in October, 1797, from Dr. Henry Hunter's translation.

ducting the Stages, put up for the night, to start before day tomorrow morning that we may go over that ground which should have been past this afternoon.

[Nov.] 17th Leave Rye in the dark & arrive at Stamford, as the Sun peeping from underneath a heavy cloud, gilded the windows of the Town. A snow storm commences before we have finished our breakfast. Call at Major Davenports. At Stratford I find that Hodgkinson has past me on the road. At New Haven where we arrive after dark, I find Mary Harding. Pass the Evening at Dr Dwights:[21] several of the Tutors were there: a man from Litchfield, a school-master called & it appear'd that much of his business was to ask "Mr President" whether he might venture to buy Dr Hunter's translation of St. Pierre's "Etude de la Nature" the Dr professed not to have read it; gave him a favourable account of it, except the *Theory of tides* which he concluded to be erroneous because opposed to Newton. The schoolmaster, said all he wanted to know, was, whether the book was on "ye right side." The president seemed perfectly to understand him, assured him that he need not fear to buy the book on that score: the Schoolmaster departed & many encomiums were bestow'd on him for his various excellencies, but above all for his piety. I was treated as usual with truly friendly hospitality by Mr & Mrs Dwight, as a brother. I slept at the Stage house that I might rise at 4 to proceed to Middletown where I determined to rest, as my purpose of passing Sunday wth Hodgkinson in Hartford was frustrated, & my hurrying to Boston would be of no avail.

Novr 18th proceed before day towards Middletown; morning clear & cold: when I came to Alsops, he was out shooting, I visited Miss Fanny Johnson, my friend William's amiable sister. dined with Rich^ds^ wife & we

[21] Timothy Dwight, D.D., President of Yale College from 1795 until his death in 1817. In 1777, he married Mary Woolsey, half-sister of Mrs. William Dunlap.

drank tea with Miss Johnson. in ye evening after our return, the sportsman returned with a brace of Owls, 1 duck and 1 snipe. We pass'd a very pleasant evening. Read a little, this day, in a Novel called ye Monk & in reviews of '96.

[Nov.] 19th Sunday. Snows a little. The conversation turning on St. Pierre "Etude &c" we sent to Mr Russell's for it. Richard & I examined his theory of tides with pleasure—as a reasoner I find him in general very Shallow. Look over reviews. What a sublime specimen of Colridges poetry! Rich^{d} show'd me a literal translation of Ugolino's story from Dante, it is the best I have seen.

[Nov.] 20th Call'd at Genl Phillips's and pass'd a half hour at Mr Whittlesea's. Go out to shoot Ducks with Alsop: there are many on the river. After dinner Richard & self ride up to Hartford in his Chair, arrive in the evening and drink tea at Theodore's where Miss Fanny Alsop now is. I observe that between Middletown & Hartford there is practised a very œconomical mode of fencing and peculiarly excellent on meadows subject to be overflowed as is the case on Connecticut River: viz: the plantanus occidentalis or Button wood tree is planted at regular distances and at common rail length and they are made to serve as posts, thus the fences are permanent, and every 4 or 5 years the tree may be cut down to common post height, thus furnishing fire wood. After passing New Haven the stone fences cease. I found the Company playing "Fortunes fool & the Launch" to an Audience of 180 Ds: such great success put them in spirits & enables them to set off for N Y tomorrow. Lodge at the Stage house.

[Nov.] 21st Some of our folks want money. I have little to spare. I gave Johnson Ds: 12.30, to pay Miss Bretts expences; to Mrs Brett I gave Ds: 6.10. Mrs. Johnson seems averse to appearing in N Y again, she resents Mrs Hallam's being call'd for & I believe fears the impression Mrs Merry has made. Johnson talks of returning to England after this season. Dine at Theodores: saw there the youngest brother of the Dwights, Edwin. Afternoon ride on to Suffield. Fences this way, zigzag or Virginian: very slovenly kind of fence, but convenient for removing. Meet at Suffield the Stage from Boston, Captn Babcock in it, he mentioned that the populace of London had insulted, while he was there last summer, 2 Regiments of Millitia, the East India Companies servants, at a parade & feast in the field near Islington.

[Nov.] 22d Leave Suffield befor day: While at breakfast it began to storm: cold rain all day. Ride thro' pine plains: ther are deer on them. Dine at Brookfield, a large & handsome town. Before breakfast this day we crossed Connecticut River at Springfield, between cakes of ice. Came on to Wooster in the evening (Worcester).

[Nov.] 23d Rain still continues & the earth is compleatly covered with ice of the most slippery kind, we have to wait untill the horses of our team are roughshod, or as the phrase is here, "calk'd" or "cork'd." We arrive to a late breakfast at Shrewsbury and have to wait the calking another team. Perhaps I shall call my *Antijacobin* the Innovator, it may not be out of date quite so soon. *Antijacobin.*

"The mane of the old black was grey with frozen rain, while from his mouth depended icicles as chaste as that so famed on Dian's Temple, each hair of his beard had its separate ornament, in size & shape resembling those ear-jewels worne by the wives of our half civilized barbarians, our Ladies—Heavens what have I written? If I had not vow'd that every word which flows from my pen should sail unskuttled down the stream of endless futurity, I would blot from my page those rude, those dreadfull words—fair reader blot out from "by" to "our" and accept the following apology.

"Evil communication corrupts good manners." I have been in habits of intimacy with an odd personage, to whom I should be happy to introduce you, who had so habituated himself to fault-finding, that nothing in the habits, customs, manners, or dress, of mankind escaped his animadversion; but above all his illnatur'd remarks were particularly levell'd at that perfect part of the creation which I so much revere the Ladies; and of all the pretty things they say, or do, or put on, to add to their adorableness, nothing was so much the object of his enmity as that pretty dangling ornament an ear ring or pendant. "They wear them now" he would say "these relics of barbarism, in three links, the first denotes pride, the second vanity & third lust"—pardon me, Ladies, it was he that said it—habituated to his misrepresentations on the subject, when the idea of an earring was suggested to my mind by poor old blacks beard jewels, the opinions of my former companion intruded themselves and the unfortunate words for which this is an apology stain'd my paper before their horrid import was impress'd on my mind."

Just as we arrived at the Inn at Shrewsbury, one of our hindwheels came off, which brought us down; we got out and I had the felicity of supporting Miss Polly Pease, the Landlord's daughter who had come on wth us from Worcester, as we pass'd over the ice. This young woman is modest & well behav'd and has every appearance of what is call'd genteel education: her dress tasty & fashionable: The Father appears to be a man of some property, owns the stages which run for several miles near him, & his sons are the Hostlers and drive them. We were to wait here untill 1 OClock. The storm continued all day & without stopping to dine, I was glad to get into Boston after 8 OClock in the evening.

BOSTON

Novr 24th 1797. I put up last night at Mrs. [Ann] Brown's in State street and this morning after breakfast deliver'd the letters with which I was charged, in doing which I saw Seth Johnson & wife at her father's, and Jedediah Morse at Charlestown: both these gentlemen spoke of the Medical repository in high terms, the first said he had been applied to by several who wished to become subscribers the latter had some communications for it & mention'd a book in his possession of Doctor [John C.] Let[t]som's which he thought might be made serviceable. I call'd at the Federal St Theatre & to my great chagrin find that Solee is not yet come to town with his company: he is at New port. I bought Mrs. [Sarah Wentworth Apthorp] Morton's "Beacon Hill" book the 1st *Quarto* 62½ cents, Mr [Royall] Tyler's "Algerine Captive" 2 vols Ds: 1.50 & some quills, ink &c. Read "Beacon Hill." I was displeased with ye beginning but afterwards found much to admire. Begin the "Algerine Captive" with great pleasure. Evening read European Magazine of 1788.

[Nov.] 25th Go to post office & receive a letter from my Wife. Send one to her & one to M Judah. Write on André. Call on Miss Morton at Mr Quinsey's. Walk to see the town. Call on Mr. Cooper (Saml). Read in "Algerine Captive." Write on "André." Miss Morton tells me y^t^ Mrs Morton is not much respected in private life, but ye contrary; but Mrs Brown my landlady says she is a very clever woman. Evening Mr Cooper call'd on me. Read "Orlando" an attempt at a Tragedy by a young man of the name of [William C.] White, who attempted playing & has published with his Drama, a head of himself in the character of Orlando, it is poor stuff.

[Nov.] 26th Sunday. Read "Algerine Captive" the authors zeal has made him scurrilous in respect to Thos Paine, and yet in the statement he makes of Mahometanism, he appears rather to favour the Musselmen. Write on "André." Cold afternoon.

[Nov.] 27th Waked by the cry of fire & ringing of Bells: there are 3 or 4 houses burnt. Write on "André." Mr Quinsey call'd on me & engaged me for Wednesday. Walk: Solee and Company not yet arrived: I find that Hodgkinson left my pamphlets at "The Boston Books store." I am tomorrow to have an account of sales. Walk over to Charlestown to dine by engagement with Mr Morse and took the oppertunity of going on Brede & Bunker hills, there is a monument erected on the field of battle, & some large houses in the vicinity. I pass'd some agreable hours with Mr Morse and he gave me the history of his prosecution of Reid, the bookseller of N: Y: for republishing Winterbottom's Hist: of Am: [22] which work avowedly contains Morse's Geography and as it prov'd by the accepted report of Wm Johnson & E H S nearly verbatim, with transpositions. Mr Cooper call'd and engaged me for tomorrow. Mr Davis who lodges in the house with me, put into my hand a poem by Mr Thos Paine of this place on the invention of Letters, it has merit: he likewise lent me, & I read it, a volume of poems, by Townsend, London very beautifully printed & ornamented, it has some poetic merit.

[Nov.] 28th Still very cold. No letter from Hodgkinson. Write on André. At a circulating library I got Voltaire's Philosophic Dictionary & read in it. Dine at Mr Coopers, with Mr Allen, Mr Jackson, Judge ———, Dr [Peter] Thatcher a priest, Mr Wells, and Mr Davis my house mate: much political conversation, high federalists, much exasperated against the French. I staid after the rest & Cooper gave me an account of the party conflicts of the Town in which he was the Federal Champion, cutting down french flags & liberty poles at the risque of his life, fighting mobs &c &c and writing down Governor [Samuel]Adams in the News papers. Came home & read in Voltaire, after supper, Dance an Irish West indian who lives in the house got quite drunk, this creature is a specimen of the West Indies & is a lesson in human nature, worn out, restless, confused & flying to brandy for relief perpetually. Cooper is a character, warm, open, eccentric: In his youth a sea officer, now a Notary public and Justice of the peace, ready to quarrel or fight & commanding the peace by a threat and an oath.

[Nov.] 29th Write to my Wife. Read Voltaire. Call at the Fed: St^{t} Theat: & see Solee, he opens on Monday next & has promised me as much as possible of the

[22] William Winterbotham's *An Historical, Geographical, Commercial, and Philosophical View of the American United States,* published in London in 1795, was re-printed in New York in 1796, by John Reid.

receits. He tells me that Hodgkinson is about opening the old Theatre New York. Mr Cooper sends me the presidents speech: read it. Dine with Mr Quincy, who is very polite: meet there a Mr Greene with whom I travel'd in Feby or March last from N Y to Stamford. Evening our family is increased by 2 more West Indian Englishmen, not making an encrease to my comfort.

[Nov.] 30th I am induced still further to involve myself with Solee, by way of getting his Company here as my only hope of receiving payment. Write on André. Dine with Dr Jedediah Morse: He read to me a letter from a Member of Congress in 1782 giving an Acct. of a Medal which Dr Franklin had had struck at Paris & 2 impressions of which he had sent to Congress for their approbation, on which he had represented France as Minerva, shielding America, a helpless infant in the Cradle, from England, a Lion: the writer reprobates the design & the designer. Morse likewise read to me letters, (I believe from Mr Adams in 1783) from Holland, in which the designs of France at that period are exposed as inimical to us & Franklin represented as the Dupe of that court: likewise a letter from [blank] in America to the Count de Vergennes in which the ill designs of France are laid open (the last was intercepted). After dinner I took a long walk, from Charlestown through Cambridge, by Mr. Pomeroys house where I intended to call but changed my plan, through Brooklyn, [Brookline] Roxbury & over the neck to Boston again. Evening rec^d a letter from Hodgkinson, directing me to send on Scenery from Boston, & informing me that he settled every thing here with the proprietors who were extreemly liberal & that there is nothing for me to do!

Decr 1st See Solee who promises me 600 Ds: on Thursday morning. See Jones at ye New Th: [23] & communicate Hodgk's directions. Write to Mason F Cogswell at Hartford to assist in forwarding ye Company's goods from

[23] The Haymarket Theatre.

thence if still there. Write to my Wife & to M: Judah. Read in Voltaire.

[Dec.] 2d Read in Voltaire. Write on André. Dine at Mr Sheriff [Jeremiah] Allen's, in company with my friend Cooper & sundry Judges, priests &c. I saw likewise, here, Mr James Allen the poet, whose manuscript poem of Bunker Hill has been so often mentioned; He is a man upwards of 50, odd in his manners & appearance & very slovenly. My Landlady tells me he is an Atheist & the popular report is that he keeps his Coffin in his bed chamber & sometimes sleeps in it: This good lady, Mrs Brown, gives a good character of Mrs Morton as an amiable domestic Woman, her husband is Perez Morton, a lawyer & democrat. Cooper laughs at his talking so much of himself at his house & attributes it to the wine. Evening read Voltaire.

[Dec.] 3d Sunday. I sigh for Home. Read Voltaire. Walk. Yesterday Mr [Samuel] Parkman, to whose daughter I brought a letter from Mrs G M Woolsey call'd on me & invited me to his house. Evening at Mr Parkman's, nothing was said or done worth noting. Home, Dance came home drunk was quarrelsome, in attempting to pursue the servant walk'd out at the Window & tumbling down broke his head &c.

[Dec.] 4th Take Burns poems from ye Circulat^g^ library & read. Call on Caleb Stimson, he suggested an Idea, that Hodgkinson might establish himself here, that, the Trustees of the 2 Theatres would unite, destroy all opposition & support Hodgk: he said something of the kind had been mention'd to Hodgk: by trustees of ye Federal Th: Call on Solee and on Jones. Write on André. Dr Morse calls on me. Evening the Haymarket Theatre was opened for the Benefit of [Charles Stuart] Powel the man for whom it was built: I went there & saw some wretched acting.

[Dec.] 5th Took from a circulating library, Hutchinson's hist: of Masachusets & read therein. Drink tea at Charlestown with Mr Morse. Evening, Cooper, Davis & Mr Bailly, one of our West Indians & a pleasant man, went on board a hulk stranded by a wharf where oyster men roast their ware & supply customers on the spot cook'd or raw: here we supp'd. I went this morning over the New State house in company with Josiah Quincy.

[Dec.] 6th A man of the name of Campell called on me & told me that y[e] Trustees of y[e] Federal Street house, had refused to let Solee have the Wardrobe untill he found a bondsman for their valuation Ds: 750 with other moveables: that he (Campbell) had consented to be bound for Solee, in payments of 30 days distant from each other (Ds 130) he (Campbell) having possession of the things: but that fearing Solee's ability to make good the contract, he should this morning retract. unless I would cover him: he mention'd many circumstances concerning the wishes of the proprietors of both Theatres form a Coalition, & I, considering that if Solee failed in his engagements it would be well to have a hold on the Theatre, told Campbell provided the things were of the worth, & could be secured to me in case of Solees failure, I would cover him Campbell. I call'd on Stimson & talked further of the Idea of Theatrical Coalition. Mr Davis carried me over to the ticket office to introduce me to Paine (Thos.) a young man of letters who is eccentric, & made poor by a marriage with an actress & his fathers consequent disapprobation. Call on Miss Morton and on Mr Parkmans family. Read in Masachusets hist:. Evening, Federal Street Theatre, Wonder & Adopted child, in y[e] house Ds 120.

Dec[r] 7th Up early & call on Solee, but get no money, he promises to be with me before noon.

To my wife.

"My dear Betsey.

December the 6th hath past and I am still in Boston. Two weeks have I been here, three from my home and family. For my coming hither or staying so long, I incur not self-dissaprobation: that I should depend upon the fortunes of another & a stranger waiting on Solee for money is owing to weakness. Hodgkinson had written that he knew not how to get away from Boston owing to the debts due from us: Solee, could not remove his Company without assistance & proposed that I should become his security to his creditors to the amount of 350 dollars payable in 90 days, he giving me his notes payable in Boston within 50 days, or immediately on opening his Theatre there: to gain time by this means I consented, thinking Solee's payments in Boston would satisfy the Trustees there & that before the 90 days were past I should be in cash from the New Theatre. After becoming security to the amount of Ds: 350 I found Solee could not yet get off, & I, by degrees became his security unto the amount of Ds 750: here is my weakness: I thought the 350 lost if he was impeded in his intended opening & went on to the sum named. I had given Hodgkinson liberty by letter to pledge my word to y[e] trustees that I would appear in Boston & give security for our debt there; when I left N: Y: I supposed he had done so, but I find that they took his security *alone* for the debt. I have let the Trustees know that our present engagement with them *cannot* be complied with, and have reason to believe that some good will arise from my being here, they being fully convinced that as long as there are two Theatres here, neither can succeed, the proprietors and friends of the one, constantly opposing the other; this is not only the opinion of the proprietors of our Theatre, but also of Solee's and both parties look forward to a junction of interests, and to establishing our Company or at least one under our direction as their sole dramatic Corps. Hodgkinson has established himself in the good opinion of the people generally; and the manifest difference in the playing and private behaviour of the N Y Company from the other players has gained them the good will of both parties in the town. If Solee's scheme fails, which appears almost inevitable, there will be but one Theatre allowed of here, and Hodgkinson will have it. Solee opened, not untill last night & then to Ds: 120. That I shall be dissapointed in my expectations of securing all I am bound for is certain, but hope I can leave the business in such hands and in such a train as will eventually secure me. If I come home dissapointed and mortified, it is you that must cheer me to that firmness which will enable me to struggle against every difficulty.

W D"

Solee pays me 35 Ds:. Campbell calls on me and tells me many circumstances concerning Theatricall business here. Mr Dance sends me the Annual Register for 1796: poor fellow he is so mortified at his behaviour Sunday last and at having "walked out of the window & cut his eye" that he has not quitted his room since: he that night discharged his ill humour on Mr Ochtholony a bostonian by birth but always a british subject & a resident in the Island of Jamaica, accusing him in broken sentences of denying his country, assuming consequence among those who knew him not &c; this is now a source of poignant regret for Ochtholony is the chosen friend of Mr Bailey, merchant of Marthabrae, with whom he is returning to Jamaica in Baileys ship & Dance had determined to solicit a passage with them which he now dares not think of. Ochtholony has been since May 1796 in Halifax as one of the commissioners sent with the Maroons and Bailey [24] having been an officer of Dragoons during the Maroon War,[25] I obtain valuable information from these gentlemen on this subject.

Dec[r] 8th Go with Cooper on board the Frigate Constitution. Campbell tells me that the Trustees of the Fed: St[t] House look towards Hodgkinson and speak unreservedly on the subject. Read in Annual Register: their American affairs are abominably stated. their account of the Maroon war is from Bryan Edwards and Bailey & Ochtholony, say, that Mr Edw[ds] who was not on the spot during the transaction, has been deceived, or has wilfully misrepresented facts & asserted falshoods.

The Authors of y[e] Ann: Reg: state from Mr E: that "from the Treaty concluded in 1738 by Gov: Trelawney, with the Maroons, it appears, that they were for every offence against the white inhabitants, to be delivered up to the common course of justice in the island *2dly* "that these people existed in the most depraved state of barbarism" *3dly* "that in the month of July 1795, two Maroons having committed a felony were apprehended, tried by a Jury at Montego Bay, & sentenced, according to law, to be shipped; which sentence was inflicted in the usual manner by the black overseer of the workhouse negroes, whose office it is to inflict punishment on such occasions." *4thly* "that on the return of the offenders to

[24] John Bailey, Capt. Lieut. and Captain, April 1, 1795, of the 19th Regiment of Light Dragoons. British Army List, 1796.

[25] For a history of the war in Jamaica, W. I., and the deportation of the Maroons to Nova Scotia, see R. C. Dallas, *The History of the Maroons,* London, 1803, 2 vol.

Trelawney town, the principal Maroon settlement, the whole body of Maroons assembled; and after some tumultuous debates they determined to send a written defiance to the Magistrates of Montego Bay, adding that they intended to attack the town on the 20th of July. The Militia assembled on y[e] 19th: but y[e] parties were prevented from proceeding to extremities by the Maroons desiring a conference with the magistrates, in the course of which the matters in dispute were settled to the apparent satisfaction of all concerned." *5thly* "that the Maroons in desiring this conference were actuated solely by motives of treachery; that they knew that the principal part of the regular force of the island was to sail on y[e] 26th for St. Domingo; and that they immediately began to tamper with the negro slaves, and to seduce them from their allegiance. Seriously & justly alarmed at this information as the fleet had already sailed, lord Balcarres lost no time in dispatching after it a swift sailing vessel, which was fortunate enough to overtake it on the second of August, and on the 4th, one thousand men and Col. [William] Fitch disembarked from the transports in Montego Bay." *6thly* "that the war now formally commenced, though it appears that there was a considerable party among y[e] Maroons themselves averse to hostility. On y[e] 12th Aug[t], on the approach of the British troops, the Maroons withdrew from y[e] New Town: but they employed this manoeuvre merely as a feint, to draw their opponents into an ambuscade, where the conflict proved fatal to the British commander, Col. [George] Sandford, and a considerable number of his party. After this affair the Maroons established their head quarters at a post which was almost inaccessible, called the Cockpits, whence at different times they dispatched small parties, who conducted this desultory warfare with the usual cruelty of barbarians. Col. Fitch, who succeeded Col. Sandford in the command, followed him likewise in his fate, & fell a sacrifice to this wily & active enemy in an ambuscade." *7thly* "that the general assembly was convened in September; and in such circumstances it was natural to recur to past experience for a precedent to govern their conduct. It was found, that in the long and bloody war which had been carried on previous to the treaty of 1738, a certain species of dogs had been employed to discover the concealment of the Maroons, & to prevent the fatal effects resulting from their ambuscades. By a resolution, therefore, of the assembly, an order was sent to Cuba to procure a hundred dogs, accompanied with a proper number of Spanish chasseurs: but in the mean time such measures were pursued as promised to render their assistance unnecessary. By the indefatigable zeal and activity of Gen. [George] Walpole, who succeeded Col. Fitch in the command, the Maroons were completely hemmed in; and the passes to other parts of the Country were effectually secured. From y[e] want of a supply of water, and the terror which the rumours, propagated concerning the dogs, had inspired, the Maroons were once more therefor induced to conclude a treaty: and Mr Edwards adds that "not a drop of blood was shed after the dogs arrived." *8thly & lastly* "that, in consequence of the treaty, the Maroons surrendered, and with their wives and families were removed in the month of June following to lower Canada, where lands were provided for them, and where they are to form a free, and, we hope, a flourishing settlement."

Judge Wendell called on me & invited me to dine with him tomorrow. Cooper pass'd part of the evening with me. Went to the Theatre, "Mountaineers & Catherine & Petruchio" Mrs S Powell has merit but not equal to what I expected. Finding Miss Morton in the Stage Box I was induced to stay thro' the exhibition: while we were in the withdrawing room a gentleman who joined the party remarked that "Catherine & Petruchio was altered from Lord Chesterfield." In the Taylor, Villiers displayed great powers of face and gave me a hearty laugh.

December 9th Snow Storm. Go with Campbell & become bound to make the payments good for which he accountable on Solee's account, he making over to me in case I am so called upon, that security which Solee now gives him, viz, the Wardrobe & properties of the Theatre, which are sold to him by the Trustees. Solee likewise agrees with Campbell to forfeit all such additions as shall be made to Wardrobe or properties, if he fails in his payments.

MAROON WAR

For the first article see [Edward] Longs history of Jamaica, for ye treaty of 1738.

As to the *second,* Ochtholony says, that the Maroons lived in their towns and settlements as quiet, inoffensive, hospitable & even usefull inhabitants of the island: that he has often resided with them and hunted in their territory: that they were not only civil, but kind & submissive: and Bailey joins with him in treating the stories which would represent them as Cannibals, as the unfounded fabrications of their enemies, or founded perhaps on their custom of treating with indignity the dead bodies of such as are slain in actions against them; a custom, common to them with other Savages, or people in part of savage manners: for man must have attained to a high state of civilization if scenes of war bloodshed & murder do not at certain moments & in certain situations throw him back to the savage state <*at least temporarily*>

I for ye present pass to y^{e} *Sixth*. Both the gentlemen state that, Col. Sandford, was order'd by ye Gov. to take post at [blank] a place beyond the New Town but not so far as the old: that the maroons were averse to beginning the work of death: that although the new town was so situated that an enemy could not approach it but thro' a defile which would expose them to inevitable destruction from the unerring fire of the Maroons, they gave a free passage to the Whites by removing to the old town with their families intending no opposition to the execution of Gov: Balcarras's orders; but Col. Sandford, with [blank] dragoons and many of the inhabitants who were scarcely half arm'd and seem indeed to have considered the expedition rather as a party of pleasure than as a serious invasion of the country of an active & intrepid enemy, having passed without opposition through the defile and the New town, instead of proceeding to take possession of the post assigned him by the orders of ye Gov. pushed forward to attack the Old town, which was likewise defended by a defile according to the custom of this people, a practise no doubt established during the war preceding the treaty of 1738. It is supposed that Sandford would not thus have deviated from his instructions, if he had not, as well as many of the planters & merchants who were with him, been heated by intemperate use of wine. The Maroons finding their retreat attacked defended that defile which led to the immediate depot of all they held dear, their aged, their wives and their children: and though the place in which they made their stand was infinitely inferior in strength to the first defile, such was their unerring aim, that after killing Sandford & the officers and gentlemen who were with him, they destroyed at their leisure the greater part of the soldiers, and it is not certain that they lost a single man. It appears that at the time Fitch lost his life, there was a plan of a general attack upon the Blacks in revolt, the militia of the South side being ordered to advance & take post at [blank] while those of the North side should encamp at [blank] in the first of these parties was Bailey in the second Ochtholony. Col. Fitch wth the main body was to advance in the center & it was while he was reconnoitering for a fit spot for his station, that in passing from one eminence to another, within view, by the advice of [blank] he fell into the ambuscade of the Maroons and with the greater part of his Companions, was cut off.

Seventhly. Genl Walpole who succeeded Fitch, was empowered to treat with the Enemy which he did, one of the express articles (tho' private) being that they should not be remov'd from the Island. As to the reasons given for their concluding this treaty, they are false: both gentlemen concurring in the assertions, that they not only were not hemmed in, but that, from the nature of the Country, they could not be hemmed in: that they could remove from place to place with facility & without danger: that they knew every defile & could retreat or advance as occasion required, in situations & by passes, mostly unknown to their enemies & when known, to them impassible: that while their comparatively enervated foes were obliged in that sultry clime to sweat under loads of provision in their marches, the Blacks knew where to seek the delicious fruits of the Country, and could kill of the herds of wild Hogs what number they pleased; the Thatch tree not only supplied them with excellent food, but by consuming it and lixiviating the ashes they at any time procured salt for their culinary purposes: and that, as to water, they had plentifull supplies of it, while their pursuers were sinking with fatigue & thirst. Mr Bailey says that he has, <*with his fellow soldiers,*> heard the murmuring of the water falls, in the deep gullies possessed by the Maroons, while <*they have been*> parched with heat & toil & unable to procure a drop of moisture, he & his fellow soldiers, have listened, longing, to the sound, without daring to advance towards it.

Concerning ye dogs I have not yet made enquiry.

Far am I from wishing to injure Mr E: a gentleman whose labours have delighted & instructed thousands, but when I see him joining with the throng to lacerate the flesh of the oppressed, I will exert my utmost power to turn aside the blow even tho' the lash should fall on his shoulders.

Eightly. "In consequence of this treaty the Maroons surrendered" but it is false that in consequence thereof they were removed to lower Canada. When the general Assembly found that they had these people in their power, they determined on their removal from the Island: this measure, Gen. Walpole strenuously opposed and threatened to return to England & to throw up his commission, justly feeling the aggravated insult of having the principal article of that treaty openly violated, which he had, under the sanction of the Assembly's instructions, concluded, so much to the advantage of the Island. The Assembly then altered their mode of proceeding and employed agents to persuade the Maroons that after the blood that had been spilt, they could never be happy in the neighbourhood of the whites; representing the intentions of the Assembly as perfectly honourable & friendly, that they should be removed & settled in some Country suitable to them & their wants supplied: <*by the Assembly,*> and by tampering with one of their leaders of the name of Smith & withal promising him and his family a place of residence in the Island, they finally procured these ignorant people to petition the Assembly to remove them: on which they voted £20,000 Sterl^{g} to remove them to Halifax & settle them comfortably, to which place they proceeded, attended by commissioners. Surely this was not the climate for an African Negroe or West indian Maroon to be transplanted to: but Gov. [Sir John] Wentworth seizing the oppertunity of speculation, represented to the Court of Great Britain certain advantages to be derived from settling these people in the province & in violation of truth, that they were satisfied with their situation, and making similar representations to the general Assembly of Jamaica offered to take the herd off their [hands] on condition. The Assembly happy to get rid of these unfortunate wretches, very readily believed that they were very happy amidst the snows of Canada and agreed to the proposals: the Maroons are therefore now left to the brotherly love of Gov. Wentworth & the commissioners are returning with petitions to the General Assembly for relief.

Disappointed by Solee who fail'd in his engagement not even calling on me, I sought & found him and he promises to meet me tomorrow 12 OClock. I dine at Judge Wendel's with company. Evening talk with Ochtholony.

December 10th Sunday. Read in Annual register.

Maroon War

Second article. There are still three settlements of Maroons remaining at Jamaica, the people of which were not concerned in the war, and indeed are not either numerous or warlike; the Maroons of Trelawney town, being the only formidable settlement: they were accustomed to the use of fire arms from infancy in hunting for food, and for the runaways from the plantations, an abominable service which they performed for the whites.

Third article. Two Maroons, in hunting, killed two pigs belonging to a neighbouring plantation, they say, mistaking them for wild pigs. They were taken, and tried by a law made subsequently to the Maroon treaty & in contravention thereof, condemned by the evidence of a slave and whipped by the hands of a runaway negroe whom they had restored to his master: one may suppose that the man who had been deprived of his liberty by them would not spare them when under his lash and it will be found difficult by the friend of Justice to pity their retributory suffering, while at the same time we cannot but be astonished at the impolitic conduct of the Magistrates of Montego bay.

Fourth article. It was this last indignity which kindled into a blaze the touch-wood disposition of the inhabitants of Trelawney town, and some among them breathed war and defiance, particularly a fellow called Palmer, who, when one of the chiefs from another Maroon settlement came by desire of the English and endeavoured to persuade them from hostility, after having in vain caution'd the old man to silence, shot him on the spot, & cutting of his head kick'd it down the hill on which they were assembled: <*crying out*> tauntingly desiring it to tell those who sent him that it was war. This Palmer is now with the tribe at Hallifax and is one of the few, who were excepted to in the private Treaty of Gen[l] Walpole, as not being to remain in the Island, but he stands not alone now, and even Smith, who was employ'd to persuade his countrymen to comply with the wishes of the Legislature, under promise of liberty to return, is now in the same predicament with the ruffian Palmer, forcibly detained by Gov: Wentworth contrary to the wishes of the commissioners. It appears from the representations of my informants that the Maroons were at this time generally desirous of a reconciliation, and that 17 of them, in compliance with the Governors proclamation did come in, but when their remaining companions saw that they were treated as prisoners, and marched, with their hands tied, down to Montego bay and their put on board of vessels in the harbour; they exclaimed "there is no trusting the white men" and justly concluded that they had no safety but in arms. The 17 men who came in before hostilities commenced, are equally exposed to all the rigours of transportation & the cold climate of Halifax.

Fifth article. There is every reason to believe that the Maroons were not actuated by treachery.

Sixth article. It appears that the Maroons had even removed their families beyond the old town, & that Col. Sandford with companions and Dragoons, an enemy quite new to the Negroes, had enterred or were enterring the old town without opposition, shouting & huzzaing in a tumultous manner, when Sandford seeing a Maroon, who had not had time to conceal himself, rode after him & discharged his pistol at him, the fugitive escaped & one of his companions instantly shot Sandford dead, on this the firing commenced, and happy were the few whites who escaped safe from the bloody field. It appears that while Fitch had the command, several attempts were made to induce the Maroons to surrender & many conferrences held with their chiefs, but as the Col. had not power to ensure their remaining on the Island, he could do nothing. Smith was generally on these conferences, & attempts were made to induce him to leave the rebels, but he told them that even if he wished it he could not bring off his family, & that, they must live and die together.

Seventh article. The Thatch tree, is low, having a very short trunk, the foliage resembling that of the Cocoa tree, it is the leaves which are eaten and resemble Cabbage, with a bitter taste. The Maroons were not apprehensive of the Dogs.

Instead of Mr. Solee, I receive a billet from him informing me that he has taken physic & cannot come out, at present, but will wait on me at 5 this evening. The evening comes but no Solee. Dance has not been from his room yet, but to night gets drunk with brandy. Read in Annual reg:. Write on André

Decr 11th Call on Solee, he was out. He calls on me, but still no money. I let him know that his note endorsed by Jones is due as well as the acknowledgement for 700 Ds:. He promises me 200 Ds or upwards to night between play & Farce, or if the receits will not allow it to raise it by aid of a friend & the sacrifice of Goods at Auction tomorrow morning.

Ochterlony & Baily go this morning to Portland, the first shewed me extracts from Gov: Wentworths letters to the Duke of Portland, published in the *Sun* London: these extracts are to be published here on Wednesday, & are to be followed by remarks on them, by Ochterlony: He has left for me the following memorandum.

"Alex Ochterlony of Sav[anna] La Mar, Jamaica, requests that Mr Dunlap will do him the favor to forward any publications to the above address that may be relative to the Maroons.

I got from the Town library by aid of Mr Cooper, a quarto History of Jamaica, I suppose Longs. I find from this that the original Maroons or Marons, were the negroes of the Spaniards disposess'd by Penn & Venables, who on the expulsion of their masters fled to the interior & continued a grievous thorn in the flesh of the Conquerors. According to the treaty of 1739 they were to remain free, to have in fee simple 1500 acres of land near Trelawney Town with liberty of hunt^{g} anywhere within 3 miles of any settlement (I suppose the author means any where without 3 miles &c) that if any white man did them injury, they should apply to a Magistrate for redress & if a Maron injured a white person, the offender should be delivered up to Justice: That Cudjoe & his successors should have full power to punish crimes committed among themselves, the punishment of death excepted, capital cases being reserved for the tribunal of the White Magistrate where the maron was to be tried like "other free Negroes." These are the principal articles mention'd by this historian who does not give the whole treaty.

I call on Miss Morton & Mrs Quincy. After noon Quincy called on me & carried me to the Hall of the Historical Society where are many valuable books & manuscripts relative to our Country as well as natural productions: by appointment I am to dine with him & his family at 1 tomorrow & proceed with them to Cambridge to see the Colleges &c. Evening Theatre, murder of Hamlet. No money for me.

Decr 12th Oppress'd with a heavy cold on my lungs. In vain I expect money from Solee: his Managerial Career seems to be drawing to a close in this quarter. After taking an early dinner with Josiah Quincy & family, he, his wife, Mis Morton & self, proceeded in a good Hack Coach, to Cambridge the afternoon very fine. We saw the library, said to contain 14000 Vols: they are elegantly bound & tastily arranged. Mr Adams the present president of ye U S has lately presented a very valuable collection of French books from his private library. They have a museum here. In a very handsome room opposite the library is the celebrated orrery made by Mr [Joseph] Pope of Boston, in this room are pictures of the benefactors of the Colledge, & of Messrs Washington & Adams, 2 of the first, one by Trumbull & an execrable thing by Savage: Mr Adams's is by Trumbull & at first did not appear to me like him, but on examination I found it accurate, except the tasty air which the painter has diffused over it. Our expedition was very agreable. Evening at Mr Cooper's, Ladies there, Mr Parsons & wife, Mr [Thomas] McDonnough, British Consul & his wife & daughters, I had some conversation with him, he is *a good sort of man*. Mr Parsons put me in mind of the young pensylvaman with whom I travel'd from Stamford in Feby or March last who gave me an account of Muir: Mr P had travelled on from N Y to Phil: with him & I had been a subject of conversation: Mr P mentioned his travelling southward from Phil: in company with Jefferson, Blount & Taswell, he says they appear'd to agree in political sentiments, that Jefferson was a polite man, but much attached to the french & their politics: Blount he said, was a "bitter fellow." Taswell mild in manners, an *ennemy to Commerce,* supposing it the bane of republics. A Gentleman from Plymouth Mr or Doctor Howard,[26] who now lodges with us, was a surgeon in our western expedition under [Anthony] Wayne, & says that had not Gen[l] [James] Wilkinson, by prevailing on Gen[l] Wayne, by repeated solicitations, to shorten his line of march, (which was extended in Indian file, each man distant from the next 6 foot,) and compress his strength, the Army would probably have been defeated, as under Sinclair.[27]

Dec[r] 13th Again disappointed by Solee. Write to my wife. Buy Mrs. Mortons Ouabi. Mr Davis presents to me, Paine's poem called "The ruling passion." Read in these poems and in "Hist: of Jamaica." There is much curious matter here concerning Negroes & monkeys a strange mass of absurdity in theory, and error in supposed fact. This is curious "A Buccanneer historian (Esquemeling) tells us that having landed with a party at Costa Rica, the toil of shooting was sufficiently compensated by the pleasure of killing the Monkeys:" they were very dextrous in eluding the arm of the *sportsmen* & he adds that "it was *high fun* to see the females carry their little ones on their backs *just as the Negroes do their Children.*" While these *gentlemen* were *amusing* themselves, the historian says, that if a monkey was wounded "the rest flocked about him, and while some laid their paws upon the wound, to hinder the blood from issuing forth, others gather'd moss from the trees (or rather probably says Long, some species of styphic fungus) & thrust into the orifice by which means they stopped the effusion. At other times they gathered par-

[26] Nathan Hayward. See F. B. Heitman, *Register of the U. S. Army, 1789-1903,* I, 517; Wm. T. Davis, *Plymouth Memories of an Octogenarian,* 162. He received an honorary M.D. from Harvard in 1819.

[27] Major General Arthur St. Clair, Governor of the Northwest Territory, was defeated by the Indians at Fort Recovery, Ohio, in November, 1791.

ticular herbs & chewing them in their mouth, applied them as a poultice: all which says he (the Buccaneer, whose words are now quoted) "caused in me great admiration, seeing such strange actions in those *irrational* creatures, which testified, the fidelity & love they had for one another."

Here we hear the animal who was amused with the *"high fun"* of shooting those creatures whose amiable & tender behaviour he bears testimony to, murdering them in sport even while carrying their young from the scene of danger, or exposing themselves to death by crowding round their wounded companions for the purposes of love; we hear this animal calling these superior beings (superior at least in this picture) *"irrational."* If these ignorant buccaneers had not been hardened by the absurd doctrine & prejudice of *instinct* may we not suppose that they would probably have acted more like rational animals, themselves, or at least have evinced some of that irrational benevolence so conspicuously displayed by the Monkeys.

The following fact, brought forward among a heterogeneous mass of fact & falshood, avowedly, to debase the negroe race, is worthy of attention in another point of view. "The unhealthiness of some of the European factories here" on the Coast of Africa or Slave Coast "has been imputed in a great measure to the abominable custom of the natives, of exposing their fish to the sun till they became sufficiently stinking, fly blown & rotten. This causes a stench which fills all the atmosphere in y[e] neighbourhood;" This blessed Author, is fully of opinion that the Europeans by buying up the Africans for their plantations have done humanity infinite service by preventing them from eating one another! there are many pages of this kind of stuff. There is a great deal of valuable information in this work tho' the Author is i[n]veterate in his errors. It appears that the Coromantins or negroes from the Gold coast have been the only slaves who have troubled the planters by what they call rebellion, these people Long describes as similar in many things to our Indians: their disdain of servitude, warlike deportment, pride, apparent insensibility to the tortures inflicted by their enemies &c these qualities, so much bepraised in the Indian are branded with every odious epithet when found in the Negroe. Two of these warriors being prisoners to their Christian adversaries are gibbetted alive & suffered to linger exposed to sun & weather and tortured with hunger & thirst untill reliev'd by death, the one living 7 days in this state the other nine, & dying in convulsions. These men never utter'd a complaint. Our Author says their insolence & obstincy continued to the last! It appears that the Maroons never violated their treaty, with Trelawney, but on all occasions assisted the planters. The Creole slaves, were generally found faithfull to their Masters, the *rebels* were the newly imported Coromantins.

[Memoranda at the end of Volume 14:]

Solee gives his order for <*350*> 700 Ds to be paid by his treasurer on opening in Boston.

I endorse for him notes payable in 3 Mo: from this date Octr 16th 1797.

To Hugh Gaine for	125 Ds:
Wm Baylis	53
John W. Gilbert....................	86.25
	95
	43.75
Atty Wentworth	38.50
Roosevelt	62
Wayman	24
Atty Wentworth....................	49
P R Livingston.....................	100
Richardson	22
90 days from Octr 21st	
Daily advertiser, Greenleaf...........	43.75
Solee	100.
	720.
M Judah	40
	760.

I have likewise given my note to J Solee payable in 90 Days for Ds 500 & have rec^{d} his, endorsed by Edwd Jones & J Williamson payable in 45 days for the same sum Ds 500

I have likewise become security for 175 Ds in ninety days from the 21st Octr 1797.

Novr 30th Boston, I gave my note to J. Solee payable in 30 days from this date for 220 dollars, and took his for 300 Ds payable in 20 days, (The 300 includes ye 220, 60 omitted in a former acknowledgment & 20 as part of my expences hither)

Jany 8th 1798, I took up the above from Berry & Rogers, giving one at 20 days from this date for the same sum, endors'd by P Ten Eyck.

Jany 31st I took up the above, having one for ye amount discounted with ye bank of N Y for 30 Days.

The above I finally paid to y^{e} Bank.

DIARY OF WILLIAM DUNLAP

December 14, 1797—June 1, 1798

New York City, Boston, and Philadelphia

(Manuscript volume lettered *Memoirs 15* owned by
The New York Historical Society)

MEMOIRS 15

Boston Decr 14th 1797

Waiting for the Stage to take me to Providence. I went to the Theatre last night, "Jew & Rosina" Sollee had promised me all the receits over 200 Ds: The house was not above 100. He changed his acknowledged with me for a note of 700 Ds: allowing me the 35 Ds: paid to me, for my journey; I went to Mr Phillips's & left with him Sollee's notes, 1 for 700, 1 for 300 & 1 for 20 dollars. I this morning wrote a note to Mr Phillips desiring him to pay Mr Caleb Stimson, the first 50 Ds: he receives from Sollee & give me notice of so doing. Call on Campbell, who appears certain that Sollee must stop very soon. About half past ten I leave Boston, the weather is now as unseasonably warm as it was uncommonly cold when I left home. Dine at Walpole: finish reading Ouabi, which has give me more pleasure than I expected. Evening very dark we stop at Attlebury where I am comfortably seated after a good dish of tea; reviewing "Beacon hill." I have often thought that to make poems of Trumbulls pictures, or rather a poem which should take in our revolutionary events only dwelling on such prominent scenes as are fit for the pencil.

Hark! on the breeze rude sounds tumultuous roll,
Fierce shouts wth shrieks commingling rend ye soul,
The Cannon's thunder erst inspiring fear,
Now, welcome, <*drowns the groans which pierce my*>
shields from groans the tortur'd ear.
See where the fierce destroyer hurls the brand
Of smoking ruin on the crimson'd strand,
The humble cottage and the lofty spire
Sink undistinguished, wrap'd in hostile fire,

While Charles's sinuous creeks and devious bays
Reflect in <*blood*> deepened red the horrid blaze.

Oerpower'd by numbers now & spent with toil
<*At length*> Heavy the rustic bands from fight recoil,
Still loath to leave the hill, again they turn,
Shake the exhausted horn & inward mourn,
Now down the <*hill*> slope & o'er the neck they <*fly*> hye,
While gallant Putnam urges them to fly.
They turn indignant, "Haste" the veteran cries
We can no more & he that lingers dies"

In firm array the Britons onward <*move*> bend <*Each footstep moist*>
Treading in blood of father, son or friend
Striding oer kindred slain they gain y[e] <*hill*> field
Our yeomen slow, to numbers only, yield.
They can no more unerring pour the fire
The means of death expended they retire

Last of Columbia's sons to quit the post
In <*thoughts*> sense of duty, <*all*> sense of danger lost,
<*Close*> Within the ken of many a well known foe,
Warren retires, indignant, firm & slow.
Not yet disguis'd, in murderous array
He look'd, a Bridegroom on his Bridal day:
Conspicuous mark, each <*ball at him is aim'd*> mercenary's aim
And oft in taunts they call upon his name.

Anxious <*for him*> his brave companions frequent turn
Ask to advance & for the combat burn.
Urged to retreat obedient they comply
When lo—the Hero falls—they rush, they fly,
With powerless arms <*their leader to defend*> to shield him from the foe
<*And o'er*>
Offering their breasts to each impending blow.

Decr 15th Arrive at Providence to late breakfast. Read Paines "Ruling passion." In having rained all night & still raining we proceed in heavy roads, but get no further than a village called *Scituate*. At Scituate we join the Mail Stage, after combating the speculative genius of the driver, who wished to make us believe that having come on in an opposition stage he was not obliged to take & would not without being paid extra: a little firmness on our part settled the matter. Wrote Mason F. Cogswell.

[Dec.] 16th Clear & cold. Arrive at Norwich about 2 OClock. I here bargain'd with the Innkeeper to put me on to New London tomorrow, as the Mail stays Sunday there. I then proceeded to the landing, where Mr Howland resides: he had company at dinner with him the Huntingtons of this place & Mr Lowthrop wth their wives.

[Dec.] 17th Sunday. Walk about on the hills & view the town & rivers. 12 OClock come on in a chaise to *New London:* walk & view the town. As I walked up the hill, I stop'd, & leaning over the stone wall of a burying place, was viewing the near & distant objects, the tomb stones, the harbour & the sound, when an old woman came pacing up the hill on a sorry nag, and having arrived opposite me she exclaim'd "poor young man! poor young man!" I thought she might be lamenting for me as I had just past the town house where a Methodist was bawling & the Church where the bell was ringing, & had not attended to either of the calls. I left my leaning place & following ask'd "Whats the matter Madam?"

"The poor young man" she rejoin'd, "for whom they are tolling the bell, Jerry Brown went into his barn last night, & there he lay on his face, as it were dead."

"Was he a stranger?"

"No, as it were, a neighbours son, a young thing of four & twenty" and the good old Dame commenced her pacing again & left me: what a notable clacker this must be, who could not pass even a contemplative stranger leaning over the fence of burial ground without telling all the news of the day to him.

Poetical copies from *Historical pictures*

No 1

The Death of Warren a Poem.

"To seize the fleeting images of the still-receding past, to give them "local habitation & a name" and present them for the approbation of the present and y[e] future, is the object of the present undertaking."

Thus from the phrygian foe young Turnus strode
In port majestic as the Warriour god
High sense of justice heav'd his labouring breast
And gave prides semblance to his loft crest,
O'er his broad back he hangs his fourfold shield
<*And slowly*>
Scorns their weak blows & slowly leaves the field.
Alas, no shield protects brave Warrens life
For him no God descends midst mortal strife!

Dec[r] 18th I leave New London before day and about 8 OClock cross the Connecticut at Saybrook ferry: arrive at New Haven before dark & pass an agreeable evening at my excellent brother Dwight's. Receive a letter from my wife dated y[e] 9th: all well.

[Dec.] 19th Leave New Haven before day, dine at Stamford & see the family at Major Davenport's arrive at Rye in the evening. Pascal N Smith came on from Stamford with us & was very sociable & pleasant.

[Dec.] 20th Leave Rye at 4 OClock & arrive at my house between 12 & 1 in NEW YORK absent 5 weeks lacking a day. See Hodgkinson, he has been playing since the beginning of last week to thin houses, except y[e] first: has engaged Prigmore Fawcet & Hogg!! Chalmers & Williamson not here. I told him I should as soon have thought of engaging a hog out of the street as Prigmore. Visit some of my friends: evening home W W W with us. Smith with me in y[e] Afternoon. At the Theatre to night Love in a Village" & A good spec" play in Boston under the title of "The Georgia spec." Am[t] 270 Ds

[Dec.] 21st Collecting mony for Dr Morse. Visiting my friends: enquiring into business.

Mr Simon Walker

Sir

About the beginning of Nov[r] last, your brother James Walker rec[d] from my partner Moses Judah, two notes, dated Nov[r] 2d, the first due in 60 days the second in 90: I did not see your brother or know of the transaction untill the notes were given; I then feared that the first note would become due at a time unfavourable to the payment & have striven hard to make collections to answer it: I have but now arrived from a journey to the Eastward for that purpose, which has been unsuccessfull: & I think it my duty to let you know that if the note is presented by the Bank for payment at the time due it must be protested, to my material injury & to the injury of the House whose agent you are, for, the second note in that case will probably share the fate of y[e] first; but, if you will grant the further indulgence, of exchanging y[e] first note for four or five hundred Dollars cash, and a note at 60 days for the remainder by thus throwing the remainder behind the second note we shall be enabled to make the whole good at the appointed times. I make this proposition to you in the plainess of good faith knowing my power to fulfill it, and/boldly asserting that I have more property in my possession than will ten times answer every demand against me: of this Mr James Walker might easily have been convinced, if, happily, he had applied for the character of *me*, the *firm*, or our *business*, to any other than a pityfull & malignant enemy. I find no fault with Mr J: Walker; & probably, the impression made is not to be obliterated by my interested assertions; but in case/the present arrangement takes place, I shall be happy to establish a mercantile character with so respectable a mercantile house as that of Wm & Alex. Walker. An answer by return of post will be esteemed a favour.

I omitted in the copy sent the words from "boldly" to "case" as marked above. The person alluded to in them is Henry Rogers, who was heard to give such an account of me & my business as immediately to induce Walker to declare that he would push us.

Mr & Mrs Kent, W W W & wife pass'd the first of the evening with us, afterwards I read in "André" to my Wife. Chalmers and Williamson have arrived.

[Dec.] 22d Attend to business and my Children. Visit New Theatre, the severe cold now impedes the work.

To Mr Ravaud Kearney

I seize an early oppertunity after a long journey to the Eastern states to endeavour to prevent the ill consequences of your depending on me for the fulfillment of my engagement <*to you*> respecting the purchase of Land. It is not in my power to make payment on the time agreed upon and my failure leaves you at liberty to conclude the bargain void, making me accountable for any real damage by you sustain'd in consequence thereof, or, to suffer the bargain to remain as at first, only deferring the time of payment, interest as before. With my best respects to Mrs. Kearny,

I remain ever Your friend

[Dec.] 27th Mr Simon Walker, complied with the request of my letter. On friday night was performed "Macbeth & Romp" to Ds: 176, on Saturday "Cure for ye heart ach" & a good spec" to Ds 231. Sunday I dined with G M W. Christmas day at home W W W & wife & mother with us. Yesterday I attended strictly to business. Write to Joseph Byrnes of Charleston South Carolina Enclosing Solee's note endorsed by Jones & J B Williamson, a notification to E Jones, Sollee's note endorsed & paid by me, a certified power of Attorney to J Byrnes, withal directing that everything be done to enforce payment; this packet I send by the Ship Fame deliver'd to y^e $Capt^n$ Gabriel Havens. Write to Jedidiah Morse enclosing 165 Ds: in notes for him. Drink tea at W W W's. Theatre "Dramatist & Waterman" Mr Chalmers first appearance in Comedy, Mr Williamson's first appearance: in y^e house 222 Ds:. $Will^{mn}$ pleased much particularly a song introduced called Nancey & sung without accompanyments.

[Dec.] 28th Attend to my Children & business.

Jany 4th 1798. Our Theatrical business is still bad except Monday y^e first of Jan a house of 494 Ds:. With much difficulty we prevailed in having the finishing of y^e New Theatre postponed and a temporary close made of

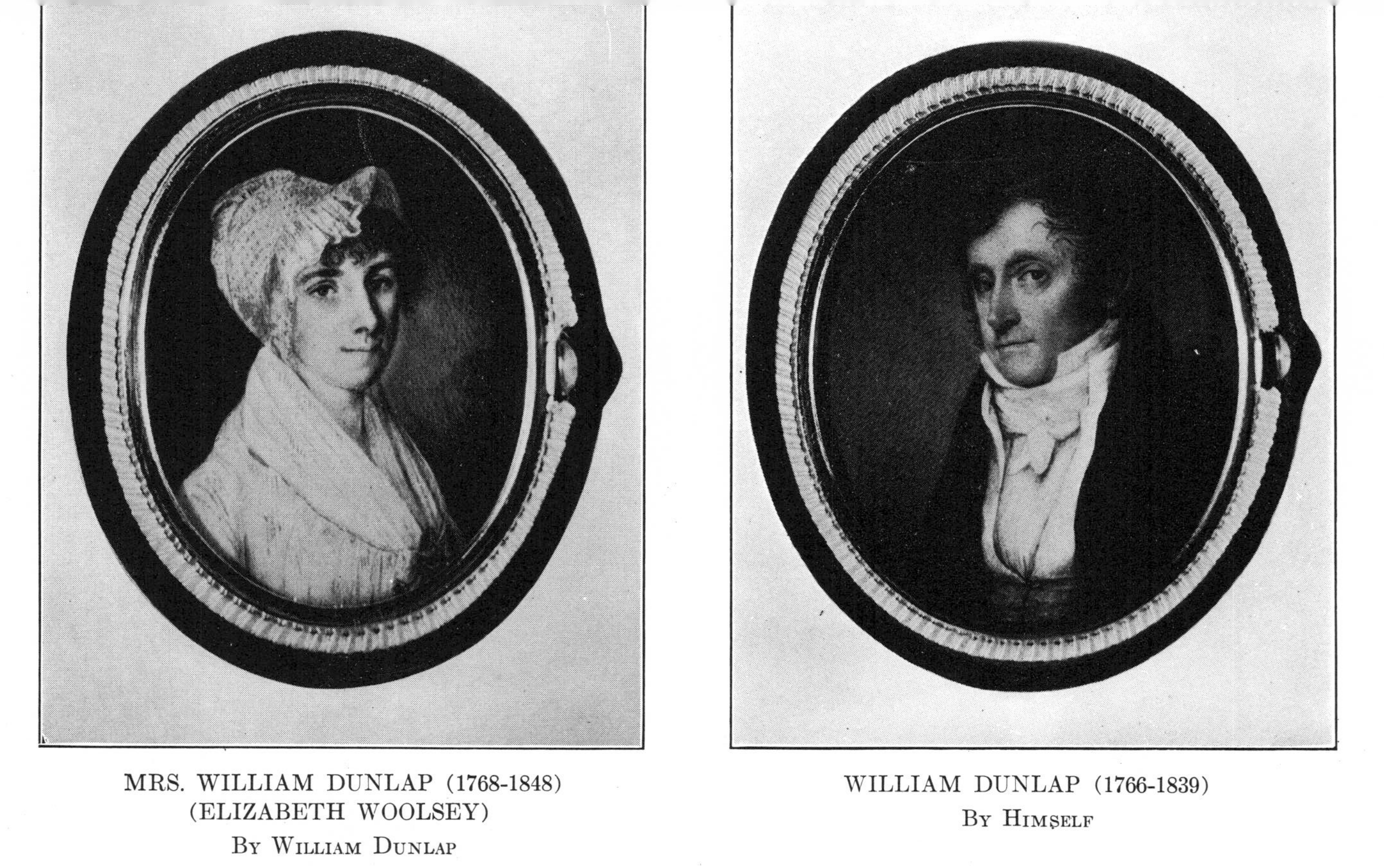

MRS. WILLIAM DUNLAP (1768-1848)
(ELIZABETH WOOLSEY)
BY WILLIAM DUNLAP

WILLIAM DUNLAP (1766-1839)
BY HIMSELF

(Courtesy of Miss Ethel Carmalt and Miss Geraldine W. Carmalt)

ye business so that we play in it, in 2 or 3 weeks. [Thomas Abthorpe] Cooper came to town on New Years day, and expresses a strong wish not to return to Philadelphia—indeed he wishes an engagement here and there are many of our young men who are very anxious for the event: they have persuaded him to play here one night for his amusement & to gratify them and last night Hodgkinson announced him for Pierre which he is now rehearsing & tomorrow night plays. I yesterday received a letter from Brown full of self condemnation, particularly for his conduct last winter: in one to Smith he says he has finished a novel or romance. A day or two ago Sharpless painted a portrait of me which I think very like, he has a good likeness of Smith and one of Wm Johnson.

[Jan.] 5th Cooper wrote to Wignell demanding the payment of a certain note given to him by Wignel & Ranaigle, which they suffered to be protested & on which he went to Jail as endorser, & asking permission to or giving notice (for I did not see his letter) that he intended to, play here a night, he received an answer prohibitting his playing & telling him that the note should be paid by tuesday, provided he was on ye spot: the time given by Cooper was untill ye preceding Saturday. Wignel likewise wrote to Hodgkinson, beginning his letter with "Mr C having informed me that you have solicited him to play" &c or words to that purport. Cooper's rejoinder I saw, it is nervous & well written: he tells him that paying the note on tuesday will not do: that he shall not fail being in Phil: at the time appointed "I might perhaps fail my friend in an appointment, never my enemy": he remarks that Wignel had written to Hodgkinson and tells him that the first paragraph is a falshood, that he <*never*> did not say that Mr H: had solicited him, on the contrary the truth is that he, C, asked permission to play &c: This evening Cooper play'd Pierre, Hodgkinson Jaffier: [28] 240 Ds in ye house. Cooper's Pierre did not

[28] In *Venice Preserved,* a tragedy by Thomas Otway.

appear so well as before, Hodgkinson appeared to play unusually well.

[Jan.] 6th Evening: Cooper play'd Penruddock;[29] in the house Ds: 160. I did not see him as the Club was with me & a very pleasant one. I have read the Reviews for Septr 1797 and Appendix: and in Gibbon. Write a little on André.

Sunday [Jan.] 7th Teach my children: read in Gibbon & N Y Mag: for Decr. Write additional songs for Sternes Maria.

[Jan.] 8th Messrs Chalmers & Williamson, instead of being with ye Company at the opening had gone off to Baltimore, with some difficulty they were prevailed with to come back: they arrived at the latter end of a week, when the plays of the week had been fixed on and advertised without them, notwithstanding which these *Gentlemen* demand salaries for that week. Write to Joseph Byrnes and enclose Sollee's note for 49 Ds endorsed by me & paid to day. Pass ye evening at W W W's; Gahn there: talk of Kosciusko. Theatre All in ye Wrong & Rosina, in ye house Ds: 125.

13th January 1798. We determined at the close of last weeks Theatrical business to play but one week more, and open on the 22d Inst. in the New House. On Wednesday last we play'd Earl of Essex, <*Fortunes fool*> Love & mony & ye Oracle to 190 Ds: and last night Wives as they were &c & Catherine & petruchio, to 265 [dollars] Some days ago Mr. Henderson mentioned to me his wish that we (H & self) would admit the proprietors with free tickets into the Theatre. Hodgkinson had mentioned that Henderson had hinted ye thing to him some time back & that he had pointedly negativ'd it & I concluded that it was a transient thought of Henderson's and that there was an end of it. I now enquired the number of proprietors he said about 130; Mr Henderson went lengthily into

[29] In Richard Cumberland's comedy, *The Wheel of Fortune.*

statements of the little temporary disadvantage, if any, that would attend such a concession on our part, and the great permanent advantage that would result by having these men "in good humour" as he expressed it. After some time I found that the "good humour" was wanted by the committee when they should call the proprietors together to state accounts and require a settlement. I made several objections, as that no such diminution of profits were contemplated in the agreement made by Hodgk: & self, with the committee: that acting upon that agreement I had suffered materially & looked upon the opening weeks as my source of compensation. Mr Henderson affected to state this free admittance as a temporary thing, to cease as soon as the Committee could be called together and a settlement obtain'd. The purpose of the Committee would undoubtedly be thereby answered, but I told him that if the <*custom of*> admittance of proprietors was once begun, it could not without offence be broken off & it would be established. He wished to persuade me that even if it was, it would be no disadvantage to us. He said there must be a meeting between the committee & the Managers and something further determined on. I left Mr Henderson somewhat troubled in mind on reflecting, that in consequence of an agreement, by which I was to have possession of a certain Theatre for three and a half years, on terms which were duly weighed & determined upon and which I thought sufficiently advantageous, I had weakened my little capital in trade, & stretched my credit, undergoing fatigue & anxiety beyond calculation, to be told, when the time for taking possession drew nigh, that the persons making the agreement with me after long deferring their signatures, concluded not to make good their engagement, but that I might go into the building & use it for one season on the terms agreed, depending for the future on the determination of others or of those who might become purchasers of it. after yielding to the necessity of taking possession amidst such uncertainties, because of the debts contracted by my reliance on these men—now to have a proposal of having a hundred dollars taken from the profits of every full house by way of smoothing difficulties for the men who had so cruelly deceived me, a proposal made at such a time, when it was known that I *depended* on the receits of the house for discharging pecuniary engagements and must therefore be in some measure in their power—these reflections troubled me. I mention'd the proposals to my friend Smith who declared them the proposals of a rascal. I mention'd them to P Ten Eyck he appear'd astonished and said he would speak to Henderson. Gamage & every one I mention'd the subject to, said to comply would be ruin. After this, I think the next day, meeting Henderson again, as usual on the stage of the New House, he asked me for the memorandum of an agreement which he had given to me, saying that he had no copy, I replied that he should have a copy, and I had one made that day, but he has not yet required it: the original is what Mr Henderson wants: This morning about eleven OClock I went with my friend E H Smith to the New Theatre, we had scarcely entered the lower boxes when Mr Henderson called to me from the third row on the opposite side & I went up thither, Smith with me, we found Carlisle Polluck with him, & reading a paper "I have just given Mr Polluck" says H "a piece to read which I have drawn up for publication" he took it from P's hand & put it into mine. In this, the Committee informed the proprietors or subscribers, that the Theatre would be opened, apologized for its not being finished in the style contemplated, and informed them that by a "temporary" arrangement or agreement with the Managers they would be admitted free of expence with "untransferable" tickets: I state from memory as to words. I returned the paper with my thumb upon the part respecting the admission tickets, P & Smith both attending, and in a pointed manner observed that "there had been no such arrangement, or agreement." Mr Hend: replied "O no! this was not intended for immediate publication, not untill the matter had been determined with us."

I took this oppertunity to urge my former objections to the measure in stronger terms and Mr Henderson went over the same arguments (if it is not absurd so to call them) in favour of it. When he mention'd the future advantages which would arise by having the establishment permanent, I told him I had, now, little prospect of any future advantages from the Theatre, and that on the emolument from the opening I relied for relief from the debts I had contracted in consequence of my agreement with them. He said I had a certainty of continuing in the possession if I chose. I gave him to understand that after what had past I had no confidence. I told the gentlemen I had no idea that the original subscribers expected free tickets, that it was now many months since the agreement wth ye Managers, that the terms were well known and that I had never heard of any dissatisfaction on the subject of admittance. I had previously remarked, that if they mentioned the subject to the subscribers, they would raise an expectation and cause a consequent dissapointment if the measure was not finally adopted. Mr Henderson now assured me that all the subscribers to whom he had mentioned the subject expected it. "I mean all those who have mentioned it to me." Thus, I presume, upon his plan of putting the subscriber in good humour that they may agree to take upon themselves the Committee's debts, Mr Henderson has already assured many of them of this great favour of being admitted gratis to view the spectacles which are to be exhibitted at an enormous expence, by the dupes of their honourable Committee. I told Mr H that I could not conceive that the gentlemen who had subscribed to the building could be so selfish as to withdraw their patronage, as he represented, from the Theatre, because not complimented with a free ticket: he said that when people employed their money they expected something in return for it & appealed to me. I replied, that if I had had such a surplussage of money as would have justified me to myself for becoming a subscriber to such a build^{g} I should never have looked for any profit from it. He said people who had the greatest surplus of money generally wished to encrease it. I said I believed it was the case, but I thought few would think of speculating in such a case as the one we were speaking of. Mr Henderson, said by way of querie, "I presume you <*would*> do not consider us as bound to fulfill our engagements" or words to that purport: I replied, "Sir, I know nothing of your engagements but as they respect myself: When two parties enter into engagements, I should think it unjust that the one should be sacrificed to screen the other from inconvenience." here they both protested that they wished only to devise means for the benefit of the whole concern. Mr Henderson repeatedly suggested that even on these terms, Mr Hodgkinson would have the Theatre on better conditions than those originally proposed by him to the subscribers. I said be that as it may it concerns not me, if I had not been induced by the terms of our agreement with you, *I*, should not have been concerned in the business nor have incurred the loss & expence which have attended the supporting the Company for the purpose. Mr Henderson said I was already engaged in the business: I said no, my engagements with Hall. & H were broken and at an end. After agreeing to meet and discuss the point at Mr Pollock's on monday at 4 in ye afternoon we parted. Smith was highly disgusted wth Henderson. Pollock was generally silent. I saw Kent, he asked me respecting the opening of the Theatre & I mentioned the leading circumstances of my situation with these men, he much regretted that I had not firmer hold of them: but I did not ask his legal opinion. I call'd on Hodgkinson & mentioned the above particulars.

Dr Dwight arrived in town yesterday I past an hour with him. He drank tea with us this evening; after which I met the club at Smith's, where was Dr Maize [Mease] of Phil:, a pompous young man, Dr Miller, Mr Kent, Wm Johnson and Mr Sharpless. We play'd this evening for the last time in the old house, "The Comet & Tom thumb" to Ds: 204.

Jany 14th Hodgkinson suggested an Idea of naming the Boxes from the principal dramatic Authors & Actors of Great Britain, I changed it to ye dramatic Authors of Europe to the exclusion of ye Actors & adopted it. We went together to ye Theatre & determined some business.

Jany 21st Sunday. On monday last, Hodgkinson & self met the Committee as appointed at Mr Carlisle Pollock's house and the result of ye meeting was that we should admit the proprietors *gratis,* the committee allowing us in return an abatement, of per centage formerly agreed on, during the time this regulation shall be in force, which is to be looked upon, as an experiment. The committee talked as if their intentions were in the highest degree liberal towards us. The remainder of this week has been passed in unavailling efforts to forward the finishing of ye Theatre & we find at the close of this week that we must wait another. The company have rec^{d} the disapointment with apparent good nature. I have been obliged to borrow money to pay Sollee's debts & have heard nothing concerning him: I took up the note of Ds: 500, yesterday. Gaine & Ten Eyk have been very friendly. Wignel and Rainaigle after keeping Cooper in suspence & without salary or employment have arrested him: he has given bail and has informed Ten Eyck that he will be here tomorrow. I had previously desired Ten Eyck to let him know that if he was persecuted he had an Assylum here. I dined on Wednesday at Mr M Rogers's with Dr Dwight and on Friday they dined with me. Dr D read to me a poem he composed for New Years verses, but did not publish. It is a bitter invective against all frenchmen innovators and infidels: I thanked him but gave no opinion. Having finished "André" I am to read it to Dr Dwight tomorrow.

Upon enquiry Hodgkinson gave me to understand that it was his intention to charge me 30 Ds: per week for his services as Manager during the Boston business! on my pointing out calmly that that business had supported him & his family while it was ruining me, he said he had not made the charge & would defer settling the accounts untill he saw how the present season turned out. This mans extravagant mode of living and what he & his companions term generosity, make him rapacious in the highest degree: he has not an idea of the nature of justice. The club met the last night with G M Woolsey, present Smith, Johnson and self. During this week, that is from Wednesday, John has been studying French, attended by one of our Musicians. Read in Darwin. Write on André, copying & correcting.

Jany 22d 1798. Hodgkinson delivered to me the following paper put into his hands by Wm Henderson, & written by him, as a substitute for the Memorandum of agreement upon which we have been acting since May last.

"Memorandum of an agreement between Carlisle Pollock, Jacob Morton and Wm Henderson on behalf of the proprietors of the New Theatre in this City, of the first part, and John Hodgkinson and William Dunlap, Managers of the Old American Company of Comedians of the second part.

The parties of the first part agree to rent to ye parties of ye second part, the said Theatre and the property belonging to it on the following terms and conditions viz

1st Possession shall be given on the 29th of Jany instant.

2nd Untransferable rights of free admission into the house, except on benefit nights, shall be allowed to the number of one hundred and thirteen being the amount of shares subscribed and paid.

3d The parties of the second part shall pay to the parties of the first part, weekly upon the gross <*amounts*> receipts of each night of performance (Benefit nights excepted) at the following rate

On any sum from	500 to	600 Ds:	7½ per centum
Do	600	700	12½
Do	700	800	15
Do	800	1200	17½
Do	1200 to any higher sum		20 per Centum.

And on Benefit nights (which are never to exceed 27 in any one season) there shall be paid 10 per centum, on whatever sum the gross receipt of each night may be.

4th No rights of free admission (except those first mention'd) shall be allowed, unless it be to performers and those to be limited as much as possible.

5th Such additions as may be necessary to be made to the scenery and machinery shall be done by the parties of the second part by consent of the parties of the first part; to be valued and paid for by the proprietors when ever the parties of the second part shall cease to occupy the house.

6th No Alterations shall be made in the scenery or machinery without the consent of the parties of the first part, and the parties of the second part shall be answerable for any damage that may be done to either: that which may arise from the necessary use of it, and fire, excepted.

7th The parties of the first part reserve the right of making such disposition of the rooms in the front of the Theatre (one for a Box office excepted) as they may judge proper, and also that of appointing a person whose duty it shall be to count the House, & see that the fires and candles are carefully extinguished after every performance.

8th The parties of the second part engage that during the time they occupy the premises hereby rented, the Old Theatre in John Street shall not be opened for any Theatrical exhibition whatever by their consent or concurrence, and they stipulate that they will not dispose of their interest in that property upon any terms in which a condition to that effect shall not be included.

9th As it is not in the power of the power [*sic*] of the parties of the first part to rent the premises for any certain <*term of time*> period in consequence of the incumbrances with which the property is charged, it is therefore mutually agreed by both parties that this agreement shall continue in force untill it shall be decided by the proprietors or in a legal manner, in what mode the debts for which the property is liable shall be paid.

I must confess I have seldom felt greater indignation than on hearing this paper read. Hodgkinson gave it to me and I engaged to state my objections in writing, and to draw up another memorandum more conformable to my ideas of the spirit of the original agreement. I shewed this to Smith who partook of my indignation.

Evening teach my children.

The objections which arise in my mind on reading the above memorandum of an agreement are

1st That the name of Edward Livingston, one of those persons whom the proprietors had appointed their Committee, & whose name is inserted in the agreement, upon which the parties of the second part have acted by expending their property and contracting engagements, is in the present memorandum omitted.

2dly That the following words, inserted in ye first agreement after due deliberation and some debate, the parties of the second part contending for <*more*> a greater extent of time and the parties of the first part asserting their powers to be limited to the term expressed in the aforesaid following words, which words, in the apprehension of the parties of the second part, make the essential part of said agreement, and without which they <*never*> would not have acted upon it, are omitted in the present memorandum viz. "for the term of three years and six months to be computed from the time the same shall be ready for Theatrical exhibition."

3dly That in respect to the first article of the terms & conditions mention'd in the memorandum of agreement now under consideration, the parties of the second part think that they ought to be put in possession of the premises, on or before the 27th of January instant as ye 29th is the time appointed for exhibition & one or more rehearsals are previously necessary.

4thly That in the second article, the following words or words to their effect, are not introduced, according to the agreement verbally made, at the house of Mr Carlisle Pollock on the 14th of Jany instant, viz. "this condition only to remain in force untill the Committee shall have obtained the concurrence of the subscribers in the measures for finishing ye buildng adopted subsequent to the first agreement between ye aforesaid parties for renting ye aforesaid building or untill the proprietorship shall be determined, the right of free admission to subscribers, then to cease.

5thly That in respect to the fourth article of the memorandum under consideration, the parties of the second part fully remember that it was discussed at the above mention'd meeting at the house of Mr Carlisle Pollock, and that it was agreed that no performer as a performer should have the right of introducing any person or persons free from the usual charges: that, the right of the performer to free admission for himself was not question'd: that the right of the Managers to introduce their wives, their children or occasionally a friend was insisted on by the parties of the second part and not objected to by the parties of the first part; and that, the parties of the second part informed the parties of the first part, that Authors who had written for the Theatre, especially such as had written for the immediate company performing & whose pieces were in possession of the Manager, were by custom immemorial admitted free: at which time it was observed by one or more of the parties of the first part, that the small number of such Authors in this country render'd it a matter of no consequence: notwithstanding which such Authors are by the present article excluded from such privilege manifestly to the discouragement of literature and genius.

6thly That by the 5th article of the memorandum under consideration, the parties of the second part would be prohibited from getting up any new piece in which a new scene was necessary without the consent of the parties of the first part previously asked and obtained, that is, without permission so obtained for employing their own money, for the purchase of scenes for their own use and the gratification of the public: nor could they bring forward any old piece or stock play in which a scene might be wanting <*from*> owing to the present very scanty store of scenery, without first ask^{g} and obtaining consent from all the parties of the first part: thus having the controul and regulation of their business taken from them, and furthermore that, after having so asked and obtained permission, after having expended property in procuring scenes to be painted and machinery to be made, the parties of the second part being (according to the memorandum under consideration) mere tenants at ye will of the parties of the first part, may be at any time ejected, at which time, by this article, all the scenery & machinery so accumulated by the parties of the second part must be sold to the parties of the first part or their employers at the valuation of the purchasers.

7thly To the 6th article it is only to be wished that after ye word machinery in the first line should be added "delivered to the parties of the second part."

8thly To the ninth article it is objected, that as it would be by the apparent free will and consent of the parties of the second part, make void and null that agreement on the faith of which they have acted for many months at an enormous expence in the expectation of remuneration from its fulfillment, they cannot in justice to themselves or in justice to what they .believe to be the honourable intentions of the parties of the first part, consent to it. Certainly the parties of the second part cannot require of the parties of the first part, that which they have not the power to do; at the same time the parties of the second part cannot conceive that the parties of ye first part would enter into a solemn contract (no less solemn for that the incidental circumstance of signatures were temporarily omitted at the wish of the parties of the first part) the consequence of which they knew to be expence, contracts & engagements on the part of the parties of the second part, without they, ye parties of ye first part, had power so to do. We are told that debts have since been contracted for finishing the building and that the parties of the first part have made themselves responsible for large sums of money, this appears to us only to encrease their proprietorship & not to diminish their power of fulfilling the original agreement. If the bargain made with us, is a bad one, having power to make it, we conceive that the parties of the first part only render up their trust to their employers with an incumbrance upon it for the term of 3 & a half years, if the bargain is equitable, there is no incumbrance. If the original subscribers do not chuse to become responsible for the engagements enter'd into by their Committee and the building must be sold, may it not be sold with this lease upon it?

If sold, will not the principal proprietors, the parties of the first part, become the purchasers? And if so, what diminishes their power of fulfilling the original lease? We are willing to rely on the honourable intentions of the parties of the first part, <*but let us not*> to fulfill the original and acted-upon agreement; let it rest: but let us not annull by signatures that which only wants signatures to be as binding in law as <*it is*> we conceive it to be in Justice.

Jan[y] 23d 1798. I show'd the above to Hodgkinson who wishes it copied & presented to Henderson, with certain amendments to their proposals, which I drew up this morning, in conformity to and obviating the objections. Cooper has arrived from Phil: & is to be with me this evening. Dine at W W W's. Evening, Smith came to me & I show'd him the papers relative to the New Theatre, afterward Cooper & Ten Eyck came. Cooper says Mr Godwin is a small man delicately formed, about 40 years of age, Holcroft a man of about the same height but muscular and aged about 54. That Mr Godwin has no fortune but from his writings: that he is at present much afflicted by the death of Mrs Godwin (Miss Wolstoncraft) whose death being in consequence of childbirth, was painful in the extreme and that she showed a distressing reluctance to quit the world. I expressed to Cooper my wish that he might continue here and set at nought the idea of a prosecution from Wignell, for giving him employment. We talked over the characters that he might have: he said he would play the Count in "The school for arrogance "Young Dornton" "Cheveril": [30] he wishes Hodgkinson to give him Romeo.

[Jan.] 24th I deliver'd the objections to Henderson, hav[g] previously mentioned them to Carlile Pollock who did not know of this second memorandum at all. Pollock, repeatedly expressed his wish that the terms should be made rather more favourable than at first, to us, than the contrary said he was aware that if the proprietors lost, it would be nothing to them, but if the managers

[30] Count Connolly Villers, Harry Dornton, and Cheveril are characters in three plays by Thomas Holcroft: *The School for Arrogance, The Road to Ruin,* and *The Deserted Daughter,* respectively.

lost, it was very serious to them and talked altogether in that liberal stile.

Dine at G M W's. Evening home: instruct the boy in french.

[Jan.] 25th Hodgkinson tells me that he had a conversation with Henderson & Morton on ye Stage of the New Theatre in which he understood that the Commissioners, met last night, that Henderson said he did not mean the memorandum as we understood it: that they pledged themselves as men of honour to do every thing for us in their power, but that they could not lease the building for a time: that some memorandum must be signed before they gave possession. I sat down & drew up a memorandum on the plan of the one last delivered by Henderson obviating however my objections to the 3d, 5th, 6th, & seventh articles, adding Edwd Livingstone's name & omitting the 9th article, inserting in its stead, an engagement on their parts to do all in their power to ensure to us possession for 3 & ½ years on terms as generous & equitable as those intended. M: Judah has gone to Connecticut to endeavour to secure a debt. I just now received a letter (in answer to mine) from Mr Ravaud Kearney, apologizing for not before answering me & acquiescing in my proposal of deferring ye payment for ye land. Hodgkinson tells me that he delivered to Henderson a Copy of the memorandum I drew up this morning, that he look'd it over and then objected to the last article in which they <*agreed*> were to engage to do all in their power to ensure our possession for the first mentioned term, but said he would shew it to the gentlemen. Smith & J Allen call'd on me; I afterwards join'd them at M: Rogers's where with them & Dr Dwight I pass'd ye evening untill 9. Sign'd tickets untill past 12.

[Jan.] 26th By a letter from Caleb Stimson of Boston I learn that something is done by Phillips on my account, or attempted, he says the last nights receits were attached. They have not yet coalesced there. To day Hodgkinson showed 2 letters from Wignel, one addressed to J H alone, in which he apologizes for having accused him in a former letter of asking Cooper to play: and one directed to Messrs Hodgkinson & Dunlap in which he sends an extract of Coopers article & warns us not to employ him. Henderson brought me an article to substitute for the last article of my last memorandum, saying he wished to "word something" so as to "meet the ideas of both parties" this is it

> "And whereas it was the intention of the parties of the first part to have rented ye premises to the parties of the second part for ye term of three years and six months if the situation of the property would have permitted it, the parties of the first part agree to use their influence to have the parties of ye second part continued as tenants but it is mutually understood and agreed that this agreement shall remain in force to the <*first*> day of [blank] next only."

I call'd at Kents & show'd him Wignels letter, he said that he thought Cooper's article was broken by their not fulfilling their contract with him, but he feared there was a deficiency of proof: he said if Cooper was liable for damages, we should be so likewise if we employed him. I saw Cooper & asked him respecting his proof, I was not satisfied as to the sufficiency: he promised to see Kent again. We are very busy at the New Theatre having advertised for Monday we must be ready: but there much to do.

[Jan.] 27th Snow storm. [John] McKesson has had writs served on G M W and me: and on my mother: a writ was out for M Judah but he is out of the way. The last I heard of this business was from young McKesson who required an account from me of what charges I had against his uncle and promised an account of ye demand against me: several times I was reminded of bringing forward this account, my immediate business prevented it at first, but I did, some time past make the statement which has lain neglected in my desk, and I am reminded of the business by a Constable. Dr Dwight dines with me. Read part of André to him and he made some judicious remarks: he approves of the sentiments attributed to André and to Washington: he corrected me in several instances.

[Jan.] 28th Sunday. Teach my children. P Ten Eyck called & told me that he had appointed 12 OClock to day to meet Mr Kent with Cooper & Hodgkinson. I went thither & found them in consultation, ye result of which was that we could not engage Cooper as Wignel might prosecute us for every seperate time Cooper play'd & would every time at least obtain costs. Evening Smith & Johnson call'd on me, after tea I took them with me to the Theatre which was lighted for the first time. The scenery had fine effect. Call at W W W's: home, read Gibbon.

[Jan.] 29th Dr Dwight leaves town. Employ Wm Johnson in my affair with McKesson. Hodgkinson told me to day that Simpson had applied to him, for the part of Leonora in the Padlock, for his wife's daughter Miss E Westray: the part is Mrs Hodgkinson's. I told him that I would not consent, for these reasons; that the Padlock was old & required strength of cast when done, that to put out Mrs Hodgkinson & put in Miss E Westray would make the piece to[o] weak to do at all. Hodgkinson seem'd inclined to comply with Simpson's request and asked what he could say to him. "Say if you please that I objected, & give my reasons"

A busy day & night, The Theatre was opened with [Dr. Elihu Hubbard] Smith's address, Milns's prelude "All in a Bustle" followed by As you like it & the Purse: the house was overflowing: great crowding & confusion; many got in without paying or without delivering tickets owing to the press: Cooper accidentally seeing the disorder; took place with a door keeper & restored order to one of the Box entrances: Every thing was received with shouts & glee, tho' I believe the inhabitants of the Gallery were not quite pleased with their abode. My returns of the house will not correspond with the appearances: Ds: 1245. The Gallery was not full.

[Jan.] 30th Busy with money & tickets. read a little in [William] Hayley while our clerk goes to his dinner from y[e] store. Saw Hodgkinson who seemed in an ill-humour. Cooper was there who said Mr Kent had told Ten Eyck that if the penalty of his articles was offerred to Wignel he must take it, & Ten Eyck & Cooper seriously think of raising the sum by subscription; £500 Sterling! Attend to accounts.

[Jan.] 31st Mr Kearney of Amboy having accepted my proposals of deferring payment, I write this morning offering to honour his draft for Ds: 100 at 5 days sight & pay the remainder on y[e] first of May. Ten Eyk show'd me his subscription book with several names at 10 & 20 Ds: I told him to put down mine 20. I mention'd to Cooper what Ten Eyck was doing & he seemed to dissaprove it. A busy day & evening, "All in a bustle" repeated; with School for scandal & Lock & Key" only 500 Ds: in the house "What a falling off." Mrs Hallam kept the stage waiting, was hissed, abused the call boy (a young man) in true billingstate [*sic*] tone, if not in words: Hodgk. quarrels with the property man—who can conceive the discontents of a Theatre? I rec[d] a letter to day from Joseph Byrnes of Charleston S. C: who writes that he on y[e] morning of y[e] 20th instant he saw E Jones "on presenting Sollees note he immediately said he would pay it with pleasure in three days & made some apologies for not having forwarded y[e] money to pay the note at maturity. I shall call on him according to appointment & let thee know the result in due time—he informs me that he has reason to expect Sollee here daily."

Feb[y] 1st Occupied with business & ill in health. write to C Brown. Pass the evening at J Murrays & W W W's.

[Feb.] 2d Evening Theatre Child of Nature & Lyar, Chalmers's first appearance in y[e] New house amount $260!!

[Feb.] 3d First Saturday in the new house, Mr Mirvan Hallam who according to my apprehension & remembrance had, when he asked for an engagement, solicited only 2 Ds weekly encrease of salary, now says he was promised by me $18 a week, an encrease of 4. Jefferson whom we have raised from 17 to 20, says he was promised 22; and Martin whom we raised to 18 from 17 says he expected as much as Jefferson. I sent to Mr Hallam by E Gill a Check for 50 dollars, accompanied by a slip of paper containing

"Mr. Hallam	20	
use of Wardrobe &c	5	
	——	25
Mrs Hallam		25
		$ 50

Gill presented it according to direction & demanded if it was right, Mr Hallam said no & refused to receive it, said that it was not according to agreement &c.

I had sent the salary to Mr Hallam as the same allowed to Hodgkinson for performing it being our express agreement with him, that he should have the same. I sent him 5 Ds for the weekly use of his half of the old wardrobe & properties; calculating thus Mr Hallam, demanded and received of the Copartnership, for his half of all the property of the Old American Company 20 dollars per week, value of which property in use £4000, as the remains of said property in use is not in value £100, $5 is a full allowance. I sent to Mrs Hallam the highest sallary given in the company. Mr Hallam is disatisfied.

Write to J Byrnes S C. "I forward with this J Sollee's notes, one for $22 one for 40, one for 24 & one for 45 making 111 dollars in addition to the sum you already have advice of. I have confidence in your diligence in my behalf. I am justified by experience when I say "put no confidence in Sollee, Jones or Williamson."

In the evening I met Mr Hallam at the box stairs at the Theatre he look'd as if he wished to quarrel if he could; he said he had no money in the house and asked if I would give him the balance of his last weeks salary.

I asked what it was, & brought it him immediately, taking it from Falconer at the ticket office, he took in a hurried manner & walk'd hastily off.

4th Feby Sunday. Read a little in Darwin & instructed the children. Copy & correct André.

[Feb.] 5th Much occupied with business: Gamage tells me that Hallam continues to growl, that he has been around to his old supporters and complained loudly: Gamage at my desire asked him if he would send any message to me: he said "no I will see him myself." I staid in my room most of the day, but he came not. Evening "Earl of Essex & All the world's a stage" in the house $317.

[Feb.] 6th Mr Hallam was on the stage at rehearsal all the morning, but spoke not to me. Hodgkinson & Jefferson had some altercation this morning about the addition which Jefferson says was promised to him by Hodgkinson for his wardrobe $2. Hodgkinson talked in a very cavalier manner, and Jefferson on his positive refusal, told him not to put his name in the bills for Friday, which Hodgkinson told him he should not & intimated or said that he wanted not his services. I afterwards told Jefferson not to determine rashly, that I would speak to Hodgkinson again on the subject, that my interest was as much concerned as Mr Hodgkinson's and that the sum in question should not by my consent part us. I had a conversation soon after with Hodgkinson, he said he minded not the money but Jefferson questioned his veracity, I said no, only his memory: he said Mr Jefferson instead of entering into a conversation of explanation had resorted to threats of quitting us &c. I plainly told him, that he, by his first words to Jefferson that morning had prohibited conversation, that what took place was mere altercation & ought not to be remember'd: he talked much of Jefferson's *insolence:* I told him that a quarrel with Jefferson at present must be avoided: he said I might agree to give him addition and so make it up, but he would never speak to him again. I call'd on Jefferson & settled the matter to his apparent satisfaction. Evening translate Telemachus with John. Copy & correct André.

7th Feby 1798. See by the Monthly Review of October that the reviewers have favourably noticed my "Tell truth & shame the Devil" and "The Archers" particularly the first. Smith's "Edwin and Angelina" is noticed in the same page not so favourably as it deserves, tho' they allow it interest, the criticism on the three is superficial. Gamage says Hallam refuses to sell the John Street property. Cooper proposed to day that he should purchase a share in our Theatrical scheme, & play as a proprietor, I told him to take Kent's advice upon the feasability of the project. The prospect of Theatrical business is so bad that we look to shutting up very soon. Write to Caleb Stimson of Boston and to Saml Cooper, desiring information from Mr Phillips respecting my business there. Write to Saml L Mitchill. To Stimson I send $50, borrowed of him. Evening in the house $345. Cold weather.

[Feb.] 8th Gamage says Hallam will sell all the property here & in Philadelphia. Margaret attempts a french lesson this morning. Smith reads to me part of his Manumission Oration, & 2 translated sonnets by Alsop from Metastasio.

[Feb.] 9th I find from Gamage that Hallam wishes to be on good terms again: he has sold the old Theatre for £115, to be pull'd down & remov'd immediately. I consulted with him what to do with the scenery: and he agreed to have the best of it taken off the frames and roll'd up, and destroy the rubbish, he seem'd quite friendly: he told Gammage that Maxwell, a scotchman, one of the subscribers had hinted to him that the proprietors or some of them thought of governing the Theatre by a Committee and arranging the business & cast of plays themselves, and that he (Hallam) had discouraged it. Maxwell & one Dixon, another proprietor, are Hodgkinson's enemies, and have found room for me: as a companion to him. There is a report that the New Theatre Boston is burnt. Evening. Mr Howland, his wife and y[e] Woolseys dined with us. It proves to be the Federal St[t] Theatre which is consumed. Theatre "Wives as they were & [blank] in y[e] house 255 Ds:

Saturday [Feb.] 10th Read in review. Dine at W W Ws with y[e] Howlands. Evening Theatre "More ways than one & Agreable surprize $373. Club at Johnson's, he reads from y[e] review, present Smith, Johnson, W W W, Miller & self.

[Feb.] 11th Read review. Write on "Rule a husband and have a husband or the way to tame him." Teach my children. Call at M: Rogers's.

[Feb.] 12th Ten Eyck shows me a little book called Pocket companion to y[e] Theatre, in which is an account, apparently authentic, of Cooper: he is said to be the son of a Surgeon, who resided in the neighbourhood of London, his father went as a surgeon to the east Indies, & dying there left a large family of Orphans. Mr Godwin, some way connected with the family, took & educated Cooper, and under the instruction or direction of Holcroft he was destined to the stage: his first appearance at Covent Garden in Hamlet is highly spoken of & much promise noted of him: his being infected by vice in the Country Theatres is noted. Write to Joseph Byrnes & enclose Sollee's note to H Gaine, paid by me for $125 & his note to Greenleaf, p[d] by me for 43.77. Write on my Comedy. Theatre, 'Fortune's Fool & Good Spec" in the house $314.

[Feb.] 13th Smith this morning told me that Burke (Bunkerhill) asserted that he had a tragedy soon to be play'd, first rehearsal on Wednesday next, called "Joan

WILLIAM WALTON WOOLSEY (1766-1839)
By William Dunlap
(Courtesy of William Samuel Johnson, Esq.)

of Arc." I reply'd certainly not, I know Hodgkinson has such a thing in his possession, but it never has been offer'd to me & cannot be even accepted without my approbation. Knowing how capable Hodgkinson of promising I thought proper to speak to him on ye subject. "Mr Burke reports about town that he has a tragedy in rehearsal called Joan of Arc." "Mrs Johnson has consented to play the part." "But it does not depend upon Mrs Johnson and Mr Burke: I have never read his play, & do not know that I should approve of it." Certainly, certainly, you had better take it home and look it over." "Besides, if it is accepted, unless its merits are much greater than my own piece (meaning Andre) I shall not consent to its being done first." "You are very right, surely not, surely not."

From this it is plain that Burke has been told that his play should be done, without consulting me, and no obstacle presented but obtaining Mrs Johnson's consent to play Joan. $Even^g$ Mr Hobson's & $Stand^g$ Committee.

[Feb.] 14th Snow storm all night & day. Johnson call'd on me, said he heard Mr Hodgkinson was going to Boston, that he & Mrs Johnson wished to talk to me on the subject—that that had no idea of being carried back to Boston at this season. I told him I knew of no such scheme: & he was satisfied. Dine at M: Rogers with the Woolseys & Howlands. Evening Theatre $224 to Spanish Barber & Oracle.

[Feb.] 15th Barret arrived in town with a letter from a Mr Blake one of y^e Haymarket proprietors, recommending to us to let him have the Theatre for the season. Hodgkinson for the first time show'd me two letters from Mr Winthrop advising him to come on immediately and establish himself there. After Barrett went away Hodgkinson declared his wish to quit N. Y. and we talked of making arrangements for next winter in which he should establish himself in Boston & leave me with a Company: thus to seperate. I raised no objections. He talked of even going down immediately, and doing something. We concluded to let the Boston Comedians have our Theatre there for a certain number of nights for Benefits, they paying so much per night, for us, to the proprietors on our account. Write on André.

[Feb.] 16th Give our consent to Barret, to let them play untill 23d March, they first obtaining the proprietors permission & paying on our account, to y^e prop: 10 p: C: on the receits. Write on my Comedy. Read Italian Monk by that poverty stricken animal [James] Boaden & Zorinsky by [Thomas] Morton. Evening, Theatre, "Earl of Warwick & Highland Reel" $402. Write on André: and on y^e Minutes $Stand^g$ Committee.

[Feb.] 17th Hodgkinson show'd me a letter sign'd by Stimson, Winthrop & 2 other trustees expressing dissaprobation in res[pect] to Barrets having the Theatre. If it had not been for my interference Hodgk: would have put Barret into the Theatre without even asking their permission! Write on the Comedy & on Andre. Club at W W Woolseys. Theatre "Chapter of Accidents & Children in y^e Wood" $242.

[Feb.] 18th Sunday. Write on André. Instruct Children.

[Feb.] 19th I rode out with Cooper to Tyler's, who now keeps the public house and Tea Gardens, [31] where Brennon formerly liv'd. Cooper gave me some account of himself. His mother going to Holland when he was between 8 & 9 years of age, left him, with Mr Godwin, he offering to take the charge. Godwin's anti-religious opinions being known to Mrs Cooper, she charged him to send Tom to church, which was at first accordingly

[31] Joseph Tyler's Washington Garden was situated at the south west corner of Spring and Hudson Streets. Kept since before the Revolution by Charles J. Brannon, it was re-opened in 1795 as the New York Garden, under the proprietorship of George Gray Jr. I. N. P. Stokes, *Iconography of Manhattan Island,* III, 977; V. 1319; N. Y. City directories; *N. Y. Hist. Soc. Collections 1906,* 196, 251.

done, but the boy finding it irksome soon contrived to pass the time in ye park with his companions and on his return to pretend that he had been at church often telling falshood to support the deceit. How common a case is this? Forcing children to attendance on religious meetings is no small portion of that education which makes men what we see them—Hypocrites & Lyars. Mr Godwin soon saw the evil, and to remedy it, told the boy what were his mothers wishes, but that he should not <*insist on*> enforce the fulfillment of them. From that time to this Cooper never went to Church. Mr Godwin was his preceptor in every thing: He instructed him in Greek & Latin, French & Italian: He regularly read to him every day after dinner: Cooper mentions "Clarissa Harlowe" and Shakespeare's work among the books Mr Godwin read to him. It was customary for Mr Godwin to dine every Sunday at Mr Holcrofts & Tom went with him. Thus Cooper lived untill he was past 16 years of age, when one morning he told Mr Godwin, that he was tired of studying Latin & Greek and thought he was able to support himself. Godwin was surpriz'd, but simply asked him what he wished to do. Cooper said he would walk to Paris & join the French Army. Mr Godwin, mildly said "we will talk further on the subject tomorrow morning. Godwin & Holcroft both talked to him & he relinquished the scheme of going to France, telling him that all he wanted was to be independant. Among other schemes he proposed being a chorus singer at one of the Theatres & Mr Holcroft appointed him to come to him that he might judge of his voice; on trial Holcroft said it would not do. Singing given up, acting was thought of, & Cooper read Zaphna to Holcroft, who declared it was hopeless, but on his speaking a speech in Richard hope was revived. It was agreed that Cooper should try some country stage & at length he was sent on the Stage Coach down to Edinburgh, to Stephen Kemble, with letters recommending him for young Norval. On arriving at the Scotch Capital Tom, assumed the dress of manhood, his dangling locks were cued & frized and in all the awkwardness which the novelty of dress and situation inspired, but full of confidence, he waited on the Manager. After one or two cool receptions, a rehearsal was called & Mr Cooper was to play with Mrs Siddons: she did not attend the rehearsal, but her husband was there: Tom, ranted, Kemble, walked up & down the stage in despair, but Cooper thought it admiration. After rehearsal, he was desired to wait on the great Man next day. No idea had entered his head yet but of self satisfaction. "This is a difficult part you have chosen, Mr Cooper" "Very difficult Sir" with a smile of confidence. "I wish we could think of something else—" Here the veil was drawn aside & poor Tom found that he was rejected. Douglas was play'd, but not by him & he remained unemployed, untill the Company went to New Castle. There he play[ed] some little parts of no consequence, untill by some chance "Malcolm" in Macbeth was assigned to him: he played it with applause, but having to speak the Tag, he became confused, at seeing the people begin to rise & go out: confusion begat terror & totally unable to proceed he stood motionless, while dead & living dramatis personae joined the prompter in giving him the word. The Audience hissed & hooted, and still poor Tom continued with his arm extended & a vacant smile on his fixed face & so might have stood, had not dead Macbeth order'd the trumpet to be blown & the Curtain dropt. This done, Kemble arose & order'd, young Malcolm to follow him: then & not untill then did Tom move. "Order the treasurer to pay Mr Cooper £5. Mr Cooper I have no further service for you." Thus finish'd our Hero's first campaign, and he was happy to find himself once more at Mr Godwin's fire side, after having expended his last penny in conveying himself to London on board a Collier. His second expedition was to Portsmouth where he met Tyler & where he supported himself & enter'd into dissipation without reserve. On his return again to London, he no longer lived with Mr Godwin, tho' he studied under his & Mr Holcrofts direction, avowedly for the Stage, and accordingly made his appearance at Covent Garden in Hamlet. His success was great & he played likewise Horatio, & Macbeth. He was now 20 years of age. There being no opening for [him] in London, in the first line of business & he refusing any other, Mr Harris gave him 50 Guineas & he went into Wales, from whence Mr Holcroft sent for him to engage with Wignell.

Evening Theatre "Cure for the Heart ach" and [blank] in y^{e} house $327.

Feby 20th 1798. Storm of rain. Write on André.

[Feb.] 21st A meeting of the subscribers to the New Theatre, when it appeared by the statement of their Committee, that after expending the original money subscribed, they have accumulated a debt of £34000. Most of the subscribers will not pay any thing further, the deed for the property is in the names of the Committee & they have mortgaged it. A Committee of 5 was appointed to report on ways & means to discharge the debt. Cooper was with me this evening & look'd over André, I pointed out Bland for him. He prefers McDonald. Theatre "Man of Fortitude & Midnight Wanderers" in y^{e} house $294.

[Feb.] 22d Cooper goes off to day with £500 Sterling in his pocket to tender to Wignell. I desired him to speak to Bernard as to a future engagement here with me, after Hodgkinson's departure. Williamson show'd me the *part* of André from Mr W Brown's (of Boston) play of West point preserv'd: there are good passages in it. Smith with me this Evening. By an advertisement in ye Phil: papers, that Wignell & Rainaigle have been obliged to shut up the Theatre (for a week only they say) they accuse Fennell of being ye cause & call him ungratefull. Coopers absence is mention'd as another cause. Write on André.

[Feb.] 23d Attend to business & write on André. Johnson requests from his wife that I will read it to her. Burke leaves Joan of Arc with me: read it with much disgust. Evening Theatre "More ways than one" "Love & mony" & "Oracl" in the house $140.

[Feb.] 24th Read Smith poetical epistle to Darwin to be prefixed to the American edition of Botanic Garden. Dip in Coleridge & Southey's works. Mr Gaine tells me that the Committee to report on ways & means to pay the debt on the New Theatre met last Evening & to day a report is to be drawn up: he supposes that it will be sold, the first subscribers agreeing to sink their payment for a silver ticket for life, untransferable. Finish writing & correcting André with its prologue. Milnes desiring to see or hear it, is to meet me at Johnsons when I there read it. Cooper has talked in terms of high praise of it, I find. Evening Theatre "Spanish Barber & Next door Neighbours in house $187. Club at Smith's, he read in Coleridge & Southey. C is the greater poet, but "poor Mary" is exquisite.

[Feb.] 25th Sunday: writing out the parts of André. M: Dangel Johns French teacher dined with us & afternoon gave me a Lesson. Evening read André to Milns & the Johnsons: it seemed to interest.

[Feb.] 26th Burke (Bunkerhill) met me in ye street & ask'd me if I had read his play. "Yes" "And how do you like it" "It wants correction." "What do you mean by correction? I am sure there are no grammatical errors." "Unless I have the book before me I can not point out what I mean precisely, there are metaphors which are confused or false, and the whole requires your severe attention before it is fit for a prompt book."

He said he had bestowed every attention on it and that he was proud of it. I objected to the incongruity in the character of Joan wherein he makes her at first appear as an inspired personage as in Shakespeare, then to represent herself as merely inspired by patriotism & at last to appear as a prophetess again & send her foreknowledge in a letter to the French, from the stake. He vehemently supported his child, & I appointed him to meet me tomorrow morning, on the subject. Even[g] Theatre, Every one has his fault & Two strings to your bow." in y[e] house $223.

[Feb.] 27th Burke came to me: I had previously looked over his play again, & was pleased with the situations &c, & more with the thing in y[e] whole than at first. I pointed out parts to correct, a character to omit &c, & he took it away to re-write it, & I gave him hopes that it might be play'd. Cooper arrived from Philadelphia. He on Saturday last, formally tendered the £500 Sterl[g] to Messrs. Wignel & Rainagle jointly & severally in presence of Mr Thos Taylor of Phil: & Mr G[ilbert] McEvers of N: Y: they refused to accept of it, but afterwards sent for Cooper who refused to return. Cooper afterwards offerred Dallas their attorney $1200 which he refused but pressed him to pay the whole sum & offer'd him his discharge, but Cooper now refused: & brought back the money. Evening at Kents. Afterwards Cooper supped with me & related many circumstances of Godwin, who was once a Clergyman.

[Feb.] 28th I procured from Mr Kent a pamphlet containing the proceedings of the Court martial respecting André published by order of Congress: Miss Seward's Monody &c. Evening Theatre "Hamlet & Adopted Child" the profits for Mr Cooper. In the house $895. Cooper's Hamlet was justly admired, I think his scene at the play the finest thing I ever saw. He was received very flatterringly.

Mar: 1st Very busy. left André with Chalmers for his determination respecting the part of McDonald. Milnes left a farce for me to look at called a "Flash in the pan or the [blank] Evening Standing Committee.

This day *Mar 2d* The committee appointed to report to the subscribers &c of the New Theatre meet again:

Just before going to the meeting Mr Gaine & Mr Henderson had some conversation wth me respecting the renting the Building. I had every assurance that they would not let it to any other person. Mr Gaine asked me if £2400 per annum might be mentioned as the sum that might be obtained for it, I objected & he then proposed £2000. I did not object, Henderson acquiesced. Mr Henderson asked me the meaning of the report that Hodgkinson was going away. I told him that such was his determination, made known formally to me, and to the proprietors of the Boston house & that his intention is to open in Boston in Sept. next. He regretted his loss as a performer. I mention'd Cooper & Bernard supplying his place. He spoke of Hodgkinson as making himself many enemies, & I said he had a pecular faculty at offend[g] people. He said he had sent a very rude message to Mr Pollock concerning the opening or keeping open the windows over the Stage door. They talked (Mr G & H) of the building being sold immediately to pay the debt: & the subscribers tickets sunk: They both agreed in the propriety of endeavouring to have a Theatre prohibited here during July, August & Sept. Evening Theatre. "King John & Romp" in y[e] house $353.

March 3d Gave Cooper his first weeks salary 20 & 5 for Wardrobe. Walk out to Tylers: Cooper came in there, we return'd together I walking he riding his Mare. I told him that Chalmers declined playing McDonald, as being incompetent to study it in time. he observed that perhaps he would play André & Hodgkinson McDonald. I said I should not dare ask Hodgkinson to exchange. He said Hodgkinson had said André was the worst part of the three. Dine at W W Woolseys with G M W & Mr Howland. Evening Theatre Man of Fortitude & Doctor & Apothecary in y[e] house $275. I saw part of the play and was mortified to find my poor much to be pitied thoughts so be-mangled.

Mar: 4th Sunday. My Friend Suckley breakfasted with me. Call on Hodgkinson by the letters from Boston which he communicated to me, I learn that Barret, immediately on arriving at Boston advertised to open the Haymarket Theatre, without delivering our Letters or consulting the proprietors: 2 days afterwards he sent our letters & the Trustees, refused him permission to open the Theatre. The trustees write to Hodgkinson inviting him to come on and immediately establish himself by way of preventing the rebuilding of the old Theatre. Wm Tudor writes to Hodgkinson that the Old Theatre will be immediately rebuilt & that he may have it for next winter. Caleb Stimson acknowledges the receit of ye 50 Ds: sent him & says he has burnt the Note. Hodgkinson return'd & we talked on the situation of the business: he proposed making a Commonwealth of the Company, but nothing was settled. Cooper came in and we talked of arranging plays & casting characters & we appointed to meet on ye business at 6 in ye evening. Cooper dined with me & look'd over my "Mysterious Monk." He says Godwin & Holcroft went with him to the Coach when he sat off for America: he saw Godwin but for a short time, while in London to join Wignell: he thinks Godwin mention'd me to him as resident in N: Y: & sent a message what he knows not. When he first knew Godwin, he still wore his parsons dress, black with a large cock'd hat, his hair friz'd at the sides & curl'd stiffly behind: (he is a small well made man weakly, thin faced, very large nose, & blue eyes) he changed his dress altogether, a blue coat, yellow cassimire waiscoat & breeches, highly blued silk stockings (the same in which he equip'd Cooper for his scotch expedition) hair plaited behind round hat & spectacles. His dress at present is plain with short unpowdered hair & so is Holcrofts.

Mar: 5th Come to a determination with Hodgkinson to reduce Salaries & expences or close at the end of this week. Evening, "King John & Doctor & Apothecary" in y^{e} house $307.

Mar: 6th Give notice to the Company. Afternoon set off for Amboy by the way of Paulus Hook taking my gun with me. When the Stage stopped after crossing the Causeway, the Sun was setting & my ears were saluted with the songs of vast numbers of birds; I looked out and saw large flocks of Blackbirds settling on the neighbouring trees, their flight was from the North west and every throat was swelled with its song. I lodged this night at Elizabeth town.

[March] 7th Up at half past 3, the sun rises beautifully and calls forth the notes of the meadow lark & black bird. I saw this day the red wing'd black bird, & black glossy plumed: robins (T: Migrat:) Blue jays, Meadow larks, Blue birds, besides the different kinds of hedge birds. Breakfasted at J Heards & proceeded to Bloodgoods, who undertakes to cultivate my Orchard on shares. Go to Amboy & visit my friends there. Compton agrees to cultivate the Lot back of the Garden: the trees in this Lot have been injured by cattle getting in.

[March] 8th Leave Amboy & return: Lodge at Night at New Ark.

[March] 9th Get home. On Wednesday the Provoked Husband was play'd & the Double Disguise to $342. This evening Theatre "Romeo & Juliet & Quaker" Coopers Romeo, in the house $735.

[March] 10th The Company agree to the Salaries being reducing to what they were last winter & the Benefit expences are fixed at $380, playing 3 times a week. Chalmers declines playing any longer with us, convinced he says that he is of no use to us. Williamson likewise goes. Evening Theatre "Young Quaker & Deserter" in the house $257. Read Sh: Henry 5th.

[March] 11th A rainy Sunday. Write on the Books of the Theatre. Teach John. Read Henry 4th 2d part: & Zoonomia. A few minutes at W W W's.

[March] 12th Go round with P Ten Eyk & prevail wth the printers to advertise for 75 Cents instead of a dollar thus we curtail every thing. Buy paper for printing André, 12 reams at 38/. £22.16.—or $57. Theatre, evening, "All in y^{e} wrong & Rosina" in y^{e} house $223. part of y^{e} evening at W W W, wth Smith, talk of the Fracas at Rome with Joseph Buonaparte. Smith shew'd me y^{e} first proof sheet of *"Alcouin"*

Mar: 13th Attend to Business, write a short preface for André. Get the Robbers and the Conspiracy of Fiesco" in y^{e} German from Sterlitz.

[March] 14th Leave André with Smith & Johnson. Smith reads me a letter from Hopkins who was in Paris attending Fourcroy's lectures. Evening Smith & W W W & G M W with me. Theatre "Battle of Hexham & No song no sup[p]er" in y^{e} house 364$.

[March] 15th Attending to various business. Look over several books to find proper banners for the Britons under Cymbeline. read Cymbeline. Evening at M: Rogers. W W W & wife there. Correct first sheet of André.

[March] 16th Take a lesson of German. Carry y^{e} proof sheet of André to Smith & Johnson for recorrection & pass half an hour with them. Walk with my Wife & Children & order 60 loads of Street Manure or 1 Boat load to be deliver'd at Perth Amboy, manure which has been in pile all winter at 3/6 ye load, & 50 load immediately from the Street at 3/. I am to pay ye boatman 2/ ye load for delivering it on the wharf at Amboy. Evening Theatre "Cymbeline & Lyar" in the house 216 dollars.

[March] 17th Walk out to Tyler's: he says he remembers Sir Wm André a tall young man, an officer, Major André's brother. Evening Theatre in the house 288 dollars to Coopers Hamlet: I saw most of it and think it the best acting I ever saw. Cooper says old Macklin attended each of his representations of Hamlet in London; asked to be introduced to him and payed him high compliments.

[March] 18th Translate a little of Schiller's Fiesco. Call at Hodgkinson find there Cooper, Ten Eyk, Chalmers, Williamson, Beekman. Evening Johnson & Smith with me. Read preface to Taming of y[e] Shrew &c.

[March] 19th Translate. Write on my Comedy. Evening, Theatre for Chalmers's benefit "Road to Ruin," & a medley consisting of speaking, read[g] & singing with which he fill'd up a flaming bill: in the House $1177. Chalmers read "Le fevre," among other affairs, among the Gallery folks hissed him & threw several things at him. The Audience in general were much dissatisfied with the species of entertainment

[March] 20th Much engaged in business

[March] 21st Rain. Write on my Comedy. Evening Theatre: Robin Hood & Next door neighbours" in y[e] house $99.

[March] 22d Correcting proofs of André: searching for information concerning the salt mines of Crakow at y[e] little town of Walietzka: Darwins Botanic Garden, is very poetic on y[e] subject & even by the note gives one to believe that there is a town underground in the mine, cut out of y[e] Salt: the Enc. referred me to Philos: transactions, from them, by visiting the N: Y: Library, I learn'd the particulars noted on y[e] opposite page.

Ph: tr: Vol: 2d p: 523.Salt mines in Transylvania, & Hungary by Dr Brown. What is cut from these mines is called stone salt & is less easy to dissolve than salt procured from boiling: it is ground for use: ordinary colour somewhat grey; some of it mixed with earth: there are some pieces very clear & transparent & so hard that they carve figure out of them. Polish mines near y[e] small town of Welezka "which (the church excepted) is altogether digged hollow underground," but it appears that the mine is much deeper than this town (even if this means than the town encaverned) for in the town is one of the descents for y[e] Miners: 3 kinds of salt here, "course & black," second "whiter" third "clear like chrystal" "the course black salt is dug out in large pieces 3 Ells long & 1 thick: these are ground for use. Colour "darkish grey with some mixture of yellow.

I drank tea at W W W's & searching [William] Coxes Travels found all I wanted, a plain account of the Mines by an eye witness: thus view'd, the town vanishes & Darwins Church with Glittering spires, is a cave cut in the saltstone, called a chapel & some Crucifixes &c, cut in ye salt. I sought this information for Ciceri our painter, for ye scene in Zorinski, which to <*night*> morrow is exhibited unfinished. Pass the latter part of the evening at G M Woolseys. Night Fire in Maiden lane 3 houses consumed.

[March] 23d Give Cox to Ciceri. Read Reynolds Comedy of Cheap living. Fawcet put a manuscript Comedy into my hands, call'd The Lad of Spirit. Evening Theatre "Zorinski & Spoil'd Child" Zorinski has been in preparation all winter & much talk'd and we had to its first representation 293 dollars!

[March] 24th Rain & violent storm. Read, with E H S, the Minister, translated from [Schiller's] Cabal und Lieb, by Lewis [*sic*] ye Author of ye Monk. This is a very wonderfull play. Correct proofs of André. Smith with me in ye Evening: No play.

[March] 25th Sunday. prepare ye Manuscript of André for a prompt book: correct & mark the written parts of ye play. Evening call on Hodgkinson: he inform'd me that Barret & Harpur had written to him informing that the proprietors had decided against them only because they thought they had no right to interfere in leasing ye building during our term & therefore praying for our full permission. Paine in a letter to Hodgkinson, says it was insinuated that *we* had written to ye proprietors wth a view that they should let Barret & Harpur have the Theatre that *we* might plead it as a breach of contract. Hodgkinson says that he has written to the proprietors of the Haymarket Theatre, that unless he can have the Federal Street Theatre for ye winter & theirs for a summer Theatre, he declines having any thing to do with either—that he will not encounter opposition—that they must look *our* contract as at an end necessarily. All this without my knowledge or approbation! He says he shall know by his next letters from Boston whether or no, he can fix there: but that he goes on no other terms than having both, or, one being annihilated. He talked of *my* Company for this place next winter. He asked what summer scheme I thought of. I told him I would not be concerned in any summer scheme. He talked of coming to an end of the season at the end of this week & beginning Benefits; I advised to see what the week would produce. He said if he staid in this place in consequence of his Boston scheme failing, he should stay as an actor merely, tho' he believed he could get more elsewhere. He says Gamage industriously spread the idea that Hallam & I are hereafter to be the N: Y: managers: From Gamages talk to *me* I believe it. He talks of André doing something for us. I bade him look what Zorinski had done. Paine in his letter says that they are roofing y^{e} Fed: St^{t} Theatre, which will undoubtedly far exceed the other. Hodgkinson says it is offered to him as the winter Theatre.

[March] 26th Correcting proofs. Evening Theatre "Zorinski & Midnight hour" in y^{e} house 485$. Cooper very imperfect in Zorinski & spoiling the scene with Hodgkinson. Hodgkinson spoke to him, I suppose rudely & they had some warm words.

[March] 27th Read André in y^{e} Green room. Some words pass'd between H & C again this morning. Rehearse André. Afternoon Cooper sent me a letter wishing André put off: I call'd on & told him I would rather see it imperfectly represented than put it off, for I knew of nothing else to enable me to pay Salaries on Saturday. I sat with him some time. I told him he was wrong in respect to Hodgkinson this morning: he laugh'd & assented. Evening W W W's.

[March] 28th Make out bill for André. I saw Henderson at Gaines, & told him it was necessary for him to make some arrangements for the renting the New Theatre for the next season. He acquiesed. We agreed that there was no time to lose. He ask'd if Hodgk: certainly went from this. I said I believed so. He said *they* ought to know. I undertook to ask him from the Committee by his wish. I am to call upon him to talk over matters preliminary to an agreement. As soon as I saw Hodgkinson he told me that he had an answer from the Federal Street proprietors, in which they expressed their satisfaction in his acceptance of their offer. "Then you wrote to them that you would come?" "Yes but the terms are not yet settled." "I ask thus pointedly because Mr Henderson required of me, this morning, your determination" "You might have told him that at any rate I would never be a Manager here" I spoke to him of the necessity of immediate arrangements: he advised me to conclude with Henderson immediately. I mention'd going to Phil: & seeing Bernard. Afternoon, Ten Eyk says the Committee will come to a conclusion wth me, they see the necessity. Mr Gaine says there will be a great house on Friday. Ten Eyk says Cooper in his rattling way made up with Hodgkinson & the miff has pass'd off. Evening: Theatre Douglas & Children in the Wood" in the House 419 dollars, my wife, her Mother & our Children were at the exhibition.

[March] 29th Call on Henderson & tell him Hodgkinson's determination: Henderson told me that the Committee had determined to proceed in leasing the house without waiting any decision as to the future proprietorship, that I had nothing to do but to determine what sum I could give per year (for which purpose he advised me to talk with Mr Gaine) and <*make*> give him my proposals which he would lay before y[e] others & come to an immediate agreement. He said I must be at all the expence of fitting the house for another season & that the admission tickets must stand as they are. He asked me who I should get to superintend the Stage? I told him I wished to engage Bernard for *that* & that I should arrange the business myself: we talked of Mrs Oldmixon to help fill up the vacancy Mrs Hodgkinson will make. He advised to keep well with the Hallams but by no means to give him a part in the Management. At rehearsal I mention'd this conversation to Hodgk: who expressed himself much pleased that the matter is so far fixed. André twice rehearsed to day. Yesterday Smith show'd me a letter from C B Brown in which he describes himself as assiduously writing Novels & in love. Smith had some numbers of a weekly Mag: [32] in which B has published under the title of "The Man at home."

[March] 30th I had much talk with Gaine and Henderson upon the terms of the lease for the New Theatre: I told them 4000 Dollars per annum was the utmost I could think of giving. I mention'd the contingency of being obliged to keep shut, & Henderson said & Gaine concurred that in such case nothing would be exacted from me: I said I was willing to make any agreement which should proportion the payment to the profits that I wanted not great emolument, but that I started from the risk of losing all my property by such an engagement. They agreed perfectly with me. Henderson mentioned a per centage on all receits; I made no objection. He desired me to consider of it & mention the rate. I mention'd the justice of being paid for the scenery at quitting the property tho' not its first cost: Henderson & Gaine both fully agreed. I mention'd that Hallam would expect something from me: they both thought I ought to give him & his wife first situations in my Company but *no more.* Rehearse André. Evening "André & poor Soldier" in y^{e} house 817$. The play was much applauded notwithstanding the extreme imperfectness of Cooper & some others

[32] *The Weekly Magazine of original essays, fugitive pieces and interesting intelligence,* published in Philadelphia by James Watters. "The Man at Home" begins in the first number of Vol. I, February 3, 1798.

but on Bland's throwing down his Cockade there was a few hisses.

[March] 31st I find Cooper's friends displeas'd with André because he cut so poor a figure in it & my friends much displeased that it was done so badly. Mr Gaine, G[arrit] Kettletas & others advise me not to repeat it on monday as intended: On consulting about the Theatre I find that general satisfaction was expressed, but our warm & ignorant people, look upon Bland's action as an insult to the Country. On considering that to withdraw the play would show as an acknowledgement of its insufficiency I determine on its repetition on Monday. Make an alteration in 5th Act, by making Bland on his repentance receive the cockade again. Evening Theatre "Zorinski & Highland Reel" 265$. Club at Smith & Johnson's.

Ap[l] 1st Sunday. Call on Mr & Mrs Johnson to talk of an engagement for the ensuing Season: they say they are to be determined by the arrival of letters from England whether they go thither or not, no other Objection was started as to engageing with me. Last night Hodgkinson having caused the Curtain to be rung up before Ciceri had got the Stage ready, the latter flew into violent passion & abused Hodgkinson & left the house where Hodgkinson swears he shall never act as Machinist more. This morning Ciceri came to me & simply related the fact, blaming himself for his passion, but withal determining not to conduct the Stage during Mr H's remainding residence in the business.

Ap[l] 2d Rain. I am told that the people are so offended at the Cockade business as to threaten to hiss off the play to night. Ciceri resigns his situation to day & I employ Morris to take the temporary direction of the department, continuing the painters. Henderson came up to the Theatre & seemed to press my taking steps for another Season: he wished me to see him tomorrow morning & settle as to the terms of hiring the house: bringing with me the average of the receits per night during the present season: on making it out I find it $387. a sum much greater than I expected. Evening Theatre "André & Midnight Wanderers" Violent storm of wind & rain, in the house $271. The play was received with constant applause.

[April] 3d Storm continues, put off the play intended for to night. Call on Henderson and talk on the agreement for the Theatre, the result was merely an offer from him of letting me have it, I agreeing to pay 12 & ½ per cent on all the receits: I objected to the rate: that or 5000$ per year seems to be what is expected. I demanded in case I took it, credit to be lent me for 2000$ to be expended in decorating the House & preparing scenery, this he gave me to understand would be granted, and a certain portion of the cost of all scenery repaid me out of the rent but how much we did not determine. Think of André for my benefit as Author next Saturday. A little while at Hodgkinsons this afternoon, Cooper there, as usual smoking segars & drinking madeira. At Swords's I saw a bungling attack upon André in y[e] Argus, answer it in the evening

Ap[l] 4th 1798. Dine at W W Woolsey, with Kent Smith &c. Evening Theatre Douglas and Double Disguise $121. Correct last sheet of André.

[April] 5th The Swords's tell me that my Assailant in the Argus is one Conolly an Irishman a partizan of Utt the Cooper. See Henderson again & we agreed, I to take the house at $5000 for the ensuing year, and in case of my not being able to keep it open 8 months in the year a proportional deduction to be made from the rent. "We want the property to pay us not you" was the expression of Henderson: He further agrees to assist me with his credit in the sums necessary or which I may think necessary in preparing the Theatre for opening next Season &

to pay for all Scenery &c which I shall have made, according to the valuation of indifferent men on my quitting the property or closing accounts. Fine day to-day. I told Hodgkinson the terms on which I was to have the Theatre & he advised me close the bargain: I mention'd to him my design of going on to Philadelphia to see Bernard: he thought I had better write: I spoke to Cooper who thought I had better go on by all means. I mention'd Mrs Oldmixon to him: he said that if I made any agreement with Oldmixon I must be very exact & very tight & specify the characters she must do: with Bernard I should find no difficulty. Evening Theatre "Fashionable Love & Farmer" in the house 216$.

[April] 6th Fine day. See Henderson: he says that Carlisle Pollock agrees to the bargain between him & me: that they could not find Jacob Morton but doubted not his acquiescence & wished me to proceed upon the firm reliance that the thing is settled: he press'd me to go to Philadelphia immediately. On the 31st of March I found, a fine specimen of the Salix conifera in flower, the Male & female shrubs near each other. Today I visited them & found the female flowers already withering.

[April] 7th Saturday. Preparing to go to Philadelphia by the way of Amboy. More abuse in the Argus to day against me. Evening Theatre "André &c for the Authors benefit in the house 329$. Speak to Johnson again on the subject of an engagement, he will not yet determine.

[April] 8th Sunday. I left New York in the Amboy Packet and after a very tedious passage arrived there, after 11 OClock at Night: sup & Lodge at Robert Rattoon's Tavern

[April] 9th In the morning I was awakened by the song of the Robin—very sweet—Saw Compton & gave directions concerning the garden and fruit trees. Breakfast with Mrs Terrill & Mrs Brown. Walk out to my

Orchard: Bloodgood is drawing in my Manure. The Apple trees put out last Fall are flourishing. of the Quince slips but three are living. The Cherry trees are most of them living. Continue my walk out to Woodbridge. The birds I saw were the Robin, Crow, Blue bird, Hedge bird, Black bird (different kinds) Meadow larks, English snipe, Quails, and Wild pigeons. I saw one Black snake, about 5 foot in length. At Woodbridge I saw Mr Patten who agreed to run the division fence between his Upland & my Meadow on the Staten Island Sound, making a straight line, to intersect both Meadow & Upland by way of saving fence, he agreed that J: Heard should settle the line for me. Dine with Heard—he pays me $7.50 for a Ton of my Salt Hay. Leave Woodbridge after dinner & arrive at Princeton about 9 OClock.

[April] 10th Fine Morning. I now wait the Stage. Talk a little with Captn Bunyan, who now resides here. Dr Morse joins the Stage & we proceed in Company: from him I learn the State of our politics. How very evident the change of climate is seen in approaching Philadelphia by the young leaves on the trees. Many pidgeons flying, the Robin & the Red Wing Blackbird very frequent. Arrive in PHILADELPHIA about 8 OClock in ye Evening: rain: Call on Bernard who was not at home: write a note appointing him to meet me at 9 tomorrow morning, and call again; he being still out I leave it.

[April] 11th After a storm it is now clearing again: Waiting for Bernard at the Indian Queen where I put up. Specimen of criticism. Two of the Gentlemen in the Stage yesterday, talking of theatricals mention'd Cooper & both agreed that his principal excellence is his being always perfect in his parts or master of the words of his Author!

Bernard sent a note appointing 12 OClock to meet. I went to Mrs Smiths & engaged a room. See Tracey. Call on Brown who goes with me to the Booksellers [John] Ormrod & [James] Humphreys & gives me some account of his "Sky Walk" he says it is founded on Somnambulism. Bernard calls: says his engagement with Wignell expires the second week of August next: I made known my intentions, and he desired me to <*make*> put my offers on paper & he would call again between 1 & 2 OClock. Call on [Thomas] Dobson the bookseller, look into "Proofs of a conspiracy &c" this is at least a curious book. Dine at Mrs Smiths in Company with Messrs Tracy, Dana, Sewall, Griswold, Bartlett & Coit: Read the papers Drink tea at Browns. Go to the Theatre & see "The Italian Monk" with no pleasure. The Stage & Scenery appeared poor in comparison with ours.

[April] 12th Leave 12 copies of André with Dobson & 12 with Humphry's. After breakfast converse with Tracey on the political state of America; mans happiness; depravity; ignorance; Godwin. I yesterday put into Bernards hands proposals to this effect—an engagement for 9 months from next Septr at 25$ p week and 10$ in addition for directing the Stage, & the same salary for Mrs B which she now receives: a benefit for each the charges of which should not exceed 390$. He promised to call on me at 10 OClock this morning, but in the stead sent a note excusing himself as unexpectedly oblig'd to attend rehearsal.

"I feel myself highly flattered & much favor'd by your polite <*offer*> & very friendly offer for *New York* but I find it impossible at present to make up my mind to the change—if I can be of the least service in procuring MS or recommending Performers now in England or on the Continent you may freely command my services, and rest assured that no man on earth will hear of your success with more real satisfaction than &c &c

J Bernard

Chestnut St[t]
Thursday
Mrs B begs her best respects

Perhaps I shall send the following in return.

I have frankly avow'd to you that the intention of my journey was to obtain your support for the New Theatre and I now as frankly confess that I should be chagrin'd to return without accomplishing my object or at least without the pleasure of once more conversing with you on the subject—another reason for wishing to see you again before I depart, is, that, in writing down my proposals I reckoned on an oppertunity of obviating any objections, explaining my intentions or of complying with any demands from you which should be within my power, in the promised interview, & therefore was perhaps too concise.

If you can meet me this afternoon at No 119 South Second St[t] I will wait on you from 3 to 5 OClock, or on your notice will attend you at any place between those hours or on any other that will suit you."

Brown carried the above for me.

Dine with C Brown: he reads to me the beginning of a Novel undertaken since "Sky Walk" he calls it Wieland or the Transformation" this must make a very fine book. At 3 I went to [Benjamin] Carrs and received a note from Bernard as follows

D[r] Sir

I havė Cheveril to *study* for to morrow evening which demands every hour of my attention as I have not been able to look at it till this morning.

I am sorry circumstances will not permit me to quit *Phila* but a promise has been extorted from me to *continue* by those friends that I cannot disoblige.

I once more return you sincere thanks for your polite offer & friendly wishes and remain &c &c

Yours truly &c &c
J BERNARD

Thursday

Mrs. Oldmixon was waiting for me at Carr having been informed at my desire, by him, of my wish to engage her. We talked over the business: she said she had received offers from Whitlock for Charlestown very great—that her benefit was here insured to her & her salary 7 guineas per week—that she was willing to do the best old women in Comedy, the Comic Singers & occasionally a serious one, and the best Chambermaids—she referred me to Sir John & I am to see him to morrow. Drink tea with Charles at his friend Paxson's. Mrs P. is a very charming woman & P a man of strong mind and good information, I pass'd the evening with them untill 9 OClock & then went home to meet Chalmers according to *his* wish, but he did not come & play'd Backgammon with Tracey.

[April] 13th Call on Brown & write to my Wife & to Joseph Byrnes of Charleston. Dine with Carr at a Mr [J. B.] Freeman's an Englishman who is publishing a work in Numbers which he calls the Thespian Oracle: saw Harwood there and spoke to him of an engagement, offerring 25 dollars the week; he made no objection, said he should certainly leave Wignell, but that Hodgkinson had previously made him offers for Boston, that he should write to Hodgkinson, & if they did not conclude, he would write to me. Ride out to Germantown in the Stage, at the Inn, I found a horse in waiting & Sir John Oldmixon's servant with a horse & Cart, I preferrd to walk—his house is about a mile from the Inn: here I drank tea & supped with him & his wife & concluded the engagement memorandumed on page 78.

Mrs Oldmixon engages for the ensuing season at N: Y: to play the first line of Opera, or such characters as she has given in a List of, the best of the Comedy Old Women the best of the Chambermaids, or at her choice in Comedies Mrs Mattock's line of playing: Salary 7 Guineas per week—she finding her own Wardrobe, & having a benefit free of the Charges on benefits. Stipulating not to sing in chorusses, unless in certain circumstances of the Company she may herself choose so to do: The Theatre is to be kept open from on or near the 1st of September ensuing, for 38 or 40 weeks except unavoidable circumstances of calamity shall oblige me to shut it & during the time of its being so opened, the above named salary is to be regularly paid.

W D

This is the substance of said agreement.

[signed:] JOHN OLDMIXON

[April] 14th I rose at 5 and walked into Phil: by 7, eight miles. At 8 I joined the stage for N: Y: and sat off for home, we lodge at Prince town after having crossed the Delaware at Lamberton in a violent gust of Wind.

[April] 15th Sunday. Proceed with the Stage to Woodbridge. Dress and Dine at the Inn & walk to Amboy: drink tea at Mrs Parkers; sleep at Mrs Terrils.

[April] 16th Set out young peach trees. After breakfast, with a bundle of Asparagus walk out to Woodbridge to join the Stage, but it was so full that I am left behind with Mr Heard. Shoot a few Birds. The birds I saw to-day were, Crows, Blackbirds of different kinds, Meadow Larks, Snipe, Woodcocks, Robins, Doves, & Hedge birds, Snow birds or sparrows. Towards evening a violent storm of wind & snow. Read in Weekly Magazine which I brought on from Phil:

[April] 17th Ground cover'd with snow, which however disappears in a few hours, tho it continues cold & windy all day. After breakfast walk to Eliz: Town. Call on Mr Williamson & at Mr Crowells: proceed from thence in the stage and arrive at New York about 4 OClock. Smith calls on me. I call at Hodgkinson's but he was out. I learn that Burkes Joan of Arc was not well attended on the first night & that it was laughed at & hissed; the business of the prophecy by letter, especially. Smith tells me that Hallam has loudly vented his discontent at my having hired the Theatre & declared that he will not be an hired Actor &c: the report is that Wignell has sent for him to come thither & that they will join in opposition to me. Pass part of the Evening at Mr Roger's W W W & Wife & mother there.

[April] 18th Shall I send the following proposals to Hallam?

"Sir

The Committee of proprietors of the New Theatre not chusing or not having power to prolong the lease of it beyond the present season, on the terms agreed to with Mr Hodgkinson and myself and Mr Hodgkinson declining all further concern in the holding or improving said Theatre, all engagements, agreements or contracts depending upon our so jointly holding & improving it must necessarily cease at the close of the Theatre.

The abovementioned Committee, have, however, in consideration of the loss sustained by me in The New Theatre, offered said Theatre to me for the ensuing year for the sum of $5000 and it is my intention immediately on the close of the present season,

MRS. BENJAMIN WOOLSEY, JR. (ANN MUIRSON) (1737-1807)
By William Dunlap
(In the Theodore Salisbury Woolsey Collection)

to proceed in decorating the house & preparing a full stock of Scenery and to open the house early in, or perhaps on the 1st of, September.

Your situation, and Theatrical character, entitle you to every consideration on a change of this kind, and I hereby offer to sell to you my lease, for the sum, which shall appear on closing the present season to have been lost by me in consequence of my having hired the New Theatre; provided I can obtain the permission of the proprietors so to do, in which case I will altogether withdraw; *or* I will for the half or fourth of my aforesaid loss sell the half or fourth of any profit, I may gain the ensuing year, you joining with me in the business, as a performer & leaving the direction to me; *or* I offer, for your assistance and the assistance of Mrs Hallam as performers, 50 dollars weekly, you both finding your <*wardrobes*> stage clothes, and in addition a weekly sum to be determined upon, for the use of your Theatrical property, to be agreed upon by us, or left to indifferent persons. Your immediate determination is solicited by

W D"

Having read the above to Gaine, Ten Eyk, & Henderson & they approving I copy it & give it Mirvan Hallam to carry to his Father. Milns tells me that Hallam affects to consider Hodgkinsons going to Boston merely as a feint & that we are still united, that Hallam said he was wait^{g} for my proposals & if they did not suit him he would make a "blow up" that would make the last appear nothing. Meet Hallam at the Box office, he took me out & said he "acceded to my last offer" and appeared perfectly satisfied, but wished me to talk with Mrs Hallam as to her business. Evening Theatre Siege of Belgrade & Two strings to your bow" in y^{e} house 705$

[April] 19th Talk to Hodgkinson on the subject of making up a Company—he wants Harwood—and Mr & Mrs Johnson—wishes me to take Mr & Mrs Barret. In walking to E Town day before yesterday I gathered a specimen of Arum the name of the species I do not know; the plant is vulgarly called Skunks Cabbage and is very common on the sides [of] rivers and wet places, but I never before saw the flower as it appears before the leaves; the leaves are now appearing & the flower decaying: the smell is rank & offensive.

[April] 20th I called on Henderson & proposed signing writings in respect to the Theatre: he assented, asked me to draw up a writing: I agreed: I mentioned or rather read from this book my conception of the terms agreed upon; he seemed to think that I ought to be obliged to pay $5000, unless the Theatre could not be opened owing to *public Calamity,* and mentioned difficulty in leaving it in my power to shut the Theatre in case of not being successfull, and then pay them no rent. I replied that unless I could receive my expences it would be in vain for me keep open the Theatre, that if I did it I must accumulate debt, without having means to discharge it & without means to pay rent: I quoted his words "We want the property to pay us not you." He acknowledged the principle. I told him I would not take the House upon any other principle than paying 5000$ provided I could keep it open 8 months. He made no difficulty but that of leaving too much in my power. He requested me to draw up the writing and see him tomorrow morning. He afterwards came up to the Theatre & shewed me a paper drawn up by the Committee, for the purpose of obtaining loans to discharge their, in this they state that they have let the house for the ensuing Year for 5000$ (without mentioning any proviso's,) they having a right to 113 free tickets, untransferrable (which is true) and they offer these tickets or rights to such as will subscribe, stating that they have become the purchasers of the property. He now seemed to wish that Hodgkinson & his wife might be engaged for next Winter, and appointed Hodgkinson to meet him at 2 to day: I am to see him tomorrow morning.

Mrs Hallam took me aside to day at the Theatre and begged me to let her have a list of characters which she was to play in the Company, complained of ill-usage, which I chose to consider as level'd against Hodgkinson, and declared she would not remain in the Theatre to be so treated another Season. I promised to call & see her.

Evening, Theatre, "The Will & A flash in the pan"

Milns's new farce, in the house 395$ the Farce was dissaproved of.

[April] 21st Write the following to lay before the Committee—

MEMORANDUM &c

1st Possession to be given immediately on closing the present Season.

2d Untransferable rights of free admission into the house except on benefit nights shall be allowed to the number of 113.

3d The party of the second part shall pay to the parties of the first part 5000$ for the use of said Theatre and property for the term of one year, beginning on the day possession is given as aforesaid; provided that the said party of the second part shall be enabled to keep said Theatre open for y^e purposes of Theatrical exhibition 8 months during said year, but if, from any cause whatever, the receits of said Theatre should be inadequate to discharge the expences and the party of the second part shoud not be enabled to keep open said Theatre for the purposes aforesaid, the parties of the first part shall deduct from the said 5000 dollars, a sum in exact proportion to the proportion which the time said Theatre shall be open less than 8 months, shall bear to said 8 months; provided it shall appear that the party of the second part has endeavoured fairly and honestly to keep the Theatre open the full time.

4th The party of the second part shall at his own expense, ornament and prepare the Boxes &c for the reception of the Audience, and complete the Stock of Scenery as far as time will permit before the next opening.

5th The parties of the first part, shall, for the above purpose, assist the party of the second part, by endorsing his notes to the amount of 2000 dollars for the purpose of procuring from the Banks a loan to that amount, if called upon so to do, this sum to be divided into four notes of $500 each one dated the first of May, one the first of June, one the first of July and one the first of August, next ensuing this credit to be lent if required untill the first day of November next ensuing & no longer.

6th Such Scenery as the party of the party [*sic*] of the second part shall cause to be made, during the time he occupies the premises, shall, on his ceasing so to occupy, be valued by 3 indifferent persons, one chosen by each of the contracting parties & the third by the first two, such valuation to be paid by the parties of the first part to the party of the second.

I carryed the above to Henderson who read it in my presence and made no objections: he is to show it to his Colleagues & I am to see him on Monday morning. Milns's Farce is very much disapproved of. I call on Ciceri to consult for scenery to my "Sternes Maria" he is to design the Vineyard. Evening Theatre "Romeo & Juliet & Jubilee" $178. At Club in Smith's room Smith & Johnson (who drank tea with me) W W W & Mr Radcliff. Smith reads in "Sky walk" which interests us all very much.

[April] 22d Sunday. At Hodgkinson's. He says Mrs Hallam was intoxicated last night & display'd her usual behaviour when so, at the Theatre. Call on Smith & Johnson & bring home with [me] "Sky Walk": begin to read it to my Wife. Barton having sent on by Capt: Hendricks the Mohegan Indian some of pamphlet entitled "Collections for an essay towards a Materia Medica of the United States" I get one. Read "Sky Walk" Evening at Hallams They complained dismally of Hodgkinson. She had been used very ill—they seemed surprized that I had no assurances of Mr & Mrs Johnson staying, thought it would be too much to lose her and Mrs. Hodgkinson. They only wished in case Mrs Johnson did stay that in casting new plays Mrs Hallam should share equally. Mrs Hallam wished to have Albina in the Will, when Mrs Hodgk: left it vacant, this I promised, and Lady Priory in "Wives as they were &c" When I returned I found Smith who read in "Sky Walk" for us.

[April] 23d Writing on Books of the Theatre. I call on Henderson by appointment to know the determina[tion] of the Committee respecting the memorandum of agreement left with him; he said that he had seen the Gentlemen individually and that they objected to the words "any cause whatever" as giving me power to shut up the Theatre at any time when the receits did not answer my expectations, that the Committee were willing guard me against public calamity, as War or Sickness, but thought I must risque bad-luck from bad houses, myself. I finally agreed to strike out the words "any cause whatever" & substitute "War sickness or any other public calamity." He said there would, he believed, be no objections to signing it; that he would see them & have it settled. Read "Sky Walk" to my Wife. This is a very superior performance.

[April] 24th Write on books of ye Theatre. Walk: Saw great quantities of the arum I found in walking from Woodbridge to E Town: the Dentdelion is in blow: saw a plant in flower quite new to me, it reared its head above the young, but looked as if its growth had been very rapid; with leaf the stem arose about 3 inches from the ground, as if jointed & a dark husk at each joint thus This plant I found near the bank of the sound below Stuyvesants house. A white flower I take to be the wood anemone I saw in blossom. Theodore Dwight is in town I call & see him at W W W's. Afternoon read "Sky Walk" Evening Theatre, "Siege of Belgrade & Modern Antiques" in the house 317$. W W W & [Dwight?] pass the evening with [us]: Smyth came in & staid after the others reading "Sky Walk" to us unto the end. I give high credit to Charles for this work, yet am I not satisfied; Is not Lorimer to much exalted—too fascinating? Why are we not satisfied as to the pistol of Avonedge? and how are we to account for the dagger, so oppertunely ready in the Chamber of Mrs Courtney? perhaps these are trifles—the work is masterly.

[April] 25th Preparing to move to John Street. Call on Henderson. he had prepared the following writing which I assented to & took with me to have copied.

"Memorandum of an Agreement between Carlile Pollock, Jacob Morton, Edward Livingston, & Wm Henderson on behalf of the proprietors of the New Theatre in this City; of the first part, and William Dunlap, of the second part. The parties of the first part, agree to rent to the party of the second part, all that building known as the New Theatre in this City, with all the property belonging to it, on the following terms & conditions *viz.*

1, 2, 3d unto "given aforesaid"

4th Should the party of the second part be prevented by War, prevailing sickness or other public calamity from keeping said Theatre open for Theatrical exhibition eight months during said year, then in such case the parties of the first part shall allow a deduction from the rent, of one hundred & forty seven Dollars & five cents; for each week the Theatre shall be closed, in consequence of such public calamity.

5th Same as 4th

6th The parties of the first part shall for the above purpose assist the party of the second part, by endorsing his notes for a sum not exceeding Two thousand dollars (for the purpose of procuring from the Banks a loan) if called upon so to do, the credit to be lent untill the first day of November next if required & no longer—the party of the second part engaging to give the parties of the first part satisfactory security previous to their endorsing any note.

7th Same as 6th wth add^n^—and the party of the second part shall be answerable for any damage done to the present Scenery & Machinery when in his possession, that which may arise from the necessary use of it & fire excepted.

8th The rent mentioned and agreed upon shall be paid in eight monthly payments, the first payment to be made one month after the House shall be opened for Theatrical exhibition."

I asked Henderson what would be considered satisfactory security, and mentioned my Land at Amboy—he said that would be sufficient, asking how we should determine its value & answering himself by adding, "What you gave for it will show. I said I could show what I gave for it & that it was since much improved.

Evening Theatre "Macbeth & [blank] in ye house 316 50/100 dollars.

[April] 26th Writing. Give Henderson two Copies of the Memorandum. Evening Pellesier brought me the additional music of "Sterne's Maria"

[April] 27th Dine at W W W's with Dwight Johnson & Smith. Evening Theatre "Lad of Spirit & Waterman" the first written by Fawcet of ye Company, the Audience received it with a degree of pleasure—it is a patch'd up thing. Meet at Mortons house, himself, Wm Henderson & Carlile Pollock & the agreement was signed in presence of Wm Johnson & E H Smith as witnesses & Mr Radcliff.

[April] 28th Call on Jacob Morton & leave with him my papers respecting my Amboy Farm, that he might be satisfied as to the security to be given to the Committee as endorsers of my notes. Not yet quite removed into my new habitation. Mr M: Rogers agrees to let me have the use of the money borrow'd of him last June, 6 months longer. We had agreed that Burk might have his play repeated to night provided he could find security for the charges, which he offerred to do. He said Brokholst Livingston had consented to be his security & repeatedly appointed times when to bring him to the Theatre: Yesterday he assured me that Mr L had promised him that morning to be his surety & had appointed 10 OClock to come with him [to] the Theatre for the purpose: neither of them appearing I wrote to B Livingston, stating Burks assertions & suggesting that a line from him would be sufficient without coming to us: he returned a note saying that Mr Burke had *mistaken* him & that he had advised Mr B not to risque the rep[et]ition of his play. We then gave out Jane Shore in its stead: in the afternoon B sent to Hodgkinson declining the favour of a night, but recommending his play for the benefit of the Stock. In the house to Fawcets play 320$. Go to the State prison with W W W, Dwight, Johnson & Smith: T Eddy went with us through the different appartments: as the workshops are not yet erected many of the prisoners are without employment, they were melancholy objects, but in the Hall & apartments devoted to those who make shoes all looked if not well at least tolerable. All was clean, decent & orderly & the appearance of the victims approaching to cheerfulness. Evening Theatre Jane Shore & All the worlds a Stage" in y^e house 160$. Club at G M Woolseys. Read to day Smiths publication of Browns "Alcuin" 1st & 2d parts.

[April] 29th Sunday. Read to my Wife, the unprinted part of B's "Alcuin." Call on Smith: he calls on me. Evening call at G M W's with my wife.

[April] 30th Quite warm. Finish moving. Afternoon walk out Williamson's Nursery. In my way thither I was accosted by Marinus Willet's Wife, who (before unknown to me) beg'd me to listen to her, I supposing her some person in distress, did so. She recounted her former marriages with [Joseph] Ja[u]ncey & [Thomas] Vardill, and her present unhappinesses & asked my advice. I excused myself from ignorance of her and her husband & gladly got rid of her. Williamson gave me a root of what is commonly called periwinkle which I have set out. I have set out a number of Lombardy poplar twigs. He showed me some plants of the three-thorned Accacia, a native, which he recommends for hedges. Evening Smith with us. Theatre "London Hermit & Gentle Shepherd for Simpson's benefit: in the house $529.' The play much dissaprov'd of.

May 1st Attend to business as usual. Hodg: mention'd on the Stage this morning this necessity of Writing to Hartford & giving up the Theatre: I wrote as follows & he sign'd with me.

"Sir

Through you as Treasurer to the proprietors of y[e] Hartford Theatre we beg leave to inform the proprietors, that on the close of the New York Theatre for the present Season, all Theatrical contracts between us, the Subscribers, by mutual consent, are at an end: that the Theatrical establishment which we have directed, is, from that time, no more: and that we conceive the contracts entered into with said proprietors, necessarily cease to exist in consequence of said dissolution of the Company

We r[em]ain &c
JNO HODGKINSON
W DUNLAP

Mr Wm Imlay

Call with Smith & my Wife to see Miss Potts, C B B's wished-for.

May 2 Evening Theatre, Mrs Johnson's night "West Indian & Wandering Jew" the last much condemn'd: in the house 832$. Cooper's Bellcour was good beyond my expectation. Rec[d] a letter from Barret offering his & his Wife's services.

May 3d Walk out to Williamson's Nursery. Many flowers are now in blow. The people, last night, hiss'd the praises of English sailors, which happening to be in the mouth of Mrs. Johnson, she is much mortified. Afternoon Miss Potts drinks tea with us. I buy of the Swords's their (of rather E H Smiths) edit: of Botanic Garden & 4th No: Med: Repository: read in the last.

[May] 4th I this morning mentioned again to Johnson my wish that he would determine on staying with me next season: he told me his only reason for not giving an answer is that, he has friends who are interesting themselves for him & his wife in London & he does not wish to engage untill he hears from them. Read Smiths Epistle to Darwin. Enc: Art: Gleditsia, the Triple thorn'd Acacia or Honey Locust, the species belonging to this climate is Gleditsia triacanthos. Afternoon walk in the fields. Read in Weekly Mag:. Evening Theatre "Love makes a Man & Selima & Azor" for the benefit of Hallam Jun[r] & Martin: in the house $647.

[May] 5th Walk. Read in Med: Rep: Evening Club met with Dr Miller.

[May] 6th Read Med: Rep: Enc: Pennant: Buffon: Dine with Sharpless, present Smith, Johnson, Miller & Mr or Dr Robertson, a polite and learned man.

[May] 7th Attending to business. Read in Med: Rep: Evening, Cooper's night, Mountaineers (his Octavian) & Old Maid, in y[e] house 773.

[May] 8th pd. 175$ for Sollee & Jones: & send on the note to Byrnes to try to recover for me. Write to Barret. pass some hours with Smith. Read in Monthly Magazine (London) and Monthly Review for Jan[y]. Evening home.

[May] 9th A Fast day, appointed by our president. My Mother goes down to Amboy. Write at the Theatre. Cooper's Octavian gain the palm from all the Octavians seen on our stage: Smith, who does not like the Character, says he was melted to tears. Smith called for me at ye Th: while Johnson waited for us in the Park opposite, we walked untill 1 OClock: Smith dined with me & Johnson came to us after dinner; he brought in his pocket Miss Hays's "Emma Courtney" and read for us untill Miss Woolsey of New Haven came in. Evening Mitchill pass'd two hours with us, conversation partly on Science & partly on an unhappy affair terminated to day. A day or two past there was a meeting of a number (say 900) young men, who call'd themselves the Youths of the City, who elected a chairman (Col^l Nicholas Fish an unmarried man upwards of 40 years of age) and passed certain resolves, addressing the president & offering themselves as the men first to be called upon in case the country should need defence. In the Argus, Greenleafs blackguard paper, appeared a paragraph in ridicule of the meeting and representing that aged men were among the youths such as Master Nicky Fish &c and Master Jemmy Jones a youth of 60, meaning Mr James Jones an unmarried man of about 50 a genteel and respectable Citizen, who as appears was not present on the occasion. Mr Jones was so much hurt that he called on Greenleaf and made him give up the Author of the paragraph whom he gave as Brockholst Livingston. Tuesday evening Jones met Livingston on the Battery and taking him aside question'd him respecting the paragraph & on Livingston's acknowledging himself the Author demanded satisfaction—irritating words passed, Livingston told him he might take satisfaction when & how he pleas'd on which Jones caught him by the nose & struck him. Henderson who was with Jones interfered. To day a challenge was given by Livingston, accepted by Jones, they crossed to Hobuck in New Jersey, Livingston's shot took effect & Jones is dead.

May 10th The above is much the subject of conversation & pretty general disapprobation. Attend to my accounts. Read "Emma Courtney" & review. Smith call'd on me. Mr Sharpless called & we settled that monday should be the day for an expedition to Haerlaem, the party Smith, Johnson, Miller, Mitchill, Sharpless & wife, Miss Johnson, my wife, myself, and Mr Mason, an English Botanist. Even^{g} Theatre; Mrs Hallam's night "School for Grey beards & Invasion" in y^{e} house 554$.

[May] 11th Attend to business. Call on Mrs. Parker [33] who came up yesterday with her daughter Mrs Smyth. Call on Cooper: he says he remembers Miss Hays (the Author of Emma Courtney) that she wrote a letter to Godwin desiring to be acquainted with him; that he waited on her & they became intimate—this must have been soon after publishing political Justice, she was then about 30 years of age. Cooper read to me & afterwards gave me a letter from Holcroft to him of which I make this Copy

"Mr Cooper, Theatre, Cheltenham

You do not like the word lamentation. You will less like the word that I am going to use. But, before I use it, I will most sincerely assure you I mean it kindly. I do not like rodomantade heroics. They are discordant, grating, and degrading. They are the very reverse of what you imagine them to be. It was not from report, but from your letter itself, (The letter alluded to was not to Holcroft but, I believe to Mr Marshall, Cooper was at that time in ill health) that I collected my idea of lamentation: and compared to your sufferings, I repeat, Jeremiah never lamented so loudly: at least such is my opinion; and I hope you did not intend by a hacknied and coarse quotation to deter me from saying that which I think may awaken your attention. If you did, it was in a moment of forgetfullness; for you know that a man of principles ought not to be so deterred. I speak plainly; from the very sincere wish, which I so long have cherished, of rouzing you at once to the exertions of Genius and the sagacity of benevolence and urbanity. It is to excercise benevolence and urbanity myself that I am thus intent in wiping from your mind all impressions of supposed rudeness, or rigour, in thus addressing you.

[33] Mrs. James Parker (Gertrude Skinner) and her daughter, Mrs. Andrew Smyth (Maria Parker). See W. N. Jones, *History of St. Peter's Church in Perth Amboy, N. J.*, pp. 427-28.

And now to business: after just reminding you that, though you did not wish me to apply for a London engagement for you it would have looked quite as friendly had you written to me without this personal motive.

Mr Wignell, the Manager of the Theatres of Philadelphia and Baltimore in America, has applied to me; offering you four, five, and six guineas a week, forty weeks each year, for three succeeding years: & insuring benefits to the amount of 150 Gs. I have reflected on the subject and have consulted your other true & tried friend, Mr Godwin: and, notwithstanding that this offer is so alluring, it is our decided opinion that, were it ten times as great, it ought to be rejected. As an actor, you would be extinct; and the very season of energy and improvement would be for ever passed. I speak of men as they are now constituted; and after the manner as experience tells me that their habits become fixed: eradicably fixed. Mr Godwin indeed expresses himself with great force, mixed with some little dread lest money should be a temptation that you could not withstand. However, we both know it to be but right that the decision should be entirely your own; and I therefore send you this information. Be kind enough to return me your answer, and without regarding my or any man's opinion, judge for yourself. It is right that Mr Wignell should not be kept in suspence.

Yours kindly and sincerely

T Holcroft

<*26th August*>
Sept 3d 1796

The above is a transcript of a letter which was dated August 26th and directed to you at Swansea where I suppose it is left. Let me request an immediate answer.

A Gentleman has just been with me on the part of Mr Daly who is to be in town in nine or ten days and wishes to engage you for the winter Season but his I think as prejudicial except that it is nearer home and not so durable an engagement as America Ireland is certainly the school of idleness However all these matters must be left to yourself."

In Coopers answer to this letter part of which he shewed me, he plead the necessity of change of Air for his health & determines for America.

After dinner Hallam called on me: he was very polite & mentioned a report that Wignell had taken the New Circus but thought it must be a ruinous scheme to come here.

Write to Harwood.

"Sir

I have been in expectation of hearing from you, and have earnestly wished that your determination might be in favour of New York: if in answer to this you can give me your decision I shall be pleased, or if you wish to make any enquiries which may lead thereto you may depend upon prompt and explicit answers from

W D"

Sharpless & wife Mr & Mrs Rogers &c drank tea with us. Call with my Wife on Mrs Parker.

May 12th 1798 Finish y^e^ Review for Jany. Call on Smith & Johnson. Read in Weekly Magazine. Attend to business. Walk. Drink tea at G M W. Evening Club with me. Mrs W W W & my Wife fav^d^ us wth th^r^ Company. Theatre "Mysteries of the Castle & Jubilee" in y^e^ house for Jefferson's benefit 607$.

[May] 13th Call on Hodgkinson: I asked him if the lots in John Street were sold, he said he believed one was sold beside the one Hallam kept & that Gamage said he thought the other would be sold to morrow. I asked him if Mr Milns had given security for the charges of the night he was to have, he said "No" I replied that he had offered it & it must be done: this passed in presence of Johnson who was making arrangements for his benefit: after he was gone Hodgkinson remark'd that he feared Cooper would not answer my expectations saying that he was shamefully imperfect last night, that his send^g^ to the Theatre on Thursday even^g^ to say he could not play was one of the most scandalous things he ever knew, as the falshood was so palpable, that, he would not play with him for 100$ a night, that, Cooper said he should like not to have played last night but then he must have kept his room for an excuse &c &c. I asked Hodgkinson if he had any news from Boston: he said he had had a great many letters. I asked for the sum of information, he said "Nothing." He asked me when I should have leisure to attend to our accounts together with him, I replied that I was now busied in making a statement of the acc^{ts} of the Old Theatre, that I wished he would make a statement of the acc^{ts} of the Boston & Hartf^{d} business when we would meet & come to a settlement: to this he agreed: I asked when he would be ready, he said, "soon, as he had nearly made his statement." Borrow'd from him Holcroft's "Knave or not" Lewis's "Castle Spectre" & Colman's "Blue beard" Read in them.

May 14th 1798 Holcrofts "Knave or not" is a fine play tho' not equal to y^{e} "Road to Ruin" "Castle spectre" is entertaining & has some force. "Blue beard" a trifle. Disappointed in our intended excursion to Haerlaem by lowering weather. Chalmers in town & says Wignell's comp^{y} are now at Baltimore & the report is that he is to go from thence to Alexandria, if so he comes not here. Evening Theatre Mrs Melmoth's night "Count of Narbonne & Double disguise." in y^{e} house 693 $.

[May] 15th Attend^{g} to business. Mrs Terril & Mrs Brown[34] dine with us, they intend to embark for New Providence the day after tomorrow.

May 21st 1798. Last Wednesday 16th I went to Elizabeth town point in the boat & walked up to the town where after receiving some money from Mr Williamson on acct of Freeman of Morristown (viz $125 leaving still upwards of £200 or $500 to be paid) I drank tea with Mrs Crowell & lodged at the Stage house. About 3 in the morning I rode on to Woodbridge & walked down to my Mother's to breakfast. in the afternoon I walked with my Gun & trimmed my trees; passed the Evening at Mrs Parkers who had just returned from N. Y. Mr Butlers family have arrived here from Philadelphia. On the 19th (Saturday) I agreed to give James Goelet £70 for his part or half of the lot & stable adjoining our house at

[34] Mrs. John Terrill (Sophia Watson-Waterhouse) and her daughter (by her first husband, John Waterhouse), Sophia (Waterhouse) Brown, wife of John Brown of Nassau, New Providence Island, Bahama Islands. See W. N. Jones, *History of St. Peter's Church in Perth Amboy, N. J.*, pp. 214, 486, 496.

Amboy: walk out to my Orchard & finish trimming & cleaning all the Trees. Bloodgood finishes planting the corn to day & dunging all the trees: walk on to Woodbridge but return with Patten & Heard to my meadow on ye Sound to settle the running a line for division fence. Dine at Heards, walk down to the orchard again & back to Woodbridge where I remain untill Sunday morning 20th when in the Stage come home. To day (21st) attend to business. Met Goelet in the Street & he told me he had sold his land to Thos Farmer "Why did not you ask £70 for it & did not I agree to give it" "Yes but there was no written agreement & he offer'd me more"! I called on Farmer he said he had a mortgage on Peter's half & bought James's to secure himself, that he did not want to keep the lot & when he had the matter finally settled he would sell it to me or give me a preferrence.

Milns had a benefit allowed him by Hodgkinson last Wednesday evening & his new play done called "Wives pleas'd & maids happy" with a large & flourishing Bill in y^{e} house 675$ & Johnson whose benefit followed on Friday had in but 416$ *not Rent & charges* to the "Will & Sicilian Romance" Johnson is much disatisfied & says he will go to England. Even^{g} Theatre Hodgkinson's night "Cheap living and the Launch" in the house 919$.

[May] 22d Johnson tells me that he has in part engaged his passage for England: She seems down-cast. I had considerable conversation with Jefferson, he said he had had offers from Wignell—he mentioned letters from Bernard I had heard that Bernard had written for him—I frankly told him my plans and offer'd him $20: he said he believed he should give me his answer in the affirmative in a day or two. Read "James the Fatalist." Evening stand^{g} Committee & at Harry Mitchell's.

May 23d 1798 Write for Stand^{g} Committee. Call on Mitchill he showed me his translation of the song Harmodius & Aristogiton. Call on Johnson & his wife, their talk was all of going, she appeared low-spirited. I profess'd my sorrow for their determination; she at length asked me to write a few farewell lines—she choked & burst choacked & burst into tears. I sat down nearer to them and with some preface offerred in case they would stay $45 per week: he & she from the beginning profess'd their wish to serve my interest &c neither of them seeming ready for an answer to my proposal I got up & told him I left him to consider & determine; he said he would determine in 3 hours. In the afternoon I again called at their lodging, they had lain down: Johnson got up, he was not yet prepared for a final answer, but gave me to understand that he thought of accepting my proposal, he appointed 8 tomorrow morning to call on me & determine the matter. finish "James the Fatalist." Evening at Mr Coits with G: M: Woolsey & Wife &c; Smith with me. Theatre Williamson's night, "Surrender of Calais, Naval gratitude, & St Patrick's day" in y[e] house 561$ he talks highly & damns N: York like a gentleman.

[May] 24th Johnson call'd on me this morning but profess'd himself yet undetermined, proposing finally $50 as the salary, I objected to the sum telling him I did not think I could with propriety promise such salaries, he fixed on 6 OClock this evening to give his final answer. I conclude that he has determined to stay. Hodgkinson complains that Cooper attends no rehearsals regularly. I received a letter from Sir J Oldmixon on behalf of a Miss Oldfield referring me to Cooper for her character as an actress which he says is nothing. Oldm: says his wife is with Wignel at Baltimore—that is reported they go to Alex[a]. Read in [William] Bartram's travels. Yesterday we had the first rain for near three weeks remarkable at this season so long a drought: it clouds over again this afternoon. Write to Sir J Oldmixon.

[May] 25th Showery weather. Mrs Melmoth called on me. She wished a continuation in the Company: promised to do every thing in her power: would give up all the young parts in Tragedy if required mentioning Calista

&c: & saying she never wished to be made love to on the Stage. She talked of having a salary as high as Mrs Johnson: I told her I would not bind myself to regulate one person's salary by another, that if I raised Salaries I could not expect success: She said she should not insist on the salary but she did not choose or think it just that she should pay at her benefit a higher salary than she received &c. At 12 OClock I saw Johnson & wife & we came to an agreement, Salary $45 to be paid certainly 35 weeks, commencing the third Monday in September, but if prevented from playing so soon he is to give me credit untill I begin: Benefit charges for him or his wife not to exceed 380: the agreement to be private: to this agreement we sign'd. They wished me to promise that in the getting up new pieces Mrs Johnson should have her first choice; I did not promise but objected to shackling myself: They wanted me to bind myself that Mrs Johnson should not play on a Saturday night if she had play'd the preceding Friday: I refused peremptorily. Read Bartram. Evening Theatre Mr Hallams night "New Peerage & Miser" in the house $410: not expences!

[May] 26th Walk out to Tyler's: who engages with me for the ensuing season at 20 dollars the week & finds his wardrobe: benefit expences mention'd at 380 dollars. He advises to send for young Darley to share the opera business wth him. Settle with Martin who for 25$ is to play, superintend the Stage & prompter; take charge of the Taylors & Wardrobe, armoury &c & make ornaments armour &c. I have been obliged to go as far as $22 in my offer to Jefferson and he has not yet accepted that. I have engaged Miller for $12 he promising to do any thing & every thing & attend to his business. I spoke to Seymour letting him know that I expected from him and his Wife the fulfillment of the original articles, the services to be performed to me: he said he was satisfied & would inform his Wife. Afternoon walk with my Wife & children & drink tea with W W W & wife. Evening write on my Comedy.

[May] 27th Sunday. Write on my Comedy. Go to the Theatre to write.

"To Mr Darley Junr"

Sir:

I have it in my power to offer you an engagement in the N Y Theatre for the ensuing Season to commence about the middle of September next & to continue untill the middle of June or longer, and tho' not personally known to you, it is with pleasure I seize the opportunity and a hope that it may meet your approbation. The line of business which is at present vacant (thro' the removal of Mr Williamson) is opera business to be shared with Mr Tyler, he resigning the young men, as for example, giving up young Meadow to you and taking Hawthorn, in short, there is a large share of business open in this line: in other business I should expect your exertions to be at my direction. The salary I can offer is 18 dollars to be paid weekly; the benefit charges not to exceed 380$. I shall be obliged by a speedy answer, however you may determine, if in favour of my proposals I shall thank you to return with yours, a copy of this with your acceptance signed on it. If there are any questions you would ask I shall answer them freely."

Attend to acc^{ts}. Write on my Comedy.

[May] 28th Rainy day. Write on ye Comedy. Mr Williams the Anthony Pasquin of London was introduced to me by Hodgkinson on the Stage: his appearance is not more in his favour than his writings. Hodgkinson is violent in his execration of Johnson, who, he says, was playing off the farce of taking his passage for England &c in order to make him & me bid on each other: he says that before his (J's) benefit Johnson gave him to understand that he would not stay in N: Y: but would go to Boston with him, giving him the preference, that he asked his terms which he told him should be for Mrs Johnson what she now enjoy'd (20) and for himself as much as any man in his Company not fixing the sum: that after the benefit he told him that he should go to England and that he said nothing more to him untill he heard that he had concluded the bargain with me. It appears to me that Hodgkinson is very much dissapointed in Johnson's not engaging with him & that he had clandestinely intrigued to deprive me of him. Mrs Seymour had some conversation wth me about next season, she wanted 5 dolls more p: week: I told her that I looked on the articles as being [in] force and that an [*sic*] any rate I would part with her rather than give any thing more: she acquiesced in the present situation. Afternoon at Smith & Johnson's. Evening Theatre, Tyler's night, "False impressions & Highland reel" in y^e house $598.

[May] 29th Rain continues. Read Smith's discourse before the Manumission Society deliver'd while I was at Phil:

"To Mrs Melmoth

Madam:

In the conversation you favor'd me with concerning an engagement for the N Y Th: under my direction for the ensuing season, tho' there was a general coincidence of ideas and an implied agreement, there was not that definitiveness (if I may so express myself) and explicitness which I conceive necessary for our mutual interest and good understanding. I was the more convinced of this when last night you consented to play Olivia in ye Italian Monk, merely on condition that you should not be required to do it again in consequence of having done it for a benefit. Olivia is a short part, true, but the character is that of a matron, dignified in sentiment & from situation, interesting and pathetic (as far as I remember). In forming a Company I would wish it to be considered that if it is surcharged with numbers the expence will clog exertion on the part of the Manager and perhaps stop the business by render^g it impossible to pay the Salaries: I therefore mentioned to you that next season it would be necessary for the members of the Company not only to exert themselves but to vary their exertions. I would wish it to be an acknowledged principle that an actress of the first abilities does not degrade herself by adding consequence to a short part or by aiding the cause of virtue in exhibiting a picture of the deformity of Guilt. In the same conversation, a certain line or description of youthfull character you even expressed a wish to give up, you with great good sense said that you did not "want to be made love to upon the Stage" but how far does this relinquishment extend? The Grecian Daughter you expressly reserved and Belvidera, I am far from asking a resignation of either of them <*altho' in Belvidera you may chance to have a very unsuitable Jaffier to make love to you, in point of age and figure during Mr Hodgkinson's absence*> but among the youthfull characters under consideration I certainly meant and still mean to reserve for my disposal not only the young unmarried women but the young married women as brides &c. by reserving to myself the right of casting these characters I by no means consider you as excluded from the cast: as to the character in the Italian Monk I shall consider you as bound to do it (either that or the Marchioness), if I direct; not the more for having done it for a benefit, but as falling within the scope and intention of your engagement and so of many others.

The next thing to be settled is salary: that which I offer is $20, the salary now paid. This I believe was agreed to: my agreement with Mr & Mrs J was mentioned in our late conversation: one of the articles of that agreement is that it shall be secret. Benefit charges shall not exceed $380 nor fall below it, therefore my engagements with others, are to be considered altogether as my affair.

If these terms suit you it will give me real pleasure: but other terms I cannot offer. I have been as plain & concise as possible in addressing you, convinced that it is my duty to you as well as to myself to have the business perfectly understood.

I remain &c

Afternoon a little while with Johnson & Smith. Evening they pass'd with me: we read again C B B 3 & 4th parts of Alcuin.

[May] 30th Read Dr Dwights 2 sermons against Infidel Philosophy: An intemperate farrago of falshood and abuse. Read on "Love for Love" & "Way to keep him." Evening at Post's. Theatre "School for Soldiers & Animal Magnetism" in y[e] house $495.

[May] 31st On going to the Theatre this morning the first salutation was from Johnson, who wished to speak to me: what he was going to say would be a terrible shock to me, but his interest was so materially that I could not think him wrong: he was absolutely determined to go to England. He pull out & read a letter, rec[d] this morning wherein his friend in London tells him, that both Harris and Wroughton have heard of Mrs Johnson, that she may [have] a situation at either house: that Mr Harris offers her a situation & a salary that will entitle her to give orders (such a salary J: says is not under 6 Guineas) and in case of success as good a salary as any woman in the Company. I told him I could say nothing; he knew what had pass'd; I should not oppose his determination. He profess'd his wish to serve me &c squeez'd my hand & left me. Afternoon walk with my Wife & little girl. Evening at M: Rogers.

June 1st 1798. This being the day on which Hodgkinson by his agreement with me, (drawn up by & signed and sealed in presence of Wm Johnson) is to convey to me by deed the property specified in the agreement. I waited on W Johnson carrying the agreement with me & asked him whether it was my business to demand the deeds. He said no it was Hodgkinson part to present them. At rehearsal on the stage Hodgkinson mentioned that this was the day on which he was to convey the property to me and mention'd the Philadelphia property, asking if I wished him to see about the deeds for that. I told him that I supposed, as he intended to leave N: Y: it had been his intention to make other arrangements, respecting our agreement that it was not merely the property in John Street and in Philadelphia that I purchased: that I supposed it had been his intention to make void the agreement; that I was willing to pay him for the use of his property & make any arrangement on just and satisfactory terms to both. He said, as he was going away he did not wish to be concerned in the Philadelphia property, that it was dead property or worse, a tax on him (thus intimating that he did not wish to relinquish the sale made to me) I said, I did not believe it was in his power to fulfill his part of the agreement. "Why?" "You are bound to convey to me this property free from all encumbrance, you have not removed the mortgage" he replied it would be remov'd to about £500. He is to have his moity of the proceeds of the sale of the lots in John Street, set off against the sum for which the property is mortgaged, but he does not consider that if he fulfills his agreement, the one half of said moity is mine & consequently only a fourth of the proceeds of said sale can be used by him. I mentioned to him that if he considered the agreement as to remain in force, the one fourth of the proceeds of the sale must be paid to me. He talked hesitatingly but seemed very unwilling to give up the idea of my being bound by the agreement. He said he had no objections, if I wished, that our connexion should continue, he being equally concerned here

& I at equal risk in the Boston scheme. I said *no,* "I have an utter repugnance to any distant scheme, I will not be concerned in any business which is to be transacted away from me: I have smarted enough." he answered "the same objections might be raised on my part as to being concerned in New York" "Certainly, but for myself, I will be concerned in no business beyond N: Y: the Theatre may be kept open 9 or 10 months here & that is employment enough for any Company." He made no reply. I told him that if he meant to hold me to the bargain that I should expect on his part a strict fulfillment of the agreement. He made no answer. I asked him if he thought it just that I should pay him £3000 for property acknowledgedly not worth it, telling him that it was well understood that it was not this property I wanted to buy, but that the money was to be paid in part for the property, in part, in consequence of certain agreements.

[Accounts and memoranda at end of manuscript volume 15:]

My Farm

Dr.			Cr.
To Cash (see p: 148 Vol: 13) [*Supra,* p. 114]	1762.18	By Buckwheat	10.—
D° for cutt^{g} salt hay	9.—	By Cash for hay	7.50
D° sett^{g} out trees	12.50	By D° D°	3.75
D° Cart^{g} post^{s} rails	2.50	By D° rent for pasture	17.50
D° Clear^{g} & ploug[h]ing swamp	4.—	By Compton for hay	9.37½
D° D° & seed^{g} it wth Grass	3.—	By Rackow D°	3.75
D° Cart^{g} rails	2.50	By Ratoon for Fresh hay	[blank]
D° D° trees from Heards	.50		
D° D° Hay (salt)	6.—		
D° D° Dung	22.—		
D° Ditching	4.—		
D° for posts	17.—		
D° Dung sent from N. Y.	78.50		
D° R. Kearney	50.—		
D° D° D° 1798 Sept. 27 (to A Bloodgood)	20.—		
D° Cutt^{g} Salt Hay	12.—		
D° Sharpning rails	4.12½		

[Estimate of theatrical expenses for season 1798-1799:]

Mr Hallam	25	
Mr Cooper	25	
Mr Johnson	20	
Mr Tyler	20	
Mr Jefferson	20	
Mr Martin	18	
Mr Hallam Jr	16	
Mr Hogg	12	
Mr Lee	12	
Leonard	8	
———	8	
Master Stock[1]	4	
Hughes	10	
Falconer	14	
		212
Mrs Johnson	25	
Mrs Oldmixon	37	
Mrs Hallam	25	
Mrs Melmoth	20	
Mrs Hogg	14	
Miss Westray	12	
Miss E Westray	12	
Mrs Collins	12	
Mrs Petit	3	
Mrs Cook	3	
Mrs Hughs	3	
		166
orchestra		140
Lights		109
Labourers		24
Doors		50
Cleaning		5
Printing		68
Properties		6
Wardrobe		15

Wood & Coal	15
Ciceri's departm^{t} ..	60
	870
Rent	145
	1015
Mr & Mrs Seymour	25
[blank]	25
[blank]	25
Mr Miller, 12 Miss Hogg, 4 & another 4	20
Manager & clerk, in this is included 7 dollars for Martin, who is [to] superintend the stage & prompter, take charge of the Wardrobe & Armoury and make the necessary ornaments, armour &c devoting his whole time to it	30
	4) 1140
	285

27	for lights less	\$ 1140
12	doors	67
17	print^{g}	3) 1073
3	prop	\$ 354.33
3	fire	Benefit Expences
5	Ciceri	
67		

Mr Hewit leader	1st Violin
Everdel	d°
Nicolai	2 Violin
Samo	d°
Henri	1st Clarinet
Libichiski	2d d°
Pelesier	1st Horn

Dupuy	2d d^{o}
Gilfert	Tenor
Nicolai Junr	Bass
Adet	d^{o}
Hoffman	Bassoon
Dangle	Double Bass

Jany 12th 1798 Destroyed

Box Tickets formerly used for the old Theatre J[ohn] St eng^{d} Hallam & Hodgkinson		135
Pit Tickets	d^{o}	80
Gal: d^{o}	d^{o}	125

Deposited with Falconer 500 pit tickets & 100 Box d^{o}

on a house of 499 we gain				99
500 we pay 37.50 therefore we gain only				62.50
599	44.92½	d^{o}	d^{o}	154. 7½
600	75	d^{o}	d^{o}	125

Copy of acct render'd by G M W Jany 9th 1798

Dr.		1796	Cr.
Smyths notes		Octr 4th By Cash Rec^{d}...	1111.11
1 Note payable 31st Decr 1796 Ds.	1062.0	2 Mo. & 27 days interest @ 7 p. c. 18.80	
1 ditto " "	3731.—	1797	
1 Year & 7 days interest on Ds 3682.68 @ 7 p. c.	262	Jany 3 Cash	1000.—
		1 Year & 4 days int: 70.78	
		Feby 7th Cash for Smyths third of damage recover'd from M & Mumford 74.7	
		11 Mo. interest...4.75	
		May 9th Cash by 2 notes of L. & Moore	1500.—
		7 Mo: & 29 days interest 69.71	164. 4
		Balance Ds:	1207.35
Ds:	5056.57	Ds:	5056.57

<Borrow'd of J H Hardenbrook Ds: 250 to be paid on Saturday ye 3 Feby 1798 & left him as security D & Judahs note endorsed by Hodgkinson for Ds: 500.>

Borrow'd of J H Hardenbrook 500 Ds: giving D & J's note endors'd by J Hodgkinson which will fall due the 21st of March.

<Jany 29th 1798, Gave my note payable in 15 days to Arthur Berryhill, to take up an endorsement on acc^{t} of Solee for 40 Ds.>

Feby 22d 1798. Gave my note payable in thirty days, to Mr Hugh Gaine, for 1500 dollars, to be endorsed by him & discounted, that Cooper may carry on the money & tender the penalty to Wignell.

The above being bro^{t} back by Mr Cooper and deposited by Gaine & Ten Eyck, they have drawn out for me $1150.

Mar: 26th put in my note for discount for 1500 to take up the above, endorsed Gaine & Ten Eyk. Borrow'd 400 of P Ten Eyk.

<Mar. 2d. 1798. Endorsed for John E Martin a note for 176 dollars, due in 30 days from this date.>

Ap^{l} 20th Endorsed for John E Martin a note for 111.19 $ due in 60 days from this date.

Ap^{l} 25th The note for 1500 $ falling due, endorsed Gaine & Ten Eyk, put in another for the same amount this day, dated y^{e} 28th. May 26th, renew'd y^{e} above.

May 12th W H draft in fav^{r} of J Mount in 60 days for 100 $

Accepted Henderson's draft payable in 60 days from the date for 58 75/100 $ dated May 14th 1798

May 25th another for $150 in 60 day from date in favour of P Allison.

Decr 26th paid Sollées note endorsed by me

Ds:	82.
protest	1.50
	83.50

paid for certified power of Attorney sent to Charlestown 1.7

1798 Jany 8th paid Sollees note end^{d} by me for 49.

$30.40 one years taxes on Old Theatre.

DIARY OF WILLIAM DUNLAP

JUNE 1, 1798—DECEMBER 15, 1798

NEW YORK CITY AND PERTH AMBOY

(Manuscript *Memoirs 16* owned by YALE UNIVERSITY LIBRARY)

MEMOIRS 16

Memoirs of Wm Dunlap or Daily Occurences from June 1st 1798 to Decr 15th same year Vol 16th

June 1st 1798. Noon. Call on Smith who was busy correcting proofs of Med: Repository: read in Weekly Mag: See Gamage, who says Gaine will not make the arrangements wished in respect to the Mortgage, by taking other security & endorsing the full amount of the sale of ye John Street property, & that in consequence one of the Lots is returned by the purchaser who will not buy with the mortgage on it. Even^{g} Theatre, Mrs Hodgkinson's night "Castle Spectre & Launch &c a pantomime" in the house [blank]

[June] 2d Write to Brewer by Johnson directing him to deliver my manuscripts to J in case he has not disposed of them. Give Johnson a memorandum, to receive them & if he thinks fit to offer them to the Theatres giving him one third of any profit that may arise from them: to see <*the*> Messrs. G G & J Robinson & if they open an account with me, to send me Holcrofts pamphlet, Massinger, & Beaumont & Fletcher & all new plays 2 copies of each, this last J^{n} undertakes for me at any rate. Write to the Robinsons that I send them 300 Copies of André & 100 of each "Archers & Tell truth &c" for which if they sell I offer to take books. I agreed with Captn Kemp to take them and Johnson has promised to see them delivered. Read Weekly Mag: & Cumberlands "False impressions" this is a very weak comedy. a little afterpiece by Jame[s] Arnold call'd the shipwreck has more merit, with some alteration I think this may be made a favourite entertainment. Write on my Comedy.

June 3d 1798. Sunday. Pellisier & Dupuy call'd on me,

the last wished & I promised his present situation in ye Orchestra, the former proposes an augmentation of salary from 15 (the present) to 18. I did not agree to it. May I not or rather would it not be better to write thus to Hodgkinson.

It is now more than 2 years since we enter'd into contracts mutually binding on each other; the outlines of which were, that for a certain sum of money to be paid by me at certain stated periods in given proportions, you should sell to me certain property putting me in immediate possession, and making on or before a given time, now passed, full and legal conveyance of said property free from all & every incumbrance; and to connect your Theatrical interests with mine for five years in such sort that all Theatrical arrangements, bargains or acquisitions should be during that period, for our mutual and equal account or advantage. During the 2 of the 5 years which have passed many untoward events have taken place, many unforeseen circumstances arisen: the time of making the legal conveyance arrived & found you unprepared to fulfill the agreement: even before the expiration of the first 2 years, you solicited from me a release from that part of the agreement, which was certainly at the time of forming it considered as the principal or most material part of it, if not the very soul; I agreed to release you conditionally that other arrangements should be made satisfactory to me. To facilitate those arrangements I now address you, for I think our mutual interests will suffer by further delay.

You have not fulfilled your agreement, consequently the penalty of the articles is incurred, if it be found that I have <*fulfilled*> performed my part up to the time present. I mention not this as a reproach, I feel not the spirit that can lead to it, <*but*> I am anxious not to be misunderstood.

It is now, in my apprehension, impossible that our agreement can be fulfilled. What remains to be done, is, that we close accounts and seperate, or remain together upon some new and different footing. I see but one mode of adjusting the account, which is, that the money paid by me in consequence of the agreement or in compliance wth it be refunded with simple interest and that I pay to you reasonable compensation for the use of your property, to be computed either by the value of the property or by the advantage derived to me from the use: the first I presume to be the true mode. I may be wrong in my ideas on this subject, if so, do me the credit to believe that I am open to conviction, ready to acknowledge error and wish to do right. If a difference of opinion should ultimately prevail, I am ready to abide by the decision of men, if not wiser at least more impartial than ourselves.

You have sometimes spoken as if your prospects in respect to

Boston were not perfectly as you could wish: You have declared to the proprietors of the Theatre here, that if you staid here it would be merely as a performer, they in consequence have let the Theatre to me but still indulge hopes of not losing you. As your principal objection to remaining here have been the trouble & responsibility of conducting the business; *that* being removed, I must so far indulge my hopes of your being prevailed upon to stay by offers of a regular income not depending upon the casualties of good or bad houses, as to conclude this letter with some proposals to that effect.

For your services and the services of Mrs H. the ensuing season, in Tragedies, Comedies, Opera's Farces, Interludes & Pantomimes, unconditional & without reserve relying upon my sense of Justice & propriety in casting characters, <*I offer $90 Salary*> both finding your own wardrobes servants & dressers, & you superintending the musical department I offer weekly salary $100–.

In case an arrangement should take place, I should look no further for any person to supply the place of Mrs Johnson, relying upon Mrs Hodgkinson to take such part of her business as I should allot & accommodating Mrs Oldmixon who was engaged upon a supposition of Mrs Hodgkinson's removal. Mrs Brett would in such case be <*likewise*> affected by my engagements with Mrs Oldmixon, otherwise her situation is at her service as heretofore & the same of the rest of the Family.

You have lately had proofs that you & Mrs H have not depreciated in public favour: with lower benefit charges your emoluments of course will be greater, and the charges shall not exceed $385: If I could offer more I would do it, I know your value.

Again assuring you that nothing is here said but in the spirit of good will & accommodation: I rest

Your friend

W D

Smith called to see me. Read in Weekly Mag:. Write on my Comedy. Evening call at M Roger's & W W W's.

June 4th. Copy the letter to Hodgkinson: & deliver it to him myself to be read at his leisure. He put into my hands a letter from Wm Imlay rec'd some time since which he answered without my concurrence, he says giving a negative to their proposal. The letter is as follows

Messrs H & D. Gentlemen

At a special meeting of the proprietors of the Hartford Theatre, the contents of your letter of the 1st instant to me, as Treasurer to said proprietors have been taken under consideration. And at their request I am now to inform you, That, notwithstanding they do not concur with you in Opinion, as to the dissolution of the contract, for the reasons assigned by you, They are willing to accede to your proposition, & release you from the Contract, upon payment of the rent for the present Year. The proprietors to be at liberty to make the best of the House from the present time. I am &c

W Imlay.

A very modest proposal! Play put off from this evening on account of altering the Gallery & for other reasons. Read in Weekly Mag: Begin an essay the Stage.

[June] 5th Write on essay. See Smith & talk of a Weekly Magazine for this place, to be printed by the Swords's & for their emolument, we having all power over it. Just before sitting down to dinner I rec[d] a letter from Hodgkinson bro[t] by Miss Harding. I will copy it, I shall perhaps better understand it before returning an answer. The words mark'd are marked in like manner in the original.

"I hope in many parts of your letter you have mistaken *yourself:* You *were* put into immediate possession *of One fourth* of the property and emoluments belonging to Hallam & myself from the day our agreement commenced: you regularly drew a *salary* for your service & you likewise drew *Interest* upon that property, from our expences, to the conclusion of last June. The untoward circumstances that attended us, had created a determined opposition between Mr. Hallam & myself, & availing yourself of this, you once signified your intention of quitting altogether; but finding that I should probably be successfull in my application for the New Theatre, you changed your opinion & in conformity to our agreement, you demanded, in future, *One half* of the emoluments conceiving you had a right to an equal participation in whatsoever I enjoyed: You were put into possession, & have received *One half* of what the Theatre has afforded: you have likewise continued to receive *interest* for the use of active property, under your purchase. You seemed to agree with me, that my situation, as acting manager, was rendered, by many circumstances, too unpleasant to support: & you agreed that I should make other arrangements, upon condition that you should, previous to any application of mine, have the power of selecting from the company, such members as you chose for your future pursuits: you never even hinted that this change would make an alteration in your purchase; you gave me reason to expect the contrary; you had a right to do so, when the determination and the regular progressive consequence, of the misunderstandings between Mr Hallam and me, had now placed you in a situation to enjoy 75 parts out of a hundred, more than your purchase only two years before had warranted: I faithfully kept my promise to make no negociation with any actor till you were first served to my great injury; for by it I lost Mr & Mrs Johnson; who told me, on board the vessel which has carried they away, my *seeming indifference* was the sole cause of their departure; for, could they have supposed I wished their service, no emolument that either England or America could at present offer would have tempted them, for one moment, even in thought, to quit me.

The nature of our agreement extended to your having legal conveyance of One fourth of the old American company's property on the 1st of June 1798: previous to that day part of it had been sold, & *sold under your own agency as an owner & proprietor*. On the first of June I took an oppertunity of telling you, that I was then ready to make your conveyance: you said a part of the property had been sold: I reminded you *how* it had been sold; and that if any overplus money had been received more than your payment to me warranted, it was at your command: you observed, our agreement extended to 5 years: I was very considerably shocked at your manner, but collecting myself, told you that in no agreement were my personal services implicated; & as to property, whatever additions were *mutually* made I was ready to employ them for our *mutual* Benefit: your answer to this was, you *did not mean to fly from your agreement if I wish'd to have it fulfilled,* but as I was busy then, we would talk further another time: You observed further that you did not wish further connection with Boston or any place at a distance. I never saw you again, that I recollect, untill the 4th of June, when you delivered me the letter which has given rise to this statement. You say the day arrived on which I should have made conveyance, without finding me capable of doing so; & that I have broke my agreement, & incurred the penalty I never sold you property till what I sold, I had paid for, & was ready to convey at any hour demanded: *Three whole days!* have elapsed since the time appointed for the conveyance; but you must recollect, I pressed you *on* the day to have it done; how then have I broke my agreement? You not only wish to evade the payment of the whole purchase made, but you say you expect to be refunded what you have in part advanced: I can only say to this: Cancel the agreement from its *commencement* & *refund* the *Salary* & the *interest* of property you have received, with the *emoluments* annexed thereto & I will agree immediately: this I think full as equitable as your proposal, for what you have done since your entrance into the company, I previously bore the fatigue of, & *partly* since; & certainly I have ever deemed your salary, the salary of a proprietor enjoying emolument rather than a compensation for adequate services; & the issue has certainly been in your favour; for tho' you will have gained nothing in two years, probably have lost; yet the expiration sees you in sole possession, & need I add, certainly placed there by your connection with me: I hope I need not remind you, that the New Theatre could have been solely mine. I beg also to call to your recollection, that when, on (I believe) the 24th of May, you made me sign a receipt for £ *500* dated *received on the first;* it was done by accommodation, for you had *not paid one Shilling* nor had one shilling been received from the sale of the property in John Street: Those who mean no ill, suspect none: I hope I should be wrong to harbour a harsh conjecture on that business. You could not mean your offer of engagement to me, a serious one surely! you could not even imagine I would remain in New York, an *Actor,* at the *entire mercy,* in my business of any man! You could not *seriously* ask my wife to stay, & give up her business to Mrs. Oldmixon, taking another range she is averse to! I thank you for the *compliment* of your offer, but conceive it an *entire compliment.* I hope no difficulty will occur to force a public appeal for justice, but that, by complying with a fair & advantageous settlement (for I cannot but think *either* the *agreement* or my *offer* advantageous as you are now situated) you will leave it in my power to esteem & professionally to the utmost assist, you I wish to know your determination immediately.

JNO HODGKINSON

New York
4th June 1798

After copying the above, I call'd on Gamage & as he is the person who has transacted all Hodgkinson business in respect to real estate and of course knows the situation of the John Street property, I enquired of him as to the nature of the encumbrance on the property, existing at the present time. He informed me, that at the time I purchased there was a mortgage on the property for £2000, one thousand of which was to have been paid on the first of May 1797, and the remainder on the first of May 1798, the time of the first payment arrived, the payment was put off, consequently at the time of making the second payment the whole sum with interest was to be paid. In respect to the Philadelphia property, Gamage tells me, that Hodgkinson has it not in his power to convey it, for that Hallam only convey'd to Hodgkinson John Henry's title in it, which title Hodgkinson cannot show and which Hallam has in conversation with Gamage denied. I showed Gamage my letter to him & his reply. Even[g] drank tea at G M W. Call'd at M Rogers's. Theatre, Mrs Seymour's & Mrs Bretts night, Italian Monk & Prisoner at large" in y[e] house $337.

June 6th 1798. Write to Hodgkinson.

"In my last letter to you I professed myself open to conviction, ready to acknowledge error and wishing to do right; permit me to consider you as <*influenced*> possessing the same disposition & being influenced by the same motives.

You assert that I was put into possession of one fourth of certain property according to agreement. Surely I never denied it: on the contrary in my letter I offer compensation for the use of it during the term of possession, that compensation to be agreed upon between us, or if our ideas should widely differ, to be determined by impartial men. I surely never have denied that I received a salary: it was a proposal from you, you named the sum, it was 14 dollars a week, 2 dollars a week more than Mr Gill's, 7 of which 14 were paid by Mr Hallam, 3.50 by the property for the use [of] which I offer compensation, and three dollars fifty cents from you. Yes, however unworthy my services to you were of the sum, I certainly did receive it. I likewise did receive what you call interest on the property, which must be acknowledged among the advantages accruing from its use, advantages which I have offered to make the standard by which to decide upon the compensation due to you. Your statement thus far is certainly accurate, but these were not disputed points to the best of my knowledge: the only difference of opinion concerning these matters appears to be, that you consider the giving me possession as giving me a right to the property, whereas I consider it as only giving me a right to use the property and receive emolument from the use, in the same manner as we now jointly occupy the New Theatre, and use Mr Hallam's wardrobe: if it had been otherwise there could have been no necessity for that part of our agreement which says "That he the said J H his heirs &c &c shall & will at the proper costs & charges of the said W D, on or before the first day of June &c &c by such deed or deeds, conveyance or conveyances in the Law as the said Wm Dunlap, his heirs &c &c shall devise & require, well & sufficiently grant &c &c &c all that certain piece or parcel of Land (describing the property in J St.) and also the one equal moitey &c &c that is to say the one equal fourth part of all Leases &c &c &c which belongs to the said old America Company &c &c freed and discharged from all Incumbrances whatever &c &c.

You next state that "availing" myself of the opposition between Mr Hallam & yourself, I signified my intention of quitting altogether, but find[g] that you would probably be successfull in *your* application for the New Theatre, I changed my mind & demanded one half of any emoluments which might arise from said acquisition.

It is always painfull to have disagreeable events past & forgotten, forcefully brought back to the cognizance of the unwilling memory, but when they are brought back let us examine them without flinching.

In the agreement before quoted <*from*>, are the following words <*and*> "that all future acquisitions to the said property and improvements thereof shall be for their mutual and joint benefit in proportion to their respective shares therein: and that all future purchases of Theatrical property made at any time during the term of five years from the date hereof by either of the said parties, shall be for the equal & joint account and benefit of both the said parties". consequently the application you mention as made by you for the New Theatre must have been an application made for our mutual benefit (and I presume with my approbation & consent) or it was an infraction of the above article. For my part I know of no application for <*it*> the New Theatre other than calling on Wm Henderson and asking the determination of the Committee you at such times declaring your resolution no longer to continue your connection with Mr Hallam. In the Month of March 1797 I was some days in Connecticut, on returning home, I called on you Mar: 14th. Mr Hallam's disatisfaction on account of his Wife's being prohibited the Stage had been openly shewing itself: our conversation turned on the vexations arising from this source and at length we enter'd upon the subject of an agreement with Mr Hallam to quit the business. You soon gave me to understand that if *you* could induce Mr Hallam to quit all title to the New Theatre, you should consider yourself as the party principally concerned, and me as holding only one fourth. This conversation added much to my knowledge. I was obliged to appeal to our agreement which happily for me, was explicit, was legal, was signed. You finally acquiesced and seemed to agree in the justice of my ideas. I here made no demand; the conversation was of a thing which might happen. You saw before you the prospect of an advantageous bargain which you wished to appropriate as much as possible to yourself, therefore before concluding it, you strove to induce me to relinquish that title to equal participation which your contracts <*with me*> had vested in me, I repelled the encroachment and you reluctantly desisted from the attempt.

When I left your house you accompanied me & meeting Dr Gamage the idea was started or revived of making proposals to Mr Hallam similar to those he afterwards acceded to, Dr G undertaking to deliver them. After parting with G you <*proposed to*> asked me <*that*> if Mr Hallam should reject our proposals if I would join in open opposition to him & endeavour to get the New Theatre: & you on part[s] professed yourself perfectly satisfied with the agreement as stipulating an equal participation. <*On*> Calling upon you the next day you revived the subject of the day before & insisted upon my having no right to an equal participation wth you in the

New Theatre: Dr Gamage came in; the subject was renew'd before him; your copy of ye agreement was taken from your desk and put into his hands and I was again forced to insist upon a right so clear, so defined, so intended; again forced to appeal to signatures & seals as my only security. This all happened before I signified my wish to withdraw from the business, not after, as you have stated, <*and took place*> It was in a conversation with you on the 25th of March, the day after you had been <*hissed*> insulted in Puff, that I signified such a wish to you, in which conversation you determined to quit the N: Y: stage & make any arrangement in respect to our bargain that should satisfy me or appear just. Your statement being erroneous the conclusion from it must of course be erroneous. It was at this time that you consented to take my Salary of 14 dollars a week if I continued to keep the books without salary. <*It appears from these incontrovertable facts, that when I signified my intention of quitting the business it was in consequence of your avowed design to leave the Stage & of the quarrels in which you had involved me with Mr Hallam.*> Here I must observe that your resolution was taken in consequence of the bad success of the business, <*a business*> consequently when you talk of leaving me in possession, you mean in possession of a losing business, a business which had not enabled its directors to fulfill their contracts, Which business you leave me to carry on under the disadvantages of a weakened Company and a fixed Rent. Soon after this the quarrel between you & Mr Hallam became such in its consequences as to induce you actually to quit the stage though without relinquishing your Sal^{y} as perf: wh^{h} I thought it just you should receive. Sitting in the green room by ourselves on the 17th of April, you proposed that I should continue to hold my Theatrical property and if we could obtain the New Theatre that we should take it on equal shares dividing the profits, I allowing you what should be deemed just for your services as acting Manager and performer: to this I acceded. Proceeding upon this foundation <*we proceeded*> the New Theatre was let to us & I was put into possession of it jointly with you by its proprietors. You now come to the business of your proposed seperation from me, a thing evidently in opposition to our agreement; in opposition both to our original agreement & to the subsequent agreement made in respect to the New Theatre in which last you contracted for your personal services during the time of holding it which we at the time considered as 3 years. I but casually mention this last agreement as it is informal & neither signed nor sealed. You say I "seemed to agree" &c. Let us recur to facts. You often, indeed continually, gave me to understand that you was disatisfied with the encouragement the Theatre received & with the little attention paid to you, exclaiming against New York &c &c: I at length understood that offers had been made you from Boston; & on the fifteenth of February last, when Barrett was here <*for*> you formally signified to me your wish to quit N: Y: if I would agree. I made no objection, the terms being understood by me, that, I should be left satisfied. In speaking of the Company to be left here, I understood that you should, not merely remain neuter, but should assist me in forming such an one as might be as compleat as possible after withdrawing yourself & Mrs Hodgkinson: it appears that I was mistaken, I am willing to suppose the mistake mine, but as to the assertion following "You never even hinted that this change would make an alteration in your purchase; you gave me reason to expect the contrary;" I must point out that you are mistaken, by bringing to your recollection, that once in particular in the Theatre, I <*did*> desired you to take into consideration the terms upon which we were to seperate, putting you in mind that our former agreement must necessarily be done away, & wishing you to inform me whether it was your desire that I should continue a purchaser of the property upon some equitable arrangement or make you compensation for the use of it. To this you gave me no answer, but leaving the room, I believe on the call of business, merely said "Yes, I will" or words to that effect. I am willing to imagine that the hurry of business and excessive study erases some things from your mind and by confusing dates causes a misconception of others. I perfectly remember likewise making this representation to you "Our former agreement must be cancell'd, otherwise you can at any time demand of me half the advantages which may proceed from my <*bargain*> lease of the New Theatre, I having the same power over you." If representations of this kind were not frequent from me the reasons are obvious—I supposed you to be in possession of the same facts which I possessed; the proposal of annihilating our contracts by seperating our interests came from you, in consequence <*of bett*> as I supposed of better prospects held out to you from Boston, I therefore expected that the proposals of arrangements equivalent to those which were to be annulled, would come from you: and I forebore pressing the subject on you, from a fear of appearing to wish your departure. <*As to my enjoyment of 75 parts out of a hundred*> As to negociations with actors, you say you made none—if by that you mean that you concluded none you <*are*> may be accurate, otherwise not; and the beginning a negociation was evidently an impediment to my concluding one with the same person. Mr & Mrs Johnson are not here.

You tell me that part of the property to be conveyed to me on the first of June 1798, was previous to the day appointed sold, and "under my own agency as an owner and proprietor" I have already shown that I never have owned the property consequently could not sell it; and it is well known to Dr Gamage <*that*> & Mr Gaine that I never pretended to own it, indeed they know that I could not own it. That I consented to the sale is certain: but as this consent seems to be brought forward as a reproach, I will examine the circumstances which led to it; fortunately I am in possession of facts, and I reconcile myself to the task by the hope of convincing you & the promise to myself that this letter will be the last on the subject.

An agreement was made between us in which the sale of ¼ of a certain property was contemplated, but at the time of the agreement the property was mortgaged for £2000 & interest. You proposed that in one year from my entering into possession say May 1796, you would pay £1000 & interest and on ye first of May following discharge the remainder, such being I believe, the tenor of your engagements with Mr Hallam. The time of the first payment arrived & was passed over the whole being put off untill the time of the second; The second was approaching with still less probability of fulfillment: I gave my consent with an express intention to assist you in removing your difficulties. This sale was in agitation and my concurrence given long before any Idea arose of your quitting your situation & by enterring into agreements foreign to my interest annulling those contracts which involved among other things the <*sale of*> conveyance of property to me. I little thought that a consent so given & from such motives, could be considered as an injury done or intended. Before the sale took place your determination to quit your connection with me was made known: my consent obtained to it & consequently to the annulling of our agreement, upon condition of other arrangements being devised & executed, other arrangements satisfactory to me were promised; you was the person proposing the change therefore from you I awaited the particulars of the change, these particulars not being communicated, I went so far as to ask for them, expressly mentioning the <*subject*> business of the purchase and asking for your desire on the subject: (this you state differently but I presume upon the circumstance being recalled to your memory; if not, we are at issue on this point, without a possibility of decision): the time of making the conveyance arrived without any proposal being made to me: for me to have demanded from you the conveyance, when I knew you had not removed the incumbrance would have looked like insult, beside that knowing your intention not to perform the other parts of y^e^ agreement, an intention avowed & agreed to conditionally I was daily looking for your proposals of accomodation. Under these circumstances I met you on the Stage, the first day of June. You told me that you should want $300 next day, I promised to see them presented to you: after some pause you remarked that this was the day on which the conveyance of the property was to be made to me "if you chuse" you added "I will convey the Philadelphia property to you, we will see about the papers relative to it immediately" and then mentioned the value of that property &c: on your pausing, I remarked, that from <*your intention of quitting the connection with me*> various circumstances I had concluded that a different arrangement was to be made in respect to the purchase: that I was willing to pay you for the use of the property or make any settlement that should be just and satisfactory to both. You said, that as you were going away you did not wish to be troubled with the Philadelphia property, that it was dead or worse a continual tax on you. I mentioned the incumbrance still remaining on the property here. I mentioned this with no other view than to show the impossibility of fulfilling the contract & to lead to some proposals. You were mistaken in supposing that I mention'd the sale as an obstacle to the conveyance on my stating that the conveyance could not be made, you mentioned the sale of a part of the property as supposing that to be the obstacle I alluded to. You now proposed that we should be equally concerned in the Boston and New York schemes: I objected: I said I would not engage in any business which I could not superintend myself, nor be concerned in any Company but for what is denominated the winter season. When the term of our original agreement was mentioned, you denied that your "personal services" were <*implicated*> intended. Your words were "my personal services are not implicated in any agreement" here give me leave to point out to you that you are in an error, for by personal services you here intended connection in business one of the express stipulations of our contract, & indeed I can see no way by which a connection in Theatrical business with me could be possibly intended at the time of our contracting without your personal services being implied both as director & performer: You will doubtless recollect on reviewing the subject that my hopes of emolument in the business you invited me to, were expressly founded on your personal services, and that it was only on the ground of not subjecting yourself to insult on the stage, that you objected to being bound in writing to exert your talents as a performer for our mutual benefit during the term of the agreement, expressly acknowledging that such was the intention of the contract, in presence of Mr W Johnson & Mr E H Smith the witnesses thereto. To return to ye 1st June. I certainly did tell you in the course of this conversation that I did not mean to fly from my agreement, if you wished it fulfilled, but I added that "in such case I should expect a fulfillment on your part," & I meant no more than a fulfillment, just, reasonable, &, (need I add?) still in your power. I will not presume to judge what will or will not shock you; but I am conscious of nothing shocking in my manner or words on this occasion. Our conversation was interrupted by the duties of your business. I afterwards attempted to renew it: we were interrupted again & you expressed a desire that I would remain on ye stage: I did so for, I suppose near half an hour, when finding no further conversation likely to take place, I walked up to you & observed that I supposed that you could not renew the conversation at that time, you said it was impossible & I went up stairs to my usual business. Before leaving the Theatre I again saw you, but the conversation was not renewed. I saw you again the next day both at the Theatre & at Mr H Gaines. The next day was sunday, I wrote to you & on monday gave you the letter.

I am sorry to observe the spirit in which your answer to me is written especially the remainder,—to the remainder, <*for*> on account of this spirit I shall be very brief in my reply. I did not say you had broken your agreements. I stated that they had remained unfulfilled past the time appointed to fulfill them & proposed a settlement on principles to be agreed upon between ourselves or fixed by impartial Men. I cannot possibly offer more. You say you pressed me to receive the conveyance—I have stated the conversation that passed already—need I repeat that the encumbrances were not removed? Need I ask you if you could convey even the Philadephia property to me at the time appointed, or if you had made arrangements so to do? <*If, (as must be true) you thought you could convey what you sold at any hour, I do not wonder at your being shocked when I told you, you could not.*> You propose to me to cancel the agreement from its commencement, I agree, nay I proposed it. as to the small portion of salary paid me by you during the first year <*you*> I cannot but think I deserved it notwithstanding your opinion, & for the interest & other emoluments, after deducting some portion for risque & for emoluments of other business given up to partake of the advantages you invited me to, I do not think we should eventually differ.

You call to my recollection an exchange of receipts, telling me that I "made" you sign a receipt for £ 500 when I had not paid one shilling. You signed receipts for me to the amount of £ 1000, taking my receipts for the same sum on account. If it shall appear that before the first payment was due from me, I had paid it all in advance, & had even paid between 2 & 300 dollars upon the second, (I mention the overplus from recollection) and that during the second year I <*was*> have constantly been in advance your assertion will appear strange that I have not paid you a shilling. At present I <*can*> shall only say that I believe your statement is not accurate; this is a business our accounts will settle.

I must confess my offer to you was serious & must be content to <*be*> remain the <*butt*> object of your cutting Irony, <*&*> the butt of your poignant ridicule. The only palliation I can offer, is that I was led to do it, by your expressions of disgust to Managership, and declarations that if you remained in New York it would be as a performer, repeated to me & sent by me as a message to Wm Henderson, added to certain expressions discouraging me from engaging performers, such as hints of the uncertainty of Boston scheme &c "there is time enough between this & September"—"many strange things may turn up between this & your opening"—with occasional "ifs" in respect to your leaving New York. <*My only fear of offending was in not offering enough, for as to business I supposed that if the terms proposed met not with approbation, you would mildly* *have told me so, & pointed out what you would agree to.*> You must know that I could have no reason to wish Mrs H to give up anything; but, having made an engagement in consequence of your determination to withdraw her, with another person, I could do no otherwise, in making an offer than to mention the circumstance. I sincerely join with you in the hope that no dfficulty will occur in our <*settlement*> adjustment of accounts. I am sorry that my letter, instead of facilitating seems to have proved a hindrance to our settlement, we will, with you[r] consent here drop intercourse by letter, <*which on my part*> and appoint a time & place to meet & either agree to some satisfactory adjustment or leave it to indifferent persons. You state as the only modes by which I can leave you the power to esteem me, a complyance with the Agreement or an acceptance of your offer to cancel: as the first appears to me impossible, for reasons which I shall be happy to give rather in conversation than by letter (tho' I believe they may be collected from this letter), my only resource is the last: <*which I hope I shall be able to do*> when our accounts are bro^{t} forward & settled, I hope we shall remove every difficulty to this last mode.

[June] 7th write a part of the above. Read to E H S. Afternoon sit down to Copy it for Hodgkinson. Write to Barrett offering him 50 dollars a week for himself & wife their wardrobe & dressers. Visit at Henry Michell's, and at Mr Fitch's, to see Mrs Holly of Stamford. Evening Theatre, "Robbers & Farmer" for Messrs. Faulkner & Miller, in the House $825.

June 8th. Jefferson concluded this morning to accept my offer (see p. 116 vol: 15) $22. The two Miss Westrays agreed with me for $13 each to do anything I order for the business expressing themselves fully satisfied. Copying the letter to Hodgkinson. Evening Cooper & Ten Eyk were with me.

[June] 9th Finish Copying y^{e} letter to Hodgkinson: read it & his, to Ten Eyk: read his letter to Wm Johnson who advises an arbitration. Wm says it will be impossible to make him understand what justice is. Buy Hugh Trevor; read in it. John reads it. Evening Theatre "Knave or not & No song no supper." gave Gill my letter to deliver to Hodgkinson. In the house Miss Broadhurst's night $202.

[June] 10th Sunday. Read Hugh Trevor with increasing delight. Noon, see Gamage in the street as I was going to Call on Ciceri G told me, without my asking him, that going to see Mrs Hodgkinson, who has had a miscarriage, H show'd him my letter: that it was a plain candid statement of facts, that it had gone some way to convince H that he did not tell him what he thought of it, but asked if I was right in respect to the property which Gamage told him I was. that the great offence was to his vanity in having an actors situation offer'd him. Saw Ciceri, agreed that I would give Massé $12 a week. talk of plans for ornamenting & Scenery. Ciceri is to have $26 & if he chooses a benefit at the end of the stock, then to quit & not add to benefit charges. Massé & Audin are to be engaged as are all in the department from week to week, at any time to be dismiss'd. Read Hugh Trevor.

[June] 11th Attending business. rec[d] a letter from Hodgkinson in quite a lowered key. He wishes me to suppose that all my letter is wrong but he refutes no part of it. "he never conceived" this, and "he was ignorant" of that, is the general stile. he says "the property could not be encumbered, because if sold tomorrow it would fetch more than it was mortgaged for" he says "when you speak of monies advanced on your part you seem to forget that I have large claims on the same grounds myself; I believe not very inferior to the *whole* of your own." He says he meant no part of his letter in ridicule or irony, but says that "a proposal stipulating, that *unconditionally* and *without reserve* one man should lay himself at the *mercy* of another, relying solely upon his sense of Justice & propriety, I hope was never before offered to the most unworthy talents." he concludes by offer[g] to leave our affairs to arbitration. Write to Hodgkinson.

Sir

Give me leave to assure you that if I have mistaken the intention of any part of your letter of the 4th or have attributed to you a spirit you did not feel, (which I sincerely hope is the <*truth*>

case,) I am ready to receive contrary impressions & to give them a much more hearty welcome, than the disagreable ideas received, whose place they shall wholely occupy.

If, as is very probable, we should still continue to hold different opinions on many past transactions, we must console ourselves with the <*idea*> knowledge that no two men can view the same object in the same point of view, or have the same perception of it, and that as the organs, habits, and <*education*> circumstances of men necessarily differ so much their <*opinions*> thoughts and the actions to which those thoughts give being.

If the assertion, that in my offer to you <*for certain salary on condition of continuing here,*> concerning an engagement for New York, my motives were far from any thought of offence can give you any satisfaction, it is offered with as much sincerity as pleasure. To the best of my remembrance at the time every article of agreement I had seen ran in the manner I expressed myself, & I had no farther thought on the subject than, "if Mr H wishes to stipulate for business, it is an after arrangement, this is a beginning proposition."

I agree with you as to the arbitration & will take an early opportunity to consult you on the mode.

I remain Your friend

W D

Evening Theatre "Tamerlane and the Maid of the Oaks" for Messrs Hallam Junr & Martin in the house $425.

June 12th Finish a short essay on y^{e} Theatre & send it to James Watters Phil:. Write on my Comedy. Meet Hodgkinson in the street, we spoke to each other as usual he complaining of illness. Dine at G M W's with Smith, Johnson, M: Rogers, W W W & Genl Gordon: we had some rallying & sportive conversation politics & morals. Walk with Wm Johnson who returns & passes part of the evening with me: we conversed much concerning Holcroft & Hugh Trevor.

[June] 13th Concluded and interchanged signatures on an agreement with Joseph Jefferson for ye next season, at 22 dollars & he finding his wardrobe. Cooper called on me to ask my interference in putting off the play to night "Deserted Daughter" because Martin is sick tho' Fawcet offers to read Donald. I declared that I thought a put off injurious & refused. About 5 OClock I hear the play is put off & I understand without the consent obtained of Fawcet whose night comes—this proceeding is Coopers, & I fear from selfish motives not being ready in Mordent. Evening Post & wife with us & W W W & wife. Write on my Comedy. Hodgkinson to day spoke to me on the ordinary business of the Theatre. Look at Biography of living Authors: Hearns travels. Stauntons Embassy.

[June] 14th Attend^{g} to business: Fawcet objects to taking his night as the Miss Westrays had put off theirs & so encroached him: it was proposed by Hodgkinson that the Company should take the risque of ye remaining benefits from the individuals, by giving their salaries on a night which was deficient—no one made open objection—Jefferson said he "should be glad to serve the performers but he should like to be earning a little money for himself, he should be idle for 2 or 3 months to come" &c. However a kind of languid consent having been given, Hodgkinson concluded the thing so settled. In the afternoon I walked out to Tyler's, Hallam & his wife were there. She enter'd into an examination of Theatrical affairs wherein Hodgkinson's management & person, Coopers playing &c &c were loaded with every species of odium. He occasionally joined in with notes of disapprobation. Mrs Tyler praised her own acting & Tyler pointed out the enormity of benefit charges & the great abuses which had crept into the Company. A more compleat picture of selfishness & envy I never saw. Evening Th: Miss Westray's & Miss E Westray's night "Deserted Daughter & Wedding day" in ye house 559 dollars. I sat in ye pit the whole time of performance. Miss E Westray exceeded my expectations in Joanna, her youth gave her more interest than Mrs Johnson, her figure was very beautifull she spoke with propriety tho' not with sufficient energy. Miss Westray did pretty well as Sarsnet.

[June] 15th We concluded to day to close the Season with the consent of the Company. ye remaining benefits to be managed so that the individual shall engage the performers necessary for his night & pay no more. I engaged Hallam Junr for 18 dollars a week he promising to do anything. Read in Recruiting Officer. Smith call'd on me: he to morrow leaves town for Litchfield on a visit. Write on my Comedy. Visit at G M W's.

[June] 16th Walk. Accidently falling in with Cooper who was alone in a chair, I joined him & rode some miles with him. We conversed of Holcroft considerably: he says that on the publication of Hugh Trevor the players of Covent Garden had a meeting & agreed to show their displeasure to its Author by withholding their society from him, ordaining that he among them who should be guilty of speaking to him should be sent to Coventry. He says Mrs Mattocks is Mrs Fishwife & that Glibly was acknowledged by a fellow of the name of Taylor: the Holcroft is apt to oppose peoples prejudices in conversation, is talkative and often offends. We talked of the Miss Westrays and of letting Miss E. play Juliet next season. I was informed on my return that Hallam had called on me to ask my interference to persuade Hodgkinson to revoke a resolution with which he had left the Stage this morning in consequence of some of the performers not attending rehearsal, *viz* not to play again. In the afternoon one of the servants of the Theatre told me that there was to be a rehearsal tomorrow, Sunday! Read & hear Jack read French. Drink tea at Post's. Evening call in at W W W's: as the conversation which took place here was curious I will faithfully set it down in the form of Dialogue.

Mr & Mrs Woolsey, Timothy Dwight Junr and W D: are the persons who speak: a young man of the name of Williams & my Wife were present but silent.

W W W. A curious affair has happened in Philadelphia. The Secretary of State has horsewhipt the Spanish Ambassador.

D: A curious affair indeed. I am sorry for it.

W W W: This, I suppose was not done officially: it is only Mr Pickering has horsewhipt Mr <*ger*> Yrijo and I daresay he richly deserved it, for he is an impudent fool.

D. Mr Yrujio may be a very great fool but I think horsewhipping no great proof of wisdom in Mr Pickering.

W W W. He was perfectly right if the affair is as stated. It is said that Mr Yrujio in a large company called Mr Pickering a traitor to his Country & accused him of receiving British Gold.

D. And Mr Pickering to prove the accusation false, horsewhipt him.

W W W. I do not speak of it as a proof. But I think that when the law does not screen a man from <*punishment*> insult he does perfectly right to inflict punishment himself.

D. It appears to me that this would lead to murder, to inflicting Death.

W W W. I should have no objections if he had horsewhipt such a scoundrel to death. (His face was now flush'd, his utterance rapid tho' somewhat confus'd, he leaned his chair back against the Wall, apparently heated, not satisfied)

T D: jun. (Turning quick upon me with some fire in his eyes) Would you Sir, suffer yourself to be called a villain in public company without resenting it?

D. I certainly think I ought.

T D: jun. Then, Sir, it would be concluded that you acknowledged the charge

D. Perhaps not. I think there are better ways of repelling an unjust charge than by passion. I should in the first place deny it. And would not my assertion ballance my accusers assertion, no proofs being adduced on either side?

T D jun. Certainly not. For it would be naturally expected that if you were innocent you would show anger at such a charge.

D. If resentment and anger are proofs of virtue, we have daily evidence of a most virtuous community.

Mrs W: I have often heard it mentioned as a proof of Bill Livingstons guilt, than [*sic*] when Captn [blank] charged him with having picked his pocket, he did not resent it.

D. I know nothing of the circumstances of this case, but I certainly think that if I was accused of being a thief I should not conceive anger or resentment necessary to my justification.

Mrs W: All the world thought that his not resenting the charge was an acknowledgment of its truth.

D. I should be conscious that the accusation did not make me a thief.

Mrs W. I do not say that it would. But the good opinion of others is of some consequence.

D. Of great consequence: but I ought not to forfeit my own good opinion, by doing what I knew to be wrong, for the chance of retaining the good opinion of the world.

Mrs W: There is not one man of five thousand would act as you describe.

D. It matters not, if I am right, tho' I should be one alone of five million.

T D jun: Do you think it unjust for a man to punish another for an injury that other has done him?

D. I certainly do think so.

My beloved brother having collected himself changed the conversation.

O, how much more might I have said on this subject if I had been in those habits of self possession which would have given me power over that knowledge, scanty as it is which I have at my command in the moments of solitude? How might I have shewn the immorality & injustice of all punishment. how might I have pointed out the banefull effects of resentment & anger <*and*> false shame & dastardly fear of the worlds misjudging. How might I have appealed to them as religionists & Christians, against principles so contrary to the morality of y[e] sermons of their God incarnate? But I felt that I could not be the advocate of forbearance without feeling passion or point out the lovelyness of temperance without causing irritation. I therefore forebore. I could not help reflecting on the situation of the poor Infidel philosopher combatting for virtue, even for Christian Virtue (for tho' I denied the justice of punishment, christians do the same, as it respects man, giving that business which is too odious for themselves to their God, "Vengeance belongs to the Lord") with the brother in law, sister & son of the President of Yale Colledge, the author of Sermons "on the nature & danger of infidel philosophy.

Nay not content with shifting an attribute so repugnant to human nature from their own shoulders, they even put it further from them by removing it from their own immediate God, <*making*> willingly allowing the God of the Jews to be the God of anger vengeance & punishment, & making his son a mediator: as if his humanized nature had taught him Justice, unknown to the perfect God his father.

17th June Sunday. In conversation with Ten Eyck I learn that Hodgkinson expresses disatisfaction at the prospect of quitting this place. Ten Eyck says he came into their store yesterday, & he said "Well you are going to leave us altogether?" "Why I don't know" says H: "I dont see how I can do otherwise now" On T: E: telling him that his freinds would be much displeas'd he said "I cant help myself now. I am *ousted.* the Committee have let the house to Mr Dunlap—and how?—Mr Hallam came in & cut short the question & the conversation. Read in [Robert] Dodsley's old plays "Adventures of five hours" is capable of being made a good play for the Stage: "City night cap" has fine things in it. Evening at Sharplesses: Sharpless & family were prisoners to the french at the same time that Mr Russel was, with whom I dined at Middletown: S gives a different port[r]ait of him from that I saw in the drawing room & at table. S: gave a humourous description of a scen[e] he witnessed in a Methodists chapel in his neighbourhood.

June 18th Read in Old plays. Attend business. Call M: Rogers's. Evening Theatre, Miss Brett & Miss Hardings night, "Castle spectre & Honest Theives," the last is the "Committee" cut down: in the house $409. Hodgkinson quarrels with the wind instruments. Martin & Simpson quarrel in the green Room. Mrs Hallam is most excessively gracious with me: wants to speak to me: Thinks it would be much better for me to employ my Company in Philadelphia in Mr Hallams Theatre untill November, but she is such a fool, she knows nothing of such things, perhaps Mr Hallam & me had better talk on the subject &c &c. Gave Hodgkinson a copy of a bond to be enter into by us in respect to the arbitration: he is quite friendly in his behaviour, the reserve is rather on my side, tho' it scarcely amounts to reserve.

June 19th Hodgkinson says Mr John C Shaw is the man he has fixed upon as an arbitrator, & appoints Thursday evening as the time: he says Mrs Hallam was *gay* last night. Call on Mr Carlisle Pollock who agrees, for the Committee, not to charge percentage on the benefits to come, or last night's. Call on W W W & get from him the monthly reviews from November 1797 to March 1798. Saw Col^{l} Burr at W's and was much pleased with him. Read Review. Evening, rec^{d} a letter from Mrs Simpson in some measure forbidding me to engage her two eldest daughters: [35] it is a well written letter: she objects to their being seperated from her, their guardian: says she will not consent to their signing any articles with me: that since they have lived where they are, (Mrs Fortune's) they have renounced all duty to her: that she has taken counsel, & knows her powers over them as minors and will exert it: that tho' of age by the laws of this Country, they cannot claim their protection as they are aliens & concludes with appealing to my feelings as a father. Take the warm bath & then go to W W W's to see my wifes mother who has just arrived from Stamford.

[June] 20th Read review. Call on Hopkins who has just return'd from Europe after a residence of one year in England & one in France. I found with him a Mr Lee of Boston, likewise just return'd from France: Mr Woolcot joined us, having arrived yesterday from Phil: and a conversation took place by which I learned that Lee had brought with him many letters from Talleyrand, to citizens of the United States: that he is fearfull of being consider'd as a french agent: that these letters have a pecular seal: that they are to Bache & others: that there were letters to Genet & Volney but not with this seal which are deliver'd. Lee offers to deliver these letters to Mr Woolcot to be sent on to the secretary of state. Mr Woolcot asks me repeatedly if there were any letters for Mr Jefferson: Answer, No: Mr Woolcot offers a receit for the letters.

[35] Juliana and Ellen Westray.

FRANCIS BAYARD WINTHROP (c. 1753-1817)
By William Dunlap
(Courtesy of Mrs. William Tidball)

I laughingly told Woolsey yesterday that his report concerning Mr Pickering was premature & he laughing replied that he had since heard that it was an affair of a similar nature between Mr Pinkney and the Spanish Ambassador at Paris.

Hodgkinson wished me to join with him in a declaration that the musicians who had quitted the orchestra in consequence of his message to them t'other night should never play in it again, which I not choosing to do, a few words rather acrimonious passed between us. I told him that I made no rash determinations, for when I had determined I should probably abide by it. He said "tho you plead their cause, by god, none of them shall set a foot in a Theatre where <*he is*> I am." In the course of the talk I mention'd my differing in opinion from him. "I am sorry you *do* differ in opinion from me" "It is not worth while, when mens opinions differ for either of them to be sorry." "You will be sorry, Sir, before next winter is over." "It is certainly kind in you to be interested on my account." I afterwards asked him the time & place of arbitration; he fixed the Tontine Coffee house 8 OClock. I called on Mrs Simpson, she went over the grounds of her complaint: he came in: I offered them a situation for next winter, they seemed to relish the idea: but she said if they engaged her youngest daughter must be engaged. They talk of expectations from the death of a relation in England and of returning in case of such an event & that the Miss W's must do so likewise. She (Mrs S) makes great objections to Mrs Fortune's as a place of residence for her daughters, & objects to leaving them here without employment while she goes as proposed to Albany.

Mr Woolcot in a polite note excuses himself from dining with me tomorrow on account of business and Mrs Woolcots illness. Call on Dr Miller. Read Reviews. Call at Sharpless's: drink tea with Mitchell, he had just receiv'd a letter from Priestley for the repository. Call at W W W's and pass half an hour at M: Rogers's.

June 21st Cooper leaves town, I paid him \$121 for 2 Theatrical dresses. I communicated to y^e Miss Westray's their mother's letter to me and told them all that had passed: they said they had told her that they would change their lodgings if she insisted on it, but gave their pointed determination, never to put themselves in the power of Simpson. Their eyes were filled with tears especially the oldest, but they said nothing improper nor gave way to their emotions. I met Hodgkinson at Gaines & he asked me for a memorandum of the money he has received this past winter. I made out for him the following—

In y^e Old house 5 weeks	
p^d Mr Hodgkinson	822.47½
rec^d from him salary 5 weeks @ 95	475.—
Ball^{ce}	\$347.47½
p^d on acc^t of Old house 5 weeks	
play^g & since closed	\$5929.35
rec^d	4557.85
Ball^{ce} due Treasurer	\$1371.50

p^d Mr Hodgkinson during stock business in y^e N: T: up to which time his acct^t is posted and no further	\$1197.62½
Mr H is credited during said time on account of salary left with y^e Treasurer say up to April 28th	890.—
	\$307.62½

Mr Hs night	920.—	10 p^r C^t on which is	92.	
Gall	50.	Ch:	380.	
	697.25		472.	
	747.25			
	472.—			
	275.25	ball^{ce} in fav^r of Mr H carried up		
bro^t up				275.25
Mrs Hs night	990.37½	p^r C^t is	99.3½	
sales	793	Charge	380.—	
	479.3½		479.3½	
	313.96½	ballance		313.96½
				\$589.21½

Messrs Hopkins, W W W, Johnson, G M W, Miller, & Mitchell dined with me. Hopkins gave many interesting particulars concerning France: it appears that the Government is a military despotism kept within certain bounds by public opinion and obliged to act offensively towards the world for its own preservation: that science is cherished & by means of national schools, the riches which the power of the nation has concentrated, is laid open to every enquirer: that the freedom of the press is suspended, but <*freedom*> liberty of speech not infringed: that the mass of the nation go to mass on sunday as stupidly as ever, while the well informed laugh at religion and make a popular day of rest of the decade-day: that agriculture flourishes and the state of the peasant is ameliorated. After tea walk on ye battery & then went up with W Johnson to the Tontine Coffee-house, where Hodgkinson met us but J C Shaw not having come to town the business was postponed untill Saturday evening. I walked with Johnson to Riley's. H was with us part of the way, he asked me some questions respecting the above memoranda: Johnson mentioned to him the propriety of having a statement of the question ready, he said in a friendly manner that he had no statement to make; he said his company for Boston was nearly compleat. I told him of my situation with Barrett.

June 22d I received yesterday the following letter from Barrett.

Boston June 16th 1798.

Sir

I have at this moment yours before me. shall be extremely happy to winter under your Banner, if other matters Can (& I think they may) be adjusted wth regard to *Business* &c &c. I cannot suppose you *mean* any But the *First* in *Each Department* next and only I shall state is that of Salary which I hope for the services of Both, *wardrobe & all,* you will not think an addition of 10 $ p^{r} week more than we deserve, when you consider the Expence of Dresses. Sh^{d} we meet, I hope you will have no objection to my regulating the stage Business of Mrs Bs & my own, which liberty I have ever had in all the Theatres I have been in. have no objection to Benefit Charges, only wish to know how they are settled, that Mrs B. & self may not

Fall *near* so as to injure Both. I had the Favor of your Former letter, but many Days after I Gave a line to Mr Jefferson. Shall hope for the favor of a line from you by the first post

&c &c G L Barrett

I hope you will not think me impertinent when I Request to know who is your *acting* manager as my Being Comfortable Greatly Depends on that.

Do you sir pay Travelling Expences which I have ever had on the Continent.

Answer

Sir

Much pleased with your expressions of readiness to "winter under my Banner." I immediately apply myself to give such explicit answers to the queries suggested <*by*> in your letter, as shall leave no possibility of future misunderstanding in case of your joining the N Y company. And here give me leave to premise that if any thing in this Letter should appear offensive from its freedom I beg of you to consider it as proceeding from the above motive: for I believe, Sir, that a situation in the N Y Company to which you have it in your power to be eminently serviceable may be made a permanent situation to you more than I intend it to be to me, & when I quit I feel assured of the power of putting any deserving man in possession of the <*business*> Theatre. The Company will be much lessened from what it has been tho' I hope no less efficient, but the diminution of numbers, without which I have no prospect of keeping the charges within those bounds which alone can give <*prospect*> hope of success, renders it necessary that the members of the company should adjust themselves to its exigencies and occasionally do such parts as in an over abounding company would fall into other hands: this is an accomodation which has been agreed to by Mr Cooper & others. You know as well as I do, what a vast range of business is left <*open*> unoccupied by the absence of Mr Hodgkinson; in Comedy the Rangers, Vapids &c &c in low Comedy a great variety, & of both these the greater part are open to your acceptance with a share of the Tragedy. I take it for granted that any part done by Mr Hodgk: <*has done*> will not be refused <*by you*> if cast to you. I certainly shall expect accomodation, and as I shall for the next season (which is the only one I at present make arrangements for) keep the direction of the business, the choice of plays, their casts &c entirely in my own hands, I shall expect usefullness to the best of your ability and I feel sure that you may expect from me, justice.

Mrs Barrett is no doubt aware, that tho' Mrs Johnson has left the Company, there remains in Comedy Mrs Hallam & in Tragedy Mrs Melmoth. It is Mrs Johnson's business, (which certainly was of the first kind) that is now vacant; & the youthfull characters which

I have agreed with Mrs M to give up; I certainly should not <*require*> wish Mrs Barrett to degrade herself, but as I said above, I shall cast <*my*> the plays myself.

As I look upon both you & Mrs Barrett as occupying the first stations of the profession so my offer of salary was of the highest grade any prospect of <*business*> profit in N: Y: will permit: but I look upon the matter of business as so very essential to the well-being of a Theatre that I can think of salary but as a secondary consideration. It is usefulness which constitutes worth.

In regulating stage business, I shall pay just deference to your opinion, and I think it not improbable but your knowledge may be rendered serviceable to me and if so by mutual agreement, beneficial to you: (tho' I by no means at present propose such an agreement) notwithstanding this I would wish clearly to be understood, that while I direct the stage my opinion must be paramount to any, or all other.

I readily agree that the distance of time between the benefits of yourself & Mrs Barrett shall be regulated to your wish to the utmost of my power.

As I engage my Company merely for the one Season, the engagement to commence on the opening, which I expect to be the middle of September, I consider myself as free from all charges of expences previous to opening: if expences of travelling were to be allowed to any one, certainly it should be to Mr & Mrs Barrett. Your further thoughts & if possible your determination as soon as convenient will oblige

Yours
W D

Put the above in the post office. Read Reviews. Evening Theatre for Fawcet & Mrs. Seymour "Lad of Spirit & Miller of M:" in y^e house $324.

June 23rd Very warm. attend to accounts. read Reviews. Evening meet Hodgkinson, Wm Johnson & John C Shaw at the Tontine Coffee house after executing the bonds we proceeded to consider the business: Hodgkinson acknowledged that I had reaped no advantage from the business I am to pay him for, but states that he leaves me in possession of business from which I have much to expect and burthen him with the dreadfull encumbrance (as he now represents it) of the Haymarket Theatre. He asserted in positive terms that when he thought of going to Boston and gained my permission, he had no idea of seperating his interest from mine: I was so shocked at this terrible falshood, that I contradicted it in the most plain & unequivocal terms & asserted that I was not only then convinced that <*such*> his intention was a total seperation of interest but was now convinced of it, and could prove it to the gentlemen. This assertion he brought forward as a proof that he had no intention of breaking dissolving the agreement in respect to y^{e} 5 years connection. He made no reply to this charge of falshood. He seems to rest his principal hope of compensation on the idea of being left with the Hay Market as a burthen upon where he expects, he says, to sink $2000 this summer! The Arbitrators are to meet again, and to give their award before the 5th July. Read Review.

June 24th Sunday. read review. I called upon Gamage & mentioned to him Hodgkinson's assertion respecting the seperation of interests: he (G) says he "cannot be enough astonished that he should make an assertion which all his actions gives the lie to."

[To William Johnson and John C. Shaw, Arbitrators]

Gentlemen

I came forward on Saturday to submit to your decision all differences between John Hodgkinson & myself, supposing ye particular question to be: What compensation shall Wm Dunlap make to John Hodgkinson for the use of certain property appertaining to <*John Hodgkinson*> him for the term of two years, <*leaving it with you to decide upon the compensation due*> to be estimated, either <*from*> by the value of the property, or <*from*> by the chance of profit from the use of it: the actual profit or advantage being out of question as it is agreed and acknowledged that said Dunlap has received no advantage?" But Mr Hodgkinson having asserted to you that he is <*willing*> is & has been constantly willing & ready to fulfill a certain agreement which was presented to, & left with, you, thereby making me appear as the person originally wishing and intending to break said agreement, I hope you will examine into the assertion so far as to convince yourselves whose original wish intention & proposition it was to seperate interests & thereby annull said agreement; and secondly, whether Mr H had it in his power or has it even now in his power to fulfill said agreement: for the purpose of making this investigation, I beg of you to call upon Mr

Hodgkinson to bring forw[d] 3 letters written by me to him since the first of June, & on me for two letters written by him to me: these letters will lead to enquiries, which nothing but Mr H's before mentioned assertion, and a subsequent assertion which I will immediately notice, should have induced me to bring forward. Mr H's second assertion is, that "in seperating himself from me, he never had an idea of seperating our interests." By this *second* assertion Mr H supports his *first;* and if both are granted, the impression is, that Mr Hodgkinson's intention in going to Boston was merely to carry on our mutual business for our mutual advantage, while I remained here for the same purpose; but that *I,* taking advantage of his not being ready, to the hour, to fulfill the letter of the contract between us, had insisted upon annulling it altogether; thereby in addition to other injuries throwing Mr H into an inferior & myself keeping possession of a superior business, and burthening Mr Hodgkinson with a contract for the H M Theatre in Boston, highly prejudicial to him. That such must be the inference from the statement of Mr H, I <*leave*> am certain you will see on examining the assertions <*themselves*> & <*from*> the letters before mentioned. <*& your own sense will*> it therefore becomes an indispensable duty in me, to attempt to *prove* to you, Gentlemen, that the seperation here contemplated, (viz. Mr H's going to Boston to take possession of both Theatres and to manage both a Summer & Winter company and leaving me, after the expiration of y[e] then existing lease of, or agreement for, y[e] N Y, here, to hire it anew in my own name & engage a Company for it) was originally suggested & proposed by him & that it was meant, consider'd & proposed by Mr Hodgkinson <*and myself*>, as a compleat seperation of interest; that, the time of seperation was on both sides so far anticipated, as that arrangements were made, by mutual acquiescence or agreement, on the ground of seperate interest; <*that Mr H has from various circumstances was not enabled*> that, <*it*> for the above & other reasons Mr Hodgkinson could not fulfill the original contract, and, that tho' I should be left by Mr Hodgkinson in a business ever so profitable, while he takes another, however inferior (not that I am by any means convinced that this is the truth), it is a change of his seeking, not mine; that he has made his election and that I am left to conduct a business of great risque contrary to my wishes, a business never of my seeking but which I was induced unhappily to engage in at the solicitation of Mr H.

And to *represent;* that had not Mr Hodgkinson, asked my permission to seperate interests & *proposed* to take upon himself the H M Theatre, I should have exerted myself to have otherwise disposed of the <*Hay-*> contract for said Theatre, which I considered & still consider as capable of being made advantageous to him, tho' heretofore ruinous to me.

In respect to Mr Hodgkinson's being ready & willing to fulfill the original agreement, and having never had an idea of seperating interests from me, he has given you assertions. Of the *contrary* I offer you proofs, in his own handwriting, from his words to others, from actions performed by him, and others by me under his sanction, encouragement or direction.

With esteem, your obliged friend

W D

Read Reviews.

June 25th Made an average of the receits of the New Theatre during the 13 weeks of stock business which I found to be $333 a night including the centage due to the proprietors, exclusive of that, 323. This estimate I gave Wm Johnson, together with a supposition that the profit on the business may be $700. I gave him likewise my letter, to himself & Shaw, & we had some conversation on the subject. Attend to accounts. After dinner Hallam called on me: he wishes the last night the Theatre shall be open & to have no assistance from Hodgkinson: he is very bitter against Hodgkinson and tells stories from which he draws harsh conclusions respecting Hodgk's honesty. Read reviews. Hopkins calls on me, we talked of Chemistry, state of manners and opinions in France; he recommends Dupuy's book on the origin of Religions. Drink tea at John Cozines, my old acquaintance Mrs Depeyster and her daughter-in-law Mrs Peale [36] were there, and Mr Peale the Painter & Museum owner. pass an hour at M: Rogers's.

[June] 26th Attend to business. Agree with Mr Hewitt, who is to lead my Orchestra next season and attend to the getting up of Opera's for $14 per week. Read in Review. Afternoon walk to Williamson's Nursery. Call on Mitchill. Miller was with him, reading a paper for y^e^ Repository, on Fever, sweating, application of water &c. Drink tea at Henry Rogers's. Evening Theatre, for Hoggs

[36] Elizabeth De Peyster, daughter of William and Elizabeth (Brasher) De Peyster, married May 30, 1791, Charles Willson Peale, of Philadelphia. *N. Y. Reformed Dutch·Church Marriages* (*Coll. of N. Y. Gen. Soc.* I), 265; *N. Y. Journal,* June 8, 1791; William Kelby's MSS. notes on the DePeyster family, in the library of the N. Y. Historical Society.

benefit, Clandestine Marriage, in y[e] house $316. Mrs Hogg played Mrs Heidelberg, and certainly with much spirit.

[June] 27th Attend to business. Mrs Melmoth call'd on me by appointment. Circumstances had prevented my send[g] the letter to her concerning her business. She agrees with me to exert & accomodate. I mention'd the character in the Italian Monk & she said she was wrong and ought not to have objected to it. I agreed to allow her $25. She again mentioned Miss R Ryder, and is to write for her to come out. I promised to pay her passage on her articling with me for the usual time in such cases. Hodgkinson let me know yesterday that he expected or wanted Everdel to go with him as his leader. I told him that E had applied to me for an engagement as first violin under Hewit, & teacher of the singers & that I had agreed with him for 12 dollars. he complained of the man, mentioned his articles, proposed giv[g] me the articles of the Seymours, he as his division tak[g] Everdels, and then compelling him to go to Boston. I told him I would not be an obstacle in his way of having E, but that I was engaged to him, and promised to speak to him. I call on Wm Henderson: he finds fault with Pollock for relinquishing y[e] Centage on benefits & prohibits it for those to come. He says the Chandeliers for the Theatre are here. I mentioned to him Hodgkinson's assertions in respect to seperating from me, and his insolence on occasion of my offer to engage him. He utter'd his surprize & contempt. Hodgkinson has engaged himself & wife to sing at the paltry public gardens [37] on the Battery. Call on Hopkins: he goes tomorrow to Litchfield: he says Trumbull had like to have been shut up in Paris last Fall, by aid of David, & showing the plates from Bunker hill & Montgomery he was dismissed with commendation. Tyler makes a rout on acc[t] of having the centage to pay

[37] Joseph Corré's Columbia Garden, near the junction of State and Pearl Streets, New York City. See G. C. D. Odell, *Annals of the New York Stage,* II, 36; I. N. P. Stokes, *Iconography of Manhattan Island,* III, 977; VI, 623.

on his wifes benefit: he has publish'd flaming bills, in which Mr Anthony Pasquin & his Masque make a figure. Look over the acc^{t} of Pasquin & Watkins blackguardism as given in ye Thespian Mag: Wm Johnson call'd on me: he says Shaw mentioned £1000 as compensation to Hodgkinson, & he, (Johnson) £500: that Shaw talks of the business in the same manner Hodgkinson did, seeming merely to repeat his crude ideas: & that Shaw had Mention'd Cozine as a third person to decide. Walk with my Wife. Read Review. Genl Heard wth us.

June 28th Attend to business. Call at Gaines: people seem to be agitated respecting the state of our political affairs & the heat of our Government. Examine with Martin into ye state of the old Wardrobe. Read Reviews. Drink tea at G M W's. Call at W W W's.

[June] 29th Attend to business. Read Reviews. Walk out of town with the Boy & Girl to see our militia parade. Evening Theatre, Mrs Tyler's night "She stoops to conquer" in which the fat old woman advertised her last appearance & *did* Miss Neville: to this was added Mr Williams alias Anthony Pasquin's afterpiece "The federal Oath or <*Columbians*> Americans strike home": this piece is certainly without rival in the Drama, unless it may be Milns's "Flash in the pan": this last by the by is a misnomer, for the *piece* undoubtedly *went off*—and never will be heard of again. The benevolent intention of the benevolent Mr Williams in his piece—of patch'd work—is to inculcate some grand and novel political truths, Such as, that, we ought to damn all Frenchmen, and that, "two yankee boys can beat four mounseers"

[June] 30th Mr Hallam took me aside and express'd his wish again to take a night after Hodgkinson is gone: I promised him the Theatre, I told him, after Hodgkinson's departure I should go to Amboy & return again to set the people at work at the House & that before they begun he could take the night which should cost him for the house, whatever it should cost me. Read in System of Nature. Ev^{g} at W W W's.

July 1st Sunday. Very warm. Write at the Theatre. Read "System of Nature" Gamage called on me to let me know that Shaw had called upon him as the third arbitrator from which it appears that S & J cannot agree.

[July] 2nd Still warmer. Running about to obtain from the Committee the endorsements they promised me. Read in System of Nature. Evening at M: Rogers's.

[July] 3rd Still intemperately warm. Read in System of Nature. Afternoon Showers. C. B. Brown arrives from Phil: last from Princeton & takes up his abode wth me. He has brought on his 2d novel but not compleated.

[July] 4th Noise & parade. Walk with Brown. Read in Wieland. Evening walk.

[July] 5th Attend to business. Write to Bates & offer him $20 per week salary. Evening Wm Johnson gave me the award of the Arbitrators: pass some time at Sharpless's with Johnson & Brown. After supper B reads his Novel to self & Wife, as far as he has gone.

[July] 6th Exceed[ing]ly busy in putting affairs into some order before Hodgkinson leaves me: see him & take from him, his book of the Boston business & some statement of Hartford. Evening at Mr Coits with my wife & G M W & wife, call at James Watson's to see Mrs Woolcot.

[July] 7th preparing accounts. Go with Hodgkinson to Wm Johnson's: I agree to buy of him all his part of the Wardrobe, Music, Scenery Musical instruments, properties &c &c to pay him $1600, in notes distantly due. Mr press'd Mr Johnson to get the papers ready a conveyance of the property free from encumbrance, & a bond exonerating me from any bargain, contract &c &c made by him in Boston or elsewhere: we parted and I made out according to promise a statement of his acc^{t} with me upon supposition as the books are not in sufficient forwardness. Gamage hinted to me that the 2 Miss Westrays were going with Hodgkinson. Mrs Hallam sent for me & told me that Miss Westray was going with the Simpsons, but that Eleonora wished to stay if she could be assured that I would employ her: I told Mrs Hallam that I looked upon myself as bound to the young Ladies —she wished such an assertion in writing & I gave it without addressing it to any one. The Hallams think Hodgkinson wishes Miss E Westray in order to injure me & Mrs Hallam says, that he said publicly at the Theatre that [I] could not keep it open 6 weeks. Thus while he was representing the advantages of the great business he was leaving me in, to the Arbitrators to enhance their award, he was trying to ruin my credit with the performers.

[July] 8th Sunday. Smith comes home. I got the papers from Johnson & called on Hodgkinson. I likewise carried the rough statement of my acc^{t}: he was at the Coffee House: we went up stairs: he by degrees objected to every part of my charge: Dr Gamage who was with him below before I came, tho' I knew it not, & to whom I had shown my acc^{t} yesterday, was call'd up: Mr H objected to paying me interest on 1580 advanced him more than a year ago. Gamage had yesterday told me that I should not do myself justice if I did not charge it. now appealed to, he said nothing: the conversation descended into altercation. I express'd my contempt of Hodgkinson very freely & left him, with Gamage. I called on Johnson again, & mentioned circumstances. Hallam sent for me: he had been with Hodgkinson before I was, & swears he is the most impudent Lyar breathing: he threatens to arrest him. Read "Canibal's progress" Afternoon Gamage called on me, & after some preliminary conversation told me that Hodgkinson had executed the bond & conveyance & he doubted not but that our account could be adjusted &c. I told him that it was Mr Hodgkinson's business in compliance with the award to present to me the papers & that I was ready in return to give him the Notes, after which I must look for security for my book debt, & if Mr Hodgk: attempted to leave town without giving me such security, I should arrest him. Gamage proposed that the ballance which appeared to be due to me on the books should be deducted from the sums awarded & my notes only given for the remainder: we pledging ourselves to settle any error amicably. I agreed & he went away requesting me not [to] go from home as he proposed that H & self should meet. After tea, Gamage returned & proposed from H that the bond & conveyance should be left with him (Gamage) untill I should be enabled to make out my account current, the particulars of which he should compare wth the books, and that he as H's attorney, in which capacity he assured me had full powers should be authorized to deliver the bond & conveyance, and deducting the ballance due me by book from the sum awarded, receive notes for the remainder & give me a full acquittal. To this I agreed. Hodgkinson proposed leaving the question of interest to any two merchants. Evening Smith with us & afterwards, Johnson & Mitchell. Gamage again called, & shewed me the bond & conveyance signed in presence of Gamage & Hyde (which last came with him, apparently to witness my assurance that I would not arrest H.) In Hyde's presence I mentioned the terms of the settlement saying, I wanted nothing more than security for any ballance due me from the books, to sett off against the notes awarded, but as the ballance was to be deducted from the notes I was satisfied. On mentioning these circumstances to Johnson he thought well of the arrangement, but wished me to be certain of Gamage's powers.

July 9th call on Gamage who shews me his powers & assures me that Hodgkinson before him & Hyde, assented to this mode of settlement saying that he would throw no obstacle in the way, by raising objections to my acc^{t} but would rather sacrifice 2 or 300 doll^{s} to accomodation. Gamage on his part assured me of his disposition to see the affair well settled. See Ciceri & put him in possession of the house as my agent. pass an hour with Smith & Wolcot. Evening Brown & G M W drank tea together my wife being out: go wth B to W W W's. Walk.

[July] 10th Examine into the state of the property bo^{t} by me of Hodgkinson. I purchased of him all his Theatrical property, as well as that which he purchased of Hallam & that which was purchased in conjunction with Hallam, as all that had been bought by him & me. I find that he has carried off with him several coats & dresses of the first description, and of Wardrobe charged to y^{e} Co. (himself & me) at $205, as bo^{t} at Boston, & of course now altogether mine, he has taken the whole: He has taken off, by express orders to his servants, who took them during my absence, a pair of Kettle drums & a double bass, (cost $200): He has taken more than half the Music, part Hallam's & mine & part mine alone: & he has taken all the prompt books of plays done the last year & some others. Went with Hallam to Gamage (his Attorney) to let him know that we should demand these things of him in form. Dine at G M W's wth Brown & Miss Moore: Drink tea at same place. Visit at W W W's & M. Rogers's. Brown & I read part of Hugh Trevor together.

[July] 11th About starting for Amboy but stop'd by rain. I find that Hodgkinson has employed a man for a long time back, in copying such Music as he intended selling and leaving, and that all the music paper used for his copies he has expressly ordered to be charged to the Co. (Himself & me) value $20. This is a specimen of the continual false charges & pilfering of this ——— Hodgkinson. Began an essay on Newspapers & their Editors.

drink tea at W W W's, then go G M W's where we take up our abode for the Night.

[July] 12th After breakfast leave G M W's and crossing Paulus hook ferry: my Wife, Children & self, proceed for Amboy: arrive at Woodbridge about ½ past 1, dine with General Heard, who with his wife attends us to Amboy. £67.15

[July] 13th Walk out to see my Farm. Corn not so forward as expected. Buckwheat sown last monday. Attend to the children. Evening visit at Mrs Parkers, the old Lady is at Bordenton at Dr Burns's with Mrs Smith of whose recovery there are no hopes.

[July] 14th Out with my gun; discharged 5 times & kill'd a snipe, a Bittern, a Dove, a High hole, and a Woodcock: the last on the wing. John writes a letter in French to Dangel. Read in Gibbon. Drink tea with Mrs Terrill. Evening wind & rain, quite cool weather ever since we came.

[July] 15th Sunday. Walk out to Woodbridge to look for a passing Stage to return to N: Y: but find that the Sunday is so strictly enforced as to prevent their running; and after passing an hour at Heards in pleasant chat with Bloomfield, I return to Amboy taking in my rout my Meadow on the Sound. John reads to me in Hume, and some Letters of J B Rousseau in y^e "Pieces interressantes." Afternoon with my Wife & Children walk out to the Farm.

[July] 16th Walk out with my Gun. At 11 OClock set off to join the stage at Woodbridge, get in one at 12. Arrive at N: Y: about ½ past 6. Lodge at W W W's, who has gone with his Wife & children to Northampton. Rec^d a letter from Barrett, complaining of my silence, from which it appears that mine had not reached him on the 9th.

[July] 17th Write to Barrett; a few words with a copy of my last; I mention that I believe Hodgkinson is my enemy to guard B: against representations which I have reason to expect. Call on Johnson: C B B there. Receive Weekly Mag: 6 numbers. See Gamage. Hallam calls on me. Read in Weeky Mags. Dr Aiken [38] observes that in june the music of the Groves has ceased in England or nearly so, and after the end of that Month no birds are heard except the stone Curlew whistling late at night, the yellow hammer, Goldfinch & Golden crested Wren now & then chirping; yet have I heard ye ignorant & prejudiced English when here complain of the silence of our groves when now, the middle of July we have the cheerfull song of the Robin (M: Thrush) the sweet notes of the Boblink, sometimes waving on the reedy grass & at others soaring like the English skylark, the whistle of the quail, the five notes of the Meadow Lark, the occasional song of the Cat bird, the King birds chatterings, with various others some of them melodious tenants of the bushes & hedges for which I have no name. Receive a letter from Barrett acknowledging the receipt of mine. Dine with G M W: Drink tea with Johnson Smith & Brown. Unwell from pain in my breast.

[July] 18th Write to Barrett.

Sir

A few hours after putting a letter for [you] in the P Office in return for yours of the 9th I recd one from you dated the 12th You give me to understand that Mr Wignel has made you *liberal* offers, believe me Sir I <*cannot*> shall not become a competitor with Mr Wignel in *offers;* if Mr Wignel's offers are more eligible than mine, the prospect of their fulfillment as good, and the business he <*will*> can give to you & Mrs Barret better, it is your duty to prefer Mr Wignel to me. However, <*Sir,*> as I said in my letter of yesterday, it is not pecuniary considerations that are of the first object with me, and as you say Salary "is more than a secondary consideration" with you, I hope we may yet meet.

Before I go any further, give me leave to rectify an error in yours in respect to a declaration of mine that I looked on Mrs B & your-

[38] "June," from Dr. John Aikin's *Calendar of Nature,* was printed in *The Weekly Magazine,* vol. II, no. 18, June 2, 1798.

self "as the first in the profession." my words were "as I look upon both you & Mrs Barrett as *occupying* the first stations of the profession"—meaning thereby, the first situations and business; if my words have not conveyed this meaning, it is an error of composition. I should not notice this but from my dread of misunderstandings.

I am fully aware of the interest of a Manager to keep up the opinion of the public in respect to the performers of his Company. it is a justice he owes to himself and to the Gentlemen & Ladies, who engage wth him. But on the other hand, how pitiable must be the situation of the Director of a Theatre who having several performers of merit cannot get up a piece because it has but one *first* character, & each says, I play that or none. As to Mrs Barrett's business, I stated generally as an example, Mrs Johnson's, and the younger parts of Tragedy which Mrs Melmouth had heretofore in possession. Of the characters mentioned in your last letter I will at once say which are at her service: "Jane Shore, Imogen, Portia, Lady Townly, Beatrice, Estifania, Violante, Rosalind." Of the characters mentioned for yourself, there are at your service "Felix, Ranger, Vapid, L[ord] Townly, C Surface, *<Alexander,>* Rover,"—perhaps some of the others as they are not engaged, but I will keep some discretionary power in my own hands at all events. I could add to your list many which I think you would not object to, such as "Nominal, Bastard in K[ing] John, Harry Herbert, Dumont or Shore in Jane Shore." I could mention many more, and many more which would fall to Mrs Barrett. Belcour in the West Indian is probably *<your>* the only part you have done in that play, yet I should expect you *<to give it up & play>* to do the Major if circumstances required it. In short, Sir, taking into consideration *<your>* the expression in your last that if you can "render" me a "service" *<you>* I "sh^{d} never find" you "retreat from the extent of your power to oblige me." I think we shall not disagree and if you can conform to my ideas of business, *<so far as to go occasionally out of your line>* the addition of Salary shall not be the bars between us. Mr Hodgkinson's return to N. Y. next Winter I look upon as impossible. My intention is to open the Theatre about the middle of September & keep it open untill the middle of June. With every sentiment of respect & sincere wish for that mutual accommodation which may bring us together I remain &c

Breakfast wth Smith Johnson & Brown. Attend to accounts. Dine with old Mrs Woolsey. Gamage with me in the Afternoon to examine my acc^{t} against Hodgk: as far as I had gone he approved. He gave me his history. Call at M: Rogers nobody home: same at Smith & Johnson's. Drank tea at W W W's: read in [Jonathan] Edwards on Free will & on Original Sin.

[July] 19th Attending to accounts. Mr Hallam call'd on me: he talks of going to Albany & playing next month. Dine as yesterday. pass'd this [evening] at Columbia in Mitchills apartments, where was formed a Society entitled "the American Mineralogical Society." We chose officers & adopted an advertisement for publication. The members are, Dr Mitchill, Edwd Miller, E H Smith, Mr Warner, Solomon Simpson, Wm Johnson, Saml Miller, C B Brown <*& myself*> Saml Hopkins & myself.

[July] 20th previous to my leaving town L Gardie had called upon me & informed me that he had some Music in his possession, the remains of what had been given him by Mr Hodgkinson to copy, and that Mr Hodgkinson had gone away in his debt $20. I told him the music belonged to the Theatre & not to Mr H & he said it was at my service; I sent for it & he was not at home. Yesterday I call'd at his lodgings about 9 OClock in y^{e} morning, he said Mrs Gardie was out & had the key of the place where the music was, asked when I should be at home & promised to call on me that day. This morning between 8 & 9, I met Hallam, he put on a woefull face "My dear Dunlap what I shall tell you will be a Terrible shock. Gardie has murder'd his wife & himself." I concluded, knowing they were poor, that it had been a matter determined between them. What I shall relate of the former history of these people I collect from Ciceri & Pellesier. Gardie was the only child of a french Nobleman the Kings receiver general at La Rochelle & possess'd of great wealth: the young man, idle in his habits from the expectation of inheriting, was sent out to St Domingo with goods & money on a trading Voyage by his father. Here he met with a beautifull Woman, the Mother of a male infant, fascinating in her manners, and as an actress, for that was her profession, excelling all competitors and charming every beholder. This Woman had lived as a wife with a performer of the name of Maurison, who was the father of her infant, but finding that he was not faithfull to her bed, she seperated herself from him, & he went to France, where, being a man of abilities & having acquired property at the Cape, he was elected one of the Municipality of Lyons, after the revolution, & was afterwards murdered with the other citizens of Lyons during the reign of Terrorism. Gardie & the fascinating Actress became united & she accompanied him to La Rochelle, certainly not as his Wife, as she continued to exercise her professional abilities. The revolution although it deprived the elder Gardie of his title, neither took from him his wealth nor his office, & he is said to be still receiver general at La Rochelle. One evening, at the Theatre, the Audience called Madame Gardie to sing the Marseillais Hymn, which she refusing, their rage was so great that it became necessary for her to fly the Country; she accordingly returned to Cape Francois, accompanied by M: Gardie. On the insurrection of the Blacks, they fled to this Country, where they have lived as man & wife, he principally supported by her salary as a Dancer. During the last Winter & spring, she had no employment, the Theatre of N Y not being able to support the enormous Company which Mr Hodgkinson had loaded it with. She however offer'd her services, free of expence, on condition that she should be entitled to a benefit; which was granted to her, but failed. Gardie had received some emolument from copying Music for Hodgkinson's private acc^{t}: Hodgkinson as was said, left town & in his debt. Gardie was now in debt & to his conception void of resource. He turned his thoughts to La Rochelle: his wife had often solicited him to write to his Father for assistance, without effect: he now wished her to return thither with him, but she remembered the cause of her flight and refused. It appears that a seperation, whether final or temporary I know not, had been determined, he had engaged his passage in a Vessel for France, and she had been the evening before her death at Mr Hallam's consulting as to the means of enabling her to return to St Domingo. On the fatal & horrible night, Gardie, <*perhaps in consequence*> occupied a small bed in third story, in the same chamber in which his wife and her boy now 9 or 10 years of age, <*like-wise*> slept in another bed. The boy awoke in the night & found himself in his supposed father's arms, who was in the act of removing him from his mother to place him in the other bed; on the child's asking why he did this, he bade him be quiet & not wake his Mama, laid him in the bed he had removed him to & the boy again fell asleep. Starting from sleep at the sound [of] a groan which he recognized as <*his*> proceeding from his Mother, the little lad in terror called out, "What is the matter papa? What is the matter with Mamma?" "Hush" was the reply "Your mama is not well, but she sleeps, dont disturb her." Again the child slept, unconscious that Death in his most horrid & threefold form of murder assassination & suicide then stood at his side and half his task atcheiv'd. A noise of falling struggling & groans a third time awoke the terrified boy, who receiving no answer to his repeated calls upon his father and mother, left his bed, and groping in the dark felt the yet warm corse of his father, on the floor in the middle of the chamber, felt the blood as it streamed from the wounds & unknowing what he did, pressed his little fingers into the gaping gashes whence life had scarcely escaped. Wild with confusion and terror the child fled from the room & leaving the door open ran down stairs & called upon the Mistress of the house. His tale was incoherent. His papa & his mama,—something was the matter with them—he could not tell what—his papa & his Mama—. His cries were not attended to, he was desired to go to bed: repulsed thus & not daring to return to the dreadfull chamber, he sought the bed of one of the Negroe servants & crept trembling to his side. Towards day the Dogs of the house found their way to the scene of blood and with the most piteous cries gave vent to their feelings. Several times they ran howling up & down the stairs, before the family were alarm'd. On entering the room the miserable murderer lay on the floor weltering in blood, his right hand above his head still grasping the knife, his face & limbs horridly distorted;

he had been obliged to inflict several wounds on himself before he fell, she had been killed by one blow & lay as if asleep. The weapon was a Carving knife, new & apparently purchased for the purpose. When I last spoke with this man, he had probably already prepared, and perhaps had concealed about his person the instrument of murder & suicide.

[July] 21st Quit N: Y: in the sloop for Amboy, becalmed. leave the sloop & cross staten Island arrive about 2 OClock. Visit at Mrs Parkers. Gardie's affair is much a topic of conversation. Susan Parker appears to be zealously a religionist & there is with Mrs Parker as a visitant, an old Lady whose religious zeal goes to enthusiasm "The principles which prevail in these days lead to suicide & every kind of sin" "Ah! this is philosophy!" I represented, a conviction of duty to his fellow creatures as sufficient to withhold man from self-murder. Nothing but the fear of God it was said could be sufficient. I suggested that Gardie might be a christian by profession; it was replied that he had not religion enough to prevent his committing these crimes; then, I rejoin'd, it is evident he had not the fears of religion sufficiently impress'd upon him to prevent the evil; upon a supposition that duty to his fellow creatures was the rule he had adopted, it is evident he had not that duty sufficiently impressed upon him: When guilty of this murder he was under the influence of monstruous error; but it neither proves the inefficacy of religious fear or philosophic benevolence, as a motive, it only proves that neither cause of action was present. The old Lady was troubled in spirit & became silent. In the course of this conversation Mrs P related a curious case of suicide which happened at Bordentown last Winter. A married Lady whose Husband was absent, but who lived in affluence and gaity, bless'd with a fine child which she nurs'd, undertook to put a period to her existence & executed it by throw[g] herself into the river through an air-hole in the ice. She had often avowed her opinions of the justifiability of self murder & disavow'd a belief in a future state. She had previous to the act been in ill health. She had been in company the afternoon preceeding the evening of her death: she dressed herself for the purpose, taking off her rings & trinkets & carefully depositing them. She was tracked in the snow to the river & the hole in the ice: returning tracks were likewise found & a servant asserts that she went to the sideboard, <*after*> at time of her supposed return, and pouring out half a tumbler of brandy took it out of the room. The tumbler was found empty in the Entry: her body was found some days after.

[July] 22d Sunday. Walk with the children. John reads a french lesson to me under the trees in my persimond grove. read Brown's continuation of "Wieland" to my Wife & in W Magazine. Walk with my Wife & Children.

[July] 23d Work in the Garden. Endeavour to ascertain the lines of lot purchased from Mr Kearney. Afternoon read and attend to ye Children. Write on a second essay for Weekly Mag: entitled "Encore." [39]

[July] 24th Walk out to Woodbridge to take my passage in the stage for N: Y: on my way pass thro' my Orchard & observed on one of the little trees 22 apples: call on Bloodgood: call on General Heard. Arrive at N: Y: at 8 OClock being long in crossing the Ferry.

[July] 25th Breakfast with S, J & B. Call on Gamage who tells me that Bates is in town waiting to see me. Ten Eyk hav^g mentioned that Bates was at Tyler's I walked out thither but he had removed. Tyler says Williams (Ant^y Pasquin) is sick & calling me aside applied in his behalf for *a situation* in the Theatre for him next season. I met Gamage there & walked home with

[39] "Encore", signed "W. D.", was printed in *The Weekly Magazine,* III, pp. 41-42, August 11, 1798.

him: he says Mrs Hallam says many true things of Hodgkinson. Hallam is about letting his house & going lodgings: he has taken Mrs Gardie's little boy & buried the man & woman, this, as his Box book is open for a benefit tomorrow night, is repeated in many ways in the papers & his humanity much insisted on. Dine with M: Rogers; Major Davenport there & two other Connecticut gentlemen: much talk after dinner on politics. Drink tea wth S, J & B, & read part of the remainder of Wieland, the first proof of which was under correction of the trio. Visit G M W.

[July] 26th Finish read[g] Wieland at S, & J's we had some conversation in respect to proposed alterations suggested to B. Attend at the Theatre; see Bates; he expresses his wish to join the Company. I agree to give the first salary or equal to any man, (which is $25). He gave me a list of characters & I am to see him again tomorrow at 10 Dine at G M W. Look over play bills to make a list of Characters for Bates. Bates is to write to Fox to engage him as second singer or to divide with Tyler: he says Whitlock desired him to say to me that he is not ingaged. Drink tea at G M W's. Evening Theatre, Mr Hallam's extra night. "Rivals & Poor Soldier" in y[e] house $520.20.

[July] 27th preparations are making to receive the president with honour as he returns home through this City where he is hourly expected. I called & asked Hallam, if, in case of Mr Adams staying long enough, he would assist me in giving a play for monday evening. He said "Certainly, ever[y] thing in his power I might command." Bates disapoints me at 10 OClock. M Judah informed me that his Father is in Town & wishes to see me; I met him between 11 & 12. What he had to impart is that Moses is married. I had heard the report but hardly credited it. The old man is much chagrin'd and well he may be. He says Moses's acc[t] is, that at his aunt Cable's he often met wth the girl (Miss Peck sister to Wm Peck Merchant Tailer) related to the Cable's, that they became intimate & familiar & in process of time the Lady told him that she was pregnant or told her brother (I am not certain) the brother demanded marriage and by the aid of menaces &c &c prevail'd. The Lady miscarried. Moses does not wish to have her for a wife & much distress it is to be presumed is the consequence.

[July] 28th Breakfast with G M Woolsey & wife & borrow his clothes. See the Judah's Father & son together. The marriage took place last April. I advised to take his wife & treat her as such: I pointed out her unhappy situation & suggested that more tenderness was necessary than even to a Wife in more fortunate circumstances I represented that if there was no circumstance of person or character in the young Lady (she is only 18) that rendered happiness improbable, it was his duty to acknowledge her, & I represented his credit as requiring it. Upon a suggestion that he had not intended or promised marriage, I represented his actions, to a girl in her situation, as implying as much as words could do, & being full as binding. I was obliged to leave them. I went down broadway for the purpose of seeing Malcolm the President's Secretary & meeting him with Mulligan & some other's, I requested Mulligan's introduction; I then mentioned the wish of knowing the president's will in regard to visiting the Theatre, he told me the Pres: would if possible leave town this evening, at any rate tomorrow morning. He told me, on enquiring the meaning of bruises on his face, that he had been assaulted last evening on the Battery, merely from being recognised as ye President's secretary, seized by ye throat & with difficulty rescued. A prosecution is commenced. See & engage Hogg & his wife & Daughter for $30. and then have to rescue him from jail, by giving a certificate of his engagement and a promise to pay 10 dollars weekly of his salary for 4 weeks to his creditor. Engage Bates, to give him $25 for self & wardrobe & 8 dollars a week for his daughters services, and if he gets up a pantomime for me & attends it, 10 Guineas. See Moses Judah and his Father again. Every thing is settled, the young Mrs Judah is to stay at his Aunt Cable's at present, he promises to be a very good husband, and as the old Gentleman says "perhaps everything is for the better." I left town in the E Town boat and landed after dark, walk up to the town, call on M Williamson, sleep at Cutler's tavern.

[July] 29th Sunday. Ride to Amboy in Cutler's chair. All well.

[July] 30th Write to M Judah. Write to Dr Gamage. Begin a regular system of instruction for the Children, John, Read^{g} Hume, Hist: Eng: writing, arithmetic, and French (pieces interesante) Margaret, read^{g} Sandford & Merton & Children's friend, & beginning to write.

[July] 31th Shoot Snipe. Teach Children. Read Weekly Mag: Walk out to my Orchard &c.

Augt 1st Write 2d Essay on Th: for W Mag: call'd "Encore." Teach children. Shoot Snipe. Visit with my Wife. Even^{g} James Palmer arrived.

Augt 2d Rec^{d} letter from Barrett which I thus answer.

Sir

I hasten to acknowledge the receipt of yours of the 25th July, & to express my pleasure that after the explanations that have taken place, we have come to an agreement without the possibility of misunderstanding.

The salary I offered was, for Mrs B. and yourself, $50, you finding your own Wardrobes, Serv^{ts} Dressers &c: you in return demand "for the services of both, *wardrobe* and *all*" $10 more. To this addition I cheerfully assent in consideration of your friendly acquiescence in my ideas of business: but you may well conceive the necessity I am under of having $25 considered as my first salary, I therefore stipulate that you, on your word engage to me, that you shall only make it known that Mrs B & yourself are on the first establishment—let the additional 10 dollars be received & enjoyed but not mentioned; let it be considered in your own minds as an addition for the expensive wardrobe Mrs B's line of acting will require wth dressers &c &c. I perfectly agree with you as to the agreement in form: although I am of opinion that our mutual letters and signatures are from this time binding. Information of Th^{l} transactions & your suggestions will be thankfully received. Hodgkinson, so wore out the "cure for the Heart ach" that I do not think it would draw half a house, but I shall take an oppertunity of writing on to you respecting study. Mr Cooper in playing Octavian, gained so great an advantage over Mr Hodgkinson, that, previous to my correspondence with you, the part was appropriated to him. Wignel, Gardie &c &c. My Tailors shall have orders to serve you in altering your dresses &c when not employ'd for me: further than this I cannot go: & indeed conceive every provision of the kind included in the allowance for wardrobe.

I remain &c &c W D

Copy of Barretts letter, above answered

Boston July 25th

Sir, yours of ye 17 & 18 Came Sat^{y} & monday. I have therefore taken the *first moment* to answer Both & as you have Comply'd with my request of Salary & your Honoring Assurances of Business &c &c, I dont Delay to say, *that you may Depend on Seeing us on or before the middle of Sep^{r}*: perhaps some regular form of agreement may be proper when we meet, not that I Entertain the least Doubt of Your *word* & Honor. I have no objection to the major in the West Indian. If I can render you any service you may command & *confide* in me. I saw the Federal Oath (Anthony P's thing) last Night here & think it might be alter'd for the better do you wish me to prepare for it near the Beginning of the Season. a very *poor house* not more I should suppose than 200$. I suppose you mean me to do y^{e} Rapid. if so I will look over it. if any other parts that you may think of for Either will thank you to mention them. I sh^{d} not have wrote of Mr Wignells letter But from a conduct I think is Due from Man to Man, of returning definative answers as quick as possible, & rest assured Sir, I did not mean it as a Stimulater, for if you wish or Doubt the Authenticity of my word I will in confidence show His letter when I have the pleasure of Seeing you. I have only to request that as soon as this Comes to hand you will favour me with the acc^{t} of it, & hope you will find ever sensible of your *respect attention* and *Friendship*

Yours Most Sincerely
G L Barrett

Wm Dunlap Esq.

I am requested to Beg the Favor of speaking to Mr Gardie sh^{d} he be with you, that if he does not send for his Goods now in a person's hands, they will be *sold*. in your next (which I hope to receive by return of Post) will thank you to mention Salary &c. & I suppose S[r] with many others you forget Octavian, as Mr C has play'd another part in the play in N Y. I have ever been allowed the Taylor of the Theatre to make or alter my Dresses, which I hope you will not object to. Believe me Sir, tho I am a man of Few words; yet you will Ever Find me *Sincere;* Success attend *you.* Mrs B <*joins*> requests to join with me in Respectful Compliments.

Teach my Children. Call on Mr Joseph Taylor and settle the line which divides his land from mine on the hill: he agreeing to its being run as expressed in my Deed. Write to M Judah in answer to one received this morning. Rec[d] a letter from Dr Gamage.

3d Aug[t] Read in [John] Robison's History of a Conspiracy &c. Attempt to take a ride to Woodbridge with a hired Horse & chair but the Creature being used to stop short of our destination, would not go on & we were obliged to yield to him. Walk on the beach with my Wife & little girl.

[Aug.] 4th After breakfast, with little Palmer and my boy each with Fishing tackling & my fowling equipage I proceeding on a sporting expedition: I got a Woodcock a Dove; a lark &c & the boys some fish. Afternoon rain. Read in Robison.

[Aug.] 5 Sunday. With my Wife & children & J Palmer walk to A Bloodgood's: We found two Tulip trees on Bloodgoods ground & one on mine (Liriodendron Tulipifera) The quantity of Grashoppers is immense, many acres of Buckwheat is cut off & much grass destroyed. Read Robison. I should think this Man's character to be similar to Dr Dwight's with more knowledge of the World.

At this time the Snipe are plenty. Dove seem to collect in flocks of five or six. The robin yet sings sweetly & the whistling of the quail is heard in every direction. Many small birds continue their cheerful song, but the songsters who take the lead in May & June are silent. The Locust now is frequent & the evening silence is broken by the Katydid & the cries of the Night Hawk as he pursues his prey, not the song of "Whipoorwill," which is only heard during the season of incubation. The seed vessel of the Liriodendron Tulip: is cone shaped, at this time ab^{t} 1½ inches long, the seeds not ripe. Read Robison.

ANTI-JACOBIN [continued]

"Eight thousand pound, you know, is, as I said a pretty thing, Mr Beardsley, and I looked that Harry should now return and go into some business that should encrease this fortune and his consequence and provide for his young family. Sure enough he came and we were all gladness and joy and thankfulness. The young couple had one or two interviews and then he with a seemingly honest frankness expressed his high satisfaction of my daughters great improvement, and of the prospect of happiness which his union with her promised. I thought this a good opportunity to talk to him about the main chance, you know, Mr Beardsley, so I asked him how he intended to dispose of the £8000. He answered with a smile that it was not a difficult thing for a young man to dispose of a few thousands, and then began to talk on other subjects; but I soon came round again, and telling him at the same time that he must not be offended at the anxiety of a Father for the welfare of his children, at the same time telling him that I considered him as my son now, which to be sure was a little premature as things have turned out—but who could have thought—however as I was saying, I came to the point again & asked whether he intended the £8000, to be used as a Capital in trade, or if he thought [of] buying Landed property and settling in the Country? But he soon knocked me all of a heap. I shall never forget his answer. "My excellent friend" said he "I fear you do not perfectly understand me, and my motives of action, which tho' adopted after the strictest examination I am at present capable of, may be a cause of discontent to you <*after*> when the union shall have taken place which will appear to you as connecting your interests more particularly with mine, therefore I will now give you a brief statement of my plan of establishment, of the manner in which I have already disposed of a part of my Uncles legacy & of the intended appropriation of the remainder.

Augt 6th I rec^{d} this morning a letter from Hodgkinson, in which he tells me that he had rec^{d} my acc^{t} current through Gamage, that he will give his ideas of it in a few days: that there were mistakes in packing up the Wardrobe: that "*if there is any*" music sent to Boston which ought not to be sent thither he will see it return'd: that most of the prompt books that are left are *his!!!*

He offers his service to mark prompt books for me & conclude[s] with requesting me to send him the Music of a long string of Opera's, which he will return before I open. I likewise recd a letter from Mr Judah, by which finding that Ciceri wished my presence in N. Y. I immediately crossed Staten Island & arrived to dinner at W W W's, who had returned home since my last visit: he brought me from Dr Dwight his Sermons against Infidels and from Theodore his 4th July Oration. See Ciceri and settle business with him. See Gamage, and learn that Cooper went to Boston and play'd for Hodgkinson on the 2d night of opening the Theatre and that the 3d night their was no Audience and the Theatre was shut. To Coopers first appearance about $300. Thus it appears that Hodgkinson's campaign is cut short. G attributes it to the Yellow Fever being in the place. See Smith Johnson & Brown & read the additions of the latter to his "Wieland." Call on G M W who is unwell. Brown & I drink tea with W W W after which W W W & I go to look for Kent & find him at Boyds where we past a very agreable evening. Kent had just been reading Mad: Roland and is highly delighted with her, my brother[-in-law] attacked her. The Millers were brought up & condemn'd as democrats: Messrs. Radcliff & Riggs were present.

[Aug.] 7th Breakfast wth S, J & B. Talk on our project of the Weekly Magazine to be published by Swords under us. Call on G M W and then depart for Amboy by the way of Paulus hook with Mad: Roland in my hand in French. Read by the way. Dine at Genl Heards, who with his [wife] being intendg a visit to my family I came down to Amboy wth them. All well.

[Aug.] 8th Call on Mrs Parker and mention to her the regimen for Mrs Smyth suggested by E H S, & mention to her Dr [Thomas] Beddoes's experiment on himself in producing and curing consumption. Take the children with me and Mr Halstead's chain, and measure the lot next to mine (Kearney's) call'd on ye map Barbarie's. I found the fence from the corner as it now stands of Mr Parkers lot (Penns on y[e] map) to Corringtons orchard, 17 c. 50 1., from thence to the road 10c. 15, I then took the 7c. 25 as measured by Compton & self t'other day agreable to the map down the road towards Amboy, from thence as near as I could judge upon the line marked in the map as running S 8 30, E. 8 60, but which I found 9 30 to the remains of the old ditch and if continued to the line as Mr Parker's fence now runs making 10 38. Teach the Children. Afternoon take my gun, and the boys with their fishing rods & go down to Sandy point. About Sun Set the Blackbirds in large flocks come from the fields where they feed and alight upon the Sand. Is this for gravel or salt? I return'd with 18 Blackbirds & Snipe.

[Aug.] 9th Before breakfast, I measured the lot called Penn's on the Map. The line marked on y[e] Map S 34. E. 14 Ch: I made 13 10. I made the distance from the corner of the fence as it now stands to the old ditch 79 links. The line running N E by N 4 degrees Northerly 23 ch. 30, I find right. The line running N W by W 4 degrees, W[ly] I find 12 ch. 14 (on the map 12). Teach the Children. Read Robison. The day very warm.

[Aug.] 10th Still Warmer. Teach the children. Finish Robison's book: a strange mixture knowledge & prejudice, truth & error, and another proof of the avidity with which we make every circumstance bend to the favorite System. With what perseverance these religionists believe or pretend to believe the necessary connection between Religion & morallity: with what impudence inculcate that without Religion a man cannot be virtuous. I yesterday read Theodores Oration. Read in his brothers discourses on Infidel philosophy & begin an answer to them. Read in Madam Rol[d] Evening at Mrs Parkers.

[Aug.] 11th Somewhat Cooler. Teach the Children. Write on answer to D[wight]. Read in Mad: Roland. M: Judah arrived from N: Y: he brought me a new No.

of Medical Repository & 2 Nos. of Weekly Mag. I likewise received a letter from Mrs Simpson requesting an engagement for herself and youngest daughter: [40] & a letter from Hodgkinson to Gamage under cover from the latter to me sent by desire of the former. I will here copy it.

Boston Augt 2^{d} 1798

DOCTOR JOHN GAMAGE

Dr Sir

I have been some time arranging my ideas of Mr Dunlap's acc^{t} current: on examination I find his charging me with the *whole* of the sums sent down to Boston is *right,* for as I *charged* him with a compleat half of all disbursements (that is losses), it operates the same as mony borrow'd from an indifferent person by *me,* which *I* have a right to pay: there are other points I shall object to: I have nothing to do with Mr Solee's transaction & if I understood Mr Dunlap right, those endorsements have been paid to his agent in Charleston; at any rate it was a transaction unauthorized by me; one in which the company was no way concerned, & I did here both for Solee & Williamson the like act of folly, but I never thought of making them a *joint* account, which I *must do,* if Mr Dunlap can substantiate *his.* his Journey to Boston being on the *same business,* is liable to the *same objection* I might with equal or much more propriety charge mine *with* the Company & *back* again, which I have not done: there is a charge of $125 paid Mr Gaine for Mrs Mechtler: Mr. Dunlap, contracted with me to pay half the interest on my remaining Bonds yearly in addition to his purchase, I beg you to remind him of this <*purchase*> circumstance, Mr W Johnson was present at the time & I have his acknowledgement of the fact during a correspondance which took place at the time I was going to leave *York* for *Philadelphia:* Mr Dunlap could not act as *Treasurer* during last summer; the few transactions he was troubled with, I could have got done from various individuals, such as advancing a little Money to those of the company who had dependencies at N: Y: the whole of which I believe does not exceed 200 dollars exclusive of what he sent *me:* Add to which it was his own request & wish to stay in York with an offer to receive *no emolument.* Also as to receiving of 5 D^{lls} p^{r} week interest; if *I* have charged interest in my account of Salary it is *right* otherwise it cannot be: to the best of my recollection *I have not:* that however is a point he can easily ascertain: 26 D^{lls} charged for Mr Hughes, given by Mr Dunlap to his wife, I have no memorandum of, nor recollection of *my ever receiving:* if Mr Hughes can satisfy me it is right I will allow it:

[40] Elizabeth A. Westray.

Mr Dunlap cannot charge me with anything respecting *Crosby,* because since the transaction he has signed him a *general release & at the time,* took the affair on himself: if I was to be charg'd with a part I ought to have [been] consulted before I *entirely gave away* the debt. *Mr. Campbell* objects to allowing the seven Dollars charged to *him.* As I never expect to ask the president, or his suite, for their places last year I cannot consent to be charged with *his half* back again; if it is ever paid, I will certainly allow it, but I understand *since,* that the President with his Suite, regards all public exhibitions when he is persuaded to visit them, as *invitations* & not meant to be accounted for: he visited Mr Chalmers at Philadelphia on the same ground:—the six suits of Armor, are not sent & therefore the charge must be withdrawn: and the *Arm & thigh pieces,* being <*sent*> sewn on some Boston stock dresses were sent & I will *take care* they shall be return'd by Mr Cooper The Breast Plates, Helmets, Belts &c are in New York: Mr Vals wardrobe Leonard packed supposing I had never render'd an account to the partnership of it, I am *willing* however to keep it at the charge made to me, tho' since I bought it, it has been used 9 months on joint account: I will thank you to communicate this to Mr. Dunlap as early as possible.

your friend J H

This is a copy exact, with the pointings and markings. On another page is the following

Ballance sent on from Mr Dunlap			1633.72
Error by Solees endorsements	750	375	
Dº Acting as Treasurer Summer	320	160	
Journey to & from Boston	60	30	
Six suits of compleat Armor	100	100	
Manuscript Cure for a heartach left in N.Y.	14	14	
President & governors suite	52	26	
Mr Hughes, no memorandum of	26	26	
Mr Crosby's debt	60	30	
Mr Campbell	7	7	
Hugh Gaine for Mrs Mechtler	125	125	
	—	—	893.—
			740.72
p^d since to John Pew	8	4	
To John Patten	4	2	
To Miss Scott	10	5	
To Mrs Brett balance	3	1.50	
To Miss Brett 3 weeks & Two nights Salary owing when Theatre closed	51 33/100	25.66½	
			38.16½
			$702.55½

Vals
Regimental suit compleat inventoried at...... 16 D^{lls}
Regimental waisc^{t} & Breeches white d^{o}....... 12.6

22

680.55½

What Mr Dunlap means by 81 D^{lls} paid to Mr Wools 54 Weeks at 1½ D^{lls} I know not & will thank him for an explanation thro' you *81 D^{lls}*

P. S. There is a general alarm in Boston respecting the Yellow Fever, & the Theatre is temporarily closed in consequence.

On examination we find not come of Mr Vals wardrobe
A Blue Regimental & New Kerseymere waiscoat & Breeches..16 d^{ls}
Also white Dimity or Jane Waisc^{t} & Breeches belonging to white Regimentals ....12 d^{ls}

Augt 12th Sunday. Write to Dr J Gamage

Dr Sir/

I yesterday evening received yours enclosing Mr Hodgkinson's letter, which I return with this.

Indeed sir I cannot but regret that you should be induced to prevent by your interference my taking legal methods to <*prevent*> hinder this man from absconding in the precipitate manner he did: not from any doubt of the goodness of your intentions or <*from any dou-*> of your strenuous endeavours to see justice done in this business, but from a fear, suggested by my knowledge of the man, that you have been deceived. My reliance is that you are a man of business, responsibility and good sense & that I have your word that I shall not suffer for my forbearance.

Mr. Hodgkinson gives a just picture of his sagacity, when he shews you that after weeks of consultation and deliberation, <*he should be*> is enabled so to "arrange his ideas" as to discover that if he received 1700$ & return'd 500, he has <*indebted*> still 1200 to acc^{t} for perhaps after a few weeks more he may enabled so to arrange them as to perceive, that any mony paid <*or to be paid*> in consequence of an agreement with him which he was unable to fulfill, was by an after agreement to be refunded, & that all engagements on my part in consequence of said <*intend*> agreement for the purchase of property, are by the subsequent agreement made nugatory. To notice any further his refusal to repay the mony paid for him to Mr Gaine would be an insult on your understanding.

He asserts that the transaction with Solee was "one in which the Company was no way concerned" such assertions are common with this man; but it is sufficient for me that I can prove the contrary: can prove that it was done with no other possible view but to serve the Company (particularly him) in the difficulties which his folly had brought it into, as described in his own letters: and that it was authorized by the same tacit agreement to be bound by each others contracts, which, and which alone could bind me to abide by his ruinous engagements at Boston & elsewhere. Any money which he can prove that he has advanced for the Company's purposes, stands on the same ground as the rest of his account. As to the infamous insinuation that the money has been paid to me or to my agent with my knowledge & then charged to him, it is of a piece with the assertion made in your presence at the Coffee house & repel'd by me with the contemptuous indignation it deserved, viz. that, I had exhibited to him an account every article of which was wrong & that I knew it to be so. I fear, Sir, this man will make it my duty to bring his actions before a Court of Justice.

You know sir why I charged for my services at N: Y:. It was by way of ballancing <*his*> in some degree his unprecedented charge for services as acting Manager. If my charge is not allow'd by him, I shall leave to a jury to say what his services were worth to me. His accounts orders & receits will refresh his memory as to the charge of weekly interest & the mony paid him by Hughes.

As to Crosby's affair it is very probable <*it very probable*> I could not substantiate any debt against Mr H for mony paid to relieve him (Crosby). I relied upon a sense of Justice in Mr H. Dont you, who know him, laugh at me?

The Armor which cost according to the best estimate I can make less than $54 & which is charged at $100, is not to the best of my knowledge at N. Y. Should it prove to be there, I may perhaps take no further notice of the affair, on the overcharge being allowed. I must be excused from having anything to do with Mr Vals wardrobe at Mr Hodgkinson's charges. I know how these things are managed, the music or the Wardrobe of a necessitous performer or musician is purchased in the lump for a trifle; the purchaser selects all the valuable or usefull articles & the refuse, is put down as purchased for the company at arbitrary prices. This is Management worth paying for.

Mr Hodgkinson affects ignorance in respect to Mr Wools. You may refresh his memory (for it is not tenacious) & mention if you please that this Stephen Wools made claim to certain property, which claim he rescinded for a certain annual sum, which sum was paid by the purchasers of the claim by weekly payments under the denomination of Salary viz $14 per week. Having been unfortunately connected in business with these purchasers it appears that one of them has supposed that I had been generously paying for him without expectation of remuneration one half of his part of said purchase money: but it is not so: I am willing to allow for the nominal services of this superannuated man $8. a week to the said purchasers, but no more: consequently I charge to Mr H ¼ of the surplus while connected with Mr Hallam, & ½ for the remaining time. I had explained this to your satisfaction before; but I pity you if you should think it necessary to explain it to the <*Querist*> Enquirer.

These remarks are made freely, Sir, for I feel no iota of respect for the person of whom I am writing; but I sincerely hope there is nothing which <*which even make*> can in any wise offend you. I shall proceed, now, with my account, and shall rely, as heretofore, on your unbias'd exertions to procure me justice. Mr Hodgkinson seems to refer our business to a law decision, if so, he is bound to you that, that decision may be had in N. Y: since through my knowledge of you & on your assurances I suffered him to escape.

With respect Your friend

W D

P. S. I conceive it to be of moment to Mr H that he should render quickly an accurate account of the Music, belonging to Mr. Hallam & myself which he has taken off with him or left with any person in New York. The idea of mistake is well enough for the present.

Evening walk

Augt 13th Shooting with M Judah before breakfast he & Jame Palmer go up with the boat. Teach Children. Read in Enc: & Weekly Mag: Afternoon with my Wife & Children walk out to Aaron Bloodgoods, 2 miles, which we make four by our wanderings to gather fruit & enjoy the scenes around us. Sup on the game of the morning.

[Aug.] 14th Rain. Read in Weekly Mag: & Enc: Teach my Children. Slips of Lombardy Poplars which I sat out in the beginning of this Month are growing vigorously. I hence conclude that any time during the warm months will answer for this purpose. I have budded 16 peach trees of last year, with buds from Clingstones, large peaches & Nectarines.

Write on reply to ye Discourses & read in the Gospel of Matth: Visit at Mrs Parker's: She show'd us a marine production often found on our Beaches a sea vegetable, in the cavities of what may be called its leaves are minute shells, shaped perfectly like the Conch. In what manner do shellfish propagate? In each of these circular bag-like leaves is an opening sufficient for the embryo Conchs to be received & as they grow they would burst this receptacle & free themselves. The shells in question are so tender that they are pressed to powder between the fingers with the slightest exertion.

Aug[t] 15th Rainy morning. Read in Med: Repository. I presume the Sea vegetable loosened from its watery bed & thrown upon the sands, the shell fish within have all perished, being too large to escape through the apperture & not large enough to burst the leaf. I find that shell-fish are oviparous and discharge their eggs (very small) surrounded by mucus like the spawn of frogs, in this state it is attached or deposited, so as to be most secure from the danger of being cast on shore. In this state the egg of the Conch has been deposited within the leaves of this Sea weed. Teach the Children. Trim Lombardy P's and set out slips. Read Enc: art: Scriptures & Matth: Write on ans: to Discour: Drink tea at Mrs Terril's. walk with Mrs B & my wife. write again on discourses.

[Aug.] 16th Write again on discourses. Rain & then hot sun. Teach children. Read Enc: art: Scriptures. Write on my Comedy.

[Aug.] 17th Rec[d] from New York a letter from Hodgkinson dated August 8th Boston, recommending a Mr Baker and his wife as performers: this letter is written with perfect familiarity as from a friend to a friend. He say "There has been as alarm here of the yellow fever which has, with other impediments, made Theatricals here wear a gloomy aspect; but the alarm has now, in a great measure, subsided & we hope to hear no more of it." Teach Children. Read Caleb Williams 2d edit:.

[Aug.] 18th Lombardy poplar slips set out within a few days thrive perfectly. Teach Children. Read Enc: & Caleb Williams. Walk with John & my Gun a little while being driven home by a gust. Rain every day this week.

[Aug.] 19th Sunday. Read Caleb Williams. Walk with John out to A Bloodgoods & with him over the farm. Receive a letter from M: Judah he says that Mrs Hallam having sent for informed him that "she had just rec^{d} a letter from Miss E Westray, dated at Worcester Augt 19th in which she informs Mrs Hallam that owing to the prevailing fever at Boston the Theatre was shut, that herself & sister were in a distress'd situation for want of money, that they had rec^{d} but 10$ from Mr Hodgkinson since they had left N: Y: & that her sister was writing to Mr Dunlap by same post to forward them money to bear their expences to N: Y:." Rec^{d} likewise a letter from Barret dated Augt 9th He rejoices in the engagement: says he cant think of finding Dressers for himself & wife: thinks he can be of great assistance to me: "I forbeire saying more about *parts* as I have not an opinion you would ask Mrs B or self to anything to injure Either or lower us in the Idia of the Audiences" he says the Theatre is shut untill September & the Company gone to Newport, "since the house has been open'd not one night half charges." "Mr & Mrs Simpson are discharged"

Write on Answer to Discourses. pass evening at Mrs Parkers.

[Aug.] 20th Pass the forenoon in endeavouring with Mr Halsted to fix the lines of my lot on the Hill. Teach children. Read Caleb Williams. Write on answers to Discourses.

[Aug.] 21st Read Caleb Williams. Teach children.

CHARLES THOMPSON (To begin it)

My case is peculiarly hard. I have become the object of contempt <*to*> and horror to all my Countrymen and of compleat <*self*> disaprobation to myself. I am condemned to eternal solitude, <*whilst*> with a mind most unhappily filled for such a state, every review of the past bringing with it <*unutterable*> the soul-sickenings of poignant regret and the unutterable pangs of never dying remorse, <*and*> whilst the prospect of the future is one unvaried fruitless blank, joyless as the parched desart without tree and without fountain.

I will record the chain of events which have made me what I am. I will take a gloomy pleasure in tracing effects to their causes: I will publish this to the world & show <*them*> mankind that my actions, so detested by them, flowed from principles avowed by themselves, & that in circumstances similar to those which make me now <*detestable to*> abhorred by society & by myself, they, if true to the principles they profess, ought to do as I did."

Took a walk with my boy & my Gun. Afternoon rode with my Wife & little Girl to Woodbridge as far as the house of the late Wm Smith's: drank tea at Gen[l] Heards.

[Aug.] 22d Walk out with my boy & girl. Teach Children. Finish reading Caleb Williams. How far this varies from the first edit: I can not point out I can not even be certain from my memory that it varies any, but I have rec[d] new impressions from it and exquisite pleasure: I have read it with a more compleat understanding of it than ever before, more pleasure from the beauty of composition & scarcely less from the interest of the tale. Read M: Roland.

[Aug.] 23d Write to Barret.

"Sir I rec[d] yours of the 9th and look upon matters as settled between us. I feel confident in myself when I assert that you may depend upon my fulfilling my engagements as expressed in my letters, & I doubt not of your cheerful performance of your part of the contract. As to *Dressers* the article was mentioned in my <*first*> letter of 7th June, my first offer to you, in your an[swer] you demand more than I offered, for your & Mrs B's services *"wardrobe and all"*. I have complied. I am immovable when a point has been settled. After the Theatre has been opened under my own immediate direction & I can judge of the *power* and the *will* of the *individual parts* of the complicated *whole;* I shall determine in what manner to proceed in respect to the future direction of the stage department. In consequence of a letter from Mr Hodgkinson I have written to Mr Baker informing him that I have not the vacancy necessary for his being useful in the Co. I will write to let you know the night of opening as soon as it can be determined. With respectful compliments &c &c

Walk with my Gun. Afternoon read.

24th Aug[t] Walk out with my Wife and Children to Breakfast at Gen[l] Heards. Jack H teaching my boy to ride. As we were about returning in H's Coachee, for they would not let us walk home, W W Woolsey arrived from N: Y: to visit us, & passed us going down in the stage. Mr & Mrs H went down with us.

[Aug.] 25th Walk out with W W W & my boy to get some butter. Very warm. Read in M Roland & converse with our brother.

[Aug.] 26th Sunday. Very warm. Read in M Roland, and converse. Visit at Mrs Parkers in y[e] evening.

[Aug.] 27th W W Woolsey returns to N: Y: I accompany him as far as tht Spa in Elis Baron's Coachee who happened to be down here on business. pleasant morning. Teach Children. Finish M R Appeal from which I have received much pleasure. Read several articles in y[e] Enc: particularly Quaker. Drank tea at Mr A Bell's where was Miss Cornelia Patterson daughter of Judge [William] P.

[Aug.] 28th Teach children. Read. Afternoon walk with my boy & Gun; some few wild Pigeons are to be seen

[Aug.] 29th Walk with the Children & bring home apples. Teach as usual. Grapes ripe in the Garden, (purple) Evening at Mrs Parker's; The Packet boat arrives from New York & brings to us Mrs Woolsey the elder & her two youngest grandsons [41] of the name of Palmer, likewise M: Dangle. The yellow fever so prevails in New York that the inhabitants are flying in every direction. W W W has gone to Stamford. I receive a letter from M: Judah who has shut up the store & with his

[41] Thomas and Benjamin Palmer, children of Captain Palmer and of Esther (Woolsey) Palmer, daughter of Benjamin and Anne (Muirson) Woolsey. Dwight, *Descendants of John Dwight,* II, 1095.

wife gone to his father's. I receive a letter from Sir J Oldmixon informing me, that he "withdrew Mrs O from W's Co. immediately on y[e] close of y[e] Theatre in Baltimore the 10th of june as" he "would not suffer her to proceed to Anapolis on y[e] terms acceded to by the generality of y[e] Co." he asks me for information as to my opening which he expects to depend "on contingencies the fever at present is as bad as possible in Philadelphia & report says you are not free from it altogether in N Y should this be the case I presume your intention of commencing the season in September will be frustrated, whatever you determine on she will be very much obliged if you will give a fortnight or three weeks notice as it will be necessary for me to go to N Y to procure a small house & arrange other business for the Winter."

[Aug.] 30th Walk out with Dangle & the boys & with Mr Joseph Taylor measure the end lines of my Sterling lot & determine the line of fence between us. Take a lesson in French & begin talking in that language with Dangle. He gives me a sketch of his history: he says that he became convinced of the falsity of reveal'd religion at 17 when studying for the priesthood & then when he enter'd the order he was reconciled to preach[g] the Christion superstition by this kind of sophistry—"You are employed to teach the people the religion of their fathers not your own opinions." He was put in the Inquisition & in suffering & sickness remained in its dungeons 16 months for having, when a chaplain at Madrid, preached the propriety of addressing prayers to God Almighty rather than to the Virgin Mary and y[e] Saints. Walk in y[e] even[g] wth Dangle & my boy.

[Aug.] 31st Write french wth Dangle. Walk with my gun. Dangle & John accompany me part of the time. I shot one Quail, of which I was glad as Mrs Smyth, long sick & very weak has for some time supposed that she could relish this particular kind of food. Write to S[ir] J Oldmixon. Read in the Med: Rep: Drink tea with Mrs Terril. Walk wth my Gun.

Septr 1st Walk with Dangle, learning to speak French. Dangle is reading Caleb Williams, he is a curious man: certainly a thinker. Hunt & talk French with Dangle.

[Sept.] 2d Sunday. Walk with my boy & Dangle: Talk french: he gives a most frightful picture of French depravity of manners & want of principle: describes to me the mode of confession, its uses abuses & great influence: confirms the pictures of the bestiality of monks & priests from forced celibacy & of the other sex from the same cause. There is much philosophy in this man. Finish read^{g} Med: Rep: Read in Botanic Garden. Converse lengthily with Dangle of Religion & Politics. Write to E H Smith.

[Sept.] 3d Walk with Dangle & my Gun & practise french. Afternoon with D & ye boy to practise with him. Visit our Neighbours. Read in Weekly Mag:

[Sept.] 4th Last Night violent storm. Study french. Walk with my Gun in the Evening shoot large Black birds.

[Sept.] 5th Walk & talk french with D. After breakfast wth D & John: sit in the pleasant little valley near Wm Taylors & read Telemaque. Receive letters & papers fr^{m} N. Y. Letter from Brown, Johnson & Smith

First in B's hand writing

"Your letter was very acceptable & seasonable: It cheared *us* poor solitary beings with this plaguey fever at our doors, in our cupboards & in our beds.

Johnson & I are pretty well, but E H S, by midnight sallyings forth, sudden changes of temperature, fatigue & exposure to a noon day sun, is made sick. perhaps it would not have been so if this Demon had not lurked in the air. Tomorrow it is hoped he will be able to answer your questions as to the prevalence & comparative malignity of this disease himself.

This afternoon I revised the last sheet of Wieland. It will form an handsome volume of 300 pages. Some ten or twelve have been added since you last saw it.

I have written something of the history of Carwin which I will send. I have desisted for the present from the prosecution of this plan & betook myself to another which I mean to extend to the size of Wieland, & to finish by the end of this month, provided no yellow fever interpose to disconcert my schemes.

Your letter bespeaks you to be happy. Why is it so? I just now asked W J. He says you are constitutionally cheerfull & having gotten rid of a certain pestering coadjutor, your constitution, in that respect is at liberty to shew itself. I ascribe it partly to this cause & partly to the congenial aspect of nature that surrounds you, to domestic happiness, to literary & luxurious leisure, rendered more pleas[g] by contrast & to health. Am I not right?

Why are your christian allusions so frequent? "Caute & timide" say I, which for your edification I translate "slow & sure". Your motto is, perhaps too much like that of a young prodigal which he inscribed upon his coatch "Nec lenti nec trepide" which a by stander interpreted into "Nec or nothing."

In Wm Johnson's hand.

W J, as you conjectured, is doing nothing: not absolutely nothing, but nothing interesting to an "infidel philosopher." Yet he rejoices in the works and fame of his friends. Charles feels all the joy and parental exultation of an Author having this day, been delivered, by the aid of H Caritat & T & J Swords of an handsome duodecimo, the offspring of that fertile brain which already engendered, two more volumes. This borders upon the *prodigious!*—300 pages in a month! Yet he is neither in a delirium or a fever! What an admirable antidote is philosophy.

But mind Charles, & let us have no allusions to the Vulgar cant of the religionists: I commiserate your situation: so destitute of intellectual food: You had better leave a dull uninteresting country scene & join us. The Town is the only place for rational beings. Under the shield of Philosophy what have we to fear? As to fever, it is a being of such unaccountable origin, such amazing attributes, and such inexplicable operations, that I deliver it over to the Doctor, to be treated of *secundum artem*. That is to say, according to *his trade*. What can we do for you?

[Alexander] Somerville has shut up shop, and eloped into the Country. The Weekly magazine is not, therefore, to be procured. The 2d edit: of Caleb Williams you have. There are *new* Books here to be obtained.

I rejoice that you are happy at Amboy. I leave the philosopher Charles to search for the Causes. If you want occupation let us hear from you by every *Amboy Packet* in *french* or *english.*

In E H Smith's hand.

These gay friends of mine have so covered the paper with their gambols that nothing but coldness and conclusion, dullness & death-heads are left for me.

Had you seen me extended on my bed yesterday, rejecting (alas the while!) half a dozen applications from the sick & confined to pills & potions, you would have trembled for the safety of your poor philosopher. To-day, however, I have sitten up 'till this hour; &, if the day be fair, tomorrow shall resume my customary functions.

Our fever has been confined to made ground and its vicinity, on y[e] east side of y[e] Town. There it is no longer safe to remain. You would be astonished at the desertion of Pearl, Water, Front &c Streets, which exceeds that of 1795. On this account the fever cannot be said to increase much, tho' some are taken with it every day: the numbers each day being less than at first.

It is impossible to estimate the mortality its comparative extent in relation to 1795: no regular acc[t] being kept. But I imagine it is less than in that year. I compute that about one in ten die; & that not more than one in a hundred would perish, with early attention & faithful nursing.

The sad Geological observations, in which there is every thing but order, consistency & novelty, are J P Smith's of y[e] Phil. Chem[l] Soc[y].

Our Mineralogical Society progresses very well. We have had within the last month a number of communications. But this Fever will prevent our meeting to night. The *thing* you brought with you was *sand* enveloped with *clay,* the Clay appeared very fine. Collect some more of it. Hopkins is out of town. Love to Mrs D.

By order of the Con
E H SMITH (this day 27)

Tuesday noon, Sept 4, 1798

Sept.[r] 6th Went out with y[e] two young Palmers to get apples. After breakfast with Dangle, shoot & study french. Receive a dunning note from Mr R Kearney & answer it. Read in Telemaque with D: by his reading it to me I accustom myself to understand the language by the sound alone.

[Sept.] 7th Write to M: Judah, to come to N. Y. according to his intention about the 11th & transact some business & if the place should in his apprehension continue at that time unsafe, to come hither. Write to Gamage. Walk to Woodbridge with my Gun & Swiss companion to put letters in the Post office: call at Gen[l] Heards: come home to dinner. Attend to french.

[Sept.] 8th Read & talk french. Afternoon with Mr Dangle, my wife, the Palmers & my children go to Sandy point to shoot & fish: a pleasant rambling excursion. Evening Mrs Terril's. rec^d a letter from Ciceri.

[Sept.] 9th Sunday. Write to G M W. Walk out Aaron Bloodgood's with Dangle & John, by the way met Genl Heard's servant with a note informing me that his youngest Daughter died that morning of the Dysentery & was to be buried at 4 OClock. After dinner rode with my Wife to Woodbridge & attended the funeral. Evening the boat having arrived we have accounts from N: Y: of the increasing state of the fever & birth [of] a Son [42] to G M W. Call on Mrs Terril.

[Sept.] 10th Walk with Dangle and my boy & T Palmer to a neighbouring farmer's: observe them making Cider. Study french. My little girl having considerable fever I call in Dr Darby.

[Sept.] 11th She is still sick. Write to Ciceri: to G M W & to E H S. Afternoon walk with Dangle on Staten Island with my gun.

[Sept.] 12th Study french. Walk. General Gates, who is here with his old lady at Miss Abbee Thorps, meeting me this evening, informed me that Kosciusko had left this Country privately & landed in France with great honours. Dangle in conversation some days back, was pointing out to me the probability of France restoring Poland to a rank among the Nations as a republic. Will not K. be the Leader & chief in the enterprize?

[Sept.] 13th Study french. Afternoon walk with my Gun, accompanied by D, B Palmer & my boy (who talks nothing but french on ye occasion) along the sound.

[Sept.] 14th. Study french. Walk with Dangle up the Brunswick road. Afternoon read C B Browns beginning for the life of Carwin—as far as he has gone he has

[42] George Muirson Woolsey, Jr.

done well: he has taken up the schemes of the Illuminati. Evening go with my wife to see Mr & Mrs Gates; the old Genl is very conversable & has information: he says Kosciusko is the only pure republican he ever knew "He is without any dross!" says the old man.

[Sept.] 15th Weather becomes somewhat warm again; after being for some time cool. The Fever in N: Y: has continued to encrease. Finding it necessary to go out to Woodbridge, I took my Gun, and Dangle accompanying me related certain particulars of his unfortunate life which have made a deep impression on me: the day is warm: we return about 4 OClock. Evening receive by y^e boat a letter from G M W who tells me of the death of R[ichard R] Saltonstall & the encreasing malignancy of the Plague: receive from him $50. Visit at Mrs Parker's.

[Sept.] 16th Sunday. Very warm. Eat the last peach from our fine Clingstone tree. Read in a view of Turkey published in 1784 sent me by Genl Gates and in Enc: and Gibbon 4th Vol. oct: edit:. Study french.

[Sept.] 17th Warm. Agree with Compton to fence my lot on the Hill. Study french. Afternoon, Bates sent for me to come to him to ye Tavern: having brought his family to N. Y. he is obliged to fly thence with them & is without money. I represented my situation to him: in debt to every body & borrowing for the present support of my family. I walk with him in the evening on his return towards Woodbridge. John Cozine is dead & many others whom I know.

[Sept.] 18th Pick up oysters on the shore with the boys. 10 OClock receive a letter from C B Brown & Wm Johnson they have with [them] in the house Signor [Joseph B.] Scandella an Italian Physician, dangerously ill of the fever under the care of Elihu. Brown wishes to come down here; I have written to him & Johnson to come down immediately. to Elihu, my apprehensions for his safety & my confidence in his doing his duty. Mr

Crowel of E T, dines with us & my mother goes wth him home. I write on my answer to Dr. Dwight discourses. Rain, for the first time for 2 weeks or more.

Septr 19th Study french & teach the children. Genl Bloomfield calls on us. We visit Genl Gates, who with his lady leaves us for Mr Garnet's at Brunswick where Dangle & self have promised to visit him. Read in Enc: art: Metaphysics. Walk with D & John. Mr Warner accidentally calls at the door and informs me that Elihu H Smith lies dangerously ill. Receive a letter from G M W. "Your letter to Smith I have not yet delivered and very much fear I shall never have an oppertunity he is now very ill of ye prevailing fever in short no hopes are entertained of his recovery by his physicians Miller and Mitchell; medicine has no power <*over*> on his system, and his stomach in so irritated a state that nothing will remain on it: he is in a stupor but as far as his mind is exercised it is rationally; he is at Horace Johnson's. His friend Dr Scandelli was taken ill a few days since & died at Smith's room." This is dated yesterday 11 OClock. Distress and sickness are hourly encreasing in the City. Notwithstanding my firmest attempts, this stroke bears hard upon me. Receive a letter from Moses Judah & $50.

[Sept.] 20th Write to G M W & M: Judah. Rec^{d} likewise yesterday a letter from Ciceri who informs that the work at the Theatre is stop'd & the people Gone away. Afternoon walk out to Bloodgood's with Dangle & John.

[Sept.] 21st Reports of Smiths death. Rec^{d} a letter from G M W who tells me that E H Smith breathed his last about 1 OClock of the 19th. Doctor Rodgers who just call'd on me, says that [Dr. Amasa] Dingley is likewise dead. Walk with Dangle and my boy to Mr Drake's a farmer on the Brunswick road. Evening receive the follow^{g} letter from W Johnson & C B Brown

N York Sepr 20th 98

How fallacious is hope! How vain is theory! When I wrote you last little did I imagine that in the short space of four days so

CHARLES BROCKDEN BROWN (1771-1811)

BY WILLIAM DUNLAP

(Courtesy of Herbert Lee Pratt, Esq.)

dreadful a misfortune was to befal me. I feel as if awakened from a horrid dream: haunted by its images—my mind is distracted—my strength subdued—I wonder how I have passed through such scenes and almost doubt the reality. That I live is matter of surprize and almost of indifference.

Forgive me! I thought to have summoned resolution to have told you the events of the last 8 days. Our dear friend Elihu is no more. The best devised & most potent remedies availed nothing. This terrible disease exerted all its malignity. It proved fatal on the morning of the fourth day. I can say no more.

Charles had gone to my brother's in Greenwich Street. Since sunday he has staid with Dr Miller. He is languid & pale but having taken Medicine by the advice of Dr. M, he wants only to be restored to strength. I wish to get out of this hateful City. As soon as Charles is strong enough to bear the fatigue of travelling, shall either visit you at Amboy or go to Middletown.

Your friendly letter was received this day. I believe we shall come to you tho' I cannot fix the day.

Poor Scandella! The paper has already informed you of his death. Elihu was taken sick the night preceeding his decease. What a day follow'd! My dear friend adieu. remember me affectionately to Mrs Dunlap & to your children. I am happy that you are at a distance & in health. Take care of yourselves. Heaven preserve you

Your friend

W J.

21st Well my beloved friend! It may afford you some satisfaction to recognize my hand once more tho' vague & feeble in a degree that astonishes myself. I can add little to what is before said by William. Most ardently do I long to shut out this City from my view but my strength has been, within these few days, so totally & unaccountably subverted, that I can scarcely flatter myself with being able, very shortly, to remove. I do not understand my own case, but see enough to discover that the combination of bodily & mental causes have made such deep inroads on the vital energies of brain & stomach, I am afraid I canot think of departing before Monday at the least.

Let me join in congratulations on your domestic serenities.

I suppose when we reach Woodbridge, a conveyance to your village is procurable

Farewell

C B B.

Septr 22d Write to G M W. W Johnson & M: Judah. Walk with Dangle to Crows Mills. Read in Telemaque. Visit at Mrs Parkers with my wife.

[Sept.] 23d Sunday. Report says Dingley is not dead. Walk with Dangle. Study french as usual. John reads Hume's hist: to me a practise discontinued for some time. Write on remarks on Dr D[wight]'s discourses.

[Sept.] 24th Dingley is certainly dead. Write on remarks &c. Ride with my wife & little girl to Woodbridge & among other places call at Gen[l] Heard's: he is preparing for publication System of manœuvres or evolutions &c for the Cavalry of the State, & solicits my corrections: return home to dinner. Hogg & Williams (A Pasquin) call on me: they say Mrs Collins is dead: I felt an indefinable sort of shrinking from Williams: after a little while with me on the stoop where I was reading Telemaque when the[y] came up, the[y] proceeded to the Tavern: they had come from dining with O Riley the schoolmaster. A note came soon after for Dangle from Hog who is his brother mason: on Dangles return he said Williams remark'd that I was cool to him & attributed it to his being a friend of Hodgkinson's. Johnson & Brown arrive having left N: Y: at 1 OClo: & crossed Staten Island: they stay with me till bed-time & then return to the lodgings I had provided for them at Miss Thorp's. Brown has quite recovered but is pale & so is William. They say the change of air & exhiliaration of spirits they have experienced on leaving y[e] city is inconceivable.

[Sept.] 25th Weather much changed. high wind. Walk with my friends. Read the beginning of Charles's last novel called "Calvert (proposed to be changed to Caillemour) or the lost brothers." Read the additions made to "Wieland" of which Wm has brought a printed Copy. My friends dine remain with me until bedtime.

[Sept.] 26th Wind abated: weather cold. Walk out, Johnson & self with guns, Brown & Dangle without. Evening visit at Mrs Terrils & Mr Kearney's with my friends.

[Sept.] 27th My friends breakfast with me Walk with Brown who recounts particulars of the deaths of Scandella & Smith. Pay to Aaron Bloodgood $20 for Ravaud Kearney by his order. Walk out with B & J to Florida.

[Sept.] 28th Breakfast with B & J at their lodgings. Walk with them to Woodbridge. Conversation on French politics, Atmospheric air, Animal heat, respiration. Brown tells me the manner in which his mother breaks off his connection with Miss Potts. Browns brother visits him from Princeton. Evening J: has letters from Tracey & others at Litchfield partly commissioned by Smiths parents to return thanks & make enquiries. Tracey in a poscript to Horace Johnson says "Did Smith die a Diest [*sic*]? if you require, the answer shall be kept secret." It appears that Mr & Mrs S. are anxious on this subject: Johnson is now happy that he can say nothing in answer, for our beloved friend was seized so violently that he was in a stupor until death, scarcely speaking & then but when roused from his sleep to answer some question which done he slept again.

[Sept.] 29th Write to Carlile Pollock & enclose notes to renew those due in y[e] beginning of Oct. Walk with my Gun, shoot Wood-pyes, alias Highholes &c. Brown & Johnson with me after dinner walk.

[Sept.] 30th Sunday. Brown's brother departs. We walk & get nuts. Afternoon, walk my wife with us.

Sept[r] [*sic* for Oct.] 1st On Staten Island, hunting Quails. I kill four, 3 of them younger than I thought any were at this season. Blue Jays are in large flocks. The quantity of Red & black butterflies is so great as to suggest the probab[il]ity of an uncommon number of catterpillars for the next year.

[Oct.] 2d Weather warm compared to last week. Write to M: Judah. Read Telemaque as usual to Dangle. Walk wth Johnson & Brown. Walk with Dangle to my nearest Meadow to divide the product wth the man who cuts it.

[Oct.] 3d Before breakfast out after Quails; kill one. Ride to Woodbridge with my Wife. Read in Staunton's acc^{t} of the Ambassy to China &c. Johnson & self wth Guns, the children with baskets for Nuts pass the afternoon in the Woods & fields. Kill two Squirrels.

[Oct.] 4th Write to Carlile Pollock & to M: Judah acknowledging his of Sep: 26th & requesting his exertions to assist me, by collecting money to enable me to proceed with the Theatre. Write to Ciceri. Dangle receives from N: Y: Mirabaud's System of Nature & Boulangers, Christianity unvieled, translations the last by Wm M Johnson, at whose grave I arrived last year on the 21st of Sept. when having left Mrs Woolsey at Flushing L: I: I walked to Jamaica: the next day in my walk to Brooklyn I fell in with Dingley (who died a few days ago) Johnson's friend & from him received a short account of the deceased: a man of genius sinking at the age of 30 under disease acquired in our Southern Climates. I read in Boulanger. Evening walk with B, J, & my Wife.

[Oct.] 5th Hunt Quails with Johnson. Evening read in Staunton's acc^{t} &c & Enc: Call at Mrs Parkers.

[Oct.] 6th Hunt on Corringtons farm, kill a brace of Quails. Afternoon Walk with my friends, & ye Children and gather Nuts. Evening sup & converse with B & J at Miss Thorp's.

[Oct.] 7th Sunday. Easterly Storm. Finish read^{g} Boulanger. Converse with B & J on Religion &c.

[Oct.] 8th Storm continues. Write on accounts. Afternoon Storm ceases. Walk with B & J & pass the evening with them.

[Oct.] 9th Read in Staunton's account &c. Write to Carlile Pollock stating the necessity of the Committee's extending ye time of credit endorsement. Write to M: Judah the propriety of removing to ye neighbourhood of N: Y: Afternoon: hunt with Wm Johnson. Brown went to Brunswick on foot. Evening read^{g} french.

[Oct.] 10th Read in Staunton. Walk with my Gun & enquire for some Cherry trees to sett out for grafting on. Walk, Johnson, my wife & self. Johnson mentions his wish that I should assist in the memoir of E H S.

[Oct.] 11th Read in Staunton. Attend to running a line of fence between my Westernmost lot & Jos: Taylor's. Shoot a large Wood Cock. Brown returns from Brunswick. Afternoon attending to the line & finishing. Read with J & B in Darwin, B. G: & Enc: art: Plant.

[Oct.] 12th Read [Henry] Burton's narration of his life & sufferings, printed in 1643: this man was one of the enthusiasts of Charles I time: this narrative is a fine specimen of enthusiasm & self deception. Walk out wth my gun & shoot 2 Wood pyes. Write on Anti Jacobin. Read Staunton.

[Oct.] 13th Read Staunton. Write on my Novel. Walk with B & J. Afternoon go with the Children a nutting. After Sun-set observe great numbers of Quails gathering in ye Buckwheat fields: shoot one.

[Oct.] 14th Write to John Kent. Walk with Johnson to A Bloodgoods. Write on my Novel which I now call Harry Colbert. Pass ye afternoon with B & J.

[Oct.] 15th Out before breakfast with my Gun. Read Staunton. Work in my Garden transplant^{g} & staking Vines.

[Oct.] 16th Out before breakfast with my Gun. Walk wth B & J: to Princs Bay, Staten Island. Afternoon attend as a Pall-bearer at ye funeral of Mrs. Smyth[43] who died, Sunday evening 10 OClock. Pass ye even^g with J & B.

17th October. Attend to my boys french. Walk to Woodbridge; hunt; return in ye evening. Sup with Johnson & Brown.

[Oct.] 18th Walk with J & B. Attend to the setting of the board fence which now encloses the whole of the town lot. At Mrs Smyth's funeral t'other day R[ichard Channing] Moore the parson preached a funeral sermon. A mass of common place sentiments, scriptural quotations, & affected attempts at the pathetic. Read Staunton.

[Oct.] 19th High winds & clouds; walk with my Gun up the sound. Teach my boy french. Read Staunton.

[Oct.] 20th Light rain. Teach french. Johnson returns to N: Y: altho' our last accounts from thence mention 22 deaths in 24 hours & many of those persons prematurely returning. Clears up: Walk. Evening visit at Mrs Parkers: the old lady tells some of her Mountain stories so as to make me wish to visit the hills of Morris.

[Oct.] 21st Sunday. Walk with my Wife & family after seeing Brown off, on his way to Burlington. Finish reading Sir Geo: Staunton's elegant & philosophic acc^t of the British Embassy to China from which I have derived much pleasure & instruction. It has appeared to me in reading this work that Essays on the Character of the Chinese: their customs &c &c might be written with great effect taking this acknowledgedly authentic Author as a kind of text book. Begin to read Edwards' West Indies; What a difference of style as well as views between this pious apologist for Slave-holders and the manly Staunton!

[43] Mrs. Andrew Smyth (Maria Parker) died October 14, 1798, aged 27 years, and was buried in St. Peter's Churchyard, Perth Amboy. W. Northey Jones, *History of St. Peter's Church in Perth Amboy, N. J.*, (1924), 471.

[Oct.] 22d Work in the Garden, setting out slips of Vines. Evening walk with my Gun & the boys. Receive a letter from Wm Johnson. Read Edwards W Indies.

[Oct.] 23d Showers. Write to W J. Work in Garden. Read Edw^{ds} W. Indies. M: Judah arrived here; he left his fathers in haste on being informed of my death. Walk.

[Oct.] 24th M Judah returns to his father's. Work in Garden. Walk to A Bloodgood's. Read in E^{s} W I. Visit at Mr John Johnsons & Mrs Parkers.

[Oct.] 25th Mrs Woolsey leaves us for N. Y. Write to John Kent. Work in ye Garden. Read Edwards.

[Oct.] 26th Work in the Garden. Walk with my Gun & Children. Read Edwards.

[Oct.] 27th Up before day & before Sun rise set off wth my wife in a hired chair for Eliz Town, where after breakfast I left her and proceeded to NewArk I there met S Boyd & sent off a short letter to W Johnson. Return to E T where we are detain'd by rain. Read in [William] Guthrie's Grammer.

[Oct.] 28th Sunday. Read "Life of [William] Glendening" a Taylor turn'd preacher who has recorded his Lunacy as visions, to support himself he quotes among others Garrison another methodist who says he saw the Devil in the shape of black cat. Leave E T about ten & after stopping at General Heards arrive at Amboy, where I find a letter from the faithful John Kent & 2 bundles of trees from Williamson.

[Oct.] 29th With a labourer setting out trees in my orchard: After replacing such as had failed the additional Apples are 25 making ye Orchard 225.

[Oct.] 30th Finish planting on the hill by putting out 2 White heart Cherries & 2 English Walnuts or Madeira nuts & 210 Threethorn'd Accacia's for tryal as a hedge. Shoot 1 Quail, 1 Woodpye & 12 Robins, the latter in great numbers are flying over since the frost which began the night of the 28th. Read^{g} Edwards: his 2d Vol: contains much valuable information well given.

[Oct.] 31st Set out in the house lot 6 Green Gages & 2 White heart Cherries. Work in the Garden. On examining my peach & nectarine trees, I find just under the surface of the earth a grub, from 1 to 12 under the bark of each tree, the gum oozing out in great quantities & some trees almost girdled. I took away the earth, cleansed the wounds, destroyed such grubs as I could find some of them half an inch long, & then poured on boiling water to kill eggs & young, covering the roots with sea weed sea sand & earth. Evening Ciceri arrived in consequence of a letter which I sent up by Dangle, who return'd yesterday.

Novr 1st Write to W Henderson requesting that the Glass Chandeliers imported for the Theatre may be delivered to Ciceri. Write to W Johnson. Walk with Ciceri part of ye way to Woodbridge on his return; talk on ye subject of the Theatre & give directions. Returning, a smart snow storm meets me from the S E. Read Edwards & finish his work: this work cannot be read without advantage, but he who trusts to the statements of a Planter on the subjects of which he treats must be credulous indeed. It continues to snow all day; night rain. Read in Enc: many articles.

[Nov.] 2d Snow on the ground but fast melting away. Walk with my gun. Teach & study french. read in Enc: Visit at Mrs Parkers. Teach french.

[Nov.] 3d Read in Enc: Cast plays. Visit at Mrs Terrills. Teach french & study it.

[Nov.] 4th Sunday. Walk with my family on the hill. Cast plays. read in Enc: Teach french & write it with John.

[Nov.] 5th Write to Carlisle Pollock & walk out to Woodbridge to send the letter. Cast Farces.

[Nov.] 6th Finish pruning my Orchard. Shoot robins. Write on my Comedy. Receive letters from M: Judah, who open'd store last thursday: & from Wm Johnson, who departs for Middleton.

[Nov.] 7th Receive a letter from Cooper who is at Poughkeepsie & wants money to bring him to N. Y. Our Servants return to town. Write to M: Judah to inform me if my Cellar has been cleans'd; & to Cooper enclosing a line to Judge Kent request^{g} his assistance for Cooper. Shoot some birds; by firing at a Hawk I procure a Quail from his talons. Write on my Comedy.

[Nov.] 8th Shoot 3 Ducks from the shore. Walk out to Woodbridge to receive M: Judah's answer, who informs me that all is ready for my reception. Shoot a brace of Quails. Read in Encyc:.

[Nov.] 9th Walk with my Gun. Shoot 1 Quail. Afternoon set off for Woodbridge with my Wife & Children all huddled in a one horse chair, we are very hospitably rec^{d} & treated by Genl Heard & Lady.

[Nov.] 10th After breakfast we leave woodbridge in the Stage; stop a few minutes at Elizabeth Town: and after a tolerably pleasant journey arrived in N. Y. at ½ past 1. No dinner being prepared for us at our house we go directly to W W Woolsey's & dine with him & his mother. Afternoon at my store. Evening Jefferson & Miller call on me. Read in Rousseau's Confessions. Pennants B Z. Find letters from various persons

[Nov.] 11th Sunday. Go to see Derry who is very feeble. Call on Ciceri & go with him to the Theatre which promises to be very superbe. C says all will be ready in 2 Weeks. Write to Barrett in return for 2 which I found waiting for me dated 16 & 23 Septr in which he tells me he shall draw on me for $75 to help him on. I write that I will accept his draft at long date, & if the Miss Westrays are at Boston, to inform them that I will do the same for them. To Sir John Oldmixon I write in answer, that the Theatre will soon be ready. Martin calls with 12 plays purchased for me, among which are the "Stranger" "Secrets worth knowing" & He's much to blame" which I read in the course of the day, as does Cooper who arrived in Town yesterday and dines with me to day. The Stranger is a bad translation from the German, & not the Copy performed with so much applause, but I think with industry I can rewrite it so as to answer & bring it forward immediately. "Secrets &c. is Mortons & has merit, it will do for playing "He's much &c" is apparently Holcrofts & is excellent tho' not his best. G M W & W W W call to see us, as does M Rogers. Evening visit at G M W & M: Rogers; at the last place, see the elegant edition of Staunton's Embassy with the plates.

[Nov.] 12th Write to Mr R Kearney. To Mr. Crowel. To Mr Kent by Cooper who is to go off & endeavour to settle affairs at Poughkeepsie. Look over prompt books. See various members of the Company. Call on Wm Henderson without seeing [him]. Call on Mr Gaine. Begin to re-write "The Stranger. Visit at W W W's & M Rogers.

[Nov.] 13th See Wm Henderson who directs me where to receive the Lustres, gives consent to making steps & door for greater convenience in the back of the Theatre, & that the new Upholstery shall be charged to the Committee. Attend to various business. See Mrs Hallam. Write on "Stranger." Write to Mr Fox & offer him $18 per Week. Agree to give Tyler 2 additional $ for his Wardrobe.

[Nov.] 14th Write on "Stranger." Rec[d] a letter from Munto, offering his services from Boston: return an answer declining. receive a letter from Carr offering the services of Mr & Mrs Shaw: return an answer declining. Receive the lustres for the Theatre. Attend to business. Write to Miss Julia Westray, enclosing a request to Josiah Quincey Esq[r] to assist the sisters with $50 on my account. Evening write on "Stranger."

[Nov.] 15th Write on Stranger. Receive an application from a Mr Ryder. Attend to the state of the music & give orders to purchase Harpsichord scores. Give 20 Dollars to redeem certain music left by Gardie: viz. Orchestra parts of Agreable surprize & Children in y[e] Wood. C B B arrives in town. Visit at y[e] Miller's where Brown is. Call on Sharpless, he is out of town.

[Nov.] 16th Write on Stranger. Meet by appointment a Mrs Halsey at Mr Hewit's who wishes employment as a singer. She has a strong voice & may be usefull. Attend to business. Evening at Seth Johnson's. He gives me some Boston papers, by which I gather, that Hodgkinson had given much dissatisfaction by endeavouring to raise the price of the pit from 50 to 75 cents, in one paper he in a pompous advertisement apologizes & mentions *his* sinking $5000 in 13 weeks in 1797, & in the next Nov[r] 10th he advertizes to take 50 cents as before. He calls loudly for support, & every corner of the paper has a puff direct. His Company is Mr & Mrs Hodgkinson, Mr & Mrs Whitlock, Mr & Mrs S Powel, Mrs Brett, Miss Brett, Mr & Mrs Harper, Mr Williamson, Mr Chalmers, Mr Turnbull, Mr Simpson, Mr Munto, Mr Helmbold, Mr Kedy, Mr Price, Mr Homer, Mr Villiers, Mr Kenny, Mr Lathy, Miss Solomon, Miss S Solomon, Miss Harding, Mrs King—who else I know not. Barret calls on me having just arrived without his wife. The Miss Westrays are at Boston unemployed & I have reason to hope will come on with Mrs Barrett. Write on Stranger.

[Nov.] 17th Write on Stranger. Write to B Carr, concerning Fox or Darley jun^{r}. Go to Theatre as usual & call at Mrs Fortune's. Agree to send $50 for Mrs Barrett & 50 more for the Miss Westrays. Bates with me talking over business. Brown dines with me. Write on Stranger.

[Nov.] 18th Sunday. Write on Stranger. Walk out to Tylers to see Barrett on business, found him with Williams & Pownal drinking & smoking. What a trio! Evening Dr Miller & Brown with me. G M W also. Finish the Stranger.

[Nov.] 19th Rain all day. Attend to business. Mark "He's much to blame" for ye prompter. Cast plays.

[Nov.] 20th Violent Snow storm. Receive a letter from Mr Gilb^{t} Fox, declining an engagement. Cast plays & mark prompt books all day.

[Nov.] 21st Write to my Mother. To Johnson, no 3 Portugal Street, Lincoln's In, London & To B Carr. Sir John Oldmixon arrives but not his wife. Yesterday Hughes shewed me a letter from Hodgkinson, demanding certain prompt books, by which I find his manuscript of "Man of Fortitude is here. I will therefore re-write my "Knights adventure" by the assistance which this stolen piece will give my memory, make the clown be driven back by Robbers who are beaten by the Knight the clown attends him & is deliver'd with him. S J O dines with me. Evening r^{d} farces & cast them.

[Nov.] 22d Read a Comedy, put into my hands by Bates written by *Beete* called "The Immigrants or whimsical Clubbists" *common.* Deliver'd the part of ye Stranger to Cooper. Call on Mr Hallam, he seem'd reserv'd. Write on my Comedy "Rule a Husband &c" Obtain monthly reviews from W W W's, & have an exquisite treat in reading the scene the reviewers have extracted from "Benyowski a Tragedy by Kotzebue, or at least attributed to him. They speak well of "He's much to blame" & "The Stranger." Write an address for opening Theatre & a squib on the *rational amusements* (so announced) of the Riding Circus.

[Nov.] 23d Reading review. Call on Brown & the Millers & show for their opinion my Address in terms of extraordinary approbation. Attend to business. R[d] Review. Visit at W W W's, & M Rogers's.

[Nov.] 24th Attend to business. Visit Mitchill. R[d] a farce call'd "Dupes of fancy" execrable. read in review. Mr W Holly visits us. Write on my Comedy.

[Nov.] 25th Sunday. Weather cold. R[d] Review. Cast plays. Write on Comedy. My Mother arrives.

[Nov.] 26th Wm Holly breakfasts with us. Attend to business. Write on Comedy. Wm Johnson having return'd drinks tea with us & C B B.

[Nov.] 27th Mr Bates returns from Philadelphia, & tho' I had cast him [for] Sir Oliver in the S for Scandal at his request he hesitates doing it for the opening, talks of tryal & first appearance, altho' he has been exhibiting himself in the Circus & City Assembly room & in all the Villages in the neighbourhood. Attend to business. Write on Comedy. Drink tea a[t] W W W's.

[Nov.] 28th Mr Tyler refuses the King in Hamlet. Bates positively refuses to do Sir Oliver & I am obliged [to] make out a bill without him by putting Martin Joseph & walking out to Tyler's to ask him to study Sir Oliver by Monday. Write on my Comedy.

[Nov.] 29th Read in Reviews. Attend to business. Cooper changes his style in respect to doing occasionally second Characters. Mr Jefferson refuses Dr Phlogiston, but retracts on *my* speaking to him. Mrs Hallam dont chuse to play Kitty in High life below. I draw up regulations with annexed forfeits, to be signed by the company. Mr Hallam refuses signing them, altho' previously informed that I should consult him as to the parts he was to do. Write on Comedy.

[Nov.] 30th Looking anxiously for Mrs Oldmixon. Write on Comedy. The Box book is open to day for the first time, & the School for Scandal & High life below Stairs advertised in the papers for Monday the 3d Decr. The disposition of the Company seems eminently hostile to each (as usual) and to me. Mr or Mrs Hallam have said nothing to me, but their conversation to others is highly disgusting, & she, I am told, is intoxicated daily. Receive a letter from Josiah Quincy, in which he informs me that he has advanced to the Miss Westrays on my acc^{t} $50 & requests me to repay it to Jacob Morton. His letter is polite & friendly. ½ past 3 OClock P M. finish my Comedy of "Rule a Husband & have a husband or The way to tame him." M Rogers & W W W & their wives drink tea with us.

Decr 1st Have a rehearsal of school for Scandal, & High life &c. Mrs Hallam very reserved. The Music of Sterne's Maria play'd in the Green Room. Mem: Ebenezer Watson's name inserted in ye list of subscribers instead of James Watson's.

Decr 2 Sunday. Preparations for opening Theatre. Reading Review.

[Dec.] 3d Obliged to get Mrs Tyler to do Lady Sneerwell & put Mrs Hogg into Mrs Oldmixons place as Mrs Candour. She arrives in the Afternoon. Open the Theatre with an apology. In the house $730. Martin spoke the address instead of Cooper who is lame. A lame beginning.

[Dec.] 4th Rehearse Inkle & Yarico & I read the Stranger to the performers in Green Room: I never saw a play affect performers so truly before. Drink tea at

W W W's. Call wth my Wife to see M: Judah & Wife. Write &c & Call on Mrs Oldmixon

[Dec.] 5th preparing for having the Stranger done on Monday. Rehearse Inkle & Yarico, "Quarter of an hour before dinner" and "Preparations for a Cruise" Hallam had last night a fracas wth his Wife, & fell into fits screaming like a fury or madman. Cooper says he is jealous of him & in consequence he (Cooper) intends moving. Evening, play the things rehearsed, to $267. Mrs Oldmixons' Wowski was very fine her songs exquisite. Bates not mellow in Trudge. He was better in the Tailor in "Preparations &c"

[Dec.] 6th Rehearse part of Hamlet & "The Stranger." Some of these scenes cannot be played or heard without tears. Mrs Barrett far exceeds my expectations: She read Mrs Haller with judgement & feeling. I commissioned Barrett, to write to Harper & offer him & his Wife $30 a week for both if they will do anything. Read Every Man in his humour with a view to have^g it done. Call on W Johnson & C Brown the latter read me proposals for a Magazine & gave me "Wieland." Drink tea at M Rogers's.

[Dec.] 7th Rehearse Hamlet & Sultan. Attend to business. prospect of a good House. Evening Mrs Oldmixon taken ill in her dressing room, goes home & is brought to bed of a daughter; after in vain trying to prevail on Mrs Hallam to read Ophelia, am obliged to apologize to the audience & return their money.

[Dec.] 8th Attend to business. Rehearse Stranger & Adopted Child, and in the evening Stranger again.

[Dec.] 9th Snow Storm all day. Read in Dodsley's old plays & others. Determine on writing a Comedy from the Honest Whore. Ciceri dines with me.

[Dec.] 10th Attend to various business. Begin the Comedy & call it "She was to blame." Rehearse Stranger & adopted Child. Evening in y^e House $641. Stranger very well received; no comic scene ever produced more effect than the last between Solomon, Peter & Barbara when she exposes them & the pathetic scenes were truly so.

[Dec.] 11th Attend to business. Write a little. Rehearse he's much to blame. Evening Mrs Barrett lets me know that she must decline playing Lady Vibrate. Determine on doing "Secrets worth knowing, before the other in consequence.

[Dec.] 12th Rehearse "Stranger & Miss in her teens." Attend to business. Evening Theatre the above pieces in y^e house 495$.

[Dec.] 13th Rehearse "Secrets worth knowing & Mock Doctor." Write a little. Evening Mitchill wth us. He tells me that R West is in town.

[Dec.] 14th Rehearse Hamlet & Mock Doctor. See R West & his Wife. Write a little. Attend to business. Evening play as above, in house $430.

[Dec.] 15th Go with my Wife to see R West & Wife: they decline coming to stay with us as they leave town immediately. The Stranger has made a very good impression. Somerville wants to publish it. Papendicks liberal translation is this day put in my hands. Rehearse Douglas & Love a la mode. Evening. Sterlitz tells me he has the German Copy of Count Benyouski. Theatre, Douglas & Preparations for a cruize is play'd, in house $208. Write on She's <*much*> was to blame.

1798			
June	5th	paid for altering the Gallery......	$23.50
	12	Lent Mrs Collins	10
		for the use of money to Dr Gamage for Mr V	24
		Lent Mr Bates	10
		D^{o} Hughes	5
		Give my note in fav^{r} of Jefferson due 30 days from y^{e} 4th Novr 1798 for	50
		D^{o} D^{o} to Cooper	50
		Accepted a draft for Barret due the 26th of December for (annull'd)	75
Nov^{r}	15th	pay for ye Orchestra parts to Agreable surprize & Children in the Wood	20
	16th	Gave my note, due in 60 days from this date, for a Large Lustre...	100
		Gave my note in fav^{r} of Mirvan Hallam at 30 days	65
	17	Gave my note at 45 days in favor of Massé	26
		p^{d} Lee (part for use of House)	4.25
		p^{d} Morris	3
		p^{d} Martin (to purchase skins)	10
		p^{d} Mr Audin	20
	19th	Gave my note to Audin due in 60 days from this date for	100
		Gave my endorsement to J Martin on a note due 90 days from this date	65
	22d	Gave my note to Wm Bates, due 60 days from this date	54
	24	p^{d} Wm Lee	3
		p^{d} Wm Blackman	1
	29	p^{d} Hughes	3
Dec^{r}	1st	p^{d} Lee to buy Wood	3
		Lent Mr Cooper	5

p[d] Miss Westray's (to J Quinsey order) 50

rec[d] from Faulkner 45

Mr Hogg $5
Martin $10
Conrad $2
Miss Vincent $28

Dec[r] 6 Mem: in my handkerch: $124

	p[d] Lee	$3.10
	Bates	5
	William	10
	Mr Martin	115.46
	Mr Oldmixon	37
	Ciceri for his people (30)	91.25
	Lee	12
	for Carting Coal	1
	for Jacket for Adopted Child ...	3
	Tailors work	2
11th	Massé	35
	Gave note due 60 days from Dec[r] 7th to Wm Dodge for Coal for.	106.35
	p[d] Wm the blackman	10
13th	Lent Dunlap & Judah	380
	D[o] D[o]	150
	p[d] Mr Cooper (Falkner)	28
	Hogg	20
	p[d] To Wm Hendersons order	27.37½
15	p[d] Beut Dangle	30
	J. Martin	10
	William	10

Hodgkinson / Bar[t]	50	30
Hallam	25	
Cooper	25	
Martin	25	
Tyler	20	
Jefferson	25	22
Hallam Jr	16	18

Hogg	12		
Miller	12		
Lee	12		
Leonard	8		
Shapter	8		
Stockwell	4		
Hughs	10		
Falconer	14		
Seymour	9		
	275		254
Bates			25
			279
Hodgkinson } Bar[t] }	40		30
Oldmixon	37		37
Hallam	35		25
Melmoth	20		25
Brett	14		
Brett	14		
Harding	12		
Westray	12		
Westray	12		
Collins	12		12
Simpson	14	Hogg	14
Hogg	4		4
Petit	3		3
Cook	3		3
Hughes	3		3
Seymour	16		16
Mr. Simpson	16	Bates	8
	532		439
Orchestra	140		140
Lights	109		109
Labourers	24		24
Doors	50		50
Cleaning	5		5
Printing	68		68

Properties	6	6
Wardrobe	15	15
fuel	15	15
Ciceri's depart[t]	60	70
Rent	145	145
	1169	1106
Mrs King	10	
	4)1179	
	$ 295 nightly 4 nights in ye week	

27 for lights less
12 doors
17 printing
3 properties
20 Ciceri's dept.
79
1 ward[be]
80

1179
80
3)1099
366.33 3 nights ye week

1107
80
3)1027
343

477
630
4)1107
278 nightly 4 nights in ye week on ye supposition of Hodgk family going & Barrets com[s]

COLLECTIONS OF

THE NEW YORK HISTORICAL SOCIETY

FOR THE YEAR 1930

THE JOHN WATTS DePEYSTER
PUBLICATION FUND SERIES

LXIII

WILLIAM DUNLAP (1766-1839)
By Himself
(In the Theodore Salisbury Woolsey Collection)

DIARY OF WILLIAM DUNLAP

(1766–1839)

THE MEMOIRS OF A DRAMATIST, THEATRICAL MANAGER, PAINTER, CRITIC, NOVELIST, AND HISTORIAN

VOLUME II

JANUARY 1 – SEPTEMBER 21, 1806

MARCH 17 – MAY 6, 1811

NOVEMBER 23, 1812 – MAY 7, 1813

OCTOBER 15, 1819 – FEBRUARY 13, 1822

CONTENTS

ILLUSTRATIONS

LETTERS FROM WILLIAM DUNLAP TO HIS WIFE

JANUARY 1—MARCH 6, 1806,

PHILADELPHIA, BALTIMORE, AND WASHINGTON

and

DIARY OF WILLIAM DUNLAP

JULY 3—SEPTEMBER 21, 1806,

PERTH AMBOY, NEW YORK, AND BOSTON

(Manuscript volume lettered *Memoirs 23* owned by YALE UNIVERSITY LIBRARY)

MEMOIRS 23

Copies of letters to my Wife made by my desire by my little girl

Phil. January 1st 1806

My dearest Bess

A happy new year to you and those around you. I have had serious thoughts of passing this day with you, nothing but the expence deterred. What a contrast this to the last. Oppressed with a debt which destroyd mind & body, but I will not think of it now. If you was but with me I should be content.

Yesterday was our first winters day, and was preceded by a storm that did much mischief in this harbour. I have nearly finished all the pictures I have begun here and if no new ones offer I shall start from this place on monday.

I look for a letter from you to day, & hope to find you have recieved the 45 doll^{s}. If it is not so you shall have another check by Saturday.

I did intend to have writen you a long letter for a New Years gift, but the morning has slipt away and I must go out to finish by appointment Mrs. Harwood's picture. Adieu my dearest

W D

Phil: Jany 3^{d} 1806 Friday

I received yours, and am very sorry Mr. P has been so negligent. I do not understand whether he has the acc^{t} and receit or not. If not, I think you had best send it to him If he has it, let him know that I left the acc^{t} with you, supposing it the same as cash and that you want the money.

The cold weather makes me more anxious for you. if

you get the money from Mr. P. provide yourself with plenty of wood while the roads continue good.

As to my pictures I have painted three for money, the fourth Mr. Bache is out of town. I have done one Washington's head & begun another: these I look on as Cash. I have painted at our friend Brown's at Mrs. Wignels and at Mr. C Clays, where I am from the kindness of Harwood & wife, and the frankness of Mr. & Mrs. Clay, quite at home. The sketch I made of Mag. is of great use to me, as it is the admiration equally of the ignorent & the Connesseur (I cant for my soul recollect how to spell the word)

I have succeeded highly with Mrs. Harwoods picture, & expect it to aid me at Washington as I am to carry letters from her to Mrs. Maddison. I have bought me a waiscoat $5.50, A box of colours, of paris preperation and very fine $10. Ivories & pencils &c. $10. Dont think me extravagant. I really think I shall never part with a dollar but for a necessary—these things were so to me.

I have employ'd a man to collect subscriptions for this City, at 16 per cent upon what he collects, he delivering the first volume & recieving the money. It is as low as I could get it done & with difficulty found a man fitting.

You need be under no apprehension for the expence of the engraving. Independent of the additional currency it will give to the Volume, I doubt not as many prints may be sold in the print shops as will pay the Engraver.

I wish you to tell Mag. to look for the 23d Volume of those little books in which I journalize, and copy in a neat hand, all my letters, begining at the 1st January 1806. it will improve hir writing, and spelling, and I will journalize by letter to you, which will add to your entertainment.

Pray sell your butter, try to get the money and buy plenty of wood, that I may at least think of your being warm, if you cant have all the comforts I wish you. Adieu my love, with best love to our mother and daughter. John has not yet written to me.

W D

Phil Monday Jany 6th 1806

I recieved yours of Saturday this morning. You see I am still here. I am very glad you have received the money; I shall not want any of it sent to me. For Mrs. W[ignell]'s child's picture I recieved 25 doll^{s} & she is so well pleas'd that I am employ'd to paint a second at the same price. I have sent by Dr. Irving, a Washington's head to D[avid] Longworth to sell for me, and am far advanced in another, much finer than anything I have done. If I do not get employ at Washington I shall not stay there, and I shall when there ask 25 doll^{s} for every head I paint—my present stile of painting will justify it. As to doing without a female servant, I say no—you must not think of it so much by way of answer.

It will be wednesday or thursdy before I leve this. Your next letter must be directed for me at the post office Baltimore.

Some days ago, a traveling quaker, a traveller and a writer of a book of travals, called to see my friend Brown, & I was introduced to *friend* Samson. Anxious to have his book praised in Browns Magazine he made his remarks and enquiries all tending to that point, but accompanied with a truly quaker self-sufficiency. I do not know wether you know what I mean, but I think there is a kind of priggish self-full smiling impudence, which is peculiar to the vain of that sect. Such a one is friend Samson. He is large, florid, healthfull, rich, has travel'd in England France & Italy; talks of Authors and Artists; has a collection of pictures; and is any thing but a wit, a Connoisseur, or a gentleman. perhaps I am too severe. it is best to believe I am. Brown carried me to see his collection of pictures. The best is a small picture about 2 foot by 1, said to be by Reubens. I never saw anything so small by Reubens. Be it whose it may it is very fine. The subject, Christ paying the tribute money, "Give (or render) unto Ceaser that which is Ceasers." He has a Magdalen said to be by Guido and some sea pieces & Landscapes.

[Benjamin] Trot[t], finds sufficient employment here,

& has raised his price from 30 to 40 doll[s]. he is a man of genious, with excentricities; has misspent much of his time, but is now inclined to make the most of the remainder; he has shown me some little things, since I have been here, of consequence in the mechanical, or preparatory part of the art.

This stormy day, the first snow we have seen I have pass'd, in steadily painting. Beginning a portrait of Mrs. Brown, and finishing one of Jefferson. I find it necessary to destroy the one I painted of Mrs. B in July last, as you may suppose. The one I have begun is, in comparison, *light* to *utter darkness.*

Tuesday [Jan.] 7th

I have painted stedily to day without going out of the house the streets being very wet. The evening has passed in playing Backgammon with Charles, and reading *Anquitil's Lewis 14th* a very entertaining and most valuable book. There is a vast display of nature both in her hideous & amiable forms. The intrigues of an intriguing Court & the characters of Fenelon & his pupil the Duke of Burgundy Lewis's grandson. The Authors principally quoted are St Simon & Madame de Maintenon, the first is remarkable for his talent of drawing characters. Maintenon's letters must be well worth reading. There is every reason to believe that she was married to Lewis & it is certain she was a great nay a good woman. But "what is Hecuba to you or you to Hecuba"?

With all love, good. my next from Baltimore

W D

Phil Jan[y] 9th 1806 Friday [*sic*]

Here I am my dear wife. And now for the why and the wherefore. After sending off my last letter Harwood called to tell me that Mrs. Jos Clay wished to sit for hir picture to send to hir husband who is in Congress. Of course my Washington's head was laid by and yesterday I began the picture at Mr Curtis Clays where to day I shall continue to work at it & to morrow finish it. I shall therefore remain here at least until monday.

I have taken my usual early walk to the Shuylkill this morning which I found frozen completely over. Winter has at length mounted his throne but I hope his reign will not be long. He has cast his white robe o'er his shoulders and shook his glassy sceptre over us in terrorum. I hate him heartily.

The good Citizens of this place are giving dinners to the Moreaus, Eatons & Decaturs. I see by a news paper that Capt Bainbridge was at one given to Decatur, and is enumerated among the guests. It has not been my lot to meet him any where. I have made three efforts to see Mrs Levy [?] but have been unsuccessfull. Last evening Harwood had a party of musical people of the Theater to commemorate his wedding day; I was with them untill a very late supper and then ran away for the party was not musical to me.

I hope to recieve another letter from you while I am here. pray take care to get plenty of wood & every thing that is within reach that is good and comfortable. With love to our mother and daughter. Adieu

W D

Phil Jany 14th 1806

My dear Bess

I rec^{d} yours of Saturday yesterday. I lament the situation of the family you allude to I see not where there misery is to terminate.

I have finished Mrs Clays picture and shall be on my way to Baltimore when you recieve this. The account of my labours here stands thus

Mrs Wignels Child...	25	A Washington sent to New York to sell...	20
A copy begun to finish on my return	25	D^{o} much superior for which I would not take	30
Mr C Clay	20		50
Mrs J Clay	20		
Mrs Crosskeys	20		

$100 certain
50 uncertain

Heads of Mrs Wignell Mr Harwood Mr Jefferson for myself

Half length of Mrs Harwood to be carried to Washington & exhibited, but ultimately to be presented to Harwood

Head of Mrs Brown for hir husband

And all this done in less than 5 weeks at a season when the days are at the shortest

I have recieved a letter from John the composition very respectable, the hand writing not so mutch improved as I expected.

I dined on saturday at Conrads with a party of *literati*. Fessendon [44] (the auther of Tractoration), Denny,[45] Mr John Vaughan (member of the philisophical Society of this place) Doctor [Nathaniel] Chapman (one of the founders of the Edinburg review) Brown and myself. Fessendon is a huge heavy fellow as big as Coll Humphrey's, with features as heavy as his person, and an address rather awkward; but his conversation, tho' fabricated *a la yankee* is agreable & evinces an amiable disposition. He is a mechanical as well as a poetical genius, and when in England was concerned in erecting floating mills upon the Thames, similer to those used in France and Germany. Denny is a small, neat man, an entire contrast in appearance and manner to the foregoing. He appears to be about 45 years old & is well bespater'd with grey hairs. Tho' a Masacusets man he has freed his conversation from yankeeism's, and speaks with as much facility and correctness as he writes. He is polite in his address, attentive to the etiquette of conversation and studious so to suit it to those with him as to elicit those sparks which might other wise lie dormant. with all this, I confess I did not hear those brilliant things which I

[44] Thomas Green Fessenden, author of *Terrible Tractoration, a poetical petition against galvanizing trumpery* . . by "Christopher Caustic", London, 1803; N. Y., 1804.

[45] Joseph Dennie, editor of a weekly magazine published in Philadelphia, called *The Port Folio.*

expected from the mouth of the editor of the portfolio. Mr Vaughan, talked much & sensibly but not profoundly.

Doctor Chapman has an agreable intelligint countinance & speaks with precision and elegance, but is not fluent, owing, as it appears, to some defect of the palate or other organ of speech. Brown tells me, he wrote the criticism on John Davis's travels, which pleased us so much last winter.

The winter has broke up with us, and I suppose the Ice of the Deleware is sunk by the rain of last night. Added to all my antipathies against cold, I was very anxious on account of Armet Brown who has a ship laden and ready to sail, which if not liberated from the Deleware would have proved a great loss to him.

Our friends in this house are well. They have repeatedly desired their remembrances to you. The boys continue to grow and to crow & to be beauties. Adieu with love to mother and Mag, who I suppose laments the flight of the snow.

I am glad you mention'd the little dutchman, who is in my feelings, a part of the family.

W D

Phil Jany 17th

Still in Philidelphia, my dear Bess, but positively to leave it to morrow at 8 OClock. After dispatching my [blank] I sat down to put a finishing hand to my Washington, when behold, his black velvet coat was pealing off from the ivory and all in holes & patches, I am obliged to give him an entire new one. Then came on snow and frost so intense as to make me congratulate myself that I was by a friendly fireside. Yesterday was an excessive severe day. The water froze in my pencil, not two yards from the fire, so that several times when I attempted to put colour to the ivory, it was mingled with icy christals. This morning is milder, I have been to the Deleware supposing it frozen over; but it was free, and the warmth of the sun at 8 OClock promised that it will continue so.

I thought yesterday of your Behama neighbours. Imagination brought their shivering figures before me; but it reminded me that you might be shivering too; for I fear you cannot keep your large open appartment warm.

In Philidelphia, where the emancipation of the Blacks originated there are more free people of that colour than in any other place in the union. Most of them are degraded & vicious but there are many useful and respectable. They are hired servants by the month, Cooks for occasional dinners or parties; Waiters of the same discription; Mechanics; (one in particular a rich sail maker, having many journimen & apprentices under him) and one Clergiman. I have seen funeral processions led in solemn state by this black and all black gentlemen. Early associations made it appear ludicrous to me. It seem'd like mimicry. Some days ago, I cross'd the Skuylkill at the great bridge and walk'd along the bank to the upper floating bridge, above or north of the City. In the way I pass'd unexpectedly through a rural cemetary beautifully situated, on a spot more suited to the living than the dead. I soon found that It was a place of rest for the children of Africa, and read the following Epitaph.

To the membory of —— who departed dis life —— eage ——

From this you may infer that in addition to my list, there [are] black teachers of orthography & black manufacturers of tombstones.

Adieu my dear Bess, with all love to those around you.

W D

Baltimore Jany 20th

I am now 104 miles further from you than when I last wrote & in health and full imployment.

On friday evening I left our friend's and lodged at the stage house to be ready for starting. Next morning, after breakfast, wrapt up in my great cloak & my feet guarded by my mockasons I left penns City for an untried route. My companions were a tall scotsman and a short scotsman, two frenchman, the one a giant the other a deformed dwarf, a little frenchwoman, the wife of the latter, and a little *Fiddy* lap dog.

The heart of the woman was in possession of the lap dog, and the occupation of hir Husband was to nurse its possessor.

After passing the villages of Darby & Chester, we entred Deleware State and arrived at Wilmington. This town has nothing of the neat & handsome style of the northern & eastern villages. It is little more than one long street on the declivity of a slope, at the extremity of which is Christiana or Christine Creek, which runs into the Deleware.

Shut up in a close carriage one gains little knowledge of a country by passing through it expecially at this dreary season. at a village called Newport we dined. About 10 OClock we arrived at the Susquehana, which is here a mile in width. It was hard frozen, and we crossed on foot, our baggage being drawn over in a sleigh by negroes. This passage and the detention of supping made it 12 OClock before we left the banks of the river. The night was by no means severe and occasionally it snow'd. It was daylight before we reached Baltimore. The country in the neighbourhood is rude & presents none of those appearances which usually indicate the vicinity of a City. About 9 OClock we were set down at the Stage house in Baltimore.

After cleaning and breakfasting, I sallied fourth to view the town whose first appearance is by no means agreable, but I must have further opportunities of seeing & judging before I attempt a discription of the Capital of Maryland.

Having been recommended by Mrs. Wignel, to Briden, the keeper of the Fountain Inn and Coffee house, I sought him and took up my abode with him, having a convenient room appropriated for painting. Before I went to bed for the first time in Baltimore I had two pictures engaged, Mr. Briden's and Mr. Jenning's. This morning Mr. Jennings sat to me & I have worked all day, having promised to finish the likeness by tomorrow night.

I recieved your letter dated 16th at the post office & was recognized as an old acquaintance by the post master Charles Burrell.

Your letter has made me quite melancholy. But the severe wether I hope is over, and I hope we shall have no more long seperations. It is a subject I wish to avoid—it is useless to dwell upon it.

I am here utterly alone. As soon as I can I will seek Elijah Rattoone. In a few days I will write again & fully as to my situation & prospects. Divide my love with Mag and my mother. Adieu

William Dunlap

Baltimore Jany 25th 1806

My dearest Bess.

I have recieved yours of last Sunday & tuesday. You before this have mine with the information of my arrival in this place. Monday Tuesday & Wednesday were employ'd in painting a picture, for which I have recieved the money.

Wednesday evening I drank tea with Mrs. Rattoon. during a part of the time, the *Doctor* was out, and she introduced the subject of his troubles in this place, which, whether, I ever heard of them or not, were quite new to me. Reports have been spread very much to the detriment of his character; which reports she attributes to the ill will of your old acquaintance Doctor Behn. Such however was the dissatisfaction of part of the Episcopal congregation that Docter R. thought proper to resign his situation, and intended to leave Baltimore but his friends insisted upon his remaining and Mrs. R. says, a church is to be built for him. I have since heard Docter R. spoken very hardly of in publick and it seems the spirit of Division runs high in the church.

Young [James] Inglis of N. Y. son to the china dealer, is settled here in the presbyterian Church, & it seems that on his introduction a schism took place & another Church was built.

The Winter appears to have flown. It is here like spring

MARGARET DUNLAP (1791-1837)
By William Dunlap
(Courtesy of Mrs. William Tidball)

& I presume is so with you, for when I came here I found as much snow & ice as I left in philidelphia: I therefore presume that when it is cold here it is cold at Amboy and *vice versa.*

The Man of the house Mr. James Bryden & his wife have both sat to me for their pictures, and I understand I am to paint their daughter Mrs Behn, wife of a german Merchant now absent, but the last mentioned is not yet engaged. I have two pictures allready engaged for Washington City when I shall arrive there, a Mr. & Mrs. [Charles] Love.

I have subscription papers out here, what will be the result, I cannot say. I have employ'd a man to collect names on the same terms as at Philidelphia, I am now certain of publishing the first Volume if no more and shall make preparations on my return to philidelphia.

I drank tea again last evening at Mrs. Rattoons, where in the conversation of Mrs. R. & Miss Bull, a fine old lady, I find something approaching to what I love most.

Your last excited a variety of sensations, but upon the whole pleasure predominated, I hope my mother may continue to find the winter a favorable one to her health. Mag does not presume to neglect the copying I prescribed for her. I feel grateful to everybody that contributes to your amusement. Tell Theodosia that if she continues good she shall still call me father.

In my next I shall attempt some discription of this very thriving city. I have as yet but a superficial knowledge of it. I fear the house I am in is a expensive one, but the people seem anxious to employ and throw imployment in my way. it is probably better than a cheaper and more obscure situation.

Adieu my dear Good night.

W D

Baltimore Jany 29th 1806

My dearest Bess

It was my intention to have written you a long journalizing letter to morrow, and it has but now occur'd to me that if I do not put a line in the Office tonight you will not hear from me until next tuesday, I therefore merely sit down to say I am well, that I may go & deposit my letter before I go to bed.

I am painting on my fourth picture; after finishing which say next Sunday I shall go on to Washington which is but 45 Miles further; a short days ride.

Direct your next of course to the post office at that place.

I am very weary of this place. I am very weary of my days work & the lack of faces in which I can take intrest. Good night. I had better seek rest that weary my self with telling you that I am weary. Adieu.

W D

Baltimore Feby 1st 1806

My dear Bess.

I shall leave this place tomorrow after two weeks residence, which has enabled me to form a pretty accurate estimate of the town & its inhabitants as compared to other City's of the United States.

Baltimore, so called from the first proprietor Cecilus Calvert, Lord Baltimore, is situated about 200 miles from the Atlantic Ocean almost at the head of the great bay of Chesapeak, and near the mouth of the river patapsco. The State of Maryland is divided into Eastern & Western by the Chesapeak and is watered by the streams which flow into it, among the largest is the susquehannah, flowing from the north & which I cross'd in coming hither, and the patowmac from the west, having its source in Virginia & dividing the two states. Among the smaller is found the patapsco which flowing from the west falls into the Chesapeak to the southward of Baltimore which is built round a bason made by an inlet from the river thus.

[Space left blank. Margaret did not copy her father's map.]

The length of the town from Fells point quite around the bason is about 3 miles; its breadth irregular. It has had the most rapid growth of any place on the continent and ranks as the fourth in size and third in commercial consequence in the United States.

Annapolis, nominally the capital of the state, is 30 miles to the Southward and is as rapidly declining as Baltimore is increasing. Fells point is the place where the shipping lie and are built, and is of course the rendezvous of Sailors and those that live by their vices. Though it is regularly laid out, it is with the exception of a few houses, a mass of wretchedness and infamy; yet through this medium flows the commercial wealth of Maryland and part of Virginia. Is not such the channel of all commercial wealth? Next to fells point comes Old town the original Baltimore, divided from the remaining and principle part of the City, by the mouth of a stream, call'd Jones's Falls, over which are several bridges. From Old town, proceading west, we enter the main or Baltimore Street, which is the seat of the retail trade of the town, is spacious, and the greater part well built; it is parelel with the head of the bason & is cross'd at right angles by streets running to the water. The present direction of the growth of the City appears to be westward. In that quarter is the market for produce which is brought in cover'd waggons, as in philidelphia, but with very inferior teams. The horses are generally small and driven 2 abreast: 4 to each team. Trucks are used for the transportation of goods, Hackney Coaches are used here more than any where on the Continent except Boston.

Of the publick buildings I can say little & I believe little is to be said places of Worship are numerous for the size of the place but none remarkable for size of structure. The Court house is a wretched old building, standing in the center of a street, with an arch'd gangway under it beautiful by a pillory and whipping post. The dansing assembly room or house, is the handsomest building in the place and the proprietors have allotted a lower [*sic*] in it to the City Library company: thus literature is kept in due subordination to dancing & card playing. This observation leads me to manners, which are such as might be expected in a society formed of commercial adventurers from all nations and in which slavery exists on the old colonial establishment. I have seen several counting houses open on sunday with the clarks at work; & Billiard tables publicky notefied by sign boards. From the first I onely infer that less attention is paid to appearances here than to the northward; & from the second that gambling is not in such *general* disrepute. A *Raffle* was held at the house I live in some days ago and many of the first merchants of the place mingled in attendance with professed gamesters & surrounded the table. Some watches & a clock were raffled for; which done, the company threw the dice for money until 2 OClock in the morning. An informer, however was present, and all gameing or betting above 5 doll[s] being prohibited by law of the corporation, these *gentlemen* had the mortification of appearing as culprits before the Mayor & recieving sentence of punishment by fine.

Having yesterday finished my painting, I walked in the afternoon to the Fort [McHenry] which commands the entrance of the harbour or bason of Baltimore. It is three miles from the town on a neck of land formed by the inlet (the head of which is the bason) on one side and the petapsco on the other. As you go to the Fort, on the left is a promontory which overlooks the town, the harbour and entrance south of the bason and the river On this height is a house called the observatory where signals are made of the approach of vessels as at the narrows of N. Y. Harbour. The Fort is at the extreme point of the neck, and is a strong fortress with brick walls surmounted by earth and garrison'd at present by a captains guard. The barracks are within the walls and could contain some hundred of soldiers. A battery is below the Fort at the edge of the water, which was formerly the only defence of the harbour, until the United States erected the present fortress.

I may have mentioned in a former letter the unimproved appearance of the country in the vicinity of this place, as we approached from philidelphia no cultivation; no country seats. But on the other side of the town and on the banks of the patapsco are many delightful villa's and snug retreats, with all the attention to decoration and delight which is usual in the neighbourhood of populous towns.

I pass'd an hour to day in the Library, which tho' small is well chosen and well arranged. My attention was principally taken up with a view of Modern Rome: another of St. Peters, and the Vatican: and a third of the inside of St. Peters. The two last well design'd and engraved.

Doctor R. has just left me. He says the subscription, is open for building him a church & filling very fast. He talks freely against his enemies & ascribes his persecution to envy of his popularity.

Groomrich is here. I called to see him and he return'd my call. He talks as much as ever and Correggio & Reubens, Titian & Claude, Vandyke & Kneller, roll off his tongue with the rapidity & incessancy of a Mill torrent. He show'd me a few good pictures; One by Sir James Thornhill (Hogaths farther in law) one by Kneller and one (perhaps) Vanduke, with two Landscapes by Italian masters, whose names I cannot recolect.

Adieu. my best love attends you and those with you ever.

W D

Washington Feby 5th [1806]

My dearest Bess

Here I am safe and well and employ'd in painting in Georgetown near Washington owing to which I have seen nobody I know. I write this in the most hurried manner that I may walk up to Washington and see Mitchill [46] & others, at a season of the day when I cannot work.

I recieved yours of the 1st this morning by walking 2 miles for it and must do the same to deposit this.

Adieu

W D

[46] Dr. Samuel Latham Mitchill was a U. S. Senator from New York, 1804-1809.

Washington Feby 6th

My dear Bess

My last was mearly intended to prevent your unesiness from not hearing of my arrival. I now sit down to communicate, what if, known before I could have given you full information would have caused you much uneasiness. I was one General Heard's securities, and could not until this moment assure you or myself that I should not be prosecuted as such; but I am now assured that no steps shall be taken against me. I have this morning seen Mr. Gallatin, the Secretary of the Treasury, respecting my situation, and recieved his directions how to act, in preasance of Mitchell, who introduced me. Mr. Gallatin has full power in the case. As to Heard, he is removed, and will be prosecuted and I presume (if not able to pay arrears) imprison'd, from which situation nothing but an act of Congress can relieve him.

You will perhaps feel hurt that I have not communicated the circumstance of my suretyship to you. When I first became Genl Heards security, I thought it but a form; it almost pass'd from my mind, and when it was brought back with some apprehensions of danger, the disorder & intricacies of my affairs, and the certainty of bankruptcy again drove it away. After I had become insolvent, I wrote to Doctor Mitchel and stated my insufficiency to be a surety to the Government, which letter he inclosed to Mr. Gallatin and assured me that other surety would be demanded of Heard, and that I should probably hear no more of the matter. Though I felt in some measure secure in these assurences I dared not mention the circumstances to you as I knew your apprehensions would be a source of torture. Heard never gave me a hint that he was in arrears, and I long flatter'd myself, that some other surety had been demanded & given. I had likewise determined upon visiting Washington and knew I could then gain information of the real state of the business. Heards arrears are $3455 so that if I had not been brought to insolvency by my own misfortunes I should have had now to undergo all its horrors, for the misfortunes or misconduct of another. As it is, I am but as I was. I seize the first moment after my interview with Mr. Gallatin to disburthen my mind and to make you secure against the circumstance of accidentally hearing that I was one of the miserable man's suretys. Now you must forgive me for having risqued property, when I had it, by becoming any persons bondsman; and for having, out of tenderness for you, kept the transaction from your knowledge until I could tell the event of it: and then I shall feel perfectly reliev'd.

Feby 8th My journy hither was performed with little fatigue, on monday last, and though it rain'd and the roads were heavy we came the 45 miles from Baltimore to George town between the hours of 6 in the morning and 4 in the afternoon. The country is poor through which I pass'd. There is said to be but one good farm from Baltimore to Washington: that is after passing the immediate vicinity of the first. About 7 miles riding brought us to a ferry over the patapsco, passed in a scow guided by a rope drawn tight to stakes on either side. Five miles from Washington we cross'd the eastern branch of the patowmac, at Bladensburgh, a poor Village once of some trade. The river is here a mere mill stream, at Washington 74 gun ships ride in security. On entring the City of Washington from the north or east the first object is the Capitol which when finished will be an immense and superb building; One wing is now finished and another carried up but not cover'd in. In the finished part Congress sits. A few houses appear near the Capitol but when you arrive at the summit of the hill on which it stands, you see all that is built of the City particularly the publick & private buildings streaching along at intervals 3 Miles to George town, which is likewise seen from this spot. I went directly to the latter place as being the residence of the gentleman who had engaged my pencil at Baltimore.

I put up at McGlaughlin's hotel, George town, where many members of Congress reside from the scantiness of accomodations at Washington & are convey'd backwards and forwards by *Hacks* which makes the *Pensylvania Avenue* (for so the road or street from George town to the Capitol is call'd) very lively. This road is a finished turnpike road with good foot paths or side walk, and planted with double rows of poplers. On tuesday I found Mr. Love, and began to paint. In the afternoon sought Mitchill, but he was out. I found Miss Templeton at Mr. Smith's the printer of the ministerial gazette [47] but as she was engaged to a party at Mr. Madisons, I return'd to George town to tea.

Wednesday afternoon I found Mitchil and made the appointment with him to see Mr. Gallatin the next morning the result of which visit I have already mentioned.

I would have you take no notice of Heards business whatever. I think I shall by this post write him, not to mention my arrangements or situation arrising from my previous insolvency, but to know his statement of his accounts & what resources he has for deminishing the debt, though I presume he has none.

Continue to direct to me post office Washington, as it is probable I shall remove to that City in a few days where I can board about as low as any where else. I cannot well raise the price of my pictures as I intended I fear it would prevent employment & Mr. Love having engaged at Baltimore at 20 doll^s had mention'd my price as such. I have another picture bespoken and more talked of.

The first part of this letter was written on the Capitol hill at the quarters of our Connecticut friends with whom I dined that day and after passing part of the evening at Mitchills quarters among the oposite party walk'd to George town to rest.

with all love to you and yours

W D

[47] The *Universal Gazette* was published in Washington, D. C., by Samuel Harrison Smith, 1800-1810. Brigham, "Bibliography of American Newspapers", in *Proc. American Antiquarian Society,* new ser., XXIII, 367, (Oct., 1913).

Washington (George town) Feby 9th Sunday

My dear Wife

This is a cold day and makes me think that you must have a return of winter with you. I have just return'd from a walk of 3 miles up the western branch of the potomac the scenery of which must be in summer extremely beautiful. Near George town is a cannon foundery [48] belonging to a methodist preacher of the name of Foxhall A whimsical combination of employments, Casting Cannon & preaching the Gospel—and casting Cannon at preasant for the Dey of Algiers.

About three miles up the river is the lesser falls of the potomac which have rendred a Canal and locks necessary. I never saw the mode of lock navigation before.

An Encyclopedia can better discribe the mode of passing boats through the locks than I can. Fifteen miles up the river I am told are the great falls and locks. By means of these produce is brought 150 or 200 miles to George town & Alexandria, which last town is 5 miles lower down the river than this place. Washington is situated in the fork made by the East & west branches of the patomac; a small stream runing through it formally called Goose creek, now the *Tiber* as it leves the foot of the capitol hill. This stream falls into the potomac about a mile and a half from the Capitol, oposite the presidents house & the publick Offices, and makes the scene very picturesque. the point made by its joining the great river reminded me of the point of Statin Island opposite to Amboy another small stream divides Washington from George town & is call'd Rock Creek; several bridges over it make communication easy. This last stream is the seat of many mills & its high banks afford pleasant scites for a number of Gentlemens villa's.

The situation of Washington is certainly very fine, but it has long been ascertain'd that people cannot live much less grow rich upon prospects, and the prospect of future

[48] The Columbian Foundry, established by Henry Foxall. See Madison Davis, "The Old Cannon Foundry above Georgetown, D. C. and its first owner, Henry Foxall", in *Records of the Columbia Historical Society,* (1908), XI, 16-70.

prosperity has not been strong enough to keep those mechanics as inhabitants who first remov'd to the City at its foundation. No houses are building; those already built are not finish'd and many are falling rapidly to decay. I believe there is not a knocker or bell to any door in Washington. It reminds me of the Cities founded by Catherine 2d in Russia; tho' it is not so bad as some of hers with houses and no inhabitants & others which exist merely in name & on the map. The shops and Stores which supply the inhabitants of Washington are principally in George town.

Feby 12th 1806 I am still in George town and have been for some days at the house of Mr. Charles Love for whom I am painting 2 pictures. I am in the family of *Love*. Certainly I am in a family of kindness & hospitality. Mr. & Mrs. Easton are next door neighbours and have been in to see me. He writes in one of the publick offices. She made many enquiries concerning her old acquaintances in Amboy & seam'd fond of the subject. She remembred and reminded me of Dangle's designating her as the "woman that talk'd night and day."

I have called at the post office Washington several times in hopes of a second letter, but in vain. I hope when I deposit this to find one. Until I leve George town I shall not be able to do anything with my subscription, tho' I will try & make arrangements this afternoon for seeing the president.

Adieu my dear. with love to our Mother & daughter

W D

[At this point the handwriting changes. Evidently Margaret stopped copying her father's letters, and the following were transcribed by a more mature and experienced hand.]

Washington Feby 13

Never, never, my dear Bess, will I be seperated in this manner from you again. I endeavor to console myself by imagining the pleasure of my return home, but all in vain. Neither does the number of Men, I see around me, who are absent from their homes their wifes & families, give me any consolation; tho it is generally supposed that fellowship in suffering lightens pain. Mitchell says he writes to his wife every day. It may be so for the members of Congress have not only opportunity but temptation for letter writing. They are seated with each one his pen ink & paper before him, & while one idle fellow is idly talking upon an idle subject, the rest who must sit, to avoid hearing him & fill up the time write letters.

I have drank tea with Miss Templeton & as you may possibly feel some curiosity respecting the *illustrious* Ambassadors from the Osages & Tunisians I will give you her account of their appearance at the City Dancing Assembly. The Indians, dressed as they commonly are among the Whites, that is in Cloth Coats & pantaloons, with their national ornaments were seated at one end of the Room. The Turk a handsome old man, with a white beard, superbly dressed & attended by his two secretaries both richly vested in the Oriental style, placed himself opposite the Osages & thro the medium of their interpreter, in the French Language, put various questions to them in this manner. Do you believe in Jesus Christ? No, dont know him. Do you believe in Mahomet? No dont know him. Are you descended from Ham, Shem or Japhet? Dont know them. The Turk then remarked that their Heads were shaved in the manner of his own, that is, all off except on the top; & that they resembled the Bedouin Arabs. He then asked one of the Osages if they had such handsome women among them as the ladies present. The savage replied "yes, But not so handsomely dress" & retorted the question to the Tunisian, who smiling & turning to the ladies, said, "they, the disciples of Mahomet, were promised such beauties in paradise." You see by this that his Tunisian Excellency is a polished courtier: Yet so little has he of diplomatic Dignity that he is a vender of Otto of Roses (& other knic knacks) which his secretaries sell at $.50 per phial. He has dismissed one of his Attendants for striking an insolent blackguard Barber of the city, & before sending him off, bastinadoed & requested to know of the Secretary of State whether he wish'd him put to Death as he was impowered (& I suppose perfectly willing) to take his life.

Mrs. Smith,[49] with whom Miss T stays was a Miss Bayard of N. Brunswick. She is clever, but very sentimental. Her husband is a little man & reminds one of C B B, but Brown has I think the air of a Philosopher, while S. looks like a Monkey turn'd Barber.

Albert Gallatin, Secretary of the Treasury is a thin man about my height or taller, with dark hair, coarse & bushy, yellow complexion, long nose, hideous mouth & teeth, but a black, intelligent & piercing eye. The day I called upon him with Mitchell about Heards affairs, he was somewhat disturbed by the news of the sailing of the Leander from New York with men & arms and a clandestine expedition under General Miranda, supposed to be against the Caraccas. Being a Genevese his native language is French, but he speaks English, with great correctness altho with a Foreign Idiom. That same day I saw the Vice president [George Clinton] in the senate chamber; he said he should be glad to see me at his house: but I have not been. I attended the congressional debates one morning, but was heartily tired. Randolph who is almost an Orator in the House of Representatives did not speak, those who did were miserable animals. You can scarcely conceive any thing so mean, as connected with a great national Assembly.

Feby 15th

I see Mrs. Eston daily. The day before yesterday, I drank tea with her. He has very politely invited me to stay at his house, but I must take a room in the City or I shall do nothing. I am now without employ—happily for some days, I have been without expense. Mr. Joseph Clay, member for Philadelphia called upon me with a polite letter from Mrs. Harwood, enclosing an introduc-

[49] Margaret (Bayard) Smith, daughter of Col. John Bayard and wife of Samuel Harrison Smith (founder of *The National Intelligencer.*) Her letters were printed in 1906, with the title *The First Forty Years of Washington Society,* edited by Gaillard Hunt.

tory letter to Mrs. Madison, wife of the Secretary of state & leader of every thing fashionable in Washington. This letter I yesterday delivered & was very politely received by the Lady, who is a fine Woman & a handsome woman, tho not a young woman. She advised my removal from Georgetown to Washington, expressed her wish to have Mr. Madison's picture (who was not at home) show'd me Stewarts pictures of Messrs. Washington, Jefferson, Madison & herself & invited me to call upon her with Mrs. Harwoods picture.

On my way back to George town I called on Mr. & Mrs. [Joel] Barlow, who appear very friendly indeed. She spoke much of you of your Mama & of your poor Brother John of whom she speaks with gratitude & the affection of a sister. She expresses a strong wish to see you & desires her love & remembrance. He appears to be a very clever man; plain, frank & intelligent. He show'd me some proofs of plates which are engraving in London for a superb edition of his Columbus. I call it Columbus tho he says it is so altered as to be an entire new work. It is to be printed in Philadelphia

I rec'd yesterday your short answer to my short letter on my arrival here. I have neglected poor John but will not continue so to do. I am glad to hear of him what you communicate. How is it for money with you? had I not better pay your postages too? Adieu.

Washington Feby 17th

After being really oppressed by a sultry atmosphere, behold to day, a thorough tho not a very cold snow storm. In my last I mentioned a visit to Mr. & Mrs. Barlow—a few more words of them before I take another subject. They had been intimate at Mr. West's & among other anecdotes relative to him Mr. B. told one in which Stewart was concerned which mark the unhappy connection in this instance of talents & turpitude. S. professing great esteem & much gratitude for Mr. and Mrs. West, painted a very fine portrait of the former & presented it to the latter. The picture was much admired & highly valued. Not long before leaving England, S pretending a wish to alter or more highly to finish some part, prevailed upon Mrs. West to send it to his rooms, & immediately sold & delivered it to Alderman Boydel, who supposed it his property. S went off & West almost by force recovered the picture. In Dublin this same eccentric & immoral Artist being lodged in Jail for Debt, began the pictures of a great many nobles & others, receiving the half price at the first sitting, & after thus getting enough to release himself, mov'd off, & left their Irish lords imprison'd in effigy.

[Feb.] 18th I rec'd yours to day in which you *lash me*. Well! I kiss the rod. With it I rec'd a letter from the miserable Heard, showing some agitation & a hope that by promises his fate may be averted. Alas it is too late. He has been a week removed & I suppose by this time, his successor Manning has received his Commision. Tho' it snowed all yesterday, the ground is already naked & the temperature mild & benignant. *Tomorrow* I am to quit the family of Love. Love is here eternally present to the sight & hearing. Every spoon, every towel, sheet & pillow case is marked with Love. But it is not *my* love. After some Difficulties, & various walks to the City, I have hired a Room at a Hotel, not finding one at a private House to suit. I am to pay $10 per Week, for lodging, boarding, fire & Candle, having a Chamber to myself.

Feby 19th This is my Birth Day. I am forty years old & you are thirty seven. Here is a theme for reflection, but I will confine my speculations to this, we are both well & I am wiser than I was. I am just settled in my new habitation, at Semmes's Hotel, City of Washington. From the Window where I am writing, I see the Capitol at two Miles distance, towering like some antique Ruin, & wanting nothing but some Colossal columns with their heads at their feet, to remind one of Rome or Persepolis. On Monday I sent Mrs. Harwoods picture to Mrs. Madison & received her compliments, thanks & assurances that it was very like. I have this morning called upon her a second time & taken away the picture. Nothing more was said of Madison's miniature being wanted. She said she had mentioned me to Mr. Jefferson & his daughter. I requested permission to copy Mr. Jefferson's picture by Stewart & Mr. Madison's; which was obligingly granted & the first immediately sent to me.

This day is sultry. The frogs have already commenced their town meetings, tho their Orators do not yet exert their throats to their full extent.

I was interrupted by a call to dinner. This is the land of Hog, homminey & hoe-cake. At the public houses they have homminey at Breakfast, homminey at Dinner & homminey at Supper, at Mr. Love's we had usually three kinds of Bread at Breakfast & tea (or supper) Vizt Bakers (& often 2 kinds of that) Hot biscuit home made & hoe cake (or as they call it Corn bread) The District of Columbia, a territory of 10 Miles square, or 100 square miles, comprehends a portion of two States, Maryland & Virginia, ceded to Congress, & placed under its peculiar government. to the North of the Potomac, in this district is Washington & Georgetown; to the south of it, Alexandria. The two first in Maryland the last in Virginia. From Rock hill, on the Banks of Rock Creek, just back of Georgetown, the three Cities, are in view at one time & make with the noble sheet of water which the Potomac here spreads a beautiful & magnificent prospect. The Potomac above George town soon dwindles & is interrupted by falls & the Navigation aided by locks, & at George town itself, the channel is injured by the deposits from the stream. To remedy this defect, the inhabitants by a stone dam have joined a pretty little Island of a mile & half in length, call'd Mason's Island to the mainland on the Virginia side, to reduce the waters to one channel with a view of deepening it & the hope of removing a Bar of sand which prevents ships from freely entering. This experiment will not receive its trial until the freshets when they expect the great flow of waters will wash away the Bar. In the mean time the people of

Georgetown are much alarmed & agitated by a project of throwing a bridge over the potomac, below them, rendering the communication between Washington & Alexandria more direct & shorter by 5 miles, and (as they fear) injuring still more the navigation of Georgetown.

Feby 20 I have mentioned that I yesterday heard the croaking of the Frogs for the first time; Mr. Jefferson informed me that he heard them 10 Days ago, & noted down the circumstance. Yes, I have seen, touched & heard the great man. A fresh sheet of paper must be devoted to him, & all he said & all he did. I this day began to copy Stewarts picture of him; so that my poor head is full of Jeffersons.

Saturday 22. I kept this till to day because by sending it one or even two days sooner, you would not gain time in the receit. I have one picture begun for pay. I have obtained the presidents name to my subscription. In my next perhaps I may guess the time I shall be on the return.

Adieu, with love to all with you.

Washington Feby 25

Thank you my dear Bess for your letter, with the detail of your family oeconomy & arrangements, I received on Saturday. I will now proceed to recount the wonders of Washington City. And first—Thomas Jefferson, is a tall man, say 6 feet & thin. His hair which has been red is now grey & is worn in negligent disorder, tho not ungracefully. His complexion is ruddy & his eye (a hazle) very animated. He converses with ease & vivacity, possessing true politeness, which places his guests perfectly at their ease. During the short period which we past with him, rendered shorter by the certainty of having interrupted him in study or Business (for he came into the room *en dishabille* & slippered) he talked of the early approach of spring, of gardening French & English, prefering the latter & praising their great taste in laying out their ground,

MRS. WILLIAM DUNLAP (ELIZABETH WOOLSEY) (1768-1848)
By William Dunlap
(Courtesy of Mrs. Henry McKeen Ferriday)

censuring Gen[l] Mason the proprietor of Mason's Island for the bad taste he had displayed in laying out that charming spot; Gardening led to notice of Mr. Parkins, an English gentleman residing in Virginia, an excellent Draftsman & skillful adept in disposing of pleasure grounds, this to painters &c.

I have been to visit a Chief of the Rickaraw Indians who was mentioned by Mr. Jefferson as an extraordinary man, speaking many Indian tongues & likewise conversing by signs. He has come to the seat of Government, from a distant part of the Louisiana territory—200 miles beyond the residence of any tribe that has yet had intercourse with us, this immense journey he undertook as a deputy from his nation & others, accompanied only by a French trader as an interpreter & guide. Mumford who had seen him before was the leader of Mitchill & myself. When we entered the house which is a boarding house appropriated to Indians, we found the interpreter, the Rickaraw & 2 or 3 Osages, in a small front room with the 2 matrasses & a Bear skin on the floor. The Osages went in & out the room during our stay or occasionally stretched on the floor. The interpreter entered into conversation with us in French. The great man was seated cross-legg'd on a mattrass scraping & cutting Guinea-hen feathers & did not deign to raise his eyes to us. His dress was a second hand blue, military coat, without facings, but with two large gold epaulets, a flannel shirt, dirty light colored pantaloons & shoes covered with mud of many days standing. He had rings in his ears & a blue cotton handkerchief, tied about his head in the French manner with a buckle disposed in the front. He is a large old man & nearly as dark as an American born negroe, but with light hazle colored [eyes]. His hair was covered by the handkerchief. After conversing some time with the Interpreter, Mitchell desired him to inform the Rickeraw that a Senator of the U. S. from the great City of N. York having heard that he was a learned traveller &c &c had come to see & become acquainted with him. This harangue the interpreter delivered in a loud & distinct voice & at great length. The learned savage continued during the whole solely occupied in cutting & trimming feathers, occasionally whistling in a whispering key as he attended to his work, & without once looking at us or appearing to hear the interpreter. The interpreter finished & the Rickeraw continued at his work. We concluded that he would take his own time & therefore turning from him entered again into conversaton with the Frenchman. By & by the old man smiled & made a sign to a young Indian who went out & brought him a pitcher of water. He then pointed to the litter he had made in cutting & the young man took it away. The Rickeraw now very deliberately put away his knife & work & began to prepare some tobacco for smoking. We continued to converse with the Frenchman. At length having prepared his pipe, lighted it, placed a chair in the middle of the room & seated himself, the chief appeared for the first time to notice us. Still he spoke not, but pulled from under his belt, or out of a pouch or pocket hanging in front, he pulled some papers & presented one of them to Mitchill who read it aloud. It was a certificate & recommendation from Genl [William] Clark & Capt Merriweather Lewis, the gentleman who has been for many months exploring that country by order of the president. When Mitchill in reading came to the Rickaraw's name, he gave an assenting gutteral sound the first he had uttered & so to the names of Clark & Lewis. The paper was returned & we shook hands with him. He then presented 3 pieces of paper, which joined lengthwise, presented a map of his rout, of his country, the course of the Missouri, the relative situations of a great many Indian nations, & Captain Lewis's encampment.

Feby 26th Wedny

I have just rec'd your letter of 22d & the tone of complaint in which it is written has changed the current of my Ideas too much for me to continue the foregoing subject. When I shall get home I do not know, when I shall leave this place I cannot yet tell. I must obtain some leading names for my Book & it is a very uphill business. If it is best that my mothers furniture be removed to Amboy, I should suppose it may be done immediately. I see no prospect of using it in New York. I shall go there on my return & wish you to go thither likewise; & from thence with me to Philadelphia.

I calculate for you to receive this letter next saturday, & on that day I think I shall put a letter in the Office to tell the day of my leaving this place for Baltimore. It is not my intention to stop to paint in Philadelphia, but to do that work on my return thither with you. I enclose $10 for fear you should be short of Cash. With love to all, Adieu.

Washington Feby 28. 1806

My dear Bess

This is the last letter I hope that I shall write to you from this place. I begin a picture of Mr. Baldwin tomorrow which I will finish on Monday & leave W. on tuesday. If there is no work waiting for [me] at Baltimore, I shall be in Phil. on Friday. Here I must buy paper for the first volume of my work & set the press a going if it can be done without delay.

Continuation of the Rickeraw

Having displayed his map, he traced his rout with his finger, & by means of signs, sometimes explained by the Interpreter, he made us perfectly understand him. So expert are the western Indians in pantomime that we are told they sometimes hold council in which not a word is spoken. "Here" says he "is my country. Then he pointed out the situations of the neighboring tribes, recapitulating their names & marking by signs their distinguishing characteristics. Among the rest he named & described a nation of whites, with blue & grey eyes & light colored hair. This the interpreter corroborated. He traced his rout to the place where he met Cap^{n} Lewis. Then told us that he guided him westward & returned again with him. When in his rout he came to a village, his sign for entering was, to raise the left hand & arch it, & then to pass the right hand with the fingers somewhat pointed under the arch, the back of the last touching the palm of the first. When he came to a mark of a River running into the great River—Missouri, he signified his crossing by the action of rowing. In this manner he marked the whole of his route, ending it by a rude figure signifying the presidents house in Washington; beyond which he had drawn a gun, a sword, powder, ball & tobacco as the presents he expected.

A part of the country on this side the Rickaraws, he described as volcanic, & near this burning soil, he had marked a cavern the properties of which partake of the marvellous. If a man was to be thrown in "says he by signs" he would be thrown out again by the force of the wind. Take a tree & throw it in, it will descend for some time & suddenly be tossed out, thrown into the air & scattered in pieces.

He had two other marvellous spots on his map & his account of them is in the true Mandevillian Style. The first is a lake in which a monstrous amphibious animal resides, with horns like a Cow &c & The second is likewise a lake, the waters of which have such an attractive relatively to stones, that all the stones for a certain distance around it have gradually forsaken their old beds & taken up their abode at the bottom of this lake. This must be all true for in the first place he saw the stones at the bottom of the lake, & in the second the Rickaraws never lie. His sign for speaking truth & the contrary is very expressive, he draws a line with his finger from his heart to his mouth & thence straight to the auditor or spectator; for falsehood the line comes crooked from any part of the Abdomen & on issuing from the lips, splits, diverges & crosses in every direction.

When he returns he says, all the natives around will assemble to hear his report; & what he sees & hears, he shall treasure up in his head & faithfully recount.

After a pretty long interview we shook hands & parted, much pleased with the novelty of the exhibition & the animation & intelligence of the old savage, who compared to the stupid Indian of the North is a civilized man. Is it not probable that these Western & southern Indians retain more of the civilization of the Mexicans & Peruvians from whom all the tribes have originated, & that the farther others have wandered from the parent stocks the more they have brutalized.

I this day returned the presidents picture to Mrs. Madison, but did not see her as she was not well. I saw a swiss artist there an old man, who draws profiles on vellum very prettily in water color & pencil lines at $3.

Doctor [William] Thornton superintendent of the patent office has treated me politely & presented me with some pamphlets. The Doctor draws very well but he writes abominably. His lady [50] paints very prettily & is an accomplished woman.

This place has been from its commencement & still is the resort of speculators & projectors. It is absolutely melancholy to see the waste of labor & materials in this speculatively great city. It is a composition of disjointed members which are falling to decay, because removed from & disconnected with the heart. First round the unfinished capitol stand some good buildings finished & inhabited at least in winter. Then proceed a mile south is the navy yard & arsenal & a cluster of mean but inhabited buildings. A mile southwest of the Capitol is a row called the 20 Buildings left unfinished & without window sashes. A mile from these directly west is Greenleaf's point, near which are 40 houses, at least twenty of Brick, some inhabited but most unfinished & decaying. In a line West from the Capitol is the pensylvania avenue, a well finished road with houses scattered along it & terminated by the magnificent house of the president, on each side of which but at some distance, are two handsome Brick buildings in which the public offices are kept. I have hardly left room to say adieu

[50] Anna Maria (Brodeau) Thornton. Her diary, kept in Washington in 1800, is printed in *Records of the Columbia Historical Society* (1907) X, 88-226, from the Thornton MSS. in the Library of Congress.

Washington Feby 28 Continued.

Around these public buildings are various clusters of Houses, an unfinished brick church & the walls of an unfinished house. On one side of the Pensylvania avenue is an unfinished large hotel without window sashes. proceeding from the Presidents house to George town northwestwardly, we find disconnected Rows of houses in Brick which are inhabited, 4 6 & 7 together, designated the 6 Buildings &c. then comes a void of half a mile which brings you to Rock creek & Georgetown. The original speculators [51] [Robert] Morris, [John] Nicholson, [James] Greenleaf & [Samuel] Blodget, failed & left the master builders to pay their workmen as they could & abandon the work to decay. Still say existing speculators if the Canal navigation is continued from the lower falls of Potowmac to Greenleafs point, abandoning the River at the falls & thus making it safe for the Canal Boats, quite to the junction of the Eastern Branch of the River, Washington must become the depot of the Western produce & with Capitallists a great commercial place. It is like any thing else at present.

March 1st Saturday

Last night it froze with a high wind & to day it is very cold. on Thursday last it was not only like spring but summer. A gentleman told me that 20 miles from this his Peach Trees were all in Bloom. I should suppose the severity of the Frost would destroy the trees as well as the fruit. Blodget the speculator called on me to remind me of former acquaintance in London & New York & to make a long talk. He is an eternal proser. He has plan'd a great national University to be established here, the Colledges to be placed around a monument erected to the memory of Washington, that the students may have ever before their eyes the image of the founder of their Liberties. Congress are called upon to erect the

[51] For early land and building speculation in Washington, with accounts of these men, see W. B. Bryan, *A History of the National Capital* (N. Y., 1914) Vol. I.

Monument & the public at large to build & endow the Universities, subscriptions he says are already obtained for $18000 which as fast as received is placed at Compound Interest by being vested in Bank Stock, the Cashier of the National Bank, *ex officio,* being Treasurer. This is a great scheme but the man is a great Talker.

March 2d Paint on Mr. Baldwins picture. Walk for exercise to the Mouth of the Tiber. Write on my Comedy of the Father &c. which I have almost re-written. It is very cold.

Tuesday evening March 6

I have this evening, this moment arrived in Baltimore on my return home & my thought running before the clumsy Carriage tells me that if I do not put a line in the post office immediately, you will not receive it before Tuesday. Therefore I hasten with this Adieu

[At this point, the copying of his letters ended, and Dunlap himself resumed daily entries:]

Amboy July 3d 1806

I have long omitted journalizing. During this interval I have travelled a great deal between this place, New York & Philadelphia; let me endeavour to recollect the principal events of the period.

In passing thro' Phil: last March on my return home I only stop'd one day. On y^{e} 25th I again return'd to Phil: to paint some pictures & my wife & daughter went to New York. I remained at my friend C B B's 3 weeks. I at this time met Cooper and he inform'd me that J. K. Beekman had engaged to purchase the Theatre for him at $50,000, & to advance 15,000 for alterations or more if required. We talk'd over his plans & he proceeded to Charleston S. C. About the middle of April I rejoin'd my Wife at New York & we return'd hither the last of the Month, leaving the town in commotion about the death of John Pierce who was kill'd by a British Frigate at Sandy Hook. The purchase having been made by

Coopers friends I have communication with them & write to him. I return to N. Y. & stay a week & bring home my daughter & Maryann Woolsey. <*Go to Philadelphia about the middle of May and return'd the beginning of June (4th)*> Visit New York in consequence of a letter from Cooper dated 2d May from Charleston which see p: [blank] Was landed in consequence of Easterly storm at Eliz: point & walked to paulus hook the storm encreas'd & drench'd me in rain. Next day got to N. Y. where I attended to Cooper's wishes in respect to performers; and then went to Phil: supposing him to be in Baltimore. C B B's hospitable mansion is filled by N[athaniel G.] Ingraham, his wife & her sister Miss Phoenix. Examine the interior of Bank of pensylvania. Meet an old acquaintance at Hardy's where I lodge, in Thos Seaman. Return home June 4th. Visit N. Y. where I find [Edward G.] Malbone and receive some hints from him in Miniature painting. I[n] consequence of a letter from Cooper appointing me to meet him in Phil: Saturday June 21st I leave N. Y. on friday, & arrive next morning, we met, & I persuaded him of the necessity of his presence in N. Y. Sunday we leave Phil: & I arrive at Amboy Next Morning. Thursday next I join him at N. Y. and enter into the business of arranging his business anew. With great difficulty make Ciceri listen to staying with Cooper on Acc^t of C's having spoken to [John Joseph] Holland to direct the alterations. Mrs. Jones engages. Johnson & wife throw obstacles in the way & the negociation being broken off, C asks me to go to Phil: & see Mrs. E B Hamilton & if I think fit engage her. On the 30th June I set off & next morning saw the lady, in ye evening heard her read & recite & next morning saw her again. I found her excessively vain, with some talents, a fine voice, and a good face, but without knowledge of the stage or of the necessary modulations to give effect to her voice, without feeling, with a clumsy person and an idea that if she appear'd on the boards all actors past present and to come would be eclipsed—and as to emolument 100 or 200 doll^s ye week seemed to[o] little. We parted & [I] return'd to Amboy arriving this morning, having written C an account of ye failure of my mission. On ye day of my arrival in Phil: I dined with [John] Watts, Denny's publisher, an Author, scholar & printer. Isaac Riley of N. Y. & Mr Meredith (I believe Wm) present. I made final arrangements for the publishing 1st Vol of my works. Cool day & afternoon rain.

July 4th. Very pleasant & cool. Walk up to the farm once mine now Aaron Bloodgood's & sell to Aa: B: an old sled $1, to James Compton An old Wheelbarrow & 2 Cart Wheels, to be valued according to the iron but not to be less than $2. Compton is likewise to have an Ox-chain at its worth. I saw some woodcocks in my walk but shot none. The Thrush, the robin & some smaller birds are still vocal.

Leave Amboy at 10 OClock & walk to Woodbridge to take the Mail Stage for N. Y. but it had already past. Sleep at Brown's tavern, finding my way to a bed chamber without being able to wake any body. ,

[July] 5th Take the stage at 6 & arrive in N. Y. at 11 OClock. Find Cooper at Hoggs and immediately go to work for him. During my absence it has been reported that I had sail'd for England, & my appearance is quite a cause for surprize.

[July] 6th Sunday. Breakfast with my son, at G M W's, whose family are at Phillipsburg. Call on W Johnson. C B B has return'd home.

[July] 7th Attending to business with Cooper Secure copy right to my work. Cooper offers & I accept a yearly salary of Three hundred pounds sterling e i 1312.50 doll^{s}, and to secure me 400 doll^{s} from a benefit. Sleep at Osborne's on a sopha.

[July] 8th As yesterday. Write by Colemans desire to see if a place can be had at Compton's, Amboy, for Mrs. Jones. Visit Mrs. Morree, to talk of an engagement.

[July] 9th As yesterday employ'd. Mr & Mrs Johnson after having broke off are seeking their engagement. Even^{g} at the Gardens or Summer Theatre. they play'd Animal Magnetism & sung some songs. About 300 people present.

[July] 10th C having insisted that Mrs Johnson should give a part of her business to a lady, if she comes from England, who was written for in consequence of <*their*> her refusal, she again refuses to engage, & he has let his house & taken passage for the family. Take a short ride with Cooper.

[July] 11th Friday. Finish & deliver to Mrs. Jones her picture. preparations are making to execute a man for murder. A regiment of militia are under arms. An execution is a very rare occurence here. I went near the County Gaol to see the crowds, it was an instructive spectacle. I am told the man Banks died with the most perfect composure & firmness—never changing countenance at any period of the preparation, & officiating to hook the rope himself.

[July] 12th Leave N Y with my son at ½ past 8 after breakfast at G M W. Read Miss Edgeworth's Leonora. "I fear I can give you but a birds eye view of this New Word tho' I would willingly dive deep enough to give you sometimes a fish eye view as somebody has express'd it e i a peep at the bottom." arrive at Amboy at ½ past 2.

[July] 13th Sunday. paint. Evening leave home; walk to Woodbridge & take the pilot stage & reach p: hook before 4 on ye 14th. Wait for ferry men. Get to bed at ½ past 5 in N. Y. arise at 8 & attend to business. Meet at 3 P M W W W & his Mother at G M W's & appoint to go with him to Bloomingdale this evening.

[July] 15th Return from Bloomingdale by ½ past 8 this morning. Write to the Palmers to send me on 400 Copies of first Volume. Make Call books for Cooper.

[July] 16th Attend to Cooper's business.

[July] 19th In the evening met Colman and walked with him to Mrs. Jones's where to our astonishment we found R. T. Paine. Coleman took his leave soon but Paine was pressing for an interview with him & they appointed an hour after. I soon retired & went in search of Cooper, whom I found & told the news to. C met P & then ran down to Hoggs & appointed to see Cooper at 9 next morning, & ran to Mrs Jones's to get the start of P whom he suspected of intending to return thither.

[July] 20th Sunday. C says he got into Mrs. J's house & had just time to extinguish the light & fasten the door when P. came, but finding all fast went off. C stay'd wth her, of course in the dark, until 12 OClock. Coleman details P's intentions to Cooper viz. to make Mrs. J. offers from Powel of 50 doll[s] a week & endeavour to prevail upon Cooper to give her up, or at least to give up 1 or 2 years of her article. P: professes to have brought a lawyer's opinion by which Mrs. Jones is to see the necessity of returning to Boston to obtain her divorce, &c. &c. Cooper determines if possible to prevent P's seeing her again and to urge the immediate setting out on the projected journey to Virginia. With these views he left me at Hoggs with Colman. Staying longer than we expected C who went to look for P by appointment & found that he had left his quarters, concluded that he had gone to the lady's & that they had met. After waiting again some time C left me & return'd saying he had met P, who told him he had been to Mrs. J's & received answer that she was gone to walk with Mr Cooper. This Coleman supposed was untrue, & that Cooper was still with at her house. Coleman again left me to go on an errand into the Bowery and soon after Paine called at the door & enquired for Mr Cooper, and Mr Coleman, questioning the boy if they had been at the house (Hoggs) to day & if they had been together. Being answer'd in the affirmative he left the house. I look'd out of the window & saw his manner hurried & agitated. Cooper now return'd and I found that in this short interval he had carried the lady off & lodged her at Hoboken. While talking on business Paine call'd again and Cooper went off to avoid him. Paine came up to me. He was agitated and heated. I was seated with Hugh Pownal making a memorandum of business to be done by him for Cooper in England. Paine enquired for Cooper? He is not here. Has he been here lately? Yes. Very lately? Yes. Within 20 min[ts]? Yes, within less time. He wanted to see me, C, & Coleman together. Where should he find Cooper? Where did he live? &c. Having received a direction to Cooper's place of residence, he departed. About 2 OClock Cooper return'd & ask'd me if I would go with Mrs. Cooper to Hackinsack. I agreed. We went to his lodgings. Paine had been there & could gain no intelligence even of the time Cooper intended leaving town for Mrs. Cooper supposed the period two days off. Mrs. Cooper immediately prepar'd to go with me. A Coach was called & we drove to the state prison Greenwich St. stop'd at a public house & discharged the Coach. We soon cross'd the Ferry to Hobocken & I hired a coachee & arrived at Hackinsack before 6 OClock.

[July] 21st Hackinsack. Walk about the Neighbourhood. Mrs. Cooper expresses her dissatisfaction at being made the companion of Mrs Jones whom she represents as the mistress of Coleman: however she determines to comply with her husbands wishes & treats her with politeness. At 5 OClock P. M. Cooper arrives with his servant in a top chaise for Mrs. J and himself & Placide in a Curricle for Mrs. C. Placide returns with me in the Coachee & we arrive at N. Y. 9 OClock.

[July] 22d Principally occupied in making an arrangement with Ciceri: a business I had abandon'd as hopeless.

[July] 23d Go by packet to Amboy. dispatch Ciceri's terms to Cooper with letter to Phil: & duplecate to Baltimore.

WILLIAM COLEMAN (1766-1829)
Attributed to William Dunlap
(Owned by The New York Historical Society)

[July] 24 paint. Fish.

[July] 25th paint.

[July] 26th last night Mrs Witherspoon died. Occupied in attending upon her family.

[July] 27th paint. read. Attend funeral.

[July] 28th Return to N. Y. with my son, Jacob Stout Junr & Mrs Terrill.

[July] 29th Receive letters from Cooper in which he negatives that part of the terms I had proposed for Ciceri by which Ciceri is empower'd to object to any other person painting for the Theatre during his engagement. Ciceri of course determines to go off.

[July] 30th See Ciceri again. He gives me to understand his wish to return & be employ'd. If Cooper chuses & I write to him he will engage for 2½ or 3 years at 40 doll^s all the year & the privilege of getting up a pantomime, for benefit, still however insisting on the disputed power: but by this arrangement any body may paint for the Theatre in his absence. C likewise brings me drawings by [blank] to judge of as an Assistant.

[July] 31st Ciceri calls on me. He will waive the stipulation respecting benefit rather than break for it. His direction "Charles Ciceri" To the care of Mr. James Vidalot No. 71 Broad St. or 10 Murray St. Duplicates to be made. Mem: Hodgkinson's last offer "You are to have the engaging & discharge of all necessary Carpenters, Scene shifters, & Painters employed in the New York Theater during the aforesaid periods & they are to be subject to your orders."

Write to Cooper. That Ciceri will be at sea before he receives my letter. That he feels himself a banish'd man & wishes to return. That he (Cooper) had parted with him rather from a determination to keep in his own hands a power pernicious to himself or at least useless. That I wished his instant answer to the question, whether he would engage Ciceri if he return'd in Jany or Feby next for 2 and ½ years at 40 doll^s ye week paying all the time—the benefit left to Mr Cooper to do the best—the power respecting Assistants as expressed in ye agreement with Hodgk:

To Cooper for tomorrow's Mail.

You will have rec'd a letter from me dated July 31st requiring to know if you will engage Ciceri from his return in Jany or Feby next for the purposes expressed in the propositions rejected by you at &c In that letter I roundly asserted that the power &c &c I will now explain. You want as your Architect, scene painter & Machinist a man of Science an Artist & a gentleman, or, if you please instead of the last a conscientiously honest man. Such a man, if such a man can be found, must labour for you con amore if he labours to any effect. His interest and your interest must be one. He not only labours assiduously himself but he is the moving soul of many subordinate parts: parts which cannot come under your cognizance, which are without the sphere of your knowledge and in short of which no person but himself is competent to judge. This gentleman if he is such as you wish has a reputation to sustain. A reputation like that of every other artist built upon years of toil and as dear as that life which it is to support & render respectable. Suppose that you had made an engagement with such a person for the purposes before stated & he had neglected to shut out the possibility of misunderstanding & had not stipulated for the full control of his department. You feeling yourself at liberty would perhaps accept the offer of another Artist to paint a drop scene or some brilliant flat & would order it for exhibition. What would be the effect of this treatment upon the gentleman you had entrusted wth so very important a branch of your business? Either he would break through his article as considering it violated by you in its spirit & intention, or he would say to you, "Sir, you can have no view in this but my degradation, for you cannot be so blind as not to see the effect this must have upon the public. The preference you give to another artist over me will be infer'd & the public judgment will be guided by you to my injury. If the Artist whose works you wish to exhibit in the place of mine is really superior to me, it is not your interest while you rely upon me for the support of your *spectacles,* to weaken me by the comparison; and if he is but my equal or even my inferior he will appear as my superior first, by the preference <*given by you*> you manifest secondly by the choice of pieces for exhibition. Certainly you must know, Sir, that <*among*> of the many plays which are perform'd some are better suited to give a painter an oppertunity of gaining reputation than others as some are better suited than others to effect the same purpose for the Actor; so likewise in almost every play their is some one scene better calculated to procure credit, as there is some one character better adapted to <*procure*> command applause; and will not this exotic artist chuse that which will most strike? undoubtedly. While the subordinate parts must be supplied by me under the pressure of invidious comparison. Sir, I consider this as <*a piece*> an act of injustice tending to my ruin, without adding to your emolument. It is true that by my article of engagement I have not stipulated for the exclusion of any artist inimical to me (for I must consider as my enemy any man who without my consent, <*or even*> nor without my request would make an offer of the nature we speak of) or for the power of engaging & discharging assistants and therefore you can legally proceed to destroy me but, Sir, you must henceforward expect nothing from me, but what my article legally obliges me to perform."

I will not prolong the speech of my imagined painter; I will not dilate or repeat; I only ask of you to read twice. What the business is which a man in this situation may be obliged by his article of engagement to perform, ask Mr Holland; who certainly spoke from his heart the last time we dined with him. He told you that an Artist was not bound to work by the hour like a mechanick. He told you true. Where is the man who shall judge of the time required for designing a picture, or the number of hours necessary for the artist to execute his design? Where is the article that can bind a man to promote your interest at the sacrifice of his own ease? Believe me my friend you can do better without the good will of your best Actor (even tho' you were not an actor yourself) than without the good will of such a man as we speak of. The Actor will exert himself before the public for the recompense of public approbation & thereby support your interest, but there is no reward for the thousand services render'd in secret by your Scene painter & Machinist except what springs from the consciousness of doing right & the pleasure of promoting the interests of his employer.

If Mr Holland could or would have consented to abandon his present situation & take all this charge upon himself, I should not have mention'd the name of Ciceri so often to you. Mr H you say is your friend, mutual confidence exists between you & I could not have doubted <*but that*> your <*have*> full assurance that every branch of this important department would be concluded to your satisfaction. But you are directed to send for a stranger, of whose competency as an artist you cannot judge until you have no resource in case of failure, & <*of*> for whose honesty, delicacy & honor there can be no voucher.

In speaking of the terms on which Ciceri will return, I forgot yesterday to mention the Assistant. He wishes to have the power if necessary to go beyond 14 dollars, as he hopes to bring an artist who is a better landscape & figure painter than himself, and he would hope you would trust 2 or 3 dolls per week to his discretion. Caton (if that is his name) can be engaged if you please for one season only if you think best, tho' it is my opinion that for the two next seasons you will want two assistant painters.

If you determine upon engaging C. my letters will follow him & reach him at Bourdeaux or Paris; If not be as particular in your instructions relative to Pownal as possible. In either case direct as to the employment of the Assistant here.

I presume my motives cannot be mistaken by you therefore I will make no apology for giving my opinions & advice. they are after all but opinions & advice & your orders shall be cheerfully obey'd by

Your french Taylor has call'd on me. How is he to be furnish'd with money.

Aug[t] 1st. Add to C's letter. "Placide has just been showing me a proposition he is going to make to Ciceri to induce him to return—at the same time ceding him to you if you desire. *did not send this addition.*

[Aug.] 12th A great deal of my time has been occupied in visits to my family at Amboy. I have been arrested by the district Attorney of the U. S. as John Heard's security. I returned yesterday from Amboy and found the following letter from Cooper.

Peterburgh Aug[t] 6th 1806

Your two letters on the subject of Ciceri I received together this morning.

[Two and a half pages blank; the remainder of the letter not copied]

Write the following as instructions for Hugh Pownal.

You will please to engage for Mr. Cooper, a Scene painter who is at the same time a Machinist, and capable of taking charge of the whole of the department of Scenery & Machinery for the New York Theatre. The terms you are authorized to offer, are, Six Guineas per week for Eighteen months from the time of his arrival, or if it is necessary to engage him for a longer period, make it two years &

six months. If possible let the engagement for the additional year be to pay only when employ'd; *that is,* to pay when the Theatre is open, certain, & as many weeks as employment can be given when it is not open. But let not this seperate you from a good artist. Rather than not strike the bargain agree to give the salary all the year round for two years & an half. You may further engage that he shall have a benefit on the usual charges to performers, & you may even go so far, *if necessary,* as to engage that Mr Cooper will secure $300 doll^{s} profit upon said benefit. This gentleman will please to procure for himself an Assistant, such as he thinks will answer <*best the purposes*> to whom you are authorized to engage a salary of fourteen doll^{s} per week. You <*will*> may likewise engage <*for*> that Mr Cooper will pay the passages of both painter & Assistant on their arrival. For a first performer capable of filling the first line of Tragedy & genteel Comedy, you are authorized to offer and Mr Cooper is hereby bound to pay a yearly salary of Four hundred pounds Sterling <*a year for*> during three years from the time of arrival; which is upwards of 40 doll^{s} p^{r} week for 43 weeks his services being at the command of Mr Cooper from the first day of Septr until the fifth of July following in each year. He will have the choice of first Comedy business & in tragedy play the counterparts & seconds to Mr Cooper. He will have a benefit each season, at the charges paid by others. His passage to be paid by Mr Cooper on his arrival & repaid by him in instalments during the period of engagement. You will endeavour also to engage a first lady, & you are hereby authorized to give the same terms as for the first gentleman. She will have the first line both in Tragedy & Genteel Comedy. If you should not be so successful as to engage either in the female or male a person of talents equal to this offer, and can engage such as from your knowledge of theatricals you judge can stand in the places, you are authorized to use your discretion & reduce the offer'd terms accordingly. If Mr Talbot can be had, you are authorized to offer him the same terms with an additional hundred pounds per year. e i instead of £400 yearly, offer £500.

There is a powder used, in Theatres, especially on the continent, for producing artificial flame, called *Licopodium.* it is collected from a species of Moss in ye North of Europe. if you can procure a few pounds it will be very acceptable.

With respect Sir I remain
Y^{r} ob^{t} Ser^{t}
W D

Mr H Pownal

P S. I should be glad of a few doz Ivories for miniatures, about 3 Inches by 2½ or larger of best quality & not East India Ivory. The best is unpolish'd & free from veins. Half a dozen pencils for Miniature painting recommended by a Min: p: would be very acceptable.

N. Y. Augt 12th [1806]

To T. A. Cooper

Yours of 4th & 6th came duly to hand, & I have in consequence given the letter of instructions to Pownal for engaging a scene painter & Assistant according to your former instructions. You do me injustice in concluding that I have not made due enquiry after Caton & might with as much propriety, at least, suppose your information respecting him erroneous. Mr Caton is not in New York, nor has ever been fixed here as a painter. The most accurate information I can obtain is, that having a fortune left him, he has settled near Albany & is now building there. With much pursuit I found a man of the name of Holmes, who has great pretensions & little merit. he would not engage except as principal & is not fit, I fear, for an Assistant. Thus you see you must rely altogether upon the arrangements you can make yourself. At Baltimore is a man of the name of Grey who would in my opinion be an excellent Assistant. He is by trade originally a Taylor but paints landscapes with excellence. He painted the views in Brydens dining [room] at the Hotel.

To T. A. C. to be sent tomorrow.

I rec'd a letter from Dykes declining the offer and recommending Barnes. I wrote to Barnes making the offer Dykes had refused. I waited upon J. C. Shaw as you request I made your apology. He said that when he saw the other gentlemen he would consult them & write to you the result. This is all buzz, fudge, or what you please. I know the man. These gentlemen have no power over the children; they are simply trustees of the money collected for them. They would not accept any guardianship, power, or responsibility for or over these children. I have seen Tyler on the subject, who wishes the children bound to you; and says that Fanny importunes him to be her guardian. On the other hand Mr Thos Hodgkinson has sworn that his brothers children shall never be placed under you, but that he will take them to his house & educate them, this Fanny opposes, & Tyler "also" Placide, a few days ago told me that Cullen alias *Carpenter*[52] (who is here & about to set up a *<press>* newspaper in opposition to his friend Colman) has declared his determination to take Hodgkinsons Children & that they shall not go on the Stage. I have now told you all I know on the subject. At present there is nobody to dispose of the Children: when you are here you must see to the *<fixing>* appointing guardians, and may I presume regulate the business to your wish. C has been almost distracted by the silence of Mrs J. Pray how is her health.

[52] Stephen C. Carpenter was the proprietor of *The People's Friend & Daily Advertiser*, from its establishment September 1, 1806, until August, 1807. William Coleman was editor of the *New-York Evening Post*.

What is her conduct. how far can you rely on her services? I think you must engage Miss Delinger to be ready to stop gaps.

Aug 13 Send off the above letter. See Mr Gallatin on the subject of my suretys ship &c. He says that the 2 sureties ought to confess judgement. That previous to an execution against them it is his duty to try every means in his power to recover from the principal. On my stating to him that Heard had an office under the State Government & had hired a house in New Brunswick within the limits & did not even express a desire to remedy the evil he had occasion'd, Mr Gallatin expressed his indignation. He advised that the sureties should join in a representation of facts to the Treasury & if they had any offer to make for liquidating the debt by instalments, to make it. That either this would be accepted or execution taken out against them. In the latter case they must go into confinement when they must apply to him for liberation upon an Assignment of their property. He profess'd his wish to alleviate the case of the sureties & promised to do all for that purpose which the law would allow.

Augt 14th To T A C[ooper]

During my search for Caton I <*have*> heard of a gentleman <*of the*> by name <*of*> Guligher[53] and last even^{g} saw & conversed with him. He is an artist of great merit as a painter generally and has been for some years past engaged in portrait painting. He was the principal scene painter for the Boston Federal Street Theatre at its first establishment (I mean the house that was burnt) and painted all the scenery. He has the manners of a gentleman & man of sense. He is willing to engage for one season as principal Scene painter and waits <*the*> your answer to this for your terms. I think you need not hesitate to engage him for the coming season as the person Pownal engages, if he gets any, <*worth having*> can not be here till late in the season, and then you know you will certainly have your choice of "Tom and Dick".

If in the arrangement of your business you can find a place for the Comedy I gave you "The father of an only child" which in getting up will only require study, you will thereby promote my inter-

[53] Christian Gullager. See the Bayley and Goodspeed edition of Dunlap's *Arts of Design,* III, 305.

est, as by neglecting it, the want of worth will be implied. I mention this with great reluctance & would not do it, if I thought your interest would suffer by it.

Yours truly
W D

P. S. I look for an answer respecting Guligher by the 23d after which I ought to start for Nantucket & Boston if I go at all. Mr Bullfinch the Architect is an object

leave N. Y. about 4 OClock & arrive at Amboy about 9, riding part of the way in Mr Carey's chaise for which ride pd. 2 doll^{s}.

[Aug.] 15th Went with Mr A Bell to Brunswick to enter special bail in the suit instituted by the Treasury against Heard, and Drake & self as his sureties. See Heard. He is very "sorry"—cant do anything—is to petition Congress for relief—" &c. Return home ab^{t} 9 OClock

[Aug.] 16th Write & read Johnson's lives.

N. Y. On Monday the 18th I return'd hither with my Wife & daughter & next day went with them to Bloomingdale where they remain.

[Aug.] 22d [John] Watts hav^{g} publish'd [Thomas] Moore's poems brings a copy here with Colman & leaves it with me. My indignation is rous'd. Amidst licentious baudy songs to meet the most rancorous & vile misrepresentation of my Country written by a man who was flatter'd & pamper'd by the fools of that country while here & has return'd to his home to vilify those who bow'd to him because he had written some pretty bawdy songs before he came here, makes me blush <*for that society*> & feel indignant. "But the lays of his boyhood had stol'n to their ear.[53a] I blush not my countrymen for you collectively, but for those pretenders to taste & science who have flutter'd round this Will o' the wisp Englishman and by assuming the characters of the representatives of your Country's literature have justly brought

[53a] From Thomas Moore's poem, "Lines written on Leaving Philadelphia."

it into contempt with this Idol conscious of his own nothingness. <*Who can blame*> The admirers of [William] Cobbett are the admirers of Moore; and Cobbett & Moore dispise them for their admiration. Though not wise or virtuous themselves they cannot but see the folly & depravity of their admirers. Well may Mr M represent that Country as "Old in Youth & blasted in her prime" [53b] whose inhabitants can relish the malignant falshoods of a ruffian like Cobbet, or the bawdy lays of a debauchee like Moore. We are glad that these bawdy poems are not publish'd by an American and cannot blame a foreigner who judging of our national taste by the avidity with which Littles poems [54] were received (by a certain class) has eagerly published the poems of Thomas Moore.

The lines written on leaving Philadelphia, were distributed among the flatterers of the bard before he left America: who but must smile at the impudence which publishes them in connection with the other more honest effusions of vanity which this Vol: contains.

The merit of Mr Moore is duly appreciated by the writer of this communication, but he hopes he shall not live to see the time, depraved as the American character is in the eyes of Messrs. Cobbett & Moore, when prettiness of versafication or even brilliancy of wit shall recommend the impurity of the brothel to the toilette or the parlour windows of the females of America.

Boston Sept[r] 15th 1806. After my Wife had remain'd at Bloomingdale upwards of a week I accompanied her & my daughter to Stamford & next day visited Shiphand & Scolly's cove & the day after return'd to N. Y. where I received notice from Cooper that the Eastern journey must be given up. Paint for improvem[t] in N. Y. Visit Stamford again & again return to N. Y. on the 9th instant. On the 11th receive from Cooper orders to proceed to Boston & bring or send off Mrs Jones Children &c. &

[53b] From Moore's poem, "Epistle VI to Lord Viscount Forbes, from Washington."

[54] Thomas Moore's amorous poems were published pseudonymously in England in 1801, with the title *Poems by the late Thomas Little.*

to be in N. Y. by Monday 22d. Started from N. Y. on Friday the 12th Arrive at 12 OClock at N Haven in co. wth Captn Mix. Start again at 2 OClock the 13th with Mix, Bliss & Bryers. Darkness, rain & Thunder. At Hartford take in Lt Humphrey. At Springfield leave all my Companions. A little further on took up B Booth (Who lost his wife & child on board the Rose in Bloom) & his brother. Arrive at Worcester at 2 OClock Sunday 14th. Stay there until Monday Morng 15th 2 OClock & arrive here about 10.

Put up at Thayers. Dine at Mrs Brown's. See [Henry] Cabot & Bourne. West. Wells out of town. See R T Paine.

[Sept.] 17th See Wm. Wells who undertakes to procure subscribers. Leave with him a Vol: for the Anthology. Go with Paine to Mrs Shamway who raises difficulties in respect Mrs Jones' Children See Mr [John] Hurd a distiller twice and the 2d time after a communication with Mrs Shamway he refuses to deliver the child that is with him unless his Bill is fully pd ($98). Shamway makes a bill of $130. I suspect Paine of deceitfully instigating this Woman while pretending to forward my views. I hope it is not so.

[Sept.] 18th Leave with John West 20 Vols: of my Works. with W: Well 20 Vols. Leave with [Joseph T.] Buckingham, printer & Editor of Polyanthos a vol: & promise him intelligence. Leave Russel a Vol:—R. T. Paine has I believe shun'd me to day. I must depart & leave the business to Harry Cabot.

[Sept.] 19th Paine calls on me early. Says that he was all day out of town after Mrs Neat, who has undertaken to accommodate matters with Hurd & will wait for the payment of her own acct Mrs Jones's time. I have given Paine 130 dolls to pay Shamway: he is [to] give his note to Hurd: to ship the furniture & send the key of Bureau to me by post: Mrs Neat is to clothe the children & find a woman to take charge of them & Paine is to send them off. Bourne wished me to stay to day & dine with him & a party but I conclude to depart at 9 OClock for Providence.

New York Sept[r] 21st 1808

Here is an Hiatus which I shall not attempt to fill up.

I was a few days ago releas'd from Brunswick Gaol (where my confinement by the kindness of Mr Gallatin was only nominal, going in to receive my release) on giving a deed for all my Estate, real, personal & mixt. My situation in the New York [Theatre] has been reduced in value from 1700 to 900 dollars (with the chance of a benefit if I choose) but my time is my own 20 weeks in the year. I open the book now rather to keep an acc[t] of my mony than to Journalize.

[There follow twenty nine pages of accounts, of household expenses at Perth Amboy, clothing, and travelling expenses, September 21, 1808 to June 28, 1811.]

[On the fly leaf, at the top, Dunlap wrote in pencil:]

To introduce Mrs. Arnold opposing her husbands treason

When I became your wife &c.

I promised to love thee, honour thee, obey thee &c. Can I honour a traitor

What gain'd my youthfull heart? Thy person? No &c. Thy honourable fame

[At the end of the volume are the following memoranda, referring to the printing and distribution of *Dramatic Works of William Dunlap,* I, Philadelphia, 1806:]

Rec[d] from T & G Palmer 392 Copies 1st Vol:

	vols.
Deliver'd to J. Osborne	110
D Longworth	10
I [saac] Riley	10
John West Boston	20

Wm Wells d°	20
W T Thayer (paid for)	1
in presents	4
Wm Blagrove Boston	5
Henry Cushing providence	5

Dramatic Works &c 1st Vol: 1000 copies

paper	80
printing	138.75
Engraving	35
D° inscription	2.50
Copper plate printing	10
D° D° paper	4.75
Binding 500 copies	30
Copy right	1.20
	302.20
printing proposals	4.
Advertising	10
pack[g] Case, Freight & Cartage	2.50
p[d] for distributing	3

Rec[d] for Dramatic works &c

From Morgan Lewis &c &c at Albany	8
Thos A Cooper for Boston	40
J E Harwood philadelphia	3
Hugh McLean	3
Supt[n] Collector	10
John Hogg	2
C B Brown	1
Wm Johnson	1
John West Boston (For Z Cook)	1
W T Thayer d°	2
Sup[n] Collector	26

DIARY OF WILLIAM DUNLAP

MARCH 17, 1811—MAY 6, 1811

NOVEMBER 23, 1812—MAY 7, 1813

NEW YORK AND PHILADELPHIA

NOTES ON THE LIFE OF

GEORGE FREDERICK COOKE

(Manuscript volume lettered *Memoirs 31* owned by
YALE UNIVERSITY LIBRARY)

MEMOIRS 31

Notices of Cooke the Tragedian [55]

New York March 17th 1811. When Coopers letter arrived announcing his having engaged Cooke at 25 guineas or $116.66 per week to play wherever directed e i in New York, Boston Philadelphia or Baltimore, and have the amount of a benefit in ea^{h} place [Stephen] Price was extravagant in his demonstration of Joy triumphantly repeating "Now is the winter of our discontent made glorious summer by this son of York" again & again. He hired a pilot Boat and went down to the Hook to wait for his arrival, but came back disapointed. At length the great man came & in the same vessel McFarland, Doige & Smalley. They came up in the evening of the 16th November 1810 & Price sent a note to the Theatre for me to join him at the Tontine Coffee House where I found the veteran of the Buskin sitting with the Manager over a bottle of Madeira. I was pleased with his appearance tho' disappointed. He lookd 60 years old. Mild & polite in the manner of the old school; his sober suit of grey, his grey hairs and the suavity of his manners gave no indication of the eccentric being who had been the theme of the English fugitive publications.

He dined the next day with Price sate late & got drunk. I saw him next day in his bed. "Cooper" says he "gave me a great many cautions when I left him, but he forgot to caution me against his partner."

On Wed^{y} the 21st Novr he made his first appearance on the American stage & play'd Richard with the enthusias-

[55] The diary entries and memoranda in this volume were used by Dunlap in writing his *Memoirs of the Life of George Frederick Cooke,* in two volumes, published in New York by David Longworth, in 1813; and in London by Henry Colburn, in 1813, and in 1815.

tic applause of the Audience. His *entré* was truly dignified. I saw no vestige of the old man. His post[ure] erect, his step firm, his eagle eye beaming fire. He return'd the salutes of the audience not as a player to the public on whom he depended but as a King acknowledging the acclamations of his subjects and yet before he went on he trembled like an aspen leaf. The amount of the house was 1820 dollars. There were 1358 persons in the Boxes. On friday the 23d he play'd Sir Pertinax M[c] Sycophant, when notwithstanding a violent Snow storm the House was 1424 dollars. After playing he sup'd & drank freely; the consequence was that next day he had no voice, but he thought that he could force it at night when he was to repeat Richard. Night came, he began, his Voice broke, the audience encouraged him, he tried every remedy, in vain—he whisper'd Richard thro' & was at the end of it pretty nearly drunk. Tho a saturday night there was in the House 1155 doll[s].

He had now removed to Price's house by invitation, where every attention was paid to him, and every endeavour made to keep him straight.

His fourth night was the 28th (Wed[y]) when he play'd Shylock to a house of $1804. On friday the 30th he repeated Sir Pertinax to $1180.

The sixth night of his performance was on Monday Dec[r] 3d the play Glenalvon & Sir Archy Macsarcasm, when notwithstand[g] a violent Storm the house was $1287.

Wed[y] the 5th he play'd Zanga to $1367. This was a failure; tho' in passages very fine. His Eighth night, friday the 7th Dec[r] he play[ed] both Shylock & Sir Archy, but in the latter his voice broke entirely. The house was $1270.

On Monday, the 9th night, & 10th of Dec[r] he performed Macbeth but was thought much inferior to Cooper. The house $1605. On Wed[y] the 12th he play'd Sir Giles Overreach in the New way &c. He was extremely great in the great scene but the play did not please. the house was $963.

GEORGE FREDERICK COOKE (1756-1811)

By William Dunlap

(In Dunlap's manuscript *Memoirs 31,* in the Library of Yale University)

He made his first appearance in the richest of the Falstaff's (1st p^{t} Henry 4th) on friday Decr 14th and was deservedly admired. I generally dined with him on play days & accompanied him to the Theatre. On our way this ev^{g} we talked of Henderson & he said his best points were only copied from him. The house was $1444. His twelfth night was Monday Decr 17th & a repeat of his Sir Giles to $798. After the play he sup'd as usual but got unusually drunk, abused Price in the grossest terms & finally caught up a Decanter to throw at him. P. seiz'd him & threw him down violently. C exclaim'd "remember I am in your own house Dont strike me" P. insisted upon his going to his room. he went sullenly and as he had frequently done sat up by the fire all night going to bed in the morning. The next day he left an excuse w^{h} the serv^{t} for not dining at home & went out. he rambled about the streets of the City, dined at Brydens,[56] got drunk & did not return to P's that night. He peep'd into the Theatre at rehearsal ask'd the prompter if all was well, & went to Prices with the determination of removing his trunks & leav^{g} the house. However he was disuaded & upon being assured that Mrs Price was not angry with him for his intemperence he was very happy to be reconciled. In the evening when he saw me, he exclaim'd "Ah Dunlap! its all over now." He was so wild from the previous excess that his Cato, to which & for his benefit, an immense audience (1878$) of the first of our people was assembled, was the most shamefull exhibition ever witness'd in N. Y. I saw him when dress'd for Sir Archy. "I was very much bewilder'd. do you know that I could not remember one line after having recited the other. I caught myself once or twice giv^{g} Shakespere for Addison. Heav'n forgive me. If you ever heard any thing of me you have heard that I always have a frolic on my benefit day. If a man can't take a liberty with his friends Who the divil can he take a

[56] James Bryden was proprietor of the Tontine Coffee House, on the north west corner of Wall and Water Streets. *N. Y. City Directory* 1810; I. N. P. Stokes, *Iconography of Manhattan Island,* III, V.

liberty with?" He play'd Sir Archy perfectly well. The words were so familiar that he could not trip in them & he was somewhat recover'd from his intoxication.

Sunday Mar: 17th [1811] Dined at [Dr. David] Hosack's with Cooke, [Dr. Hugh] McLean, E[dmund] Pendleton, Cochran's, (James & Walter) T Morris &c: Cooke by H's permission began his wine drinking again but was moderate & himself moved to return home about 8 OClock & I left him in his bed room appointing 9 as the hour to wake him next morning to prepare for his Journey: next morn[g] when I call'd Bryden told me that he would have a parting bottle w[h] him & had sat up late & gone to bed intoxicated. He however got up but was restless & complain'd of pain in his breast. I sent off his baggage & McLean & self walk'd with him to the packet: he was now cheerful & chatty and sat on the Windlass till we were nearly thro' the narrows. When the waves running high & sometimes breaking over us, he went down, chill'd with the east wind. he became sick but instead of the usual nausea had chill & violent pain in the breast. Sam gave him some strong rum & water & it reliev'd him. He landed at Amboy cheerily, eat heartily of Beef Steak & while I took tea drank 5 or 6 glasses of Madeira: I took him from the wine under pretence of seeing the Hotel &c and on his return he sat cheerfully chatting to my wife & daughter with great pleasantry till 10 then ate some roasted Oysters drank 4 or 5 glasses more & went to bed. At 8 on tuesday the 19th he arose delighted with having slept (as he insists on it) better than since his arrival in America and after a hearty breakfast We began our land journey very pleasantly. At Princeton we dined drank a little beer & a little wine & proceeded to Trenton. The beer made me sick, filling me with gas, I thought tea would help me he join'd me & while we were taking it Price & Beekman arrived. My sickness increas'd to chill or ague & vomit & I went to bed when after fever & sweat I slept and got up well. Cooke had sup'd with P & B with moderation & was next morning in good order. We walk'd with Commodore Hunt & saw the spot where the Hessians were taken & after breakfast proceeded, arriving at Phil: ½ past 2. The old man was a little peevish about the time of our arrival & somewhat wild. He saw in the Phil: paper at Trenton that the Managers [57] had apologized to the public for his absence & had advertized him for friday to play Richard. "I'll be damn'd if I do!" he exclaim'd, "if I am too unwell to play Wednesday how do they know I shall be well enough to play friday?" After dinner Wood & Warren call'd. Cooke persisted in his determination & nam'd Monday as a day when he would probably be recover'd. Wood went away to announce the further disapointment to the public & Warren stay'd to show us to the Theatre. The appearance of Cooke in the Boxes took off all attention from the players who were perform[g] the Busy Body. the adjoining boxes were crowded with curious impertinents until he went to a private Box. I left him, took a walk, look'd into the green room & when I return'd found him at supper with a glass of punch. "So" says he "this is the widows third choice. he is not the Warren I remember in England. What a fop he is. did you notice the tassels to his garters? I never saw any body else wear them. Upon my word the good lady seems to descend with every husband: first Merry, then Wignel & then Warren!" He went to bed at eleven.

Thursday the 21st March we breakfasted at 9 previous to which I had taken a walk. Cooke attended a rehearsal of Richard, during a part of which he threw out his voice to the astonishment of those around him, whom he commanded & reprov'd occasionally with some asperity. I visited Trot & Sully, and pass[d] some minutes at Mr S Levy's. We dine by appointment with Wood. Rather a Theatrical party & almost of course stupid. Cooke, tho' he profess'd in the morning that he would only drink wine & water, soon began to pour down port wine so

[57] William Warren and William B. Wood, managers of the New Theatre, corner of Chestnut and S. Sixth Streets, Philadelphia.

as to convince me he was determined to be drunk. I went to Mr S[ampson] Levy's to Tea & return'd to Wood, between 8 & 9 & found C completely mad & Wood nearly intoxicated. [Stephen] Price, [Benjamin C.] Wilcox & Irving had drop'd in. "Ah my dear D. I was mistaken. I prophesied that you were in bed but you have been taking your tea. he owns himself a tea sot. He's the only man that shall command, I put myself under his orders." Wilcox who had been plying him with bumpers of port, says to me "then I suppose your orders will be sailing orders." These last mention'd three now went off professing to prepare for a Ball. "A ball!" exclaim'd C "if ever I have an oppertunity of quizzing the Americans I'll remember this. Going to a Ball in Boots, just like everything in the damn'd Country." Wood who was loquaciously drunk explain'd that they now only went [to] dress. "Don't talk to me Sir, pretty fellows for the company of Ladies, just from the tavern & the bottle, they dont know what belongs to genllmen, my dear D. sit down by me, dont leave me. didn't I throw out my voice this morning. I gave it to them. I'll show these people what acting is." "You frighted'd some of our young men. they are clever lads tho' " "Are they? I wonder how you are to find it out. But you're all alike." "But Mr Cooke I've seen you act when you were surrounded by dire dogs" "The worse of them better than the best of you." "Jack Brunton now, he's a clever lad, but you wont say he's an actor; I love Jack, he's my friend but he's a dire dog." "He's your friend? You take a damn'd queer way to show your friendship. I feel inclined to be severe D. I'll cut these fellows. dont leave me. Oh the night I slept at Amboy I never slept before in my life. poor Billy Lewis is dead. Sixty five. dont leave me." "Ah he was an actor!" "How do you know?" "Why my dear Sir I have seen him many a time" "You see him where should you see him?" "In England Sir" "And what the more would *you* know from seeing him. My dear D. didn't I throw out my voice this morning? I'll show these fellows what acting is, they talk of their Cooper their Idol, their Wooden

God. Haven't I stood the trial with John. What is your Cooper?" "But Mr Cooke you are supposing a comparison that no one thinks of. Mr Cooper is a gentleman & a scholar." "A scholar is he? How do you know it?" "but as to a comparison with you nobody thinks of making it." "They do Sir. I have heard it. A scholar. Sir he's no scholar. he's no actor. A ranting mouther that can't read a line. I appeal to you D." I look'd seriously & said Mr Cooke, Mr Cooper is my friend." He said little of Cooper after this but abus'd Wood as an Actor tho' he [had] never seen him play, abus'd Price. Abus'd the Country & continued to drink what was officiously poured out for him, while a servant by his request went for [a] carriage. "Why don't you drink? to Wood "You dont drink Sir." "I am waiting till this wine cools Sir" "So, and give me the warm, damn'd polite!" The weather was summer warm & required the precaution of Coolers. "You are all alike by God, Cooper & Price & you, all alike, a set of Scoundrels!" "Sir, I never allow any man, whatever his situation may be, to make use of an appellation of that kind to me." Cooke had used an expression which convey'd the Idea of unfair conduct as it regarded him & While he now seem'd conscious of having said something wrong Wood proceeded, "if you think there is any thing unfair in my conduct in your engagement I relinquish it, Sir." Cook made some apology. "Sir you have made use of an appellation which I will not suffer any man to apply to me." Cooke disavow'd every thing, back'd out most manfully, & they shook hands: I tried to prevail on him to walk home, he refus'd. he ceas'd drinking & turn'd his glass bottom upwards. the carriage arrived. with the assistance of Hardinge I got him in & drove to the Mansion house, H with us. Going out he ask'd who he had quarrell'd with? "Where is our host?" Wood having hold of his arm answer'd & another. nothing can give an Idea of the wildness, the repeatitions, the incoherencies, of his drunken eloquence. The time of the ride was taken up in professions of esteem for me, requests that I would promise him another nights sleep in the same bed at Amboy, praises of my Wife & daughter & requests that I would permit him to send them Heaven knows what as presents. He would not go to bed till Hardinge went away. he would take my hand & turning to H say "this is my commander." "Sir you have no commander." "Sir, but I have, but by my own choice tho', Sir." I requested H to go & soon after he went to bed, on condition that [I] would let him stay two days & nights at Amboy & send ear rings, bracelets &c &c to my Wife & Daughter & stay with him until he was in bed. I assisted him to his room. "Sam did you ever hear anybody say any thing against that gentlemen?" "Who Mr Dunlap Sir?" "Aye, this good gentleman." "No, Sir." "No, nor you never will. Sam get me a glass of brandy." Sam went for it. "Dunlap it is strange but I can never say or do any thing to offend you. I can't. we were born gentlemen, but that bullying fellow. before I leave the country—I'm the best shot in great Britain. I never miss my man—tho' its 20 months now. Sam brought the brandy & holding it in his hand began in his way to persuade him not to take it. Cooke listen'd & then smiling says "Sam you make a damn'd long preamble, set it down. get me another. go" Sam went & I persuaded him not to take any. Sam return'd. I saw him in bed & carried off the brandy.

Friday the 22d March. To my great surprize Cooke was up by ½ past 8 and ate a hearty breakfast. "Come to day we dine at home, dont we? I drink no wine. this ugly pain in my breast troubles me. We'll see [James] Fennel at Masonic Hall (I think it is) this evening. I never saw him." It was accordingly arranged *<that>* and Price calling in agreed to dine with us. In the evening he sat patiently under Fennells intolerably bad recitations, but unfortunately Francis who we met there return'd with us & sup'd. Cooke began by Cider & Francis declared he would drink nothing but beer. However a bottle of Madeira must be call'd for—"only to mix a little Wine & Water warm with a lime in it." Old times when he & Billy Frances were together furnish'd an inexhaustible topic & I seeing the Wine mixture made & in use went to bed, but alas the friends couldn't part till one oclock & Cooke got drunk to bed by two.

[March] 23d I had had my walk before C. got up. He was ashamed to complain. "This pain troubles me a little tho'. I must begin the water system. nine days were we on water alone during our passage and I never was better in my life. this is in favour of the Water system. Ah, I noticed then when your mother gave me my tea her hand was perfectly steady but mine was not so in taking it. I ought to be asham'd. in truth I was asham'd." He had staid the whole time at Fennell's reading room merely because he knew he was observ'd, but he was very weary of him. "mere school-boy ti-hem hem-ti—school boy? Nay I would have whipt a boy that could not have done better." We had a great deal of chit-chat to day, that is he talk'd a great deal as he always does, an incessant flow of anecdote & observation.

I call'd yesterday a second time on the widow of my friend C B Brown & found her in & company with her mother-in-law who is likewise a widow since my last visit to this place. I saw the twin boys who used to be my play things. I took them on my knees. I kiss'd them & remember'd former days. poor things! Charles has left another boy besides these & an infant girl. I wrote a note to day to Mr. P[aul] Allen who is engaged by B's friends to write his biography appointing a meeting.

"What's that?" says Cooke "I am remarking" says Francis "how well Mr Dunlap looks" "How can it be otherwise" rejoins C "when he is under my care." "I remember John Henry. He was once in the army. He was one of three officers that for some youthfull prank in Kingston Jamaica were brought to court Martial one broke & the other two suspended for short periods, Henry the shortest, but he took leave of the service. He play'd one season at Drury lane. he made his first appearance, an odd choice for a young man, in Adam in As you like it,

I remember—in Adam when he made it the first part in the piece, but it was odd choice for Henry" and so he runs on "sans intermission." He went to bed early & sober to day & was up by 8 OClock on *Sunday the 24th March.* After breakfast we walked over & beyond the Schuykill bridge his tongue running incessantly with a stream of pleasant & rare anecdote. "Digges was a very pleasant & easy man when himself Manager but when he became the agent of Daly he was the very reverse. perhaps he thought to please Daly. he made himself so hateful to the actors that they had a custom for many years after his death when ever they went to Cork to go & piss on his grave. it was abominable—some low-comedy genius began it. yet it was common to ask one another, "well. have you been to visit Digges yet? His grave is near the north wall in the Cathedral yard at Cork. Many of the Monuments in Westminster are very beautifull; there is one of General ——— which I never liked, there is an Angel blowing a trumpet to represent the last day, and the general is represented as rising at the sound—the clouds around put me in mind of pieces of paste—an old soldier who knew the general—perhaps had serv'd under [him] when visiting the monuments, seeing this; took out a pencil & steping up to the base wrote

"Keep quiet if you're wise;
You'll be damn'd if you rise."

John (e i Kemble) says to me one day, you are older than I am. Am I, says I, I think not.———says you were born on the [blank] of October 55. does he? I was born in October, but not 55 no not 55. My lady must be 57 or 58. Sarah—Sarah Siddons." Our walk was pleasant tho' it was rather windy. At 2 the old man sate down to his dinner, hav^{g} after much debate declined an invitation to C Ingersols. At this time hard rain. He was much pleas'd to hear of the great press to obtain boxes which took place yesterday morning and tho' I was present when the particulars were told him, he afterwards repeated them to me, exclaiming "Why this is equal to Siddons' first tour." He dined at home & alone to day. I dined at C J Ingersols. I return'd to my tea. Cook was out walking but soon return'd & made me remark that he had left half his bottle of Wine. In the evening Calbraith who lately made his debut here in Zanga intruded himself & finding Wine sat till supper & after supper & after I, heartily tired with his stupid impertinent talk went to my bed. Cooke however got to bed by eleven in pretty good order.

Monday [March] 25th I arose to meet Mr P Allen at 7. The veteran was up by 8: lively & loquacious as ever. He told me that Calbraiths errand was to get the part of Othello. "Why I think Sir he shows no great promise for Othello." "No, nor any thing else. I'm glad Wood is to do it. Iago depends upon Othello & indeed Othello upon Iago. I remember———said he had seen the play better done than ever it would be again. Barry play'd Othello, Garrick Iago, Woodward Roderigo, & Cibber & Pritchard the two Women. Palmer play'd Cassio gentleman Palmer as they call'd him." "What John" "Oh no! before him. John I believe had not play'd then." "How does Bob Palmer stand?" "Why pretty fair. Bob is a thick headed dog, but the youngest, Bill, was the worst of them, a stupid fellow, & he grew worse & worse. he died in Ireland, of Whiskey I suppose, quite a driveller before he died. if he got a few words beat into his head the sight of Daly would drive them out again. one night in Alexander he play'd Hephestion, Daly was listening to him & in the line "O reverend Clytus father of the War" he splutter'd out O reverend Clytus father of the World." Speaking of G Colman the younger "poor George he has the rules of the Kings bench & I suppose must remain there. Young Arnold was the first I believe that arrested him. he heard that Colman was down at some Country town & he took a bailiff & two post Chaises & went after him. after he had arrested him he says he cried at what he had done & when they were to return to London he ask'd Colman if he would ride in the chaise with him. "No Sir" says George "You may stick your nose in that chaise & I'll take your bum with me in this. He's a merry undone dog—comes out & cracks his jokes in term time & then goes in again. Goes to bed drunk every night. ——— call'd on him one day—saw his boy—"Where's your master?" "In bed Sir" "What was he drunk last night?" "Very drunk Sir." We got "John Bull act by act as he wanted money, but the last act didn't come & Mr Harris refus'd to advance any more, at last necessity drove him to make the finish & he wrote the 5th act one night—in one night—on seperate pieces of paper as he <*wrote*> fill[ed] one piece after the other he threw them on the floor & finish[g] writing & drinking went to bed in the morning. Tired of waiting <*for*> Mr Harris sent Fawcett to him & he insisted on going into his chamber & waking him "My dear Sir remember your promise we are all at a stand for the last act." "There it is" "Where" "There on the floor—pick it up. dont disturb me" Fawcett pick'd up the scraps & brought them to the Theatre in his pocket handkerchief." "Is this Mr Calbraith in business now?" "No I suppose he thinks it easier to be actor as that requires no industry talent or education." "I suppose so. Thats the last resource. Any thing can be an actor. Foote dismiss'd his old prompter but gave him the same salary & sent him on for little things. James Aikin says to him one day. "So Sir we have lost our old prompter" "Yes" says Sam, "the fellow couldn't read so I made an actor of him."

Walk with Cooke & Ben Wilcox. call on A[rmit] Brown, see his wife. Call at Curtis Clay's.

Cooke & self dined together without interruption & [but] that he was anxious to have the first night well over he did not lose his chatty pleasantry. "I remember a story of two men travelling together who observed profound silence for many hours at length the[y] arrived at cross roads. the driver was at a loss. they stop. "Pray Sir" says one, "do you know the road?" "Damn you Sir what do you mean! I'll quit you, Sir, I'd as soon you should break wind in my company as break silence" About 5 we proceed to the Theatre and he was pleas'd & surprized to see at that early hour (and we were told it had been so for hours before) the street fill'd by the crowd waiting for the opening of the doors, but when we found the back door of the house beset & the people who had taken places crowding in by that passage, he exclaim'd "Why this beats Sarah!" We could not get in, and the young men finding it was Cooke surrounded us with impertinent curiosity. I led him off & leaving him in High St^{t} ret^{d} to find some mode of entrance. I met Francis & C Ingersoll & the first undertook to prepare a way while I went with Ingersol to bring up the object of admiration. he had been invited into a confectioners shop where we found him & returning the people at the door open'd to right & left & let us pass. "Aye, aye, they understand their interest now, for, as the fellow said who was going to the gallows, "there will be no sport without me." I took place with Ingersol, his brother, Anderson, Dennie, Peters & others in the Orchestra. The reception was great & his return to it dignified as usual. All passed off with the utmost applause. I found him after the play a good deal exhausted, however he recover'd his spirits at supper & after some Cider, Wine & Negus went to bed.

Tuesday [March] 26th Mr. P Allen again met me at 7. Cooke up at 8, a little stiff, but pleasant and gay as usual. I visit Mrs Brown. Call at A Brown's store—out. Walk with Cooke to see Wertmuller's Danae. Dine with him at B Wilcox's. He repeatedly express'd his fear of dining there & hi[s] determination of coming away with me to avoid wine. "You'll come home to tea?" "Yes" "And so will I, I'll take tea with you. we'll come home as soon as the candles are lit." He was cautious & silent during dinner. After W introduced port Wine & he drank freely. We dined ¾ after 4 at ½ past 7 I moved off, but alas! Cooke took no notice of my departure and I left him. I went to bed before 10. About 6 this m^{g} $(Wed^{y}$

March 27th) poor Sam who had been up with [him] all night came into my room, told me that Price & Beekman came home with him and that he had sate by the fire in the parlor all night refusing to go to bed. "I have had the worst night, Sir, that ever I had with him. He wants a carriage Sir." I went to him, he was conscious of his condition, and on my requesting him to go to bed said "I will do anything you bid me." I persuaded him to bed. He call'd for brandy &c but was easily put off. Rail at Price and Cooper incessantly. "Compare me to Cooper, I that have play'd with John. I'll leave them to worship their wooden god. he suits them. Cooper & Kemble. A devil to a God! John is an actor, he is my superior, I acknowledge it! I'll never play at New York again, no by God. He ask'd me to dine with him. Not in his house. You must promise me one nights rest at Amboy. Your dear Wife and Daughter. I know you want to persuade me to play in N York. No never under the power of Price &c &c" I reminded him of playing Richard here to night. he said he would do it. I left him dropping to sleep.

P Allen brought me Brown's Novels. Rec[d] a letter from my Wife. Write my 4th to her. Coming from Wilcox's yesterday, Doctor Chapman express'd his dissapointment in Cooke's conversation which he had expected to find brilliant. Indeed he was at table first dull and then indecent. Price has just call'd on me. He says that about 10 last evening Charles Ingersol endeavour'd to get Cooke off by offering himself as a guide but Cooke defer'd his departure till Eleven then promising to go & Charles left him. Cooke then remark'd that he knew what Ingersol was about. "He was left by Wood & the tea Sot to get me home." He got in a passion with Sam this morning. "Who are you? I know you Sir, you are Mr Price's spy."

As I return'd home last night Armit and E[lijah] Brown met me. they had been to see me & I promis'd to take tea at A's this evening.

The character & actions of George Frederick Cooke

are certainly object worthy of attention as suggesting reflections of abundant utility in the conduct of life. A man bless'd by nature with Herculean strength & iron constitution, quickness of perception & facility of combination, is reduced by vice at the early age of 55 <*to*> without the intervention of disease or accident to the situation of a drivelor. A coward, a braggart, a hypocrite a backbiter, a man of repentance without amendment, forming resolutions only to break them, fearing death with womanish pusilanimity yet rushing on to meet him with the frenzy of desperation, form'd by nature for the attainment of every virtue without possessing one —I fear not one!

Meet old Judge Benson—plan of the city of Germany in Pensylvania. Sam says that Mr Cooke drunk two bottles of madeira during the night after he came home. Mr. Cliffton, Mr. [blank] call on me Mr Hopkinson, Dr Chapman & C & me.

As I was sitting down to dinner Cooke bounced into the room with an attitude "So this is economy Dinner & breakfast in one" eat his dinner drank a pint of Madeira & rode to the Theatre as gay as eighteen. In playing this evening his voice was not so strong, but most of the gentlemen who had seen him both nights say he play'd best the last. This was not so, for he was the worse for wine. I went to bed before he return'd & he got beastly drunk again & to bed about 1 OClock.

Thursday March 28th I arose at ½ past 6 to meet P Allen. At ½ past 8 I breakfasted & Price calling on me I went to the Theatre. The crowd wait[g] for the opening of the door to take places was a riotous mob. When I return'd at 11 Cooke was up, but could not be prevail'd on to go to rehearsal. he walk'd with me to the Museum [of Rembrandt Peale] & loiter'd there till 2. We dined alone, after dinner Dennie & Waterman call'd, & later Sully. I was seiz'd with an ague & tried to shake it off by a Walk with Sully. Dennie cant drink wine. Brandy! I return'd still sick & Cooke & Waterman went to Fennell's reading, I to bed. He got to bed drunk at 3 OClock this morning.

Friday March 29th I was too unwell to meet Allen at 7. Cooke did not return home last night until 1 OClock & then very drunk accompanied by Waterman, who I believe is a brandy drinker. Dennie, the editor of the Port folio, the american Addison, a driveller & a sot! While with us yesterday I had leisure to contemplate the ruin of a tasteful & polish'd edifice. His conversation was little more than tokens of assent & impertinent (tho' not so meant) anticipations of what others were saying. "Yes Sir—right—exactly so—very true—beautifully remark'd —excellent &c" Read Arthur Mervyn—poor Charles— his belief that he was fated to die early & by consumption is fully express'd here. About 2 OClock my old drunkard puts his head into the room. "How do you do to day? I'm glad to see you better. do you know I could not help thinking of you in bed. if anything should happen to you they'd swear that I kill'd you. come come. damme I cut. no more of this. early to bed to night." I took the oppertunity of representing the necessity; but he took care to anticipate me & promise amendment. After dinner he drank his pint, chatted incessantly & then rode to the Theatre to play Sir Pertinax. People are applying to him for money & he gives merely because he has not firmness to refuse, tho' he regrets parting with the cash. He told me yesterday that he had lost the money out of his pocket the night before & suspected the dresser at the Theatre—sixty five dollars in bills wrap'd in a paper—to day he tells me he has recover'd the money— that he made a great noise at the Theatre about his money & that the dresser laugh'd & said he had taken it to take care of it. Now he was not at the Theatre yesterday or indeed since the time he says he lost it.

Saturday Morn^{g} Mar: 30th 1811. Cooke came home last night & without excess went to bed at 12. Wood tells me this morning that he never saw such an enraptur'd

Audience as that of last night or such fine playing and that the anxiety for places is greater than ever. The house was 1480 the first was 1344 the second 1100. As I walk'd up to the Theatre about 10 OClock a brawny fellow issued from the crowd surrounding the door, his face flushed & clothes disorder'd. "Well Charley" says an acquaintance "did you get one?" "To be sure I did" "What box?" "My old box No. 3." "You were up all night again" "yes." These robustious fellows are paid 5, 7 & 10 or more dollars and they tie handkerchiefs about their heads & remain at the Th: door all night. Rec[d] a letter from my son mentioning Cooper's arrival. Cooke receives a letter mentioning same. Goes to rehearsal & from thence to Sully's to sit for a picture for Wood. Goes in good health & spirits to play Shylock. Allen & self proceed in our work till dinner. Cooke return'd about ½ past 9 OClock & after supper & a glass of punch went to bed at 12.

Sunday morn[g] Mar: 31st Cook dont get up to breakfast. Sam says that he dont appear so well this morning. "Indeed Sir he dont appear so well in a morning when he goes to bed *right* as when he goes to bed tipsey." I ask'd Sam for an explanation of the money business and he told me that Mr Cook met the man who dresses him at the Theatre, at Fennells and the man then told him that he had given him the money to take care of when he came to dress for Richard the night before. This accounts for the whole. Cooke was so wild as not to remember giving the money & getting drunk again at Fennels thought the next day that he had seen his dresser at the Theatre & then receiv'd the money. Cooke sends to request me to write an excuse to Fennell for declining to have his company to dinner, & I go to Woods to excuse his going to him. pass some minutes with Sully. call on Trott who says Waterman bro[t] C to his room last Thursday even[g] & wanted him to go to Fennells supper, that he declined, that Fairman went only in hope of preventing mischief, that Cooke invited Waterman & Fairman to dine with him to day. Wood tells me there was 1160 [dollars] in the house last night. Cooke dines alone wth me & only takes a few glasses. Reads in C B Browns Jane Talbot. Afternoon Trot, Sully & Waterman drop in. All quiet & pleasant. They go. He takes a dish of tea. I leave him after his supper taking Negus & read^g^. Goes to bed ½ past 11.

Ap^l^ 1st The old gentleman is up & joins me at breakfast. Finishes Jane Talbot & writes letters. I walk.

Mend^m^ given me by Price. Half after 375 for the first five nights. The sixth paying 375. half of the next 6 paying 375 each. The whole of the thirteenth & half of next three pay^g^ 375.

Dine pleasantly & soberly & Cooke goes at 5 to dress for Richard. I am employ'd with Allen. The old man eats his supper temperately & goes to bed at 12.

Ap^l^ 2^d^ Up & with Allen. Cooke rises & breakfasts at 9. Receive a letter from Price. Extract—"Cooper is well with the exception of a lame hand." "I want you to remit me on Thursday whatever may be due me—dont neglect it for Cooper has run me in debt most damnably. Cooper commences on Monday next, in the mean time we close." Walk to Theatre. Wood tells me there was $1180 in house last night. Write to Price. Meet Mrs Bainbridge and Miss Heiliger in y^e^ Street. Call on Mrs C B B & Mrs Mead. the last I found at home. She seems much attach'd to Spain. Cooke sate to Sully, walk'd & then dined at Francis's. The company was players consequently dull & noisy. But for the presence of old Anderson the time would have been very heavy. Cooke was dull. We came away at 9 perfectly well. After supper he was chatty & pleasant at intervals reading C B B's Clara Howard. "In 1800 I arrived in London to fulfill my engagement made with Mr Lewis by letter. Mr Lewis came to the Inn & found me in the Coffee room surrounded by people & tho' he had never seen me he came directly up & call'd me by name. This was monday morning & friday I play'd for the first time in London." He was born Ap^{l} 17th 1756. Holding up a ½ p^{t} decanter of Wine "You see" says he "I have left off drinking in a great measure."

Ap^{l} 3^{d} Wood calls & we arrange the business for a Week to come. Sit with Cooke at Sully's. Walk. Afternoon: Go with Sully to the Academy of Arts. Even^{g} Cooke plays S Pertinax to $1202.

Ap^{l} 4th While we are at breakfast Holland enters & breakfasts with us. Go to Theatre to settle with Warren and Wood to this time. Copy of Statement.

"Mr Cooke's Acct. with Philadelphia Theatre"

1811 March	25 R[ichar]d y^{e} 3d	$1348.15
	27 D^{o}	1114...
	29 M[an] of y^{e} World	1474.34
	30 Merch^{t} Ven^{ce}	1159.62
Ap^{l}	1 R^{d} y^{e} 3d	1187.50
		6283.61
	Expences at 390 p^{r} N[igh]t	1950...
	½	4333.61
	Mr Cookes share	2166.80½
1811 Ap^{l} 3d	Man of the World	1202.50
	Expences	390...
		812.50
	Mr Cookes share of y^{e} above 5 n[ig]ts	2166.80½
		2979.30½

Payments

Cash to Mr Price	1200
Mr. D	200
D^{o}	1579.30½
	$2979.30½

sign'd Robt Pullen
Ap^{l} 4th 1811

I told Mr Warren that Mr Price understood the charges as 375. He said it must be an error, he went & spoke to Wood, then ret[d] & said Mr Wood had stated them at 390 in his letter to Mr P. Wood tells me that Cooper is at Trenton & has sent for him to come to him. Visit at S. Levy's. Holland dines wth us. After dinner [Benjamin] Trot[t], [Gideon] Fairman & Waterman drop in: pleasant chat. Cooke takes tea with me. We go to the Museum & attend the lecture & experiments on Gasses. Hydrogen or inflamable mix'd with oxygen—bubbles from both seperate & united, ignited—inflamable air from Coal us'd as lamp—Aether—inflam'd &c.

Ap[l] 5th Wood returns disapointed—no Cooper at Trenton. Cook is up at ½ past 6 reading. Walk with Trot. Dine w[h] Samps[n] Levy. Miss Jackson. Mr McKean—charming man. 5 OClock find Cooke beset by a circulating library keeper formerly a barber to the Bath Theatre. He goes to Th: for Lear, plays to 996 dolls.

Ap[l] 6th Cooke up before 8. I was up at ½ past 6 to meet Allen. The other day when Holland & Trot were sitt[g] with us Holland said to Cooke "Cooper expects to see you in New York by such a day according to appointment. "He'll see me, but not on the boards." He is bitter against Cooper—he thinks he has not been fairly dealt with. He heard yesterday that Coopers baggage was in his possession but that *his* was in the public stores. "Why did he not claim them as his own?" Wood replied "It would be necessary to swear & he might not chuse to take a false oath." "Damn him I believe he'll swear to anything." I sounded him this morning as to another year in America & stated his profit, over all expences at 12000 in addition to wh[t] he would make this year—he evaded said "Money could be made in England too—besides you'll have another hero—George will be here." meaning [Joseph George] Holman. he was not displeas'd at the subject but it pass'd off without further notice. He told me he had received a letter from Twaits with great offers for Charleston for the month of may. Holland tells me that Cooper says he dreads to meet Cooke—justifies Prices system of treating him—that Harris, Kemble &c were incensed to a great degree at him for sending Cooke away & repuls'd all attempts at explanation. That Cooper is conscious of using undue means to get him off—rails at him as an old worthless drunkard—says he would not undergo again for *any sum* what he did for that purpose.

Sunday Ap[l] 7th Alas Cooke is again a wretched drunkard. He return'd from playing Sir Giles Overreach very finely & I took some supper & wine with him. Holland who was preparing to return to New York sat with us till ½ past 10, Cooke in high spirits, pleas'd with every thing, talking of the pictures taken & to be taken of him. "I shall go to Boston again, I have promised to finish their season. I will sit to Stuart again & send you the picture." After 11 I left him. I was restless & occasionally heard him still up. Heard the Stage go at 3 OClock. near 4 Sam knock'd and ask[ed] me from him to get up. after some hesitation I got up & slipping pantaloons without stockings & a surtout coat I went to him. "Ah Dunlap! I am glad you are here" grasping my hand "I have been rambling thro' all hell to night." "Then you must be tired & its time to go to bed." "I'll do any thing you bid me." "To bed then" and I lifted him by his arm from the chair. he looks at Sam "How came Mr Dunlap to be disturb[ed]?" "You order'd me to call him Sir." "Oh Dunlap I am not drunk, I am insane, promise me that I shall rest one night at your house. stand away, Sir, Mr Dunlaps arm is sufficient. Lights! Dunlap you are not angry! I hope you are not angry!" "No. But I must return to bed. I am not clothed & shall take cold." "Go to bed, but dont be angry." I left him having seen him seated by his bed side, & I return'd to my bed. I heard him for some time after talking to Sam who having at length got him to bed left him. During my breakfast he join'd me, in high spirits but could not eat. he acknowledged his folly of last night but is in fact under the influence of it yet, tho' full of chat & anecdote. B Wilcox dined with us & Sully, Wood & a Mr Massy. I had tea at 6 & all stop'd drinking but Cooke. they went away & he continued drinking. he wanted me to walk, I understood him & would not leave him. he order'd a Coach while I was out of the room, he thinking me off, but as I return'd he ask'd me to ride wth him, I did so. on his return ab^{t} 8 he wanted supper & began to drink again uttering his eternal round of bragging drivelling nonsense. Whenever he is drunk he returns to the blow Price struck him & his determination to shoot: to night he was very systematic "He thinks I have forgotten it. no by God! I wrote the next day to Captain McLean of ye 34th at Quebec & he has promised to meet me on the 24th at New York. The bully will be surprized to receive a note from me. I'm the best shot in England. I am sure to kill him, but then the dear little Woman—that ever I should —it's not a trifle that can bring tears into my eyes—to think that I should—" and then he chokes & blubbers like an idiot boy. at ½ past 9 I left him & went to bed. I heard him go to bed making his usual noise & look'd at my watch it was 2.

Monday Ap^{l} 8th Up at ½ past 6 & walk with Sully & Trott. The old drunkard sallied forth again while I am eat^{g} I took little notice of him. he observ'd it, and said he hoped he had said nothing at any time to offend me. he drank 4 cups of tea & afterwards want^{d} brandy. I objected, and ask'd him pointedly if he had not taken brandy yesterday morning. he confess'd. I told him I knew it from the smell of his breath & the wildness of his conduct. he promises me never to do it again. his promises! Wilcox, Wood, Warren call, he is lively. after they go I at his request allow him some Cider. Goes to rehearsal. Wood says Sat^{y} was 1050. "I had a strange dream last night" says Cooke "I thought an ugly old Woman was dragging me to a precipice. she pointed down the frightfull pit. I struggled & got from her." "I wish you may" said I "the dream is a warning." William & Washington Irving arrive from Washington they call on us with Charles Nicholas. Cooke drank his pint of Wine after dinner & play'd Falstaff in the evening. I took an early supper & walk'd after it. when I return'd I found him with [John] Phillips the libraryman he was more intoxicated than when he left me and complained much of his breast. "Oh Dunlap if you had not prevented me from taking brandy this morning I should not have got through this evenings play. as it is—my voice—hah!—there are pins & needles. I must send for a physician." I prescribed bed & he promised if I would sit up with him ½ an hour he would go to bed. I did so. got rid of the man who was with him. he prepared for bed, & promised it should not be many minutes before he follow'd me. I left him.

Tuesday Ap^l^ 9th 1811. Sam tells me this morning that shortly after I left Cooke, he grew worse, was much alarm'd & sent him for Doctor [Thomas] Park[e], who when he arriv'd found him much oppress'd & breathing w^h^ great difficulty. he bled him copiously, and the old victim is now asleep & has slept soundly all night. He got up about 2, weak & low spirited. We talk'd over the incident & its cause. He promises amendment, seems convinced that nothing but temperance can save him from death in the form he has so recently approach'd. I said every thing that I though w^d^ add to the impression made by his fears. He took a light dinner & I press'd 2 glasses of Wine on him. He reads the afternoon & evening. I pass the evening at Mr S Levy's with Mr McKean, Miss [blank] Miss McKean, young McKean, Dr. Rush part of the evening.

Wed^y^ [April] 10th Up to meet Allen. Cooke up to breakfast at 9. Goes to Sully's. He takes a few glasses at dinner and goes to play Shylock. I pass the even^g^ with Mrs C B Brown. By letter from Price Cooper plays to

1270 Hamlet & is very flatteringly received. Holland writes that he is drilling the players stiffly. Cooke goes to bed by eleven.

Ap[l] 11th Cooke & self breakfast at 9 & he goes to rehearsal. Rainy day. read Shee's Rhymes.[58] Cooke is well but not chatty. Goes at 5 to play Macbeth. It was to have been Lear but Wood is too ill to play. He return'd in high spirits, said there was a good house & the play went off charmingly.

[April] 12th When I rose at 7 I found him up making a memorandum for his benefit bill. Rather low spiritted & chilly. He went to rehears[l] at 10 & found no one there. he was vex'd & left word that he would not return. I join'd him & called at Sully's who was out. he was waspish. I led him to the Academy of Arts & back to Sully's where I left him. He was pleasant after dinner & read. Even[g] I pass at S Levy's the McKeans there & Mr M[oses] Levy. Cooke takes about as much pleasure at a picture exhibition as a blind man would. He call'd R[aphael] West's picture of Orlando saving his brother from the serpent & the Lioness the rescue of Andromeda by Perseus. of course the rough & masculine Oliver was to his eyes the beautiful female chain'd to the rock. The 2 last houses were Wed[y] 870 Thursd[y] 778. He received to day an anonymous letter from New York of whose contents he was not communicative. he exclaim'd "If he says so he is a liar." He wrote a note & sent Sam with it. This was an answer to Fennell, who was teazing him to play Iago to his Othello. The night he sup[d] & got drunk with Fennell this was all settled in their cups & the artfull James wished to take advantage of it & reported the engagement about town with hints that Wood opposed it. He did not communicate the corresp[ce] to me because asham'd of the commencement of the business.

Sat[y] Ap[l] 13th After Cooke went to rehearsal I rec[d] a

[58] Sir Martin Archer Shee's *Rhymes on Art.*

letter from Price saying Wed[y] nights house was very bad 560 dollars: A letter from Cooper to Cooke accompanied it, which I carried to him. He read it in the green room but said nothing of its contents, except compliments to me &c. He went as usual early to Theatre & play[d] Glenalvon & Sir Archy well to 1200.

Sunday [April] 14th I walk before breakfast. Cooke goes to Sully at 11 & remains till dinner time sitting for Richard. After dinner Washington Irving introduced Hopkinson & Meredith just as we had nearly finish'd our bottle of Madeira. this caus'd the bringing of a second of which they drank 4 or five glasses, he drinking fast & talking stupidly, they went & young Harris of y[e] Th. came by appointment to rehearse *Cash* with him. I drank tea walk'd & return'd. Harris went. Cooke drank until the 2d bottle was finish'd by him, except some that I threw away when he left the room. The wine gone, I requested him to take no more & urged every reason. he promis'd he would only take wine & water. he could not eat supper, but must have a basin of gruel which he takes with brandy in it. he put half a large wine glass of brandy & set down the remainder by him. I took it up & under pretence of smelling it, kept it till I had an oppertunity of pouring it on the carpet. He was now very loquacious and drunk enough to open his mind fully & talk of his grievances without being so mad & incoherent as he usually is when drunk. I sat with him until 12 OClock being determined to prevent further drinking & knowing that after that hour he could get nothing more as y[e] bar w[d] be shut. During this time he said that Cooper had inveigled him into an agreement when he was drunk, that he was drunk tho' not entirely so when he went on board ship, that he would have return'd to be sure but he was ashamed to return after having gone so far. "I came away without preparation, without my stage clothes as if I was running away like a criminal. Now Holman will come out after making every preparation & making a bargain by which he will put that money into his own pocket which I have been putting into the pockets of those scoundrels. Sir, I shall have lost money by coming here, & when I go back how do I know I shall be received. To come away without seeing Mr Harris, my best friend, the man who did every thing for me, who pitted me again them all. His Son too is my friend notwithstanding he in anger published my letter fixing the time I was to play in London. No by God I will never play in New York again! Cooper has treated me unlike a gentleman. he writes to me. when? After his second night had fail'd. he writes me a fulsome congratulatory letter. they think I am a fool. He send me to this Country. never writes to me. He comes himself & remains within a 100 miles for 2 or 3 Weeks, never writes to me, takes care that I shall hear of his great first appearance by other hands, and when he fails in his second attempt he writes to me a damn fulsome letter." I combatted this idea but in vain & he proceeded "That letter I received, that enormous letter I kept from you.—I'll show it you tomorrow mor[n]ing—that warns me against playing again in New York. I am to be hissed for not playing the last night I was advertized for. the writer signs himself my friend & countryman. he advises me not to submit to be hiss'd by an American Audience. An American Audience. No by God by no Audience! They'll hiss me because I deserted them. dident they desert me first? didn't they leave me to play to empty benches. God blast them! God blast me if ever I play for them again." he says "Cooper tells the people at N. Y. that I am engaged to him for three years! Am I? I'll show him! Coopers a ferocious fellow but not so bad as Price. did I ever tell you that he struck me? He says he was drunk. I dont believe it. I hate! hate him! O I'll write such a pamphlet on my return, on the American Theatres and I'll not forget the Managers. Cooper! play with Cooper, the Wooden God! He's no player. Send me to America to play under the direction of Mr Simpson. Mr Simpson! He & Mr Cone should draw an Ass-Cart together—a fit pair! I've got among my papers a journal of my life, I wish you

GEORGE FREDERICK COOKE (1756-1811)

By William Dunlap

(Courtesy of The Players, New York)

would digest it & write my biography. it will be a strange one. My father was a Captain in the 4th Dragoons, a high Irish gentleman. he left me a little fellow to the care of my mother but I was soon my own master. that was my ruin. at Eleven I was enter'd a midshipman & went aboard a man o' war. O it will be a strange story. I'll give you all the papers. will you? Oh! Dunlap how I delight in conversation such as this, over a glass of water. I hate drunkenness. I detest it, for its consequences you'll say—true but not alone. I dislike it for itself. many an hour have I spent in studying my profession—alone—when the world has thought me drinking. I have studied the passions, Sir and all their various grades. There, Sir, is fear, so I distinguish it from surprize. now suspicion. There's attention—now rage—that is the most difficult of all. Anger, the expression is different according to the object—from the Wife to the lowest menial." I went to my room, & soon heard a loud slam of his door & then all was still.

Mond^{y} 15th Sam tells me that as soon as I was gon[e] he sent him for brandy & the bar keeper being gone & none to be had, he in a violent rage bounced to his room & bolted Sam out. He has gone to rehearsal without coming into our breakfasting room or seeing me. he took some Cider & bread & eggs in his bed Chamber. The day pass'd pretty well & he play'd Kitely [59] well to 1364 [dollars].

[April] 16th Cooke got drunk last night & to bed this morning at daybreak. Warren tells me Cooper intends to be here Sat^{y}. Wood accepts my Comedy of 40 & 20 to be play'd at his pleasure & the remuneration to be according to its success. Cooke sitting to Sully; Mrs Hopkinson present: he exerting himself to be agreable and is really so. His anecdotes rather stale. Letter to Incledon in praise of Price & America & American Theatres, in

[59] In Ben Jonson's comedy, *Every Man in His Humour.*

short in praise of every thing he curses & condemns (Mrs P excepted). Call on Trott & go to [David] Edwins to see drawings of Cooke, Jefferson & Blisset by a youth [Charles Robert] Leslie attach'd to [Samuel F.] Bradfords store This young mans talent & acquirement in original composition almost amounts to miraculous. Visit the Pensylvania Hospital. Dine at Francis's. Warren mention'd to Cooke the publication of his letter. he was anxious to see it. read it. acknowledged it & pretended to find fault with Incledon for publishing it. I left Francis's & returnd about 9 when I found him drunk & still drinking. he would not come away with me, but consented to return if I w^{d} send a coach. I did so. he came home about 10 with young Barret & Harris order'd wine, but on their going & my expostulating with him he consented to drink no more & to go to bed, which he did very quietly. The letter being before the world he now shapes his conversation to it: and his incoherences to night were repetitions of the question "Is there any thing that can offend in it? Didn't I speak of Mrs P[rice] kindly & gratefully? &c &c.

Ap^{l} 17th Walk thro' the boasted Phil^{a} Market before breakfast. Meet Arm^{t} Brown & walk to his house for a file of Englis[h] news papers. Sam comes to me for 50 doll^{s} for Mr Cooke & I find y^{t} instead of going to bed as he promised he went immediately out to a Mrs Smiths where he still is. One OClock Sam tells me he has just left the brothel & gone to Sully's. He sat to Sully but was wild all day & communicates to every one his being out last night as if he prided in it. He was moderate after dinner & went to the Theatre at the usual time, but he play'd Lear very wildly—the house thin. I saw him in the Green room & being apprehensive of further debauch I went in search of Doctor Park, who join'd me at Wood's & I sent him to the Theatre to alarm Cooke by feeling his pulse & prescribing bleeding. Carpenter & Dr Chapman at Woods. I went home & Cooke soon came. told me he had seen his Doctor & "it is well I have. do you know? he found my pulse as it was before. he says I must be bled if there is not a change before sunday. I was going out again to night. I promised it, but I'll stay now." I went to bed.

[April] 18th The old wretch went out to his Whores again as soon as I was gone. About 10 OClock I walk'd in and found him at his breakfast. Quite sober & no hint of his having been out. I visit Mrs Brown, Mrs Mead. At the Academy. A Ceres by Wertmuller, very poor. A Street by Strickland, Views on Schuylkill by Birch junr. some Groupes of figures very abominable bad. At Sully's: Cooke sitting. Go by invitation & appointed to the Fish house on Schuylkill.[60] The ride was pleasant. we arrived at 2 & found the gentlemen of the Club Cooking beef steaks of which we partook & then walk'd with Mr Rundel[61] to see his house & grounds on the high ground above the fish house. At 3 we dined on fish Cooked by the club who serve themselves & dine under a long shed. The Mayor of the City presided, Mr [Robert] Wharton, and was very attentive to us. Curtis Clay, Jos: Clay, Messrs Worrell, Bradford, Capt Carr, Leslie (the young artist), Rundel, Wood (of Manchester: Singer), Cooke, Francis, Warren, Hardinge, &c a company of 40. The free sociality was admirable. just before sunsetting I walk'd on the bank of the river shaded overloping hill behind which a summer sun was declining. the opposite bank of Schuylkill was strongly illuminated & the objects vividly reflected in the unruffled Water. Thro' the trees which had only the scanty foliage of the season every object of the landscape was visible. Nymphlike forms in White, clambering the rocks, ploughman driving the team, distant villa's & gardens & the windings of the stream far below. One Thrush, the first I had

[60] For an account of this society, and biographical notes on its members, see *History of the Schuylkill Fishing Company of the State in Schuylkill, 1732-1888,* (Philadelphia, 1889).
[61] Richard Rundle (1747-1826).

heard this year, warbled his evening song in contrast to the boisterous sounds which reach my ear from the company carouzing in the shed. Cooke was merry & pleas'd his companions, but was drunk before the company seperated. Hardinge drove us home, as our Coachman was likewise drunk. By exerting all my influence over Cooke I got him to bed at 10 OClock. He appeal'd to me to day thus "Did you ever hear me say a word against Price?" What a strange Animal. I was call'd out to Doctor [Charles] Caldwall who interceded with me to use my influence to prevail on Cooke to play Iago wh Fennels Othello. while I was absent C thought I had gone to bed & order'd a Coach to go to the brothel. he was in high dignity abusing Sam for not flying to obey him, when I enter'd the room, he instantly changed his deportment, and soon agreed to go to bed.

[April] 19th He gets up well at 12. I walk to Academy & Panorama of Boston. Wilcox invites me to dine wh Cooper at 5 tomorrow. Cooke sits to Sully. George Bowen our Coachman arrives & McLean & Jones with him they take their Wine with us. Cooke to Theatre at 6 & plays Sir Pertinax Well. gets to bed drunk at 12. C's Story of Kemble offerring to bribe a person to write him down. Lord [blank] writing his brother the bishop of Durham sermon to be preach'd before the King. the repetition of this story to Mr Hopkinson & others. no Library. where is it? at Durham. Damn you have a kitchen here? "Dunlap, I'm damn'd sarcastic. I wonder I have escaped with my life. you are my preserver. independent of the obligation I owe you for your advice & kindness, I owe my life to you. they see you wh me & they think I can't be bad. they spare me for your sake. Who's that with him? Dunlap. Ah its all well. Who's that? Dunlap. Who's that? &c &c repeat—repeat—repeat.

20th Apl Still like June or July. To Theatre to settle to this time with Warren. Copy

1811 April 5th	Kg Lear	995.75	
6	New way [to pay old debts]	1035. 6	
8	Henry 4th	1020.50	
10	Mercht of V[enice]	870.50	
11	Macbeth	778...	
13	Douglas & Love a la M[ode]	1196...	
15	Every man (Ben J)		1365.25
17	Kg Lear	668...	
19	Man of ye World	948.25	
		7512. 6	
	8 n[igh]ts @ 390	3120...	
		½ 4392. 6	2196. 3
			$3561.28

Paymts

Cash for Mr Cooke	1.12	
Dunlap	250...	
Do	3310.16	
		½)1365.25
	$3561.28	682.62
	682.62	
	2878.66	
	2979.30	

$5857.96 is the gain of Cooper & Price, from which to give the nett profit, the expences of my journey & Cookes saly must be deducted & the remainder is clear on ye Phila engagement.

"I have gone fifteen nights without bolting out of the course. I shall go the sixteen now. Never did such a thing before. Yes I did & more. The summer after my London engagement I play[d] 36 nights in 6 weeks & travel'd 2000 miles. I swept the grass the summer."

The average of the 15 n[igh]ts past is 1091 dollars. Meet Cooper at Wilcox's. Marcoe, 2 Ingersolls, 2 Wilcox's. Cooke play'd finely to night. Cooper went behind scenes to see him: he was first a little strange but soon got over it. Before Cooke came home Cooper & C Ingersol came & found me. Cooper proposed the scheme of playing here 4 nights with Cooke beginning friday night which would detain me until 1st May. I told him I would do everything to further the interest of the Co. Cooke, Cooper, Wilcox, & Ingersol sit down to supper while I go & settle with the Treasurer.

Copy

Ap[l] 20th Rich[d] 3[d]		997.40
Expences		390...
	½	607.40
		$303.70

A bill for Musick to Warren	36...
Mr Dunlap	267.70
	$303.70

16)17360.32
1085. 2

The average recets of the 16 nights is 1089. When I return'd I found that Cooke had cheerfully agreed to stay & play with Cooper & then return to New York & play with him. This & a variety of good humour'd chat past until Cooke becoming tipsey I left them & went to bed first ordering Bowen's carriage at 5 to carry me to Amboy, Wilcox promising to *keep* Cooke until my return.

Sunday [April] 21st The day proves showery with thunder and the roads wet. Cooper overtook me near Princeton. he says Wilcox got drunk with Cooke & they stay'd till 4 OClock. he saw Cooke before he left Phil[a]

THOMAS ABTHORPE COOPER (1776-1849)

Attributed to William Dunlap

(Courtesy of The Players, New York)

(in bed) & appointed to dine w[h] him at 5 on thursday. Wet & dark. can get no further than Brunswick.

[April] 22d Arrive at home at 8. John left home for N. Y. at 7. All well at Amboy.

[April] 24th Wed[y] leave home for Phil[a] & arrive at ½ past 8. Day very warm but a violent thunder shower as we pass Frankf[t]. A lively girl in the stage which I join at Trenton. Miss Richmond of Brunswick. Find Cooke in bed. He got drunk at Mr Head's on Monday in company with Wilcox, & his spasms coming on a Physician in company bled him & he stay'd at Heads that night. Tuesday he however dined out again with Wilcox & got him [home] at 8 but was pressed to the St. George's Society which dined at Mansion House. he however got to bed about 12 & has remain'd there since. I crack'd a joke on him at the Fish house which I believe he has forgotten. I hope he has for it was not delicate before strangers altho' his propensities are so well known. Curtis Clay overset a decanter of Wine which ran down the table from Cooke. He laughing observed that it was very odd that Wine should run away from him. this attracted attention & gain'd a laugh. I ask'd "Do you know the reason?" "No, what is it." "Because you abuse it."

[April] 25th Thursd[y] Up at ½ past 6. The old man dont rise to breakfast, but about 11 Rides out. I visit the Academy & Dr [William P.] De Wees collection of pictures. Mr Lewis's with Sully to see S's copy of Mr West's Mentor & Telemachus on the Island of Calypso. A very fine copy of an exquisite original. I have a fresh remembrance of this picture as I saw it in Mr Wests rooms 25 years ago. Sully painted this & others, copys to repay those who advanced him money to go to England. he was so scanted that he could only stay 1 year & during that time lived on bread potatoes & water. We waited dinner for Cooper till ½ past 5. after dinner Wilcox & Ingersol join us. Cooper arrives at ½ past 7, having broken down

& been delay'd. I left him & Cooke & when I return'd ½ past 10, Cooper was gone & Cooke in bed. Wilcox says that in his ride with Cooke on Sunday they found at a tavern a drunken <*pedlar*> umbrella maker who recognized Cooke & told him of seeing him in England. they embraced & C play'd his antics over & would have given the fellow all his money—105 doll^s but that W held out his hand & received the money. Next day C did not remember it.

[April] 26th Luxury of the Warm bath. Cooke Cooper & self breakfast at 9. All go to rehearsal, where parson Abbercromby [62] attended in the stage box with Meredith & Pennington. All dine together e i C C & self. Evening I look at Theatre & find it very crowded.

[April] 27th Walk before breakfast. Meet Warren Who says the house was upwards of 1500. Call on Cooper walk with him. Find Cooke "How do you do, Sir?" "Oh not at all well, feverish all night, didn't get to sleep till after day light. Went to bed before 12 too. Ah tuesday night will come & then see when I'll tread the boards again—at least for some time. In London two nights a week was enough at three I grumbled, four I would not do. I complain'd of four nights awake to Mr Harris. I said its too much Sir. Why yes, said he, its almost as much as six at a race week in Country. there he had me. but consider Sir what I get for the race week. I do & I consider that what you get comes from here. if you hadn't play'd here you would get nothing there." Cooper requests me to write to Price that Cooke still talks of an engagement to play in Boston the 14th May & to desire Price to write to the Boston Managers on the subject & assert his claim to Cookes services at that time. Cooke & self dined alone. "I'll tell you what, Tom & I were not very clear at rehearsal. I hope we shall not do as Kemble & I once did in this play. We play'd a scene of the 3d Act

[62] Rev. James Abercrombie, D.D., assistant minister of Christ and St. Peter's Churches. *Philadelphia Directory for 1811.*

in the 2d. I was frighten'd out of my wits. we are wrong says I—go on—says he—when we came off I cried "Good god do you know what we have done? we have play'd the scene of the third act" "I know it" says John very cooly "and what shall we do in the 3d Act?" "play the second." We did so. And the best of the Joke the papers never noticed it. After his pint of wine he went off to play Stukely. He says Abercromby was at rehearsal again to day. Call at the Theatre. The house appear'd about 1200.

Sunday Ap^{l} 28th Walk to the Southward of the City down the River. Dine with Wilcox present his sister brother, C Ingersol, Cooper, Cooke, Wood. We had some sprightly nay witty flashes & stories. Owen Owen—o,n,o,n, —n,o,n,o, Cooke told me long since of his having introduced the exploded lines in Falstaff (Merry Wives), of remarking that it pop'd into his head <*to tell*> & he could not resist the wish to repeat them. he tells the story to day as being the effect of a wager or bet which he gains by so doing. He left Wilcox's with me about 10 perfectly sober, sat down to read, eat a slight supper, drank some wine & water & went to bed.

[April] 29th Walk. The old beau got up to breakfast. Doctor Caldwell call'd to ask him to take leave of the Audience. Cooke told him he should not play at New York, that his next playing would be at Boston, 9 nights to close their Theatre. Have a consultation with Cooper as to the means of inducing old whimsey to change his purpose. "If he will not play at N. Y.—very well—there's an end—but I'll be damn'd if he shall play in Boston." He began a letter to Cooke proposing to him to play 4 n[igh]ts in N. Y. one of them for his benefit as before but warranted to yield him 1000 & then to play till 10th June at Baltimore & only to play henceforward 2 n[igh]ts a week. I advised him to see Wilcox & get him to talk to Cooke. When I came to dinner I found from Cooper that he had had some talk on the business but while he is telling me Cooke came up. At Dinner Cooke mention'd that he would go with Cooper in his carriage. in the morning he was resolv'd that he would not. He abuses at dinner time the House the servants &c in the most blackguard style & eats scarcely any thing. Blast the meat & the Cook. God eternally blow up &c &c. At supper this was repeated, or rather while waiting for Cooper. I left him. He has given a clear proof by his conduct since Wed^{y} ye 24 that he can command his desire for Wine or spirits & restrain himself tho' even his belov'd port is before when the motive is to him sufficient. To be able to play in his best style by the side of Cooper he has abstain'd from drunkenness, the fear of sickness is not sufficient, even death he thinks he can put off because bleeding has reliev'd him so instantaineously. However it must be confess'd that the bleeding & fright of Monday the 22d may have operated somewhat to this time.

Tuesday Ap^{l} 30th I send to know if he breakfasts with me. he returns answer that Cooper breakfasts with him at 10. Now as Cooper sup'd with him I augur favourably. Cooper breakfasted together. I left them. Mrs Levy call'd me in. Mary Jackson came in. Cooper call'd on Mrs Levy & when I was going made an appointment with me "sur le pavé" in Chesnut Street. I visited at Mrs Meads, she reads to me her husbands account of the late (1st March) battle near Cadiz. Meet Cooper he says he began by convincing Cooke that his 10 months engagement with him even if the voyages to & from Europe were to be included left him till July in this Country & engaged & that consequently his Boston engagement for 14th May was a nullity. This agreed to, Cooper began to point out his plan of operations, first so many nights New York, then to Baltimore "No! damn me if I go to Baltimore. Curse me if I go to Baltimore. I'll be damn'd if I go to Baltimore. I wont go to Baltimore" After letting him go on till tired it was only to state, the am^{t} of salary during the time, the am^{t} of Benefits, the injury that would occur if he dissapointed the people of Baltimore &c & he yielded without difficulty, so all was settled.

Cooper is to drive him to New York Tandem & then back here & on to Baltimore Tandem & all is as cosey as possible. At Dinner he talks to me of going to Baltimore with all the sang froid imaginable. Evening Cooper's benefit, Othello, in house 1292.

Wed^{y} [May 1] preparatory business to departure

Copy

"Mr Cooper's engagement

1811 Ap^{l} 26th Othello	1504.76
27th Gamester	1193...
29th Venice preser^{d}	1312...
	4009.76
3 N[igh]ts Expences @ 390	1170...
1/3	2839.76
	946.58

Ap^{l} 30th Othello	1292.30
Deduct Expence	390...
	902.30
Mr Cook	116...
	1018.30
	946.58
	1964.88
P^{d} Cooper	502.63½
	$1462.24½

Robt Pullen, May 1, 1811

Leave Phil^{a}. Cooke goes with Cooper. arrive at Brunswick 11 OClock night.

Thursday 2d May. Embark in Steam boat at 6 & arrive at home Perth Amboy at 9 OClock.

I came up to N. Y. Monday the 6th May the night of which Cooke was advertised for Richard & Cooper for Richmond. Price told me he (Cooke) had been very drunk last night & that he was afraid of him this morning. I call'd on him about 12 OClock & found him drinking Wine & intoxicated from the last night. He apologized for the early drinking & said he had eat Beef & consider'd himself as having dined & would not eat or drink until after the play. He rode with Cooper. I dined at Prices & return'd to the Coffee house to Cooke before 5 found him drink[g] & in fact drunk but good natur'd & I did not leave him till deposited in the dressing room with Cooper. He got through the business without betraying himself to the Audience. He kept it up tuesday & tuesday night & Wed[y] I went to look after him again at 11 OClock he was in bed & in high spirits. appointed 2 to go & visit Mrs Price whom he had not seen since he quitted the House. I reminded him of having Price & Cooper to dine with him which he had forgotten. He was much pleas'd with getting over the interview with Mrs Price & we all dined together but could not control his drinking & at ½ past 5 he came drunk to the Theatre Cooper frighten'd at the prospect of his destroying the business and disgracing himself. he however recover'd & play'd charmingly. in house 1578. on Monday 1374.

This strange animal when pleasantly gay will take up a chain of subjects, one always suggesting the other & go over them day after day with a little variation without any apparent consciousness of having told the listener the same thing again & again. Talk of a fire that has consumed a house in N. Y. and he begins. "Was it not very odd that Drury should be burnt so soon after Covent G[n]. I was absent from London on both occasions. Incledon swears I had a hand in both & kept away. I was at —— When Covent Garden was burnt & I had just arrived at —— when the news of the destruction of Drury Lane arrived. Wilkinson says to me—young Wilkinson you know—Tates son—Have you heard any news from London? No, I dont expect letters till tomorrow. Drury Lane is burnt. my blood ran cold. Was it not very strange so soon after the other. There's a mystery about it. I firmly believe they were both set on fire on purpose—by whom I do not pretend to say. The bookseller is firmly of that opinion. it was a noble thing of the Duke of Northumberland, he lent John [Kemble] thousand pound and what was most extraordinary, on the day that the corner stone of the new House was laid he sent him the bond. For he was always noted for closeness. you knew him—your Lord Percy at Lexington

—Col[l] of the 5th red faced with [blank] His mother gave him a rub once. she wrote to him to know why he did not draw upon her agent for money. he answer'd that he did not want it—his pay was sufficient. She replied that such œconomy might be very commendable in the Col[l] of a marching Reg[t] but was very unworthy the heir of Northumberland. His officers play'd him a trick when he first join'd his regiment. It is customary for the Col[l] to give a dinner to all the Officers. He order'd one at [blank] a head. The officers told the Landlord to provide at [blank] a head. His Lordship was surprized to find every delicacy that the Country afforded, but when the bill came he saw the trick, bit his lip & paid it. John deserves his good fortune, he's a noble fellow. He says if he had been made a priest he would have been a Cardinal. Yes, says I, a pope. And thus he runs on and the same idea's produce each other at all times without the smallest attention to his having before repeated them to the same person again & again.

the bottle, that omnipotent leveller of distinctions as well as men

in 1811 (Aug[t]) the difference between Bank of Eng[d] Notes and Specie was as £414 to £317 of gold.

O, Sir, thats nothing—a London printer advertized a Lying in Hospital for the Soldiers of the Life Guards only making the Trifling omission of "the Wives of".

Nov[r] 23[d] 1812. Cooper ask'd me for an additional verse to my song of Yankee Chronology [63] to be sung in my interlude of "Huzza for the Constitution" on the 25th. I write the following

'Twas the year eighty three twenty fifth of November
Saw the Armies of England to these shores bid adieu
Ye Men of Columbia with an honest pride remember
That the blessings *then* purchased *now* depend upon you.

[63] Nine stanzas of "Yankee Chronology" were written by Dunlap for the Fourth of July, 1812, and a tenth, with an introductory interlude, was added in celebration of the victory of the frigate *Constitution* over the British frigate *Guerrière*. These were printed by David Longworth in December, 1812, in a sixteen-page pamphlet, called *Yankee Chronology; or, Huzza for the Constitution,* together with this additional stanza, sung on November 25, 1812, the anniversary of the British evacuation of New York City.

May the Sons of this City, each return of this day Sirs,
When Washington led home their brave sires by the hand
On the Altar of Freedom swear for ever and aye Sirs
That a foreign foe shall never rest his foot on this Land.

Dined with Cooper for the purpose of taking down memoranda of Cooke.[64] Waited upon Mrs Cooper [65] to her father's. Evening an hour at the Theatre.

[Nov.] 24th Make out for Inskeep the title page of the Memoirs of Cooke for advertising. Inskeep offers me for the Work (and I accept) a sum from 4 to 500 dollars not to be less than four.

Memoirs of the life of
George Frederick Cooke Esqr
late of the Theatre Royal Covent Garden London.
Composed, from Manuscript journals &
notes written by himself and from other
authentick sources of information by
William Dunlap

For number of lines & words in Tate Wilkinsons pages see p. 76. [From page 76 of the manuscript:] 35 lines of 7 words makes 245 words to a page duodecimo. 290 such pages made a vol: of Tate Wilkinson
One written page of mine on letter paper make 27 lines of 10 words e i 270 words.

Novr 25th The usual military parade & rejoicing took place to day. Our volunteers appear like soldiers in reality such is the effect of the spirit created by the War.

[64] George Frederick Cooke died in New York City, September 26, 1812, and was buried in St. Paul's churchyard, where Edmund Kean, in 1821, erected a monument to his memory. *N. Y. Evening Post,* Sept. 27, 1812; Dunlap's *Memoirs of the Life of Cooke,* II, 383 *ff.*

[65] Mrs. Thomas Abthorpe Cooper (Mary Fairlie) was the eldest daughter of James Fairlie (1757-1830) and of Maria (Yates) Fairlie. She married the actor, June 13, 1812. J. N. Ireland, *A Memoir of the Professional Life of Thomas Abthorpe Cooper* (*Dunlap Society Publications,* no. 5, N. Y. 1888); *The N. Y. Weekly Museum,* June 20, 1812; John Schuyler, *Institution of the Society of the Cincinnati . . with extracts . . from the Transactions of the N. Y. State Society.* (N. Y. 1886), pp. 199-201.

MRS. THOMAS ABTHORPE COOPER (MARY FAIRLIE)

By William Dunlap

(From the Collection of The Cleveland Museum of Art, Cleveland, Ohio, the gift of J. H. Wade)

[Nov.] 27th Paint & write on Cookes memoirs. Since I moved my family to town I have begun but two portraits, now nearly a month.

When mentioning the Fire at Richmond, notice the attacks of the time on the Theatre. Millers &c. refutation.

When Cooke in his cups used to rail at American Managers & Theatres & Actors he used to exclaim: I'm preparing a pamphlet, when I get to London I'll blow up your Managers and your Theatres & your actors and your blasted Country. I can hold a pen. I scourge your damn'd yankee manners &c" We were safe enough from Cookes abuse because of his indolence, otherwise he might have added to the list of Dunces who have visited us and thought to make themselves acceptable at home by abusing a Country that all Europe envies and that England hates Europe envies the New World a prosperity and freedom which its age & vices renders it incapable of rivalling and in addition to the motives common with all Europe, the envy of England is turned against the vigorous younger brother who prosperously resisted an elder brothers tyranny and wresting the rod from his hand with which he threaten'd chastisement, bestow'd <*it on himself*> the lashes on the threatener.

The list of Dunces who have made themselves ridiculous by or contemptible by the weak or malignant falshoods publish'd as descriptive of those whose hospitality they receiv'd and abused while in the Western hemisphere may with propriety be here given. George Frederick even if he could have had virtue enough to work, I think was not vicious enough to have added to the contemptible list.

Here the names

part of Garricks prologue to Shirley's excellent Comedy of the Gamester which he revived, is with a little alteration so much in point that I must insert it.

> When ever Englishmen take pen in h[an]d
> To give a sketch of you and this our Land,
> One settled maxim through the whole you see
> To wit—Their great superiority!
> Urge what you will they obstinately say
> That you ape them—and are less wise than they:
> Tis thus these well bred Journal writers use us
> They trip o'er here with half an eye peruse us
> Eat with us, drink our wine, and then abuse us.

C [illegible] feasted flatter'd & lampoon'd

perhaps that account of America in Quarterly review a good note

Novr 29th 1812. I yesterday [gave] D Longworth my Interlude & Song of Yankee chronology to publish. Paint on Mrs Price's picture. Cooke appears to have been absent from London the season of 1807-8. M[onthly] M[irror] Vol 3 Decr 19th 1807. Kemble play'd Iago in consequence of Cookes absence first time. preference given to Cooke and his absence lamented. page 51 to 53. Cooke said to be in Appleby Gaol. p: 60. Cooke is said to have been liberated by Rock & playing at Glasgow. In his journal he says he played at Glasgow Decr 30th 1807. 1st Vol M[onthly] M[irror] O[ld] S[eries] 1795. "They lament the absence of the *excellent* and *unfortunate* Cooke. Same Vol 373 congratulates the public on his return to Manchester. "His irregularities while in Dublin &c. M M Vol. 2, 1796. p. 507. Married Mr Cooke to Miss Daniels, both of the Chester Theatre.

Decr 6th [1812] Murphy's pages, Life of Garrick are 19 lines of 8 words that

19
8
———
152 words & from 4 to 16 such pages make a chapter.

[Dec.] 7th Receive the glorious acct of another Naval victory gaind by our gallant tars. Decatur in the United States has brot in the English frigate Macedonian having taken her in <*17 minutes*> after a cannonading of 1½ hours. Afternoon wh Cooper writing of Cooke.

[Dec.] 8th By request for the Theatre a Song called American Tars.[66]

<*Sound aloud the trump of Fame*
Again repeat each Hero's name!
Whose manly breasts by wrongs arous'd
Their injur'd countrie's cause espous'd>

[66] Printed with the title "Yankee Tars" at the end of Dunlap's *Yankee Chronology; or, Huzza for the Constitution* (N. Y., Dec. 1812, pp. 16). A printed note states that it was sung by Mr. Yates at the New York Theatre, December 10, 1812.

When nature kind goddess first shap'd this <*round*> big ball
In fanciful mood <*she flooded the Earth*> good and ill she bestow'd
Assured that she never could satisfy all
<*Her own fav'rite clime she with blessings*>
She one favourite Land with all blessings endow'd

2d

She call'd it Columbia and swore before Jove
That the rest of the world <*should but labour for that*> for this Country should toil
Thro' Asia & Afric & Europe her love
<*And collect*> Sought for us choicest gifts from each clime & each soil

3d

<*She made us the*>
<*But chiefly from Europe she graced us with good*
As the refuge for Liberty, science and laws,
As the Country of arts and the [blank] *of arms*
Then as surety for Truth Justice & Liberty's cause
She planted our bosoms with true Yankee hearts.>
Our Country she made the Assylum of laws
The home of <*proud*> fair liberty science and Arts,
Then as surety, for <*injured*> Truth & Humanity's cause
She planted our bosoms with true yankee hearts.

4th

She then <*thus address'd*> with these words made the Welken to ring
You have now every blessing that I can bestow
Tis yours to preserve and a Navy's the thing
That <*shall*> your rights shall <*preserve*> protect from each insolent foe.

[5th]

She said & twas done. Then the Barbary shore
Saw such daring as rival'd Antiquity's <*fame*> name.
But the war for the rights of our Tars <*on the sea*> gives once more
<*Gives*> To our Tars <*to renown*> a fair field to outdo ancient fame!

6th

<*When Britain the prince first of her frigates sent out*
And threaten'd a beating to all Yankee boys
On her mainsail the gueriere all proudly appear'd>
<*her name seemed the breezes to flout*

& with challenger words &c> <*occasional noise*>
See the Cruisers of Britain with threatening air
Sweep the seas & defy us with thundering noise!
The Gueriere <*in letters all painted*> her name on her mainsail so fair
<*Threate*> Cries death <*& destruction*> or submission to all yankee boys.

7th

But <*the brave*> <*gallant*> bold Captain Hull and his <*brave*> <*gallant*> bold yankee tars
<*Show'd his*> Prov'd her masts were all <*damaged*> heartless and heartless her men
And the Gueriere soon <*saw the end of her*> bad farewell to all wars,
Justice triumph'd & justice will triumph again!

8th

Next <*came*> brave captain Jones <*in*> met the frolic one day
And her masts too prov'd weak & <*her men were all sick*> too weak were her men
<*At least so it seem'd for she yielded the fray*>
At least very soon men & masts shot away
<*seamen a chill pretty quick*>
<*And our shot*> Valour triumph'd and valour shall triumph again prov'd that Yankee must triumph &c.

9th

The Hero of Tripoli next met the foe
And twas just the same story told over again
Of fighting they scarcely could make out a show
When <*her*> their masts were all gone, kill'd or wounded her men!

10th

Tis thus <*our brave*> Yankee tars shall th^{r} Country protect
And the rights of the seas on a sure basis place
The vauntings & threatenings of Britain be check'd
<*While*> And a Navy & Commerce <*our Country*> Columbia shall grace

Decr 9th [1812] W W Woolsey arrived last evening & takes his home with us. The weather is almost summer. We look for Decaturs Prize the frigate Macedonian to day. I was much pleas'd yesterday with the hearty joy express'd by many at this succession of proofs that our Navy is so efficient as to individual officers & ships. O

Woolcot was as ever heartily a rejoicer, but alas there are many of our citizens who had rather the triumph had been with the enemy!

[Dec.] 10th Inskeep gave me the follow^{g} saying he had been making a calculation about the book

2 Vol^{s} 600 pages print^{g}		$300
60 Reams paper @ 5		300
bind^{g} 2000 Vols 25 cts.		500
		1100
Engraving		50
		$1150
1000 Copies @ 2	2000	
	1150	
	$850	

from this I infer that he does not <*conclude*> think that any bargain is concluded between us.

Decr 21st I had some days ago an explanation with Inskeep & find that he did not consider himself as at all bound to me & that he would not even give me $200 for the work.

Jany 1st 1813. The weather mild. The wind long at West changed yesterday & this morning the United States & her prize the Macedonian through *Helle Gat* & safe into Harbour. I dined a few days ago at Mr O. Wolcots in company with Hull & Decatur but had not an oppertunity of conversation with either.

[Jan.] 5th Cookes life. Millers sermon—pure adoration, not prayer, adoration which lifts the heart in thankfulness to its incomprehensible creator & sinks it in humble submission to his will. I call'd on David Longworth and talked over the business of publishing the life of Cooke, having before mention'd it to his son Thomas. He offer'd me three hundred dollars and if highly successfull another hundred. I promised him an answer in 48 hours.

[Jan.] 6th Call at Inskeep's & found him return'd from $Phil^{a}$ after some conversation respecting the book he offer'd me as his ultimatum two hundred dollars. Both Longworth & Inskeep exclude themselves from any right to interfere in my publication of the same in England. Dine at Mrs Bradley's by invita[tion] of Mr Roe, my son with me: he return'd home from Genesseo the last day of the last year and is assisting me by copying Cookes life for England. I was [with] Cooper yesterday and he is to write to Marshal & engage him to publish the work in London on a sharing scheme in regard to profit.

Jany 8th 1813. This is the first severely cold day we have had this winter & it is not unpleasant. Send a letter to James Marshall, No. 3 Southampton Street, Cambden Town near London with an introductory line from Cooper, and mention my wishes respecting the publication of Cooke's life in England. Made the following bargain with David Longworth. He is to give me for the first edition of Cookes life not exceeding 2000 copies, $300. I am not to publish a second ed^{n} until his first is disposed of & am then to give him the refusal in making a bargain for such publication.

"As my admiration of the german dramatists was not influenced by the english writers my opinions have been unchanged by them: and as I never appreciated these saxon bards higher than the old English play writers, I feel no inclination to join with the hue & cry against them & deprecate them to a level with the modern drama manufacturers of <*England*> Britain. I can proudly say that I translated for my Theatre the german dramatists as preferable to the modern english play makers but neve[r] in preference or to the exclusion of the old english dramatic writers or of the better specimens of the talents of Cumberland, Holcroft & the Colmans or of any production of R B Sheridan.

Jany 11th Write to Warren and S Powel for information relative to Cooke:

"One of the most extraordinary traits in the character of this extraordinary man is <*his*> that ability which he possessed of seizing the perfect image of the <*character*> person he would represent and identifying it with his own feelings so as to express every emotion designed by the author as if that emotion was his own. And all this as if by intuition for nobody knew of his studying except in that hasty & desultory manner which his journal at times indicates. But his perception was uncommonly quick & his earlier observations on men & passions must have been uncommonly accurate. I have before observed that in seeing actors their faults were lessons to him & suggested by a representation of the <*wrong*> false what the true must be. His perception of the natural & his power of seperating it from the artificial must have been originally very great. And as <*an*> a friend, highly distinguished in our literary world most ingeniously remarked to me, Cooke when he improved his own playing by what he had seen excellent in other players did not imitate those players but only seized what he saw natural in them and made it his own in his own manner.

Had a pleasant interview with Washington Irving this morning preparatory to writing a letter to Peter which I now do.

Jany 14th Our first Snow Storm. I yesterday received a note from J. H Payne & went to see him. He is going to England in the Cartel ab^{t} sailing. 2000 d^{s} have been advanced by friends to carry him thither, as his passport expresses it "for histrionic purposes and literary pursuits connected therewith." He has a plan for publishing a book on the manners Society literature Drama &c of America.

[Jan.] 17th Mild & beautiful weather. Wrote yesterday a second note to P. Irving, stating the size & materials of my book & pressing an immediate bargain for it.

23^{d} January. Still spring like weather. Receive a notification that I am elected an honorary member of our Academy of Arts. Ride to Greenwich to see Mrs Cooke. she was in town.

Sunday 24th Jany 1813. Rain. Warm. For Cookes release from Appleby see Cabinet Vol. 3d p: 110. Cooke & Young. Cookes benefit, Edinburgh. D^{o} London. p: 426. Kent p: 428.

[Jan.] 25th Sent first sheet of Cooke's life to the press. Wrote to Twaits. Weather rainy & warm. Price gives me anecdotes, at Simpson's lodgings where I accidentally met him, of Cooke.

[Jan.] 26th Snow storm. Write Longworth a memorandum of our agreement.

Charles Incledon dress'd in the room with me, but as I <*couldn't*> cant sing & he cant act we didn't interfere in our dressing. If he <*play'd*> went on for any thing the same night I play'd it was after I had done or if he was in any of the Sing song things of first pieces I had nothing to do at all. Cooke desired that a ring which he had from C[harles] Kemble might be sent to him & Mrs Cooke gave it to Mr Price for that purpose. Mrs Cooke has sent the marked book of The Man of the World to Mr [John Philip] Kemble.

Cook's Mother & Aunts. The Miss Renton Daughters of the Laird of Renton liv'd at Lamberton. The Aunts were his mother's sisters with whom he lived.

Horatius Drunk 1808.

Return'd from Phil^{a} 1st time May 1811. Play'd in N. Y. Went with Cooper to Baltimore play^{g} till 10 June. N. Y. 3 N^{ts} 4th July Rockaway. ret^{d} N. Y. went to Albany (sat out) saturday by steam boat. drunk & quarrelsome. 1 Week at Albany & 3 at Greenbush. To Ballston for 2 days & then to Saratogo and Lake George. At this time Doige was at Albany & Cooke relieved him by employing a physician for him and giving him money. New York in Fall 1811, Sepr 2^{d}

Fourth July 1811 at Rockaway at Tylers.

At what time married.[67]

Up to Albany, Green bush, used to cross over & get in scrapes

To Lake George Ballston

Goes to Boston Novr 1811 [*sic* for Philadelphia]

Came back in dec^{r} to take his baggage & go to E. Returning from

[67] Cooke married Mrs. V. M. Behn, daughter of James Bryden, keeper of the Tontine Coffee House, New York City, in New York, on Thursday evening, June 20, 1811. [N. Y.] *Commercial Advertiser,* June 24, 1811.

Lake George he staid a week drunk at Albany beyond the time intended.

5th July 1812 sat off for Providence by Water was from Sunday to Wed^{y} After one frolic play'd 9 N^{ts} regularly [Snelling] Powel[l] & [James] Dick[enson's] Man[age]rs business good often 150 D^{s} shared half & had a clear ben^{t} began on Monday play'd 9 nights 3 times a Week & then to Boston for 3 days; Before he left N Y the dropsical symptoms had encreased and they continued 8 Weeks in bed eating & drinking but w^{d} not get up. When he got up to have his bed made complained of giddiness but sometimes would get up & sit up part of the night.

Allison Renton

To Holland w^{h} an Uncle a brother of his mother.

Sent his love to Harris, C Kemble & M Brandon on his death bed

In September (early) returned to N. Y. and died.

26th $1400

Used to be cross to Powell & Dickenson & curse them to their faces.

Moll I'm shot, but Cooper is down. always believed that he was touch'd by the ball & they dared not undeceive him.

I wont fall to night. I'll give it to Simpson & they would have to throw him down (in Richard)

After coming from Boston agrees to play but will not. goes to bed & will not get up & orders the doors lock'd. Price bursts the door. "What do you mean Sir &c. Cooper comes all in vain. he will not play or get up.

Appleby. Westmorel^{d} Marquis of Lansdown's tenant Sign of the Weathercock. [illegible] in his Lordships [illegible] This is the old Weathercock.

Foote & my Lords cape wine. Very old. small glasses—you dont drink. I am thinking my Lord how very little it is considering its great age.

Cooke 29th Sepr 1806. Richard allusion to misconduct of last season. play left unsupported. "Is this tragedy so miserably attended to in the cast because Mr Cooke plays Richard? Well be it so. The *Kings name* is a tower of strength which they upon the adverse faction want."

Jany 30th 1813 Cold & clear with about 6 inches of snow on the ground which [fell] on the night of ye 28th

Cooke invited to a pleasure party in a sail boat declines—he <dont> has an antipathy to Water.

When his dropsy was confirmed. "How the devil doctor should I come by this Water—I never drank any.

"Titty, Tiffin,
Keep it Stiff in;
Fire drake Puckey,
Make it luckey;
Liard, Robin,
You must bobin."

Drury Lane was built 1662: destroyed by fire 1672: Rebuilt 1674: pulled down 1791. rebuilt 1794: Burnt down 25th Feb[y] 1809.

Covent Garden built 1733 enlarged 1792: Burnt 1808.

20th of June married by Barry, Bryden not knowing it.

Second visit to Boston he was attended by Powell. They had a terrible Snow Storm & put into New London. Powell goes on to Boston & advertises him. Cooke stays and Powell has to come back for him.

Feb[y] 2[d] 1813. Walk to Greenwich to see Mrs Cook and bring home with me (or rather send by Stage) a trunk of his books. get more Manuscript.

[Feb.] 3[d] Walk again to Greenwich look over Mr Cookes letters & select a bundle & bring home. Get more Manuscript.

[Feb.] 4th A Thaw. Cooke's Dream. He asleep & drunk. The Characters passing in review. some inviting him & pointing with fear to Kemble, others prefering Kemble.

Sign of Washington. you could not do it worse. Cookes laugh know[g] me to be an Artist.

Feb[y] 9th "Estimate of the expence of printing a monthly publication of 64 pages in the form of the London Mirror. Calculation for one number. by Mr [David] Carlisle.

Printing 1000 copies including covers for d°..	70...
9⅓ Rms paper @ 5.50	51.13
paper for covers say	2...
Folding & Stitching 1000	6...
	$129.13
plate & printing	30.87
Extra's	10.
	$170...

500 Subscribers @ 50 cts each number	250...
200 Subscribers obtained by Longworth, at 50 pr Ct	50...
100 Copies sold Do	25...
	325...
deduct	170.
Gain per Month	$155...

and 200 Copies unsold.

If I lose by bad debts 55 dollars I still make 100 per Month.

Feby 10th Had proposals printed for the work whose expence is estimated on the last page. To be called the Monthly Recorder.[68]

[Feb.] 13th According to agreement made with D[avid] Longworth this day, he is to publish the Monthly recorder & to obtain subscribers & sell the work for 33⅓ on his receits. He to obtain subscribers & deliver copies & collect money at his expence.

printing &c		129.13
plates & printing		35.87
Distributing & collecting		10...
		175...
500 subscribers	250	
200 Do D. L. @ ⅓ off	66	
100 sold @ ⅓ off	33	
		349...
		174...
Deduct bad debts		50...
per month		$124...

[68] Five numbers of *The Monthly Recorder* were published, April through August, 1813. They were re-issued, with a title page reading: *A Record Literary and Political, of five months in the year 1813,* By William Dunlap and others. New York, printed for the Proprietor, by David Carlisle.

[Feb.] 14th Write Doctor Irving.

Cooke I observe that you always claim your part in Shakespere. What part has an American in Shakespere

D. If a descendant from Englishmen, the same as an Englishman. I have as full participation in old English glory as you. Shakespere & Milton, Locke Bacon & Newton, the Harry's, Edwards, the Marlsboroughs &c &c were the contemporarys of my ancestors as of yours, and all the glow which animates an Englishman on hearing those names is mine as well as his.

C. So, so, so, & when do you make the line of separation.

D. The year 1776. I have no participation in Britain since then. Yet still her language, her monuments, her best fame is the fame of my forefathers. Of what has past since 1776 I may admire but I do not envy. I am content with the happiness of my Country.

Feby 15th Deliver this day to Thos. W. Moore to be deliver'd to Mr Baker if Mr Baker will promise to deliver the same to Peter Irving & Co at Liverpool, or Geo: M: Woolsey, a Bundle containing the 1st Vol: of "Memoirs of the Life of George Frederick Cooke, late of the Theatre Royal Covent Garden. By William Dunlap. Composed, principally, from Journals and other Authentic documents left by Mr Cooke, and the personal knowledge of the Writer." consisting of 287 written pages exclusive of preface. A Miniature of Cooke & 2 letters 1 to P. Irving the other to G M Woolsey. *Not deliver'd.*

Drury Lane 20th Sepr 1747
When Learnings triumph
Each change
Existence saw
His powerful

[Feb.] 17th "When learnings Triumph o'er her barbarous foes first rear'd the stage.

Doctor Johnson thought that to rear the stage was a triumph over barbarism. The invention of a new mode by which to communicate knowledge to men, he thought, was a triumph gain'd by learning over Ignorance. And he thought justly. Doctor S. Johnson was a moral man, a religious man, a learned man & a wise man. He saw in the stage the second great engine by which mankind were to be instructed, the third followed in the regular progress of human improvement and secured the triumph of learning, the press was the completion of the triumph of learning and the security. But for the press, the "triumph of learning over her barbarous foes" would have been vain, and the Stage ere this with Music, Statuary, painting & poetry would have been swept from the earth by Ascetick fanaticism or barbarian ignorance.

How deplorable the state of a man who knows his weakness yet deliberately rushes on to crime. Makes preparation to guard against part of the evil instead of refraining from the cause of the whole. C <*would*> put his money out of his power by way of preventing himself from robbing himself when in a state ubriation. Then go and produce the madness & endeavour to undo the caution he had taken. In 1809 on his arrival at Liverpool he gave his money in charge to the lady who kept the board^{s} house at which he staid, charging her not to give him any if he demanded it when drunk. This making provision for vice is absolutely more abominable than any degree of accidental crime. The wretched man thinks he may now safely proceed to the filthy stye because he has secured his money, & health & reputation are deliberately put out of the account. So in this instance C goes to his old haunt—some Kearney's —and <*late*> at night comes to his lodgings & demands 50 g^{s}. the Lady refuses—he entreats & threatens & then goes off & procures a warrant & police officers & returns to demand the money it was still refused & the doors shut on him. The next day he came back in all the shame of fruitless repentance, beg'd pardon & return'd thanks to the lady of the house.

Feby 19th 1813. I am this day Forty seven years of age and enter upon my forty eight year.

[Feb.] 20th Another naval victory [69] having been obtained I have another application for a verse in addition to my "Yankee Chronology" for the Theatre. I gave the following

After Hulls verse

In october the Wasp met the Frolic one day Sirs
And her masts too prov'd weak and too weak proved her men
At least masts & men very soon shot away Sirs
Proved to Justice & Jones a fair triumph again.

69 The U. S. frigate *Constitution,* Captain William Bainbridge, captured the British frigate *Java,* December 29, 1812.

The hero of Tripoli next met the foe Sirs
And, tis still the same story told over again,
Of Battle they scarce can make one hour's show Sirs
When Decatur rode Lord o'er the lords of the main.
Then Huz[a]

See our tried constitution, Sirs, again in December,
Sustaining the rights of mankind on the Sea,
When Bainbridge gave Britain, Sirs, a cause to remember,
That sailors fight best when they fight to be free!
See the Java so proud full of brave British hearts, Sirs,
All fierce to contend for the garland of fame,
And in vain! See our thunder, how it rends & disparts her!
And the wreathe is entwined with brave Bainbridge's name!
Then Huzza!

Wealth and luxury abound in our country and in no part of it more than in this great commercial city. Taste does not go hand in hand with them, but ostentatious luxury is little less than ridiculous without taste. A great house may be procured by the possessor of wealth which shall be if he does not interfere too much with his Architect free from ridiculous misproportions or monstrous ornaments, household furniture may be procured which shall be of the newest patterns from France or England and ostentatiously display at first view the costliness of their fashion & material, but after all this when you look for those indications of true taste which combine instruction with delight & approach the splendid frame in hopes of seeing an effort of art worthy of the ostensible wealth of the Host, you find a chinese copy of an european colour'd print or some tawdry mishapen pieces of needle work figures with daubed faces or the awkward copies which Miss made from her drawing Master's models while at boarding school.

March 1st 1813. In summing up remember Cookes orthoepe-acting manner of studying marked parts—intended play.

[March] 5th Breakfast with [Dr. David] Hosack and he engages a letter for my life of Cooke—description of his decease & death & anecdotes communicated to Dr [John W.] Francis by Cooke on his death bed.

[March] 10th [James] Eastburn's reading room: became a subscriber on the 5th. He promises to forward my Recorder. Mr O Wolcot says that Captn Hull asserts that there were (I think) 30 American seamen on board the first 2 English frigates taken. When Captn. [James R.] D'Acres came on board the Constitution H asked him "are there any Americans on board?" D'A. said yes & set down & wrote the names of 12 from memory (of course known to be Americans) 17 were found on board— 12 acknowledged & immediately set free & 5 set free by Habeas Corpus on their arrival at Boston. 1 was killed in the action. only one went below.

March 28th See "The War" for Jany 26th for Naval Estimates.

[March] 29th Story of Kemble & D'Egville pantomime Robinson Crusoe. Poll, Poll

Ap^{l} 5th On the 27th Mar: Govr [Simon] Snyder laid before the Legislature of Pennsylvania a letter, dated at Harrisburg Mar: 25th from Genl Arthur Sinclair, expressing his thanks for the unsolicited aid given to him by a grant &c Nat: Int: Mar 23^{d} Verses.

> To strive against bad education's in vain
> See the lufs how he's got at his old tricks again!
> If I didn't see, would I believe that he took it,
> See! See! how the luf swims away with the bucket.

Mar: 31st the English landed on Barnegat & killed & carried off a number of Cattle.

Ap^{l} 3^{d} 2 English Frigates showed themselves in Boston Bay. Govr Shelby. Mar: 16th 1500 men, and Genl Clay for Chillecothe.
Wm Newton aged 73
New York Gaz 3^{d} Ap^{l} Fort. S. Hook

Ap^{l} 10th I Gave to Captn Brown of the ship Braganza for Lisbon a packet containing the whole of the proof sheets of "Cookes Life" and he is to send the packet by the best oppertunity to P Irving or to G M Woolsey, Liverpool. I wrote directing, as before immediate publication. One week ago I sent a similar packet by the Ohio, favour'd by Mrs [blank], And three weeks ago I sent by Mr Guest a passenger in the Pacific the compleate Manuscript with letters & to the same gentlemen.

May 7th [1813] Yesterday the first number of the Monthly recorder made its appearance. This first number will cost me

Postage	1.12½
Paper	60...
Do Covers	4...
Folding & stitching	6...
Plate & printing	30.87½
Printing 1200	75
Proposals, advertisemts distributing &c	25
	202

```
       16
1200)20200
     1200
     ----
      8200
      7200
      ----
      1000
```

seventeen pence each number

Ferguson	W[illiam] C. Rhinelander
T[homas] Hammersly	Ph: Rhinelander
Dr [William] Hammersly	John G Leake
Batten	John M D Lawrence
Roger Strong	Nathanl McVickar
John Broome	Archibd Bruce
Clement Moore	Thos M Harvey
W[illiam] P. Van Ness	Edmd Pendleton junr
Dr Mitchill	Wm Van Ness
B[enjamin] W Rogers	Walter Willis

NIAGARA FALLS, SEPTEMBER 8, 1815

BY WILLIAM DUNLAP

(In the Theodore Salisbury Woolsey Collection)

DIARY OF WILLIAM DUNLAP

OCTOBER 15, 1819—APRIL 28, 1820

NORFOLK, VIRGINIA

(Manuscript volume lettered *Memoirs 24* owned by THE NEW YORK HISTORICAL SOCIETY)

MEMOIRS 24

New York Friday Octr 15th 1819. Steam boat, on my way to seek business as a painter, first at Burlington N. J. then westward as circumstances direct. I have left $400 with my family, I have $150 in my pocket. Arrive at Trenton 10 OClock & next morning ride 3 Miles down the river to Steam Boat, Captn Jenkins formerly of the Raritan. Land at Bristol & call on [Thomas Abthorpe] Cooper who is at New York making an engagement. Go over to Burlington and call on Bloomfield. No prospect of business. Ellis B has brought from Spain a collection of pictures, which as his uncle says cost him the price of a Farm, and I say are worth nothing. Dine with Mrs Cooper and go down to Philadelphia

Sunday [Oct.] 17th See Sully. he advises me to go to Norfolk & thence to Richmond for Miniature painting at the last place. Remove my baggage to Sully's.

[Oct.] 18th Take the Steam boat for Bristol to see Cooper for information respecting the south & for letters. Sully has not had a portrait to paint for Phil: since May last & but four for Strangers. he is painting Washington crossing the Delaware, for Exhibition—a fine Composition. In conjunction with [James] Earl[e] he has erected a Gallery & they Exhibit some good pictures but with out success as to profit. Leslie's Death of Rutland, bold, broad, fine. Horse & Snake. Landscapes by Shaw, good, colouring like Loutherburg. A small Landscape by Gainsborough beautiful & bold. [Charles B.] King is at Washington he will show me some machines for preserving Colours when ground. I called on Warren yesterday, who is always the same good natured, fat, friendly creature, he has 4 or five children by his last wife—politely invites me to the Theatre & greenroom. They have played 12 nights to some profit. I understand that it is to Newcastle 40 miles, by land to h^{d} of Elk 18, by water to Baltimore.

Arrive at Bristol & find that Cooper had gone to Philadelphia. Walk to the Shamony & returning to Dinner, find Cooper landing from Steam Boat and return to his house with him—pass the day & follow^{g} night. He gives me letters to [blank] in Fayetteville, Newburn, Wilmington, Raleigh.

To ask S respecting Mr S's push I did so, and he said he began the business unknown to Trumbul, but soon told all & T appeared pleased to instruct him.

Octr 19th 1819. Bristol. C. tells me that Price is losing money every night the Theatre opens. C. is to play in N. Y. Boston & Phil^{a} & goes south 27th of Decr. Expects Keene [70] will come out. See 2 young Scotch Women, Misses [Wright] the eldest (24) the Author of Altdorf play'd at N. Y. last year, now to be play'd in Phil^{a}. C. to play Altorf. He reads the plays to me & I find much to praise.

Morse is the Oil painter of Charleston, Fraser the Miniature. Make preparations for Norfolk. See Mr Wests picture of Christ healing.[71] At my entrance I was disapointed, the effect was not as great as I had anticipated. The figure of Christ positively had no grace, no expression. The hand very fine. Composition improved as I look'd on, but the principal figure if Christ can be called the principal, remained bad. St. John had on [illegible] The priests too black, otherwise well expressed, perspective bad, [illegible] men pasteboard, principal groups fine beyond any praise, paralitic woman & attendants good, kneeling figure good. Maniac fine & his father Exquisite. Two females his sisters perhaps as fine as possible. Female

[70] Edmund Kean did not appear in New York until November, 1820.

[71] For a description and reproduction of Benjamin West's painting of "Christ healing the sick in the Temple", and an account of its presentation to, and exhibition by, the Pennsylvania Hospital, in Philadelphia, see pp. 305-321 of Morton and Woodbury's *History of the Pennsylvania Hospital* (Philadelphia, 1895).

head near the paralytic beautiful, in the extreme. Old & Young Woman on the left very fine. Infant perhaps good but not to my taste. Blind man & boy leading perfect nature & feeling. Blind girl & group fine. I am much dissapointed with all the distance as Candlstick &c.

Oct[r] 20th Write to my Wife. prepare to depart. Visit the [Pennsylvania] Academy [of Fine Arts] & am astonished by the strength & beauty of Alstons picture.[72] Rayberg's is good. Frasers miniature of Cooper, flatt & hard but good mechanical touch. See Trott who is about starting for Savanah & Charleston, he is starving in Phil[a]. Call at S. Levy's & see Mrs P. of Amboy. Get on board Steam boat for Newcastle before 12 OClock. The grandour of Alstons picture, the force, the nature, the colouring, the expression is fine, very fine; it is surely beyond Mr West's Christ Healing—it is highly finished in every part but the touch is woolly. The faces have a certain angularity, is it hardness? West's faces are better, except the Christ which is good for nothing.

Go by Steam boat to Newcastle, cross the land by Stage to French town & embark in another Steam boat about 9 OClock about 50 passengers.

21st Oct[r] 1819 between 4 & 5 in the morning arrive at Baltimore. I meet Mr Lawrence formerly of N. Y. whose miniature I once painted, he now resides in Augusta. A French physician De Norris, with 2 mulatoe Children, one a young woman, whom he says he had educated with all the accomplishments of a Lady in France, having sent her to his mother. He is going to settle in Fayetteville, but last night had nearly departed for another Country. As the steam boat past another vessel, her boom sweeping over deck the rope hanging below it, caught the Doctor under the chin & lifted him up in the air, he caught a railing of the St[m] B[t] which gave way, & he fell with it on the Deck, he escaped unhurt. We left Baltimore about 7 & at the Fort were received on board the steam b[t]

[72] "Dead Man Revived by Elisha's Bones".

Virginia for Norfolk, a very large Vessel. We stop'd an hour at Anapolis, & I visited the Town State house & mounted the Balcony of the Cupola from which the view is fine & extensive, at 1 OClock we proceeded down Chesapeake Bay and at 7 in the morn[g]

Oct[r] 22d we arrived at Norfolk, 210 miles in 24 one hour of which we stop'd at Anapolis & half an hour at the Fort where the physician visited us in consequence of the late Yellow Fever at Baltimore. I walked to Gosport (the Navy Yard) to Thos. R. Swift's house (Capt[n] Swift & deliver'd a letter from Cooper, of introduction, to him at Portsmouth where I found him attending at the Court house as a Grand juror. My new acquaintance Doct[r] De Norris before parting this morning showed me a Jewish Shekle. I see H[ugh] Reinagle at Mr [John] Crawley's: Walk in the afternoon with E[lijah] Brown of Phil[a].

[Oct.] 23d Write to my Wife and to Gilfert. Speak to the keeper of the Hotel [Matthew Glenn] respecting my plans & show him & family my miniatures. He soon after came into my room with a Miniature set in gold which he said the owner had left with him for a debt 10 years ago & asked if I could make a portrait of some one of his family to suit the setting. "Yes" "How much" "Twenty dollars" Agreed & thus I have something to do. Commence on Monday. Walk. Call to see Crawly. Coming to Hotel find Fred[k] Lewis, who has been stationed here this three years at Old Point Comfort where the U. S. are now erecting great fortifications. I have heard the cost estimated at some millions. I find that Thos. R. Swift Esq. is Capt[n] of Marines, from Philadelphia, a bon vivant & generally liked. I find a volume of Rousseau's Confessions, in french, Promenades, & find amusement in them. I see little to indicate a change of climate except the tree called Pride of China growing in the streets as an ornamental shade-tree. The black faces, and dirty patched clothing of the Servants only indicate the state of slavery and manners attendant on it. The appearances of the well dressed people, made & female is the same as at New York & Phil[a]. From Ph[a] to Norfolk is 338 miles & the journey is performed in 42 hours. I am now from home about 430 miles.

Sunday 24th Oct[r] 1819 Weather clear & mild. I went to the [Christ] Episcopal Church, a spacious Brick building, plain without & within, but neat & having a large & ornamented Organ. The Music was good. The Assembly genteel. The preacher Mr [Samuel] Low, eloquent above mediocrity. In another clergyman, reading the church service with a voice of musical thunder, and with a discretion, modulation, truth, dignity, & cadence far beyond any one I ever heard, I recognized my old acquaintance Morse,[73] whom I have known, a Lawyer, a player, a Captain in the Army, a lecturer, a schoolmaster, and who when last I saw him was in sickness & in poverty. He is now well dressed, full of flesh, health and strength & as handsome a figure as can well be imagined. After Church I joined him & he recognized me. He told me that he arrived here in June in the United States frigate, had been since to the Northward, was now in the Barracks at Gosport. He is a Chaplain to that frigate. Bishop Moore is at Richmond. Mr Low, the preacher is dying of consumption. He studied law, became a player & finally a priest. He is said to be the son of a clergyman, who resided near Fredericksburg. Sam[l] Low, who was one of the first clerks in the N. Y. bank, published a volume of bad poems, a bad play, became a drunkard, abandon'd his wife, came South and (as I hope) reformed & became a clergyman of the Church Episcopal. I will enquire if the father of this gentleman is or was poet Low. I was pleased to see several well dress'd negroes of both sexes at church, and to see that the general appearance of that race was on this day clean & indicative of enjoyment. I walked in the afternoon down the bay & round the

[73] Ebenezer B. Morse. *See* Abner Morse, *Memorial of the Morses* (Boston, 1850) 51, Appendix note LII. He died in Providence, R. I., August 14, 1824, aged 40 years. *Providence Gazette,* cited in Arnold's *Vital Record of Rhode Island,* XIV, 121.

Fort north of the Town. The Market here is wofully poor compared to the Cities of the north. The Butchers' meat looks poor, the venders of country produce pigs, poultry, butter, milk, vegetables, are Blacks, principally Women. Our Table is amply supplied, but the Butter is poor or worse, potatoes scarcely eatable, Sweet potatoes pretty good, Hominy (at Breakfast) Hams very good Fowls pretty good, Bacon & Cabbage is a common Dish & corn'd Beef & Turnips another, Fried Eggs & Sausages (at Breakfast) poor roast Beef at Dinner and Oysters in profusion at Breakfast, Dinner & supper or Tea. Oysters are carried through the street for sale opened & in the shell & I observed boats at the wharves loaded with them open'd & in large Firkins from which they are ladled & sold by the quart.

The Country round Norfolk is a flat sand level & the Woods are Ceder and pine. A little good soil and some gardens and corn fields appear here & there.

Monday Oct[r] 25th 1819. Prepare to paint a Miniature, but to my great chagrin my Landlord tells me he cannot give me employment, for if one is painted all must be painted. Morse comes to see me & mentions a little loan of money I made him when I last saw him, with promise of repayment before I go. F. Lewis calls to see me. Morse says his situation in the Navy is secure, it is 55 dols p[r] month. He only needs an arrangement with his former creditors in Massachusetts, to enable him to take orders & obtain a good living. They call him here Doctor Morse. Glenn my Landlord comes to tell me that he will have his two daughters painted in Oil, the Girls so preferring, and I am to do them at $25 each. This restores me again. Returning from a walk to the north over the same arid plain cover'd with pine which is seen in every direction except where water diversifies the prospect, I found the following polite note

Chas H Graham will be pleased to see Mr Dunlap at the Theatre, whenever that place offers any amusement for him.
Monday afnoon 25th Oct[r] 1819

I wrote a note in answer and leaving it at the door of the Theatre went in & saw a Comedy new to me called "The sons of Erin. I was pleased with it, and found unexpected good acting in some men whose names I had never heard to remember. Mr Finn is natural, has good judgment, good voice, pretty good person, expressive countenance, an easy genteel manner without being graceful. Mr Brown played an Irish servant extremely well. Mr Dalton, a coxcomb in pretty good style. Mr Thomas was above mediocrity. The ladies were my old acquaintances Mrs Young, Mrs Clarke (formerly Miss Harding) Mrs Hayes (formerly Claude & once Miss Hogg) Mrs Wheatley. Mr Pritchard, whom I met yesterday, is to play Othello on Wednesday, first time of appear^{g} here.

[Oct.] 26th [Daniel W.] Crocker who kept the Wash[ing]ton Hall is here Captn of a Steam boat to Petersburg. I remember him Captn of the Washington troop of Horse at N. Y. The state of society here is marked by the shops where articles of contrary kinds are exhibited together as in the villages of the north, by the want of a Circulating library of any kind or of a Book Store (a mistake there were two) I have been endeavouring to procure 2 Mahogany pannels to paint on & the Cabinet maker having no business & his journeyman no work can hardly be bro^{t} to do this trifle. 1 OClock, I beg Norfolk's pardon I have found 2 Bookstores tho' small ones. I have said that nothing indicates the change of climate but the *pride of China tree,* which grows large & luxurious in most of the streets, but I should add that the verdure of these trees, the lombardy poplars & the few Oaks seen round the town, at this late season, shows a different habit from the poplars & oaks with us. Norfolk is an improving place. That part of the City which lies north west is handsome, the houses give an idea of wealth & their are several with gardens attached to them.

Wed^{y} Octr 27th I observe that since my arrival the Thermometer has been at 8 OClock in ye morning from

48 to 58, at 2 OClock Afternoon from 67 to 65 at 6 in the evening from 63 to 60. Commenced a portrait of Miss Glenn. Evening walk & after tea went to Theatre but was denied admittance in presence of two or three people going in, the Doorkeeper saying "Your name is not left to night." I remark'd "If I had not had a general invitation I should not have attempted to come in." He repeated, & added if you wait sir I will send to Mr Graham." He called a person to send. I refused "It is a matter of no consequence & walked off.

[Oct.] 28th Write to my Son in answer to one received yesterday. Therm: yester: 53, 65, 61. Began the portrait of Miss Matilda Glenn. Morse calls on me and reads two letters from his creditors in Massachusetts agreeing to his proposals, this opens views of prosperity to him; he says Bishop Moore is friendly to him & apprehends no impediment in the way of his ordination. Read in [Robert] Bloomfield's Farmers' boy. It appears to me very poor. Therm: to day 56, 69, 67. Norfolk is said to be a religious place. I stopt at a Baptist meeting this evening. A french man was preaching fluently in broken English to a crowded Auditory.

[Oct.] 29th At the reading room adjoining my quarters, to which I was introduced by Captn Lewis, & where are News papers from all parts of the U. S. I was presented by Graham with a letter from Gilfert, discouraging my coming to Richmond. Graham apologized for the affair of my stoppage at the Th: door, says he positively told the doorkeeper to admit me always & requested my visits anew. Paint on both my portraits. Afternoon make a sketch of part of the Harbour, Fort Nelson & Fort Norfolk with Craney Island in the distance. Evening visit the Theatre & see Lear. [Nahum] Tates alteration of Shakespere appeared to me more than ever bald, disjointed, Lame. Pritchard not studied even the words of Lear, occasionally gave good passages. A petite piece called Married Yesterday, poor & of vile tendency. The door keeper makes his clownish apologies & Mr Graham is again very civil. Thermo: 61: 76½: 75.

Oct[r] 30th A tall swaggering young man who came yesterday from Petersburg, drinking Cocktails at the Bar and talking & swearing very loud, was accosted by the black barber with "Will you have your beard taken off, Sir?" "Hay! Yes! By God! I'll have any thing taken off; Damn me! by God I dont care if I have my head taken off!" The negroe grinning & at the same time looking down with a kind of mock humility replied "very happy to serve you, Sir." Capt[n] [William] Wilson of the Artillery who says or rather swears, for he swears to all things, that he is not only the oldest captain in the U. S. service but in the world, Swears that the play they called Lear last night was no more like Shakespere's Lear than it was like the history of John Rogers & his ten Children. "Damn me, Sir, if I had gone in without seeing the Bills, I should as soon have thought of Tom Thumb as King Lear. Such scoundrels ought not to be encouraged! By God I'd rather give my dollar to the first beggar I meet in the street than to such a set of strollers! Why Sir! they cut out the Fool altogether, the fool is the most important part in the play. I'll be damn'd if I wouldn't for a dollar set fire to their damn'd barn of a house!"

Paint. Afternoon walk. Evening see "The curfew" perform'd & prisoner at large. It is singular that Mr [John] Tobin should have stumbled on the story of my "Feudal Baron" if he did not take it from my play which was published years before the Curfew was played.

A man dressed as a quaker and apparently 70 years old called to see me to day, and asked me if I did not remember a *frolic* we had had together 40 years ago in New York when I was going to England. I denied the 40 years (it is 35 tho') acknowledged the frolic, but did not recollect him He told me his name was Seaman. I then remember'd Tom Seaman, a youth with curling black hair, laughing eyes & a frame, countenance & manner full of elasticity and animation. I looked in vain after we had sat down to talk over former times, in the shrivel'd skin, furrow'd cheek, sunken eyes, grey hair, & meagre limbs of this old man for my friend Tom. He thought we had not met since the period he mentioned, but I remember meeting him in travelling somewhere, perhaps 13 years ago, then not much changed. He has been married 30 years & (as E Brown tells me) his wife was a fine fashionable card playing Lady & is now a Methodist. He has resided at Edonton N. Carolina as a Merchant, then in Norfolk keeping the Exchange Coffee House, & now is a trader again. Ther: 66, 63, 61.

Sunday Octr 31st. Write to my Wife. Go to Church. Walk to Gosport & Portsmouth with Brown return by the Ferry. All Blacks at the Ferry. B. tells me that the west branch of Elizabeth river (& we cross both branches on bridges going to Gosport) joins the Canal from the Great Dismal in N. C. About twenty miles from this on that rout is a Lake (Drummonds pond) about 6 miles by 4, the country around it healthy. This canal leads to Elizabeth City, it is to bring the produce of N. C. to Norfolk. Ther: 54. 55. 55.

Monday Novr 1st 1819. Clear frosty morning. Walk & visit Steam Boat in which I arrived here. Paint. Evening with E Brown at Theatre. Road to Ruin. Fin very good. "Where shall I Dine." Dalton quite clever. The piece very faulty even as a trifle.

Novr 2d Paint. My friend Morse introduces to me Mr Brimhall[74] Quartermaster who engages his portrait to be begun day after tomorrow. Walk in the afternoon. The insects still sing in the fields.

[Nov.] 3d In my mornings walk hear a bird singing cheerfully on a tree in one of the Gardens of the West

[74] Elisha Brimhall, 1st Lieut., Corps of Artillery. *Register of Officers . . in the Service of the United States on the 30th of September, 1819* (Washington City, 1820), p. 59.

part of the Town. Paint. Afternoon Lieu^{t} Delany [75] engages his portrait to be begun the day after tomorrow.

Novr 4th Write to Sully, to MacLean & to my Wife. Begin Lt. Brimhall's picture.

[Nov.] 5th E. Brown leaves us. Paint on Brimhall. Begin Lt. Delaney's picture. At dinner a Midshipman accosted me by name & introduced himself as Fairley [76] of New York. These two afternoons or even^{gs} I have extended my walks at least two miles on the North road. Go to Theatre & see "Lady of the Lake" & part of "Love laughs at Locksmiths."

[Nov.] 6th Weather continues fine gradually becoming cooler. This morning the frost (hoar frost) lay on the fields like snow. After painting on Brimhalls picture he introduced me to Lieu^{t} Fraser [77] from N. Y. son of old Donald and brother to Major [Donald] Fraser whose polite behaviour on our rencontre at Schlosser on the Niagara I remember always with pleasure. Evening. Theatre. Poor Gentleman & Falls of Clyde. The first very well played. Mrs Clarke's Miss Lucretia is very excellent & Fins young Bramble, the latter piece is very interesting. Donald by Fin, shows amazing versatility & great judgement.

Sunday Novr 7th In my morning walk I found the streets swarming with negroes, laughing, talking, sporting, & some bringing in to town milk & vegetables to market. Not that the Market is not on other days but these people, principally women carry these articles on their heads about the streets for those who want & a few expose them near or on the Market square before break-

[75] Probably Henry Rozer Dulany, 1st Lieut. in the 4th Regt. of Infantry. *Ibid.*, 64; Heitman, *Historical Register of the U. S. Army*, (Washington, 1903), I, 387.

[76] Robert Y. Fairlie. *Register of Officers in the service of the United States on the 30th of September, 1819.* (Washington, 1820), p. 89.

[77] Upton S. Fraser, 1st Lieut., Corps of Artillery. *Ibid.*, 59.

fast. I have found out another walk over the Common which after passing by a bridge one of those inlets that make Norfolk almost an Island, leads among Gardens well cultivated & pleasant country houses, neat, not splendid, forming an interesting promenade.

At Church hear an excellent Discourse from Richard Moore Bishop of this Diocese, my old acquaintance of N. Y. Write to Gilfert respecting my letters & to post Master Richmond. Write to Major Vandeventer at Washington. Afternoon walk with Lt. Brimhall, and by passing through wood observe that the timber trees are not so much confined to Cedar & pine as I before thought, oak, gum, poplar &c are mingled with them. Stop at a public Garden, where five or six groupes of Idlers were pitching dollars, those winning who placed the dollar in or nearest a hole of its size.

Evening at Church and hear the Bishop again. I waited for him as he came down the aisle and after a warm greeting promised to call & see him tomorrow.

[Nov.] 8th Call at Mr Southgates (to whom I was last night introduced) and pass half an hour with Bishop Moore. He is visiting his Diocese, returns here in about a fortnight & then goes home to Richmond. I am to paint his picture gratuitously, he being pleased with the offer, to be given to some friend to the North. He has children in Philadelphia. He recommends my being in Richmond during the session of the Legislature, promisses me his assistance & thinks I shall have employment. Mrs Southgate talks of a picture. Paint on the two Misses Glenn. Evening meet Gilfert at the Theatre. He says he can promise me 2 or 3 portraits to paint in Richmond. I have engaged a room to paint in, at a house but a short distance from my Hotel.

[Nov.] 9th The weather is still dry mild & hazy. Last night Mr Fin performed Lord Ogilvy, with great cleverness, but made him too old, it was however well in keeping. Paint on Delaney's picture. Afternoon ride with him four miles, to the termination of the northern road, at a paltry Tavern on a point of sand opposite Craney Island. Receive a letter from my Son in answer to mine of the 28th Octr. Evening go to the Lancasterian School house & hear Lancaster himself in a lecture of two hours explain his system. He speaks interestingly as a man understanding his subject, but has the Cockney dialect as it respects h, v & w in all its imperfection. He has been in this Country 15 months, principally in Phil^{a}. Landed in N. Y. His plan is in operation in every quarter of the globe.

[Nov.] 10th Write to Sully to employ Doughty to send me 8, 30 by 25 & 4, 36 by 30 prepared cloths on strainers, 10 oz Vermillion, 2 bladders of White, 10 oz light red, some lithrage & some gum mastic. Paint on Brimhall. Receive a visit from Captn Swift, friendly, with apologies, invitations &c. Dine with *Doctor* Morse at the Marine Barracks, Gosport. They have snug quarters & the Mess, consisting of L^{ts} Alcot,[78] Mackie,[79] Dulany[80] (of the Marines) & Morse, make a pleasant society. We had a good Dinner &c in handsome style. Swift joined us. I walked home to tea & then went to the Theatre.

[Nov.] 11th Morse, by invitation of the Bishop goes with him to visit the residue of his Diocese. This he thinks augurs well. Paint on Dulany. The weather has encreased in warmth this 3 days & is to day at summer heat.

[Nov.] 12th Finish Brimhal's picture & both the Misses Glenn, a hard long days work. Walk. Go to the Theatre. Robbers & Irishman in London. Both pieces

[78] Henry Olcott, 1st Lieut., U. S. Marine Corps. *Register of Officers . . in the Service of the U. S. on the 30th of September, 1819.* (Washington, 1820) p. 100.

[79] Aeneas M'Kay or Mackay, 1st Lieut., Corps of Artillery, *Ibid.*, 58.

[80] William W. Dulany, 1st Lieut., U. S. Marine Corps. *Ibid.*, 100. The designation of this Lieut. Dulany as belonging to the Marines, leads to the assumption that the Lieut. Dulany whose portrait Dunlap was painting was Lieut. Henry Rozer Dulany, of the 4th Infantry Regiment, as noted *supra.*

well performed. Mr Fin, tho' wanting figure or rather size, plays Charles de Moor well. Weather perfect summer. All windows open this two days.

[Nov.] 13th Norfolk is in Lat 36.55, 116 mile S of Richmond, 389 S by W. from Phil[a] 231 from Washington. So says [Joseph] Scot[t']s Geography. Write to my Wife. Paint on Delany. Receive a letter from my Wife of 8th inst. Take a long walk. Visit Crawley. Weather becomes colder but not yet frost. Mr Fin call'd on me to day & was introduced to me.

[Nov.] 14th Paint. Go to Gosport to call on Swift. A painter late from Europe but last from Richmond introduces himself to me.

[Nov.] 15th Paint on Delany. Walk. Theatre. See John H. Paine's Tragedy [*Brutus*] perform'd with much pleasure. The whole interest is in the part L. J. Brutus which was played with great force & judgement by Fin. Perhaps the passion of the Father should have been more repress'd. The afterpiece was Matrimony.

[Nov.] 16th Tuesday. Summer weather. Begin a portrait of Mr Glenn. Mr Fin who call'd on me, tells me that when a boy he wrote a letter to me proposing himself for the Stage & endeavouring to persuade me that he might prove a second Master Betty, and that he brought his letter himself, but I gave him no encouragement, but advised him to abandon all thoughts of the Theatre. He then went to the Grove Theatre & play'd Little Pickle. He has play'd in London & Edinburgh, says Keene is not a great player, except in Sir Giles Overreach. That he is a drunkard & fond of low Company. Write to my son & send on a note for $84 to renew one of 105 in part, due 7th Dec[r]

[Nov.] 17th Still warm. We have had among the boarders at our hotel; some officers of a privateer under patriot commission of Spanish Am. who lodged at one end of the Gallery into which my apartment opens and at the other end the Agent of a slave ship from Baltimore, Mr Price fitted out for Guinea. The privateer has gone out of the Capes to wait for the Slave ship to make her a prize.

Write to my daughter. Paint on Delany and Glen. oppressively warm sitting at my Eazle. Strong S. Wind. Afternoon Gust from the N. W. and the first rain since I left home. Evening clear. Wind W. Mild. Read this two evenings in the 1st Kings with commentary.[81] Some of the comments are puerile some learned, some curious. But do not these commentators unsettle belief? When the unlearned reader sees that there are many versions differing in the reading, that many words, phrases, passages, are on all hands allowed to be mis-translated, that the most learned differ as to the meaning of words & phrases, what is the inevitable conclusion? A curious note is given respecting the mother of Asa, with various readings as to the nature of her guilt. Surely the note is at least injudicious. Is it not wonderful that repeatedly the word Sodomites is used as the translation of a word literally and only meaning *holy or consecrated persons,* e i consacrated to Idolatrous worship? Again it is said that the word translated raven in the story of the prophet Elijah, means Merchant, or inhabitants of a place called Orbim or Arabians!!! What latitude does this give to the reader, what uncertainty is suggested! Notion supported that Elijah or Elias, or Elihu, was an angel incarnate by his ascension to Heaven. The word translated prophet means likewise priest & perhaps poet, the word *Naba* prophecy means to pray, to supplicate.

[Nov.] 18th Mr More, the painter above mentioned as introducing himself to me, hearing that I was going towards Richmond, suggested my stopping at Surry Court house to paint the family of a Mr Price & a Doctor Graves, who wished him to do it, but he had no oil

[81] By Adam Clarke.

apparatus, he asked 50 dolls for a portrait. On talking to Mr Glen he knowing Price, I write to day to him, & offer to come thither on an engagement for at least 4 portraits at 30, 50, or 75 dolls according to size. Paint on Glen. We have in the house Mr Wrifford a teacher of writing, a New England man, a character, he affords me entertainment, by shrewd remarks & eccentric manners. He is a singer & has a noble voice. Evening read in Kings. How does Elisha's words "take my life for I am not better than my fathers" agree with the notion of his being an incarnate Angel? The book says 7000 had not bowed the knee to Baal, the Commentator says 7000 does not mean 7000 but a great many thousand, a majority of the nation, soon after the fighting men of Israel are number'd at 7000 & the commentator laments that Israel was so thinned, so reduced in number. "A Wall fell upon 27000 men & crush'd them" says the Com: "probably a burning wind is meant" We are told that what is translated ashes may mean *bandage* or *fillet*. Again *"Gan Yirek* may mean Garden of herbs or Grass plat. "Naboth did blaspheme God & the King" may be render'd "Naboth hath blessed God & the King" and the word *barac* may mean either bless or curse. How then is a sincere man to read this book? Again Ahab walked softly may be "barefooted" or groaning or with down hanging head. This curious Book must then it would appear be read with constant doubt as to the meaning of the original independent of all other doubts.

Friday [Nov.] 19th Colder. I have been in N. 4 weeks. Mrs Butler & her daughter Harriet & son Jon: arrive on their way to Elizabeth City N. C. Harriet is going to her father's for the Winter. I found from the meeting of Harriet & Matilda Glenn that they were acquainted & Harriet told me that she had staid at Mr Glens with her Child & received much kindness from the family. Mrs Butler told me that in travelling without a protector Glen had been very kind to her during the late War. I call'd on Mrs Southgate & took old Abraham one of Glenn's black Waiters wth 3 finished portraits to show. They were admired. I was invited to call & see the Bishop on his return. The Lady's portrait was spoken of & that was all. Paint on Glenn. Call on Mr [Thomas] Williamson, Cashier of the [blank] Bank & requested to see a portrait by Stewart lately arrived here. He very politely showed me that & many other pictures. Stewarts is the portrait of [blank] Brookes a gallant young officer who distinguished himself last war & is bold almost to extravagance & very fine in effect—some dozen portraits by Thomson, a man who clear'd 3700 dolls in 5 months in this place some years back are vilely bad—a large picture by Crawley of three Children is horrid, the rest of Mr Williamsons collection is made up of indifferent Landscapes, and bad copies. He appears a frank liberal man. Paint on Dulany. Mr Williamson calls on me with Mr [blank] & engages a picture, promising to look out for a painting room for me. Captn Watson of the Navy calls on me & engages his portrait. Lt. Zanzenger [82] of the Navy calls on me & mentions some one who is coming to me. Receive a polite note from Fin with tickets for his night. Evening. Th: Merchant of Venice & High life &c. Fin came to my Quarters with me & we talked over Theatricals. He related his early biography. He is an interesting man thus far. Receive a kind letter from Sully. He has no business yet. Thinks he must travel soon. Trott is at Charlston S. C. & his prospects bad.

Sat^y 20th Novr Weather very pleas^t. Paint on Delany, Mr Glenn, and begin a picture of Graham the Manager. Even^g Th: Blue Beard.

[Nov.] 21st Mild & pleasant weather, almost summer warmth. Paint on Graham. Walk with Wrifford. Evening read in Kings. It appears that Ahab, Jehosophat & others the first among the Israelites & Jews consider'd the prophets as having power over good or evil, not merely

[82] John P. Zantzinger. *Register of Officers . . . in the service of the U. S. on the 30th of September, 1819.*

foreseeing but willing and bringing to pass. What must we at this time think of such a people. Teachers are appointed for them by Heaven, the word of God comes direct to them & enforced by miracles & prophecies, yet they act in opposition to warning, & entertain the notions above noted of God, prophets & prophecy. When the Bible says God did an evil thing, it is only to mean that he permitted it. Where is the difference. If I permit an ill knowing it to be so which I could prevent I am as guilty as if I did it. Ahab says "put thou on *thy* robes" The commentators say it is put on *my* robes. *Hazonoth rachatsu* may either mean "washed his armour, or the whores washed themselves &c. Besides these almost innumerable variations & contradiction in translating words & phrases, we are told that there are many evident mistakes in the MSS. owing to ig[no]rant or careless transcribers. Elisha & the *little children,* cursed & destroyed. We are told that the text may mean *young* man or servant or even *soldier:* and that probably these 42 young men, servants or soldiers had been killed bears whelps, and that the two she bears came out of the wood & destroyed them for having killed their cubs. Is not this too much?

Novr 22d Write to Dr Gillespie. I understand that Jarvis advertises at N. Y. to make likenesses of paper &c this looks like a push. Receive a letter from my Wife. All well last monday. Prepare to remove my painting room or rather to go to another room, to be still attended by Glen's servants. The privateer that went to watch the Guinea Man Slave dealer, has got aground near the Capes. Both vessels are nominally Spanish & both officer'd & man'd by Americans.

[Nov.] 23d Established myself in my new painting room. The Bishop & Morse have return'd from praying & feasting. Morse says it was all one continued New England Thanksgiving day. Began a picture of an old Lady Mrs Marsden for her Daughter Mrs Hopkins. Mr

Cox engages to sit tomorrow as does Mr Pennick. Paint on Delany. Lt. Shubrick talks of his Wifes picture. Many Visitors. Receive a letter from Alex^{r} Robertson.

Novr 24th Still mild & pleasant. I last night saw Mrs S. Wheatly formerly Williams, play Violante. She is a very fine Actress but has a spice of Mrs *Overdone*. Begin a letter to my Wife. Begin a portrait of Mr Coxe of the Navy & paint on others at my new apartment. Bishop More come to see me and gives me assurances of his services for Richmond.

[Nov.] 25th Finish letter to my Wife & Begin portrait of Captn Watson of the Navy & paint on the others. Mr Dennison and Captn [Ethan A.] Allen engage portraits. Mr Triplet of this place politely visited & invited me to his house. Warm as summer.

[Nov.] 26th Warm. Begin Mr Dennison's portrait and paint on Cox and Mrs Marsden. Watson suspends sittings until I am prepared to paint a larger size on Canvass. Evening write to Alex^{r} Robertson, and request pictures, frames &c to be sent to me.

[Nov.] 27th Finish the above. Summer still. Paint on Dennison, Dulany & Graham. Receive a letter from my wife dated 21st & 22d. All well. Osborne likely to recover $50 from Pemberton of New Orleans. B W Rogers has another son & his wife ill. Evening read in Kings "talmidey nebiyaa" sons of the prophets or Disciples. A good note by Dr Clarke on the power of parents over children & creditors over Debtors. He admits the Jews to be barbarous when he speaks of the Romans & Greeks, although for the Hebrews it must be considered (I suppose) as the law of God. In speaking of the Shunamites Child Clarke says "the doctrine of reprobate Children had not disgraced the religion of the God of endless compassion & the Miracles of Elisha are very much like the Miracles of the New Testament. The same words mean either "and it has been sought" or "it was borrowed." "Dove's dung" may be "peas" a little further on we are told that several words are *added* by careless copyists.

[Nov.] 28th Sunday. Practise on Miniature painting expecting to begin one tomorrow of a French Woman. Write to my son to send on Gilferts Picture & enclose order on J A Graham for 25 dolls. Rain. Read 2d of Kings. The Story of Jehu is beautifully told. This history reminds me of Bruce's Abyssynia. Dr. Clarke calls Jehu's conduct Brutal & him an "incomparably bad man" but the book makes God say "thou hast done that which is right in mine eyes" & "according to all that was in mine heart" & promises to reward him to the fourth generation. Reward or punishment in another state is never hinted at. It appears by the History of this brutal & barbarous people that the priests were the rulers and directors of revolutions in the name of the Lord & those Kings who rebelled against them were the men who made Israel to sin. It is plain that the Kings strove against the priests & to secure their own authority induced the brutish multitude to worship other Gods than the God of the Prophets & set up other priests in opposition to them, but the Old Stock of priests had the telling of the story & that must be a key to it.

Monday [Nov.] 29th Cold. Paint on Cox, Dennison, Glenn, & Mrs. Marsden. Walk. Read in Kings & St John. When Christ says "I and my Father are one" or "the Father" the Jews beleived doubtless that he made himself God, but in his answer does he not say as much as that he only meant to assert the sameness of intention when he alludes to the prophets or Judges being called Gods by the Law? Clarke endeavours to show that Christ meant to say that he was one with the Father, but it cannot be made out.

Novr 30th Tuesday. Mild. Began portrait of Captn Allen of the Artillery & paint on Mrs Marsden & Mr Dennison. Call on Crawley. Walk. Even^g read in Kings.

MRS. AARON OLMSTED (1757-1826)
(MARY LANGREIL BIGELOW)
(Courtesy of Miss Mary O. Marshall)

MRS. DE MOTTE OF LONG ISLAND
(Courtesy of The Rhode Island School of Design)

Wed^{y} Decr 1st. Mild. Paint on Dennison, Cox & begin a picture of Watson 36 by 30 for which I agree to take 60 dollars, stating my price as 75, as in N. Y. Wrifford attempts to give a lecture on teaching but no one comes to hear him but myself & two others. Captn Allen whose picture I begun is the son of Ethen Allen of famous memory, he is however a sot.

Thursday Decr 2d. Mild. Paint on Graham, Allen, Coxe, Watson & Dennison. Evening cold & threatens snow. Receive a letter from my Wife. All well at home. She says she has laid in her winter stores & will have 200 dolls to begin Decr with, this is independent of 20 sent & an order for 25 more. Read in Kings. Clarke says the simile of the Dish 21 Ch: 13 v: is likewise render'd, by wiping out that which is written on tablets. That word translated "Grove" means an Idol. Ch: 22d It appears by the text that the High Priest found "the book of law" & sent it to the King. And Shaphan the Scribe read it before the King & he rent his clothes &c. It appears that the law had been lost. The King for the first time heard it. (Could he read himself?) When he heard the judgement denounced against Israel & Judah for their Idolatries, he sent to a prophetess to know if all this was true! The history of these people makes them out the most ignorant stupid, foolish, vile race that can well be conceived of. Dr Clarke however interprets this finding the Book into finding some part of the law & says Josiah had this book with him from the beginning. Ch: 23. The King reads the new found Book to the people.

Tomorrow will be seven weeks since I left home & six since I arrived in Norfolk. I have enjoyed good health. I have had my mind wholesomely employed generally, and I believe more uniformly so than for a long time before I left home. I have drank no wine & no spirits in any shape except a very moderate portion with my dinner. I have been better in mind & body than when I took wine at my dinner. I think I have improved in my painting. I have more confidence in my power, more facility a better style generally. I have begun Eleven portraits amounting to $315. I have finished of these Seven. My Expences in travelling, Board, materials for painting &c &c is $155 leaving a balance, if all is paid for as I think they will be, of $160. For all this and much much more, I thank my Creator & incomprehensibly great & good Benefactor.

Dec[r] 3d Cold morning but clear & it moderates to mildness during the day. Paint on Allen, Coxe & Dennison. receive a letter from my Wife which has been a Month in Richmond. Morse is going to Williamsburg, he & Dennison sit with us the first of the Evening and promise me letters to the Naval people at Washington. Read in St. John. Resurrection of Lazarus. Martha Whatsoever thou asketh of God &c Here it is acknowledged by Clarke that Martha looked upon Christ as *man,* but he says Christ in his reply tells her he is the *Author of existence.* No such thing. "I am the resurrection & the life he that believeth in me though he were dead yet shall he live" Surely this is nothing more than an assurance that eternal life is the consequence of believing in him e.i. adopting his precepts & following his example. "He that believeth shall never die" that is perish eternally. And he asks "Believest thou this" She answers "I believe thou art the Christ the son of God, which should come into the world" e. i. thou art the prophet whose coming was foretold. He is satisfied with the answer, it was what he had taught this family. "Father I thank thee that thou hast heard me" &c &c if all this is not plainly teaching that tho' acting by direction of God & having immediate communion with him, yet that he pretended to nothing in himself, I cannot read. "Thou shalt see the glory of God" or the *miraculous power* of God. Yet after all this Dr Clarke says at the end of the Chapter "His (Christs) eternal power & Godhead are manifested in the resurrection of Lazarus." Surely he might have said the same of Elijah & Elisha, and made Gods of them.

Begin letter to my Wife.

Saturday Dec[r] 4th Mild & pleasant: Finish & send letter to my Wife. Paint on Allen & Watson. Wrifford embarks in the Marktime Capt[n] Post for Charleston, his passage 15 Dolls to be charged to me by Graham as part payment for his portrait. He otherwise could not have gone on. He is to remit the money to my Son in N. Y. Morse goes to Williamsburg. Evening read in the foolish egotistical Rousseau. Graham & Pennock sit with me a while, the first about departing for Charleston.

[Dec.] 5th Sunday. A morning like October. Capt[n] Allen having been order'd to Baltimore I finish his picture to day & paint on Denison & Watson. Even[g] read. Capt[n] Duncan [84] was yesterday introduced to me by Brimhal & engages his portrait. Write to Bishop Moore to prepare my way in Richmond.

[Dec.] 6th Monday. Mild. Paint on Cox & Watson. Even[g] Read in Rousseau & St John. Rousseau says his uncle Bernard plan'd the City of Charlestown, Carolina, and went thither to build it. Dr Clark quotes a remarkable passage from the Hindu & compares it to Christs saying "If any man serve me let him follow me &c him will my father honour" and compares it as similar, to *Chreesh*[*n*]*a's* saying beginning "If one whose ways were ever so evil &c" but the Hindu incarnate God calls on his follower to adore him—not so Christ. "Father glorify thy name" Some manuscripts read "Father glorify my name, others "glorify thy son. Any of these readings amount to a disavowal of equality with God. As to what is called the mystery of the death of Christ, it is not only incomprehensible to me at present but contradictory to all my notions of God. The miraculous interference of God is incomprehensible to me & his partial interference is contradictory to my ideas of his Justice or benevolence. That men should see such miracles as are spoken of and not believe the mission of the performer is con-

[84] William Robert Duncan, of the Corps of Artillery. Heitman, *Register of the U. S. Army.*

tradictory to reason, if they were convinced of the truth of the facts. To say that God "blinded their eyes & hardened their hearts" appears to me blasphemy against the all benevolent Creator. Does Christ any where say so? "Now is the Judgement of this world: now shall the prince of this world be cast out." The Devil & Death, are called severally the princes of this world. Does not the passage mean, "Now, through me, is the world justified: and by my triumph over death; his empire abolished?" And I, if I be lifted up from the earth, will draw all men unto me" if I go, as I shall, to Heaven, I will draw all men thither to me—this agrees with Clarke whose note on the passage is beautiful, both in the allusion to Joves golden Chain & the chain of Justice of the Hindu King. Christ's conclusion of his address at the end of Ch: 12th "For I have not spoken of myself &c is plain & is the key to what precedes. I am God's messenger, prophet, I speak not of myself. He refers all to God, he assumes nothing to himself.

Tomorrow will be two weeks since I came to my painting room in the Navy Hotel. In those two weeks I have begun Five portraits.

Decr 7th 1819. Tuesday. Warm, Gentle rain in the afternoon. Finish Graham's picture. Mr Reardon calls to see my pictures & immediately sits. This is my 12th port^t in Norfolk, the 6th in my present room. Even^g Read. Rousseau. St John. "Ye call me master & Lord. These titles were given by the Jews to their teachers, Doctors. A very remarkable quotation from the Institutes of Menu ending "Sacred knowledge and devotedness to God are the means by which a man can arrive at *beatitude*. This is the saying of a heathen.

To my astonishment Wrifford enters my rooms and says the schooner is still in the harbour, that they have been beating about in the most uncomfortable situation & he has determined to go to Richmond. Graham he says treated him very cavalierly & he has again got footing at Glenns.

Dec[r] 8th Wed[y] Paint on Reardon & Watson. Lyfford Keeper of the reading rooms says Graham told him that he had given Wrifford his passage. I told him the circumstances of my paying Wriffords passage to Graham agreeing to credit him 15 dolls on his acct. due to me for his portrait. Lyfford repeated the fact & the particulars—Graham representing Wrifford as an object of his charity. Evening, I have had a multitude of Visitors to day. Let me remember some of them. Capt[n] Allen & his father in law Mr [John] Johnson. Mr Lyfford, he wants a portrait & a miniature but fears his power to pay. My Landlord Glenn and his brother who keeps a boarding house. T. Glenn has received some Boxes & trunks from N. Y. The boxes, as the vessel sailed last Saturday may contain my pictures. They have only a chalk mark directed M: Glenn. Mr. Zantzenger & Mr Allman. Mr Williamson Cashier of y[e] Virginia bank & two Mr Taylor the old Gentleman lively & pleasant invites me to his house as does Williamson with assurances of endeavours to serve. Mr Thos. L. Graham who says he is purser's clerk at the Navy Yard and pays off all these fine fellows (looking round at Watson Cox &c) and wishing to his picture & to serve me engages a small portrait at 75 dolls. Several others whom I cannot designate. The weather being drizzly I see no Ladies. I settled today with Smith & Osborne for strainers & pannels. Straining frames 36 & 30 long & clothes cost me $2.25 ea; pannels (24.20) $1.45 ea: Read Rousseau & St John. 9 & 10th v. 14th Ch: is I presume the strong text of the Trinitarians "He that hath seen me hath seen the Father" "I am in the father & the Father in me" and yet it is plain from the whole that Christ speaks figuratively as having shown them God by showing them the will of God, of being in the father & having the father in him as being in the counsels of God acting by his inspiration for he says immediately after "I speak not of myself" & again "the word which ye hear is not mine but the father's which sent me. "I am in the father, & ye in me, & I in you. "For the Father is greater than I." Besides all which he says "I will pray the Father & he shall give you &c e i after he has returned to God who sent him he will pray to God, if he was God or wished to say so, would he not have said I will send"? Can we comprehend his praying to himself to do his own will? As far as I can yet see, the Unitarians are right.

Thursday Decr 9th Warm & springlike. Paint on Reardon and Watson. Several visitors, some Ladies. Lyfford agrees with me for a portrait & Miniature, to be paid for in Hams & other produce. Mr Maxwell [85] a second. time call'd on me & introduced the Rev^d [blank] & Mr [blank] Maxwell is a Lawyer of eminence here & he & his friend the Clergyman are both pupils of Dr Dwight. Mr Williamson who appears very friendly says old Mr Taylor will sit to me. I see a good deal of character in my sitters & visitors. Evening high cold wind. Read in St John. Christ says *all things* that I have heard of my Father I have made known unto you." He arrogates nothing to himself & all is from God. He is alone Gods messenger & so pure & full of love to mankind that he lays down his life for them. Why this was necessary I can not understand. Was it that by submitting to crucifixion in testimony of the truth of his precepts he would cause a more general belief & confidence in himself & his doctrine? That such might be the determination of a just man I can conceive & that a man would thereby become more deserving of the love of God & man. But as a scheme of redemption planned by *God* I cannot understand it.

Friday Decr 10th A Winters day cold & clear. Paint on Reardon & Watson & begin a portrait of Mr Lyfford. I have been in Norfolk, today, 7 Weeks, I have begun 13 portraits, finished 9. Evening Milder. Begin letter to my Wife. Wrifford departed this morning for Richmond. I dont know what to make of him. He has been very at-

[85] William Maxwell (1784-1857). See Dexter, *Yale Biographies, 1792-1805*, 5th ser., 520-22.

tentive to me, almost troublesome notwithstanding that any attentions are flatterring, but I began to think he had selfish motives for his attachment.

Saturday Dec[r] 11th Finish & send off letter to my Wife. Read presidents Message. Mr Osbourne frame maker calls to negociate for a portrait for a friend to be paid for in Frames, pannels &c. Paint on Reardon Watson & Lyfford. Receive letter from my Wife. On Sunday Nov[r] 28th Snow in N. Y. in y[e] Night which lay 2 days, here it rain'd gently & was mild & y[e] next day was cold & on tuesday mild. In N. Y. it was a winters day on Sunday y[e] 5th inst. here it was mild as October. My wife has got in her Winters wood & has 200$ in store. My son is doing successful & profitable business in partnership with [James A.] Hamilton. My daughter is well & happy. For these and the infinitely great blessings bestow'd on me & my fellow creatures, may the all benevolent God be thanked. Evening set down to read in St John. As far as I have yet seen, Christ teaches Unitarianism, in this Ch: 16th he speaks of what is called the 3d person in the Trinity, "the Comforter, or Spirit of Truth. Christ says "this spirit" "shall not speak of himself." Is not this an acknowledgement or assertion of this person being an inferior Agent of the Deity, this appears plain as it respects the third person in the Trinity, but here follows a passage respecting Christ himself which Clarke thinks decides as to his equality or identity with God. "All things that the Father hath are mine." But as such an assertion would contradict so many other plainer assertions, we must read this passage with latitude, it can only mean that the things of the Father are given to him and that *spirit of truth* which had emanated from the Father through Christ would after his ascension or death, be bestow'd immediately upon the Disciples, they then standing in the place of Christ between God & the world. In the remainder of the Chap: he speaks plainly of himself as one sent by God & returning to God. Mr Lyfford call'd & sat with [me] till 9 OClock.

Decr. 12th Sunday. A very fine winter morning. Walk. Paint on Watson. Afternoon. Walk. Evening read St. John.

[Dec.] 13th Springlike morning. Paint on Cox, Reardon & begin a portrait of Mr Corrigen. Afternoon Cloudy. Send two hams to my family. Write to my Wife. Evening read St. John & Ferdenand Count Fathom.

[Dec.] 14th Some rain last night. Warm cloudy morning. Send letter &c by Schooner Jane Maria Captn De Groot. Clears up mild. Receive 2 packages, a bundle of papers & letters & 2 Jugs of oil by the Tell-Tale from N. Y. Letters from my wife, daughter, Alex. Robertson, Jos: Osborn, S. M. Hopkins, Maj^{r} Vandeventer & D. Gillespie.

[Dec.] 15th Springlike morning. Painted as usual yesterday & to day on Corigen, Lyfford & Reardon. Preparing to remove to the East part of this old building. The beautiful Mrs Denison calls on me & the handsome Misses Brown, with some other pretty girls. Evening read N. Y. papers.

[Dec.] 16th Beautiful weather. I learn by my letters from N. Y. that Price has large executions out against him & has gone to England. Paint on Corrigen & Watson. Many Visitors, Mr Hyndes & his daughters, the youngest very handsome. Other Ladies, Mr Strong, Mr Hill Lottery Office Keeper agrees for his portrait to be paid in Tickets e.i. 3 Tickets, he to share in any prize of 500$ or upwards, one half. Open my packing cases. find Cupid, Susanna, Lady in blue & red, Lady & Looking Glass, Two Children grouped, Gilferts portrait, Frames, Cloths, Brushes, & some linen, and Gallery of British portraits. Receive letter from my son. Even^{g} read N. Y. papers & study portraits. I have great pleasure from reading a No. of The American. The affairs of Germany have arrived at an interesting Crisis.

Dec[r] 17th Friday. Cold & cloudy. This makes the 8th week I have been in Norfolk. Paint on Corrigen, begin Lyfford's Miniature, paint on Watson. Many visitors. Hang up my N. Y. pictures. Crawley brings [Joshua] Shaw the Miniature painter to see me, he is just from Baltimore, travelling to procure subscriptions to American views, engraved by [John] Hill, painted by Shaw with letter press descriptions which he says is to descriptive a *Sentimental* Journey & very funny. He is an ignorant, conceited English blockhead. Talks of being once consumptive & the Doctor told him he must change his *hair*. Evening. A fire in my neighbourhood & all the Town to looking at it. When discover'd it was a small affair in the roof, by the time an Engine came the roof was in flames, 2 other engines came & the house was burned to the ground.

Dec[r] 18th Sat[y] Removed to more convenient rooms under the same roof. Paint on Lyfford & Watson. Mr Brunette engages his portrait to be begun at 2 OClock Monday. Weather mild. Afternoon rain. Even[g] Write. Receive letter from Doughty with bill of lading & acct. of things sent from Phil[a] 12 Cloths $17 & colours, making in all 19.58. Begin letter to my wife. Read in The American. N. Y. Census near 120,000 in y[e] City, encrease in 3 years 19,700, decreas of slaves 300.

Dec[r] 19th Sunday. Paint on Lyffords Miniature & Watsons portrait. Weather pleasant. Walk. Even[g] Finish letter to my Wife. Read in American.

[Dec.] 20th Send off my letter by [Edward] Wyer whom I found in Boston in 1813 (Cooke's Yankee Gentleman whom Sam was order[ed] to show down stairs with candle lighted at both ends) he has since been Consul at Gottengberg or Hamburg. Paint on Corrygen, Lyfford & began Mr Low & Mr Hill. Williamson came with Low and went home to send me an Eagle left here by Thompson. he then came again & staid the sitting. I have head ach and tooth ach. Walk. Evening read.

Decr 21st Finish Denison & Reardon. A beautiful morning and my good feelings restored. Judge Parker introduced by Mr Allman, talks of 2 pictures. Paint on Mr Low. Receive a letter from Morse, who is teaching elocution at Williamsburg. No encouragement for me to come thither. Evening 7 or 8 Creek Warriors & Gen[1] [William] McIntosh sup with us, on their way to Washington. Go to an Amateur Concert at Crawley's, & wish the Indians were present, to see the movements of the fiddlers, especially the leader.

Wed^{y} 22d Decr Fine morning. Walk. Paint on Lyfford & Cox. McIntosh & his Indians to see me. They expressed surprize & pleasure. Invited to Dine at Captn Swifts on Christmas day. Receive letter from my wife enclosing order from J Osborne N Orleans for 50 Dolls on Minturn & Franklin, being debt recovered by threatening Pemberton: all well at home on the 16th. Many Visitors this Afternoon. The order sent on by my friend Osborne is Jos: Byrnes on Franklin & Minturn in my favour.

Thursday Decr 23d Write to my Wife & send back Osbornes Order endorsed. Paint on Hill. Finish Corrigen, Paint on Lyffords Miniature. Commodore [John] Cassin calls to see me introduced by Mr Henry. The Misses Whitehead call w^{h} Mr Zantzenger. One of these Ladies a Deaf & Dumb. The youngest very pretty. Mr Triplett call'd & introduced Mr Smith lately appointed paymaster to this district in place of Major [blank] who was killed since I came here by the overturning of a Stage in going to Washington. Mr T. gave a positive invitation to call on him this afternoon. I did so & found him & Smith with T's mother every thing very genteel, nay elegant. I took wine & after Tea. Mrs T the younger joined us, rather handsome. Evening call'd at Williamsons found Shaw & Crawley with him. He had taken Shaw to his country seat & S had made some sketches.

Friday Decr 24th The Country folks flock in with provisions for keeping Christmas & the Market Square &

Main Street resemble a Fair. I have been here 9 Weeks. The warmth of the weather is against laying up stores, or Norfolk might be provided with Turkeys for the rest of the Winter. Yesterday was a clear Spring day, last night it rain'd & it is wet & warm this morning. Paint on Mr Hill. Write to my friend Osborne & to Mr [Asher B.] Durand Engraver of N. Y. Mr Williamson calls to invite me to dine with him tomorrow. Mr Maxwell introduces Mr [blank] Southgate. There were in Market to day, Lyford says, 311 Carts. The produce is here bro^{t} in one horse Carts. I receive a letter from Richd Channing Moore Bishop of Va: He says his son will look for a room for me & my success will depend on the pictures I can show as my work. People are poor &c. The letter is very friendly. Evening read in American.

Decr 25th The order of the morning is Egg:nog, not for me. Walk. During last night violent rain & wind from ye North. Fine morning. Mr Williamson introduces General [Robert B.] Taylor to me. Dine at Gosport with Swift. Some Sea Captain & Officers of the Navy, some Ladies & the beautiful fading Mrs Denison. I walk to Gosport & back: take tea at my Hotel, go to my painting room, make up my fire, light my spermaceti candles & read. Swift is a genteel man, whose early life has been wasted in dissipation & he is of course ignorant, his father in law Coxe an intelligent old Sea captain, his brother in law Coxe, a good natured sailor. Mrs Swift a handsome clever woman, & an old maid sister a fat notable lady. These with two spoiled children form my friend Swifts family.

Sunday Decr 26th a very fine frosty morning & mild day. Begin a picture as a design for Mrs Denisons port^{t} Paint on Low & Coxe. Walk. Ev^{g} Read. Samuel.

Monday [Dec.] 27th Mild. Cloudy. I walk every morning before breakfast after attending to my fire at my painting room. Write to Doughty & send him 19.58 dollars for Cloths & Colours. Paint on Hill, Low & Lyford. Walk. Evening at Mr Maxwells.

Tuesday [Dec.] 28th Mild frosty morning. Paint on Lyford & Low. Maxwell calls & engages a small picture of his mother, Mrs Reed sister to Mrs Marsden. Walk as usual. Evening read.

Wed^{y} [Dec.] 29th Clear cold winter's day but I think the even^{g} promises milder weather tomorrow. Paint on Hill, begin Mrs Reed, paint on Low. Mrs Reed was accompanied by her daughter Mrs Holmes, a fine lively widow.

Thursday 30th Decr Last night a little snow fell which melted in the morning & it rains steadily. In the evening it clears up windy & cold. Receive a letter from my wife. All well ye 25th. On the twenty-fourth it rained & snowed & Christmas day was clear with the ground cover'd slightly with snow in N. Y. Paint on Lows portrait. Even^{g} read Count Fathom.[86]

Friday 31st Decr 1819. A Cold winter's day but clear. Crocker, capt^{n} of the Steam Boat Petersburg says there was a violent snow storm on the Bay. Paint on Low & Watson. Afternoon visited by Mr Wright Southgate who expressed his admiration of Low's portrait & almost engaged a portrait of Mrs Southgate who I am told is a beautiful Woman. Even^{g} finish Count Fathom & write to my Wife.

Saturday Jany 1st 1820. Finish & send off letter to my Wife. The morning is clear & cold. The creeks & inlets frozen, & fresh water hard & thick. Boys & young men Skating. Paint on Low. Afternoon Walk. Ev^{g} at Williamson's. Neilson there.

Sunday [Jan.] 2d Walk. Call on Neilson by appointment. Am engaged to copy a portrait of Miss Neilson by Sully.[87] Go to Church with Williamson. It is clear & cold

[86] Smollett's novel, *The Adventures of Ferdinand, Count Fathom* (1753).

[87] Thomas Sully painted a portrait of Miss Neilson in May, 1814, and after her death, made two copies from it, in May 1818. Biddle and Fielding, *The Life and Works of Thomas Sully.*

but some degrees warmer than yesterday. Mr Low preaches.

I saw yesterday a scene which reminded me of a Slave Market. Those slaves who had not been hired out by the year in private, stood in the publick street to be hired, while whites bargained for them. This morning I saw a black driving or leading a small Cart drawn by a miserable mule with a coffin composed of thin white boards nailed together, to bury, as I presume a poor slave in the potters field, which is about a mile from the populous part of y[e] Town & near Fort Barber. This afternoon walking over the common towards potters field, I saw a procession come from a large house near the Common. A hearse cover'd with a canopy of black drawn by one horse, preceeded by six black men well dressed, one of whom had a book in his hand, & followed by 25 or 30 black men & women. I attended their movements & proceed to the burying ground. The six who preceeded the hearse sung as they walk, a Hymn the lines of which were read line by line, in a loud sonorous voice, by the booksman: All was solemn. As I approached the ground I perceived another crowd & another hearse similarly adorned was just moving from it. I drew near & heard a preacher from the midst of this second congregation, likewise all black, vociferating in the manner of the Methodists in a monotonous tone at the top of a harsh discordant voice with great rapidity and no pauses but those required to catch breath. I listen'd in serious mood and heard what but for the occasion & the sobs & wailings of the females of the assembly would have been very ludicrous. "Wo! Wo Wo! Husband who have wives look here. Moders look here, broders & sisters look here. Your own times must come. To go to Heaven or to Hell, to the blessed Lamb or to eternal fires. it was only a few days ago, when I was going by this Lady's house, she was standing at the door. How do you do madam says I. How do you do uncle Bob says she. (The orator was an old grey woolled Negro whose face was distorted by his incessant bawling, for such it was & all in one note) O

Uncle Bob I am just going. Dont be afraid madam says I dont give over. O but I am give over. I have but just a little breat left. What can I do for you madam. Nobody cant do nothing for me, all I ax of you Uncle Bob is to preach my funeral Sarmon. &c &c &c. By this time the first procession had come up & they surrounded the Grave in silence. I walked away & passed up the road about half a mile on my return found the Baptists, for such the singers were, in full chorus. It was now almost dark & I passed down Church Street on my return home. I soon over took three blacks vociferously merry & perceived that the loudest was Uncle Bob who had a scanty scarf over his shoulders about the size of a large towel & another round his hat. I slacken'd my pace to learn the subject of their mirth & found it was Death and immortality. Uncle Bob with loud laughter assured his two companions that he was certain of immortal happiness in Heaven, and the three wth with peals of laughter continued to treat this subject in a way contrasting strongly with the earnestness of the preacher at the grave. Evening at Mr Maxwells.

Monday Jany 3d 1820. I moved my painting establishment to a house nearly opposite. Afternoon Walk. Evening read in Acts.

[Jan.] 4th The weather is uniformly cold & clear. Walk. Begin a portrait of Lieut. Kennon.[88] paint on Mrs Reed.

[Jan.] 5th Same weather. Walk. Paint on Lt. Kennon. One of the Zantzengers engages a portrait. Mr [blank] says he must have portrait for his daughter. Begin copy of Miss Neilsons portrait by Sully for Mr Neilson.

[Jan.] 6th Same weather. Paint on Kennon. Evening read in Acts.

[88] Beverly Kennon, commissioned Lieutenant, U. S. N., July 24, 1813, and stationed at Norfolk, Va., in 1819. *Register of Officers . . . in the service of the U. S. on the 30th of Sept., 1819.*

[Jan.] 7th Clear & mild. Receive a letter from my Wife 31st Dec[r] Cold & deep Snow. Williamson invites me to his Country house. Says he will build a painting room & a Dwelling house for me rent 250 dollars on Fenchurch Street. Paint on Kennon. Evening write to my Wife, on the subject of breaking up in N. Y.

[Jan.] 8th Mild. Finish letter & send it off. Finish Kennon's picture. Rain. The lower part of the house I now paint in, is occupied by a Black Barber & an Irish Dancing Master. Hearing this Ev[g] something that ressembled preaching below stairs, I went to the head of the stair & found that O'Sullivan was under the influence of the Spirit converting or confirming Tom Knight, to or in the holy Roman Catholic faith. Of course as in the case of Uncle Bob I only heard part of the Sermon. "They pretend that we worship Idols, pictures & Images, but its no such thing, we only look on the picture of our blessed Saviour, for example, and it puts us in mind of his sufferings for our sakes, that's all Tom." "Yes to be sure Sir" "And if we pray to him then is that praying to the picture?" "No to be sure Sir" "Why I could take a bit of a piece chalk & make a cross on the Wall & draw a man on it, & because it put me in mind of what I owe to my Redeemer, and I kneel'd down & said my prayers would it be to the Wall and the chalk?" "No to be sure" "We only hold to the customs taught and handed down from the Apostles to the popes in a straight line through the holy Catholic Church" "Yes Sir & dey all say we believe in the Holy Cholic Church." "Right Tom, & they would never seperated from the Catholic Religion but for two German Priests Luther and Calvin who set up a new religion because the Bishops would not trust them with the Church's money, & they were patronized by a petty German prince who was no better than a Deist." "Yes Sir" "And Henry the 8th of England, who was a Roman Catholic, wrote against Luther & Calvin and shew'd that they were Heretics & the pope in consequence gave him the title of Defender of the Faith which the

Kings of England bear to this day" "Yes Sir" "But he for the sake of woman quarel'd with the Holy See." "Yes Sir. Jack see that water dat boil over." "Then Tom there is Transubstantiation" "Yes Sir" "We believe that the bread & the wine is the real body and blood of Christ, but they say how can it be, dont we see it is bread & wine & not flesh & blood, but you know, Tom, when our Saviour turn'd water into wine, it was a miracle, & he commission'd his apostles to perform miracles & he gave the same power to their followers & this is a miracle." "Yes Sir" "And then for Extreme Unction—"Halloo Tom! will you shave me?" "Yes I suppose I must" Tom Knight went into his shop & O'Sullivan into his. I went to my Tea. On my return the preacher was fiddling and another set of hearers were & are still profitting by his labours.

Sunday 9th Jany 1820. After a rainy night a clear mild day. Work on Kennon & finish higher. Williamson calls & invites me to dine. Pays me 40 dolls on acct. of Low, leaving balance due to me 25 for picture & frame. Kennon pays me 50, due to me for frame 17. Williamson shows me a letter from Shaw, containing specimen of his intended Sentimental journey in prose & verse & concluding with a wish to borrow 50 or 100 dollars. Presumption and ignorance marked on it as on his conversation: paid Mr Glenn up Jany 7th 1820. Dine & take tea at Williamsons. Ev^g call at Maxwell's.

Monday [Jan.] 10th Hard rain. Finish Hills picture. Ev^g read in Acts.

[Jan.] 11th Cloudy & somewhat colder. Paint on Mr Low, & Mrs Reed. Night colder.

[Jan.] 12th Frosty morning. Paint on Mr Low, Mr Hill, Finish Mrs Reed, paint on Miss Neilson. Ev^g quite cold. Rec: a letter from A. B. Durand Engraver Declining to share in publishing D. D. Bishop Moore's picture, agrees to Engrave it, size of Bishop White for $500, half y^e^ sum paid at commencing. The size is 15 by 17 Inches, price to be asked 5 or 6 dollars. Cost of printing & paper 15 the hundred. Thus 500 would cost me 575 dollars & 125 dollars to deliver & collect e i 700—a subscription of 500 @ 6 is 3000, of 400 is 2400, of 300 is 1800, of 200 is 1200. Go into Williamson's & play back Gammon.

[Jan.] 13th A very cold morning but clear. Walk. Paint on Lyford & Cox and began a Mr Reardon brother to the one I had painted. A Mrs Roberts & Miss Taylor her niece call on me & talk of picture of the latter. After noon Crawley's calls. Williamson had mention'd that I thought of coming here to live & C is uneasy: Williamson, Neilson & somebody else come in. Take tea with Mrs Williamson. Even^g^ write to Robertson.

Jany 14th Mild. Cloudy. Rain mixed with Snow & Sleet. Paint on Reardon, Cox and Mrs Reed. Williamson calls & engages a groupe of three Children. Even^g^ Write.

[Jan.] 15th After a rainy Night a wet morning & cloudy. Paint on Reardon. T A Cooper calls on me, on his way to Charleston. Afternoon go w^h^ C. to Gosport to see Swift.

[Jan.] 16th Sunday. Beautiful springlike morning. Rainy &c in Afternoon & Evening. Begin a portrait of Cooper. Williamson invites me to Dinner. Go. in the Ev^g^ he suggests his own plans of grouping the Children's picture, and finally tells me he cant afford to give more than 70 or 80 dollars for the picture & concludes by saying that if I have other business I may defer beginning it until my return. I told him I should not go further with the business, changed the conversation, & so ends Mr Williamson & his patronage.

Monday morning Jany 17th After a night of rain & wind a clear morning positively warm, in ab^t^ ½ an hour wind changed to W. blew a tempest at first with violent rain, then clear & cold comparatively, not frosty, & so continues thro' the day. Paint on Cooper & Reardon. Cooper & Williamson with me in the afternoon. Gilfert, Nelson, Green &c arrive on their way to Charlestown S C. Call to see them & Cooper at Davis's. Even^g read.

Tuesday [Jan.] 18th Fine clear frosty weather. Paint on Kennon, Cooper & Reardon. The Actors &c depart. Even^g Walk & read. On Saturday ye 15th I received a bundle by water contain^g Stockings, Newspapers, a letter from Saml M. Hopkins on the Indian character & a letter from my Wife. I rec^d yesterday a letter from my Wife by Mail.

Wed^y [Jan.] 19th Fine morning. Receive a letter from my Wife. See by reading room book the 400 houses in Savannah are burnt. Paint on Cox, Hill & Reardon. Mr Cocke engages his picture. Mr Neverson a young Lawyer is introduced to me by Williamson & lends me "Fanny" a poem [89] by Drake of N. Y. (Croaker) & I read it with great pleasure. Even^g read American & Humphry Clinker.

Thursday 20th Jany 1820. A Mild & Spring like day. Paint on Reardon & Watson & begin Mr Cocke. Lt Bell of the Navy engages his portrait. Afternoon Mr Neilson engages his portrait. Even^g at Williamson & afterw^ds write to my Wife.

Friday [Jan.] 21st A most spring like day. Write to my Wife & sent a draft on Mechanics Bank for 150 dolls payable to my son. I have been in Norfolk 13 Weeks, from home 14. I am preparing to go to Lyn Haven bay wth Williamson.

Sunday 23d Jany 1820 at 12 OClock arrived at Norfolk in a violent Snow Storm. Our ride on friday was pleasant

[89] *Fanny* was written, not by Joseph Rodman Drake, but by the other author of the "Croaker" poems, Fitz-Greene Halleck. It was published anonymously in 1819, but Halleck's name appeared on the title page of the second edition, in 1821.

over this level country thro' woods, principally evergreens. Trees of pine & underwood of Myrtle, with occasional plantations until we arrived at Ferry-ville, Williamson's house & plantation, situated on an Inlet called a river & looking like a beautiful small lake. After dining with Mr & Mrs Low, we went shooting, the parson with us, but having no dog found no game but one snipe which I shot. A supper of very fine fat large Lynhaven Oysters with coffee & draughts closed the day. On Saturday every preparation for duck shooting having been made we proceeded notwithstanding light showers of rain, in a Boat with four oars down the river to the great Bay of Chesapeake. On tuesday last an East Indiaman had been wrecked on Cape Henry and as we approached the bay we found the black pepper floating past us on the water. We landed on a point and saw the line of black formed by the pepper corns on the beach as far as the eye could see & the inhabitants collecting it & conveying it off in carts or canoes. Our oarsmen began to collect pepper & Low & myself went to shoot ducks, only one having been killed on the way. We return'd to the beach unsuccessful & found that Williamson had gone down to the Cape by the beach & we followed, making a walk of 6 miles, to Cape Henry Lighthouse, all this distance was strewed with pepper & as we approached the fragments of the wreck were seen strewed on the sand. Labourers were collecting the pepper & conveying it to the Lighthouse for the owners: A number of small birds in flocks were eating the pepper. Wild Geese in great numbers were both in the bay & the Inlet, but they were not to be approached. A Hard rain drove us, wet, for shelter into the House by the Lighthouse, where we found W. Directly opposite the Light was the hull of the Ship. The rain ceasing we walked our Six miles back, having seen Cape Henry, the Sea, a wreck & the beach strewed with the spice of India. Some Coffee was among the pepper, but that article was yet principally in the wreck. We embarked again near sun set & arrived cold & hungry to enjoy the hospitalities & luxuries of the Mansion at

Ferryville. I have seen a person who was on board the wreck since our return, he says they were dismasted on Monday by the squall I have mentioned. Went on shore altho' they saw the light, not judging of the distance owing to haze. I first saw in my ride the long waving Moss streaming from the branches of the trees or forming festoons. Evening Write & read, the storm of snow continues.

Monday [Jan.] 24th Cold & clear & all is covered wth snow. Finish my letter to Robertson. Paint on Hill, Reardon & Watson. Even[g] read Humphrey Klinker.[90]

Tuesday 25th Jan[y] 1820. Clear and mild. Paint on Watson, Cocke & Miss Neilson. Doctor Kennon engages a portrait. Mr Cocke says he will have a portrait of his sister. Even[g] read Humphry Clinker.

Wed[y] [Jan. 26] Cold with thin clouds snow like. Paint on Cocke & Miss Neilson. Evening Hail. At Williamsons.

Thursday [Jan.] 27th Mild & Clear. Paint as yesterday. Evening at Maxwells.

Friday [Jan.] 28 Paint on Cocke, Mrs Read & Lyfords Min: Mild. Even[g] rain. Send Grahams picture to Cooper at Charleston. Write to Cooper & send him a draft on Graham.

Saturday [Jan.] 29th After hard warm rain all night, a misty morning. Mist all day. Receive a letter & bundle from my Wife date Jan[y] 15th at that time moderate weather in N. Y. with a great deal of Snow on the ground. Paint on Hill, Reardon & Watson. Maxwell & Southgate call, the latter now talks of his own portrait. Williamson and McCormick the Commissioner of Wrecks who we saw at Cape Henry call on me. Evening at Williamsons & reading Americans rec[d] to day.

[90] *The Expedition of Humphrey Clinker,* a novel by Tobias George Smollett, 1771.

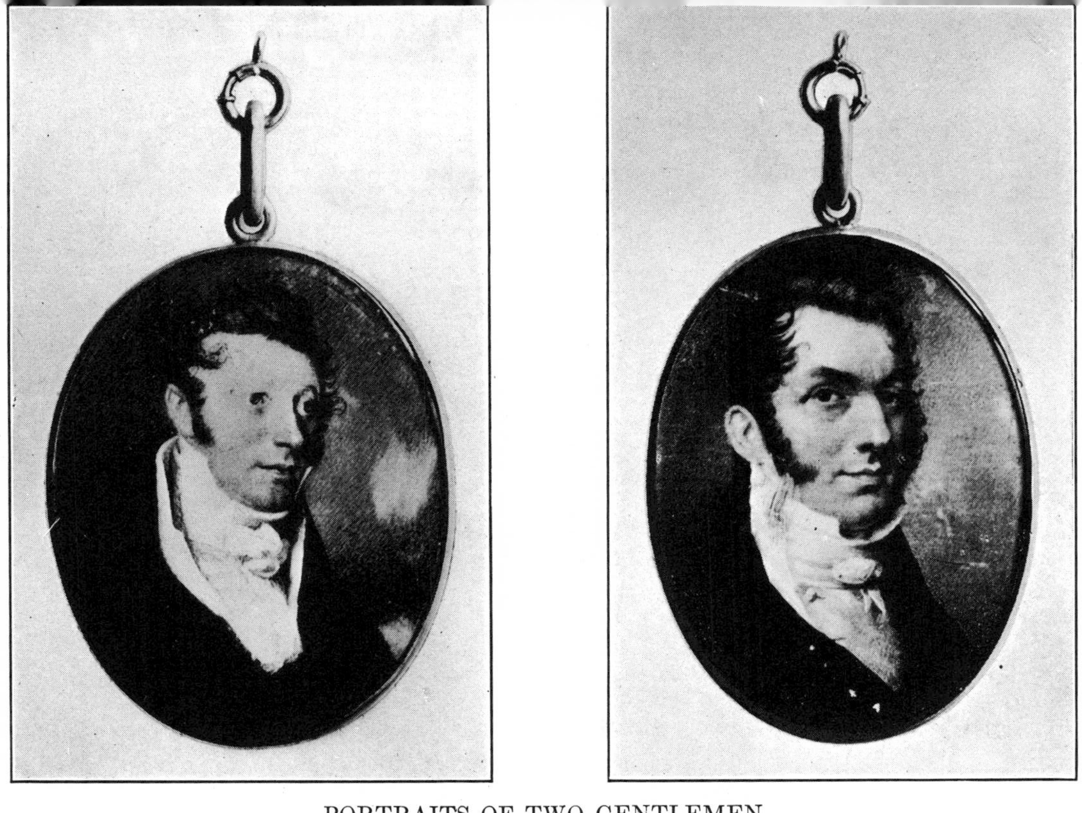

PORTRAITS OF TWO GENTLEMEN

BY WILLIAM DUNLAP

(Courtesy of Albert Rosenthal, Esq., of Philadelphia)

Sunday 30th Jany Rain in the night & this morning steady. No colder. Paint on Miniatures. Read. Even^{g} write to Cooper & send order on Graham for $31. Write to my Wife. Read. Still rainy.

Monday [Jan.] 31st Clear & mild. Receive a letter from my Wife date 21st. Paint on Miss Neilson, Mr Cocke, & Mr Hill. Even^{g} read Acts. It grows colder.

Tuesday Feby 1st. Very cold. Paint on Miss Neilson. Afternoon Walk 6 or 8 miles. Returning find a large party of gentlemen seeking me. Mr [blank] who had been introduced to me by the Bishop introduces Mr [blank] who is the intended successor of Low, & others, and engages his own picture to be begun the beginning of next week. Even^{g} read in Acts.

[Feb.] 2d Milder & pleasant. Paint on Miss Neilson. At my request the Misses Glenn sate anew, I wish to make two bolder & better pictures than the first. While they sat I had to refuse admittance to three companies of Ladies & gentlemen, as many as 14. In the afternoon 3 other companies visitted me & Mr [blank] engaged his picture to begin tomorrow.

Thursday 3d Feby 1820. Summer warmth but begins to blow between 9 & 10. Showers all day & night rain. Paint on Miss Neilson. Evening Messrs. Hill, Chapin & Dykes with me.

Friday [Feb.] 4th. Clear & mild. Meet Mr [blank] who renews the subject of his daughter's picture, if she does not come here, I to go to his house on [blank] River. Receive a letter from my Wife all well Sat^{y} last. Paint on Miss Neilson & two Misses Glenn. Mr Neilson is to sit on Sunday, Mr Hunter Tomorrow. Walk with Crawley. Even^{g} read.

[Feb.] 5th Mild & clear. Begin Mr Hunter's picture, at 8 OClock. Paint on Misses Glenn. My room throng'd with visitors. Afternoon by appointment call'd on Mr Farmer & went with him to see Mrs John Taylor & Miss Roberts her niece. See a head by Stewart & a number of pictures by Gessner a son of the poet. Engage to paint a portrait of Miss Roberts $75 size playing on the Harp. Ev^g at G. B. Hills.

Sunday [Feb.] 6th Dissapointed by Mr James Neilson who was to have sate. Mr Robertson calls in & engages a picture & sits. The weather is still clear & warm as spring, rather summer, for after sunset the inhabitants were sitting at their doors and windows as in July. Evening call at Williamsons & then read at my room. Mr Powhatan Robertson is a young lawyer and has the blood of Pocahontas in his veins. The family are among the rich of the Land.

Feby 7th Still warm but cloudy. Paint on Hunter & Robertson. Begin a portrait of James Neilson. Many Visitors. Afternoon clear & warm. Walk

Feby 8th Clear & mild. Paint on Hunter & Robertson & Neilson & begin another portrait of Cox.

[Feb.] 9th Clear & mild after a rainy night. This afternoon summer warm. Even^g windy. Paint on Robertson to finishing, & on Neilson and make a sketch of Miss Roberts at her Harp by going to Mr Taylors (her uncle) Even^g call at Maxwells. Write to my wife.

[Feb.] 10th A rainy day. Paint on Hunter Neilson & Miss Roberts. Receive a letter from my wife of the 4th & 5th inst. at that time cold & stormy in N. Y. Even^g read Tom Jones. Violent wind & rain.

[Feb.] 11th Friday Fine clear morning. Send off Powhatan Robertsons picture to Richm^d Paint on Coxe & Miss Roberts. Even^g at Williamsons.

[Feb.] 12th Saturday. Paint on Hunter & Miss Roberts. Afternoon walk. The weather is clear & perfect Spring. The red bird is singing & the Frogs are in full Chorus. By invitation take Tea & pass the evening at Mr Taylors, Miss Neverson & her brother & Mr Farmer present. Taylor is a strange original & Farmer another tho' perfectly opposite. Miss Neverson a fine woman & Miss Roberts both Musicians, with Mrs T's politeness & the oddity of her husband make an agreable evenings entertainment.

Sunday Feb[y] 13th 1820. Still spring. Walk. Paint on Miniatures, and draw. Last friday (y[e] 11th) I had been in Norfolk 16 weeks & I paid to day to that time. It appears that since I left home I have expended in

Travelling	50
Materials as Strainers, colours &c	76
Lottery tickets by agreem[t] taken for a picture	30
Frames	40
Sent home	175
personal expences & rent	233
	604

Thus my own expences in Norfolk (including rent of painting room) has been $14.57 per week, but I would not have agreed to pay so high for board, but that Mr Glenn has given me work to the am[t] of $125, part done, part engaged.

Afternoon & part of Ev[g] at Williamson renewing subject of Exh[n] paint[g] & House rooms. He engages for 300 rent & to take a part in pictures. Read Tom Jones.

Monday [Feb.] 14th Clear & warm as spring in the morning & the heat encreases to summer temperature. Paint on Hunter, Neilson & Miss Roberts, and draw for the latter at Taylors. Receive a letter from [Alexander]

Robertson by which I find the Salary of the Keeper of the A Academy is taken off and a disposition manifested to change the keeper owing to his absence. I will write to decline being a Candidate for the Office. Write accordingly to the Directors & my son.

[Feb.] 15th Tuesday. Perfect summer in warmth. The grass growing, birds singing & gardens making. Paint on Neilson & Miss Roberts. Among my Visitors to day Mr & Mrs Wright Southgate. Evening still Summer. Read. Three fifths of the slaves in the Slave States are added to the free persons represented. So that we have in Congress 20 representatives of Slaves. Virginia has 582,104 free persons & 392,518 slaves. Thus while it requires 35000 free persons to send a representative from N. Y. 25,559 free persons in Virginia do the same (or are equal). Of the Territory ceded to ye U. S. North W. of ye Ohio, it was determined in 1787 and ratified under the present Constitution That there should be neither slavery nor involuntary servitude within s^d Territory. Ohio, Indiana & Illinois, are the States formed on this compact. Kentucky formed out of Virginia was admitted without prohibiting Slavery, as the Inhabitants were considered as Virginians, & Vermont was admitted without this prohibition, because she had already herself prohibited. The western Territory of N. Carolina & Georgia was ceded to U. S. under the express condition that Slavery should not be prohibited, & as that territory was included in the original compact am^g the States which admitted existing Slavery, the new States of Tennessee, Alabama & Mississippi, are of course Slave States. But in all these transactions not only was the power of Congress to prohibit Slavery in the New States *not denied,* but positively admitted.

Wed^y [Feb.] 16th Still summer. Receive a letter from my Son. Writ to $Alex^r$ Robertson. Paint on Neilson & Miss Roberts. Mr Low tells me that the Therm: is at 75. I have had my flannels off for two days & still too warm. I sweat sitting at my work. They say it is very uncommon here. By a N. Y. paper I see that on the 10th the[y] had the severest snow storm known for years. At that time nothing here indicated Winter. Afternoon write to my son. Walk. Therm at 79. Evening read.

[Feb.] 17th Send letter to my son. Same warm weather with high wind. Call on Mr [James] McGibbon who had called on me some days past. He is apparently a worthy man but he is a very bad artist. He says he reside[d] 15 years in Boston & 9 in Baltimore. That there is not portrait painting enough done in Balt: to support one artist. That if he had heard of my being here he would not have come here. Finish Mr James Neilson. Rain & clears up very pleasant. Afternoon Walk.

[Feb.] 18th Clear & Springlike. Paint on Mr Hunter, Miss Neilson & Miss Roberts. Receive a letter from my Wife. Afternoon ride with Mrs Taylor & Miss Roberts to T's country house & make sketches of scenery for my picture of Miss R. Miss Wilson of N. Y. with us. Call at Mr Lamb's. These seats are on the E branch of Elizabeth River 3 Miles from Norfolk. The novelties resulting from the climate are the robin now pairing, the Holly tree with its evergreen leaves & red berries of a bitter sweet taste, & the "Fair maid of February a beautiful species of Iris.

[Feb.] 19th This day I am 54 years of age. Many reflexions might be suggested by that circumstance. The day is a cold spring day. I put on my flannels again. Paint on Miss Roberts. Afternoon walk. Even^{g} read Tom Jones.

Sunday Feby 20th Warm & showry. Paint Miniatures. Write to my Wife. Williamson calls on me & I go to Tea wth him.

Monday [Feb.] 21st Clear & cool. Send off letter to my Wife. Paint on Cox & Miss Roberts. Evening at Maxwells. James Dwight came here on his way to Richmond.

[Feb.] 22d Hoar frost. Clear & mild. Paint on Neilson & Miss Roberts. Many Visitors. Crocker engages for his & his Wifes & from 1 to 3 more portraits. Even^{g} read in American.

[Feb.] 23d Clear & mild. Paint on Miss Neilson & Miss Roberts. Afternoon walk. So warm that I discard my flannel shirt again. Even^{g} with Hill, Capron & Dykes.

[Feb.] 24th Summer heat. I yesterday first observed peach or Apricot trees in bloom & to day see more. Paint on Miss Neilson, Mr Neilson & Cox. Afternoon at Neilson's. Even^{g} read Buck tail Bards [91] &c

Friday [Feb.] 25th Last night a thunder storm & to day clear & very warm. Paint on Miss Neilson & Miss Roberts. Even^{g} read American & Tom Jones.

Sat^{y} [Feb.] 26th In my walk this morning I heard for the first time this year the melody of the Thrush. Green fields blooming trees & singing Birds now announce the spring & the temperature is summer. Paint on Hunter & Cox. Afternoon walk tho' the heat is oppressive. Read Don Juan (Byron's) lent by W Nivison Esqr on whom I call'd to day & was introduced to Messrs. Myers & Parker

Sunday [Feb.] 27th Rain in the night and showers this morning. Finish Don Juan. 2 cantoes. Strange, powerful, good & evil. Paint Miniature. weather cooler.

Monday [Feb.] 28th Cold & windy but not frost. Paint on Neilson and Miss Roberts. Yesterday as I took my afternoon walk, a little boy came from a genteel looking house & in the name of Mr Myers asked me in. I accepted the invitation. I had seen the gentleman at Nivi-

[91] "Bucktail bards" were poets who wrote in praise of the N. Y. Tammany Society. Kilroe, *Saint Tammany and the Origin of the Society of Tammany or Columbian Order in the City of New York* (N. Y. 1913), 148, 165.

son's office. I was now introduced by Mr Sam[l] Myers to his brother John & another gentleman & took some wine in pleasant conversation. In the even[g] I mentioned the circumstances to Williamson & found him very bitter against Myers, calling him Murderer. S. Myers is the man who shot Bowden for striking his (Myers') father. The elder Myers has been one of the first merchants here, but failed last summer. They are jews, well informed, genteel & uncommonly handsome in the younger part of the family. Evening write to my Wife.

Tuesday Feb[y] 29th Winter cold. Give to Lyford to send by the Alligator Capt[n] Hart a bundle & letter to go with 10 Hams to my wife. Write to my wife by Mail. Paint on Miss Roberts. Walk. Even[g] it has become milder. Write to my Wife. Read in Maxwells letters from Virginia.

Wed[y] March 1st Fine Spring morning. Finish & send off letter to my Wife. Paint on Miss Roberts. Ev[g] colder. Read Maxwells letters.

Thursday Mar: 2d High wind & winter cold: no ice, I presume only from the effect of the wind. The cold increases towards noon with violent Snow squalls. Paint on Miss Roberts' picture.

[March] 3d After a very cold & windy night a clear calm cold morning. Water freezes in my painting room at noon. Rec[d] yesterday a letter from my Wife: all well last Saturday: then mild in N. Y. but snow still in the streets. Paint a little on Miss Roberts. Ev[g] at Williamsons.

[March] 4th After a cold night a mild March day. Paint on Neilson & Miss Roberts. Many Visitors. Ev[g] read Tom Jones.

Sunday March 5th A mild moist day. Paint on Lyford & Miss Roberts. Even[g] r[d] Tom Jones.

6th March. Monday. A warm spring morning. I do not see in my walks the effects of the late frost. All looks fresh & blooming. Paint on Miss Roberts. Ev^{g} read Tom Jones.

Tuesday [March] 7th Cold rain. Paint on Miss Roberts. Even^{g} read in Scots Visit to Paris 1814.

[March] 8th Wet & foggy. Afternoon & evening hard rain. Paint on Miss Roberts. This sweet little girl comes generally attended by some young Lady of her acquaintance & seems as much pleased with the business of sitting as she could be by any amusement whatever. In the afternoon Williamson call'd and we talk'd over the business of my next Winters establishment. Even^{g} read "Visit to Paris.

[March] 9th After violent rain thro' the night, a fair morning. At noon rain again & continues. Paint on Miss Roberts.

[March] 10th Last night excessive rain & the morning wet. Clears up in the evening & the night frost. Paint on Miss Roberts.

[March] 11th Send off letter to my Wife. A cold morning & black frost. Passed last Evening at Mr Caprons. Painted a little on Miss Roberts. Even^{g} read Williams' France.

Sunday [March] 12th Another cold morning. Write to my wife in answer to one from her received yesterday.

[March] 13th Cold & cloudy. send letter to my wife by Jon: Butler. Write note to Mr Bowden to fix my engagem^{t} wth him. Paint on Miss Neilson & Miss Roberts. Read: Dict: of A & S [92] art: Statues, proportions of the Venus de Medicis, Length 10 faces and 2 thirds. From the bottom of the right ear to the clavicles 1 face. From the center of the left patella to the sole of the foot, 3 faces. breadth of the face from ear to ear 2 noses & 3/12—thick-

[92] G(eorge) Gregory, *Dictionary of Arts and Sciences,* first American edition, Philadelphia, 1815-17.

ness of the neck 2 noses. Shoulders 7 noses $\frac{9}{12}$—breast 5 noses $\frac{5}{12}$. a little above the naval 4 noses $\frac{9}{12}$: of the hips 6 noses $\frac{4}{12}$: of the thigh 3 noses $\frac{6}{12}$: of the knee 2 noses $\frac{1}{12}$: of the leg $2\frac{2}{12}$: of the ancle small of y^{e} leg $2\frac{3}{4}/_{12}$: of the bones of the ancle 1—$\frac{5}{12}$: of the foot at the roots of the toes 1—$\frac{9}{12}$: Length of the lower arm 4—$\frac{11}{12}$: of the upper arm 7 noses. Thickest part of the arm above the elbow 1 nose $\frac{11}{12}$: below 1—$\frac{8}{12}$: of the wrist 1 nose $\frac{1}{2}/_{12}$: From the center of the wrist to the middle finger 1—$\frac{10}{12}$: middle finger 1—$8\frac{1}{4}/_{12}$: breadth of the hand 1—$4\frac{1}{2}/_{12}$:

Mar: 14th Warm & cloudy. Paint on Mr Neilson.

Wed^{y} [March] 15th Paint on Miss Neilson & Miss Roberts. Receive a note from Mr John T Bowdoin & answer it giving my opinion on the subject of his childs picture & my prices. Even^{g} read "Hermit in London.

Thursday [March] 16th Fine spring weather. Paint on Miss Neilson. Afternoon go to Portsmouth. Ev^{g} read.

Friday [March] 17th Spring like but cool. Yesterday rec^{d} letter & newspapers from my Wife: A letter from Alex^{r} Robertson & a letter of Thanks from the Directors for faithful services &c as keeper of the Academy. Paint on Watson, Miss Neilson & Miss Roberts. Even^{g} read.

Saturday 18th March. I have been in Norfolk 21 weeks & one day. The weather to day is cold & damp. Clear evening. Paint on Mr Neilson & Miss Neilson. Read in American. Walk.

Sunday [March] 19th Fine clear morning & white frost. Out of town the water in the ditches frozen over. The day pleasant. Paint Miniature. Receive letter from my wife. Dine with Saml Meyers. Walk.

Monday [March] 20th Mild & cloudy. Write to my wife. Rain in afternoon & night. Paint on Cox & Miss Roberts.

[March] 21st Clear & mild. Becomes cloudy & evening rain. Paint on Miss Neilson. Even^{g} read N. Y. papers. It is now long since I have begun a picture & I look anxiously to the close of my stay here. I have many Visitors, much praise or flattery. I have been constantly employed & after all shall arrive in N. Y. perhaps as poor as I left it. I have supported myself & my family & perhaps open'd a source of employment and support (or more) for the future. I ought to be thankful. I am, altho' my spirits sink sometimes.

Wed^{y} [March] 22d Paint on Miss Neilson. Weather cool & damp. Receive letter from Sully who says he will be on here ye 31st & wishes me to find a room to Exhibit his "Washington at the Delaware." Busy myself in looking at public & private buildings. See Mr [John E.] Holt, Mayor, offer of the Court house.

Thursday 23d March. Paint on the Misses Glenn. Look for room for Sully. None high enough. Ev^{g} at Maxwells.

[March] 24th Find a room at Orphans Assylum that may do. Write to Sully. Springlike clear morning. Begin a picture of Mr Robt Taylor, father of General Taylor. Mr [Thomas L.] Callender, M: Judahs partner arrives from N. C. We hear of the Duel of Barron & Decatur. Walk to Portsmouth.

[March] 25th Sat^{y} Warm. Begin a picture of Mr Callender. Walk.

[March] 26th Sunday. Beautiful morning. Write to my Wife in answer to one of yesterday. Paint on Callender. See y^{m} culling Asparagus.

[March] 27th Write to Sully. Paint on Callender who departs. Paint on old Mr Taylor & Miss Roberts. Very Warm. Walk. Evening Thunder shower. Call on Williamson.

[March] 28th Very pleasant. Paint on Mr Taylor. See Asparagus in Market at 6 cents a bundle: but not like N. Y.

[March] 29th Wed[y] Cloudy, a little rain. Paint on Miss Roberts & Miss Glenn.

[March] 30th Thursday. Cold. Paint on Mr Taylor & Miss Glenn. Read Ivanhoe.

[March] 31st Friday. I have been in Norfolk 23 weeks. Sully's picture arrives without him. He writes me he is painting in Baltimore. Paint on Mr Taylor. Weather cool but pleasant. Begin a portrait of Math: Glenn: jr.

April 1st 1820. Saturday. Warm. Evening Thunder, hail & rain. Rain all night. Paint on Miss M: Glenn, & on Watson. Receive letter from my Wife of 26th March. Then warm in N. Y. as here.

Ap[l] 2d Sunday. Cold & wet. Write to my Wife. Storm increases. Paint Miniatures. Aft: r[d] Clarke's Matthew. Mathew the same as Levi. This Gospel (Godspel) written in Hebrew & translated into Greek. The translator unknown. The Christ or the Messiah is the anointed, whether King, priest or prophet. The Genealogy of Christ accord[g] to Matt. is thro' David to Joseph who found her with child before "they came together." Isaiah gave as a sign to Ahaz that his enemies sh[d] not prevail against him. "A virgin shall bear a son." This is s[d] to be a prophecy of the Christ, if it was a sign to Ahaz, it occurred in the time of Ahaz. John y[e] Baptist was 6 mo: older than Christ. There is a very remarkable passage from the Hindoo scriptures quoted here by Clarke on the performance of moral duties. In the Temptation, What is translated "If thou be *the* Son of God" should be "*a* son of God" Prophets were called the Sons of God, & even sometimes God. Evening read. The storm continues cold & violent.

Ap[l] 3d Monday. Cold, cloudy & a little Snow. Afternoon & Even[g] clear & cold. Paint on young Glenn.

Walk. Sully's picture is finer than I at first thought. The Horses are admirable. The whole composition grand. The distance sublime. Ev^{g} read. I find in Gregory's Dict: of Arts & Sci: a good Treatise on paint palette from Vandyke & Remb^{t}

1. Flake White, 2 Yellow Oker & its tints. 3 Light red & its tints. 4. Verm: & its tints. 5 Lake, Vermillion, & White. 6. Rose tint e i Lake, a little Indian red & White. 7 Blue tint e i Ultram. & White (it follows the yellows) 8 Lead tint e i Ivory black & white. 9. Green tint Pruss: blue, Yellow ockre & White. 10. Half shade tint e i Indian red and White. 11 Shade tint e i Lake, Indian red, black & white, this is Murrey colour (half tint). 12 Red shade e i Lake & Indian red. 13. Warm shade e i Lake & Brown Pink. This is for the first & second painting. Dark shade is Ivory black & a little Indian red.

Palette for Finishing for Flesh requires in addition, Carmine & its tints, Lake, Brown pink, Ivory Black, prussian blue. Meaning I presume to glaze with these pure.

To Dead Colour Flesh

Make out the whole with the shade tint (composed of Lake Indian red black & white) and the Light red tint in different degrees of lightness & then strengthen (after sweetening) the shadows by the Warm shade e i Lake & Brown pink. *Next* (still the first painting) improve the red & yellows, put in ye blues & so of the shadows.

Second Painting

Oil the work & wipe off (*Bad*) Scumble light red & yellow tints over the corresponding light parts, & glaze the shadows with the shadow tints, then touch lightly with the virgin tints the reds yellows & blues.

Third Painting

Correct the glazing, then touch upon the light parts.

April 4th Tuesday. Clear & cold. Last night a hard frost. Paint on Miss Glenn. Visit Sully's picture both yesterday & to day. Even^{g} clear & cold. Read Painting.

Drapery.[93]

General rule. Make out the first lay with three tints, light middle tint & shadow (ye same colour as the middle tint, with less of the light in it. Reflections warmer than the local colour.

93 Continuing the abstract of the article "Painting", in Gregory's *Dictionary of Arts and Sciences.*

For White Sattin

Four degrees of colour. 1. White. 2. White & a little Ivory black. 3 Middle tint, or pearl, e i White black & a little Indian red. (The second must appear always between the 1st & 3d) 4. The shadow tint which is the Middle tint with less white.

Second lay.

Is the reflections, which are made by brown ochre and white (or yellow ochre) and for dark reflections the middle tint and Brown ochre.

Blue Sattin

Paint it in with white & Black & white. First lay 3 tints of prussian blue & White. The middle tint of these 3 is azure. In finishing add or glaze Ivory black for the shades & brown oker for the reflexes.

Velvet

May be painted at once. Make out the first lay with the middle tint & shade tint on which lay the high light with light touch. Finish the shadows as of sattin.

To make a Blue Velvet by Glazing, first paint it black & White, then when dry glaze with pr Blue, or glaze the lights with Ultramarine & the rest wth p: B.

Scarlet & crimson Sattins and Velvets. A tint of yellow oker, light red & white is the ground of scarlet, and the Shadows Indian red, and Indian red & Black. Second painting Vermillion & white for Sattin & Velvet (*Vermillion alone for cloth*). The Middle tint is vermillion and a little lake or Indian red and add black in the darkest shadow. The difference between Scarlet & Crimson is that the high lights of Crimson are made whiter & the Middle tint is made darker. The reflects are light red & vermillion. When this is dry glaze with Lake & improve the shadows & reflects. The Scarlet requires one very thin glaze. The Crimson *two* stronger.

Pink Sattin

Lights, Carmine & White, middle tint Lake, carmine & white, Thin Lake & Indian red, reflects vermillion. (Deepest shadows V. Brown)

Yellow Sattin

Ground, Yellowish white shaded by yellow & brow[n] oker. Then paint the lights with Kings yellow, first tint yellow ochre & pearl tint, Middle tint is yellow, Brown ochre & pearl tint. Shade, Brown pink and Brown ochre. Finishing, The reflects yellow oker & sometimes yellow oker & light red & the shadows are strength[th]en'd with Brown pink & burnt umber.

Green Sattin

Ground, yellow ochre, a little white & pr: Blue. Brown pink & p: Blue for shadows. Paint with: 1. Kings yellow & a very little p: Blue. 2. add more blue. 3 Shadow, add more blue & brown pink. Darker, the Brown pink & blue. Querie, What is equivalent to Kings Yellow.

Black Sattin & Velvet

Ground. Light red & Indian red & black for the shadows. Finish[g] For y[e] lights Black white & a little Lake, middle tint less of y[e] white. Shade, lake, Brown pink & black.

Process. Glaze the shadows with the Shade tint & add Black for the deepest, then lay in the whole of the light with the middle tint & touch the high lights on it. The reflects are Burnt umbre or brown ochre.

Linen

The same colours as white sattin except for 2. take Ultramarine ashes instead of Ivory black. Dead colour with pure white broad for the lights & the pearl (black white & Indian red) for the shadow. Finish by glazing the lights with white with as little oil as can be, then lay in the middle tint & shade, touch then the extreme lights & last put in the blue tint. Let this dry & then put in the ref[l]exes and finish.

Black Grounds.

Tint 1. pearl. 2. Lead. 3 Yellow made of Brown ochre & white. 4 Olive, of yellow ochre, Pr: Blue & white 5. Indian red & white. 6. Murrey, which is pearl with more Indian red. 7. Stone of white, umber, black & Indian red. Dark shade of Black & Indian red. With these tints Harmoniously mingled most grounds for portraits may be made & if a curtain is introduced, lay it in if a colour approaching y[e] finishing colour & whe[n] you finish let it partake of the ground. Landscape in background should be likewise broke with the other colours & sky broke with the Lead (black & white) and Flesh (Indian red & white) tints. The Murrey tint is good for distant objects (Indian red, white & a little black) Umber and Dark warm shades in the near ground. (Terra de Cassel is the same thing as Vandyke brown In the foregoing directions it is not mentioned altho' it is the best & richest shadow & glazing colour known.

Raw umber & white is the best Drab for cloth. Claret colour, Vandyke Brown, Black & Lake. Lilac, Carmine, pr: blue & white.

April 5th Wed[y] Clear & mild. Hoar frost in the morning. Paint on Mr. Taylor & Matilda Glenn. Afternoon found a room full of Company viewing Sully's picture. Walk. Ev^{g} Read.

[April] 6th Thursday. Paint on Matthew Glenn, & on the Drapery of Miss Roberts.

[April] 7th Friday. Paint on Matthew & Eliza Glenn. Walk. Ev^{g} rain.

[April] 8th Sat^{y} Paint on Matthew Matilda & Eliza Glenn. Receive letter from my Wife. Even^{g} rain. T Brown is again Norfolk.

Sunday [April] *9th* Write remarks on Sully's picture for the Herald, & write to my Wife. Afternoon Walk. Ev^{g} at Crawley's. Shaw came in, just return'd from Savannah, Augusta &c and represents the South as a paradise of riches. He says he obtained more subscribers to his work in Savannah, and that after the fire than in any place in ye U. S. Trott he says got nothing to do in Charleston, Shields a great deal.

Monday [April] *10th* Pleasant but cool. Paint on Matthew & Eliza Glenn. Visit from Mr John Myers. Mr Low calls & says he will go to N. Y. next friday.

Tuesday [April] *11th* Cold rain. Paint on Matt: Glenn. Afternoon clear. Walk.

Wed^{y} [April 12] Clear Warm: Afternoon Summer heat. Paint on Mr. R. Taylor & Matt: Glenn.

Thursday 13 Ap^{l}: Clear and very pleasant: Paint on Mr Taylor & Matt Glenn and Miss Roberts. Afternoon walk. Even^{g} write to my Wife. Sully's picture yields here 116 dollars (Washington $64, Baltimore 240)

Friday April 14th 1820. I have been 25 weeks in Norfolk and 26 from home. Paint on Mr Taylor Master & Miss Glenn. Night rain.

Sat^y [April] 15th Paint on Mr Taylor, finish Matt: Glenn jun^r paint on Miss Glenn. Warm day. Night violent Thunder & Rain.

Sunday Ap^l 16th Cold & wet. Paint Miniature. Afternoon Walk. Ev^g read in Matthew with Clark.

Ap^l 17th. Cool. Finish Mr Lows picture, Mr Brimhalls picture & Mr Glenn's miniature.

[April] *18th.* Preparing to depart. Williamson says he will get old Mr Taylors picture sold for me at 75, frame 25, & I am to paint one of myself for him. Paint on Mr Robt. Taylor, the Misses Glenn & Miss Roberts. Walk. Call on Moran. Ev^g at Hills.

[April] *19th.* Summer. Paint on the Misses Glenn. Even^g read in Matthew & Clark.

[April] *20th* Summer. Paint as yesterday General Taylor a Visitor. Expressed himself pleased with his father's picture. Williamson a long while with me. Begin to pack up. Afternoon reading over the beginning of this volume. Every thing being then new, is noticed. Now, my journal is scant. I observe a query respecting Mr Low. He is the son of John Low, & directed me to his abode in N. Y. at his Uncles at the Union Bank. Morse is at Williamsburg teaching Elocution in the College. The Bishop is expected here tonight. My remark on the want of Book Stores &c shows how little a stranger can know, or does usually know of a Town. There are two pretty good Book Stores, a neglected Athenaeum & a subscription Circulating Library. Afternoon take a long walk partly in the woods. A very large Black snake gazed at me & then fled. A lizard of a size & kind different from any had seen, did the same. I presume it was 7 Inches long. The only new bird I have noticed is a beautiful Bluebird of plumage & note altogether different from the Common bird so called. The Dog wood & yellow Jessamine entwin[e] the woodland.

I consider the following persons as having engaged to

employ me on my return next Fall. Some are positive. I have given Williamson a subscription paper, & shall leave one with Lyford & another with Hill.

Mr Williamson	2
Mr Steed	1
Mr Nivison	2
Mrs John Taylor	1
Mr Francis B Lawrence	2
Mr Broughton	2
Mr Brimhall	2
Mr Garrison	1

Of the Tickets taken of G. B. Hill for his picture by previous agreement, Nos 4748 & 3180 have come out Blanks, 2279 is still in the wheel.

Friday Ap[l] 21st Extremely warm. Pay all my accounts. I have in Cash

Silver	4...
Northern Notes	10...
Virginia notes	85...
N. C.	69...
	168...
W's Check	60...
	228...

Due from Mrs Taylor	150	150 p[d]	
Wm Neilson	50	50 p[d]	428
Lt. Dulany	25		
Graham S. C.	25		
Callender N. Y.	25		
Lyford	20		
		295	
		523	
Mr R Taylor to be sold by Williamson picture & frame	100		

Friday Ap[l] 21st Continued. Call on Nivison & borrow, Quarrels of Authors." Meet Bradish [94] of N. Y. (Gibbs' brother in law) he is going to join the Columbus (I suppose as Chaplin). Call this morning on Bishop Moore who declines setting at present on acc[t] of business. Chat a pleasant hour with him. Ther: this afternoon 85.

Saturd[y] Ap[l] 22d Extreme heat yesterday & to day 85 to 87. Pack up. Change money &c. Read in Quarrels of Authors. Receive letter from my Wife of 16th, all well.

Sunday April 23d The early morning very pleasant. It is completely summer and the red Clover is in bloom. Read in Quarrels. Go to church & hear my friend Moore preach a weak Sermon with vile Orthoepy. Read again.

Monday April 24th 1820. Leave 2 packing cases, 2 Jugs, 1 belt & my Trunk to be sent on by Water, Mr Lyford taking charge of them. The morning is warm & clear, summer heat. Shake hands with Williamson & a few others. Good bye to Norfolk for the present. Commodore Bainbridge goes with us to Old Point Comfort & there on his Barge proceeds to the Columbus in Lynhaven bay. Mrs Bainbridge goes on to Baltimore. Renew acquaintance with them. He is going to Constantnople & perhaps into the Black sea. As we pass the constellation in Hampton Roads, Comm: Morris comes on board & I see the ceremony of manning the shrouds & tops & cheering. The Sailors in their White Jackets & trowsers clustering to the tops of the Mast was picturesque in the effect. The Wind springing up fresh from the North changes our temperature to almost cold & the boat passing near the center of the great Bay, every appearance is sea-like.

[94] Luther Bradish (1783-1863). See *The Eclectic Magazine,* LX, 112, Sept., 1863; *Dict. Amer. Biog.,* II, 567. He married in 1814, as his first wife, Helen Elizabeth Gibbs, daughter of George Gibbs, of Newport, R. I. She died in Boston, Mass., April 7, 1816, aged 29. (*N. Y. Gazette,* April 12, 1816). Dunlap was incorrect in the assumption that Bradish went as chaplain, although he sailed on the *Columbus.*

Tuesday [April] 25th A fine mild morning & at Sun rise, 16 miles S of Baltimore, near 200 miles from Norfolk already. We have several Methodist preachers on board going to *Conference.* I enquired of Comm: Morris respecting Young Fairley that I might report to his friends. The report is favourable & the Commadore expressed himself very much pleased with his conduct in every respect, as an officer & a gentleman. he mention'd [James H.] Clinton (DeWitts son) but said no more than he was well. Chamberlain likewise from N. Y. *Provost* he left well. A steam boat meets us & takes some of our passengers on to French Town. Land at ½ past 7. I go to [Rembrandt] Peales & thence to Sully's room, his palette at present No. 1 B. Sienna & White 2 Vermillion & White 3 as No 1 4 as No 2 5 No 3 & Cobalt 6 D[itt]o & Cobalt 7 Vermillion 8 D[itt]o & R Umber 9 R Umber & White 10 R Umber 11 Brown madder 12 Burnt T & Sienna 13 Asphaltum 14 Vandyke 15 Cobalt 16 Lake. No 16, 14, 13, 11, 6 used in the finishing.

I find Peale inferior to my preconceived notion of his merit & very much beneath Sully. [Jacob] Eickholtz makes the third port[r]ait painter at present in Baltimore & has the most business painting at $30. The City is very much improved since my visit of 1806. I stoped at the Fountain Inn where Bryden entertained me at that time in splendor—he has since died in poverty. In the afternoon found Sully painting Rembrant Peales portrait. At the Fountain Inn I found Jacob & Tho. Lewis. See Warren, Jefferson & Burke.

Wed[y] 26th April 1820 leave Baltimore in Steam boat. Messrs. Arch[d] Gracie & Stephen Van Ransaelaer in company. The weather is perfect summer. Gracie tells me that James A Hamilton has been deprived by y[e] Clintonians of his office of Master in Chancery.

The weather continues Summer & the passage to French Town 70 miles is pleasant. The ride from French T. to Newcastle we made in ab[t] 3 hours, arriving at the

Delaware & again embarking at ½ past 4. At 9 in y[e] even[g] arrive at Phil[a] & call on Mrs Sully.

Thursday 27th Ap[l] 1820. Judds Hotel. Cloudy morning. Walk. Meet Messrs Gracie & Van Ranssaeller. Pass the morning at West's picture & at the Academy. See no reason to alter my opinion respecting West & Alston as expressed last Fall.

Friday [April] 28th leave Phil[a] & arrive at home about 7 OClock in the Even[g] All well.

I have in my pocket	$366.	
Delaney owes me	25.	
Graham	25	p[d]
Lyford	20.	p[d]
I may expect from Williamson for Mr R Taylors picture	100	p[d]
I find at Home	150	
	686	
The Academy owes me	140	
Lott owes me		
I owe House rent	118.75	p[d]
Taylors bill	55	p[d]
Grocers	32.49	p[d]
Deposit 340		
Draw out 151.24		
May 5th 1820 $188.76		

[William Dunlap's expenses in Norfolk, 1819-1820]

Coach hire N. Y.	.75
To Bristol	5.25
Brandy, Bed at Trenton	.37½
Breakfast Steam boat on Del	.50
Shaving & ferriages	.37½
Steam boat from Bristol to Phil	.50
Porterage &c	.31½
Judds Tavern Phil 1 day	1.50
Porterage &c.	.37½
Steam boat to Bristol	.50
Breakfast	.50
Brandy &c. at Bristol	.12½
Steam boat & breakfast [Oct.] 19th	1.

Pencils & paints		5.50
Wests picture		.25
Coach hire to Boat [Oct.] 20th		.50
Steam boat, Dinner and Stage, to Frenchtown		3.75
Steam boat & supper to Balt:		3.50
Steam b[t] &c to Norfolk		15.25
Porterage, toll bridge		.37½
Norfolk, 4 Mahogany pannels		5.
	Oct[r] 25th [1819]	46.19
Nov. 1st	An Eazle	1.
10th	painting pannels	1.
10th	postage	.50
11th	Washing	2.
	Balsam of Fir	.25
	Bridge tolls	.25
Nov. 15th	paper	.37
	painting pannels	1.25
	Varnish	1.
		53.87
Nov[r] 20th	postage porterage, Wash[g]	2. ½
21	postage & advertizing	2.25
25	Vermillion &c	.50
27th	postage	.25
30th	Comb, Clothes brush, post[ge]	1.
		59.87½
Dec[r] 2d	postage, Washing &c	2.25
6	Wafers, & suger of lead	.37½
8th	Soap & Candles	1.
	Pannels & Strainers &c	17.59
11th	Postage	.25
	Board, painting room, Lodging, fire &c &c 7 weeks to 10th Dec[r] @ 12	84.
12th	Washing	1.
	Hams	5.
14th	postage	.25
15th	Cleaning	.50
16th	postage	.50
17th	Freight from Phil[a]	1.50
	Drayman	.12½
	Nails	.25
18th	Freight from N. Y.	6.41
	Woodward for pannels	6.
23d	postage & Tailors charge	.50

Decr	25th	Candles, Washs Servants	4.50
	27	postage Servt	1.25
	30th	postage	.25
	31st	Amt of Doughty's bill for Clothes & Colours	19.58
			212.96½

1819
[*sic* for 1820]

Jany	1st	Mr Osborne for 6 pannels & 2 stretching frames	7.50
	3d	Moving & 10 pannels	10.50
	7th	Washing & postage	1.25
			232.21½

1820

Jany	7th	Board to this date	54.
	12th	postage	.50
	14th	Frames (5)	40.
	15th	postage & porterage	.50
	19th	prussian Blue	1.
		Lottery Tickets	30.
	20th	Washing & servant	1.50
	21st	Sent home	150.
	2 [blot]	postage &c 50 boots 2.50	3.
Feby	[blot]	paper, postage &c	2.
	5th	a packing Case	1.50
	11th	Board &c	65.
	13th	Shoes, washing	4.
		omitted Jany	19.25
	14th	Servants & postage &c	1.
Mar:	6th	De Revere for frames	40.
		Washing, Servants &c	5.50
Mar:	20th	Tailors bill	4.50
	27th	Sent Home	50.
Apl	3d	2 Frames & prints	6.
		10 Hams for N. Y.	15.
	10th	Colours & Varnish	1.
	23d	Frames & Strainers	15.50
		Board in full	102.
		packing	2.
		Loss on money	1.80

Cash Dr	&		Cr
Brot fr: home	150	Novr 30	59.87½
from Morse	5	Sent home	20.
Mr Hopkins for Mrs Marsden	25	postage	.62½
		&c &c	1.62½

Mr Dennison	20	D°	.37½	
D[itt]o	19	Soap & Candles.	1.	
Mrs Hopkins	9	Osborne for pannels & stretchers	10.20	
Capt. Allen	39	Smith for Cloth & preparing &c	7.38½	
Mr Reardon	15	Board &c	84.25	
Mr Glenn	65	Sundries to Decr 31st as enter'd in former page	46.61½	
Mr Lifford	5			
Mr Corrygen	15			
Mr Reardon	15			
Mr Coregen	10			
D°	5			
	397	Jany 7th 1820	231.95	231.95
	232			
balance Jany 1st 1820.	$165	Board &c	54.	
Low	40	Sundries	19.25	
Kennon	50	[Jan.] 15 D[itt]o	41.	
D°	17	19th D°	31.	
Reardon	15	21st D°	151.50	
Hill	30	Feby 11th Board &c	65.	
Low	25	13th Sundries.	10.50	
Reardon	15	Mar: 6th D°	42.	
Cocke	39	27th D°	60.	
Cox	39	Ap^{l} 10th Hams	15.	
Robertson	20	Frames	6	
Brimhall	34			
Maxwell	17.50			
Poll- [blot] for Robertson	20			
Callender	25			
Lyford	15			
	566.50			
	495.25		[495.25]	727.20
Ballance	71.25			
rec^{d} from Watson	85.	Frames	11.	
Coxe	23.	D° &c &c	4.50	
Hunter	39.	Mr Glenn for board in full to Monday Ap^{l} 24th	42.	
Crawley	7.			
	225.25		57.50	
	57.50			
	167.75			

Mrs Taylor ..	150.
The Neilsons.	110.
	427.75
	63.55
	$364.20

Osborne for pack^{s} &c		2.
Loss on N. C. notes		1.80
Last day at Norfolk, Washing & Serv^{ts}		5.50
Books		2.50
Baltim. Peales &c		.75
Dinner		.25
Supper and bed .		1.
Porterage		.50
Ap^{l} 26th		
Steam boat from Baltimore to French Town.3.		
Breakf^{t} .... .50		
Stage to Newcastle ..1.50		5.
Steam Boat to Baltimore		15.
D^{o} Newcastle to Phila. Dinner &c.		3.
Bill at Phil^{a}....		4.
Stage &c. to N. Y.		7.25
Colours & Brushes		15.
		63.55

[Portraits painted by William Dunlap]

Norfolk

Miss Glenn	25 pd 25 order'd fr[ame]
Matilda Glenn	25 pd 25 d^{o}
Mr Brimhall	25 & order'd frame pd
Mr Delany	25
Mr Glenn	15 pd 15 order'd fr:
Mr Graham	30
Mrs Marsden	25 pd 34 order'd fr.
Mr Cox	30 & 9 pd order fr
Captn Watson	60 order'd fr: 25 pd
Mr Dennison	30 pd 30 order'd fr:

Captn Allen	30 pd 39 order'd fr
Mr Wrifford.	—
	315
Mr Reardon	30 pd 30
Mr Lyfford	30 pd 5 & 15
Mr Corrigen	30 pd 30
Mr Lyfford Min:	10
Mr Low	50 pd 40 & 10
Mr Hill	30 pd
Mrs Reed	15 pd & 2.50 for fr.
Sold Mr Low a frame	15 pd
Mr Kennon	50 pd A frame 17 pd
Mr Neilson	50 50 pd
Mr Glenn	20 pd
	—
T A Cooper	650
Mr Reardon	30 pd 15 & 15
<*Mr Williamson*>	<*150*> countermanded
Mr Cocke	30 pd 15 & 24 fram'd
Mr Hunter	30 order'd fr: & 9 pd
Miss Glenn	
Matilda	
	—
	750

Feby	5th	24 of them for pay	$750.	
	6th	Mr Robertson	30	pd 20 order fr pd
	7th	Mr James Neilson	50	pd
	8th	R Cox	20	pd 9 pd
	9th	Miss Roberts	150	pd
		P. R. frame & packing	10.25	pd

Mar: 24th Mr Robt Taylor (for Mr Williamson) who expects to sell it for me to some of the family for $75 (and did so)

25th	Mr Callender	50	pd 25
31st	Matt: Glenn	30	pd

DIARY OF WILLIAM DUNLAP

APRIL 27, 1820, AT PHILADELPHIA

AUGUST 9, 1820—OCTOBER 24, 1820.

MONTREAL, CANADA

NOVEMBER 14, 1820—JUNE 15, 1821

NOVEMBER 30, 1821—FEBRUARY 13, 1822

NORFOLK, VIRGINIA

(Manuscript volume lettered *Memoirs 26* owned by YALE UNIVERSITY LIBRARY)

MEMOIRS 26

Thursday Ap[l] 27 1820. My impressions on seeing West's Christ Healing &c is the same as in Oct[r] & the same or greater my admiration on seeing Alstons resuscitation of the Dead man.

I have passed my day in seeing these pictures (& others at the Academy) Stewarts Washington appears worse. Sully's Cooke still better. Sir Peter Lely & Netscher lovely. Sully is *now* colouring better.

1820

It is to me a melancholy reflection that the influence of the sordid or selfish feelings of mankind should be so much more frequently and ostentatiously displayed, than the effects of that natural, that unsophisticated love of the good and the kind, which lurks in despite of the world in every human breast. Surely it is better even in an interested view, to bestow our acclamations on the benefactors than on the destroyers of the Human race, on those who have enlightened or ameliorated the rugged path of Life than on those who have encreased its gloom or added to its asperities. Yet how quietly & unfeelingly do the herd of mankind receive the news of the good mans death who has laboured successfully to exalt our common nature, with what [illegible] those who not only have in common with their fellow men been benefitted by his labours but have received personally and immediately at his hands the gratuitously bestowed fruits of his labours.

These thoughts are forced upon my mind by the recent death of our illustrious countryman B West.[95]

It is the pride of Americans that he is an American, yet the American Academy of the Fine Arts, <*at the periodical*> not only does not convene its members to devise some token of public respect to his memory, but at the periodical return of their annual Exhibition proclaim a festival & turn their gallery into a place of revelry instead of a "House of mourning.

What a noble sacrifice to the art was this, for a fiery youth of 20 to resist the pomp pride & circumstance of War & abandon his struggling co-patriots in the hour of danger, to study painting in y[e]

[95] Benjamin West died in London, March 11, 1820.

Capital of ye Enemy. but he saw with the prophetic gaze of exalted genius the future glorious success of his present depressed countrymen & withdrew with a most heroic self immolation from a participation of their laurels that he might qualify himself for immortalizing their faces & their future victories on canvas. Born in Pennsylvania while it was a province of Britain, West by the force of genius removed himself to the old world when quite a youth, and immediately took a stand among the first Artists of Europe.

Mr Editor

In addressing a few lines to you on the subject of B West, I feel that it must be acceptable to the people of this great & growing Empire to peruse a tribute <*of gratitude*> to the memory of their illustrious countryman <*Benjamin West*>, and a few notices respecting him & some of his many pupils, recalled to my mind by the event of his death. In however homely guise I may express the feelings of my admiration & gratitude, my effort must be particularly pleasing to the members of the American Academy; who have done themselves so much honour on a former occassion by their exertions to procure the finest possible portrait of this patriarch of American painters, the gallant soldier & accomplished Artist, who relinquished the sword only that he might immortalize his brother Heroes by the efforts of his pencil, and who equally successful on the canvas and the field, is one of the most brilliant. To this Academy and its amiable president and gratefull of the pupils of West, I dedicate these desultory notices.

B. W. was born in Pennsylvania & notwithstanding this early removal from his native land; and his eminent success under the protecting patronage of his sovereign & the still more powerful influence of his own talents enthusiasm & industry, which place him among the luminaries of Europe, he always sighed for the simplicity of his native land, gloried in her prosperity & wished to be gathered to his fathers in her republican soil. Every American was as a brother to him, and his open doors & open heart ever received them as such, while to those who applied for his advice or instruction in the art over which he presided, freely received both, given with the kind full perfect wisdom of the sage & the simplicity of the child.

To the fame of his great success must be attributed that predilection which so many of our American youth have shewn for the art of painting, and to his benevolent liberality the astonishing efforts made by American genius in this sublime branch of the Fine Arts. That many of the aspirants failed is true & was inevitable, but a list of the names of those who participated in his bountiful instructions, which fell like the mercy and the dew of Heaven, upon the good and the bad, but like that mercy was "twice blessed" blessing "him that gave and him that took"—a simple list of names would prove to the astonishment of the reader, how great the influence of genius is when guided by benevolence.

My imperfect recollection gives me the names of—all Americans *—and every English Artist of [word omitted] for the last half century felt the influence of this Sun of the West. How delightful it must have been to this good old man to see his pupils prosper & to reflect that he never shut his heart or his mouth to the ingenuously ambitious youth. He had no secrets or mysteries, he told all he knew & added, "Work, night & day, draw from the Antique, paint from nature. Study the masters but copy nature." If there is any one of his pupils who imitated his paintings & not his conduct, who copied him as a painter and not as a man, who received his instructions in hopes to succeed him in fame & fortune by shutting up the treasure close for his own use alone—O how I pity him!

This venerable man, blessed by God with a sound constitution and a sound mind which told him and with wisdom to know <*the*> that temperance was the only guardian given by Heaven for the prolongation of health & life, saw several generations of men pass away while he still encreased in the vigour of intellect, and produced the surpassing works of his experienced genius. His last works Ch[rist] rejected & D[eath] on the pale Horse. Many of his older pupils & most of his contemporaries sunk before he terminated his delightful labours. His enemies (for even West had enemies) were silenced either by the grave or by <*the*> conviction. He has at length sunk in a good old age. He, as every good man & every man who exerts his talents for the benefit of man, rendered Earth more like Heaven, and I trust has his reward, tho' not snatched away in a Chariot of fire, his mantle during life covered many of his followers, and now rests in an especial manner upon his countryman Alston. Yes Alston—the accomplished Alston—if I had not seen the sublime picture of the Dead man & the bones of the prophet, I should have thought of Leslie & Sully as the Elijahs of our Elisha, but Alston is the man. Yet the mantle of Genius is ample, and Sully (the prince of American portrait painters) and the bold and excellent Leslie, may claim a share. Long may they continue to strive, *in Love,* for the greater share!

The three last named Artists all possess the irreproachable moral character, and the liberallity in diffusing their knowledge to others, which render'd their great master so amiable.

New York Augt 9th 1820. Wed^{y} afternoon 4 OClock leave home for Montreal in the Steam Boat Richmond. Secretary Thompson, Dr Bronson & others of my acquaintance on board. Again I miss the scenery of the Highlands by passing in the night.

* On the inside of the cover of this manuscript volume, *Memoirs 26,* Dunlap wrote the following list of artists: "Stewart, Wright, Trumbull, Mather Brown, Peale, Earle, Dunlap, Fulton, Malbone, Sergeant, R. Peale, Waldo, King, Sully, Leslie, Alston, Morse, Newton."

Aug[t] 10th From Hudson to Athens they have open'd a passage or canal, through the low Island which Interven'd. The Congress Steam boat leaves Whitehall every Wed[y] & Sat[y] at 2 P. M.—passage 9 dollars to St. Johns. I arrive at Albany at ½ 1 OClock, and took up my quarters at Fobes'.

[Aug[t]] 11th At 4 OClock proceed by the same rout as in 1816. They are rebuilding the part of Troy which was burnt. cross the river in a boat moved by 2 Horses on circular wheels. Lansinburg has grown. We find the Canal in progress and so on all the way. Schuyler's Village has Bourgoyne's Meadow. the Canal is cutting through it. Arrive at Whitehall about 9 OClock in the Evening.

[Aug.] 12th White Hall has grown—new houses, Stores & Inns built since 1816. a fine Lock commences the Canal Navigation of hewn Stone. Take my passage for St Johns. At Sandy Hill meet Mr Moore, son of Dr. Moore. here meet Birdsal, one of the Haerlaem height detachment. Moore joins us at W H & goes on. Embark at 2 P. M. The scenery at this place still pleases me. The Ships of War appear going to wreck. Have a view of Crown Point. The scenery of the Lake about sunset was beautiful.

[Aug.] 13th At sunrise I find myself between Cumberland head and Chazee, a poor village. The morn[g] Cool. We pass Rouse's point where the U. S. have expended $300,000 in fortifications & now find them within the Eng: line.

All is now new to me. We pass the Isle au Noix where the English are erecting military works to the amount [of] three millions according to estimate. Here are various Vessels of War half finished left as the peace [of] 1814 found them. We land about noon at St Johns, a neat village & taking Stage for La Prairie pass over an extensive plain the farm houses extending almost all the way, 18 Miles. This is the Seigneury of St John,

WILLIAM DUNLAP (1766-1839)
BY HIMSELF
(In the Theodore Salisbury Woolsey Collection)

the seigneur receives 4½ pr. cent <*of the products*> on all property transferred. It being Sunday we met the peasants returning from Church, families in Carts, men on horseback & some of both sexes on foot. All unmixed french peasants—it is compleatly a foreign country. The small horses & cattle, peculiar dress & physiognomy of the people, manner of building both the stone houses & log cabins, mode of cultivation, all is foreign. La Prairie is a large French Village of Stone houses with tin roofs & a church of the same materials. We are now in view the Falls of La Chine to the W & Montreal to the N. E. with a noble expanse of Water between. Batteaux & a Steam boat in waiting. cross in the Steam boat to Montreal in about 40 minutes—9 miles.

Montreal. Here the same style of building prevails, all is French at first view, but the English Soldiers and other persons of that nation, & Americans make a medley, all appearing to retain their own dress and manners. French is however the prevailing language. Visit the parade & walk over part of the town.

Monday Aug[t] 14th Walk. Write to my Wife by Mr Wilcox. Visit the Cathedral, an imposing effect—pictures all bad. Woman at Confession—here & there a devout individual. deliver letters to Thos. A. Turner (Alliston Turner & Co) president of the Bank of Canada. pleasantly received. deliver letter to Doctor Paine who introduces me to Mr Barrett, very pleasantly received. See the landing and military reception of Governor Lord Dalhousie, who with his lady & suite come to the Mansion house. Visit Cuninghams Book Store & Reading room, & see Bouchette's Map [96] & topographical history of Canada. Evening amused at an Auction room. retire at 9 but obliged to get up at Eleven owing to the noises of a Mason's Lodge over my head. at 1 OClock I get to bed for the night or morn[g]

[96] Joseph Bouchette. For a list of his maps, see Philéas Gagnon, *Essai de Bibliographie Canadienne* (Quebec, 1895), 659-660; Henry J. Morgan, *Bibliotheca Canadensis* (Quebec, 1867), 41-43.

Tuesday [Aug.] 15th At 6 OClock begin a walk to Finlay's at lower *Lachine* but taking the turnpike go to the Village of upper Lachine. on rising from the Flatts I have a fine view of the level on my left & the rising ground & mountains on my right. meet many men women & boys of the Cochnewagha's coming to town, most wear a black mantle, some blanketts, little differing in appearance from the tribes in ye State of N. Y. Opposite Lachine is their Village. I reach Lachine at 9 and breakfast at a Scotch Inn. I find most of the Inhabitants of Lachine, Scotch, Irish or English. there are two small French Villages between Montreal & Lachine. To reach Finlay's I turn back down the bank of the river abt 2 Miles, King's Stores, barracks &c form a little village called Lower Lachine. here I was most cordially received & agreed to stay to dinner, but threatening rain started me at ½ past 1. On the road along the water which commands a fine view of the Rapids, a Canadian peast overtook me with his trotting little horse in a small cart & politely invited me to mount. I did so, and standing up in this rough jolting machine, with a rope to hold myself up, I rode into town abt 6 miles, in a pelting rain. after changing my clothes receive a friendly call from Docr Paine,[97] who had call'd on me last night. He advises to commence painting at Montreal. so does Finlay. F. has 8 fine children & is fixed in a good office as Commissary with a good farm & handsome house. I had occasion to exercise my french to day & universally found the french inhabitants polite & friendly, if two peasants pass each other in their carts, they bow & lift their hats. as we rode past a cross, my friend notwithstanding the pelting storm reverentially lifted his hat. The crosses are very frequent, some carved with a cock & one at Lachine was ornamented with a cock at top, a little lower a scroll with INRI. The cross piece of the figure was surmounted with spikes, pincers, hammers, &c & below were other devices.

[97] Martyn Paine (1794-1877) removed to New York City in 1822, and became a leading physician there. Kelly and Burrage, *American Medical Biographies* (Baltimore, 1920).

No 439 Greenwich St N. Y. John Halsted gives information respecting Dr See's plaister for Rupture.

[Aug.] 16th A Rainy day. See Paine & make unsuccessfull efforts to obtain a room to paint in.

17th Augt There is a gloominess about this place which is very appalling. The narrow streets of grey stone houses with iron doors & windows shutters are forbidding in the extreme. The wet prevents me from <*seeing*> visiting the subburbs toward the mountain & the mountain & my walks are confined to the narrow side pavements, the bells of the Roman churches are almost incessantly ringing & are particularly annoying in the morning.

Augt 18th Friday. Walk through the subburbs and upon the rising ground under the brow of the hill. The[re] are several large houses along this slope with fine gardens & meadows & orchards, commanding a view of the town & river. I am introduced to several of the gentlemen of the place. Finlay sends an apology for not waiting on me. As Commissary at Lachine, from whence all the stores & men appertaining to the government are embarked or landed on account of the rapids, he is now sending on emigrants to upper Canada. These are Scotch peasants, $Govern^{t}$ <*allows*> lends £10 to every individual of a family, transports them to the place of settlement after landing in Canada, gives them land [blank] acres p^{r} h^{d} & working tools. Notwithstanding all this I saw a sloop load of them going to Whitehall. I presume such as had some property & sought independance as well as land. Engage a painting room & board at the Mansion House, a splendid Hotel, but cannot take possession until Monday 21st.

Augt 19th Saturday. Having now had some cloths strained, I am to day to prepare my colours at Doctor Payne's, who appears a sensible amiable man & interests himself in my affairs. Walk on the bank of the river.

Montreal from the water, when near, makes a poor appearance. The front Street has a dirty ditch of a brook running through it with bridges over it. the next Street is St Pauls (all are Saints) & it is the principal Street of business, winding in a crooked line with the river, narrow & gloomy. the next, called the upper town, is Notre Dame, it is more airy, better built, & has the Court house, Jail, and 2 Churches in it. small streets cross between these & beyond them are the suberbs, containing more inhabitants than the Town. Evening remove to the Manion house. Meet there Mr Dan: McCormick. Finlay called on me to day & introduced some gentlemen:

Sunday Aug[t] 20th Walk with Dr Paine round the Mountain by the north & over a part of it; my friend botanizing & I enjoying the new & beautifull scenery. The whole Island of Montreal is a plain except this hill & it is all capable of the highest cultivation—a great part is so, and farms, orchards, villages & spires appear in every direction. We took Shrub & water & Cakes & bread, at a Canadian (e.i. a french) small public house, & were served by a neat polite & pretty Landlady. About 4, on our return we called on Mr Barrett, the Doctor wishing to leave his Specimens, and Mr & Mrs B: detained us to dinner. Mr Cunningham, bookseller & Librarian, present: after a pleasant afternoon return to the Mansion House to tea. Find my former travelling Companions, Moore, Grey &c returned from Quebec.

Monday [Aug.] 21st The above gentlemen & Mr McCormick depart. Not being yet put in possession of my painting room I go to the mountain & Sketch. Returning meet numbers of Scotch Highland Emigrants on the road to Lachine from whence Finlay, as Commissary forwards them to Upper Canada. The hard favoured dirty scotch women and children looked wo: begone on the jolting Canadian one-horse Carts, the men were generally on foot. Write to my Wife.

Tuesday Augt 22^{d} The weather remarkably fine. Walk through the Market & buy 10 Canada plumbs for a copper. This fruit is not known in ye City of N. Y. prepare to paint. Mr S. Barrett whose portrait I was to have begun not coming I begun a picture of George 4th from the engraving of [Thomas] Phillips's picture of him. Make an acquaintance with an intelligent Scotch gentleman, Mr Wm Thomson, who is well acquainted with pictures & painters.

Wed^{y} [Aug.] 23^{d} Col^{l} Bouchet, Surveyor General of the Canada's, introduces himself to me & invites me urgently to Quebec. He says he will take the King's picture. He has published magnificent maps &c of Canada by which he says he has sunk £1700. He is the Nephew & successor to Major [Samuel] Holland, whom I remember in 1774-5 at Amboy & whose son Jack, my playmate, was too wild to succeed his father, but is now established at Prince Edwards Island. Mr Cunningham invites me to the freedom of his Library & reading rooms. Begin Mr Barrett's portrait.

Thursday 24th Augt Write to my Wife by Mr G. Howland. I have several visitors both to day & yesterday. Paint on ye King & Mr Barrett. Go with Mr Biggelow at his request (& the lady's) to see Miss Smith, a young woman of merit, who has taken charge of a large school of females, is patronized by the Canadians & priests & has turn'd Roman Catholic. She wished to see me & show her attempts at painting which are clever copies of poor pictures. A Mrs De L'auberney & her daughter were present at the meeting, they are of the first & richest of the French Canadian Citizens and are vulgar gentlefolks. am to visit them & see pictures. Mr Thomson leaves a journal in manuscript of a journey to France & Holland in 1818 with sketches, very neat & good, & observations on pictures—all doing him much honour.

Friday Augt 25th At Cunninghams reading room before breakfast. Paint as usual until ½ past 4. we dine at 5 or ½ past every day. Walk with Thomson, who has the Scotch prejudices in perfection & places unhesitatingly all other people & particularly English far below Scotchmen, and that in serious conversation.

Trimbee, an englishman at our house who has come from N. Y. says "at Montreal he begins to find civilization."

Saturday 26th At Read^{g} Room. Paint all day. Heavy rains. The sketch opposite is from the back of the Mansion House Hotel, which overlooks the St Laurence. Grants, or St Helens Island a little down the river.

Mr Thomson communicates a memorandum of the cost of the Elgin casts, which I copy

Large Trunk Unknown	£ 4. 4.–
2 Small Trunks, Bas relief, Temple of Victory	–. 5.–
2 Arms d^{o} from Frieze	–. 5.–
3 Horses heads from D^{o}	–. 7.6
Part of large trunks supposed to be Jupiter	3. 3.–
Fragment of head	–. 5.–
Female arm from one of the large groupes	10.–
Bas relief of male Trunk from frieze	–. 7.–
Arm of Metops	–. 3.–
3 small fragments	–. 3.–
Bas relief	–. 5.–
4 Bas reliefs of Frieze @ £2.10	10. –.–
High relief figure fighting wth Centaur	7. 7.–
Large female arm	–.10.–
Mask of Bach[hus]	–. 5.–
4 fragments from high relief Metops	1.10.–
Large female arm	–.10.–
3 Large Bas relief friezes of Horsemen	12.12.–
Young Theseus from high relief	2.12.6
Leg of Metops	–. 7.–
Bas relief of Frieze	1.10.–
High relief of Centaur	7. 7.–
Fragment of Metops	–. 7.–
Bas relief of Horses head	–. 7.–
2 Small Bas reliefs from Temple of Victory	1. 4.–
Large arm, supposed to be Neptune	–.12.–
Large figure of Neptune	10.10.–
Dead figure from high relief	2.12.6
Large piece of Breasts from Female groupe	2. 2.–

Theseus 10.10.–
Horses head large.................................. 3. 3.–

£85.15.6
Packing Cases for the above cost.................. 30. –.–
Say 382 dollars for casts
189 for packing cases
———
571

Sunday Augt 27th 1820. Walk along the bank of the river past the shipping & steam boats &c. All is rude & dirty. Four or five Ships & Brigs & ten smaller vessels would be the utmost amount of the apparent navigation of Montreal, exclusive of Steam boats. The parade of a few companies of the 37th seems to be the only public amusement of Montreal. Go to the English Church, a neat handsome building with an excellent organ well play'd—a thin audience to a pretty good preacher. It is long since [I last heard] his Majesty George &c prayed for. Surely there are parts of the service which ought to be expunged, & 5th repetition of the Lord's prayer might be omitted if not two more. Walk—sketch on the next leaf [of a grove of birches]. The steeple is the French church by the Mansion house, to the left the reservoir on Citadel Hill, to the right the Flag Staff on the Champs de Mars, next to it the prison & next the Court house,—distance Chamble mount^{n}.

Monday Augt 28th Walk & begin a sketch of Montreal on the side of the river, paint as before. receive a letter from my Wife.

Tuesday. Employed as yesterday. Mr & Mrs Barrett call'd in the Evening & I went home w^{h} them to tea. The Earl of Dalhousie has return'd from Upper Canada & is at the Mansion house Hotel.

Wed^{y} Augt 30th Work as yesterday. Doctor Paine tells me that Mr Hedge has determined to have his fathers picture painted. Thomson speaks in raptures of Paul

Potter's picture of the Young Bull—it is exquisitely finish'd & natural.

Thursday Augt 31st Write & send letter to my Wife. My portrait of Mr Barrett strikes with admiration. Mr Proctor, an Englishman long resident in America, expressed unqualified admiration & my friend Paine is almost in raptures. I yesterday addressed the following short letter to the Governor.

"His Excellency
Lieu^t^ General The Earl of Dalhousie K.C.B. &c &c &c
An American Artist, encouraged by the accidental circumstance of having his Painting Room under the same roof with your Lordship, solicits your attention to a few specimens of his art, at any moment when your Lordship may have leisure.
W Dunlap
No 16 Mansion house Hotel."

I have this morning received a verbal answer from his Excellency by Lord Kerr, that he had received my letter, and would visit my room, between 4 & 5 this afternoon.

Visited accordingly by his Excellency & Lord Kerr one of his Aids. Lord Dalhousie, is a plain gentlemanly soldier. he spoke of himself as a stranger in this country as well as myself, and after some pleasant chat said he should be glad to see me at Quebec & I must call upon him. I assured him I would, but, he added "I shall not be there until the end of the month." He did not think my prospects very flattering in Canada. speaking of the King, he said he was enormously fat, very much changed, one of the biggest men &c" upon the whole I have reason to be pleased with the Earl's visit tho' I do not see that any advantage will accrue to me from it. Mr McCormick returns here to day & with him Mr Le Roy & Son & daughter & Son's wife. My new acquaintance Thomson is a fine specimen of the Scotch character. He is of the "Commissariat" in which he tells me is now included the pay Department within 5 years, and the Commissaries act as such and as paymasters, having charge of the Milatary Chests. He is a determined Batchelor & has formed a plan of life altogether centered in, if not confined to self. He intends remaining in service until he attains a rank, the half pay of which is sufficient for his wants and then he is to retire on half pay. He is sober, regular, methodical, calculating, has an instinctive bowing awe for all in power, a civil ingratiating manner for gentlemen & ladies, though by no means that easy behaviour which thorough education or feeling produces, but for the poor & dependant he is rough, coarse, indelicate in manner & word & does not even disguise his thorough contempt & real unfeeling selfishness. This is harsh drawing, not from any unfriendly feeling on my part. he is towards me assiduously polite in *his* way & strives to impress me with a good opinion of himself. Why? I cannot answer, unless it be that [he] really respects, or is pleased with certain propensities & attainments in me, which he has or wishes for himself. He has some knowledge of music & painting, had read a little & cultivates a taste for the liberal arts. I borrow of him [Henry] McKenzies "Man of feeling" (for he has a small collection of books) & now sit down w^{h} a candle to read.

Friday Septr 1st The Govr departs amidst Drums Trumpets & peals of Cannon. Mr Moffatt engages me to copy a picture 31 by 25. Mr Colt visits me & is introduced by Dr Paine. Mr Cunningham calls & advises me to begin a second picture of the King. I do so. Even^{g} a pleasant game at Whist with Messrs Proctor, Bowyer (a young Frenchman) & Bulow of South Carolina. Watches are sent from Geneva to U. S. & sold at 2 & ½ dollars and yield 5 per cent profit.

Sat^{y} 2^{d} Septr Cool morning. walk & sketch. Visited by McCormick & the Le Roy's male & female. Mr McGilvery visited & was introduced to me. He says he has some good portraits & I have accepted his invitation to breakfast on monday. Go with Dr Paine & a large party to the Hospital of the Black Nuns. There is a very clever little picture in the Apothecary's Hall, of the persons of the Trinity crowning the Virgin. The pictures in the Chaple are abominable. They shew there a curious specimen of Goblin Tapestry from a picture of y[e] Nativity. They have about 40 patients attended by these religious females. Two young Ladies who had not yet taken the black veil, were handsome, one of them of a most beautiful complexion. Work-Baskets, pincushions & other toys were exhibited for sale & the purchases rewarded in some measure the charitable sisters for the trouble we gave them. Mr McGilvary was introduced to me & I have promised to breakfast with him on Monday morning. Mess[rs] Bulow & Lance & the Ladies of y[e] party go to Quebec.

Sunday 3[d] Sept[r] Three weeks in Montreal. Not well, walk. Write to my Wife. A young [man] enter'd into conversation with [me] at breakfast whom I found to be very intelligent. His name Skene son to the former owner of Skenesborough, now White Hall, he was born in England & is in the English Army. He is well inform[ed] as to pictures &c & appears full of observation. My friend Paine prescribes 8 grains of Calomel & 24 of Rhubard for me, if this Diaroeha continues—after, if necessary, Lodanum in very small doses.

Monday Sept[r] 4th Walk to Mr McGilvary's. He has a good house & elegant Garden situated on rising ground and commanding a superb view of the River & intervening rich level. He has a fine head of himself by Stewart, very fine, which he finds fault with because the coat &c are slighted. He has a portrait of his brother by Martin Archer Shee much inferiour to Stewarts but it is admired for the Highland Military dress, a vile figure of an Angel black & ill drawn, is very fine & very old, & a St Cecilia & Angels well coloured but badly drawn probably a poor copy of a better picture, is supposed original & almost invaluable. He has employed me to expunge a figure from a groupe and paint another in its place.—

it is his portrait full length. A lady with an infant & two dogs form the groupe. I have a number of visitors after my return, among them Miss Smith, Madame de Lavaunire & Mr Roland, the latter wishes his fathers portrait. Miss Smith engages me to tea tomorrow. A Mr Gibbs invites me to see *his house*. Send off a letter to my Wife by Mr McCormick.

Tuesday Sept[r] 5th 1820. Very warm weather this two days. Paint on my two pictures of George 4th. Drink tea with Miss Smith: Her friend Madame De Lauverniere with her, the Scotch French Canadian Lady born in Schenectady. a very warm night.

[Sept.] 6th Wed[y] Very warm. Walk. My friends Barrett & wife and Cunningham come hither (to the Mansion house) to board, B: having broken up House keeping. Making an arrangement for another painting room. Receive the portrait I am to copy for Mr Moffatt. Rec[d] a letter from my wife dated 30th Aug[t]. Mr Griffin a young gentleman introduced to me by Mr Cunningham calls & engages his miniature. Mr Gerard [98] of the house of Richardson Forsyth & Co. calls & talks of a picture. Paint on the King. Walk over fields out of town & return thro' the [blank] suburb just at dusk. A long closely built street of French houses with such casements or windows as we see in the flemish pictures, with the swarming population of peasants presented a scene totally unlike America.

Thursday Sept[r] 7th Walk. Begin Mr Griffins miniature & the Copy for Mr Moffatt. Mr McGillvray called. I show'd him a sketch & he is to send in the picture. Yesterday the N. W. Co.'s Voyageurs arrived & they add to our motley population. they are Canadian peasants with the additional wildness of half sailor, half savage. Many are quite Indian & all look quite as dark.

[98] Samuel Gerrard.

Friday 8th Septr Walk to McTavish's [99] house & a little up the Mountain behind. This gentleman died & left his house & plans for a superb establishment on the side of the hill unfinished. The view is beautifull beyond my powers of description, few terms which may be applied to the finest scenery but are appropriate to this. Paint on Mr Griffin. The heat very oppressive. Paint on the King's 2d picture. M: [blank] French Consul at Charleston & self have an animated conversation. Eveng extremely warm.

Saty 9th Take my walk to the Race Course about a mile from Town or 2 miles from my quarters. Paint on Mr Griffin. Weather pleasant, but warm. Paint on Copy for Mr Moffatt. Afternoon & Evening extremely warm. Ther: for some days from 82 to 94.

Sunday 10th Septr 1820. Morng very pleasant. Mr Proctor sends to invite me to walk but am engage[d] to Thomson & Barrett to visit Grants Island or St Helens, Proctor joins the plan. This Island, St Helens, is called Grant's, from having been owned by a person of that name. it is abt ¾ of a mile long, contains 100 acres, and the English Government have bought it by bartering for it, several Lots and Houses in Montreal. they are erected public edifices & intend quartering their troops there. Messrs Barrett, Thomson, Bowyer, Proctor, George Proctor & self took a Batteau and cross'd to St Helen's. visited the house & gardens formerly Grants, and encircled the Island. the center is a rocky Hill cleft by a ravine. on the north end the English have stores, & Barracks. no troops on the Island at present. crossed to Montreal Island below the town & walk'd up. During our absence Genl [Jacob] Brown & Suite & a many other Yankees arrive.

[99] Simon McTavish (1750-1804), one of the organizers of the North West Company.

Monday 11th Sep: Write to my Wife. Preparing to move. Introduced to Captn Bing [100] of ye R Navy. Read at Cunningham's. Extremely warm. Evg rain.

Tuesday [Sept.] 12th Rain. Leave Martinant's Mansn Hotel & breakfast at Annesly's. Bouchet returns and as I judge will not take the King's picture. At Mr Annesley's (who is a frame maker & picture & Lookg Glass dealer, and a Batchelor) I am to live & paint at $5 pr week. at Martinants it has cost me $13, both exclusive of Washing & extra's. Paint on Griffin. read at Cunningham's.

[Sept.] 13th Rain still. Clears in Afternoon. Paint on Griffin, on Moffatts friend & begin Revd Mr [John] Bethune the E: priest.

[Sept.] 14th Paint as yesterday. Lovely cool day. Walk with Thompson; talk of Naesmith, Wilkie, Allan, & Thompson the Engraver, Uncle to this gentleman. Evening at Barretts rooms. Mrs B: plays & sings, Thompson accompanies on Violin.

Septr 15th 1820, Friday. One of the great Market days at Montreal & the only day on which they have a fish market. Roman catholic influence in this. It is remarkable that at Montreal & Norfolk, the extremes of my travelling on this Continent, they have two similar customs not found to my knowledge elsewhere. They sweep their Chimneys by pulling a rope up & down with brush wood attached to it, & they bring their country produce in One horse Carts which are arrange[d] in order on the Market Square. Another lovely morning. Paint as yesterday.

Septr 16th Saturday. Paint as yesterday & on Barrett. After dinner walk with Annesley to McTavish's House & up the Hill to the Mausoleum & pillar erected to his memory by the McGillevray's. They are embosom'd in

[100] Hon. Henry Dilkes Byng.

Trees, surrounded by a paling, & the pillar on higher ground behind the Tomb. The whole is impressive. We mounted the Mountain clambering, & gained a very extensive view of Montreal the River & plain.

Sunday [Sept. 17] Having been unwell again for 3 days, I at last take the medicine Dr P left for me when he went away & confine myself to the house. Work on Griffins Min: & write to my Wife. Weather Cool.

Monday 18th Septr Unwell. Walk. Cool weather. Paint on Mr Bethune.

19th [Sept.] Tuesday. Cooler. Unwell. Walk. Work on Min: Mr [Harman] Blenerhassett call'd to see me. This Man made notorious by his connexion with Burr, is now here practicing Law for a living. He is a polite & apparently well informed man, appears at least 60 years old, and is very near sighted. Yesterday Mr McGillevray sent the picture & called on me. Mr Hare, D. Com: Gen. who was introduced to me by Finlay, call'd by McGil^ys request to talk over the alterations. Several visitors to day.

Wed^y [Sept.] 20th Cold. Walk. Still unwell. I saw a little up the river an encampment of Indians, 8 or 9 Tents of the rudest kind, Birch-bark suspended over poles & a birch canoe near, or making part of each Tent. Dirty & squalid they appeared to pig together in their wretched, little, imperfect shelterings, hugging themselves in their blankets; a fire of sticks at the entrance of several of the Tents. I amuse myself with studying the prints in Ackerman's Repository. De Lampré & Berzy[101] are the painters who have preceded me here, the first has been to see me, he now declines painting portraits, & paints large Historical pictures for the R. C. Churches at 100 dollars a piece, the other who had some little merit as a painter is dead. There are two others here beneath notice. Went in the evening to See Mr Charles perform his slight of hand & hear his ventriloquism. Both very good.

[101] William von Moll Berczy.

Thursday morning. White frost. Fine day. Paint on Griffin. McKenzie (Moffatts) Bethune & McGillivray. Walk.

Friday 22^{d} Septr 1820. Very pleasant. Finish Griffin & receive 30 doll^{s} the first money I have rec^{d} since I left home. Paint on Bethune.

Sat^{y} 23^{d} Mild with high wind. Even^{g} & night rain. Paint on McGillivray.

Sunday 24th Clear & colder. I am still unwell. Work a little on McGillivray. Walk. Afternoon mild & very pleasant. Walk. Night rain.

Monday 25th Septr Windy. Write to my wife by Captn [John] Garland to whom I was introduced last even^{g} at the Mansion House H: He & his wife are going to Virginia and have come from Green-Bay, an U. S. Garrison ab^{t} 200 miles beyond Michilimackinack. Paint on Bethune & McKenzie. some visitors. Afternoon quite cold. Walk. Evening reading by the fire. See & eat a poor peach, the only one I have seen. they can be raised as wall-fruit, but are not for sale. Grapes are plenty & good and apples abound of the finest. The delicate plover are brought to Market in great quantities. They come up ye River in flocks. Pheasants are brought to market. The partridge (Quail of N. Y.) is unknown here.

Tuesday 26th Septr Frosty morning but very fine. Receive letter from my wife. Morning wasted in waiting upon Mr McGillivray, who came too late to sit & appointed tomorrow. Afternoon walk. See strawberry vines in blossom. There are no Robbins, no meadow Larks & no partridges in the fields or woods here. I have mentioned the similar customs of Norfolk & this place as to Chimney sweeping & attending Market, there are other customs common to the two & not found elsewhere to the best of my knowledge. Supplying the inhabitants with water by carting it in casks, here from the river, at N. from a pump as formerly in N. Y. from the tea-water-pump. Young men going out to shoot on Sunday. But how different are the two places in many respects. The cold close cautious inhospitable manners of the motley & jarring population contrasts strongly with the free open warm hospitable virginians, as the solid prisonlike hybernacle stone houses <*with*> their deep retiring windows & doors with Iron shutters with the light open summer habitations of the children of the south. But then here is no slave population! O what a paradise would Virginia be, if it had instead of its slaves the hardy ignorant french peasants of Canada, if it had the intelligent population of the middle or Eastern States of America it would be still more blessed.

Wed^{y} 27th Septr Walk. Summer morning. Paint on Bethune & Barrett. McGillivray has his first sitting. Afternoon parade of the troops.

Thursday 28th Septr Up at 4 OClock & took some Tea. At 5 thro' a thick fog ride down to Long point & stop at [William S.] Leney's. Mr Annesley & myself took shooting equipments & it clearing up (with Mr Leney) we went in search of plover over the plowed Lands up from the River. We saw a few & got one. They are the same Bird that is found on Long Island. After dinner we went in a Canoe to Busherville's Islands some miles down the river. We there found more of these Birds, shot a few Ducks & Geese & return'd to Leney's about sun-sett. Leney has given up engraving and turn'd farmer. He has purchased 400 acres of Land at Long Point 4 & ½ miles from Montreal, the situation delightfull & the soil good. Montreal up the river, w^{h} Grants or St Helen's Island, down the river Boucherville & *Point aux Tremble,* with Islands, Farm houses & a fine country over the river, make a rich Landscape terminated by the Mountains of Chamblé.

Friday [Sept.] 29th Walk. A fine morning. Paint on McGillivray & Bethune.

Sat^y [Sept.] 30th The weather resembles our Indian-Summer. Walk on the very pleasant ridge of the Hill which forms the 3d step from the River, the 1st is the bank or level of St Paul's Street, 2d, level of Notre Dame, then come the beautiful intervale land of meadows, gardens & Orchards crossed by the streets of the Suburb Saint Lawrence & you ascend the third level or step on which is Sherbrook Street, which looks down on the Town & appears as if at some period it had been the bank of the river. the 4th 5th & 6th steps take you to the top of the mountain. Paint on McGillivray. Afternoon walk.

Sunday Octr 1st 1820. A fine clear morning. Go on board 2 of the Steam Boats for Quebec. I wish much to go thither before my return & good health and good weather next Saturday will perhaps tempt me. At 1 OClock Thomson & self cross'd to La Prairie in the Steam Boat, stemming the rapid current in a curious and pleasing manner. We were 2 hours going the 9 miles. We walk'd round the Village & enter'd the Church, where the kind of miserable pictures & Images, with tawdry decorations disgust the sight as in Montreal. We then walked down the river to Longueuile, a very pleasant walk, fine road, substantial farm houses in uninterrupted succession, and rich farms extending in lines back from the river, over a perfect level. After a walk of 10 miles we sought food & refreshment at a tavern in the Village. They agreed to give us, having nothing else, some bread, eggs & brandy. The brandy came first in dirty tumblers & proved to be miserable rum. The Landlady brought in six eggs in a soup plate and one large pewter spoon, she then went out & brought in a part of a loaf of sour brown bread grasped in one hand and a saucer with some salt in the other, and with the spoon she ground the salt from coarse to fine in the saucer. This was our dinner & apparatus, no plates, no knives, 6 eggs to be eat as we could with one large spoon. This amused me much, and with great difficulty we got two knives & another saucer, tea-spoons were not to be had. We soon dispatched the eggs, and went off to the Horse boat which plies between this place & the Cross, 2 miles below Montreal. The crossing was very pleasant, and after a walk to my quarters, my Tea, bread butter & cheese were very acceptable. I found and brought home some Mushrooms. The Haws are really a pleasant fruit in this country and to day we found a fruit in appearance like a small apple, but sweet & totally unlike the crab apple. It must be noted that this Canadian Tavern, so utterly devoid of comfort was not a Hovel, but a decent looking House, with large sign, several apartments, pictures of Saints, virgins & abundance of crucifixes, and immediately in front of the Village Church.

Monday Octr 2^d. A Summer day. I yesterday saw a procession come out of Notre Dame Church. First the Beadle in his Livery coat then 3 Boys bare headed with white Linen over their shoulders & black gowns under, the center boy carried the Crucifix of silver & the others, each a candle, next came 8 boys 2 & 2 dress'd as the first but with black caps on night cap shaped, & last 8 or 10 Priests, with the same kind of caps. Paint on McGillivray & my 2 Kings pictures. Place the first at Cunningham's reading room for sale.

Tuesday Octr 3^d Summer like morning. Walk on the Ridge or Sherbrooke Street. These 3 or 4 days past the trees have put on their variegated coats. Paint on McKenzie & King. Miss Smith & Mad^m De L'Aubigne w^h me, the first to see me paint. Walk with Thomson.

Wed^y [Oct.] 4th Quite warm. Indian Summer. Walk up the river. Paint on McGillivray. Afternoon Misty Rain from S. E.

Thursday 5th Rainy day: quite warm. Paint on McGillivray & McKenzie.

Friday 6th It clears mild. Paint as before.

Sat^{y} 7th Octr 1820. Clear and slight frost. Finish McGillivray & McKenzie. The first brings his sisters, daughter & friends to judge the picture & the verdict is favourable. Pack up. Even^{g} call on Dr Paine & with him pass the evening with the Barrett's.

Sunday Octr 8th Fine clear frosty morning, prepare for a walk to Lachine to Finlay's, as I hope to embark for Quebec tomorrow or to-night. I walked to Lachine by the River & enjoy'd much pleasure from the Scenery. Finlay out, his Lady after confinement pretty well. stay ½ an hour & walk back, making a walk of 17 or 18 miles at least. take dinner at Col^{l} Fleets who now keeps a Chop-house.

Monday [Oct.] 9th Wind S. E. a little rain. Rec^{d} from Mr Moffatt an order for 50 dollars and left it with Mr Annesley. Embark at 9 in ye Telegraph for Quebec. Lower Canada is betw^{n} 45 & 52 N. L. and 63 & 81 W. Longitude. Discover'd by J Cartier in 1534 in 1759 it becomes permanently Englands. population 1815 335,000 of whom 275,-000 are Can[adians] to whom their laws religion &c were secured. it is govern'd by Governor, Executive Councill & Legislative Council appointed by the King & has a third house elected by the Freeholders. The Govr may prorogue or dissolve at pleasure and the King may annul any Law within 2 years. They are notwithstanding in their present state actually free & free from taxes, except those flowing from the necessity of buying all manufactures from England. England must indulge them in every point for fear of the U. S. Canada owes its freedom to us and our Revolution. Some one told an Irishman that he <*was much more free in*> had more liberty here than in his own Country. "Liberty" says Pat "Liberty! when I'm six months in the year up to my knees in Snow." After dinner we land at Berthier, a pretty village, wooden houses, a fine Island opposite to it used as a grazing place for the cattle of the village. Women paddling over in canoes to milk the cows. Head wind & we anchor in Lake St Peters.

Tuesday Morning [Oct.] 10th Cold cloudy morning and going down Lake St. Peters with a head wind, at 7 OClock we are abt 70 miles on our way, (out of 180). Lake St Peters is 25 miles long & 9 wide. At a ¼ past 9 we arrive at the Town of Three Rivers at the mouth of the river St Maurice. Bouchet states this to be the third in rank in Lower Canada. Its appearance is poor & not larger than La Prairie. We stop here an hour. In the afternoon we come to Anchor in Storm & Rain, and tossing with a river-sea.

Wedy [Oct.] 11th The Storm continues & we remain at anchor until after 4 OClock in the afternoon. The scenery then becomes very fine as gilded by an evening Sun. We arrive at Quebec about Ten OClock and sleep another Night on board The Morning of Thursday I go on shore.

[Thursday, Oct. 12] The Coup d'oeil of Quebec even from the boat at the Wharf is striking. after depositing my baggage at the Union Hotel, I walk over a part of the rugged town, through two of the Gates or passages which pass through the fortifications and enjoy a wild prospect from various points. After breakfast call on Bouchet. I found him in his office & he looked as if he saw in me one risen from the Dead: He soon recover'd and was very glad to see me & after being seated enquired if I had finished the Kings picture. I answered "Yes, and I have brought it with me and expected it to pay my expences from Montreal & and back again." "That will be $40 at least" said he. "Yes, but if you take the picture you shall have it for $30, cash if not I shall try to Raffle it off for $50. He said he must have it, and then began the old story of his losing 1700 guineas by his Maps concluding by offerring me in lieu of cash, an order on James Thomson of N. Y. for $16 due for a set of Maps, and two setts of Maps complete, value 7 Guineas each.

I accepted his offer and was introduced to his Lady and four sons who were so fully employed in putting a squirrel into a cage that they could scarce attend to me. All was truly French. They had half finishe'd Breakfast when the New Cage came home & all was left in disorder. B. Demanded why he was not called to Breakfast, the Lady cried, "Bun, Bun, pretty Bun," I was invited by him to sit down & take Tea. "Adelaide I am astonished at you." The Lady sat down to Table pouting & frowning. I paid my prettiest attentions to her and smiles were restored. M: Charles had given her the squirrel. he was a charming man, &c &c. Arrangements were made for one of the young men to attend me to the plains of Abraham and show me the Lions of Quebec. On the plains of Abraham and in the prospect of Wolfes Cove I enjoy'd feelings from recollections & Associations truly enviable. On return[g] we visited the principal Fr[ench] Church. A picture of the Annunciation is worth notice. From various points of the Fortifications the views are beautiful and some, sublime. In the afternoon I went again to Bouchet get the order on T and the Maps, having delivered the picture to his servant. He wrote the order but could only give me one complete sett of Maps and one imperfect sett. 10 sheets making the great Map of Lower Canada, the general or two sheets including both Canada's on a smaller scale, and the volume of Topographical description, making one complete sett, valued by him at 7 G[s] and the same sett of the Large Map (10 sheets) and the book. He added 3 maps of the District of Gaspé. On returning to my Lodgings I found that the order was not addressed to any person. I went back. Bouchet had gone out. I was ushered up stairs and found Madame in great trouble. The squirrel had been let out of the Cage to play, and would not return but took refuge in the Window Curtain & was gnawing it to pieces, the servants were called to catch Bun, who flew from one piece of furniture to another she crying "Bun Bun pretty Bun" when he was at a distance & shrieking when he approached. this farce continued an hour with intervals of a few words to me.

Bouchet return'd, finished the order and I, declining their invitations to Tea, took my departure. The behaviour and language of this family are amusing, a mixture of French & English in both, and full of the English affectation of interlarding every thing that is said w[h] "You know" and "Do you know."

I had an opportunity before Dinner to go through the Lower Town & St Roque's suberb. Nothing can be finer than the effect of the rock and Ramparts of Cape Diamond lowering over the Houses & ships below. St Roques suberb is the filthiest miserable place I ever beheld, but the frowning battlements even here repaid me for wading thro' the filth below them. The upper Town is one complete Fortress, encircled by Walls, ditches, towers Battlements, *herissé* with Cannon, and only accessible from the Lower Town and Suberbs, through arched gateways threaten'd by towers & guns. It is altogether a wonderful place and so unlike any thing in America that I can scarcely imagine myself on my Native Continent.

Friday Octr 13th At 6 OClock, I began a Walk to the Falls of Montmorency, distant 9 miles from Quebec, by Dorchester Bridge ove[r] the River St Charles. After passing the bridge and over a low plain, I ascended for miles passing through the long irregular village of Beauport. At a Canadian Inn, I got some bread which I could not eat, some Tea & Eggs & then proceed to view the Falls and adjacent scenery and to make sketches for my portfolio. This falls are said to be 200 feet high or more & the river being very full I saw them to advantage. The scenery in various directions is picturesque & truly grand. In one of my sketches I have the brow of the Fall & over it the aqueduct lead[g] to the Great Saw Mills on the West side, with Points Levi and Quebec in the distance. I resumed my walk, turning to Quebec & reached my lodgings before 3 OClock after a ramble of 18 or 20 miles.

Saturd[y] [Oct.] 14th Before open daylight I embarked on board the Steam Boat Quebec for Montreal and about ½ past six we under steam & sail. I sketched the views of the Town as we passed up the river which are in this book. I yesterday saw a Canadian country Funeral. Four men bearing the corpse the coffin cover'd by a coarse sheet, 10 or 12 others attending in disorder & all talking, laughing & shouting through the Village of Beauport. One man follow'd some yards behind, with a handkerchief to his face, he was unnoticed, and the only mourner

The fine weather to day and the ample accommodations of this Quebec recompense me for the sufferrings on board the Telegraph in going down the River. All is to day cheerful & the banks of ye River have almost a summer aspect. A Band of Music composed of the Waiters contribute to the cheering effect. In the afternoon the wind changes and rain follows for the night.

Sunday 15 Octr Lake St Peters. Here we anchored for the night and now proceed with fair wind & cloudy sky. Travellers on this river are principally from the U. S. or Europe. Going down we had 1 American (for so we of ye U. S. are designated when not called Yankee) 3 Scotchmen & one Canadian priest. Now we are 2 Americans, 2 Scotsmen, 2 Irishmen & three American Canadians (as I suppose) one of them is Chrysler on whose Farm [102] the battle was fought in 1813 which stopt Wilkinson. Upper Canada is fast settling with Scotch and Americans, the latter in greatest proportion and (I speak from hearsay, the conversation of those who envy & hate them) thriving in every undertaking so as to promise ultimately to make the whole country American.

		miles
Distance from N. Y. to Alb[any]		160
Alb: to Whitehall		74
Wh: to St Johns		150
St J	Mont^t	27
M^l	Quebec	180
Q.	Montm^y	9
		600

102 Chrystler's Farm, near the head of the Long Sault Rapids, on the St. Lawrence River, where American troops were defeated November 11, 1813. C. P. Lucas, *The Canadian War of 1812* (Oxford, 1906).

Off Wm Henry at 12 OClock that is, 46 miles from Montreal. rainy Ev^{g} 6 OClock clears is W. N. E. The Saw Mills at Montmorency employs 80 labourers, cost about £60,000 St^{g} At Three Rivers is a Fall of the River St Maurice at which are great Iron works. The owner Ball is on board. it is a great establishment for Cast Iron ware, &c. Arrive at 8 OClock at Montreal but for darkness, & Storm cannot Land.

Monday morn^{g} [Oct.] 16th Still rain or thick Mist. At Montreal. Go to Annesley's. McGillivray refuses to pay $120, tells Annesley in a note that my demand is founded on his not making a bargain. Write a note addressed to Annesley rebutting the charge & asserting the fact that $150 would have been my price, to which if he had not agreed I should have [been] at home two weeks ago. Call on Cunningham he has not disposed of the picture of the King, takes my directions to do it at any price & remit me the money before 1st Novr. Receive from Barrett $15. Annesley again calls on McGillivray & he refuses to pay more that $100. Prepare to depart and go down to the Boat for La Prairie, leaving the boys w^{h} the handbarrow laden to follow. Annesley with me. Annesley turns back for my Great Coat. I proceed and go on board the Boat. Wait in vain for my baggage. Jump on shore as the Boat pushes off. Messrs Colt & Ogden advise me to look for my baggage on board the Quebec & other Steam boats. I do so, in vain, return to Annesleys & find that he seeing the Steam boat go off & supposing me with her, took my baggage to the New Market & embark'd with it in a canoe to overtake me at La Prairie. Thus he will have a long journey in pursuit of me while I am by his fire-side. Ab^{t} 8 OClock Annesley return'd; He having seen me on board supposed that I had gone on, & stopping the baggage took a small boat below, while I was seeking him above, crossed to Longueile, got a carriage & arrived a[t] La Prairie before the Steam Boat, not finding me he left my baggage, rode to Longueile & cross'd again in pursuit of me.

Tuesday 17th Octr A fine frosty morning. Write to McGillivray in a manner that if it does not produce my money will at least make him feel his inferiority. Shew the letter to Dr Paine. Go to La Prairie to look to my baggage. We are two or three minutes on the Rocks. See for the first time one of the N. W. Indian Bark Canoes man'd by 18 or 20 Voyageurs 9 or 10 on each side. With each a paddle or short oar all keeping time to their Choral Song. All the oarsmen or paddlers dress'd in dark blue with round black hats and a steersman with a paddle, dress'd in figured Chints or Calico. All looking like Savages. See for the first time the sabot or wooden shoe on the peasants of La Prairie they are used as our goloshoe. At ½ past 2 we go to Fleet for a dinner and then to Annesley. Evening with Dr Paine at Mr Barrett's.

Wedy 18th Octr 1820. Frosty morning. I have before mentioned the New plan of Ship-building invented by Mr Annesley's father [William Annesley]. I have this morning heard read a letter from him to his wife dated Augt 18th last, in which he states that he has proved his theory by 20 vessels, from a Wherry to a ship of 360 tons, & that now, at Hull a ship is building of upwards of 700 tons burthen, after the completion of which he will publish a pamphlet with engravings, now preparing, and then sell his patent, for England, & return to his Wife & family in America. The letter is a plain, sensible, excellent letter from a Husband who had been long seperated from his family & struggling for a great object against, power prejudice and the interest of many individuals. At Cunninghams at Paines. Go to see some miserable paintings sent from France to sell to the Churches here. Go to see De Lampré who is painting from prints for the Churches. Afternoon Annesley tells me that McGillivray has sent for his picture & tells him to call next week for the $120. Ride with Annesley. afterwards take a walk and see a Crayon picture said to be done by Copley 50 years ago, the head of a lady beautifully painted with great breadth & simplicity.

Paint at Montreal

Mr Barrett	25 pd	
Mr Griffin	30 pd	
Mr Bethune	30 pd	
Mr McKenzie	50 pd	
Mr McGillivray	120	
Prince Regent		for [which] I rec[d] Maps inst[d] of money promised
D°	D°	sold for 50 by Mr Cunningham

Expences of Journey to Canada Bro[t] forward	196.7½
voyage to Quebec	10...
At Quebec	4...
Steam boat Quebec	12...
D°	2.50
Mr. Annesley	15...
and an order on Cunningham for $22.25 from the proceeds of the Kings picture	
Oct[r] 17th Expences to La Prairie &c........	1.25
18th pd. printers	3.25

Thursday 19th Oct[r] A Mild morning. Take what a hope will be my last *Walk o' the morning* in Montreal at present. Leave Mont[l] at 10. At 12 arrive at La Prairie. At 5 arrive at St Johns on the Richlieu or Sorrell or Chamblee whose mouth I pass'd a few days since. Capt[n] Bing of the R Navy who commands at Isle au Noix in company. Some interesting conversation with him respecting the affair in Chesapeake Bay last War. I am favoured with a summer like day for this part of my return Journey. We are to sleep at Johns and embark after breakfast.

Friday Oct[r] 20th A fine morning with white frost. Embark at 8 OClock and enjoy a summer voyage on the Lake. Mr Garden a Scotch gentleman of Montreal contributed to my pleasure by his conversation. Mr Bowyer from the Mansion House is with me. The sunsetting in the broad part of the Lake was almost as fine as I saw it in August, both were truly beautiful & sublime.

Saturday Oct[r] 21st We arrive at 6 OClock at Whitehall the morning foggy & promising another summer day. I landed at Burlington last evening & saw part of the town by the light of a clear full moon. We had previously stopt at Plattsburg but I did not go on shore. All the scenery from Plattsburg to the time of sunsetting when we were approaching Burlington was truly superb, the clouds of the most varied brilliant & soft tints and the Mountains partaking of every hue of the pallette, while the nearer points, Islands & headlands shone in the vivid colours of an American Autumn. We leave Whitehall & ride over hills with bold scenery in every direction by the same road which I pass'd in the Fall of 1816. Arrive at Albany ¼ past Eleven.

Sunday Oct[r] 22[d] Obliged to stay at Albany. Chancelor Kent has just gone to N. Y. Walk around the Town. It is perfect summer. Afternoon walk with Boyer.

Monday [Oct.] 23[d] Prepare to embark. A fine morning. Meet C[harles] Rhind on board y[e] Paragon. Sit up to see the passage of the Hudson through the Highlands and by that means see the Towns of Poughkeepsy & Newburgh.

Tuesday [Oct.] 24 Arrive at N. Y. and am struck by the contrast between the beauty & richness of the City Harbour & shipping and the appearance of the cities of the North. Find my family well.

Leave New York on Tuesday the 14th of Nov[r] [1820] with my Wife for Norfolk. Leave my son & daughter to keep house in Leonard Street. We arrive same evening at Phil[a] & took up our abode with Mr Charles Chauncey. Go on to Baltimore the 19th and stay at Barnums Hotel until 20th.

Our abode w[h] Mr Charles Chauncey & his amiable family, his Wife [103] & her sister Miss [Charlotte] Chester

[103] Charles Chauncey (1777-1849) married Hannah Chester (1781-1821). Her sister, Julia Chester, married Matthew C. Ralston of Philadelphia. See Stiles, *History of Ancient Wethersfield, Conn.*, II, 216.

are of Wethersfield Con: Another sister is married to Mr Ralston of Phil^{a} & Mr [Henry] Chester a brother is likewise settled there. We pass'd our time until Sat 12 OClock, in visiting friends & seeing the City, new to my Wife, then took leave of our friends, and arrive in Balt. 3 OClock Sunday morning, the 19th Novr at 7 OClock we are well lodged at Barnums Hotel

Monday 20th Novr Leave Baltimore in the Steam B^{t} Norfolk for Norfolk after passing a pleasant day in Baltimore, showing my Wife the beautiful buildings of that City.

Tuesday morning 21st Novr Squally & Rain as we enter the Harbour of Norfolk. Land being received by Mr T Williamson who politely accompanies us to his house & insists on our staying with him until suited with Lodgings. Engage lodgings & board at Mrs Murphy's at $12 p^{r} Week.

Wed^{y} [Nov.] 22^{d} Still summer. See Lyford who says Mr Broughton will have 3 pictures painted at $25. Dinner party at Mr Williamson's.

[Nov.] 23^{d} Summer with clouds. Hope to have my painting room ready in about a week.

[Nov.] 30th A Snow Storm. I am still without painting or Exhibition Room but hope to have the first finished in 2 or 3 days. We left Mr W's on monday y^{e} 27th and are in Granby Street.

Norfolk Decr 1st A fine Winter morning, the earth cover'd with Snow.

Sunday Decr 10th I yesterday return'd from Williamsons hav^{g} walked out the day before with my gun.

Monday 11th Decr Began a portrait of Mrs. Williamson. I have finished my Historical picture which I call "Christ's first Teaching in the Temple."

[Dec.] 12th Write a Catalogue. Finish my picture of Susannah at the Bath.

Wed^{y} [Dec.] 13th Paint on Mrs W. Busy in preparing my Exhibition Room.

Thursday [Dec.] 14th Finish my picture of Mahomet afte[r] his return.

Friday [Dec.] 15th Warm as summer. Work on pictures for Exhibition. Finish Mrs. Bourke's picture. I have borrow'd from Mr Glenn, Dr Clarke's Bible & read therein.

[Dec.] 16th A Violent Storm. Ev^{g} Snow. Work all day on the picture of Mrs Cooper & child for my Exhibition.

[Dec.] 17th Rain & thaw. Work a little.

[Dec.] 18th Monday. Rain. The snow has disapeared entirely: Work on my pictures for Exhibition. The floor is at length laid of my Exhibition Room & I hope to open it on friday.

Thursday Decr 21st Last night & to day violent rain. Yesterday was perfect summer. I have been busily engaged in painting on and arranging for Exhibition in my new Gallery. I have advertised to open it on Saturday next. My Catalogues are printed. I shall show near 60 pictures of my own painting.

Friday Decr 22^{d} Finish hanging pictures & making other arrangements for my Exhibition.

Sat^{y} [Dec.] 23^{d} Open my Exhibition. The rec^{ts} \$2.25. An additional Setter engaged. This is (as Christmas Eve) the great market day. Weather very fine.

Sunday 24th Weather Still warm

25th Christmas day. Raw & cold. My Exhn recets $6.12½ Begin to copy Mr Hunters picture for Mr Owens. Yesterday Mr Cammack & to day Coll Armistead engage portraits. The Herald speaks in high praise of my pictures particularly my largest or "Christ's first teaching."

Decr 26th Snow Storm with rain. Eveng cold & clear. Begin Wm Cammack's & Wm Armisteads portraits. Receive a letter from Earl of Phila with a Box of Frames. A letter from Sully from Baltimore, saying he is doing well & a letter from my daughter. My friend Holland [104] is dead.

[Dec.] 27th A fine frosty day. Paint on my Copy of Mr Hunter

[Dec.] 28th Rain all day. Receive 3 frames from Earl priced 9, 12, & 14 dollars, which with Box Freight & Cartage makes them cost me 9:50, 13:50, 16:50. My prices must be 11, 15, 20. Paint on Captn Cammack & a View from Queens Town heights.

[Dec.] 29th Very warm, with high wind & showers all day. Curious effect of damps upon some of my pictures even so as to make them appear utterly ruined. restored by drying them near a stove. Paint on Captn Cammack.

[Dec.] 31st Sunday Pleasant.

Jany 1st 1821. Slight frost, very pleasant. Begin Broughtons portrait. Dine at Williamsons.

[Jan.] 2d Threatens snow but clears in the evening. Paint on Mrs Williamsons portrait. My Exhibition increases in value & my principal picture pleases. Become acquainted with Genl [James Patton] Preston the late Govr of this state.

[104] John Joseph Holland, scene-painter and artist, died in New York City December 16, 1820, in the 45th year of his age. (N. Y.) *Commercial Advertiser,* December 18, 1820.

JOHN JOSEPH HOLLAND (c. 1776-1820)

Attributed to William Dunlap

(Courtesy of Miss Elisabeth Marbury)

[Jan.] 3^{d} A most pleasant day. Work on the portrait of Mrs. Williamson

[Jan.] 4th Cold. 5th Very cold.

[Jan.] 6th Violent storm of rain all day. Paint on Broughton & a little on the Play scene of Hamlet.

7th Sunday. Snow. 8th Clear & Cold. 9th Clear & Mild.

[Jan.] 10th Wed^{y} Springlike. Last even^{g} past the evening in company with Tazewell; a most extraordinary man. Eloquent unaffected, mathematical, quick as lightning, sportive & cool.

[Jan.] 11th Rain. Yesterday 2 pictures engaged.

12th A Spring day of sunshine.

13th Saturday. Rain all day.

14th Sunday. Clear & Summer heat. Evening at Doctor Barraud's with Genl Taylor & others.

15th Clear & mild. 16th Cold and threatning snow.

17th Wed^{y} Snow 18th Thursday Clear & cold, the ground cover'd with snow. The 19th is the same. I finish Cammack to day & paint for 2 days on Crocker.

Tuesday [Jan.] 23^{d} The first fine day since the 14th.

24th Very cold & Snow. 25th The cold is excessive for this climate 2 degrees of Farenheit. 26th it begins to moderate 27th Sat^{y} Moderate & the harbour which had been closed is open. 28th Sunday Warm as Spring. 29th Still warmer & 30th still warmer, and the three days clear & beautiful.

I have begun a picture of Captn Warrington on speculation. Last even^{g} pass'd with the 2 Parson Lowes [105] and there Wives

[105] Rev. Samuel Low and Rev. Enoch M. Low.

Feb[y] 19th 1821 Monday. A fine clear day. I am this day 56 years of age. This is my second birthday in Norfolk, yet since the last what a variety of scenes have I pass'd thro'! I sate down yesterday to answer a letter from my amiable friend Doctor Payne of Montreal which revived the events of last Fall & may perhaps lead me again to Canada. But in all thy will be done Oh God! And may I remember that if I truly wish thy will to be done I shall strive to do thy will, and that thy will is truth and love!

Norfolk, Friday April 27th 1821. Rec[d] the following letter

Private

D[r] Sir

Should the Theatre not be appropriated in a few days, the proprietors will have it conducted on their acc[t]. If so, would you be willing to go as their Agent to London, to Embark at New York on 10 of May or Earlier.

Should you like the suggestion, an early meeting would be advisable. I leave this about Wed[y] for Phila[d] where I may stay two or three days (at the Washington Hall). You'l have the goodness to write me immediately both to Phil[a] & N. York.

With regard y[rs]

John K Beekman

Baltimore Barnums Hotel
W Dunlap Es[q]

to this I answer'd

Friday Afternoon
Ap[l] 27th 1821

D[r] Sir

I have but just received your letter from Baltimore. I did not [intend] leaving this place until July; but upon receiving your answer to this, saying that you will pay my expences to N. York, and (in case an arrangement for the Voyage suggested does not take place) my expences back to Norfolk, I will immediately embark in the Steam Boat for the purpose of an interview with you in New York.

If this should reach you in time to admit of your reply's coming to my hands on or before Sunday 6th May, I shall have it in my power to be in N. York on the 10th.

Y[rs] &c. W D

John K. Beekman Es[q]

May 13th [1821] I recd an answer to the above dated the 5th saying that this day Mr Simpson had concluded his agreement for the Theatre & that Beekmans plans were at an end.

[May] 29th Leave Mrs Murphy's boarding house & settled with her. My Wife goes with Mrs Williamson to Ferryville & I go to W's town house. The heat is now in the afternoon of 2 days 88 of Farenheit. 1 day said to be 92.

June 1st 1821. Go down to Ws plantation. Evening rain.

2d So cold as to require fire.

3d Ride to the Bay-side.

4th Return to Norfolk. See a picture said to be a Rubens "St John's head presented to Herod. Introduced to Mr Roberts Cashier of Bank of Fredericksburg.

Monday [June] 11th Last week mostly at the Ferry. Return'd to day. Of the forest trees of this part of Virginia I have remark'd many kinds of Oak not seen with us, the Willow-oak is very beautiful, the live oak, post oak, Chesnut oak &c. The Chinquepin makes a figure.

Thursday & Friday 14 & 15 excessive heat. Painting Miss Nivison

Novr 30th I went home to N. Y. with my Wife the last of June and remained there until the 22d of Novr I am now again in *Norfolk* for the third time, the place becomes more & more desolate, but I Hope to find portrait painting enough here & in the neighbourhood to support me while I finish my picture of Christ Rejected. If I can do so, & accomplish that object in May next I hope I may be better off in pecuniary matters hereafter.

Decr 1st A Wet day. I have a prospect of employment in Elizabeth City N. C. I am preparing my rooms here for the reception of my paintings & materials.

Sunday 2^{d} Decr Wet day but still mild. Even^{g} rain. Hear Mr [Joshua T.] Russell the presbyterian preach. Read Wirts life of Patrick Henry. Meagre & inflated.

[Dec.] 3^{d} Write to Earle for prepared cloths. Clear mild weather. I find that the room which Mr M Glenn had intended for me is now occupied as a place [?] for Negroe slaves bro^{t} here to ship by the Slave dealers. I am therefor off from that place. Dine at Neilsons.

[Dec.] 4th Mild rain. Go to Ferryville and live 3 days on Oysters & Hoe cake, shooting partridges. 7th Return to Norfolk.

[Dec.] 8th Saturday. Rain all day. Hear from home. Write to J. K. Beekman respecting an Exhibition room in N. Y. to be built for me.

[Dec.] 9th Sunday Clear & cold not freezing.

10th Decr Cloudy & cold not freezing. On the opposite page is the inscription for the Crucifixion as given by Clark.

ΙΗΣΟΥΣ *ο Ναζωραιος ο Βασιλευς τωη* ΙΟΥΔΑΙΩΝ

IESUS NAZARENUS REX IUDAEORUM

W. receives a letter from Elizabeth City N. C. declining my professional services, except for one picture.

[Dec.] 12th Yesterday got my picture up. Williamson has written again to Elizabeth City.

13th Hard Rain. Write to my Wife. Preparing to paint. 15th-17th Frost. Work on my great picture and begin one portrait. To day a thaw.

18th Rain which clears up mild

19th Clear & warm. Williamson goes to the Ferry.

[Dec.] 20th Thursday clear & warm. Paint on Garrison & on the great picture, as I do every day. Receive a final answer from Elizabeth City; I am not wanted.

21st Warm. Cloudy & evening hard rain. Not well. Williamson returns.

[Dec.] 22^{d} Saturday. Warm Showry. Clear & like May. Change to cold rain and a stormy night. 23^{d} Sunday. Cold & cloudy. 24th Cold damp weather. 25th At day break hail, $morn^{g}$ cold but clears. Write to my Wife and paint on my picture.

Decr 26th Clear & cold but pleasant receive a letter from my wife. all Well on the 17th

Thursday [Dec.] 27th Work as usual. Crawley has open'd his Museum in conjunction with one Griffith & for first 3 days & evenings rec^{d} an average of 18$ 4th day 5.

Saturday [Dec.] 29th To day & yesterday are perfect Spring days pleasant as May.

30th Mild, cloudy & showers.

31st Clear & Mild. I have advertised that my Gallery is open, without mentioning my large picture. I will let it be seen in an unfinished State & the other pictures are as last Year.

Jany 1st 1822. This is my third New Years day in Norfolk. The weather is clear & mild. Receive 12 frames from Earle of $Phil^{a}$.
Evening at McIntoshes with W. & Judge Parker, an Egg-Nogg party.

[Jan.] 2^{d} Wed^{y} Clear & warm as May. Receive a letter from my Wife, all well the 26th Dec: Thank God! McLean better & thinks of coming this way.

3^{d} Clear and warm. Agree with Major Cooper for board at $6. p^{r} Week & to have fire every evening.

4th A Snow Storm. 5th Clear & cold

Sunday [Jan.] 6th Clear & mild. Remove to Major Coopers Write to my Wife. Lame with Rheumatism. Sleep still at Williamsons as he is out of town.

7th Clear & warm. Nearly finish Garrison. W. comes home. I am very Lame.

8th Warm Rain. I am better.

[Jan.] 9th & 10th Clear & mild. I am to paint 3 pictures for Shiels & Co.[106] who are to print for it. Begin 1st Mrs Shiels.

11th Clear & very cold. Begin 2^{d} Mrs S.

12th Saturday. Clear & mild. Begin Mr Ashburn of ye firm of Shiels & Co.

14th Sunday was cold & clear & to day clear & cold. My Exhibition yields a little, partly owing to advertising in the Beacon which I do on acc^{t} of painting for the printers. I received a letter from my Wife by which I find that the 1st 2^{d} & 3^{d} of Jany were in N. Y. as here. Receive a letter from J. K. Beekm^{n} saying a corner Lot in Broad Way cannot be purchased &c.

[Jan.] 15th Tuesday. Clear & mild. Shiels expresses himself in high & warm terms of praise & admiration of my picture in ye Beacon of to day.

16th Clear & cold. Shiels (H.) engages his portrait, paint on Ashburn & Mrs H. Shiels & on C[hrist] rej^{ted}

17th Paint on Mrs W. Shiels. receive letter from A. Robertson & packet of papers by ye Tell Tale.

18th Perfect spring. Lame with Rheumatism in both knees. Begin Mr Shiel's picture.

106 (Hamilton) Shields, Ashburn, and (William C.) Shields, printers of the *American Beacon,* which Hamilton Shields founded in 1815.

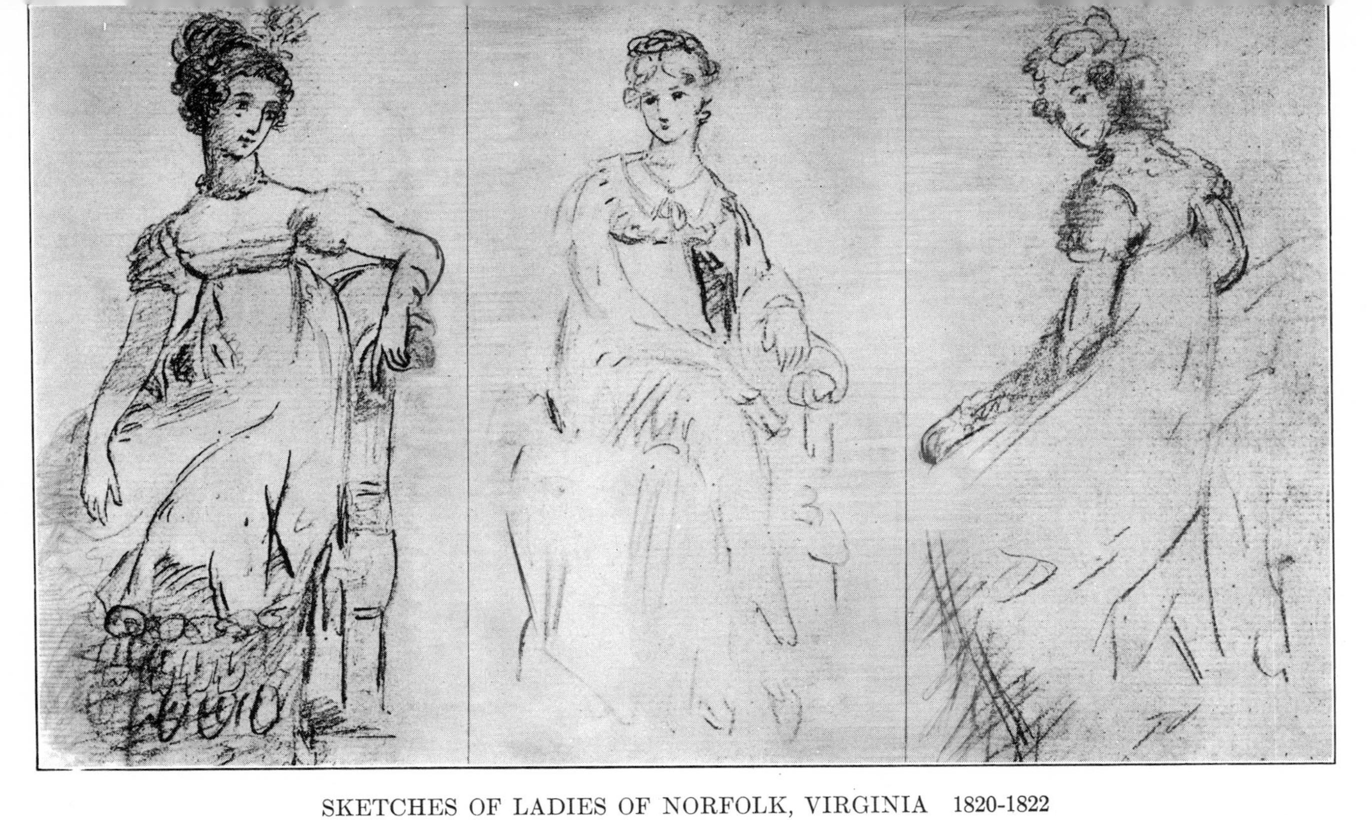

SKETCHES OF LADIES OF NORFOLK, VIRGINIA 1820-1822

By William Dunlap

(In Dunlap's manuscript *Memoirs 26,* in the Library of Yale University)

19th A Lowering & Showery Spring day. Dine with Hamilton Shiels his brother & Mr Ashburn present. Very pleasant evening. The Shiels's are from Phila

[Jan.] 20th Sunday. Warm Rain. 21st Mild & damp

22d Clear & summer like. 23d Clear & cold Spring Weather.

24th Clear & very cold. At night a slight chill

[Jan.] 25th Clear & intensely cold. Quite well again & my Rheumatism almost gone. Afternoon the weather begins to moderate. At Neilson's, introduced to Messrs. Brown & Armistead of Petersburg.

26th Very cold but moderates to a pleasant mild evening. Part of last evening with Williamson & part of this with Lowe.

[Jan.] 27th Rain all day. A few days ago Mr Ogilvie, a presbyterian Minister call'd to see my picture. After warm praises he said he would preach on the subject. To day he calls & shows me a written Sermon which he leaves with me, for remark & correction.

28th Rain. Begin Major Coopers picture.

29th Moist & chilly. Receive letter from my Wife & one from Cunningham of Montreal. Write to both.

30th Rain. Paint on Major Cooper. The picture is for Mr Richd Archer, and is painted as a Sportsman, Cooper being a remarkable Shot.

[Jan.] 31st Rain. Mr Sheldon of Wmsburg engages his miniature.

Feby 1st [1822] Mr S. says he must go home & cant have it done. The rain ceases but it is cold & cloudy.

Saty 2nd Feby A fine clear mild day but Sunday Rain all day & evening. I yesterday got in wood for the Winter. My picture continues to grow and my Exhibition yields something daily.

[Feb.] 8th Ever since ye 2d it has been either rain or very cold. Ogilsvie has made known his intention of preaching & printing a Sermon on my picture.

[Feb.] 9th Saty Clear & mild. Last Saty Wmson sat out for Douthat's & got there on tuesday eveng 4 days & 3 nights. I am bless'd that I did not go.

11th Last night it snow'd but scarce a vestige is left this evening. Receive a message from Wmson which induces me to resolve on going to Westover. Write to Douthat & to my Wife.

12th A Spring day. Receive a letter from my Wife all well 5th.

[Feb.] 13th Spring weather till evening, then Winter again.

April 21st 1822. Norfolk. The continuation of my journalizing is in a red morocco cover'd book.

Dr	Exhibition in Norfolk 1820				Cr
[1820]	posting Bills	.50	Decr	23rd Recd	2.25
	Freight of pic-			25	6.12½
	tures &c	15.		27	1.25
	Osborne's Bill ...	45.		28th	.25
	Greens Do	10		29th	1.
	Broughtons Do ..	27.50		30th	5.75
	Rent	10	1821		
	Brocksholme's		Jany	1st	6.75
	wages	12		2d	2.50
	Cleaning	.25		3d	.50
	Paper	.25		5th	75
	Loss in chang-			8th & 9th	3.50
	ing	.50		10th	.75
	Cleaning door ..	.25		11th	.75
[1821]				12th & 13th	2.87½
Feby 1st	B's wages	12		3 weeks	35.00
Mar 1st	Do	12			
Apl 1st	Do	12	[Jan.]	15	4.
				19	.25
		157.25		23d	2.

May 31st B's [wages] & print^{g} 15

172.25
111.37

Sunk $ 60.88

[Jan.]	25 to 29	4.87½
	30th	4.25
	31st	1.50
Feb^{y}	3^{d}	3.25
	6 weeks	55.12½
[Feb.]	8th	3.75
	15th	1.37½
	17th	.75
	8 weeks	61.
Mar	1st	6.12½
Rec^{d} to April 1st		
	14 weeks open	91.12½
Ap^{l}	10th	.50
May	29th	19.25
	31st	.50
		111.37½

Dr Painting at Norfolk Cr

Dr

To Expences in coming hither & residing to this time Decr 27th. 143.
[Dec.] 28th Freight & Cartage ... 2.12½
1821 Shovel & tongs 1.25
Board .... 20.
D^{o} .... 6.
Jany 15th D^{o} & washing .... 15.
22^{d} D^{o}D^{o} &c.. 14.
30th Sp: Turp: &c. & Board &c. 14.50
Due James Earl ...... 14.
Feby 1st Fixing & repair^{g} Stove 1.50
5th Board 13 Sent to N. Y. 10 & postage &c. to 8th 24.25
12th Board &c. . 15.
19th D^{o} &c. .... 13.

Cr

By T Williamson charged .... 50.
p^{d} W Cammack .... 75.
p^{d} Owens .... 30.
p^{d} Broughton 41.66
Lost Wilton Hope .... 20.
Col^{l} Armstead ... 50
p^{d} 40 p^{d}
p^{d} Mr Osborne .... 30.
p^{d} Capt Crocker ... 40.
p^{d} 20
(if one it must be 50)
p^{d} Doctor Fernandes. 10.
From W Cammack for frame .... 20.
p^{d} Broughton (2^{d}) .. 41.66
p^{d} Feby 17th Judge Parker .... 50.
Rec^{d} of Mr Broughton
Cash 40
Bill p^{d} 27.50
—— 67.50
p^{d} Wadsworth ...... 5.
p^{d} Mrs Cosby ...... 50.

Feby 26th D^{o} &c. 14
Mar 5th D^{o} &c. .... 15.
9th Freight &c. of 11 Frames . 5.50
12th Board &c.. 14.
16th Mr Green for Cloths &c .... 4.
26th Board &c. . 28.
Ap 2^{d} Rent ..... 15.
Board &c. . 14.
9 D^{o} &c. .... 14.
Stove pipe. .50
23 Board &c. . 27.
May 7 D^{o} .... 26.
Green for cloths ..... 3.

463.62½

May 30th Board &c . 45.

Dr Barraud (Williamsons charged.. 50.
1 May Fran^{s} S. Taylor.. 30. p^{d} 15 p^{d}
p^{d} Geo: Loyall with frame .... 65.
p^{d} F. S. Taylor frame .... 10.
p^{d} Robt Douthat 2..100.
E Low .... 50.
Lost Miss Neveson .... 50.
Mrs Crocker ..... 40.

Dr Painting in Norfolk &ca. 1821 Novr Cr

Travelling Expences 30.50
Wood 1.00
Sawing 50/100
Cart^{g} 25/100 .... 2.25
Snake Exhibition . .25
Dec^{r}
3 p^{d} Captn Cammack for frame .... 15.
8th Serv^{ts} & postage.. .75
10th Freight & Cartage. 6.
12th Washing &c. 1.12½
22th To Green for frames & pannells. 10.75
D^{o} for work on rooms .... 9.
25 To Wattles for services in full.... 5.
Servants 1.50
postage .50 .... 2.
Sent to my Wife.. 20
31st paid Cartage ..... .18

By Cash from Judge Parker .... 40.
Dec^{r}
15th Garrison .... 25.
p^{d} 20
17th Exhibition .... .50
from Green ...... 3.
(money lent)
Rev^{d} E Low...... 50.
p^{d} 25 & 25
27th Exhibition .... .25
31st D^{o} .... .25
1822
Jan^{y}
1st D^{o} .... .50
7th D^{o} .... .50
8th D^{o} .... 1.
12th 1.25 ....
14th 2.50 .... 3.75
Mr A Taylor his fathers portrait framed ....100.

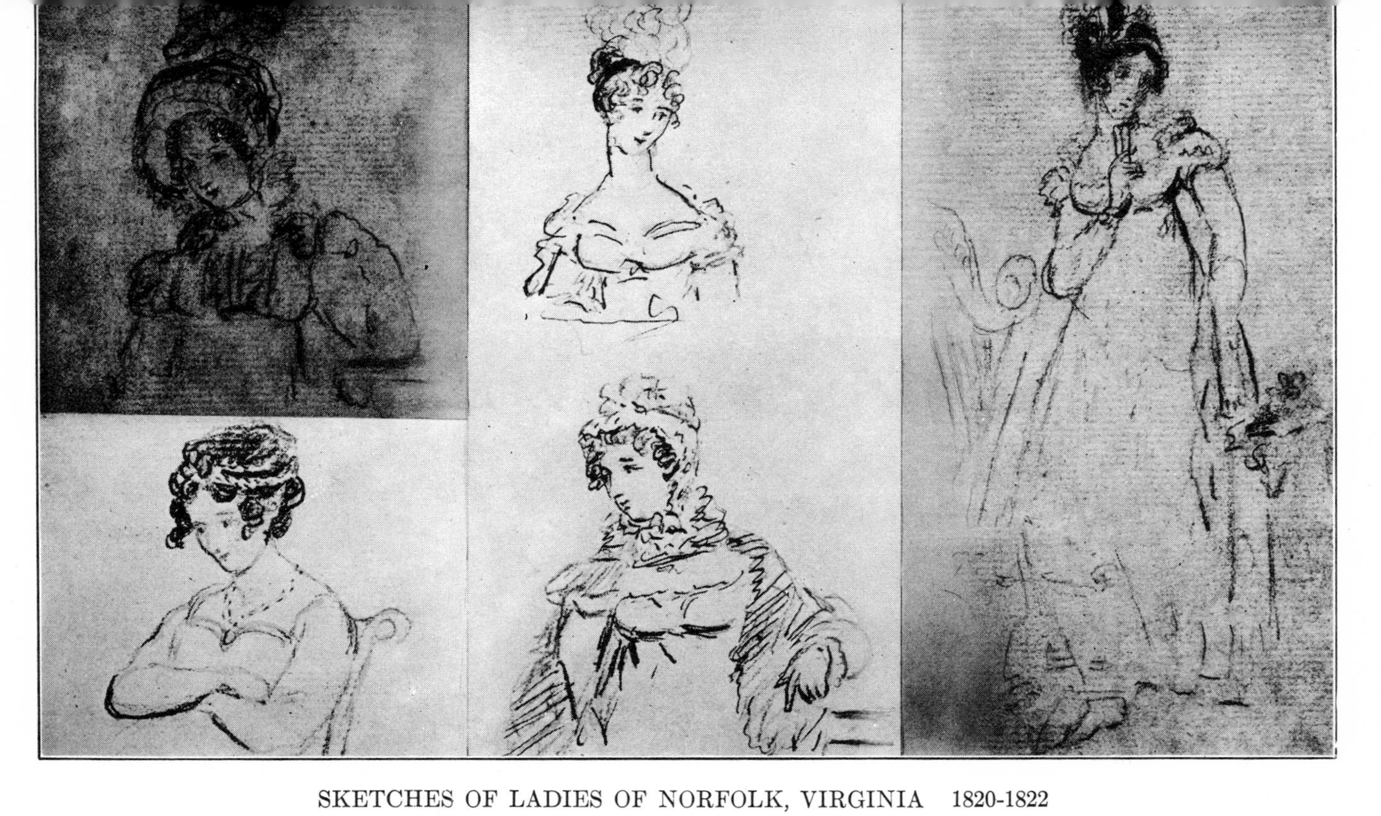

SKETCHES OF LADIES OF NORFOLK, VIRGINIA 1820-1822

By William Dunlap

(In Dunlap's manuscript *Memoirs 26,* in the Library of Yale University)

1822 Jan^y		
1st	Freight of frames.	6.75
	postage	.25
2^d	D°	.25
7th	Washing	2.
14th	postage	.50
	D° & Frank	.50
15th	postage	.25
17th	D°	.50
19th	Board 2 weeks to to morrow	12.
21st	Green for Wattles board in full......	4.
	Postage	.25
29th	Paper, Postage, Shoes	3.50
31st	Sent to my wife..	40.
	Discount on money .25 postage .50....	.75
Feb^y		
2^d	Wood, Cart^g Sawing &c	2.25
	Mending boots 12½ Shoes 2.50	2.62½
		178.93
	Sent home	60

My Expences & Expences of p[ainting] Room 118.93
Rec^d & to be received on account for 386.62

[Balance] 267.69

15th	Exhibition	1.
16th	D°	.75
17th	D°	1.25
18th	D°	1.75
19th	D°	1.50
21st	D°	.25
22^d	D°	1.25
	Messrs Shiels Ashburn & Shiels 3 portraits (for which I am to receive in payment printing in Bills, advertisem^ts & pamphlets)	75.
	W. Shiels portrait p^d...	25.
[Jan.]		
23^d	Exhibition	3.50
24th	D°	1.
25th	D°	.25
26th	D°	2.12½
28th	D°	1.
	Major Cooper a portrait	40.
29th	Exhibition	.50
31st	D°	2.
Feb^y		
1st	....	1.75
2^d	....	.75
4th	....	1.25
		386.62

Dr Painting in Norfolk 1821-2 Cr

1822 Feb^y		
5th	Washing	2.
12th	postage .25 Washing &c 1.12½	1.37½
Mar		
12th	Journey up James River	24.75

	By Balance	267.69
Feb^y		
5th	Exhibition	2.
7th	D°	.25
8th	D°	.25
9th	D°	1.75
12th	D°	2.50
13th	D°	2.50

12th postage & Draymen .... .75
Sent to my Wife..100
& D. Gillespie 80 180.
Gum mastic & Sponge .... .50
15th postage .25
Green for Cloths. 10.75
28th Wash^g 2.2
Ap^l
3^dt Sully for Canvass. 45.
Lucas for Lamps. 35.
9 Staples &c for Ch: Rej^d .... 1.
Freight of Lamps &c .... 1.
12 Gilding .... 3.
22 Screws &c. 62½
Stove pipe 6.50.. 7.12½
Frames (Earle) . 150.
Green Baize .... 10.
Sending Douthats pictures off .... .25
27 My Wife 75
D Gillespie 50 .. 125.
Baize 2.50 Spikes .50 .... 3.
postage &c .... .50
31 Washing .... 2.
May
5th Baize 4.37½
Sund^s 4.25 .... 7.62½
printing .... 75.
10th Sundries for Exh^n. 4.37½
Maj^r Cooper to 2^d May .... 42.
D^o D^o .... 40.
20th Shoes & Vermillion &c 6.50
25th Washing 2.50
postage &c .50.. 3.
Cylender for Christ's first teach^g 2.50
27 Trousers & stockings .... 4.

14th D^o 5.00
From Thos Marshall .... 60.
Robt Douthat ... 180.
Mar.
13th Exhibition .... .25
14th D^o 1.50
28th Mr Baker of Suffolk p^d .... 50.
Exhibition 1.75
Williamson for Spencer .... 5.
p^d Mr Baker engages a frame ... 16.
(p^d 10 & 6)
Williamson frame for Dr B .... 15.
p^d Mr Hall portrait .... 25.
(p^d 10 & 15)
(and 25 to be taken in Books)
Exhibition .... .25
p^d R Douthat
4 portraits & 6 frames .... 270.
Ap^l
20th T. Moran
a portrait p^d .... 50.
22 Ham: Shiels D^o.. p^d 25.
27 (Exhibition has yielded to this time $46)
May
25 Exhibition of Christ Rejected from 1st of May. 67.87½
Mr E Low a frame .... 15.
p^d Mrs Crocker's portrait .... 40.
p^d frame .... 16.

1120.56½

31st	Frames 28$ & Sundries .50	28.50	Frame Major Cooper.	16.
			2 do Williamson ..	36.
		818.50		1172.56½
1822 June				
1st	packing Boxes ...	7.25	1172.56	
	printing	25.50	1003.65	
	Hams	24.40	168.91	
	Owens for Candles	2.50	115	
	Drays &c. .50			
	Rent 150	150.50		283.91
		1028.65	Mr Taylor 100	
	Rent unpd	25.	Low 15	
		1003.65	Garrison ... 5	
			Moran 1	
				121.
				162.

Dr T[homas] W[illiamson] Cr

Dr		Cr	
Cash Apl 1st 1821.......	25.	Cash	176.
Do Johns Exps	94.78	Rent from Jany 1821 to July 1822	150.
Mrs Ws picture	50.		326.
Frame	15.		
Dr Barauds Do	50.		
Frame	15.		
portt Spencer	5.		
Frame for John's Copy of [illegible]	10.		
Frame for the Sketch of Christ rejected	25.		
Frame for W Ds portrait.	11.		
Balance	25.22		
	326.		

Recd Norfolk April 6th 1821 from Willm Dunlap Fifteen dollars in full of all demands whatsoever up to this date.

$15. Joseph Orsborn

[On a separate sheet laid between two leaves is the following receipt:]

Norfolk April 2, 1821. Received of Mr Wm Dunlap Twenty five dollars for One Quarters Rent of the Exhibition Room due 31st Ulto

Thom Williamson

COLLECTIONS OF

THE NEW YORK HISTORICAL SOCIETY

FOR THE YEAR 1931

THE JOHN WATTS DePEYSTER
PUBLICATION FUND SERIES

LXIV

WILLIAM DUNLAP (1766-1839)
PAINTED IN 1838 BY CHARLES C. INGHAM
(Courtesy of the National Academy of Design)

DIARY OF
WILLIAM DUNLAP

(1766–1839)

THE MEMOIRS OF A DRAMATIST,
THEATRICAL MANAGER, PAINTER,
CRITIC, NOVELIST, AND HISTORIAN

VOLUME III

MARCH 16, 1832 – DECEMBER 31, 1834

INDEX TO VOLUMES I – III

CONTENTS

ILLUSTRATIONS

DIARY OF WILLIAM DUNLAP

MARCH 16, 1832—JUNE 25, 1833

NEW YORK AND PHILADELPHIA

(Manuscript volume owned by YALE UNIVERSITY LIBRARY)

Journal or Memoranda of Daily Occurences by W Dunlap

March 16th 1832. The last book similar to this concludes at the 8th inst. I have continued to Lecture. on ye 13th an Audience more than usually numerous. Dr Lyel & Revd Mr Clark [107] expressed great satisfaction on hearing my Lecture on my picture of Christ Rejected. last evg lectured on histy of ye Fine Arts. Write on Lecture upon the Bearing of the Cross. The Harpers sent a supscription paper headed by a prospectus for my Histy of Theatre. Last night Sketch Club resolved to publish an Annual. Painting on second portraits of Mr & Mrs Benninger. Begin a Holy Family on the design suggested by Michl Angelo's unfinished Alto Relievo.

Saturday [March] 17th Violent Rain. Write. Then Lecture on Bearing of ye Cross at 1 OClock. Violent rain all day. Evg Snow Storm. Lecture.

Sunday 18th ground cover'd with snow. Ther: 31 in ye usual place in my house. Write on hist. of Theatre.

Monday 19th Clear. Very cold. Th: 28. Call on Messrs. Harpers & receive printed propls histy of Th: Send some abroad. Write.

Tuesday 20th Milder. Evg Bryants Lecture (last evg) this evg I lecture on Death on ye pale Horse.

Wedy 21st I had last evening a numerous Audience to my Lecture. Weather is wet. Paint & write. Dine at W W Woolsey's.

[107] Rev. Thomas Lyell, D. D., and Rev. John A. Clark were ministers of Christ Church, New York City.

Thursday 22^{d} Hard frost. Ther: in ye house 34.

Friday 23^{d} Mild. Paint. Write on Lecture for the picture of Calvary. Thursday's Lecture was well attended, Some of the Clergy visit me.

Saturday 24th Mild. Write on Lecture for ye Calvary. Ev^{g} Lecture on Bearing of ye Cross to a full room.

Sunday March 25, 1832. Mild. Write on Lecture for ye Calvary. Walk over the town of Brooklyn. Evening at Mr [William T.] McCouns.

Monday 26th Finish my Lecture on Calvary. It is a hard rain but mild temperature. Yesterday I fell in with Wood the former Manager & still actor of Phil^{a}. He promises me notes for my History of Am: Th: His son is now Editor of the C-[illegible] Courier. Warren is at Baltimore dying in poverty. Wood joined Wignel about 1797.

Tuesday [March] 27th fine day. Ev^{g} Lectured on the Calvary to a full room.

Wed^{y} 28th Fine day. Yesterday McGavin with me wishing to join in an exhibition. Go to Brooklyn to see his new bought and mended pictures. It wont do. Paint. Think of Lecturing on my pictures in the Lecture Room of the Mercantil Ass^{n}

Thursday 29th Fine day. Wm Shaw Botanic Garden asks a subscription paper for Hist. T[heatre]. Go to Niblo's. he could not be spoken to as he was at Breakfast. The Harpers have done nothing with the proposals.

Thursday. [*sic*] Pleasant. Lecture in y^{e} evening to a large Audience. Note for 75 protested through inadvertence & no notice from Bank. Get the expence remitted & deposit note for 50 dated 29th for 60 days to be paid when due. Deposit $23. Have in Bank now $22.

Tuesday April 3^{d} 1832. After some windy days we have to day hard rain. I have painted steadily. Afternoon cold wind. Clear. rain. Ev^{g} Clear & cold. Lecture on Bearing of the Cross.

Wed^{y} Ap^{l} 4th Hard Frost. Write on Hist^{y} Th:

Thurs^{y} 5th Ice. McGavin anxious to open Bowen's building as an Exh^{n} Go with him. He can have the upper story for $300. Will give me a painting Room if I will exhibit my large pictures successively in y^{e} Gallery & lecture on each, taking half receits each lecture.

Friday 6 April 1832. Ice still. Lectured last night. Yesterday painted. Paint to day & write on Hist^{y} Th: Ev^{g} attend Nat^{l} Acad^{y}.

Sat^{y} Ap^{l} 7th No Ice. White frost. Write on Hist^{y} of Th: Evening Lecture. Sands tells me that he, Bryant, Leggett, Paulding, Miss Sedgwick & others are to publish a volume of tales.[108] Paulding is engaged on another Novel.

Sunday 8th Paint. Write. Still cold. Ev^{g} W. W. W.

Monday 9th Hard frost. Water freezing in ye streets at 8 OClock. Paint. Write. Ev^{g} Nat^{l} Acad^{y}.

Tuesday [April] 10th No ice but piercing Cold. I would to day see Paulding, the Harpers, Sands. I would write on the addition to American Company bro^{t} from Boston, Johnson & wife, Tyler & wife, Jefferson, Mrs Buel & Bell her daughter. Paulding was engaged. The Harpers have done nothing & it appears only mean to publish when the list of subscribers is full without any intention of exertion to help me, as professed. Dr [Hugh] McLean only procures 8 exclusive of himself. Write on however. Ev^{g} Lecture receits 5 dollars. Weather moderates.

108 *Tales of the Glauber Spa,* published by J. and J. Harper, N. Y., 1832, two volumes. The contributors were Robert C. Sands, William Cullen Bryant, William Leggett, James Kirke Paulding, and Catherine Maria Sedgwick.

Wed[y] [April] 11th Still cold enough to require cloak. See Dr [John W.] Francis by appointment respecting Hist[l] Society for my work. Pay 75 cents freight & porterage for pictures from Boston, for the Nat[l] Acad[y]. Meet Paulding & receive apologies for not seeing me yesterday, professions & offers of Am[n] plays. Looking in Hist[l] Soc: No Boston papers. Find N. Y. Mag. with Th: Register. [two words illegible] Mirror of Taste. Weather becomes warmer.

Thursday [April] 12th Th: 55. Rec[d] yesterday a letter from Rob[t] Gilmor Esq. Baltimore saying he had put my proposals in y[e] hands of Booksellers but the Theatre has lost its interest with the public & many people abandon it altogether. Letter from Wm B Wood saying he is collecting materials for me & will send or hand them to me with all speed. Pay freight & cartage to day for Nat[l] Acad[y] $1.75. Afternoon at Hist[l] Society. Evening Lecture & then Sketch Club. Advertise to day to close my exh[n] on Saturday 21st.

Friday April 13th 1832. Th:60. Dry weather. Rec[d] the following

> "I dont know what arrangem[ts] the editor has made respecting the Article on Theatres but have forwarded him your letter & have no doubt he will be much pleased to be favoured with one from you. He will write you & will answer all your enquiries.
> D[r] Sir I am very respectfully
> H. C. Carey

Rec[d] from Jacob Benninger $50 the balance due me for portraits. He says he will have his & wifes. Paint & write. Ev[g] S. M. Hopkins' wife, daughter, B W Rogers, Arch[d] Rogers & Wife, W W W's daughters with us. Ther: 70

Sat[y] 14th. Th: 64. In my work shop before the clock strikes 6. Pay Jno. Allen 87.50 for rent due 1st Feb[y]. Afternoon sultry. Ev[g] Thunder, rain & cold wind. No Lecture.

Sunday Ap^{l} 15th 1832. Paint. Write. Cold & windy.

Monday, 16th Cold rain. Paint & Write. Attend Council meeting but ye violent Storm prevents a quorum.

Tuesday 17th Storm continues. Th: 44. Receive letter from Williamson, from Darley, from Wood, very friendly and requesting queries which he will answer. Paint. No Lecture.

Wed^{y} 18th Cold Storm continues. When I look over my Journals what a retrospect does it give. Oh God! may it operate on my thoughts on my conduct. May I love thee & thy creatures more & think less of myself! O help! help us God of Mercy! Support me in the struggles I have to go through! Help by thy influence to keep my mind on thee!

Thursday [April 19] The rain has ceas'd, the cold continues. No council meeting yesterday ev^{g}. Ev^{g} look'd over old letters preparatory to writing to day. Paint to day & write. Ev^{g} S. Club at Remb^{t} Peale's. Rain.

Friday April 20th 1832. Still cold & showery. Write. Evening Council of N. A.

Saturday 21st At length we see the Sun. Still cold. Write to W B Wood. Write on Hist^{y} Th: deliver lecture in the ev^{g} as the closing. Rec^{d} from Jany 23 to April 21st $258.75.

Sunday April 22^{d} 1832. Write on Hist: Th: Still cold but clear. Have my five large pictures taken down & rolled up. Afternoon walk. Ev^{g} at Dr M[artyn] Paine's.

Monday 23^{d} Still cold. Write on Hist: Th: Paint. For the two Academies see E. Post 1828 July 2^{d}, 14th, June 21st, 14th, & May 17th. American June 4th.

Tuesday 24th Pleasant Write on Hist: Th: Paint on Holy Family. Geo. Bowen proposes that I take the Exhibition Room or Upper Story of his house corner of Broad Way & Anthony street. We agree to share profits; Write the particulars of Agreement. Receive letter from W. B. Wood answering queries.

Wedy April 25th 1832. Receive Bowen's assent to the written agreement, with a trifling modification respecting the expence of preparing the room for Exhibition. Write on Hist: Th: Paint.

Thursday 26th warm. Write to W B Wood. Queries etc. Paulding. Mrs Powel. Give Mr Peter Alair a subscription paper at his request (with Wm Shaws name)

[April] 27th Quite warm. Write Attend to moving pictures receive a very pleasant letter from James F. Cooper.

Saturday 28th It rain'd last night & it is cold with a high easterly wind this morning. Write & attend to moving.

Sunday April 29th Cold. Rain. Write. Let me remember to look in Minerva of 1798 for acct of Gardie & wife July 21st & 31 the opening of Boston Theatre: Sept. 20 Character of E H Smith. Look to Minerva of Fall of 1797 for close of ye 2 Theatres in New York. To look in [Alexander] Wilson's Ornithology for Butcher bird, Lanius Cinereus Shrike. To request Wood to try for a copy of Contract.

Tuesday morning ½ past 5 at Clinton Hall [109] as usual. Still wet & cold. Yesterday moving to 6th Avenue from Leonard Street. Last evg Council meeting. Get my family removed to No 64 Sixth Avenue [110] by noon on this

[109] Clinton Hall, built 1829-30, on the southwest corner of Nassau and Beekman Streets, was occupied until 1854 by the Mercantile Library Association. Stokes, *Iconography of Manhattan Island,* III, 956.

[110] No. 64 Sixth Avenue was between Waverly and Washington Places. Dunlap's Leonard Street home was between Church Street and West Broadway (then called Chapel Street).

first of May 1832 after living in Leonard Street No 55 for 16 years. Clears off warm. Costs me to move $10. Receive from old Mr Benninger $100 for the second pair of portraits. Deposit $100 draw 15. In bank $105. Evening in 6th Avenue.

Wednesday May 2[d] 1832. Clear & cool. Up before 5 & walk out of town. At 8 at Clinton Hall writing. Home at 3. afternoon call on Hilson. Ev[g] Annual meeting of Nat[l] Acad[y], reelect officers &c.

Thursday May 3[d] Preparing to Exhibit at corner of Anthony St[t] & Br[d] Way. To be called Museum of paintings. McGavin hires the use of part of y[e] room for a sale of pictures for 2 weeks for $30.

Friday [May] 4th Paint. write. attend to Exh[n]

Sat[y] [May] 5th Write. Attend to Exh[n]. See Mr Harper on y[e] subject of y[e] publication & understand that they will deliver the copies subscribed for to me or on my order & I am to receive the mony therefor—they further remunerating me if the work sells well—they talk of an edition of 1500. They want the work out.

Sunday 6th clear, cold. Writing at 5 OClock. Painting at 9. Writing at 2 P. M. This afternoon 2 of the clerks of Phelps & Co. were buried, they & many others being crushed to death on friday evening by the fall of a 6 story store in which they were employed.

Monday May 7th 1832. Clear & cold. Write. Attend to Exh[n]. Afternoon write. Ev[g] Attend Council meeting. Every visit to Clinton Hall makes me 3 miles walk.

Tuesday [May] 8th Clear & cold. Go to Market. Write. Paint.

Wed[y] 9th After a rain warm. Occupied as yesterday.

Thursday 10th Clear & cool morning writing after going to market at ¼ past 5. Write to J. K. Paulding. To look in Monthly Review of October 1798 for notices of Tell truth, Archers & Edwin & Angelina. Begin to hang pictures for N. A.

Friday 11th Clear & cool. Have in Bank $5. Paint and write.

Saty 12th Clear & Cool morning, warm noon. Paint. move my painting materials to Broadway & Anthony St. Write.

Sunday 13th Writing. Reading Bulwar's Eugene Aram.

Monday 14th Writing. Attend at Clinton Hall.

Tuesday 15th Writing. Attend to pictures &c. My note for 150 dated 31st May is indorsed by W W Woolsey in readiness to take up the note for 50 indorsed by T Callender & leave funds until I receive from my literary labour. Give extracts to the Mirror. I have in Bank now $77.

Wedy 16th Write. G Bowen having let the room under that I am preparing for an Exhibition room (& which he asserted should only be let for quiet & reputable purposes, instancing reading room, or place of deposit for Harpsichords &c) to a man for Exhibiting an Ourang Outang, I suspend my Exhibition.

Thursday 17th May. Warm & pleasant. Write. Gave to [George P.] Morris & [Theodore S.] Fay of the Mirror, some extracts from the Hist: &c. Evg at N. A. & Macgavins sale of pictures. Received Letter from J. K. Paulding.

"N. Y. 15th May 1832

Dear Sir

"It certainly is an unpleasant business to collect subscribers but you must employ some person who understands such matters and I am in hopes you will not have any trouble in the sequel. I advised you to accept of these terms because I believed them on the whole to be better than you would get elsewhere in these times when there is considerable falling off in the trade. And as you had already so far advanced in your work it would have been a pity to lose the reward of your labours entirely. By this arrangement the publishers in fact take the risk of publication allowing you the entire proceeds of the subscription should they not exceed 500 dollars. And though I fully believe this risk is not great; Yet it is impossible to say (see) the fate of the work on a subject of this kind. The whole arrangement was intended to be highly friendly to you and is an exception to their to their [*sic*] general mode of doing business, which is never to publish a work, nor contract for its publication until the work is compleated and has undergone an examination.

I am Der Sir Yours truly

J. K. Paulding

Friday [May] 18th Rain.

Zsokke [111] is a native of Magdeburg early left an orphan, educated by relations "a very unhappy unloved & therefor unloving boy." In crossing the Alps in order to visit Italy (in early manhood) being accidentally detained, he was perswaded to abandon his Italian scheme (whatever it was) and take charge of a school. Having brought this school from a deplorable state into a flourishing condition he was rewarded with the honour of Citizenship. His peaceful & usefull life was interrupted by the French invasion and making himself useful to his adopted fellow Citizens, he was employed by several of the Swiss Cantons in Administrative offices but finally withdrew from public life, married & commenced Author & editor of a Newspaper. He wrote Abaellino upwards of 40 years ago. His principal works are Novels which have been very popular.

Saty 19th May 1832. Write a note to Geo. Bowen respecting the Exhn Room which was not to [be] impeded by other exhibitions & is now render'd useless by the letting the lower room, same entrance to a man with an Orang-outang. See Bowen who agrees to my wishes & I purpose arrangeing Exhn but not opening until free from *other shows*. Eveng Rain. Send letter to W B Wood.

Sunday 20th Rain. Note to ask Wood respecting the play of a Wedding in Wales by Doctor [112] [blank] play'd in Phila in 1799.

Monday 21st Exhn of N. A. Opens. A Fine display. Cool & much company. Write.

111 Johann Heinrich Daniel Zschokke (1771-1848), author of the novel *Abällino der Grosse Bandit,* which he dramatized, and which Dunlap translated. O. S. Coad, *William Dunlap,* 239, 292.

112 By Thomas Stock. Wegelin, *Early American Plays.*

Wed^{y} 23rd May 1832. Cloudy & cold. Write. I am preparing for Exhibition in Broadway but wait until the place is clear.

24th Cold rain. Storm. Write. Mem: to look for Th: in Mercantile Advertiser of Augt 1801, & to look for a Critique written by P. Irving about 1st April 1802.

Friday 25th The rain is over. It is still cold. I am dress'd in my winter clothing & fire is necessary. Write. See Morning Chronicle of 24 or 25th Novr 1802. See Ev^{g} Post of Novr 26 or 27th 1802. Call on Washington Irving he was out. J Kent on the same errand.

Sat^{y} 26th Clear and Cold. In bank 57 dollars. Rain all night.

Sunday [May] 27th Cloudy & cold. Write. Walk for exercise.

Monday 28th Clear. Ther: 60 at noon. Write & look over newspapers.

Tuesday 29th Clear. Pleasant. Write & walk. Up every morning at & before 5.

Wed^{y} 30th rain last night. Clear & pleasant. Offer my note for $150 indorsed by W W Woolsey to the Bank of New York. Write. Evening at [John] Barne's Theatre sometimes call'd Richmond Hill. The house was formerly the country residence of [blank] & since of Aaron Burr. it was on a hill & is now lower'd to the level of the City plan. Wilson play'd Hastings Mrs Barnes Jane Shore Mrs Green (is it W Green's wife Miss Wilelms) Alicia. None good but Mrs Barnes.

Thursday [May] 31st rain again & cold still. Write.

Sunday June 3^{d} 1832. Yesterday was Warm a part of the day, but now it is cold & cloudy again. I have been some days looking over files of Newspapers. My work on Th: is almost written.

Monday 4th Cloudy & cold. Write.

Tuesday 5th rain & cold. Write, the last of the Hist^{y} of y^{e} American Theatre. My note with W W Woolseys endorsement done for $150 dated May 31st

57
150
———
207 deduct Note for 50 and 20 drawn out
70
———
$137 perhaps 135 in bank this day.

Wed^{y} 6th June 1832. Cloudy & cold. Fires are needed to y^{e} sedentary.

Sunday [June] 10th Rain. I am bow'd down & humbled by an affliction almost beyond bearing. Has not my own conduct been the cause? May God forgive! May my mind be purified by the thoughts this blow has suggested & may I henceforward do the will of that God who has decreed that all error must cause sorrow. I may have been the cause unknowingly of this misery, but there are two beings suffering with me who are free from any act or thought connected with that which overwhelms us. How is this?

Monday 11th Endeavor to attend to business leave Manuscript with the Harpers.

Tuesday June 12th 1832. Thank God we are relieved from a dreadfull State of uncertainty & anxiety.

My Gallery of paintings is now ready only awaiting Gas lights. Write. A warm day. Ther: 80.

Wed^{y} 13th Again cool & windy. I am to copy in large a Miniature of Genl Santandor for Mr Castillo

Friday [June] 15th Paint yesterday & to day. Write. Receive a very pleasant letter from Mr [James Nelson]

Barker of Philadelphia giving an account of his Dramatic Works, & one to day from the veteran Matthew Carey ordering 12 Copies of my Hist: of A: Th: It has been warm to day Ther: 78; and now ev^{g} Rains.

Sat^{y} 16th Ther: 3 P. M. 84. Paint & write to day. In Bank, according to their acc^{t} $137.20 draw out to day 20 leav^{g} 117.20, according to my acc^{t} less

Mond[a]y 18th Ther: 82 <*falls to 70*> Paint & write. Attend to getting up Exh^{n}. Great alarm from anticipated appearance of Cholera.

Tuesday 19th Ther: falls to 70. Attend Council. Receits of Exh^{n} N. Acad^{y} to this time 700. All paid out & a debt of $1000 left. Harpers have begun my book.

Wed^{y} 20th Ther: 68. Paint & write.

Thursd^{y} [June] 21st Ther: [blank] Preparing for Exh^{n} Rec^{d} the following.

Wm Dunlap Esqre
My dear Sir

Yours of yesterday is before me with the receit for 18 dollars for which am^{t} I in[close] a check on the Penn: Bank.

It affords me a high gratification to furnish this small accommodation to a gentleman who has devoted so much of his time to literary <*pursuits*> objects with the too frequent barren result.

I have been myself a sort of Devotee to literary pursuits. I have labour'd hard for the public & "worked for nothing & paid myself." I have been in the Vineyard for 53 years, and never wrote a line with a view to profit although some very few of my productions were slightly profitable. I have written as much as would fill 20 or 25 octavo volumes, such as they print in London. On the single subject of political oeconomy I have written above 2000 pages, two thirds of which were given away gratuitously at my own expense.

I shall try to induce my sons to subscribe for some of your books.

Remember I consider you bound to send my books among the first that are despatched for this place.

Yours very respectfully
Matthew Carey

Philad^{a} June 19th 1832.

Draw from Bank 16.74 leaving say $100.

Friday June 22[d] 1832. In Bank $98. Ther: 76. Dr Hosack sends me letters respecting Holman: & directs his name for 6 Copies of my Work.

Sat[y] June 23[d] Ther: 78. Getting ready Exh[n] Write.

Sunday 24th Write. Paint on Miniature of Santandor

Thursday 28th It has been very warm for two days Ther: 80 to 84. Paid Jno Allen 50 dollars on acc[t] of Rent. In Bank 48 doll[s]. Exh[n] open 4 days—2.37½, 2.25, 7.12½ & 4 dollars.

Sunday July 1st 1832. Friday exh[n] yielded 5 & Sat[y] 6.25. Ther: This 2 days 74. This morning walked out to Cato's.[113] Correcting 1st proof of Theat[l] Hist[y]. Ther: rises to 80.

[July] 2[d] Ther: 85. We are told by authority that the Eastern Cholera is in our City. 14 Cases yesterday & to day to 1 OClock & of them 11 deaths—a terrible proportion. We have been preparing for the enemy, but we are not prepared.

[July] 3[d] Ther: 85. The 14 cases of Asiatic Cholera in one day are reduced to 14 cases of various disorders in 10 days & doubts of any Asiatic malady, but alarm has spread & the town injured.

[July] 4th No Cholera. Little spirit for celebration. Ther: 82. Write on Hist: Th: Read Colly Cibber who had been almost forgotten.

[July] 7th Ther: 76. The cases of Cholera increased on the 4th 5th & 6th Yesterday 37 reported, 19 deaths. Generally understood that the sufferrers are imprudent or intemperate persons. The number of deaths in the City

113 Cato's Tavern, East 54th Street, east of Second Avenue. Stokes, *Iconography of Manhattan Island,* III, 977.

is less than usual at this time of the year. Business is much suspended & many hundreds have left the City. The same disease is at Albany. I am engaged in making a Catalogue of American plays & Dramatists for my History.

[July] 9th Monday. The alarm of Cholera continues, business at a stand. I believe if the minds of men had not been prepared by the accounts first from Europe & Asia & then from Canada that the disease as now existing here would not have been noticed. Report of Board of Health, in private practise 18 cases in 24 hours & 4 deaths, in hospitals 10 deaths and in the Alms house Bellevue a greater number of cases & deaths.

July 10th rain. Cool. My exhn good for nothing. My book dragging slowly.

Thursday 12th July 1832. Ther: 67 & out doors 62. There has been hard rain. Last report of what is call[ed] Cholera in 24 hours 35 cases private practice 6 deaths, Hospitals 30 Cases 10 deaths, Bellevue (Alms house) 53 cases 25 deaths. Many leave the City & stranger[s] avoid it.

Friday 13th Ther: 58. Clear. Report 27, 10 private practice, C. Hospitals 39—22, Bellevue 35—17, in all 101 cases 49 deaths in 24 hours. Read "Count Robert of Paris" [114] what a falling off is here!

Saty 14th Ther: 68. Clear. Report 43 new cases 15 deaths in private practice, 43—29 Hosp: 29—22 Bellevue. Business stoped. The weather & every appearance of Nature beautiful

Tuesday [July] 17th Ther: 72. Sunday the Cholera acct stood 133 new cases 84 deaths, Monday 163 new cases 94 deaths. of course more panic. I began on Saty

[114] A novel by Sir Walter Scott, published in 1831.

two portraits for Sidney & Gilbert McCoun, long since paid for, & my prospects are very gloomy for the means of subsistence. I hear nothing from the Harpers. Nothing from Exh[n]. To day Tuesday the acc[t] is more favourable stand 66—19: 63—18: 22—13 or 145 new case[s] and 50 deaths. The Harpers send me proof sheets.

Wed[y] 18th Cholera acc[t] stands 118 new case[s] 58 deaths.

Thursday [July] 19th I go daily down to the corner of Anthony street & Broad Way & paint or transact other business, but no business is to be expected as the Citizens are removing daily & strangers shun the infected place. I feel thankful that my family were removed from Leonard Street to this open & clean place. In the house I left three or four cases of cholera are reported and two deaths. The report made to day is in the City 114 new cases and 42 deaths, Hospitals 77 new cases 28 deaths, Alms house (Bellevue) 11 new cases 12 deaths. Total cas[es] in 24 hours 202. Deaths 82. And it is known that several physicians do not report. Francis (who brought me the stomach of a Cholera patient in his pocket wishing me to make a drawing of it) says he does not report. This pestilence or infected atmosphere, is a most incomprehensible affair. One thing is plain the greater number of victims are the vicious the dirty the depraved—and the places where death is most rife are the low grounds once water, marsh & swamp—the houses crowded filthy receptacles of the unhappy people above noticed. Read A Russian Gil Blas by [blank]

Sat[y] July 21st 1832. Yesterday Ther: 78 at noon. To day 76 at 5 OClock A. M. Yesterday C. Cases reported 132 in private practice in y[e] City & 48 deaths. Hospitals 56 & 36. Bellevue 28 & 10. total 216 new cases in 24 hours & 94 deaths. In addition 10 cases & 6 deaths at Yorkville 5 miles on the Haerlem road. Thus the mortality encreases although the diminution of people is very great by death & flight.

Sunday morning cool & pleasant. The report of Yesterday makes a total of 311 new cases & 104 deaths. In the City 191—61: Park Hospital 22—8: Greenwich Hosp: 22—8: Crosby St^t Hosp: 12—4: Rivington St^t Hosp: 10—6; Corlears Hook 5—3: Belvue 20—10: Yorkville & Harlaem 29—4. Ther: 73. I have neglected to answer the following letter

Paris March 16th 1832

Dr Sir

I got both your letters[115] and this last. The death of a Nephew who had lived with me for several years, a greater press of business than common and other causes that I need not mention have prevented my writing many letters this winter. You have been often in mind and often in our mouths notwithstanding.

As to the group[116] I should be glad to comply with your request but it is altogether in the hands of Mr Greenough and I had hoped it was already at Washington for I have been stirring all my interest at home, which I fear is not much however, to obtain him an order from Government. My attacks are pretty direct being on the president and secretaries. We may succeed if we can keep off the Quacks. I have not seen your resolution of thanks to which you allude, and consequently can not yet know your opinion of the Cherubs themselves. If you have thanked the Artist you must of course think well of them.

As to what you say of my pen belonging to mankind it is very flattering coming from an honest man and an able man but I am greatly afraid the opinion is pretty nearly limitted to two or three of us. I know not why it is so, but all that I see and hear gives me reason to believe that there is a great falling off in popular favour at home. I rarely see my name mentioned even with respect in any American publication, and in some I see it coupled with impertinences that I cannot think the writers would indulge in were I at home though their insignificance would in truth be their shield, were I at their elbow. There may be better writers than I in the country, but there is certainly no one treated with so little deference. It is no crime not to be the best, in or out of the country, and as I commonly support sound political doctrines and always good I can claim to be alluded to as not disgracing the attic excellence of American Literature. I ask no puffs—they disgust me, but for God's sake let me have not deprecatory praise & pealing censure. But I sicken of the subject & sometime of—I will not finish the sentence.

115 Dunlap's letters to Cooper, dated September 20, 1831, and January 30, 1832, are printed in *Correspondence of James Fenimore-Cooper*, (Yale University Press, 1922), I, 240-45, 258-59.

116 Two cherubs, sculptured in marble by Horatio Greenough at Cooper's commission. Dunlap, *Arts of Design* (1834), II, 418-422.

If I had seen one frank manly gentlemanly allusion to myself as a writer in a single American publication in five years I would not have thought of it. One fact is beyond dispute—I am not with my own country—the void between us is immense—which is in advance time will show.

We are all well thank God though Mrs Cooper has been seriously ill this winter. We have not much apprehension of cholera, though there is little doubt that it will come here. Should it not come or should it prove light as elsewhere in this part of Europe it is my intention to come home in June without my family, which I shall leave for two years longer. So much, however, depends on the political state of Europe that all these plans may be changed.

You may see by the papers that Gen: Bernard and I (as supporters of La Fayette) have had a controversy with a Mr Saulnier, on the subject of the American Finances. The design of the Ministary was to bring America into discredit all over Europe, and to crush La Fayette. Our first letters stagger'd them—but they came out with an answer that M: Perier proclaim'd at the Tribune to be triumphant. I stepped in promptly and in a few letters demolished all their hopes and cries of victory. More shameless subterfuges never disgraced controversialists and I might add more shameless lying. Bernard stood by me like a man, and he deserves great credit for it, while there are Americans here, who not only aid the Ministers but effect to add weight to their testimony by saying that they have held *Office* at home! I am afraid that some who hold office now are not quite innocent of encouraging the enemy in order to encrease their own importance in the French Saloons. Never was a people more humbugg'd than the American people in this particular. One half of our Agents abroad are scarcely American in feeling. Having now said so much I will add that the Minister[117] here is a tolerable exception, though far from taking the course he sh[d], and that the Consul[118] though much abused, is positively one of the most patriotic men that holds office in Europe. Oh! the volumes that I could write and speak on this head! Well, now I have driven this M: Saulnier into a corner, his American supporters say it is beneath the dignity of a man like me to appear in a Navy paper! My answer to them is contempt, and to all others, that it is below the character of no man to advance the cause of truth.

There was also an awkward affair which grew out of this controversy by M. Cassimir Perier stating at the Tribune that Mr Rives affirmed that M: Saulnier was right; and that M: M: Bernard, La Fayette and Cooper wrong. Now it so happen'd that Mr Rives never said any such thing, and if he had, his opinion was not worth a button, for he knows about as much of Statistics as you do of Hindostanee. Well, there is yet to be some halfway explanations of this

[117] Hon. William Cabell Rives.
[118] Isaac Cox Barnett.

blunder of M. Perier by La Fayette, and God knows what will come of it all. Here have our Ministers in France & England both been quoted in public and [as] no one would dare to quote a Minister of a Hanse Town! So much for the sneaking policy that our people act on abroad. Shades of Jay, and Jefferson be still! I quit the subject in disgust.

You and I, my dear old friend are Artists, and we will turn to the Arts. I have not forgot you as you will soon see, for there are now on the way to your Academy some casts from me. Morse, has in addition, some excellent engravings & books that he has chosen, for though possessing the trifling advantage of a few thousands the most, I am not yet thank Heaven, Ass enough to believe I have the best taste. All the Casts, but the Vase were also chosen by Morse, who is just as good a fellow as there is going. He is painting an Exhibition picture that I feel certain must take. He copies admirably and this is a (picture) drawing of the Louvre with copies of some fifty of its best pictures.

I get up at eight, read the papers, breakfast at ten, sit down to the quill at ½ past ten—work till one—throw off my morning gown, draw on my boots and gloves, take a cane that Horace Greenough gave me, and go to the Louvre, where I find Morse stuck up on a high working stand, perch myself astraddle of one of the seats, and bore him just as I used to bore you when you made the memorable likeness of St Peter. "Lay it on here, Samuel —more yellow—the nose is too short—the eye too small—damn it if I had been a painter what a picture I should have painted."—and all this stuff over again and which Samuel takes just as good-naturedly as good old William. Well there I sit and have sat so often and so long that my face is just as well known as any Vandyke on the walls. Crowds get round the picture, for Samuel has quite made a hit in the Louvre, and I believe that people think that half the merit is mine. So much from keeping company with ones betters. At six we are at home eating a good dinner, and I manage to get a good deal out of Morse in this way too. We had Greenough up here for three months in the Autumn and then we had a good time of it. I have cut all Kings & Princes, go to no great Officers, and jog on this way from the beginning to the end of the month.

My children are good, amiable, and clever—and I may add accomplished. They give us great satisfaction in every respect. Paul is a fine boy, and among his other accomplishments can tell the subject of any statue he sees, and should it be a copy, will discourse you of the original better than half the travelled Monkeys one meets, and that too like a child.

I pick'd up a capital portrait the other day, in the street, of the time of Lewis XIV. It is Flemish, and beyond dispute an original—but of whom? The best account that I can get is that it is a portrait of Teniers wife by Teniers himself. I do not believe it. It is colour'd like Titian with Corregio's delicacy. Really it is exquisite though a little injured. It cost just $5! The honour of purchasing it lies between Samuel and me. The profit is all mine as commonly happens to him who has the most money.

The judges here pronounce Brevoorts Madona a Copy. One says the face is original. I do not believe it a Raphael but I think it a composition *after his manner* and *of his time*, by one of his scholars of great merit. There is a compound of manners & expression in it which I never saw in any original of Raphael. He has however found a picture that I believe to be an early work of Claude. It is a sea-port with some beautiful water, and some damnably rigged ships. But Claude was a Cook and what should a Cook know of the sublime art of a rigger. It took *me* years to get through its mazes with my hands cover'd with tar, instead of paint.

As to politics, nothing is settled in Europe. The Governments have agreed to let each other alone, and the wish and the hope is to cheat the people. This cannot be done long. France is a Volcano, that may break out this week or ten years hence, as it shall happen. Germany is coming on like a Giant & is very likely to do something. La Fayette says, and he is likely to be right, that Perier is pledged to carry France back to the charter of the Restoration, which with a weak Prince is it to carry it to a most vile Aristocracy. My own opinion is that there will be a turn up this summer.

Mrs Cooper unites with me in best regards to Mrs & Miss Dunlap and I desire to be mentioned to my old school-fellow young Dunlap. I believe I have made myself understood about the group. Should they not have other employment for it, take it of God's name.

Adieu, truly yours
J. Fennimore Cooper
Paris March 16, 1832

W. Dunlap Esq[re]

Write me often and depend upon answers written with a better pen. I am like the young man in the French Vaudeville who could never spell with a bad pen."

Report of to day (Sunday July 22[d] 1832) City 154—50, Hospitals 74—34, Yorkville 9—5, Bellevue 2—1. Total new cases 239, deaths 90. (Yesterday total 311 & 104)

Monday 23[d] July 1832. Ther: 74. pleasant. The report to day is City 163—46. Hospitals 42—17. Bellevue 26—10. Total 231—73. Go as usual to my painting room & paint until 1 or 2 P M & then come home. Write on Zeb: Spiff: [119]

[119] Zebediah Spiffard, hero of Dunlap's novel *Thirty Years Ago; or, The Memoirs of a Water Drinker,* printed in 1836.

Tuesday July 24th 1832. Cool & Cloudy. Paint as usual. Report to day 188 City cases 57 deaths, 51—22 Hospitals 22—7 Bellevue 5—1 Yorkville 30—9 Haerlem. Total new cases 295 deaths 96. Ther: afternoon 73. Read in Foreign Review. In respect to Cholera—the experiment injecting salt & water into the blood when the patient is in the last stage has been tried here with success. Camphor given 3 or 4 drops in a dose & repeated at intervals of ½ an hour, & friction meantime is said to be efficacious. A published prescription for an ointment for friction is

1 lb strong Merc: ointt
7 oz Camphor finely powder'd
7 oz Cayenne pepper.

A thick paste to be rubbed with a strong hand over the body.

Wedy [July] 25th Last night violent rain & Thunder. Day clear. Call on Dr McLean as my son has diaroeha. Stay at home. Read & write. Report to day 99—21: 45—32: Bellevue 10—5: Yorkville 3—3. Haerlem not reported. Total new cases 157, deaths 61.

Thursday July 26th Clear & cool. Ther: 72. Attend at corner of Anthony St & paint. Report to day City 75—23: Hospitals 48—21: Bellevue 14—7: Yorkville 2—3. Harlaem 2—1: Total 141—55.

Friday 27th Cool & pleasant. Report 73—23: 46—18: 3—5: Total 122—46. Receive proof of H[istory] T[heatre]

Saty 28th Finish G. McCoun's portrait. John Howard Pain call'd to see me. Report 93—37: 49—36: 1—4. Harlaem 2—1. [James E.] Dekay says he does not report & has not lost a patient. A Young man died with the disease nearly opposite to my house some days ago. Another (R. Bruce) to day after a few hours illness. Ther: 76.

ANTHONY BLEECKER (1770-1827)
By William Dunlap
(Courtesy of The New York Society Library)

Sunday 29th Reading Stones Masonry.[120] The [William] Morgan murder has interested me, perhaps, the more from being in the West when the first excitement occurred & seeing masons who from their words & conduct forced me to believe that they were criminals in ye affair. Stone's book is valuable as an authentic document. Attend the funeral of Bruce. Go by request to see Leslies copy of Hogarths "Gate of Calais" which I remember he sent home some years ago. It is in the hands of a person who bought it of a boy, who purchased it at a sale of pictures for 75 cents, it being without even stretching frame. Write to J. F. Cooper. Finish Stone's book on Masonry. Ther: 75. Report City cases 61 deaths 19. Total 122—39. But the Inspector reports interments of dead by Cholera 85.

Monday July 30th 1832. Last Evg & night rain. As usual at my work. Report City cases 62 deaths 14: Hosp: 35—19. Belvue 3—3. Yorkville 3—3. Total 103—39. But we know all are not reported: and the deaths reported by the Inspector are probably the truth. His amount by Cholera in 24 hours ending 8 this morning is 47 this is to be recd as a real abatement. Harlaem is not reported by the Board of Health & it is understood that the mortality in that village is frightful. Ther: 77. More rain with Thunder.

Tuesday 31st Finish letter to J. F. Cooper & put it in post office. Deposit with J. J. Boyd, Wall Street, Agent for Havre packet 3 first sheets of H of A: Th: directed to Cooper which promises to give to ye Captn of packet sailing tomorrow with request to put it in his Trunk & take it to Paris. The report of to day is City: new cases 59 deaths 23: Hosp: 52—20 Bellevue 1—3 Yorkvill 6—2 Harlaem 3—0. Total 121—58. Read Ct de Gramont.

Augt 1st 1832. Offer B of N. Y. note for 150 with W W W's endorsement to meet one of same. drew out yester-

[120] William L. Stone, *Letters on Masonry and Anti-Masonry*, N. Y., 1832.

day 10$ leaving 38. Correct proofs. Report 47 city practice 13 deaths. 39 Hosp: 24. Yorkv: 4—3. Bellevue 2—1 Total 92—41. Cloudy & some fine rain. Read Write on Zeb. Spiff.

Thursday Aug[t] 2[d] Note done this day. In Bank $26. Attend to business as usual. Report 47—14: 24—17: Bellvue none. Yorkville 10—2. Harlaem no cases, 1 death. Total 81—34. In Phil[a] last report 21 new cases 8 deaths. Dekay says the saline injection is not to be relied on. Small doses of ca[m]phorated Alcohol (3 drops) is good practice. Ther: 78 Reading Chev: de Gramont & Foreign Quarterly. Write on Zeb Spiff.

Friday Aug[t] 3[d] Kept as a Fast by Corporation recommendation. Report 48 cases city practice 14 deaths. Total 90—24. Inspectors reports 33 interm[ts] of Cholera. Ther: 78

Sat[y] [Aug. 4] Clouds rain. Paint. Report City cases 48 deaths 17, Hospitals 35—21: Bellevue 3—1. Yorkville 2—1: Total 90 cases 30 deaths.

Sunday 5th Write on Hist[y] of A. T. and on Zeb Spiff. Report 57 city cases 21 deaths. Total cases 96—29.

Monday Report 60—21: 38—13. Total 98—36.

Tuesday [Aug. 7] Rain & thunder. Report 57—19 City practice 31—12 Hospitals, Bellevue 1. Total 88—31. Read Reviews. Correct proofs & write. Ther: 78. Close & warm. Jno How[d] Payne.

Wed[y] Aug[t] 8th 1832. Wet & warm. Some rain. Read & write always going to Anthony St Corner. Dekay reads me letter from J. Fennimore Cooper. Report 52—12: 39—9: Total 84—21. Afternoon Violent Rain.

[Aug.] 9th Violent rain all night & to this time—Noon. Read in Eng: Annual Register What a dreadful picture of human nature as depraved in society does this book give. What a wretched view of the character of Sir E. Codrington as presented by the Court martial on Captain Dickenson! Read in Reviews. Write on Zeb Spiff. Rain all day. Walk to Harper's in the interval between two showers. Report 41—18: 26—10: Total 67—28.

[Aug.] 10th Clear & pleasant. Joseph Jefferson Comedian dead at Harrisburg pennsylva [blank] 1832. Charles Kemble and his daughter Fanny are announced as engaged by Price for America. Miss Fanny Kemble is the daughter of Miss De Camp. Miss K appear[ed] in 1829 in Juliet her mother playing Lady Capulet (see Ann: Reg: of yt year). This young Lady published a Historical tragedy called Francis 1st of great merit see Quarty Review of 1832. Go to Anthony corner & to Harper's. Report 60—18: 34—7: Yorkvill 3—1: Total 97—26. Interments 34 by cholera.

Saty [Aug.] 11th Clear & Cool. Ther: 72. Report 33—18: 41—15: Yorkvle 2. Total 76 cases 33 deaths. Cholera Intermts 47. Phila 173 cases 47 deaths. I saw to day a portion of a new Novel by Wm Godwin in Manuscript with a letter the last line of which (after expressing ye wish for assistance from the publication in this country) is "a de[s]titute man of letters between 70 & 80 years of age."

Sunday [Aug.] 12th Foggy morning: fine day. Reading Fredk Reynolds' amusing book,[121] to me interesting as of my own time e i 1784 &c in London. See Balloons, Dancing dogs &c The address to the Bath [Theatre] Audience in the Epilogue of Reynolds' Werter. "Who rear'd the tender bud whose dawn now draws on Juliet & Euphrasia just applause." complimentary of Mrs Merry [Vol. I: 182] Doctor Wilson see Reynolds 2d p: 70. Godwin see Reynolds p: 121. 2d Vol: Merry. School for Scandal "I

[121] *The Life and Times of Frederick Reynolds. Written by himself.* (Philadelphia, Carey and Lea, 1826.)

wish &c R: p: 128. Report City practice 33—12. Total 57—23. The story of J. Palmer dying after saying There is another and a better world" is a fiction as asserted by Whitfield see R: p: 146 2^d Vol: Sheridan in altering Kotzebue's Pizzaro Introduced a Comic servant & was obliged to cut him out again. Twistleton see R: p: 156 2^d Vol:

Monday August 13th 1832. Foggy morning. Reynolds relates that Godwin having called on Mrs Inchbald (a visit) left the room soon after H. Siddons, a youth enter'd & she asking him if he knew that the gentleman who had just withdrawn was Mr Godwin "Siddons fell on his knees" & kiss'd the chair which the philosopher had been sitting on; rapturously thanking Heaven that he had seen the Author of the best novel in the English or any other language. Mr Godwin has been a writer & publisher half a century—his benevolence & philanthropy have been all his life conspicuous—his life has been one continued series of attempts to be useful to mankind & an unbroken example of purity—however writes &c (*why* is he poor & destitute?) because he has opposed the Aristocracy & hierarchy of his country & shown the evils of that accursed system which has plunged man blindfold into guilt & misery. He is a reformer without being a demagogue. Let the reformers honour & reward him. Doctor Wilson. In this literary club they had a rule that "every member on publishing a literary composition should give a dozen of claret to the Club." Topham, Merry, Morton, Rogers, Reynolds, Andrews regularly paid the fine, but "the choice spirits of the club" to use R's words asserted that Wilson should pay the penalty for an Advertisement announcing the commencement of his Course of Lectures & by a majority of votes it was decided that the advertisement was a literary composition & the unwilling Author was author was co[m]pelled to pay the fine.

Merry On the first night of the school for scandal said "I wish the *dramatis personæ* would leave off talking &

let the play begin." Report 63 cases in city practice 16 deaths. Hospitals 41—7, 1—1. Total 105—24.

Tuesday [Aug.] 14th Very Warm Th: 81. Paint. Report 18—8: 24—7: Total 42—15: Ints 33 Phila 130—49.

Wedy [Aug.] 15th Very warm. Th: 83. Write at Anthony corner. Report 33—14: 29—8: Yorkvill 13—4. Total 75—26. Ints 27. Phila cases 111.

Thursday [Aug.] 16th Very warm. Changes. Correct proof. Report 39—14: 37—11: 3—1: Total 79—26: Ints 34: Phila 73—23.

Friday [Aug.] 17th Cool. Rain all last night & to this time 12 OClock. Report 28—11: 25—8: 10—2: Total 63 —21. Interts 32. Rain all day. Ther: 74.

Saty [Aug.] 18th Clear or nearly so. Ther: 68. Clouds. Write on Zeb Spiff: Report 38—6: 32—10: 3—. Total 73—16. Send by Messrs. Bolton, Fox & Livingston who undertake to put it in their private letter bag for Captain J. B. Bell of the Havre packet Francois 1st A packet containing 6 sheets of my history of the Theatre, directed to James F. Cooper. I had sent the 4 first sheets by Captn Funk through Mr John J. Boyd. Write a letter to J F C & put in post office. Read in Ann: Reg: & Scotts last Tales of my Landlord. Draw from N. Y. Bank $25. Nothing left. Rain.

Sunday Augt 19th 1830 [*sic* for 1832] Still clouds & rain. Th: 74. Send off another letter [122] to J: F: Cooper. Very warm S. Wind. Afn Rain. Evg rain. Report 28—9: 28—9: Total 56—18.

Monday [Aug.] 20th Clear. Pleasant. Ther: 72. Remove my pictures which employ'd all the morning having consented that Bowen shall let the lower room for the Ex-

[122] Printed in *Correspondence of James Fenimore-Cooper,* I, 277-78.

hibition of a strange animal contrary to agreement provided I receive 10 dollars per week. Correct proofs. Report 24—8: 20—6: Yorkvill 8—4: Total 52—18: (this is Tuesdays report) Reading Scotts last poor novel.

Wed^{y} 28—15: 18—5: 2—2: Total 48—22. Int^{ts} 22. Cloudy variable.

Thursday 23^{d} Augt 1832. No business but attending to proof sheets. Report 33—18: 36—7: 3—3: Total 72—28. Int^{ts} 31.

Friday 24th Report 18—8: 17—9: 3—1: Y[orkville] 4—1: Harl. 1—1:B. Total 43—20. Int^{ts} 30. Phil^{a} 28—14: Alb^{y} 33—10. Cool & pleasant. Ther: 74. Rain.

Sat^{y} 25th Clear & Cool. Ther: 67. Correct proofs. Report 20—5: 17—9: Total 37—14. Int^{ts} 16. Read in Tales of the Alhambra. Almost cold.

Sunday [Aug.] 26th Clear. Cold. Ther: 64. Report 50—23:

Monday 27th Clear. Ther: 70. Report 40—14. Read Tales of the Alhambra. Very slight stuff. [D. E.] Williams life of Sir T[homas] Lawrence.

Tuesday 28th Ther: 72. Read. Correct proof. Report 23—9: 17—10: Total 41—10.

Wed^{y} 29th Warmer. Clear. Report 4—1: 16—9: Total 21—12. Interm^{ts} 16. Write. Read. J. H. Payne with me some time. Leaves his "Opera Glass" &c.

Thursday 30th The Board of health ceases reporting. Write to J. F. Cooper & prepare to send him sheets to page 240.

Friday [Aug.] 31st send my letter but the sheets are detained until next packet (10th next month). The Harpers suspend printing my book for a week; to supply the demand for Mrs. Trollope.[123] Paint. Mr Castello tells me

[123] Mrs. Frances Trollope's *Domestic Manners of the Americans.*

that by the Jewish law a woman at the time of marrying shaves her head & no longer wears her hair. He was born & educated a jew. Those Jewess[es] who adhere strictly to the law, in Europe wear wigs. Hard rain in the even^g & night.

Saturday Septr 1st 1832. Cool & clear. Receive a letter from James H. Caldwell, wishing to communicate respecting American History. Write him. Paint. Write. Read Williams's Lawrence.

Sunday Septr 2^d Cool & clear. Ther: 68. Walk out of town. Read Lawrence. For his opinion of Miss F. Kemble see 2^d Vol: p. 520. Read Irvings Chronicle of Granada.

Monday 3^d Cool. Ther: 68. Light clouds. Maynard [124] known & esteemed in Utica died Sat^y of Cholera. [Jacob] Woodhull of the Theatre the same day. More people known to me die now than when our Corporation reported. Rain.

[Sept.] 4th Rain. Read J. H. Paine's Opera Glass. Ther: 68.

> "Time rushes o'er us; thick as evening clouds
> Ages roll back: what calls them from their shrouds?
> What in full vision brings their good & great;
> The men whose virtues make the Nation's fate,
> The far, forgotten Stars of humankind?
> The Stage—the mighty telescope of mind!"
>
> Croly

Rec^d notification from R. H. Waller that he had collected note against Solomon Root & wishing to know where he is to send it. Answer to 64 Sixth Avenue.

Wed^y [Sept.] 5th Cool pleasant. Afflicted beyond measure. O God forgive me—forgive him—help—Why do I write this? Agony is relieved by it a little.

[124] An obituary of the Hon. William H. Maynard was printed in the *New-York Commercial Advertiser,* Sept. 3, 1832.

[Sept.] 6th Clear. Cool. Ther: 66. Do little or nothing.

10th Monday. Mr John J. Boyd undertook to send a packet containing 240 pages of Hist: of Th: to Paris for James F. Cooper.

13th Thursday. Th: 65. Clear & cool. Paint a little for a few days past. Think of opening an Academy for teaching drawing & painting.

17th Monday. My son commences anew in James A. Hamilton's Office as an Assistant. I am painting a portrait of Mrs Manly. Weather warm.

20th Thursday. Still warm. Messrs. Livingston & Co. take a packet of 3 sheets for J. F. Cooper & I send a letter by Mail. Monday Charles Kemble made his debut as Hamlet & Tuesday his daughter as Bianca in [Henry Hart] Milman's Fazio. See Evg Post of 18th & 19th.

[Sept.] 21st Friday. Warm rain. Bowen offers the Gallery &c at up[p]er part of the Museum for $150 to May. Mr Gouv: Kemble writes (20th) "Mr Paulding was correct in saying that I would guarantee the sale of 100 copies, Being desirous to assist in the first publication. I am happy to know that the object has been attained, and although I have pretty much failed in my subscription list at West point & this place, yet I by no means desire to retract the promise, and I would wish 50 copies sent to me as soon as the work is out, and I will send you the amount, or before, if you desire it. The remainder you can keep for the present, or if you have a demand dispose of them until I may want them"

[Sept.] 22d Saty Warm Rain. Painting portrait of Mrs Manly.

26th Wedy Cool. Send off copy of portrait of St Ander for Castillo to send to Columbia for sale. Give the last copy to ye Harpers for Appendix to hist^{y} of A. Th. A great collection of pictures are putting up for exh^{n} at the A[merican] A[cademy] Barclay Street, Mr Bret giving 150 per month for the room for 3 months.

Sunday Septr 30th Cloudy. On thursday Sketch club met at Hoboken with Sands. Paint on Mrs Manly's portrait & head of boy in my Holy family, Castillo's Edmund the model. Friday receive a draft from Gouv^{r} Kemble for 100 dollars p^{d} in advance for 50 Copies of my book. He desires 1 Copy to be sent to Charles Hoffman Assistant Ed: of American, 50 to be sent to Coldspring & the remainder 49 to be kept by me for the present. There is a project to get up a benefit for J. H. Payne at the Park Theatre & I am invited to attend a meeting on the subject tomorrow. Send off sheets of my work to J. F. Cooper up to page 384 & a letter by the Havre packet Captn Lee. I have for 2 days past the first uneasiness or pain in Urethra since the operation 1831 (July), still there is no stricture but inflammation of the parts & parts adjacent.

Sunday October 7th 1832. During the last week I have deposited with Mr John J. Boyd a letter [125] for J. F. Cooper begging him if not already done to announce the work for publication & arrange to have it done—deposit w^{h} the same a packet containing the work complete. I have painted on Mrs Manley's picture & the Holy family I had intention to go to day to West Point & Cold Springs & to morrow to Albany but the morning threatens rain. I have advertised that I am ready to receive applications as a teacher of Drawing & Painting but without effect. I renew'd last Thursday the 4th my note in Bank of N. Y. for 150 dollars and have now in bank 48 or 50 dollars. In France if an Author produces a successful play on any Stage, no other is allowed to represent it without remunerating him. Sent by T. Cummings some leaves of my book to Robt Walsh jun^{r} Phil^{a}

[125] Printed in *Correspondence of James Fenimore-Cooper,* I, 298-99.

Monday Octr 8th 1832. Embark at 7 OClock in ye Champlain St[eam] B^{t} for Albany. Meet Mr Joseph Henry ass^{t} at Dr Becks Acad^{y} [126] He has been to Princeto[n] N J where he is elected professor. Mr Henry is one of those men who do honour to our Nature. Men who by the force of what is called genius, by the ardent love of knowledge & desire to obtain rise superior to circumstances which would seem to have doomed them to ignorance & vice and become luminaries as well as examples to others. Born of poor parents he was left in childhood an orphan with a widow'd mother who had not the means of educating him, perhaps not the wish, he was bo[un]d apprentice to a silver-smith, here he learn'd to use tools & became acquainted with a portion of mechanical knowledge, his desire for learning urged him to read for improvement & he qualified himself for the situation of a teacher in the Albany Academy. Dr Beck encouraged and aided him. After 7 hours of labour as a teacher he devoted the remaining hours to teaching himself by study & experiments. He has succeeded in attracting the attention of the Scientific in both hemispheres by discovering additional powers in the magnet, and by making his discovery subserve the purposes of further research into the secrets of Nature. He has received his reward in part by being advanced to a situation of comparative leisure where the oppertunities for pursuing his studies are encreased at the same time that he has more power to communicate instruction to others. His name will be enroll'd with those of Franklin, Silliman, Rittenhouse & other Americans who have transmitted light from the West to the East, from the region to which light has been travelling for ages to that whence it emanated. After Mr Henry left me for West Point, which I again pass without landing, Mr J. F. Sibell [127] introduced himself to me. He has lately returned home from Europe & in the same vessel with Mr. C. Kemble & his daughter of whom he

[126] The Albany Academy, T(heodore) Romeyn Beck, M. D., LL. D., Principal.

[127] John Frederick Sibell, stationer, of 56 Wall Street, New York City.

speaks highly both as private & public individuals. Kemble says Price ruined him by his system of Management at Drury Lane at the same time that he ruined himself. Kemble inherited his brothers property in Covent Garden valued at 45000£. He accuses Price of seducing his Actors from him and otherwise injuring the Drama. Miss Kemble is represented as a most charming woman without beauty. Educated in France, she return'd home on the failure or embarassment of her father & devoted herself to the Stage for his support.

Albany Monday Ev^{g} Octr 8th arrive at 7 P. M. Take up quarters at Cruttendens. He tells me no effort was made to obtain subscribers for me on acc^{t} of Cholera. There are three names on the paper, three copies subscribed for. subscription for seven were offer'd me to day on board the boat J. F. Sibell 6, Jos. Henry 1.

Albany Tuesday Octr 9th 1832. Mr E Croswell has promised to publish extracts & circulate by an employed man my subscription paper. Mr S Dewitt Bloodgood subscribed & received extracts for his brother in law Van schaiks paper. The Albany subscription now is Stephen Van Ransaeller, Joseph Henry, E. Croswell, L. Cruttenden (two copies) S. D. Bloodgood (pd) Van schaick. Wm. Page. I purpose going to West Point this afternoon.

West Point Wed^{y} [Oct.] 10th I arrived at 1 A. M. and alone after the Sergeant on guard took my name, clamber'd up to this Hotel. Literally clamber'd at first, for missing the path I went up the bed of a torrent over rocks until stop'd by one which told me that I was not in a pathway. I returned to the water & then found the circuituous way that leads to the brow of the hill & the house. Slept ill & in the morning found it raining. Genl E. Laight greeted me on the piazza & pointed out the objects of note. After breakfast call on [Thomas] Gimbrede and on Cadet [Thomas H.] Williamson. The Library was lock'd & the key borne off & I could not see

Sully's Jefferson or the books. Made the sketches adjoining. Afternoon took the North America steam boat at 4 & landed at N. Y. at 7.

Thursday Oct[r] 11th 1832. Clouds. Received a letter from Rob[t] Gilmore of Baltimore saying that he was mortified (on calling upon Robinson) to find only one copy of my book subscribed for in addition to the 2 opposite his name. "Robinson said however that many persons said they would probably buy the work if it was published & at hand & he thinks he could get off ten or a dozen copies." M[r] G concludes with regrets that he could not induce others to follow his example.

Saturday [Oct.] 13th I yesterday wrote a little on Zeb. Spiff. Saw that the title page of my book had been deposited in the Clerks office. The Harpers have the Certificate

On board a Steam boat for phil[a] I read in the Mirror an Acc[t] of Mount Vernon wherein it is stated that John A Washington is a descendant of the *General*—is not this strange ignorance in America? After a rough ride of 15 miles and a smooth on a piece of railroad of fifteen more & 2 hours steamboating on the Delawarre I am in Philadelphia. My friends Mrs [Titus] Yerkes & the Red Lion, whom I expected to find in the same place have vanished. I walk ab[t] some time in the rain & then take refuge at [L. W.] Rykemans opposite the Stateh[se]. I am in a snug bedroom, the lower part of the house is filled with noisy & drunken Electioneerers. At tea I hear a most delectable critical conversation on plays & players. Geo: Wash[n] Custis said to be over 50 and the Author of several plays all very bad. His 8th of Jan[y] was brought out by Dwyer in Phil[a] C is said to be an Orator & a painter! Hamlet a poor character & play! John Inman who travelled in company with me to day says the *prima Donna's* of the Op[a] are wretched, the Managers dismiss'd the first Cinderella & substituted a second as bad. R. Walsh [128] in his

[128] Robert Walsh, Jr., editor of the *National Gazette and Literary Register*.

paper of to day condemns Milman's Fazio & praises Miss Kemble in equivocal terms. Rain all night.

Phil[a] Sunday Oct[r] 14th 1832. A cold damp, chilly morning. I am in uncomfortable hous[e] The Independance Hotel. See Cummings & H[enry] Inman. See Sully who goes to y[e] Unit[n] Chapel & I go to Wm B Wood who promises me a list of names for to morrow which I hope by aid of Carey & Lea to put in hand for obtaining subscriptions. Must tomorrow see Inman's partner Childs [129] & remember the steel plates for Morris & the picture for Exh[n] at my room if to be had. I must call likewise on J. N. Barker & if I can find Mrs C. B. Brown or any of her children I must see them or Elijah or the Widow of Armit.

I have walked to the Water Works & find the grounds beautified. The Afternoon proved clear. The State prison I could only look at from a distance. I walked slowly over the Skuylkill upper bridge & thence to the lower ascending the hill. Recross'd the Skuylkill & stop'd at a public Garden called Botanic & Horticultural. Glass of ale & a crust of Bread formed my dinner. My breakfast was slight for the coffee was wretched. I have walked with little interruption from 10 to 4. My Inn is thronged with what are called politicians—men who gamble by betting on elections & men seeking (or seeking to keep) office. It is a melancholy degrading picture. Remove to the National Hotel.

Philadelphia. Monday Oct[r] 15th See Childs (Inmans partner). My Subscription paper lost. No names on it but two, Inman and one more not named to me. See McMurtree. No chance of engaging the picture for my Gall[y] Call on Jacob Keim 187 Cherry St[t] who says he has only received Mr Morris's order to day and the plates will be ready on Sat[y] next. Mr [John Augustus] Stone the Dramatist calls on me & promises any assistance in

[129] Cephas G. Childs, of the firm of Childs & Inman, engravers and lithographers.

a continuation Th: Hist: Go with him to Arch St^{t} Th: and see both the brothers Forrest. Edwin is to call & introduce R[ichard] Penn Smith. Mr [Louis A.] Godey, proprietor of the Chronicle undertakes to further my views. Call on H[enry] C. Carey who recommends Mr Bernard Donnan (Dornan) N. 10th St^{t}) as a collector of subscriptio[ns] Receive from Sully the paper sent to him with his name & C K Kane's. Seek in vain for Bernard Dornan. Call a second time on M[atthew] Carey & find the veteran of 72 years in his library. He presents me a Vol: of his Miscellanies. His son H. C. Carey is a polished gentleman. He invites me to dine but my engagement with Forrest & Richard Penn Smith prevents acceptance. He press'd my coming after dinner & joining the party which was prevented by business. H. C. Carey orders 12 Copies of *the* work. See Wood at the Chesnut Street Theatre & he gives me a list of names which with the paper from Sully (on which I wrote the above two with Inmans & Frazers and H. C. Carey for 12) I deposited with Mr Francis Godey an elder brother but subordinate to Lewis Godey, of the Chronicle, and Ladies Book Office. Godey undertook to advertise for a Collector of subscriptions; terms 50 cents for name, delivery of book & collecting of money. Maywood & Rowbothem and the Messrs. Forests invite me to the respective Thea^{s}: I went to the Chesn^{t} St^{t} Th: and found it crowded. Maywood introduced me over the stage to the boxes, but I could only find a place in the third tier with boys & prostitutes. Saw the Kembles in the first act of Romeo & J: He appeared to[o] old but correct, she appeared elegant and artificial. Went to Arch Street and found it crowded so that I only saw a few scenes of Orooloosa. Forrest appeared to rant. I saw not enough to judge and retired sick of a playhouse. A new Farce by Richard Penn Smith was to be performed. He and Edmond Forrest were with me in the afternoon. Smith reminded me of his having called upon me some years back & says that he offered his collection of materials on the American Theatre. I remember the visit now although I had forgotten it, but think he then told me he intended to publish & I remember no offer of material. He now promises to send me his manuscript notes &c. Forest in private appears frank, intelligent, shrewd simple & prepossessing. He has engaged a tragedy from Smith and another from Stone & makes the encouragement of Dramatists conduce to his own interest. He says Stone alter'd Pauldings play of the Lion of the West for Hackett before its appearance.

The Carey's father & son live adjoining in Walnut Street No 116 & 118. I talked freely with H. C. C. of J. F. Coopers last novel & our opinions coincide. I told him I had written & advised the Author to write more for the million. He said he was glad of it, that he had done the same. J. F. C. was at his last letter in Brussells so I fear for my plan of European publication.

Tuesday Octr 16th 1832. Returned to New York. Find all well and a letter from T. Williamson with a list of Norfolk subscriptions am^{g} 28. His sons John & William are settled in Norfolk. Gabriel is acting as L^{t} in U. S. service at sea, the younger ones at home.

Wed^{y} Octr 17th 1832. Write to Lewis Godey respecting the Book & subscribers. Call on Paulding who is to share in the second 50 copies of my work for which Gouv: Kemble is pledged if Kemble consents: if he does not Paulding is to add to the number subscribed for in his own name, how many not mentioned. He says Hackett proposed putting "the Lion of the West" into Stones hands to which he (Paulding) assented. That Hackett overcharges the part for which the play is written and fills it with every cant phrase he can pick up. Paulding puts into my hands for my opinion & correction a manuscript Comedy called (as appears by pencil writing) "The Stranger in England or the Sons of the West" and in another hand writing "The Bucktails or Americans in England." He suggests our uniting to produce Comedies and upholding the American Stage.

Geo: Bowen tells me he can let the Gallery I occupy for 300 dollars to 1st April. I told him if those who wished it w[d] remove me, I would give it up: He or they must pay for my fixtures. This scheme of Bowen's fails.

Friday [Oct.] 19th Write to J. F. Cooper & direct the letter & former packets to be forwarded to him. Barnes tells me that in letting the Richmond hill Th: to the Managers of the Italian Opera he neglected to secure admission to the proprietors & they are suing him. Evening Sketch Club with me. J. H. Payne promises to write to a friend in London to negociate with Colburn for publishing my book in Case Cooper has done nothing.

Sunday Oct[r] 21st Weather warm for some days Th: ranging from 65 to 70. To day 68. Read Pauldings "Westward ho" with great pleasure. Payne reviews it in the Mirror. Write a little on Zeb Spiff. Afternoon Walk to Bloomingdale, not quite to the Village.

Tuesday 23[d] Yesterday a hard Rain Storm. Write & read. Affliction—to day it is clear & I prepare to go to the occupations of the day with a heavy heart.

I have sent off a copy of my book to London by the way of Liverpool with a letter to Frank Ogden our Consul requesting him to forward it to direction. It is directed to Mrs Winter Chester place Cumberland (something) Regents Park London & accompanied by a letter to her directing her through various persons in case one or other should be out of the way. to make a sale to Colburn in case J. F. Cooper has done nothing & offerring ¼ to the Agent of the Sale. Payne is quite disatisfied with the notice of himself in my book & I strike out passages at his wish. Receive a letter from R. H. Waller of Rutland V[t] with a draft on the Allens for 30 doll[s]. Saying he offers it in full for my Note taking as charges of Collection the interest on y[e] money while in his hands & the price of the Morocco case sent to him last year.

Friday Octr 26th 1832. Ther: 50 and out of doors *Ice.* The Harpers advertise to publish my book this day. I yesterday began a portrait of Danl Kissam a youth of 16: for $25. I have now in Bank 49.

Sunday 28th Cold, clear & windy. Ther: in the house 50. I am agreeably disappointed at finding the New York American noticing my book very favourably. Write T. Williamson, Jos Irwin, Lewis Godey & Andrew Bell Esqres

Thursday Novr 1st 1832. For three days warm & misty. Indian summer weather. I hear good report of my book. Finish portrait of Daniel Kissam a youth of 16 who sails to day for England. Tuesday evening I witness a play at Bowery Theatre (now called American) called The Cradle of Liberty, foundd on J. F. Cooper's Lionel Lincoln. All that was good was Coopers, the rest trash. This is called a "celebrated drama" by Capt. S. P. Glover. (A Mr Taylor has been the Dramatist for this Th:). If this is to be called "The American Theatre" par excellence I hope it may have a thorough reform. A Battle of Bunker hill introduced worse than Burkes. *Job Pray* was effective & well play'd. Miss Waring displayed powers & genius in *Nab,* but Nab was transform'd to a kind of Meg Merriless & Helen McGregor. The Mirror & Albion are very complimentary to me. My friends press a continuation of the Work & the Artists are subscribing for a History of the Arts of Design.

[Nov.] 2d Same warm, smoky weather. Sending out books to subscribers & little else. Evg at Ingham's S. Club.

3d Do Do Deposit 122 dollars. Now in bank 170.

8th Thursday. Cold after two hard rains. On Tuesday I commenced translating Talma's essay on Lekain & his Art. Yesterday recd a letter from Henry J Finn on Theatricals & my book. To day a notice that my name is on the free list at ye Park Th: the Kembles to play to night: I have in Bank 190 dollars.

This Friday 9th deposit 90 making 280.
On the 8th recd the following

"Dr Sir
I have the pleasure of informing you that your name is on the free list of the Theatre.

Yr Obt
J[ohn] Blake Treasr
Wm Dunlap Esqr Novr 8th

This *favour* was extorted from Simpson by repeated applications from Mr John Evers.

Sunday 11th Novr 1832. Two days ago recd a pleasant letter from H. C. Carey respecting publications. Yesterday recd a Journal called the Constellation with praises of my work from E. E. Langdon Assist Editor publish[ed] by Eustis Prescott & Co. Merchts Exchge. Receive a letter from Geo: Watterston of Washington City frank'd by James L Hoalyes (What ye name is I know not) compleme tg & wishing me to notice that he had written certain plays. Write to him & to Finn. In the E. Post of yesterday see acct of S[ir] W. Scotts death: funeral &c &c. I have attended on the plays of Fazio & Sch: for Scandal & have noted my remarks in another book for a continuation Theatrical history. Call on J. H. Payne. See J. A. Sidell & make an appointment with him. Evg at Wheatleys & make some notes.

Monday Novr 12th Two days of warm weather. Receive from Messrs Harpers the follg "About a week ago we sent to all the persons on the list you first gave us, on which there were only 12 set down for Godie. These we sent. We have sent to Washington, Baltimore &c. Collins & Hannay have sent to New Orleans. They have it by this time all over the Country. The Editors in all the principal Cities have been supplied." From M. Carey "I have read 300 pages of your Book and shall read the remainder this evening. It is extremely interesting and recalls to my mind many various scenes which time had effaced from its tablets. To those who have any taste for the Drama it must afford a rich treat. It sheds more light on the arcana of the sanctum sanctorum of the Theatre than any other book I have ever seen. The other collators of reminiscences the Okeefes the Kellys the Bernards, the Wilkinsons et hoc genus omna, have drawn largely on their imagination for their facts, one third of which at least carry internal evidence of falsification as fully as the Munchausen Tales of [one word illegible] Barrington. Your work in every page has evidences of its being genuine.

Y^{rs} respectfully

Matthew Carey"

Tuesday Novr 13th Another warm day. Last Ev^{g} could not get in at the Park. Saw Miss Vincent at the Bowery. Deposit 60 making 340 (122 of this sum is not enter'd in my Bank Book)

Saturday 17th For three days cold. In ye house Th: 44. Out Ice. I see by ye papers S. F. B. Morse arrived yesterday. On Wed^{y} last I had pain in back & hips Thursday even^{g} increase night diaroeha, took medicine, remaind by the fire fasting yesterday, to day better. The E Post says Miss Kemble gained no credit by her Mrs Beverly & her father's Beverly was bad: This is just as I should expect. Comes on to rain & weather warm.

[Nov.] 18th Warm rain. I have written to Washington Alston to announce intention of writing Hist^{y} of the Arts of Design in U. S. & ask his Aid. same effect to C. B. King & Frazer. Th: in house 55. Out doors higher. Call by appointment of Foote 23 McDougal Street in a cellar. He is not at home. *Conway.* The name of his mother his father having seduced her & instead of making her his Wife made the mistress of a Boarding house in Bath. He was a sprig of Nobility & privileged. The boy was apprenticed to a Linen Draper but educated above that standing. As a young man, tall & remarkably handsome his ambition soared above making a shift to sell a shirt and he aspired to that dignity in the mimic world which was not to be hoped for in the real. He appeared in [blank] at [blank] and was successful. was invited to Dublin at £5 a week and much admired. Here he first played with Miss ONiel and wish'd to marry her. He made his debut at Covent Garden in [blank] in [blank] and Miss ONiel following he again play'd the hero with her if not the lover. He was awkward & continued so until some years playing *here*. The London journalists persecuted him & he fell from the hero of Covent Garden to the prompter of the Haymarket. Hilson has mentioned symptoms of his derangement. He threw himself over board at sea & when hencoops &c. were thrown over to help him, he plunged beneath the wave to show the determination of his purpose.

Monday Novr 19th Fog. Th: 55.

Friday 23^{d} I have done little in this interval. I do nothing. I have seen & noted the acting of the Kembles. I have announced an intention of writing a Hist^{y} of the Arts of Design in this country & continuing hist^{y} of Th: Yesterday a hard rain all day & I staid home & read Spark's Governeur Morris. Fay has published in ye Mirror a biography of J. H. Paine to help the Great benefit getting up for him & has let out a little of John's discontent at my notice of him in my book. For this Benefit see papers of the day with my name as one of the Committee tho' I have not attended a meeting as is the case with many others. A Notice of Miss Ellis will be found at the other end of this book. See Sparks' Gov: Morris (Diary) for anecdotes of Hudon.

Sunday [Nov.] 25th Cold enough for ice all day but clear & pleasant. Reading Spark's Morris.

26th The usual celebration of the retreat of the British from N. Y. I think I never remember an Anniversary of the day when the weather was so warm, although frequently it is as much so in December.

27th Still warmer. Finish reading 1st Vol: of Sparks. It is right to cast a veil over obvious faults in the Subject of which the Biographer treats? I think not. Truth is injured by hiding defects as much as by inventing them. Mr Morris obviously neglected to use the power he possess'd to rescue Tom Paine from prison & threaten'd death. He is excused by his biographer. There is no excuse for him. Paine's vices do not excuse Morris. There is falshood respecting Morris's long continued health only interrupted it is said by the Gout. Mr S: must have known better. Doctor Hosack or any of Morris's acquaintance must have inform'd the biographer of the chronic disease which terminated his life. The disease which kill'd him is said to to be sudden attack. All this is false. Is it of no consequence that we know the truth in this respect? I think it is. Besides when we know we are deceived on one point we lose confidence relativly to others. The disease which by improper treatment on his own part caused his death had been a visitant for years occasionally and was one that abstemious living or simple food & abjuration of stimulating liquids, with care in other respects, might have removed or render'd harmless. Morris never stinted his appetites. When attack'd by stricture he used the most harsh means for relief if in distress of urgent nature. Such attacks and such applications were common for years, and finally a mortification of the parts killed him after a season of Agony.

Receive a letter from James Fennimore [Cooper] dated Paris Octr 14th My last letter with my book complete was sent off the 10th Octr: The copy sent to Liverpool was sent off 23d In his usual sportive style he writes

"My good young friend

I regret a thousand fold that your sheets should have arrived during my absence from Paris. On my return three days since, I found them, with three of your letters. I wrote to Bentley (Colbourn having retired) that night and sent the sheets wth as earnest a request as man could make that he would give a £100 and print. You will perceive that there was no time to negociate, or I think I might have got more; as it is I am not sure I can get this. Still I hope the merit of the work (which by cutting out matter that is too local, will do pretty well for England) and my prayers may do something. You are not to imagine I got down on my knees, but I wheedled charmingly. A very few days will give me the result. If he refuses, perhaps Rich (Rid) might publish on shares. If these fail, I have no hope. I have scarcely any connexion with any European publishers. They get the sheets of my works and there the matter commonly ends. I never saw Mr Bentley, and Colburn but three or four times in my life. So that after all it is rather up-hill work. Nous verrons.

You will soon have Morse with you. He will tell you how we look, how we feel, I need not say, as respects you & yours. I shall write you again the instant I have any thing positive to communicate. Remember me to the ladies and to old Jack.

J. Fennimore Cooper

Mr Wm Dunlap

You cant imagine the pleasure I have in thus patronizing youthful talent, but you young rogues are so apt to look at the world en couleur de rose, that I feel forced to caution you against critics and all the evils to which flesh is heir. Ask old John about this, and he will give you a useful homily on hope."

Novr 28th 1832. Clear warm morning, change to cloudy at noon. [Thomas] Cole calls to see me just arrived from Leghorn. To days paper announces the death of Mrs Duff at Cincinattee of Cholera.

[Nov.] 29th Warm & clear. To night the great Benefit for J. H. Payne, pit laid into boxes & all tickets $5 except Gallery $1. People enquire of me why is this? Some say the reasons for a public demonstration of the sort and a benefit are all more applicable to me. I have been silent —but I know that if the payment is due to the American Dramatist, the man who translated by contract for a foreign stage & wrote nothing for ours, is not the man. I have spoken to Wm T. McCoun, Walter Bowne & R[ichard] Riker, offering myself a candidate for painting Govr [Enos T.] Throop's portrait. The first will write to 'T.' I expect nothing. Deposit $26 making in Bank $367.

HON. WILLIAM TOWNSEND McCOUN (1786-1878)

ATTRIBUTED TO WILLIAM DUNLAP

(Courtesy of Miss Elisabeth Marbury)

[Nov.] 30th Clouds. Last evening at Bowery Th: & see a part of Booths Oroonooka. Rant. Play uninteresting. I never saw it perform'd before or any part of it. Read it in boyhood. Hart met me & Stone. The first full of indignation at the benefit of Payn. Says that G C Verplank, Swartwout, Governeur &c &c rail at the *Humbug* as they call it. That the benefit is to be followed by a dinner at which the check for the amt is to be presented in form. The [that] G C V was appointed to preside but declares off. That the Duke of Devonshire had on application sent Payne £50 when he was in the Kings bench & the Committee talk'd of sending it back to him, but it was remark'd if *all* so obtain'd is return'd there will not be enough even if 5000 dollars are netted. That P was always in difficulties & had been in the Fleet as well as Kings bench. That he would return to England as he was attached to & had lived with Mrs. Glover the Actress. Such is now the talk. At noon my friend Doctor McLean call'd on me "I was at Payne's Benefit last eveg I said to [blank] if any one should have a Benefit as a Dramatist I think it is Mr Dunlap" "Yes by —— I'm glad you mention'd—wait a little—it shall be done." Pell was by and he and [blank] swore it should be done. I dont think added the Doctor that they will go 5 but 3 dollars a head. "I have just been to see Francis who joins heartily in it." I call'd at the Mirror Office & Morris says the receits of last night are 4800. A nett 3000 will be Paynes. "I think says he that is a Benefit for any man." "It would be a benefit to me" I replied laughing. He told me that Mrs Duff is not dead.

McLean said P. Hone had evinced the same feeling respecting me & the benefit.

Saty Decr 1st 1832. Last evg wrote my friend McLean to say that if anything is to be done by those who wish me well, the Spirit must not be let to evaporate. Go to Park Theatre. Am introduced to Dr [Robert Montgomery] Bird & see his Tragedy of "The Gladiator play'd. The weather cold with high wind.

Sunday [Dec.] 2[d] Very cold morning. Hard frost. See the rising sun during my Walk. Write on Zeb Spiff. Afternoon McLean calls—says that he & my friends think that any Benefit must be delay'd. He says he sees in a Phil[a] paper a notice of Paynes intended benefit with the remark that such a thing should be done for Wm Dunlap. This is certainly remarkable and unexpected by me. Read in Quarterly.

[Dec.] 3[d] Last night snow follow'd by rain & rain continues. At this time in 1831 Our rivers were frozen indeed all Nov[r] was winter. By McLean suggestion I write to Wood on the above subject. I will write likewise to Godey & Barker—have done so. Draw out Bank $11.62 leaving in Bank $350.

Tuesday [Dec.] 4th Mild & partly clear. Write to R Penn Smith. Reading Cox on the Columbia River.[130]

Wed[y] [Dec.] 5th Clear & pleasant. It is curious that U. S. Gazette, the Phil. Chronicle have started the idea of a Benefit to me as the pioneer American Dramatist & that it is actived by the N. Y. American & E Post. Deposit note for 150 dollars dated y[e] 6[th] to meet the accom[n] note—direct to A[nthony] P. Halsey the newly elected Cashier.[131] Draw out $10 leaving 339, & 5 more leaving 334. Lawson offers his assistance in collecting Theatrical materials. Cole calls on me—long & very pleasant talk on painters scul[p]tors and Italy. With few exceptions our painters the best in the world—delighted with Leslie —abominates Remb Peale who he saw & *knew* in England & Italy—highest opinion of Greenough. Ev[g] Park Theatre. See M[r]. Stones play of Metamora. I went disposed & wishing to be pleased. I was not.

Thursday Dec. 6th 1832. The president Message appears to me, on the Tariff & S. C. businesses moderate &

[130] Ross Cox, *Adventures on the Columbia River*. (London, 1831; N. Y., 1832).

[131] Of the Bank of New York.

proper. Threats surely ought to be used by him towards the excited Southerns. Mem: of distances. From S. point Batt^{y} to N. point Sandy hook 14 Nautical 16¼ statute miles: to Quarantine 4⅜:5⅛: to Telegraph 6½:7½: to Highlands Nav[esin]k 18:20⅛. The Naut^{l} mile is 6120 feet; the Statute or land mile 5280. The morning cold & clear. Moderates. Write a notice of Morse & Cole for E. Post & give it to Bryant. Hear that Morse is sick & go to see him: find him in bed. He reads passages from J. F. Coopers letters to him from Switzerland. C & family are to return to Paris for the winter & come home next spring or summer. Talk over C's antipathy to Washington Irving. C. feels sore on account of attacks on him. He reprobates as his letters to me show, Irvings writing for the English Aristocratical Quarterly when he was there as the representative of the Government of America in character of Chargé des Affaires. M says that the acc^{t} of the dinner given to Irving caused a burst that was frightful. We lament his indiscretion. The attack of Cooper in the American when his Bravo appeared was attributed immediately by him to a Frenchman & Lt. Paine of ye Navy discover'd by accident the Author M: [blank] who sent it to America for insertion. Since M:s arrival it has been asserted in his presence that the Author is an Am^{n} & known as such to G C Verplank. Morse asserted the knowledge of the French Author one of the Editors of Le Journal des Debats. The thing is to be sifted. Ev^{g} see a few minutes Mr & Miss Rae as Cicely & young Rapid & then go to Sketch club. Project of an Annual the designs & letter press to come from the club & the engravings by members.

Friday Decr 7th draw out 10 & leaving 324 dollars in Bank. Deposit a copy of my history of Am. Th: with the District clerk (the title was deposited by the Harpers the 9th of Oct^{r}) One of Jacob Morton's sons was present. The clerk asked me if I would have a certificate & pay 50 cents for it. I asked if it was required by law. "No." "I only wish to comply with the law. Receive letter from

Jos: Irwin Fort Monroe Decr 3^d^ with a draft for 21.50 for 11 Copies deducting charges. he says "2 of my subscribers died with Cholera on their march against the Indians" Receive likewise $19.32 from Edm^d^ A Wetmore (Utica) for 10 copies. Receive letter from Wm B Wood. He says Payne will "after his $5 benefit think himself the public idol" "The hint respecting your claims I have heard in several companies" but he thinks nothing will be done without that solicitation which I cannot submit to. This he thinks P. used. "In his early years he accustomed himself to look for naked *patronage* from any quarter, and invoked it on some occasions by such crooked means that I think he only could have humbled himself to use. How *are you prepared* for personal solicitation of all the insolent wealthy & the ignorantly vain? If you are not dont venture to hope that your just & well founded Claims will ever be attended to. The judicious & thinking part of the community consider the late *festival* as the most consumate triumph of unfounded pretension & ostentatious prodigality; and I hear from many of your townsmen that this opinion is not confined to Philadelphia. The Entertainment too was, as might be supposed quite dull & unsatisfactory." I was told last night that at the Dinner (for there was a dinner for the Committee & the receiver of the Benefit) my health was drank, standing, with *three times three!* Alas my countrymen, alas! alas! Another passage from Wood "I have ever held the Baby-acting in infinite scorn & finely have I been abused for laughing at the pretensions of Burke & C. Fisher, but if I give an opinion upon my profession it shall be the honest truth." Even^g^ Go to the Park Th. & see & hear Oraloossa.

Sat^y^ Decr 8th 1832. Rain. Write a notice of Oraloossa in a large book among other Th^l^ notes, & a short notice for E. Post. Deposit 19 dollars making my C^r^ 343.

Sunday [Dec.] 9th Rain. Cold in my few remaining teeth read Cox's Columbia river with pleasure. Write on Zeb Spiff.

Monday [Dec.] 10th Receive a very pleasing letter from Robt Gilmor with expressions of gratification from my histy of Th: & some information respectg Old Th: Baltimore He requests Autograph's to add to his collection which according to his letter must be a very curious one amounting already to 5 Vol: quarto. Mr McCoun call'd & left the following

Auburn Decr 5th 1832

To the Honourable Wm T. McCoun Vice Chancellor
New York

Dear Sir

I acknowledge the receipt of your polite letter commendatory of Mr Dunlap. If the Corporation of the City should make the request of me which you anticipate I shall not be unmindful of the merits of Mr Dunlap.

I am very respectfuly Your Obedt Servt
E. T. Throop

This is in answer to my friend's mentioning me as a portrait painter (as I suppose worthy of employment) in case of his complying with a request of the Common Council to sit for his picture. Read in Henry Wheaton's Histy of the Northmen.

Tuesday Decr 11th 1832. Last evening Mr Cummings called & brought me the Phila Daily Chronicle of Saty last, in which is a paragraph recommending the Philadelphians to get up a benefit for me as the American Dramatist & supposing that N. Y. & other cities would follow the example. Very painful night & I am still unwell. John L. Morton call'd & wished me to see Walter Bowne on the subject of his portrait, the Corporation having appropriated 300 dollars for it. I called on him but nothing definite passed. He mentioned Throops picture as wishing me to have the painting of it. Genl Morton came in & notified Bowne in a semi official way of the vote of last night. Evening Dr [John] Neilson & Mr Durand with me, we being a Committee on the Sketch club book.

Wedy 12th Pay C. Judson $137.50 half years rent. Draw out Bank $125. leaving 218 dollars. Doctor Francis calls, is full of the American Dramatists benefit, promises me assistance in prosecution of my *Continuation*. Kean, Conway, Bartly &c. &c. Rain all last [night] & to day.

Thursday [Dec.] 13th Cloudy. Clayton introduces & urges the Dramatists benefit. If anything is done that will put me at my ease & give me leisure to go on with literary works intended I shall be pleased & I hope gratefull where I ought so to be. Write a little on Zeb Spiff. Evg Sketch Club at R[ichard R.] Ward's Bond St. Rain.

Friday [Dec.] 14th Clouds. See the Harpers & tell them I have deposited Copy according to law & require the certificate (which is promised) of the copy right. Buy of them 15 copies at 1 33/100 the copy & pay 20 62½/100. draw 30 for suit of clothes making 50 62/100 leaving in Bank $167.37. draw out 6.25 leave 161.12.

[Dec.] 15th Hard rain. Do little but read papers (news) at [Mercantile] Library Clinton Hall & home. Evg Post of to day reprints from the Chronicle the recommendation of Benefits for me in all the Cities of ye Union, with some additional lines. Another journal has something on the same subjects. Evg write on Zeb. Spiff.

Sunday [Dec.] 16th A Walk before sunrise. Write. Read Hazlitts Northcote (convns) [132] Speaking of Cooper's Pilot: N. asks is it Irvings. "Oh no, he is a mere trifler, a fillagree man, an English litterateur at second hand, but the Pilot gave a truce &c" Morse told me that when in London he was looking over a mornings paper & was attracted by a piece headed *"Patronage"* and reading it was determining to purchase the paper when to his surprize he found at the bottom that it was my address to the Natl Acady. Write on Zeb Spiff.

Monday [Dec.] 17th At this time last year we had had a months winter. Part of November & all December cold.

[132] William Hazlitt, *The Conversations of James Northcote, R. A.* (1830).

17th Ther: in ye house was 26: the 18th 21. Snow on the ground. We have now mild weather but much rain. Hard rain again to day. Finish Hazlitt's convns of Northcote. Write to Robt Gilmor & promise Autographs for his collection. Write on Zeb Spiff. Cummings calls to shew me in ye Phila Chronicle a repetition of the invitation to get up a Benefit for me. In the Evg Post is another of the same nature for N. Y. only expressly calling for a festival in imitation of that for Payne. The death of Robt C. Sands is announced, a co-editor of the Commercial Advertiser, one of the Sketch club and a scholer of no mean standing. He was as thousands are a victim of intemperance & died of apoplexy.

Wedy 19th Decr 1832. I yesterday recd from Chas Fraser of Charleston manuscript notices of G. Stuart. A very pleasing letter from Henry Inman. Read Sparks' Morris. Evening at Charles P. Clinch's. To day paint. Cummings shows me a fine likeness he has just made of Forrest. Receive letter from Matthew Carey. He says that a wrote to the Harpers for an imperfect copy of my histy Th: and they wrote in reply that "they had no imperfections" he therefor requests me to send him a complete copy. I must write to him that I have not a complete copy, as every one has not only my imperfections but those of the Messrs. Harpers, for mine let him find them out but for the printers p. 236 makes me say that my countrymen the new Jersey-men <*that they*> had retired before their enemies "to await the time of resurrection & p: 241 and Smith of Drury land play'd "the Baron" in a tragedy where no Baron is known—a beg of him to substitute retribution for resurrection & Biron for Baron. Write Henry Inman (Sterling Farm, Mount Holly N. J.) I am told that the *piece* in the Phila Chronicle was copied into the N. Y. American of last night.

Thursday [Dec.] 20th Write to M: Carey. We have a hard frost & a clear morning. Read Spark's Morris. Write for Hist: Theatre.

[Dec.] 21st Colder. Paint. Read in [Timothy] Flints Geo: & Hist of the Valley of ye Mississippi. Write on Zeb Spiff. Write to Sully & Neagle.

[Dec.] 22d Very cold. Ther: in house 30. Send off a copy of hist Am: [Theatre] to M: Carey by his desire and pamphlet to Wood & letter as above. Write on Continuation Hist: Th: Receive from Robt Gilmor his Catalogue of Collection of Autographs. Write on Zeb Spiff.

[Dec.] 23d Sunday. Clear. Cold. Th: in house 34. Read Flint. Write on Zeb Spiff &c. Walk some miles.

Monday [Dec.] 24th Warm pleasant. Council meeting in ye Evg. Morse, Inman, Cole &c. Write & read.

Tuesday [Dec.] 25th Cloudy morning. Warm pleasant clear day. Write on Zeb Spiff. Read Flint.

[Dec.] 26th Clear. Clouds. Snow & rain. At Cole's room & see his paintings done in Italy. See Ball Hughes Monument of Bishop Hobart. Cole has improved more in figures than in landscape. His Tivoli & his roman Aqueduct are very fine. The Monument places Hughes higher in my estimation as a sculptor. At library find the American Quarterly and in it a review of my Hist: Am: Th: very favourable. Examine News papers for Continuation. Drew from B: $15 leave $152. Evening & Night Rain. Write on Z. S. and Conn Hist: Ther: 40.

Thursday 27th Decr 1832. Rain. Th: 40. Did not leave my house until the fine weather of the afternoon induced me to take a walk Write & read as yesterday.

Friday 28th Fine clear frosty day. At my room in Broad way sit down to write [133] to J. F. Cooper on the political aspect of the Country & other subjects, the after part of

[133] Printed in the *Correspondence of James Fenimore-Cooper,* I, 305-7.

this day very pleasant & warm. G P Morris invited me into his Editorial office and after saying that J. H. Payne was much annoyed by the notices in the E Post of intended benefit for me, offer'd to join my friends in any plan for the purpose. He said he carried P's through and would do as much for me. Advised postponing until near Spring. that the persons who had stirred in it should form a committee, name others & organize the thing. He would be one &c. John Inman sent word to Cummings that he would aid. Even^g at Park Th: Richard 3^d Mr C Kean.

Sat^y [Dec.] 29th Snow. Write notice of last nights play. I received yesterday a letter from Charles Fraser of Ch^n with notices of himself & Malbone. The sprinking of snow disappeared & the day proved very pleasant. Write and read. Governor Hayne the successor of Hamilton has answered Jackson's proclamation eloquently but not conclusively. There is an extract from a pamphlet attributed to Mr Duffie (when published?) in the Ev^g Post strongly supporting the stand taken by the U. S. Government. May this conflict end in greater union!

Sunday [Dec.] 30th Another clear pleasant day. Th: 40, always meaning in ye house. Read Flint. In 1828 An Academy of Fine Arts attempted in Milledgville. Mean^g probably a place of Exhi[bi]tion. Write on Zeb Spiff.

Monday [Dec.] 31st Another warm day, even warmer than yesterday. Received a note from Cummings & calling on him he said that Mapes had been to him to announce the death of [Thomas] Gimbrede suggesting the idea of my applying for the Situation he had fill'd.[134] Call'd on Mapes who confirm'd the intelligence. See Charles King who advises to write to Verplank & Gouv^r Kemble. Write to Verplank to present my wishes to the Sec^y at War. To Kemble to do the same to Col^l Thayer.[135] Call on Paulding & find that Kemble is in Town & leave

[134] As teacher of drawing at the U. S. Military Academy, West Point.
[135] Sylvanus Thayer, Superintendent and Commandant of the Military Academy.

the business with him. King undertakes to write to Thayer as does S Swartwout. See at Francis' J. O. Hoffman who talks over my Hist Th: General Fleming does the same. Send off letter to J. F. Cooper. Read in Mus[eu]m of Foreign Literature.

January 1st 1833. A rainy day. I make no visits in consequence. Ther: 48 and it is warmer out of doors. Write on Zeb. Spiff. Call at C. P. Clinch's. Th: 52.

[Jan.] 2d Clear & warmer than yesterday. Paint. Read. The Italian Opera having closed Barnes re-opens his Richmond Hill Theatre. A daughter of [Jacob] Woodhulls [Clara Woodhull] announced as a pupil of Mrs Barnes. I met T A Cooper in the street & scarcely knew him. A red bloated face, red nose, feeble walk, attenuated limbs, formed altogether so great a contrast to the man I formerly knew, that I parted from him although our converse was friendly & cheerful, with mournful impressions. He had been sick, recover'd, travel'd to Boston to play, taken sick again, played two nights, had lost all the season all his engagements, wished to go to Charleston S. C. O, What a monument is he to warn others. He is 57 nearly the age Cooke was when he came here & he is now lower in health & strength & in reputation as a player quite gone. It is now little more than a year since I met him in Albany & he has sunk 10 years down the vale. he then professed the necessity of stimulating, wonder'd at my tea system. we touch on the subject to day. Probably we never meet again.

[Jan.] 3d Morning misty. Clears, warmer than yesterday. Th: 50 but much warmer out. Paint. Sidney McCoun call'd with a list of names headed by his father as a Committee to get up a benefit & to ask me to suggest names. See De Bouef's Adam & Eve & Expulsion,[136]

[136] These two paintings by C. M. Dubufe were exhibited in the gallery of the American Academy of the Fine Arts on Barclay Street. See *The New-York Mirror* (X, 306-7), March 30, 1833.

very beautiful. Mr [Ithiel] Town Architect promises me notes on Architecture & Architects.

[Jan.] 4th Friday. Still warmer. Ther: 54.

[Jan.] 5th Sat^{y} Still warmer. The sun oppressive. Several friends pressing to serve me by writing to Washington for the place at W[est] P[oin]t. Judge Hoffman, Morgan, Inman. I write on ye subject to Williamson & Sully. Ev^{g} at Wm. T. McCoun's, the Masquera's there, Castello, Dekay &c and many Ladies. Ther: 56.

Sunday Jany 6th Cloudy. Ther: 58. Last year at this time the weather was warmer than it had been for weeks the Th: ranging from 35 to 40—on ye 12th it was 30, 16th —40, 20th—48. On the 28th down to 18 (and out of doors 2) 31st, 32. From this date the Th: rises but snow & rain alternately. Heretofore this Winter of 1832-3 has been uncommonly mild: Snow has not lain on the ground & has only fallen like a covering of white frost. The sun comes out bright. Walk after writing on Zeb Spiff. till 1: OClock & make an Afternoon visit to Bloomingdale where I have not been for years, I believe not since W W. Woolsey lived there, the house he used to own brought recollections very dear to me.

Monday Jany 7th 1833. Windy. Ther: 52. Council meeting of ye Nat^{l} Academy. Appointed one of 3 to meet a committee of 3 of the Am^{n} Acad^{y} as proposed by them. The design is an Union, they giving up the direction of the United Acad^{y} to the Artists & all right of voting in its concerns, their Artists to become Academicians & their Stockholders hon^{y} members. Ev^{g} a proposition is made by their sect^{y} to have a meeting of the two Comm^{tees} tomorrow morning previous to the notified meeting of the Am^{n} Acad^{y} for the Election of Officers. Received from Mr Verplank the following—"The Secretary of War's compliments to Mr Verplank and acknowledges the receipt of his note of yesterday in favour of William Dunlap as

Professor of Drawing at West Point, which has been placed upon file for consideration. Department of War Jan: 3[d] 1833."

And from Mr Sam[l] Swartwout the following "With Mr Swartout's respects 5th Jan[y]. the enclosure

"Military Academy West Point
Jan[y] 2[d] 1833

My dear Sir

I have the pleasure to acknowledge the receipt of your communication recommending the appointment of Mr Dunlap to the situation of teacher of Drawing at this Institution. Altho' I have not the honor to be personally acquainted with Mr Dunlap I have long entertained a high respect for his character as well as for his talents as an Artist. Not knowing however who are to be candidates for the situation nor whether I will be consulted as to the appointment I can only say for the present that in case reference shall be made to my opinions in the matter your communication shall receive my most respectful & favourable consideration.

I remain very truly yours
S. Thayer

Col[l] Sam[l] Swartwout"

Receive the following

"Paris Nov[r] 14th 1832.

My dear Sir

You have no doubt received my letter explaining the reason of my long silence. The delay as you will readily understand placed me in a great measure at the mercy of the publisher. I fear too you have adopted a little of the prevailing error concerning the interest which is felt in England about America and her literature. Certain individuals have been willing to turn us to account if possible and their puffs and notices have, quite evidently, thrown dust into the eyes of our credulous people, always too much disposed to receive impressions from abroad, when in truth the English reading public would greatly prefer reading abuse of us than anything else. Mrs Trollope has made three times as much (I happen to know her receipts) by her travels than I can get for a Novel. I tell you this that you may understand one reason why England is not quite a mine for us Americans.

The answer of Mr Bentley was a proposal to publish on condition of giving a note for £100 when he had sold 450 copies. I did not like this for it gave us nothing certain. I press'd him as much as circumstances would allow, but under very unfavourable circumstances, for I did not know Mr Bentley personally, and as you will readily understand, I possess no great influence in England, or, for that matter I might say any where else. I was greatly afraid of losing the chance of getting something for you, and accepted the second offer of Mr Bentley. He sent me his note at six months for £50, and has agreed to give another for the same sum and at the same time when he shall have sold 450 copies.

All the book has arrived, with the duplicate copy & all has been forwarded to London. By an oversight of the printers Sig: H of the duplicate copy is sig: H of Mrs Trollope! This mistake might have been serious, but being a duplicate it is no great matter.

The note is in my hands. I very well know you would like to have the money but there are two reasons why I cannot cash it for you. In the first place I do not happen to have so much money invested in America, and secondly if I did I should scarcely know what would be precisely your due. I will however do what I can. Mr Wilkes who was kind enough to take care of my funds, has given up all his affairs on account of ill health and he remitted to me, all the money of mine he had; but a small sum of $150 has since been paid him. Now whether this money is in his hands or those of Mr P. A. Jay, I cannot tell for the latter gentleman has consented to be my trustee for a little while, and he may have received this sum. I have drawn for the $150 in such a way that you will be able to obtain it. For the balance we must calculate. You will give me credit for *seven francs, eleven sous(!)* paid for transportation of sheets to London, make an estimate of the difference of exchanges, first on England where the note is made payable, secondly on France where I am to pay the balance, deduct interest from the day of probable payment here, and from the time you receive the $150, at 5 p^{r} C^{t} and draw for the balance on me at sight. Now here is a pretty job for old John these long evenings in which we young fellows will not meddle. You will remember to draw in francs, and that the exchange on England where the note will be paid must be materially in your favour. The note is payable the 5th of May 1833 being dated the 2^{d} of Novr 1832, at six months. I wish master John joy!

You treat poor Heidenmauer very tenderly in your letter. The Evening Post I had not seen, and it is a paper I do not see once in a year. I thank you for your wish that I may go on & prosper. In answer I have only to say I have done. The book on which I am now employed will probably be the last. I can stand no longer what I have received from home for the last four years, and have made up my mind to retire while I can do it without disgrace. Europe, I think would sustain me a while longer but I cannot forget that I was born an American gentleman. The idea of becoming a hack writer in a foreign land is not to my humour. Were I [to] tell you that my plans are not deranged and my hopes cruelly deceived I should mislead you & myself. But opinion is too strong for me. I think there has been foul play and that the truth will one day be known, but I cannot continue to court a public which repudiates me & my efforts as that of America has done, for the last four years. Some of my friends say that opinion is not represented by those who affect to represent it, in America, and that the mass of the nation will still sustain me. I know full well that there is a set, and a pretty large one, of quasi litterateurs at home, and soi-disant men of taste, who have no sympathies with the real opinion of the country, but then these men are in possession of all the reviews, do all the talking, and give the ostensible tone to all things, and it is too much for me to put these men down: besides "failing houses" as you would say in your book, is a symptom not to be mistaken. My booksellers have been cutting me down gradually these four years, and they have lately written me such a letter, as they would not have written to a man, who had a cordial, or even a respectable support from the public.

We are coming home next season, whether in June or October I cannot now tell you. What we shall do with ourselves it is hard to say. The joint fortunes of Mrs Cooper & myself will not support a family like mine and with the connexions & habits of mine in New York. Besides, to own the truth, we have none of us much heart to mingle in so heartless an affair as mere town society. I shall probably be driven into the interior, but where, Heaven only knows. I shall certainly be forced (even were I disposed to idleness) to do something to eke out an income, for the property of Mrs Cooper, never large, is nearly unproductive as yet, and mine will be sadly reduced by this abandonment of public favour. I have written you freely, my good old friend, but it is not my intention to make a parade of my retirement. The next book will probably be published like the others, sneer'd at like the others, and forgotten like the others, and the world may ask a year or two after what has become of our annual novel. It will then be a nine days wonder and the Athenians will babble of something else.

Tell Morse to pursue his fortunes where he can. We were both born thirty years too soon. Tell him also that Mr Cary quotes the influence of the Journal des Debats against me. He will understand me. Add to this that I have been in the Gallery but once since my return. Habersham looks thin but seems to work hard. But our old set is quite broken up. Frick has gone home, and, indeed, I hardly can name any common acquaintance that is here.

Mrs Cooper desires to be remember'd to the ladies [as] well as myself. I would also put in a word for old John. I shall shortly write to Morse

Yours as ever
J. Fennimore Cooper

W. Dunlap Esq[re]
&c &c &c

I ought to say that Mrs Cooper has offer'd to draw on her trustee for the balance of your note, (a thing she never has yet done for any wants of her own) but I cannot tell what this balance ought to be. I think you will get the money, by showing this letter, very readily from any one who wishes to remit so small a sum."

This letter was accompanied by a draft on Charles Wilkes & in case he had not received the money, another on P. A. Jay.

Tuesday Jany 8th Hard frost, clouds & snow threatening. Touch on a miniature of Washington painted by me many years ago. Meet Henry F. Rogers, Mr [John] Glover and Mr [Pierre] Flandin,[137] on the proposed Union of the Academies. We started the notion of dissolving both & forming one anew. They agreed that it was the only feasible mode. They agreed to the Academy being govern'd & constituted on our plan, all their stockholders having their free admissions (Rogers said that was an evil). They seemed to apologize for having been directors. They did not raise one difficulty, but are to report to their board, & if that approves, call a meeting of Stockholders. We calling a meeting of Academicians for the same purpose.

I saw Mr Jay who said the 150 dollars had been lent by Cooper to Nathl P Willis of the Mirror to bring him home, but the money had not been paid & Willis' draft on his partners protested. Jay however honour'd Coopers draft & I deposited the money making my bank credit $302. Receive the following

West Point found[r]y 7th Jany 1833.

Dr Sir

I have your letter of the 30th Ult^o^ respecting the professorship of Drawing at West Point and have seen Col Thayer on the subject, he tells me that he thinks no appointment will take place earlier than May next. The appointment is, as you know, made by the Secretary of War, and although on some occasions the opinions of Col^l^ Thayer are consulted, it is not always so. It may therefore be well to send an application to Washington. I understand that

[137] Of the American Academy of the Fine Arts. For an account of this unsuccessful attempt to effect a union between the American Academy and the National Academy of Design, see Dunlap's *Arts of Design,* (1834) II, pp. 335 *ff;* and MSS. of the American Academy owned by the New York Historical Society.

Mr Morse has also written to Coll Thayer strongly recommending your appointment.

Your truly
Gouv: Kemble

Wm Dunlap Esqr

Wed^{y} Jany 9th The clouds of yesterday dispersed and the sun was almost as warm as the previous day. Ther: 50. To day Th: 48 Clear & very pleasant. I have the assurance of many letters to further my views on W. P^{t}. Drew $8 from Bank leave $294.

Thursday [Jan.] 10th Threatening snow. Th: 44. Clears up. Morning wasted. Read aftern^{n}. Write on Zeb Spiff. Even^{g} High wind & snow. At Sketch Club. Some news paper gives Charles Leslie of London as successor to Gimbrede!

Friday [Jan.] 11th A little Snow on the ground & a very cold wind. Th: 38. In Mercantile Adv^{r} it is announced that my hist^{y} Am^{n} Th: is in the press of [Richard] Bentley 2 Vols. Write to Verplank requesting information respecting the time of the appointment for W[est] P[oint] and advice as to my going to Washington. In the Mirror, published to day(dated tomorrow) is an editorial article noticing arrangements made for a benefit (festival or grand Theatrical festival) for me. Read Reviews. Write on Zeb Spiff. Some deaths by Cholera said to have happened.

Sat^{y} [Jan.] 12th Th: 34 Very cold out. Library mak^{g} notes. Read reviews. Write Zeb Spiff to conclusion—not finish. Walk for exercise pleasantly as there is no Snow & the cold not sufficiently severe to prevent walking for pleasure.

Sunday Jany 13th 1833. A notice in last ev^{g} Post for a meeting of friends of American Literature & the Drama on account of an intended *complimentary* Benefit to me —signed Wm. T. McCoun, Hugh McLean, G. P. Morris.

MRS. WILLIAM TOWNSEND McCOUN (c. 1791-1845)
(EMMA JACKSON)

Attributed to William Dunlap

(Courtesy of Miss Elisabeth Marbury)

The Th: to day 33. Read Reviews. Correct Zeb Spiff. Walk.

Monday 14th Jany Clear. Ther 36. Evening Council meeting N. A. Appointed one of three to meet Dr Hosack & Messrs [James] Herring & Flandin on the part of Amn Acy

Tuesday [Jan.] 15th Th: 40. Paint. Yesterday I am told a meeting of 41 of our principal gentlemen took place to organize the complimentary Benefit for [me]. I see paragraphs on the subject in ye Courier & Mercantile of to day. Draw from Bank $10 leaving 284$. Write for John C. Hamilton a description of the personal appearance of his father Genl Hamilton. Evening Com: of 2 Acadies meet & unanimous agreed on ye basis of a junction in a new one. Judge Hoffman tells me that Sully is a candidate for the West Point professorship. This evening Morse gives me information which explains the mention of Leslie & Sully in the business. Morse says that before he went to Europe he was offer'd the situation (Gimbrede to be displaced) he of course refused. He says further that a person from Washington was present when [Charles] Gratiot, chief Engineer, nominated, to ye Secy of War Chas Leslie, Thos Sully & S. F. B. Morse. It was observed Leslie will not accept—answer we will try. It was said Sully would not probably & an assurance given that Morse would not (which assurance he confirms)

Wedy 16th Jany 1833. After a night of wind & rain it is clear with Th: 40. Evg colder. Cole & Cummings with me. Go to Council meeting respecting the New Acady. Write to Cooper.

[Jan.] 17th Doing nothing but read. Clear cold day. Send off (or rather put in post Office) letter to Cooper. Knap shows & reads from Voyage of Mrs Abby Morrel [138]

[138] *Narrative of a voyage to the Ethiopic and South Atlantic Ocean in the years 1829, 1830, and 1831.* By Abby Jane Morrell, who accompanied her husband, Capt. Benjamin Morrell, Jr. (N. Y., J. and J. Harper, 1833).

(the wife of Captn Morrel who accompanied him [on] the voyages he has published a book[139] about) which he says he has written—he read from the proof sheets. Read in [William W.] Campbells Annals of Tryon County & Fraser's Magazine.

Friday [Jan.] 18th Walk. Read. Beninger (the son) engages his wife's picture. Write. Th: 36. Clear & cold out. The papers all have extracts from minutes of the meeting on the "Dunlap Benefit" & notice to meet this afternoon. The Committee of the Nal Acady met at Dr D. Hosack's but none of the other Comtee met them except the Doctor. The prospect of merging the two into one appears to me more distant. If not done now it must be defer'd for six months as we must have an Exhibition.

Saty Jany 19th Clear & cold. Yesterday recd from G C Verplank the followg

"Dr Sir

The nomination of Leslie has been actually made to the Senate. It was done on the representation of his brother a paymaster of the Army that Leslie would return to this Country. W. Irving however does not believe it nor can I. Leslie cannot have meant more than a visit. However that may be, all further action on the subject is suspended for some months—when I cannot but believe that the offer will be declined.

Very truly yours

Recd by same mail a letter from Robt Gilmor, dated 16th He says he has applied to a friend for dramatic knowledge, that it may be in his power to assist me as the Work of Arts &c—advises to send printed queries all over the continent. Acknowledges the receit of the packet of Autographs. "Everets & Verplanks I had before being in intimate correspondence with those gentlemen but Godwin's, Holcroft's & Kotzebues were really treasures I had not looked for." He says he has received from "Mr Stuart Wortley the M. P. a letter of his family

139 *A Narrative of Four Voyages . . 1822 to 1831*. By Captain Benjamin Morrell, Jun. (N. Y., J. & J. Harper, 1832).

connexion the celebrated lady Mary Wortley Montague." He says relative to my application for the West Point professorship that he has written to his friend General [Alexander] Macomb "and also to Benjn C. Howard our member, who married my niece and who *has the ear* of the President as much as any member of Congress, in your favour, and begged them both to exert themselves in obtaining the professorship for you. I shall rejoice if these letters prove of service, and I am sure they will engage the interest of two persons as well fitted as any others to succeed with the President."

Cummings tells me he was at the meeting last ev^{g} on the Benefit business. That there were upwards of 50 present & other names answer'd for. It was agreed that pit & Boxes sh^{d} be at $3 the ticket. All present to take not less than five. Some 25. They & their families to go in the pit. No stars or extra to be called for. The Park to be the house. A Committee of 7 appointed to carry the affair through. Wm T McCoun the chairman & Charles King the secretary are two of the 7. Tickets to be had of Wm T. McCoun. A Committee appointed to wait on F G Halleck & request an Address for the occasion. Mr Dean, Mr Cutting & others spoke. Mr [Francis B.] Cutting read a paper of resolutions to be published with names of the persons meeting affixed which resolutions were agreed to.

Dr McLean called to tell me the result of the meeting. He is one of the Committee. He said it was thought best to have it soon & without extra aid. The play Fraternal Discord the Farce Bonapart in England. Ev^{g} Write on Zeb Spiff.

Sunday Jany 20th 1833. Rewrite a great part of my Farce of Bonaparte in England. Th: these 2 days 36 & 37. Clouds.

Monday [Jan.] 21st Fog. Th: 40. Write on B in England. Meet Committee at Dr Hosacks. Agreed that the Stockholders of the A. A. sh^{d} in ye N Acad^{y} be still stockholders but with[ou]t vote. All power being in y[e] Acad[ns]. Morse & Herring to meet & draw up a paper to be submit[d] to the Committee tomorrow. Col[l] Stone calls on me.

Tuesday [Jan.] 22[d]. Fog. Th: 42. Write on Bon: in Engl[d] Afternoon at Dr Hosacks committee not yet prepared.

Wed[y] [Jan.] 23[d] Fog Th: 42. Hosack has written for the Kembles for y[e] Benefit, contrary to my wishes. Write as yest[y] Ev[g] at Hosacks. The two Committees [of the two Academies] agree on terms of Union & they are adopted by the Council of the Na[l] Academy.

[Jan.] 24th Fog & rain. Ther 44. By arrangement the Directors of the Am[n] Acad[y] was to [have] call'd at 5 this afternoon to adopt or reject the Agreement. Herring writes to our Sec[y] that [John] Trumbul says no meeting shall take place without his previous consent. He adds that he has called a meeting notwithstanding. The com[tee] of the Nat[l] Acad[y] meet at Hosacks at 7. Draw out $30 to pay for clothing, leaving $254. Rain & an increase of a heavy cold prevent my attending at Dr Hosacks or at the Sketch Club at Mr Wards. The American of tuesday & E Post of to day talk of Extra performers for the Complimentary benefit.

Friday [Jan.] 25th Rain all day & last night. Th: 44. Write on Bonaparte in England & finish it.

Saturday [Jan.] 26th Th: 40. Out door hard frost. Read in For: Quarterly & Journals. Write on 2[d] copy of Zeb Spiff draw out $10 leav[g] in Bank 244.

Sunday [Jan.] 27th Morning cloudy. Th: 40. Read in Foreign Quarterly article Goethe. Writen surely by a German—full of mysticism. Clear & mild after 9. Write on 2[d] copy of Z. S.

Tuesday [Jan.] 29th Yesterday & to day Th: 40. Yesterday wrote a little. Ev^{g} at Hosacks with Morse Durand & Cummings Hosack & Flandin came in from the meeting of their Directory & told us that Trumbull had come prepared with a writing which he read to them, & which the Directors approved & order'd to be printed—that the Agreement of the Committees was put on file. Flandin was convinced that Trumbulls discourse was unanswerable & show'd that the Stockholders could not give up their right of voting for Directors. Hosack said little. I remarked to him that he had asserted that Trumbull was out of the way. He laugh'd. The conversation was desultory, I said the business was at an end—Morse said the same—an appointment was made for a Council meeting for this evening & I left them to go & see a part of Forest's Hamlet. This Ev^{g} (Tuesday) at Council meet^{g} directing preparations for our Annual Exhibition.

Wed^{y} [Jan.] 30th Ther: 42. Out of doors warmer. Wrote on 2^{d} Copy of Zeb Spiff. Dine at Arch^{d} Rogers. Ev^{g} & night Rain.

Thursday 31st Jany Storm, rain & hail. Th: 42. Becomes a Snow Storm. Write on Zeb Spiff. Read [Timothy] Flint's Francis Berrian. Remain at home all day.

Friday Feby 1st The ground is cover'd with a few inches of snow. Go to Library &c. G. P. Morris requests Bonaparte in England for the Festival Committee. Meet Placide who says he will play it or any thin[g]. Forest has volunteer'd. Read in Mirror &c & Write on Zeb Spiff.

Sat^{y} Feby 2^{d} Clear. Th: 33. Note for 150 due Feby seventh or Thursday next. Write & read. Vathek.[140]

Sunday [Feb.] 3^{d} Ther: 33. Write on Zeb Spiff.

Monday [Feb.] 4th Ther: 32. Give Morris for Mirror a note [of] encouragement for J. F. Cooper. The Editors are all against him owing to his defiance of them. Write a

[140] A romance by William Beckford.

description of the inauguration [of] Washington for Stone. Attend to Note due 7th Weather clear. Read [Sir Thomas S.] Raffles' Java.

Tuesday [Feb.] 5th Clear. Th: 34. Write to John Williamson of Norfolk. Read [Etienne] Dumonts Mirabeau. Write on Zeb Spif. Talk with the Harpers on the subject of publishing it.

Wedy [Feb.] 6th Th: 36. Slight snow & rain. Clear at Noon. Write on Zeb Spiff. Read. Evening cold & windy.

Thursday [Feb.] 7th Clear. Ther: 34. Very windy & cold out. See Morse's picture of the Gallery of the Louvre and several other pictures beautifully painted. He is engaged in answering Trumbuls weak and false publication respecting the National Academy. Read in Mrs Radcliffes memoirs Note p: 72 Carey & Lea's edition. Raising of Lazarus by West. Evening Sketch Club at Clinton Hall, T Cole's night. Look in at Theatre & see Miss Kemble in Juliet's great scene of madness & taking the draught. It appeared to me exaggerated & the celebrated slide altogether pantomimic. Mr Mason I saw in the Apothecary scene & thought him the worst Romeo I ever saw.

Friday [Feb.] 8th Clear. Not so cold. Pay Quarter's rent to C. Judson $68.75 drew out of Bank 48.75 Leaving 194 dolls Receive letter from T. Sully to aid in my Histy of Fine Arts.

Saturday Feby 9th 1833. Spring like clear day. Th: 40 & warmer out of doors. Write on Zeb. Spiff. Read Mrs Radcliffs last romance with little pleasure or profit. At Barclay Stt Exhibition. Much concerned respecting Henry Eckford's death.

Sunday [Feb.] 10th Clear. Ther: 44. Write on Zeb Spiff. Walk. After my dinner, I answered the bell of the Street door, as our only servant had gone to church. Two gentlemen presented themselves & one of them presented his card, supposing probably that I was not myself—that I was my servant is certain. It was Mr Charles Kemble & his nephew Mr J. Mason. Mr Kemble presenting the card, mentioned my name. I said I am Mr Dunlap—"he had come to return my call." I invited & they came in sat perhaps 20 minutes, Kemble & myself in chat respecting Theatres (of which he said there were many in London at 3d & 6d entrance) painters, players &c. "Mr Whitlock in fine health and as young as ever" They took their leave & I must now call on Kemble & daughter *which I have not yet done.* The occasion of the call—the acknowledgement or assertion of my having called on him—is all unknown to me.

Monday [Feb.] 11th Th: 44. Clouds & storm threatening. Call at B. W. Rogers's whose wife is dying of consumption. Call on C. Clinch to know if any tiding respecting H. Eckford is received. See the Harpers respecting Zeb. Spiff. Offer for 500 dollars one editn of 2000, retaining rights of Copy & to publish in England. See that Barnes announces Miss Fanny Kemble's Frances the first. Evg read in Miss Austin's Emma with pleasure. Snow.

[Feb.] 12th Th: 41. Clouds & the ground cover'd slightly with Snow. In ye E. Post of yesterday is republished a letter of E Forrest denouncing the Courier & Enquirer in which he implicates his friends of the Post probably without intention. Forest has in the most libberal manner volunteered to the Committee for my benefit. I call'd on G. P. Morris, he tells me that Bryant has furnished him with a biographical notice of me for the Mirror. Morris undertakes to write an Address & when I left him was going to C Kemble to settle respecting his appearing on the above occasion (& his daughter) or not. The Harpers incline to publish the Novel & I am to leave it with them for decision.

[Feb.] 13th Yesterday ev^{g} & night rain & so to day. Th: 42. Write on Novel. Rain & hail all day. Read in Emma. Receive a letter from Mr Lines of New Haven requesting my decision of the question whether Desdemona [meant] that she wished Heaven had made such a man as Othello for her, or made her, instead of a woman a man similar to Othello. I shall say the latter.

[Feb.] 14th Clear. Ther: 40. Write Mr Lines. See the Harpers & leave 1st Vol: of Zeb Spiff. Call at Office of Mirror. The Kembles are engaged for my Night. Call on Mr C Kemble. Not in. Call on Cummings. Morse has written his answer to Trumbull. Call at B. W. Rogers's. My daughter still there & Mrs R still lingering. Henry Eckford's family have rec^{d} the confirmation of his death in Constantinople. Receive the London Edition of my Am^{n} Theatrical History, in 2 vols price 28/ (sterling of course) Ev^{g} Sketch club at Doctor [William Walton] Verplanks. Bryant, Weir, Nelson, Mason, Ingham &c &c.

Feby 15th 1833. Th: 40. Clear. Write to J. F. Cooper by Peter Gassner. Afternoon Snow Storm. Read Miss Austens Emma with much pleasure.

Saturday [Feb.] 16th About 10 inches of Snow on the ground. The day mild & clear. Ther: 40. Every body apparently in sleighs. Have an explanation with Harpers respecting copy right of my Theatrical History which I feared they considered as theirs. All settled satisfactorily. Mr Clark gives me hopes that for 150 doll^{s} the Brooklyn Insurance will release their claim on me for $150. I find from the Harpers & from Paulding that there [is] disatisfaction between them. "Westward ho" dont sell well. It has not been republished in England owing (Paulding says) to its being sent through the post Office & Bulwer refusing to pay £5 postage. P. says he will have nothing more to do with them.

Sunday [Feb.] 17th Confined to the house owing to a fall on the ice yesterday evening which hurt my back &

has given me besides lameness a sick headach. Write on Zeb Spiff. Read "Swallow Barn" [141] with pleasure. Read in [John] Taylors records—a queer book about every body. Rain in ye night.

Monday [Feb.] 18th Th: 42. Thaw & Fog. Wet. Do not walk until 5 P. M. Snow gone in town. Write on Zeb. Spiff. Read Taylors Record. Curious opinions. 1st Tristram Shandy "Contemptable nauseous & obscene Rhapsody" Wolcott after twice conversing with Curran declared he "would not insult his magpie by offering her that fellows brains for a dinner" Taylor himself speaks contemptuously of Curran. He tells a story of Merry to make him infamous. Doctor Monsey is eulogized yet calls Mrs Garrick a bitch at her own table & Garrick laughs! There are other instances of *manners* highly improving & the general State of morals between the sexes is truly edifying. Warburton is insolent impudent & a knave. Voltaire broke open a ladies escritoire at whose house he dined. Boswell is a fine fellow & they got drunk together (that is he & Taylor). The Revd Mr Bate Editor of ye Morning Post fighting a duel & shooting Richardson another Edr. That Lord Chatham died in consequence of rage while the Duke of Richmond abused him in Parlt, C choking. Copley's picture. The peers never debate in their robes. Duchess of Kingston without religion or decency Appears at a masquerade nearly naked. Mr Burke hard, uncharitable, irritable and not admirable as to talent. Peters the portrait painter studies divinity because Wilson the landscape painter was in distress for money & P. thought he could make more by preaching. Gifford & P. quarrel & are the bitterest enemies. This book is a satire upon human nature & English society; the author a silly fellow. A letter being left with Lord Grosvenor to frank, was accidentally without seal and his *Lordship* opened & read it! Peters & Gifford each accuse the other of mean subserviency to the vices of Lord Grosvenor. Hopner a satirist & enemy to Peters as a painter.

141 By John Pendleton Kennedy.

Peters painted indecent pictures for his patron Lord Grosvenor!

Tuesday [Feb.] 19th 1833. Th: 46. Foggy as yesterday but clears as yesterday. I am this day 67 years of age & enter of course ye 68th My health generally good: my activity little impaired. My pecuniary circumstances better. My blessings many and my thankfulness not adequately strong, but I am thankful & hope to be more & more so, whatever my state bowing in gratitude to my creator. Write on Zeb Spiff Read Taylor's record & write a notice of it for E. Post.

Wed^{y} [Feb.] 20th Took up my note of long standing due to Brooklyn Insurance Office. Leave in Bank 23 dollars. See C Kemble & have a chat at Office of Mirror. Call at E. Post Office. Henry Eckford's remains arrive from Constantinople.

[Feb.] 21st Frosty out. Th: in its usual place 46. Write on Zeb. Spiff. Ev^{g} See a scene of Miss Kembles Frances 1st Go to Sketch Club at Ingham's. full & pleasant meeting.

[Feb.] 22^{d} Th: 42. Out of doors Spring. I received a letter from Williamson desiring me to draw on Hall for 40 dollars he says "I wrote to Genl Gratiot in your behalf & received an answer that your recommendation stood as high as any other candidate but that the place had been promised to Mr Leslie." Receive letter from H Inman desiring me to secure him a place on the 28th the letter is feeling & friendly. Write to Williamson, Inman, Neagle, James Thackara & send Williamson a copy of ye Mirror with Bryants Biographical sketch of me.

[Feb.] 23^{d} Th: 44. Perfect spring. Write on Zeb Spiff. Walk. Read.

Sunday [Feb.] 24th Cloudy & colder. Finish revising Zeb Spiff. Afternoon Springlike. Walk. Ev^{g} Hard rain. Snow. Cold Wind th: in y^{e} day 50. Read Taylor. I will not say silly fellow but odd. Read in Swallow Barn. Said to be by Dr. Kennedy of Baltimore. Great cleverness.

Mond[ay Feb.] 25th Snow in drifts. Clear & cold. Read. See Taylor's Records for Sheridan & Kemble p. 381. Forrest is to play in $Phil^{a}$ Wed^{y} night 27th yet be in N. Y. to rehearse next morning. Read Swallow Barn.

[Feb.] 26th Clear & cold. Th: 36. Finish Swallow Barn one of the best productions of the country. The Harpers have had my Man^{t} of Z. S. some days & dissapointed me repeatedly by not giving a decision—it is in the hands of some one who has not given his opinion. Morse's examination of Trumbulls address I read to day. It exposes it fully—but who will read?

[Feb.] 27th Ther: 39. Clouds. Clears up. Give a few lines to Clayton and Van Orden for a pamphlet containing opposite passages from my Address to the Nat^{l} $Acad^{y}$ & Trumbuls address to Am^{n} $Acad^{y}$. Call it Conflicting Opinions or Doctors differ.

[Feb.] 28th Clouds. Th: 39. Out of doors cold East wind. Noon begins to Snow & continues to March 1st

March 1st 1833. Th: 36. Violent Snow Storm. On the evening of the 27th ult: received the following.

"New York Feb 27th 1833

Dear Sir

At a meeting of the Committee of the Citizens of New York friendly to Literature and the Drama, held this evening at the Shakspeare Hotel it was unanimously resolved that ten tickets, seats secured in Box No. 16 be presented to you and the members of your family for the Benefit to take place at the Park tomorrow Evening.

We are with sentiments of Esteem and great respect yours

Chas King Sec^{y} David Hosack Chairman

To Wm Dunlap Esqr

Answer

New York Feby 28th 1833

Gentlemen

I have received with sentiments of profound gratitude your favour of yesterday announcing that &c

I regret that I cannot avail myself of this delicate attention, for which, and the honour the Committee have done me in the eyes of my fellow Citizens I have not words adequate to the expression of my feelings.

I must request of you gentlemen to present to the Committee the assurances of my grateful sense of what has been done for me, and to receive with them my thanks.

With sentiments of the greatest respect &c

The Harpers return my Manuscript (e i the portion left with them) with the following

"W D Esqre

Dear Sir

Our literary friend has turned in your M. S. but declines giving an opinion. He says that he cannot form one until he has read the second Volume, and he will not advise us until he has read to the end. We regret that we could not get out of him something more definite and satisfactory. As the business now stands we can do nothing. If therefore you can procure from Carey a satisfactory offer you had better accept it. If however you should not succeed in procuring such an offer, the attempt shall not operate against our taking the work afterwards. That is their declining shall not influence us at all in the case. Were we not situated in our business as we are at present we should probably pursue a course somewhat different.

Yrs. J. & J. Harper

Read in Ed: Rev: Correct Zeb. Spiff. Doctor Francis calls and tells me that he was at the Park Theatre last night and all went well. That Miss F. Kemble was a poor Belvidera, her father a so so Jaffier and Forrest a superb Pierre. Hundreds of the Audience of last night would see him for the first time & hundreds prejudiced against him, therefore his exertions for me will be rewarded by well earned reputation. Mrs Sharpe spoke G P Morris's address well, and it was received with enthusiasm. The Doctor avows the intention of calling me out, this I foresaw & avoided.

I saw Charles Judson yesterday & he agreed that I should have the house No 64 Sixth Avenue at $275 the next year & expend 25 of it in paint & repairs. Snow continues all day. Read & correct Zeb. Spiff. The Ev^{g} Post has a letter from Charles Kemble to the Committee refusing compensation for himself & daughter for the benefit.

March 2d 1833. Ther: 34. Clear. Ground cover'd deeper wh snow than any time this winter. Write a letter to H. C. Carey to accompany M. S. of Zeb. Spiff. offering it on his own terms with or without copyright—send him Harpers letter. Th: falls to 28 High wind. Snow squalls & drifts. Leave the M. S. & letter with B. W. Rogers who living at the American Hotel with his family undertakes to forward it to Carey. Every one tells me that the Festival of Thursday went off greatly & Blake of the Theatre says the company was not only twice as numerous as at J. H. Payne's benefit but in better style & the satisfaction expressed much greater. The amt received & expences not yet known.

Sunday March 3d Clear: Th: 25. G. P. Morris's address spoken by Mrs Sharpe has gain'd him credit. All speak highly of Forrests Pierre. His enemy of the Courier blackguards him. I see by my memoranda that this time last year the weather & temperature were warm & pleasant & on the 19th cold (Th: 28) and snow on ye ground.

Philosophy—Metaphysics—Natural Theology—now are more free in their enquiries than within my recollection. Men, who see at all, see that it does not derogate from the character of God or limit his power, and that it is much more stimulating to mans religious feelings to consider the Deity as all benevolent & the enemy of physical as well as moral evil, than as all powerful & permitting even the most trifling physical evil. We can only conceive of God by ourselves. His goodness in our minds can be only our goodness infinitely magnified; his power can only be our power infinitely extended & incomprehensibly greater but still limitted, or evil could not exist. That there is a prevalence of good we see, we enjoy & ought to be grateful for, that there is progressive good we see & exult in the hope that man will be hereafter incomparably better & happier; but this view of the subject serves to prove the existence of great present evil, without detracting from the loveliness of the character of an infinitely benevolent God. The will of God is love to all. Reason tells us this. But Reason the greatest good gift bestowed on man is progressive as is all other good. The Will of Good is communicated by reason. Every truth discovered by reason is a Revelation from God. Self (Ego) is the *subject,* any thing perceivable by self is an *object.* My foot, my hand, my pen, are equally objects—self (the faculty of perception) is distinct—the *subject* perceives the *object,* and reflecting on both conceives the bond of union in a first cause. Is this the process that leads to the knowledge of God?

We may conceive of Evil as necessarily inherent in matter & of matter as improvable; consequently evil as *finite* and God as infinite. This view of our creator encourages hope as well as gratitude & makes religion a system of consolation & thanksgiving. Paley, Butler, Balguy, all in the main agree in the above view respecting good & evil. The last has these words "men must be gradually formed to that capacity and temper which are to make them happy for ever." Now I interpret this *thus.* The infinitely Benevolent would if within the limits of possibility have made all things perfect instantaneously, but that being inconsist[ent] with the qualities of matter or the material, the state of perfection or happiness is progressive. We & those who preceeded us are necessary links in the great chain which is to become brighter & brighter by a law, the best possible, impressed upon creation from the beginning. The present is the effect of the past and the cause of the future. Could any thing be changed without changing the whole? Yet whatever has been, or is, or will be of evil, is contrary to the will of God, yet *is* of necessity. God is only the cause of Good. Yet through evil good ultimately will come, as the omniscient seeing, design[ed] his universe.

Cummings & Mapes call on me. The latter saw the Farce of B: in England and from his repeating portions & describing effects I judge it that it pleased.

Monday March 4th 1833. Clear & cold. Th: 26. Said to be 6 out of doors. This commences another term of ye presidency of Andrew Jackson. The enforcing Bill and the Bill for modifying ye Tariff both passed. It is supposed that the profit from the Festival will be 2400. It is announced in the papers at 2800 and 3000. Afternoon H Inman & Cummings with me. Receive the following

2 Pine St March 1st 1833

William Dunlap Esq

My dear Sir

As I am conscientiously opposed to the Theatre I could not join in the late exertions of your friends in promoting your benefit at the

Park Theatre but I cannot let the occasion pass without giving you some testimonial of the high respect and esteem I entertain for you as a gentleman an Artist and a personal friend. I beg you will therefore accept the accompanying copy of *Raphael's hours* from your sincere & well wisher

Saml F. B. Morse

Tuesday [March] 5th Clear. Th: 26. Afternoon light clouds. Negociating with Niblo respecting my exhibition pictures. I understand that Debuff's pictures of Adam & Eve have been unusually successful many days yealding 100 dollars ye day. Reading in Beachy's Narrative.[142]

To Edwin Forrest

I cannot be content that the Committee who have evinced their regard for me, should alone return thanks to you for your prompt offer and efficient exertions on that occasion. I beg of you to accept my warmest <*thanks*> acknowledgements & assurances that I feel deeply & <*deeply*> gratefully not only the service but the manly frank & unostentatious manner in which it was performed. It gives me pleasure to add that my personal friends <*feel*> express the same sentiment; and the public joins with them in praise likewise of your professional skill and full complete success on the occasion.

Respectfull & gratefully Your friend
W D

Receive the following by the hands of my good young friend W Sidney McCoun

New York March 5th 1833

Dear Sir

It has become my pleasing duty as the Chairman of the Committee appointed by the Citizens of New York who were convened to express their deep sense of the services render'd by you to the promotion of the Fine Arts and to the Dramatic literature of our Country to inform you that a Benefit has been appropriated in which many of your fellow Citizens have had an oppertunity of expressing their estimate of those services & bearing their testimony to your character as a private citizen—for the proceeds I refer you to the Hon^{bl} Wm. T. McCoun the Treasurer.

Allow me in the name of the Committee to congratulate you upon the success that has attended their efforts and to add their fervent

[142] Frederick W. Beechey, R. N., *Narrative of a voyage to the Pacific . . . 1825–28.* (London, 1831; Philadelphia, 1832).

wishes that the evening of your life may be as happy as the former part of it has been usefully and honourably employed in the advancement of the cause of virtue—accept Dear Sir the expression of my personal regard & respect

David Hosack Chairman

Wm Dunlap Esqr

Answer.

March 5th 1833 N. Y.

Dear Sir

I acknowledge the rec^{t} of y^{r} letter & with pleasure your communication of this morning.

Of the many very gratifying testimonials which I have received, <*of the esteem*> evincing the good opinion of my fellow Citizens connected with the event you allude to none will be valued more highly by me than the approbation of my conduct through life <*expressed*> manifested by the Committee <*of*> appointed by the Citizens of New York who were convened to express their sense of the services I had render'd to the Fine Arts & the Dramatic literature of the Country, <*through you their Chairman in this letter*> manifested through you their chairman

<*Let me*> I must beg of you, Sir, to find language wherewith to <*express*> communicate my deep sense of the honour the Committee has done me <*in the eyes of my fellow Citizens, and to tender my thanks*> I cannot find words to express my sense of the feelings shewn towards me. For yourself Sir accept the expression of my <*respect and*> esteem and best wishes <*that you may long continue your benevolent exertions*> for your welfare

Wm Dunlap

March 6th 1833. Snow. Clears away. Th: 30. Write to Hosack & Forrest as above. G. P. Morris tells me that he & others are endeavouring to excite the Philadelphians to follow the example of N. Y. and get up a Benefit for me.

Thursday [March] 7th Clear. Th: 34. A deep snow on the ground. G. P. Morris tells me the Festival will net me 2517 dollars. The proprietor of the Knickabacker Mag^{ne} engages me to write a brief biography of Gilbert Stewart. Read Beachy's Narrative. Ev^{g} go to Nelson for Sketch club find it postponed & sit with him & [illegible] Col Fish & the ladies a few minutes.

Friday [March 8] Clear Ther: 36. Write on Stewart. Receive from Thos Williamson through Mechanics Bank $40 which he rec^d from Hall of Norfolk for me. Now in B. N. Y. 53.40. Th: rises to 40. complete thaw. Begin Biography of S.

Saturday March 9th Clear. Th: 42. The Vice Chancellor gives me the following

Dunlap Committee

Money received		
669 Tickets sold @ 3....................	2007	
241 D° sold by members of the Committee.	723	
4 Gallery tickets	4	2734
96 Box tickets sold by Mr Simpson.......	288	
50 Gallery	50	388
Donations		
From James G. King....................$	20	
Moses Field	5	
Edmond Simpson	50	
Rec^d by Charles King and Genl Fleming....	47.50	122.50
		$3194.50
Monies p^d Out		
To Mr Simpson Charge for house.........$	561.04	
G[eorge] P. Scott & Co (for tickets &c)...	65.87½	
Amos Butler[143] (advertising)..............	19.12½	
Sundries	30.92	676.96
		$2517.54

Note Mr Simpson's 50 dollars donation is a deduction from the charge of the house. Mr Amos Butler's bill was 38.25 & he deducted half. All the other Editors gave the whole of their advertising. Among the sundries paid was a present of 25 for a dress to the Lady who spoke the Address.

rec^d 111	$2517.54
250	361.
361	$2156.54

remaining April 1, 1833
with Wm T. McCoun

[143] Amos Butler was editor and publisher of the *Mercantile Advertiser and New York Advocate.*

Write on Biography of Gilbert Stuart for the Nickabacker.[144] Read in Atheneum

Sunday March 10th Clear. Th: 44. Finish sketch of a Biography of Gilbert Stuart for the Knickerbacker. Look over [John] Galt's [*Life of Benjamin*] West. A sprinkling of Snow in the night.

Monday [March] 11th Th: 44. Clear. Make enquiry respecting an Annuity for myself & family. Not yet answered.

Tuesday [March] 12th Th: 45. Mist & rain. Write on biography of West. Received from Knickabaker $25.

Wedy [March] 13th Clouds. Th: 44. The above sum was enclosed in a note from Messrs. Peabody & Co.

To Mr Thos Wells
No 111 Fulton Street Brookly[n]
Sir/
I acknowledge the receit of a note from you accompanying a letter. The Style of that letter precludes an answer. To you, from whom I acknowledge the civilities of intercours and with whom I have before communicated on ye subject, I will state, in reply to your note, that I consider myself under no obligation in law or equity to the person alluded to.
I further state that I have just and acknowledged demands upon me for more than I can ever possibly possess of property: and that the monies accruing from the liberality of my friends as a testimony to my literary efforts will not be placed at my disposal & is now in the hands of the Vice Chancellor

Respectfully &c W. D.

Recd 111 dollars. Pd E. Bennet in full $10. Deposit in N. Y. B. $30 making in bank $83. My Note in Bank will be due April 10th I offer'd to take up a note given to Pendleton for $65 but the person who presented it demanding interest, which I refused, he is to see me tomorrow.

144 Dunlap's "Biographical Sketch of the late Gilbert Stuart" was printed in *The Knickerbocker,* I, 195-202, April, 1833.

Thursday [March] 14th Clear: Th: 41. Write a letter to go by H: Inman tomorrow to H. C. Carey respecting Zeb. Spiff. Mrs B. W. Rogers [145] died this day. Write on Biography of West.

Friday [March] 15th Clouds. Clears pleasant. Pay Parker & Clover a balance of $62. Pd Yesterday 65 to take up note to John Pendleton. I have in Bank to[day] $21. Wm T. McCoun holds in trust for my Wife, the money from ye Benefit & is to put it on interest at 6 per cent taking Bond & Mortgage Security. See Mr Peabody & mention publishing. I have paid outstanding debts

To Insurance Co	366
Jnoo Allan	25.50
Jno Pendleton	65.43
E Bennet	10
Parker & Clover	62
	$528.93

Saturday March 16th 1833. Clear. Th: 44. Write on Biography of West. Read. Ingham called to tell me that Weir had been applying for the West Point situation & that the interest of Mr Forsyth has been solicited for me.

Sunday [March] 17th Clear. Th: 45. Read. Write. Evg at Mr McCoun's. Th: 44. J. H. Payne can't get up benefit in Boston.

Monday [March] 18th Th: 46. Clouds clear off pleasant. Pay E. Post $6.87 (4.75 for Bowen & self) in Bank $14.12½

Tuesday [March] 19th Clear. Th: 56. In Bank 4.12½. M. M. Noah is about setting up an evening paper.[146] He says to prevent Mat. Van Beuren from becoming presi-

[145] Mrs. Benjamin Woolsey Rogers, *née* Catharine Cecilia Elwyn.

[146] The first number of the *Evening Star,* of which Mordecai Manuel Noah was editor and publisher, was printed September 25, 1833.

dent. Noah's friends advance the money "So" he says "if it fails I lose nothing." G. P. Morris talks of an even^{g} paper too. Noah rattled away very pleasantly in Morris's private office. Read. Ev^{g} Rain.

Wed^{y} [March] 20th Rain. Ther: 54. Write letters of introduction for Wm Sidney McCoun to C. B. King & Doctor [Robert] Greenhowe of Washington and to Robt Gilmore of Baltimore sending to the last Autographs for his collection.

Thursday [March] 21st Mist. Th: 56. Read Dumonts Mirabeau. Ev^{g} Sketch club. Emerson tells me that Charles F. Hoffman mentioned that I was engaged as Editor of the Knickerbacker. I set him right. In Bank $254.12½.

Friday [March] 22^{d} Clear. Six A. M. Th: 59. Call on C. F. Hoffman and explain respecting the Knickabacker stating that Peabody had asked me to contribute & I had assented. He says P: used him ill & that he seperated from him after receiving a years salary. P: first mentioned me as the Editor & then as combined with others. I assured H. I had not undertaken or even been offer'd the Editorship. He said on P's mentioning me, he (H) had written a notice of his declining & expressing his pleasure that the work would be conducted by me. Hopkins McKracken is the author of articles on language in the work.

Sat^{y} [March] 23^{d} Clear. Yesterday the Frogs were in full concert in every pond & pool. Th: 59. Call on Verplank—out. Inman has return'd. Carey has not yet read Zeb Spiff. Read [Peter] King's [*Life of John*] Locke.

Sunday [March] 24th Clear. Th: 58. Write on 2^{d} Vol: Am^{n} Th: Read King's Locke. Walk to Dry Dock.

Monday [March] 25th Clouds. Th: 55. Clears. Taking down my pictures from Br^{d} Way. Read Locke.

Tuesday March 26th 1833. Clear Th: 55. Write. I have in Bank $234. Remove my large pictures to my house. Finish reading Locke.

Wed[y] [March] 27th Clear. Th: 50. Ice out of doors. Write. Call on Doctor Francis. Read.

In Bank 200 dollars	
Bring forward debt p[d].......	528.93
p[d] Judah & Callender	33.47
	562.40

Thursday [March] 28th Clear. Th: 50. Read. Write recommendatory letters to R West & J F Cooper for Mr Phillip. At Morse, Durand's, Library. Read Mrs Hutchinson: Ev[g] Wright's Sketch Club.

Friday [March] 29th Clear. Th: 48. Receive papers from Rich[d] Penn Smith on Th: Hist: from Peabody on the Dunlap Festival with a wish of Doctor Hosack that they be published in y[e] Knickerbacker. I don't wish it. Write to R. P. Smith & Charles Fraser. Write on Hist[y] Am[n] Th:

Sat[y] [March] 30th Clear. Th: 48. Write to Alston—to Sargeant. Call on Inman who shows me my Address to y[e] Students published in a London Work on y[e] fine Arts. Receive the following

My dear Sir —&c—

having read it (Zeb Spiff) I fell much at a loss what to say respecting it. The use of the names of Cooper & others would have a strong tendency to make it sell, but it appears to me very doubtful if it be proper thus to use those names, and I should hardly be disposed to publish it with them although I consider them important aids to the sale of it. If published as it stands I believe it will sell & am persuaded that you could hardly fail to derive an advantage from it & that Harpers could readily dispose of a considerable edition, although we should hardly like to do it. We are at this moment exceedingly crowded with light books for publication having as many as will carry us at the rate of one per week, far into the Summer & it would not be easy to find a place into which to insert it. I regret very much that it is not in my power to make a liberal offer for it &c &c &c. Under existing circumstances I must return it &c &c.

H. C. Carey

Phil. March 27th 1833.

The parcel will be sent in a Box we are packing for Messrs Carvells.

Read in Mrs Hutchinson. Stewarts Sandwich Island.[147] Cunninghams West[148] &c.

Sunday March 31st 1833. Clear. Th: 50. Walk. Write on Histy of Painting. Afternoon walk & view the excavations & embankments of the intended rail road to Haerlaem. Finish Mrs Hutchinson. Read Stewart.

Monday April 1st Clear. Th: 56. Dept. pd . . 560.40
pd Advertisers . . . . 10.
$570.40

I have in Bank $190.

Received my M. S. of Zeb Spiff. Received John F. Watson's book of "Tale of ye Olden time" with a complimentary letter from him & a request for contributions respecting the old time of N. Y. & its vicinity. Evg meet council of N. A. at Clinton Hall.

Tuesday [April] 2d Cl: Th: 59. Write to John F. Watson, Germantown & James R. Lambdin, Pittsburg. Write on Biography of B. West. Evg at Wm T. McCoun's & at a meeting of the Academicians & Associates of the National Academy. Morse deliver'd the premiums to the Students & address'd the Academy. I moved Resolutions which were adopted & signed by all the Artists present & order'd to be published. Th: rose to 62.

147 Rev. Charles S. Stewart, *Private Journal of a Voyage to the Pacific Ocean and Residence at the Sandwich Islands in the years 1822, 1823, 1824, and 1825*. (N. Y., 1828).

148 In Allan Cunningham's *The Lives of the Most Eminent British Painters and Sculptors* (N. Y., J. & J. Harper, 1831) II, 5-53.

Wed[y] [April] 3[d] some clouds. Th: 58-60. Clear. Ev[g] Rain. After paying note in Bank I have there $30. Write of Wests biography. Peabody asks for 6 or 7 pages for next Knickerbacker to be paid at my own price. Read Miss Kembles Francis 1st which has good passages but it improbable in incident & monstrous in the motives of the dramatis personae—characters it has none.

Thursday 4th April. Clearing after rain. Th: 60. Write. Read Stewarts Sandwich Islands. Receive the following

"New York Ap[l] 5th 1833.

D[r] Sir

We should be happy to receive from you a short Article upon any subject that may suit you for our next No. of the Knickerbacker. Any compensation for the favor will be held subject to your wishes by Y[s] very truly

Peabody & Co

To Wm Dunlap Esq[re]

Walk to Bloomingdale & back.

Friday [April] 5th Clear. Th: 62. C: Leslie is announced as professor of Draw[g] at West Point to be out in Sept. next. See Peabody who says he pays two Editors for the Knickerbacker. I promise a communication for next month. Read Stewarts second voyage to the Sandwich Islands & strictures on Beauty and Kotzebue.

Sat[y] [April] 6th Clear. Th: 60. Write on Biography of C. W. Peale. Walk. Mr Castello calls on me & tells me the portrait of St Ander has not sold at Caraccas that he takes it himself & has order'd it to Bogota for sale. He pays me $20 for it.

Sunday [April] 7th Clear. Th: 59. Write on biography of B. West Walk Read Cab[t] of Nat[l] Hist: Even[g] at W T McCouns Mr Woods there. Write John F. Watson. Rain.

Monday April 8th 1833. Rain. Th: 56. Write on Biography of Archibald Robertson. Evg Council of Natl Acady Clinton Hall. Read Natl Hist:

Tuesday [April] 9th Clear. Th: 60. Post Office with letter to H. C. Carey. Bank. Clayton & Van Orden's. Library. The Harpers. They agree to print Zeb Spiff: it is to be submitted to John Inman who is their hired reader & saw part of it before. I showed them Carey's letter. They are to take their time as to publishing. Dekay asked them 1500 for his Constantinople & they offer'd him 750—he took it to Carey & brought it back to them for that sum. Verplank is editing Sands' works & publishing a vol: of discourses. Receive the following

Cambridge Port Massachusetts
April 6th 1833

William Dunlap Esqre

Dear Sir

The following answer to your first letter was written some days previous to the rect of your last. I owe you many apologies for having so long delayed it, and, with the assurance that not the slightest disrespect was felt or intended I must beg you to pardon it.

Dear Sir

Though I have not the pleasure of your personal acquaintance, your character has long been known to me through several of our mutual friends; I need not add that I could not have this knowledge without feeling towards you the most sincere respect. I will therefore reply to your letter with the frankness of a Friend, assuring myself that you will give this a friendly reception.

I had some years since an application similar to yours from a gentleman of your City, and my first intention was respectfully to decline it; but I suffered myself to be guided by the advice of a friend and consented to supply dates, and some other—but *what* particulars I cannot now recollect. I had partly however sent my answer to this effect when I regretted that I did not adhere to my first purpose; and when the work for which the Biography was required was afterwards given up I then made up my mind to decline all future applications of a like nature.

In common with all Artists I am always gratified when I hear that my works are well received by the Public and especially when they are approved by my brother Artists. Farther than this I have no wish; on the contrary I have such an invincible repugnance to every thing like personal notoriety that I should at once (respect-

PORTRAIT OF A LADY

BY WILLIAM DUNLAP

(Courtesy of The Worcester Art Museum, Worcester, Mass.)

fully) decline the honour you intend me could I do it without subjecting you or myself to unpleasant misapprehension. For the omission of my name in a Work professing to treat of *all* American Artists, would if unexplained very naturally subject *you* to the suspicion of personal hostility towards the individual omitted; and *if explained* would inevitably draw upon *me* another kind (and no enviable kind) of notoriety. I know human nature indeed too well not to be aware that my exposition of my motive, for declining what has become nowadays so common a compliment, would be met by many sneers. I should hear not a little of my fastidiousness or affectation. Under these circumstances and with the real desire to gratify you, I will therefore furnish you with the dates and such facts as I may state without "egotism."

When I tell you that I have had many troubles, I trust you will pardon the lateness of this reply.

With sincere respect Yours
Washington Allston

P. S. To your second letter allow me to say briefly that I will with pleasure reply to the questions proposed in it as soon as the state of my Wife's health will allow me to do so. She has been for some time ill, and still continues so, confined to a dark room, with a distressing inflammation in one of her eyes. I will not delay it however longer than I can help. Of Copely's connexions here I have no personal knowledge. If I can gather through my friends (some of whom I believe are acquainted with them) any information respecting him, I will transmit it as collected. Concerning Mr West, besides his kind reception of me, I do not think I can add any thing to what is already known to the public. Should any new particulars occur to me, I will note them down: the same also of Stuart. Of Bembridge I know only that he left many portraits in South Carolina, but I have no recollection of their merits. I have no knowledge of Ramage.

Will you do me the favour to present my best regards to Mr Morse, with my thanks for his present of colours by Mr Mason.

Perhaps it may gratify you to know that in a conversation I had some years since in London with Charles Lamb, the Author of Elia, he spoke highly of your "Life of Cooke."

Wed[y] April 10th 1833. Gave two short essays to Peabody. Read. Write. Walk. Ther: 60.

Thursday [April] 11th Receive news of the death of Mrs G. M. Woolsey.[149] Move my pictures up to 6th Avenue. Th: 60. Left Zeb Spiff with the Harpers. See Knap there who says that the passage over which the New

[149] Mrs. George Muirson Woolsey, *née* Abby Howland.

England troops carried their cannon & took Louisburg, is a soft mud that would not then or now bear a boy, but that he (Knap) found the Engineer or Artif[ic]er an old man and had from him the explanation. The troops brought snow shoes with them which enabled them to keep the surface & they drag'd the guns on platforms. Knap & [James] Frothingham concur'd in representing G. Stuart as a very passionate man & a great Liar. Knap said he was agent for a company or subscription to get a picture of a Mr Taylor for the Roman Catholics in Boston. Stuart Engaged to paint for 200$ but presented the picture unfinished & unlike & required 300 saying it was the agreement. The money being refused (even 200) until he amended the picture he did so & made a fine one. Fr: says Penington had a journel which S commenced in Ph: in which he frequently notes "to day Quarrel[d] with Tom" the appellation he gave his wife On another occasion he agreed to paint a picture for 200$ & appointed a time, it being to be painted in 3 days, the sitter going away. The sitter called & was put off from day to day until he left his card announcing his departure next day. S. complained of ill usage & a creditor to whom the money was promised had to remain a creditor of the improvident painter. He was undoubtedly an imprudent man, a bad Husband & father. Receive notes for my Work from [John] Neagle & [David] Edwin.

Friday April 12th 1833. Th: 64. Warm out. Read Life of a Sailor.[150] A little rain & Thunder.

Saturday [April] 13th Ther: 58. Much colder out. Write on Hist[y] of painters &c. Write to John Neagle acknowledging his with Edwin's notices.

Debt paid bro[t] forw[d]	570.40
p[d] Bank of N. Y.	150.
	720.40

Sunday [April] 14th Read Life of a Sailor. Write of Hist[y] of Arts. Afternoon walk to Assylum of Deaf &

150 By "A Captain in the Navy" (Frederick Chamier).

Dumb along the excavations for Rail road. Th: 54. Out doors this morning Ice.

Monday [April] 15th Clear. Th: 54. See G. C. Verplank at the City Library & he promises me notices of Houdon & Ceracchi. Smybert is noticed by him in his Historical discourse. One of his pictures in Columbia College. Get a vol: of Cunningham from Harpers with memoir of Copley. Leave letter for Neagle with Inman.

Tuesday [April] 16th Clear. Th: 52.

To Lord Lyndhurst.[151]

In the year 1784 I presented letters to your father from your Aunt Startin[152] whose portrait I attempted in Crayons as an introduction to him. He received me kindly & I dined with him & probably with you, a boy, at his house in George Street, Hanover Square. Having thus introduced myself I will introduce the object of my letter.

At the request of many of the Artists of the United States and with the assistance afforded by them I have undertaken to publish a History of the rise & progress of the Arts of Design in this Country. Your father must occupy a distinguished place. I have Allan Cunninghams notice of him & I have other material. Your letter to my friend Sam' F. B. Morse is before me. I want from you the date of your father's birth. The place. The time of his marriage. Of your birth. Of his departure for Europe—and other particulars which may be agreeable to you to communicate for such a purpose. Any remarks on Cunninghams notice shall be attended to.

I ask this, upon the full conviction that you <*would*> must wish a biographical notice of your father to be as accurate as possible.

Of his merits as a man & an Artist I <*am*> have ample testimony & my own knowledge. Any communication you may favour me with will be used as directed by you.

I remain respectfully

Your Lordship's Obt Servt

Recd from Wm T McCoun $141 being the balance after investing 2000 in Bond security with him. I have now

151 John Singleton Copley, Baron Lyndhurst, son of the artist, John Singleton Copley and Susannah (Clarke) Copley.

152 Mrs. Charles Startin (Sarah Clarke), sister of Lord Lyndhurst's mother, Susannah (Clarke) Copley. See *New England Historical and Genealogical Register,* XLVI, 16.

in Bank $160. Meet Washington Irving for the first time since his return from Europe. He is in fine health and our meeting was a very pleasant one. Of the Hist: Th: he expressed the pleasure he had received & exclaimed "Peter will be delighted with it." Peter is in good health & residing in Paris. Washington anticipates a second edition of my book and volunteers assistance. "I can give you a great deal" was spoken with glee. G. P. Morris has promised anecdotes of Kean. Met John Inman at Morris' & talk over Zeb. Spiff. Receive letter from John F. Watson with some hints respecting early painters & Wests early pictures.

Wednesday Ap^l^ 17th 1833. Rain. Th: 54. Write & read Cunningham's painters.

Thursday 18th Clear. Th: 54. Write read & Walk.

Friday 19th Clear. Th: 58. Go to Brooklyn—get my picture of my Father & mother painted in 1788 repaired & put on Hamilton's Esel. Seek materials for hist^y^ of painters &c. Evening McCoun, Castillo & families with us. Read Miss Austin's Novels.

Sat^y^ [April] 20th Clear Th: 60. Write to John C. Hamilton respecting his father. To Judge Bacon Utica for a copy of Copley's bill & receit for a portrait of his mother. In search of a periodical called "the friend" I am told D[aniel] Coolidge 304 Pearl Street has it.

Sunday 21st of Ap^l^ 1833. Clear. Th: 64. Walk. Read & write.

Monday [April] 22^d^ Clear. Th: 66. Walk to [Thomas] Hogg's Nursery & flower Garden before breakfast. Write. Go to Mr Coolidge but find nothing in y^e^ Friend. See to the progress of Exhibition or collection for it. Evening attend Council at Clinton Hall.

Tuesday April 23[d] 1833. Clouds—thunder—Rain. Th: 64. Rec[d] yesterday the following without date.

Dear Sir

Your letter has reached me. Mr Wilkes had, and probably has now the $150, but you are getting too rich for trifles. I agree with you perfectly that European odour is the one thing necessary. We shall see the difference between you and Mr Payne. But what is character, or service, or fidelity, with our people. How did I come forward in defence of Lafayette, when the paid Agents of the Government were serving the enemy. I sacrificed time worth at the very least, a thousand dollars and now the American papers are abusing me for occasioning abuse to which I answered. Rives is at the bottom of all this, and he may ride to the presidency on this and a few other expedients of this quality. Well, I have done.

Mr Jay will pay you the rest of the money. The note is payable March 5th for £50 sterling. You have only to calculate interest and exchange and to take the balance. By the time you get this Mr Jay will have cash enough of mine and the matter had better be settled at once. I shall be in England this Spring and I will look into the sale of the book. As yet I can tell you nothing, not having even received a copy sent to myself.

We are all surprized that Morse has so soon forgotten us. Not a line from him since he sail'd. You can tell him I am too proud to write to such a Recreant, but I will send him some news.

I have had the womans head cleaned. It has come out beautifully and four connoisseurs have pronounced it a Teniers without hesitation and without hearing any thing in advance. The Rembrandt is pronounced pure Gold by all who see it. One dealer said, at first, it might be by a scholar of Rembrandt, but on looking closer, he said no scholar of his could have imitated the half tint. Three have valued this picture at $2000, and one at $5000. I am afraid I am too poor to bring it to America. I have bought a noble half length, small size, Holbein. It is a beautifull & a very perfect picture. This I think I shall get to America.

With love

J. Fennimore Cooper

In a former letter he says "the note is due the 5th of May being dated the 2[d] of November. This is correct.

Write to Judge Hopkinson & to John F. Watson. Call on Verplank—see him in the street—see Bryant & go with him to Rhind's where he is sitting for a portrait & to Agate's. Go to Cumming's, to Post Office & Bank. Leave in Bank $150. Receive letter from John F. Watson. Write on Hist[y] of Arts. Read.

Wed[y] April 24th 1833. Rain. Th: 60. Write. Read in Life of a Younger son—a vile book. Ev[g] Council meeting.

Thursday [April] 25th Clear: Th: 58. Mrs Amelia Gilfert (Miss Holman) died the 19th in Phil[a]. Call on Hamilton who assists me in repairing my old family group of 1788. At Library. Meet Bryan & afterwards Morse as spectators of the fire at the City Hotel & go with the last to the roof of Carvills (the house in which M: has his pictures) a[nd] view the fire until it is got under. At W W W's. At Arch[d] Robertsons with him & Charles Rhind. Both the Robertsons remember Trumbulls telling us that Rumford informed against him in 1780 & the story of West's procuring assurance from George the third that no harm should result. Ev[g] read Watsons Annals. Rec[d] letter from James Cochran says he will pay in the Fall.

Friday [April] 26th Clear. Ther: 56. Read Watson. Write to Vanderlyn for information respecting himself. To [Jacob] Binninger to borrow the portraits of his father & mother.[153] Call on Verplank & obtain documents respecting Hudon, Ceracchi & Le Trobe With Morse & Cole. See Mount's full length of Onderdonk.[154]

Sat[y] [April 27] Clear. Th: 54. Write. Go to y[e] Library to seek extracts from Sparks Governeur Morris. Vol. not in. Find it at Carvils. Go with John L Morton to see Freemans picture. Home by ½ past 1 & write. Receive letter from H. C. Carey referring me to Encyclopedia Americana for Art: Leslie written by Miss Lesley & to

[153] These two portraits were shown by Dunlap at the 8th Annual Exhibition of the National Academy of Design, in 1833, nos. 71 and 73 in the catalogue (printed at N. Y., 1833). They are briefly described, in a critical note on the exhibition, in *The New-York Mirror,* X, 387. The parents of Jacob Bininger were Abraham and Catharine (Embury) Bininger. See *The N. Y. Genealogical and Biographical Record,* XXXIII, 137.

[154] William S. Mount's portrait of the Right Rev. Benjamin T. Onderdonk, Bishop of New York, was also exhibited at the National Academy of Design in 1833, no. 75 in the catalogue. See *The New-York Mirror,* X, 387.

Mc Murtrie for Bembridge. Receive Nos. of The Friend from J. F. Watson.

Sunday [April] 28th Clear. Th: 58. Read & write. Evening with Charles Rhind and then with C. P. Clinch. He tells me that J. F. Cooper dramatized his Pioneers & that it did not succeed.

Monday April 29th 1833. Clear. Th: 66. Give G. P. Morris an introduction to review of ye Exhibition. Go to Clinton. The library. Dekay has published another pamphlet to forward his election & it is pointed. Bring Mrs Dwight my wife's sister & the relict of Dr Dwight to my house. Write. Afternoon Th: 70 & out of doors much warmer. Watsons story of the man who procured money to ransom him from the devil might be introduced perhaps be the denouement of my Morristown-mony-finders.[155] My hero being detected by Mrs C, whether by bringing him down the chimney or otherwise, might confess his imposture & excuse it by bolding [*sic*] avowing himself the bought of the Devil.

Old Captn Anthony Rutgers commanded a privateer in the french War & in ye revolutionary retired near Newburgh. Mr [Charles] Clinton the father of Govr George & General Clinton was well known to Rutgers. Mr Clinton was an Irish gentleman & man of education but had married below himself an Irish drab. The merits of Clinton recommended [him] to Governor Colden & he employed him as a surveyor. Afterwards Clinton opened a school (after he had purchased a tract of land now invaluable) and Rutgers, [Samuel] Provost (afterwards Bishop) with other lads of good families in the City were schoolfellows with Clinton's after distinguished sons.

Among the earliest pictures that I remember were some in oil on cloth without frames of Huntsmen, dogs & horses. Heaven knows where they came from or where they went. They made a deep impression on me & I recol-

[155] Probably the story printed in *The New-York Mirror,* XIV, 157-58, Nov. 12, 1836, as "Tom Bell, a Tale of the Good Old Time."

lect them still with pleasure. This must have been in 1772 or earlier—and when I saw Heard's hounds from Woodbridge enter Amboy surrounding the black Huntsman with his Jockeycap, broad belt, & hunting horn, he appeared to me a most dignified and enviable personage. The drawings of the Chief justice Smith & these impression[s] & his appearance & after life must be noticed. The Race ground at Amboy—races & reviews on it. Ev^{g} Council meeting of Nat^{l} Academy and begin to hang pictures.

April 30th tuesday. Clear. Th: 70. Write. Read. Let me remember to procure at least the sight of the caricatures mentioned by Watson p: 169 "Tales of O. T." A contested election for Trustees of the City Library. I hope to find Ceracchi's trial. Receive $81.10 from P. Jay being the ballance due me on Bentley's Note I have now in Bank $231.10. M: M: Noah met me "I am settling or removing a Bond connected with my former office before commencing an Evening paper to be a tea table source of information & amusement. When you wish a corner for literature or the arts it shall be always at your service, all I stipulate is—never pay any bill and I will send it to you as long as you live." Ev^{g} at Clinton Hall. High wind. In the night four squares burnt between Hudson & Washington Street extreme North.

Wed^{y} May 1st 1833. Clear. Th: 68. Make preparations to paint. Finish reading Watson's "Tales of O. Times." Ev^{g} Annual meeting of Nat^{l} Acad^{y}.

Thursday [May] 2^{d} Clear. Th: 68. Write & read. Pay $68.75 to Charles Judson in full of rent. In Bank $162.35. Ev^{g} at Clinton Hall.

Friday [May] 3^{d} Clear. Th: 62. H. C. Carey refers me to Mr McMoutrie (James McMoutrie or Murtrie Phil^{a}) and Mr James Coxe. Write to both. Go to Library & examine article West in the American edition of Edinburgh

Encyclopedia adopting a few paragraphs. Clinton Hall with Morse Cole &c. At Mirror Office. G. P. Morris says that John H. Payne has insinuated or said that M's exertions for P's benefit were not disinterested—and expressed decided hostility against him for exerting himself in my behalf in conjunction with McCoun Clinch & others. Paine is in town & avoids Morris. Peabody has published at Hosack's desire the papers relative to my benefit in the Knickerbacker [156] omitting the Names of Morris & Forest & Morris says abusing him on the cover of the book. I must in self defence publish a denial of my being the Editor of that Journal as the report is still in circulation. Afternoon. Walk out of town.

Sat[y] [May] 4th Clear. Th: 62. Received yesterday from Chas Fraser further communications respecting painters. See Mr [Henry] Gahn who promises me accurate information respecting Wertmuller. In Bank today $147.35. On the 3[d] of April Peabody (as mentioned under that date) requested 6 or 7 pages for the *Knickerbacker* of May. I have been so often accosted as Editor of that work that I put a line in y[e] Ev[g] Post denying the being such. As Peabody in his note making the above request <*offer*> says "Any compensation for the favour will be held subject to your wishes" I to day on taking the No for May, told him to give me check for what he consider'd the communication worth. He said he did not expect to pay any thing as he had paid me for the previous essay at more than 3 dollars a page. I asked him if he remember'd the note promising whatever I might demand? He said "Yes" he had a copy of it. And then asked me to say what I expected. I replied "Under these circumstances—nothing" & left him. Assist Morse in making Catalogue for Eig[h]th Exhibition. Rain. Return to Clinton Hall & remain writing until 9 in the evening; and the[n] leave Morse & some of the Council at work for the public good.

[156] "Correspondence of the Dunlap Benefit", printed in *The Knickerbacker*, I, 323-329, May, 1833.

Sunday May 5th 1833. After a night of rain, thin clouds Th: 62. Read. Write. Afternoon walk to Bloomingdale. Every thing in the face of the country lovely. F[rederic] Depeyster jun. met me accidentally & I returned with him in his Gig. Cummings & Mapes with me in the evening.

Monday [May] 6th Clear. Th: 62. Attend at Clinton Hall. Write for the Mirror. Receive letter from Judge Hopkinson [157] respecting Pine. Evg again at Clinton Hall for the 3d time. Adjourn'd meeting of the Academy.

Tuesday [May] 7th Clear. Th: 63. Write on Pine's life & for Mirror. Attend to Clinton Hall affairs. Th: 69. Evg Rain & Thunder.

Wedy [May] 8th Th: 72. Begin portrait of Balivar from a plaister cast. Exhn Clinton Hall opens. Write for Mirror. Afternoon attend a Committee at Clinton Hall .Evg Rain.

Thursday [May] 9th Paint. Write for Mirror. Th: 72. Clear. Receive a letter from Henry Sargent Esqre in answer to one of mine of March last. After apologies he declines "altho' he would feel highly flattered by any notice" of mine, yet feels "greatly embarressed in attempting to furnish any facts for such a publication." He says he can scarcely claim to be more than an Amateur Artist. Bembridge & Ramage he never heard of & refers me to Doctor [Benjamin] Waterhouse of Cambridge for Copley & Stuart. He says he was well acquainted with Copley & a townsman of Stuart's. Write to Doctor Waterhouse of Cambridge.

Friday [May] 10th Paint on Bolivar. Read N. Amn Review. Write for Mirror. Write Henry Sargent. Th: 66. Rain Evening & Night.

157 Part of this letter from the Hon. Joseph Hopkinson, of Philadelphia, is printed in Dunlap's *Arts of Design,* I, 317-18.

Sat^{y} [May] 11th Clouds. Th: 62. Afternoon warmer. Paint on Bolivar. At Library & Clinton Hall. Receive letter from J. McMurtrie. He tells me that Bembridge was his mothers half brother but little more that I did not know before except that his name was Henry. He speaks highly of Krimmell and I know with justice. He will furnish more respecting him. Of Trott he speaks harshly "he drew badly & knew nothing of the anatomy of the *head* which was all he had to do with. I have by me several of his miniatures a disgrace to any man who painted them. Birch he says has deteriorated. He promises to consult with Sully & furnish more for me.

Sunday May 12th 1833. Write to James McMurtrie. Write for Mirror. After another rainy night, Clouds. Th: 64. Read Madame Junot. Even^{g} at W. T. McCoun's.

Monday [May] 13th Clouds. Th: 70. Read. Got to Clinton Hall—at McCoun's. Receive letter from Honble Edmond Pendleton saying the great grandmother's picture painted by West is w^{h} Mr Chas Fraser at Trenton & at my command. Read. In Bank to day $137.35. Ev^{g} Finished at Clinton Hall the adjourned Annual meeting. Showers in y^{e} day.

Tuesday [May] 14th Clouds. Ther: 68. Applied to yesterday to paint flags & Standards with devices for the Hibernian Society. I today make sketches & calculations for them.

Thursday [May] 16th Clouds. Rain. Th: 64. Yesterday & today paint. Write for Mirror. Read Mem^{r} Madame Junot. Rain.

Friday [May] 17th Clouds. Th: 62. Finish review of ye 8th Annual Exh^{n} of N. A. for Mirror. Write to Edmond H. Pendleton, Hyde Park & J. F. Cooper, Paris. Receive a letter from Henry Sargent still avoiding the giving facts & dates respecting himself but promising to see Doctor Waterhouse. Write on Hist^{y} of Arts. Ev^{g} Clinton H.

Saturday [May] 18th Moon changes: clears up warm Th: 72. Paint on Bolivar. Read Quarterly review. E[lias] Hicks called on me & told me that John McDougal Lawrence the son of Judge [John] Lawrence & grandson of Genl [Alexander] McDougal had letters & papers in his possession which he wished to be used as the basis of a biography of the Genl & that Sparks had applied for them. He wishes me to undertake the subject.

Sunday [May] 19th Clear. Th: at 5 A. M. 72, at Noon 78. Write on Hist: of Arts. A. Robertson details the transaction of Trumbull relative to West when he quarrel'd with his master about the panorama. Walk. Read Quarterly Review.

Monday [May 20] Clouds & rain. Th: at 5, 72 at noon 69. Paint. Finish Bolivar. Begin Dr [Hugh] McLean.

Tuesday [May] 21st Showers. Th: 70. Paint: read [Caleb] Cushings [*Reminiscences of*] Spain Bank to day 127.35. Thunder & hard rain.

Wedy [May] 22d Clear. Th: 68. Write. Read. Afternoon Walk & enjoy the beauties of the country in great perfection.

Thursday [May] 23d Th: 68. Paint. Read. Walk. Receive a very pleasant letter from Washington Alston with promise of more and a packet from John Neagle with like promise.

Friday [May] 24th Th: 65. Windy. Read & finish Cushing. I owe him thanks. Write. Go to Library, Clinton Hall, Morris's. begin a pencil sketch of Morris.

Saturday May 25th 1833. Windy. Th: 62. Read in Mirror & Stuart's America.[158] Last Evg at Clinton Hall with Morse Ingham &c. Rain commences at 10 & continues hard until

[158] James Stuart, *Three Years in North America* (N. Y., 1833).

Sunday morning at daylight. Th: 64. Wrote yesterday on Fine Arts & read Stuarts America. Write to Alston. Write on Hist: Fine Arts. Read. Th: this afternoon 70. There is opposite my dwelling the process of removing a 3 Story brick house which after some days preparation commenced yesterday & moved ab^{t} 2 feet when y^{e} rain stop'd the work.

Wed^{y} [May] 29th Clouds. Th: 64. Clouds, mist & rain this 3 days. In Bank to day $117.35. I have written on Hist^{y} of Fine Arts & read Stuart's America. To day at Library. Receive letter from C. P. Clinch offerring me $100 if I think it will pay for materials for a picture, cabinet size from Scott's Talisman. I will do it.

Thursday [May] 30th Clear. Th: 63. Write on H of Arts. Francis brings me [John Payne] Collier's Hist: of Dramatic Poetry. Answer Clinch. "I will *canvass* the subject." Making sketch for M.

Friday [May] 31st Clear Th: 64. I received yesterday a letter from John F. Watson of Germantown with one from Joseph J. Lewis Attorney at Law, West Chester, son of Enoch Lewis the Mathematician who wrote West's biography for Enc: Am^{a}. Read Stuart's Am: Afternoon Rhind & Castello with me. Ev^{g} at Clinton Hall. Morse tells me he has letters from J. F. Cooper & La Fayette. Cooper comes home in the Autumn (October)

Sat^{y} June 1st Clear. Th: 64. Green peas & Strawberries plenty for a week past. Finish reading Stuarts Am^{a} There is much good information in the book, many facts collected & many observations made by the writer that are just. But there are gross errors or want of observation. He hears no swearing until he reaches the South & West —he sees no prostitutes walking our streets—&c. there is too much praise & too much twaddle—but there is a mass of information.

Sunday June 2[d] Clouds. Showers. Th: 68. Read Scotts' Talisman. Colliers Annals. Received a letter from Key West from W. A. Whitehead (Collectors Office Key West Florida) requesting information relative to my native place Perth Amboy; particularly its early history & that of its inhabitants. The Exh[n] of the Nat[l] Aca[y] open'd last year on the 21st May & was check'd by Cholera the 21st of June doing little After. The receits were to 19th June $700. We open'd this year the 8th of May and to the first of June have rec[d] $800. Five or six weeks more may give an additional 700. The A[n] Acd[y] has not yet opened, but they let their rooms to profit to Adventurers. [James] Thom's statues of Tam O'Shanter [159] &c are now Exhi[d] there. Very hard rain in the evening.

Monday June 3[d] 1833. Clear. Th: 70. On Saturday last the workmen accomplished the removal of the large three story brick house & placed it on its foundation prepared for it about 3 feet higher than it originally stood. It was by 3 screws, turned by 3 men, one at each, moved 100 feet. Read Scott's Talisman, a second or third time since the publication. Go to Bank & leave $107.35. Go to Harpers' repeats the engagement to publish Zeb. Spiff. Receive letter from J. F. Watson & from Enoch Lewis disclaiming being the E. Lewis who wrote in the Enc: Amer[a] & the Friend. Ev[g] [Th.] 66. Am[n] Acd[y] open an Exhibition to day.

Tuesday June 4th Clear. Th: 66. Finish reading "The Talisman with a view to the picture for Clinch. Receive a letter from C. P. Clinch saying he is glad that I "will canvass the subject" & enclosing $100. Go to Bank & leave $207.35. Call at Library & Morris's. Read Colliers Annals. Ev[g] at Clinton Hall with Morse & Joscelyn. Write to Neagle.

Wed[y] June 5th Clear. Th: 65. Read Collier. Go to A. A. Exhibition, to Clinton Hall, to Morris's, to Library. Ev[g] again at Clinton Hall. Leave in Bank $157.35

[159] The four statues are described in *The New-York Mirror,* X, 371, May 25, 1833.

Thursday [June] 6th Royal H. Waller of Rutland employs me to copy the miniature I painted of his Wife. Leave wh Morris some remarks on A. A. Exhn Read Mirror & Collier. Rain. Th: 66. Read Collier.

Friday [June] 7th Rain. Th: 65. Unwell. Read Collier. Afternoon Clear. Paint on miniature of Mrs Waller. Read.

Saty [June] 8th Clear. Th: 65. Health better. Paint on Miniature. Read. Write a little.

Sunday [June] 9th Clear. Th: 64. Read Collier. Finish Miniature of Mrs Waller. Read [Edward] Gibbon's Memoirs.

Monday [June] 10th Clear. Th: 62. Read Gibbons memoirs. One OClock. Paint Miniature study. Miss Deming with us for the night.

Tuesday [June] 11th Clear. Th: 64 at noon. Wind N. W. & cold. I had fever last night. I have taken a Walk of a mile Paint. Read Gibbon. Walk again. Paint. Write. Read. No return of Disease.

Wedy 12th June. Clear. Th: 64. Write to Wm Whitehead Key West & to Mr Lewis Godey. To the first I promise information, of the last I ask what he owes me. Ride down town to make calls but every body is gone to meet the president. Go to Library, Clinton Hall, &c. & ride home. Not yet well. Read Miss Austin's Sense & Sensibility. Walk. Academy receits now $1000.

Thursday [June] 13th Clear. Th: 66. Not yet well. Walk. Read. I rode down town. Charles W. Woolsey arrives from London. The night Thunder & hard rain.

Friday [June] 14th Clear. Th: 72. Read. I have [Cadwallader D.] Colden's Life of Fulton to examine. 1 OClock P. M. I have walked to the Library & back visiting various places without inconvenience.

Saty [June] 15th Clear. Th: 72. Godey writes that he has not collected *a cent* for me & he believes *they* (those who bought the book) must be *sued!* Read Coldens Fulton. Draw and study for the Talisman picture. Read Gibbon's Rome. Ev[g] at Beach Lawrence's. Read Prince Pückler Muskau. I only walk in the Square.

Sunday [June] 16th Clear. Th: 72. Draw. Read. Write a line to Waller of Rutland Vt. Julius, Augustus, Tiberius, Caligula, Claudius, Nero, Vespasian, Titus, Domitian, Nerva, Trajan, The Antonines, Hadrian. The Coliseum was built by the successor of Nero. The Laocoon was found in the Baths of Titus.

Monday June 17th 1833. Clear. Th: 70. The german prince is very amusing. Gibbon though an old acquaintance is more instructive. Walk to Post Office, Bank (& leave 147.35) Library, Clinton Hall (see Mr [William] Goodacre there) Morris's &c. &c. Prepare to go to Phil[a] tomorrow. 2 OClock P. M.

Tuesday [June] 18th Up at 4 & leave N. Y. at 6. Arrive at Trenton at ½ past one. Cost 1.50 & 37½ for breakfast. Go to Mr Charles Fraser & see a portrait of his grandmother (Dinah Marmion married to Peter Bard) painted in 1758 by B. West. It is much injured but was a firmly painted & well drawn bust. The drapery good. There is in the family a portrait of the same person in youth by a very inferior hand & a picture of Mr Wm Bard by another hand. Two of Sharpless' Crayon portraits of Dr [John] Bard the elder & his Sister, quite good. The morning was quite cool, the sun now scorch[g]. I got up with headach & it Continues. I had for Companions Messrs [James Barton] Longacre, Mason & Earl. Mr L. who was a pupil of Murray says he [i.e., George Murray] came from Scotland a destitute lad, was taught eng[g] by Anker Smith in London, got entangled with the liberty boys & came to Am[a] in consequence. Was a trader in the Southern States & failed. Having married while there he came to Phil[a] with a family in poverty. His talents as an Eng[r] now stood him in stead & he soon was employed by Bradford for the Encyclopedia. Then came the Bank Note business & his association with [Gideon] Fairman in 1811. Longacre then with [John F.] Watson & soon after with Murray who was the man of business of the Co. & speculated with the money & spent & lost it. His opposition to the P. Acad[y] & association with Trott. Take a dinner of tea. Walk about the Village, sleep half an hour. Walk in another direction. Take tea and at 9 go to bed, after sitting a silent observer in the Bar Room of the Rising Sun. They promise me a stage at 5 tomorrow morning to carry me to the Steam boat which carries me to Philadelphia—fare 25 cents. It is but 12½ from N. Y. to N. Brunswick.

Trenton Wed[y] June 19th 1833. Clear. Up at 4 & prepare for proceeding to Philadel[a]. Pay at Trenton for tea twice & a nights lodging $1.25. Leave y[e] place in a stage at 5 and reach the Rail road at 6 arrive at Bordentown & take the steam boat at ½ past and soon leave the wharf. The ride through a cold fog. Fare to Phil[a] 25 cents, breakfast 50 cents, whole expence $3.87½. At 8 OClock the fog dissipates & we see the flat borders of the Delaware & soon after the beautiful towns of Bristol & Burlington. Hart who sat to me for a portrait in 1817 & never came to have it finished, and in 1830 bought his brother McCurdy's picture of me and never paid for or took it, accosted me with smiles & compliments inviting me to his Cottage at Bristol where doubtless he resides in affluence and perhaps self content. Arrive *at Philadelphia* at 10 and see Judge Hopkinson at [James] Earls & Judge Baldwin. Hopkinson repeats much that was in his letter. Go to [John] *Neagles.* Born in Boston 1799. Apprenticed to a coach painter. Desire for portrait painting. Begins in Phil[a]. Goes to Lexington Kentucky in hopes to practice, discouraged by finding Jouet there a good painter. Money exhausted & determines to return home by way of New Orleans—offers himself to work his passage and narrowly escapes flogging by the boatmen who think he is quizzing them.—meets an acquaintance who assists him—sells part of his clothing. Arrives at N. O. & meets a man whose portrait he had painted who buys a Washington's head of him & enables him to get home.

Go to Edwins. The Doctor [William] Smith mentioned by E was provost of the Phil^{a} College.

Stuart, Trott & Edwin were neighbours near ye falls of Schuykill in 1798, yellow fever time. S. says I can make that picture of Judge [Thomas] McKean look like his son, takes chalk & removing the wig & scratching over the face does it though before remarkably unlike. "When I [David Edwin] carried him the proof of Judge [Edward] Shippen's portrait, he had a sitter & it was sent in, he came out. You may consider it the greatest compliment ever paid you when I leave my sitter to tell you how much I am pleased with your engraving of this head." "I enter'd Boston in the evening in a Stage & next day waited on S. "I knew you were in Boston say[s] S. Why Sir I only came last evening. "I saw you—you came like a criminal back foremost." I had been sitting on the front seat.

Jarvis was in Boston. I knew S. did not like him—declined going with him to S's. When I waited on him afterwards I said "You had a visit from Mr. Jarvis yesterday. "Yes Sir and he came in Buff Sir he had buff gloves, buff waistcoat, buff Jacket & trousers & buff shoes." I told Jarvis and he dress'd himself carefully at his next call & wore a black coat. I told S that I had repeated his remark on the buff & reminded him of Jarvis's black coat. He clapt his hands & laugh'd immoderately at the notion of J's dressing in black to visit him. Instances were mentioned of S's painting portraits from memory. He had so painted his own mother and others with great success—this is owing to his observation of expression rather than feature. "You have Hull's likeness, he said to Edwin. He always looks as if he was looking at the sun & half shutting his eyes.

Decline N's invitation. Take a small bowl Clam soup. Engage Board & Lodgings at Champions Arch Street. Sleep an hour. Dress & after tea go to Sully's.

West gave Sully a letter to [blank] W[h]arton, governor of ye Hospital (& a plan for a place for the picture of The Healing) Warton told Sully that he introduced Stuart to West. He was with other Americans dining with W, when the servant announced a person as wanting to speak to him. "I am engaged. Who is he?" "He says he is from America." That was enough. W left the table & on returning said "Here's a young man says he is from our City, go Warton & see what you can make of him. I went out & saw a handsome youth in a fashionable green Coat and I at once told him that I was sent to see what I could make of him. "You are from Phil[a]" Yes. "Your names Stuart?" "Yes" "Have you no letter to Mr West?" "No, Sir" "Who do you know in Phil[a] ["Joseph] Anthony is my uncle." "That's enough—come in" and I carried him in and he received a hearty welcome. At one period of S's London life, he had as an attendant a wild boy the son of a poor Widow & another attendant was a Newf[d]land dog. The boy & dog were attached to each other & when one was sent on an errand the other accompanied him. Tom was a terrible truant and played so many tricks that S threaten'd to dismiss him, but he still found some way to hold on his eccentric master. One day, as story tellers say, Tom staid when sent with a message until S out of patience posted off to the old Womans to announce her sons dismissal. On entering she began first "Oh Mr Stuart! Tom & the dog have been here!" "So I supposed & I shall send him to remain here." "O Mr Stuart the Dog!" "Well he has been here too." "Yes Sir! look there he overset my mutton pie, broke the dish, greased the floor & eat the pie." "I'm glad of it. I come to tell you that your son will not do for me. I dismiss him." The mother entreated & told over the story of the pie again & again until S. getting over his displeasure conceived the project of a joke founded upon dogs pie-dinner. "Well, well, say no more. I will try Tom again provided you never let him know that I came here to day or know of the dogs having eaten the pie." The promise was given of course & S posted home. Tom found him where he left him & had his story ready to excuse his delay. "Very well, Sir, I shall know whether you tell me the truth—go & bring in dinner." S. sat down to his beef, & Towser took his place by his side as usual, Tom as usual in attendance. S. addresses the Dog "Where have you been Sir?" puts his ear to the dogs mouth, "I thought so, and you have had your dinner?" "Bow." "Yes I knew it, what have you been eating, put your mouth nearer Sir" "Bow" "Pie, very well, Sir, You & Tom have been to Mrs Jenkins's and eat her mutton pie" "No, Sir, I didn't touch it, he had it all." From that time Tom concluded that if he wished to deceive his master he must leave Towser at home, but rather thought that between the Dog, the Devil & painter he had no chance for lying.

Sully tells the anecdote of Alston & himself going to Mr [George] Gibbs to see Alstons Elijah in y[e] Wilderness, and Miss Gibbs showing them her father's portrait by Stuart. Sully exclaim'd I never saw a Vandyke, Rembrant, Titian or Rubens to equal it. I committ myself &c what say you? "I say that all combined could not have equal'd it."

It was at Norfolk that *Sully* knew *Bembridge*. He has a book of engravings bo[t] after his *death in Phil[a]* with his Autograph. He died poor, about 12 years ago. He was a portly pleasant gentleman somewhat like Stuart in manner & told a good story.

[Ralph] *Earl* who painted in N. Y. and Connecticut in 1788-9 had an older brother [James] who painted many good portraits in Charleston when Sully as a boy was there & Sully saw his Widow in London & gave an acc[t] of his [illegible] & his death by yellow fever when his property was shipped for his return hence. [Ralph E. W. Earl] The son of Earl who painted in N. Y. painted in London when Sully was there, very badly & is now in this country with an appointment under Jackson.

Call'd with Neagle on Mr [Christian] Gobrecht a dye sinker & engraver who has promised notes on dye sinking. Go to bed at 12 OClock. Rain.

Philadel[a] Thursday June 20th 1833. Clouds. Up at 5.

Sully says once calling on *Jarvis* he was left alone & took up a book. It was a life of Morland. When Jarvis returned to the room Sully sat with the book open on a table & his hand on it. "Do you know why I like that book?" says J. "Because it is the life of a painter." "No. Because I think he was like myself."

Sully says that *Alston's* embarressments are owing to his great picture of Belshassar which he has said he could finish in 6 weeks. S has heard him say that he holds the greater number of shares in it. Perkins holds 2000 dollars in it, which he would willingly sink but dares not hint it to Alston. S. has heard Alston say O never undertake any thing that cannot be accomplish'd by your own means. He is poor. It has been suggested that Congress might be induced to employ him to fill the 4 panells at W. left open by T. & he has been written to, to know if he would accept the order. His reply was "I will undertake one only & chuse my own subject. No battle piece." Verplank has a letter which I must see.

Sully relates the story of *Stuart* being employed in London as an Organist in a church as told him by Stuart & given me by Fraser and says that he has heard him play well on an organized pianof[t] which he had in his house. He told an anecdote relative to Trumbul's having lost the sight of an eye thus. T. brought him a picture for his instruction when they were with West and S says "I was puzzled by the drawing and after turning it this way & that I said "T this looks as if it was drawn by a man with one eye" T replied "I think it very unkind Sir to speak in that manner though I have lost the sight of one eye." "Now I never knew or suspected the thing." Stuart would then go into a theory to prove that a man with one eye could not possible draw true. I have heard of this theory & his remarks on T's drawing in Boston among S's companions. Sully considers it merely as one of Stuarts whims. Stuart would lecture on any subject from the Divinity to a corn-cob. Sully considers his pictures in Boston as his best & the best old Mr Gibb's.

Speaking of Inman Sully said "I remember going around your Exhibition room at N. Y. and seeing a fine Landscape. Who painted this? 'Inman' Then I came to a beautiful group—ah this is very clever—lets see who is this? 'Inman' Then some Indians. 'Inman' By George here is the finest Miniature I ever saw—it was a Lady in Black. Who is the Miniature painter? 'Inman' Monsieur Tonson! His large portraits I knew, but he is a most extraordinary man for rapidity, diversity, & excellence."

Breakfast at ½ past 6. Go to Godey's—not in. Read Leslie (art: in Enc: Americana). See a print from a miniature by *Anson Dickinson* from a picture by Peal painted in 1772 of Washington as a provincial officer. Write to my Wife. Call on J. Hopkinson see Pine's picture of H's father. H promises anecdotes of Stuart.

Mem: S., West & Copenhagen Jackson. "No eyes" "It is not nine days old yet." Wager & 3 pictures 300 dollars drank up & 200 in debt.

Meet Cooper (T. A.) He says the benefit here netted 1800 dollars but has ruined him & if he cannot arrange something for his relief with "these people" he must advertize his furniture this afternoon. I made him promise to call on me for advice & assistance if anything is done for him in New York. O! it is melancholy! Call on Matthew Carey who was an active man for ye Cooper benefit —he says the sum is between 17 & 1800. Says he is no favourite & but for the Children nothing would have been done. Call on Longacre Whose engraving of Judge Washington & Andrew Jackson I have seen.

Stuart. Lord Mulgrave whose name was Phipps employed S[tuart] to paint his brothers' Genl Phipps portrait previous to the Gen^ls^ going abroad. On seeing it he said "What is this? This is strange." "I have painted your brother as I saw him" "I see insanity in that face" The Genl in a short time went mad and cut his throat. A proof of Stuarts accuracy in respect to expression. (This Hopkinson told me).

I call on J. B. Longacre as above mentioned. He is joined in the portrait Gallery publication with [James] Herring. He was with Neagle when [he] asked Stuart for a pinch of his snuff. "You had better not take it. It is pernicious." "Your practice contradicts your theory Mr Stuart." "Shall I tell you a story? You were never in England so I must begin by describing an English Stage Coach." This he did, concluding "all this being filled they sometimes stow some in the basket. With such a load & one fellow in the Basket we went on our Way, and Coachee contrived to overset us all in a ditch. We got up none much hurt & after examining ourselves we thought of the man in the Basket. He was found apparently senseless & his neck twisted awry. One of y[e] travellers had heard that a dislocation might be removed if promptly attended to & seized the man by the head began pulling & he began roaring out let me alone! Let me alone! Nothing's the matter with me! I was born so! "Gentlemen I was born so (taking a pinch) I was born in a Snuff mill." He said his father lived at Kingston town Rhode Island and manufactured snuff. Mrs Pollard said he kept a snuff shop in New port.

Make an appointment to go to Germantown tomorrow 2 OClock with Longacre. Dine at S. Go & see the Germantown Railroad & locomotives.

Go to Sully's.

In 1799 he return'd to Richmond from Charleston S. C. At Charleston he had been placed with his brother in law [Mons. Belzons] a very poor miniature painter who ill treated him. S repels brutallity & leaves him, sleeps in the Exchange, next day taken home by a friend. Mr Read offers to procure a midshipmans warr[t] for him, but his brother Lawrence inviting him to Richmond Mr Read advises him to go. No money. Capt[n] Leffinwell takes him to Norfolk & to his house & forwards him to R. In 1801 began to paint miniatures in Norfolk where his brother then resided. In 1802 copied Angelica Kaufmans picture & painted his first portrait in Oil, Mr Wm Armsted of Norfolk. In 1802 Lawrences business failed and he went to Richmond to seek employment leaving Tom to take care of the family in Norfolk & if possible pay arrears of rent. It was near Christmas, a time at which festivity is rife & every housekeeper provides for the coming cold weather. Tom had neither provision or money and a hoe cake and some sweetmeats which made the family Christmas dinner. Tom contrived to pay most of Lawrences debts but the furniture was sold for the rent & his sister & children went up to Richm[d]. Tom now began the world for himself & Brown, Taylor & himself took a house in C°, his years earnings were $120. They lived in Church St[t] and Taylor falling [in] debt was imprison'd, Tom attending & relieving him. When Sully became eminent, T boasted that he first patronized him at Norfolk. *A patron.* In August 1804 S. went to Richmond & join'd Lawrence again who work'd in ornamental work. Tom painted Miniatures. He now determined to go to England. His plan was to paint first at Petersburg, save money, go again to Norfolk and then take advantage of circumstances. He went to Petersburg, but while working there, his brother Lawrence died & he returned to Richmond to assist his Widow and children. He took charge of them, and from a sense of duty, in due time married his brothers Widow & became the father of his children which he has faithfully been to this day. In Sept[r] 1805 Cooper was playing at Richmond & sat for a portrait in Oil to Sully (small) and in 1806 induced him to bring his family to N. Y. by insuring his employment to the amount of 1000$. This started him in the world. When S presented himself "Here I am Mr Cooper" "Well I am ready for you, work is engaged, you shall have a painting room in the Coffee room front of the Theatre. Call on Dunlap for money; you have a credit for 1000 dollars. In 1807 Sully began to keep memoranda of events. The generous disposition of T. A. Cooper has not been guided by prudence he is now (1833) a worn out actor, a victim to intemperance—poor to desperation with a large family of children for whom 1700 dollars has been raised by a benefit & placed out of their fathers hands by his consent to which benefit S. gave 100. In 1807 with the kindest disposition Cooper play'd his tricks with boyish glee on his friends. Sully had nearly finish'd a portrait of James Harw[d] of Phil[a] when Cooper came & looked over him. "It is very like—but you have strangely colour'd it." "How?" "Dont you think it is very green?" "No." &c. Then Harwood the junior, then Twaits, "James looks as if the green fat of the turtle had stain'd him." Goes to Stuart in 1807 leaving his family in Hartford. Carried letters to A[ndrew] Allen, Perkins &c none to I[saac] P. Davis. Allens cordiality P. coldness—throws away all the other letters. Allen introduces him to Stuart who was painting his portrait. S paints Davis' head & shows to Stuart who looks a long time & says nothing. S in terror at last "Keep what you have got and get as much more as you can." Stuart instructed him in everything. Comes back to N. Y. with his family much improved & has nothing to do. Jarvis then in full business & S asks employment in working on his draperies &c & copying his pictures for which Jarvis paid him & treated him generously. B. Wilcox[160] of Phil[a] invites S. thither and he removes. Trott & S take a house together Feb[y] 1808. Embargo stopt S's first business at 50$ & he by Remb[t] Peales advice offers to paint 30 at 30$ it succeeds and he continued successfull. He felt at

160 Benjamin Chew Wilcox (1776-1845).

that point at which a visit to Europe was necessary for further improvement and it was proposed that the P. Acad[y] should furnish 3000$ to be repaid by pictures copied from masters. This was agreed to & he announced his intended departure & declined sitters. He was then told that the Academies funds would not allow an advance of money & perhaps in a year it might be done. Thus disappointed B. Wilcox opened a subscription at 200 dollars each for each sum a picture to be sent from London copied from a master. Sully's inexperience made him insensible to the inadequate price he only thought of improvement [blank] shares were subscribed, money raised & leaving the greater proportion with his large family he sailed for London. Charles B. King had then been [blank] years studying in that capital & with a letter to him Sully went for advice. "How long do you intend staying here?" "Three years." "How much money have you got?" So & so. "Why that is not enough for three months. I'll tell you what—I am not yet ready to go home and my funds are almost gone. Before I saw you I was contriving a plan to spin them out. Can you live low?" "All I want is bread & water" "Well, it will do. We will hire this room, take in milk & bread, keep our Landlady in good humour by a little present now & then, and work away like merry fellows." So they did and made themselves excellent Artists by a system of labour, oeconomy & independence that does them infinite honour.

Go to bed at 9. Rain.

Friday June 21st 1833. Champions Hotel Philad[a]. Hard rain. Up at 5. Breakfast at ½ past 6. Look over a book of memorandums put into my hands by Sully. Remember to ask of Robt Sully. Who is Bowman? Many passages of Sully's book will be valuable if distributed under different h[ds] for the Hist[y] of ye Rise & progress. Stuarts picture of himself in possession of Dr Waterhouse is marked on the back Æ 24 AD 1778 of course he was born in 1754. Clears at 2 OClock. Call on Neagle. Rembr[t] Peales letter from Paris published respecting his *liquid flesh.* I remember well his wax pictures. In 1804 he advertised that he must be known as *Rembrandt* & disclaims the Peale. Just before his last departure he wanted to sell Neagle a secret respecting painting or preparing pigments. Neagles first meeting with Jarvis in a stage coach—description of dirt & tobacco juice—shows a miniature &c &c "I am Jarvis" meets him at a ball at

Washington in full black. Story of his sitting up with a corpse & cutting off the head & carrying it off—&c &c. Call at the Mint too late to see Dr [Samuel] Moore. Go to bed at ten.

Phil[a] Sat[y] 22 June. Up at 5. Punch. A boy in Paris having seen Punch strangle his wife &c took the oppertunity of the absence of his parents to try the same joke on his infant brother. Earl in London with a house in a square & a great business. Franklin Peale has been sent to Europe to gain information on Mints & Dye sinking: Sully gave a model to the Manager of y[e] Mint here for a new liberty's head but they prefer'd the old one on the half dollar. When Congress bought Remb[t] Peales vile Washington they might have had Stewarts original of the General & his Wife for 1500$. Call on Sully. On McMurtrie, out—on Longacre—he draws well & his portraits are very true. Go to the West picture. There are two of his earliest on pannel. A Sea piece copied from a print; and a Composition of a cow, trees, houses, a Ship, men &c mere boys work but a curiosity. My early impression of the head of Christ is made stronger—it is very poor & so is John & Peter no great things. The principal Group exquisite. There is a print from a something pretending to be a head of Christ painted by order of Tiberius & passing to the Emperors of Constantinople, from them to the sultans & then to the pope. Rigmarole. I have not seen it. Call at the Mint & deliver Verplanks letter to Dr Moore who promises me every information in his power as does Mr Nease [161] the Engraver & Dye sinker of the establishment. Moore goes with me through the building & explains as the workmen perform, all the processes of coining from the forming ingots of the alloy'd metal from the furnace—rolling them (by passing under successive rollers) into slips the thickness of the coin—cutting out the circular pieces (leaving the perforated remainder to go again to the furnace)—milling the circular pieces & last stamping them into money or coining. The

[161] William Kneass.

rapidity with which all these operations are done is astonishing. The Machinery moved by an invisible power and of a structure beautiful to my sight but incomprehensible to my ignorance. Walk to the Rail road depot & take some bread & cheese & Ale. Longacre by appointment joins me & at 2 OClock we are drawn by a Locomotive Engine to Germantown. Pass the Afternoon with John F. Watson & family. See a portrait of a Gentleman (half length) by West before leaving home—it is even better than the one seen at Trenton. Return by Rail road to Phil[a]. Very Warm.

Philadelphia, Sunday, June 23[d] 1833. Clear & warm.

Barralet. Was an Irishman. Had practice at home. Was a man of talent. Made designs for Books. Longacre when a boy with Murray was sent to assist B in painting a transparency commemorative of Perry's victory. B. took snuff & told stories instead of working.

Go to Sully at 8 and make notes until 12.

When *Jarvis* was a boy in N. Y. & with his father, as he pass'd an unoccupied house in his way to school munching a piece of bread of butter he was attracted by sobs & looking in the place saw a little fellow crying bitterly. "Whats the matter?" "I've lost my father & I am hungry." "Hungry?" "Yes I have had nothing since yesterday." "Take this" The boy fell to eating & Jarvis sat down by him. "Where's your father? "He went to sea in y[e] Sally while I was playing on the wharf." The boys father was mate of the ship & supposed him on board at the time of sailing. Jarvis forgot school & took the boy to his father who found out the owners of y[e] ship & took care of the boy until his fathers return. We may judge of the Sailors feelings whe[n] he found that his child was left behind & his gratitude to the father of Jarvis.

Sully when painting in y[e] Theatre N. Y. began a portrait of Mrs Warren & had appointed a sitting at 4 P. M. Displeas'd with his work he began to repaint it at noon & lockt himself in. He heard footsteps & a knock & Mrs Warrens voice "Mr Sully" "He is not here" said his companion "Yes he is for his key is on the inside—he must be asleep." He determined to be asleep & they went away. He made his alterations & was ready for his sitter at 4. "Why Mr Sully you are a sound sleeper." "Yes that I am" But to sleep here before your Esel—& we made noise enough to rouze the dead. "I never sleep before my Esel—the truth is I was preparing for you. I

GEORGE SPALDING

By William Dunlap

(Courtesy of The Worcester Art Museum, Worcester, Mass.)

did not want any one to come in—you gave me the hint that I was sleeping, & I determined to sleep you away." They had a hearty laugh & she excused his first deception as a reward for his confession.

Sully & his brother in law. The boy had been directed to attend to the cleaning of a Gallery & was so doing but employed himself at one end while the cleaner scrub'd at the other [Belzons] came in & seeing S. at his painting look'd no further but furiously swept his box of paints from the table dashing every thing to the floor, assailing him with opprobious words. Tom replied & the master advanced as to chastise him but was instantly floor[ed] by a blow —he arose only to be knock'd down but at length seiz'd the boy active boy when Toms sister interfered & separated them. S. seized his hat and left the house.

Sully & Chester.[162] C. had tried the Stage but it would not do—he then shipt himself as a sailor & went two voyages but was disgusted with his companions & on arriving at Norfolk left the ship & at ye age of 19 bound himself to a Cabinet maker at Gosport. After Tom Christmas dinner he met Chester & they were comparing notes as they walk when C stopt & said do you go on. I must turn this corner—wait for me at ———. Tom obey'd and by & by C. came to him flush'd with colour & explain'd. He had been abused on shipboard by two sailors & promised that when he found them on shore he would punish them—he saw them at a distance & not wishing to involve Tom sent him on & then turning the corner gave chase & hailed his ex-shipmates. Now my lads fair play & I thrash you both!" Spectators gather "Gentlemen dont let them both come on at once—take care of that fellow till I finish this" "Aye aye, we will" C soon satisfied himself that he had punish'd one enough & then turn[ed] for the second, but he seeing the beating his companion had received broke from the crowd & ran. Sully & the frolic at his friends wedding at Petersburg—the Horse—the bridge —His habitual temperance only violated them, & at Coopers—when we retreated over the fence into Catherine Alley.

Sully first in Boston. Met I. P. Davis's at Fields and received great kindness from him. Saw Stuart paint a portrait strange mode of marking hard lines & scumbling over them. Asks Stuart a general mode. "I'll show you"—brings a mirror "How many times do you see yourself." "Three, the furthest indistinct." "So begin your pictures—then come up to the second—& if you *can* to the third."

When Sully went to England he took but 400$ leaving with his Wife 1000 & paying his passage. B. Wilcox gave him a credit to any am^{t}; but he only drew for his passage money to return. On June 18 went to sea & July 13 arrived at Liverpool. Went to Birmingham to see his aged Grandmother (90) & shows me a sketch then made of the house in which he pass'd his infancy. Revival of recollec-

[162] Chester Sully, one of Thomas Sully's brothers.

tions. Old lady who had known him a boy & her wonder at him & his coming from America. Carried letters to West from Wm Rawl[e]. Went with C. B. King and W. came out to them to the Gallery. S surprized to see a little man in y[e] great painter. Painted a head of C. B. King to show West what he could do: who pointed out a want of know: When he 1st saw West he was painting the Healing for P. Hospital. The Directors of Hosp[l] charge against the receit of that picture $14000, whereas the building costing that sum is appropriated to many other uses which ought to reduce the charge to 7 or 8. West intended this picture for the use of students but the Hosp[l] Managers deny access to it for that purpose & receive money from Artists as others. Sully calls on Hopner who was gouty: he professes willingness to aid him & answer questions. S. asks what yellow he uses in flesh. "Yellow! None" "I thought yellow was necessary to balance the blues & red's" "There is no yellow in flesh Sir." Beechy very kind but rough in manner. C. B. King & Sully have a bed room in common, and a good painting room in common, in Buckingham Place Fitzroy Square, a room occupied at times by Alston, Leslie & others. They live on Milk, bread & potatoes & thus S. makes his 400$ last 9 months with the aid of something for painting copies of Penns landscapes for John Coates. John Hare Powel then in London offer'd him any assistance, but the painter only availed himself of the generous offer to get access to the collections of the Aristocracy with whom Powel was intimate. Sully arrived in July & having seen the Lions thought to fulfill his contracts by copying pictures, but who would lend works of Value. He spoke on the subject to West & he offer'd all he had whether old masters or new. But for this offer, finding english collections out of his reach he was about going to Paris. West advised him to remain & made all easy to him, by allowing him to remove his most valuable pictures to his lodgings.

Daily W had a levee of young Artists for advice on their productions which was given with amenity and encouragement. As a proof of his indulgent manner Stuart tells of his having had the first Camera Lucida ever seen left with him & showing it to Stuart with explanation. He attempting [to] examine it let it fall on the hearth & broke it to pieces. Stuart stood with his back to West & his eyes on the wreck in despair when West said "Well Stuart—you may as well pick up the pieces." Sully's practice was to work steadily to the time of y[e] Academy & then go thither & draw. When he put down his name the Students went to the book to see who the newcomer was and the cry was "What, Another from America. *Marshall* was at this time playing at the Haymarket. S. met him in y[e] Streets and introduced him to M. A. Shee. S never saw play or heard Concert except such in private as at Mr Collards who as a musician appreciated Sully's musical taste & knowledge. *Shee* and experiments. Mastic will not crack if used over colour that is dry.

The Lithrage used in making drying oil is granulated: Oil kept over it & occasionally shook will be good.

Trumbull in 1809 was living in a splendid establishment in Argyle Street & painting portraits. West painted his Amor Vincet Omnia in Rafe's Room while the Christ healing was in the Room below at the end of the Gallery. Sully calling on him took up the wing of a Mackaw to look at: "That said West is the wing of one of my genii, I never paint without the object before me if it is to be had." Sully made a copy from Coreggio & carries it to West. "It is very exact, but what ground did you paint it on?" "A Tan colour." "That accounts for the difference, the original was painted on a lilac ground." Sully begs to have the original again, takes it home & made a second copy on a lilac ground. C. B. King and Sully have a living model to study from in their own room. Sully introduces by Powel to the collections of Behring and Angerstein. At the latter, his attention was arrested by Hogarths' Marriage a la Mode and Titians pictures did not please him, until Beechy directed him to the Ariadne. West's criticism upon the head painted by C. B. K. led Sully to severe study of Osteology which he pursued by candle light to the injury of his eyes. Having made 7 Copies for subscribers, painted 4 Landscapes for Coates & studied diligently besides, Sully in March 1810 sailed for N. Y. In April they were in peril from Ice Islands. West asked Sully to visit his native place "Enquire for Springfield Meeting house—2 miles from where road crosses you will find the house." On this road he quarel'd with the boy who was willing to be a Tailor. Sully went & found the house occupied by an old man in his dotage who could not comprehend what he wanted & would but for his son have turn'd him & his companions out of the house. S. left his companions & went out to draw the view of the building of which he sent two sketches to Mr West. When he return'd the old man was reconciled & show'd the room in which the great painter was born. (The road crosses from Springfield & it is 2 miles forward) Alstons colouring is more like Titian than that of any other modern.

To pay his passage home S. drew on B Wilcox for $200 & the same friend advanced 300 to Mrs. S. On his return to Phil[a] he & Trott occupied the same house. S. was full of employment & his improvement much spoken of, but he says his difficulty in recurring to y[e] portrait style was great & no improvement until he could apply his theoretic knowledge. (The owner of West's birth place was Croker by name) In 1811 S. out of health & goes to Richmond. B. Wilcox when offer'd the 500$ refused it and insisted on pictures. S painted & sent to the amount of 700. In 1811 he made a study of a head in the Style of Rembrandt to instruct *Charles Leslie* in Oil painting, shewing him the management of y[e] materials "for which" says S. "he has never ceased paying me by presents of prints, drawings &c." Doctor [John Syng] Dorsey agreed to attend S's family & receive pictures of the value of 100 a year—the Doctor said he must break off. "Why" "Because none of you will be sick." "Let us remain so & I am willing to paint three times as much for you." Old Doctor Lewis was sitting to S. when Abercrombie came in. "So sitting for your portrait." "Yes. I have settled all my affairs & have nothing to do but have my likeness taken & die." In 2 months he was corpse. Dr. [James] Abercrombie sitting to Sully challenged him to paint as long as he would sit. "I can paint all day." "And I can sit all day" Trott came in & finding a sitter retired. After the longest time allow'd for the operation he return'd, found the Doctor & again retired. He came a third time after a longer interval and there still sat the Doctor. "Well Mr Trott, dont you think I am a good sitter?" "Good, why you sit like an old hen." Samuel Coates a Manager & afterwards president of the Hospital was painted by Sully as a present to the Hospital & the Managers afterwards employed & paid him for Doctor [Benjamin] Rush's portrait—both full lengths size of life—this was in 1813. He had in 1811 painted a large full length of G. F. Cooke & given to the Penn. Academy. (Gold leaf as a ground prevents cracking) The first year after his return S. earned $4500. and the same for 2 years following. By invitation S. went to N. Y. to paint Decaturs picture for the Corporation. Stuart had been requested to paint Bainbridge but had disagreed with Bainbridge & delayed the work. The Corporation applied to Sully to go on & paint the picture in Boston assuring him that portraits of all the Officers to be complimented would follow. S. wrote to Stuart saying that he had heard him express his aversion to painting backgrounds, draperies &c and that now if he would paint this succession of Naval & military men, Sully under his direction [would] do the accessories. Stuart never answer'd the letter. Sully declined going on to paint Bainbridge on the ground of interfering with Stuart. Jarvis was applied to & went on & did it (*Was it not Hull*) and all the rest followed. Some years afterward Sully being in company with Stuart he proposed to Sully to paint in company with [him] taking draperies &c & said "We can carry all the continent." Sully replied that he should be delighted with it and then asked him if he remembered his letter to him in 1814 but he denied any knowledge of it. "If we had undertaken it, Sir, we should have painted"—Stuart interrupted with "All those full lengths that blackguards painted." (For Decatur S. received 500$) *Stuart* was written to by Hopkinson to paint a full length of Washington for the Penn. Acad. and offer'd 1500 dollars. He never answer'd the letter. Among painters anecdotes this may pass. Mons: Brugere came to Sully and engaged his portrait, the transaction to be a secret as he meant to surprize his wife with a New Years gift. While this was in process Madame Brugere called on the painter who thought the secret had been let out. "Monsieur Sully I would surprize my husband with a New

Years gift. He has wished my portrait, I have said 'No' a long time, you will paint my portarit & keep it very *very* secret." Accordingly both were painted & both secrets kept & Sully contrived to place both in their parlour after they had retired to bed on N[ew] Y[ear's] eve—the same pretence answering for each. Mons: Brugere came next day "My God Mons: Sully how we have all played trick. My Wife gets up and goes into the parlour & I listen. & I hear her exclaim & laugh! and I went to her "Aha my dear is it like?" "Look if it is like!" and there I find her portrait by my side. I trick her. She trick me. You trick both." In the years 1815 & 1816 Sully's receits were $4120 & 4133. (I spoke of Lawrence being in debt. S said he was extravagant in purchasing pictures & scarce prints. Was not a gambler, lived in style, was a religious man & told anecdotes of going & reading to an old sick servant &c) After 1818 Sully's business declined. He lost much time by undertaking a drawing of Wests picture for the Hospital for an engraving to be paid 500. He found the money would not pay him & beg'd off the bargain or an addition of 200 to the price—they chose to let him off & all the time employ[d] was lost. This was in 1818 July. In October he received an order from N. C. for two Washingtons but he preferring to paint one historical picture fixed on the crossing the Deleware. it was agreed to. he wrote for the size of the place it was to occupy & receiving no answer went on to paint without. When it was finished there was no place large enough for it & it was left on his hands. It was exhibited without success. The picture of Crossing y[e] Delaware was sold to [John] Dogget for $600 & sold by him to [John] Greenwood of the Boston Museum. S. painted two small panelled studies of 4 feet by 3 before painting the large, one was purchased by [blank] and is now in Edinburgh. In 1824 S's business had declined with distress of the monied interest in Phil[a] and having been strongly invited to Europe he determined on a plan of subscription for portraits of Eminent men in England originals & Copies of portraits of Locke Newton &c. Carried his plan to Gen Cadwallader who had been civil & highly lauded—the result of the conversation was that when he left his house he tore up his prospectus & threw the pieces in the Gutter. He now thought of going to Boston to seek work & packed up for the purpose; But [Gideon] Fairman, [Cephas G.] Childs & [Gilbert] Fox (Engravers) came to him and said you must not leave us. "I have no business." "If you had gone to England you w[d] have come back—if you go to Boston you will stay there. Will you paint our portraits." "Certainly." It was agreed, he unpacked and from that time to this has had uninterrupted success.

(Look to McMurtrie & Neagle for Krimmel) In 1820 built in conjunction with Earl the picture Gallery in Chesnut Street. In 1821 went to Monticello to paint T. Jefferson & after 12 days left the place with the greatest reluctance. A friend suggested making a copy of the Capuchin Chapel [by Granet] for exhibition & this year in July stop'd from going to Boston by Fairman Childs & Fox engaging portraits in 1824.

Six OClock Sunday Ev^{g} [June 23, 1833]. I have written as above and am somewhat tired—it is a warm day & I have been confined to the house writing in my bed chamber with the window up & coat & waistcoat off. I must go out this evening & fear walking for my disease (irritation) continues.

In July 1821 Sully went to Boston having obtained Mr [Benjamin] Wiggins consent that he might make a copy of the Capuchin Chapel. He then first became known personally to *Alston*. He painted in Mr Wiggins's house. Sargeant gave him four months to make his copy—Alston said five—Stuart said six. He finished it in less than three—he worked ten hours every day & one day fainted with fatigue. He told Alston it was done. "You have made a sketch." "A careful finished copy come & see." It was acknowledged to be such. *Sully* says Trott was in all things extremely sensitive in many things generous & righthearted. S. first knew *Eichholtz* at Lancaster as a Tin man and attempting to paint pictures very miserably. Eichholtz invited him to use his painting room for painting the portrait of a public man by order. He advised Eichholtz not to leave the tin ware but he persevered, went to Stuart, and in 3 years from that time produced good portraits and is now independent & return'd to Lancaster. *Murray* Sully was obliged to quarrel with from his asserting untruths respecting him relative to the Artists & Academy. Trott was under Murrays influence & then broke off the intercourse with Trott who lost ground in Phil^{a} as a man & artist & finally ruined himself by his conduct towards the woman he married & deserted.

Walk. Take tea. Call on McMurtrie from whom I rec^{d} a note of invitation this morning. He promises me notes on Krimmel. He has several of his drawings which I see. A fine head of a lady by Inman. Alstons mother & child. Leslie's copy of Guido's head of Christ. Promises me files of Leslie's & Alstons letters tomorrow even^{g} when I am to take tea with him. [Benjamin R.] Hayd[o]n's picture is travelling. I offer Our Nat: Acd^{y} room but no reply on the subject. Call at Longacres but he was in bed. Go to bed after ten.

Phil[a] Monday June 24[th] 1833. Up before 5. Clear. I must finish my enquiries to day in this place at present. To meet Longacre at y[e] Atheneum. To see Mr Lawson on y[e] subject of Wilson. To enquire respecting Ceracchi's trial at Atheneum. Library & elsewhere. To see Edwin ab[t] Baralet &c. To see Godey. Neagle. Sully & with him to McMurtries. Come to dinner after calling on those above & on Reeder [163] who came to America with Krimmel in 1810.

Krimmel was born at Edingen in Wirtemberg in 1787. Was taught drawing by [blank] the Dukes painter a man of talents. K's brother a merchant in Phil[a] sent for him but K prefer'd the fine arts to merchandizing and left his brother throwing himself upon the world with nothing but his talents as a stock in trade. At his first boarding house he painted the inmates in payment. The picture in his peculiar style which attracted attention was his pepperpot Woman. He made a picture in colour from Wilkies blind fidler & soon after painted his Blind mans buff. He & his companion Reeder taught drawing. Krimmel was frugal & industrious & reserved money enough to enable him to visit Europe. He landed in France, visited Vien[a] & other parts of Germany sometimes travelling on foot saw many good pictures & return'd to Phil[a] with a little money remaining. He painted for his friend [Alexander] Lawson who has his best picture an Election scene at the State house Phil[a] which is a great composition. He lost his employment as a drawing master because he was honest enough to refuse to cheat parents by finishing the works of his pupils. None had taste enough to employ him in a style which would soon have equal'd Wilkie & he remained neglected and poor. His friend Lawson advised him to paint without waiting for orders & exhibit his pictures for sale. He did not follow the advice. At length a picture of Penn was order'd & he prepared for the execution but going to visit a friend at Germantown he went with the boys of the family to bath in a Mill pond. He separated from them & when on preparing to return home they sought him, only his lifeless corpse was found in the Water. His character was faultless, his talents extraordinary, his life blameless, his love of truth exemplary. Mr Longacre introduced me to Mr Lawson the friend & teacher in drawing as far as stimulating him to the trial, of [Alexander] *Wilson.* They were intimate & often visited [William] Bartram: both attached to study of Nature. Wilson was melancholy, even talked of suicide, wrote verses & played the flute & indulged in solitude. Lawson suggested drawing to him—he thought it impossible he could draw but consented to try—copied

[163] Alexander Rider.

some small figures very badly & was confirm'd. L suggested flowers as his subject & gave him to copy, he succeeded & persever'd, then tried to draw a bird from nature & was delighted himself & surprized his friend. Bo[t] Reeves colours & painted from nature a bird he had shot. Thus was as far as man can be self taught. His biography is attached to his work. *Lawson* came from Scotland to Manchester at 16, to this country in consequence of love of liberty in the year 1794. Always fond of engraving he attached himself to [James] *Thackara* & in despite of his ignorance progressed in the Art. Studied drawing. Work'd for [Thomas] Dobson. Engraved the plates of the Supplement to Enc: Engraved for Baralet and work'd in conjunction with him. *Baralet* an Irishman the son of a French man had been a teacher of drawing in Dublin. Was most extravagant & eccentric. An Irish-French-man. A great beau though lame. Powder'd & ruffled. [Edward] Savage a New England man found [blank] working as a dull engraver at half a guinea a week and engaged him for four years at the same *and found* for America. The poor fellow found he had been deceived and after engraving Savages Washington family, took legal advice on his thraldom & was set free. Lawson is a tall raw boned man full of animation, athletic & an incessant talker—shrewd—satyrical though full of good feeling. Krimmel & Wilson he speaks of with rapture both as to talent and moral worth. Murry on the contrary he represents as a cunning knave. M on his arrival offer'd himself as a journeyman to Lawson who recommended him to Bradford by whom he was employed. *Barolet* kept himself poor by extravagant & grasped the earnings of Lawson when they laboured conjointly but did it openly & as if he might do it & still kept Lawson his friend. B made designs for [John Blair] Linn's poem, Lawson engraved them & Barolet would retouch & sometimes spoil them. If Linn was discontented with B's design he feared to speak to him knowing his passionate manner & outrageous oaths. In one instance he asked Lawson to represent his wish for alteration in a design—he did so & B raved like a madman. Lawson says that Audubon is a liar & impostor. That he is a frenchman by birth though professing himself a Louisianian. That he told Charles Bonaparte that his father was an officer in y[e] french Marine & came out to America bringing him with Count D'Estaing. That after various adventures & manoeuvers he was placed in the Western States & on a certain occasion Mr [blank] a quaker of respectability told Lawson that a wonderful man had arrived from the Back Woods bringing paintings of Birds beautiful beyond praise colour'd with pigments found & prepared by himself. At this time Lawson was engraving for Charles Bonaparte. One morning very early Bonaparte rouzed him from bed accompanied by a rough fellow w[h] a portfolio. They were admitted & the paintings in pastel displayed. L. thought them extraordinary for the work of an untaught wild man. Bonaparte admired & Audubon sat by silent. At length they came to the portrait of the horned owl. Bonaparte declared it superior to Wilsons on the same subject. "Its twice as big" says the Scotchman—and examining it he thought it very like Wilson's. "Here my dear" to his daughter "bring down the horned owl." It proved a copy reversed & magnified. Lawson spoke freely of the pictures, said the birds were ill drawn &c. Audubon said nothing. Bonaparte said he would buy them & Lawson should engrave them. "You may buy them, but I will not engrave them" "Why not?" "Ornithology requires truth and correct lines here are neither." In short he refused & Audubon departed with B not having spoken to Lawson: who says that all his design then was to sell the paintings. After a time B came again bringing one which he said he had bought and beg[d] Lawson to engrave it for his work. He consented but it was too large. B wanted him to reduce it. "No. I will engrave it line for line & will not correct any thing. It is wrong." in this & that part "let him reduce it & I will engrave from his drawing." Audubon came to Lawson and said "I understand you object to engraving this." "Yes it is too large for the work." "And you object to my drawing." "Yes. This leg does not join the body as in nature this bill is in the Crow straight, sharp, wedgelike—yours is cro[o]ked & waiving —these feathers are too large." "Sir I have seen them twice as large." "Then it is a species of crow I never saw. I think your work extraordinary for one self taught but we in Phil[a] are used to seeing very correct drawing." "Sir! I have been instructed seven years by the greatest painter in France!" "Then you made dom bad use of your time!" He measured me with his eye, said L, and but that he found a big fellow I thought he might have knocked me down. Lawson insists upon it that Audubon is a bold impostor, says that Charles Bonaparte now laughs at his pictures & tells a story of his exhibiting to him a picture of a *new* bird and on B's insisting on seeing the original—it was not to be found and such lamentations over the loss as amused the young man. He says that in the *turkey* he has given a flat foot the thumb or hind claw flat whereas in nature it is not & cannot so be used & mentioned other proofs of ignorance. "I would expose him but that I am the engraver of Wilsons work." Lawson has promised to write for me on Krimmel, Wilson & Artists generally as he knew them. He claims to be an American Artist, knowing nothing when he came hither. Complains of the great difficulty he met in having printing done, pretty much as *Edwin* does. Says Trumbulls portraits in y[e] declaration are caricatures particularly mentioning Mc Kane. [Thomas McKean]

Rain begins about 1 OClock & continues. I fear I shall not reach McMurtrie's this ev[g] nor get off tomorrow. Ev[g] go to Sully's receive material from him & his testimony in favour of Audubon as far as his drawing & painting birds. Not to his veracity. When he came to Phil[a] in 1824 he wished to paint portraits, applied to Sully, took a room opposite to him, received instruction, but gave it up a[nd] offer'd remuneration which was refused. His birds very fine. The reed bird & Wren & young. Go to McMurtrie in the rain. Meet there Longacre. Watson sends me word that Mr Taylor painted in Phil[a] in 1760 & a miniature of O Cromwell by him is in y[e] Mus[m]. McMurtrie testifies to Audubons drawing & paint[g] birds accurately. Receive some letters. Get back near eleven.

Phil[a] Wednes[y] June 25th 1833. Up at ½ past 4. Make an Abstract from Neagles Memd[a]. Meet Longacre at 6. Breakfast. Call on Godey, not up. Call on Neagle & receive Manuscript & promise of more. See L. A. Godey and receive six dollars p[d] Board & Lodging 7.25. Steam boat & rail road to N. Y. 3 Whole expense of Journey $15. Embark at ½ past 9. Leave Phil[a] at 10. Find Capt[n] Jenkins the first steam boat commander I knew still in the business—22 years between N. Y. & Philadelphia. We are two hours to Burlington, one more to Bordentown and arrive at South Amboy at 5 OClock. At N. Y. ½ past 7. The day has been so cold as to require overcoats.

I find my family Well & commence Journalizing in Another book—marked "Memoirs" & number'd 30. On Wednesday June 26th 1833.

The book commencing Wed[y] June 26th 1833 is of a leather Cover & marked with gold leaf on the back.

[The following memoranda were written at the back of the book, turned upside down:]

Sully at school in New York with Mr Stanford in 1793 & part of 94 when his mother dying at Richmond he went to Richm[d]

May 1833 Covent Garden Th: shut unable to pay and the performers playing at the Olympic. Hackett Falstaff &c at y[e] Haymarket. Kean at the point of Death.

Phil[a] Dec[r] 4th 1804. Remb[t] Peales advertisement [know]ledge of the anatomy of the head.

In 1799 the 1st Fed[l] St[t] Th: was burnt.

1797. Marshall & Mrs Marshall at Boston (I believe at Fed[l] Street under Williamson) & Cleveland & Wife. Burke had 100 Guineas p[d] him for Bunker hill & 6 Guineas a week thro' the season. Notwithstand[g] that this wretched thing drew great houses to the Haymarket, they could not pay their players.

Mirror of Taste. Biography of Cooper—bought the New York Theatre at a vast expence—false

Lewis Hallam who came out in 1752 is said to be the son of Hallam Macklin kill'd. false

Hodgk[n] made his first appearance in America on the stage of the Theatre in Southwark Phil[a] True—in 1792—in the character of Belcour.

Carpenter in Mrs Merry's biography (Vol 1st M[irror] of taste P: 118) places her in Phil[a] playing in opposition to the Old Am: Company the first season of opening the Chesnut Street Theatre (false) she was brought out by Wignel in 1796 with Warren & Cooper.

Warren's first appearance Friar Lawrence & Mrs Merry's Juliet. Morton one of the first company of Wignel play'd Romeo.

Hodgkinson in Charleston S. C. in 1805 (true) see M of Taste. His death falsely told in Vol: 2[d] [page 338]

Wood's biography Vol 2[d] [no. 5, November, 1810, pp. 230-235] In 1799 appointed Wignel's treasurer & so continued till 1803 when Wignel died in Jan[y]. Warren becomes Manager Wood goes to England, brings out Twaits.

John B. Linn commences Dramatist (Mem[rs])

1796 Wignel arrived in N. Y. with Cooper Warren

Mr & Mrs Merry & others on y[e] 19th Oct[r] Mr & Mrs Whitlock in N. Y. in Sept[r] On the 5th Dec[r] Wignel opened with Romeo & Juliet Mrs Merry: Juliet. Wed[y] 7th produced his Ballet dances Mr & Mrs Byrne, and Friday Cooper made his first appearance in America in Macbeth.

1797 Fever in Phil[a] Wignell & Company in the circus Greenwich Street New York. Fennell, Moreton, Cooper, Harwood, Marshall, Blessitt, Francis, Hardinge, Bernard, Fox, Warren, Wignell, Mrs Merry, Mrs Marshall, Mrs Oldmixon, Mrs Hardinge, Mrs Francis, Mrs Wignell, Mr & Mrs Byrnes.

1798 [Illegible] first appeared on y[e] Stage in Annapolis Mr Merry died at Baltimore. Moreton died. Mrs Simpson's letter respecting the Miss Westrays June 19th

Querie? Did not Whitlock & wife come out with Wignell's first Company? Yes. Settled.

1800 or 1801 Wignel converted the Building now the post office (always devoted to letters) in Washington D. C. and opened the first Th: in y[e] Capital of y[e] U. S. with Venice preserved. Pierre, Cooper—Belvidera Mrs Merry.

[Robert] Merry's play of the Abbey of St Augustine was play'd & perhaps written in America.

1803 Mr Wood return'd from England & brought out Twaits. Jefferson join the Phil[a] Company. Mr Wignell died of injury sustained in being bled. Mrs Wignell Manager, resigned the management to Warren & Reinagle.

1806 Beekman & Astor purchased the New York Theatre for 50,000$ Fennell reading in Phil[a]. Boston Company—Bernard, Darley, Usher, Kenney, Twaits, Powel, Mrs Powel, Mrs Darley, Mrs Darby, Mr Fox. Vauxhall N. Y. Th: Twaits, Sully, Youngs, Hogg, Mrs Young, Mrs Villiers, Misses Dellinger & White.

1808 Mrs Warren (late Mrs Merry & Mrs Wignell) died suddenly at Alexandria.

Miss Smith afterwards Mrs Bartley appear'd and is compared to Mrs Siddons!!

1810 Theatre opened in Phil[a] 26th of Nov[r] & 28th Mrs Twaits play'd Lady Macbeth. White's play of "The Clergyman's daughter—from McKenzies Man of the World.

1810 After the death of Reinagle, Wood propos'd for a share in the Management & in this year commenced as such at Baltimore w[h] Fennell as Othello. Oct[r] 26 open'd the Phil[a] Theatre and in March 1811 Cooke played in Phil[a] (20th March). That season (1810 & 11) the number of nights was 88 and the receits $71,052 or $807.40 per night. The Circus in Walnut Street Phil[a] opened as a Theatre. Theatre in Richmond burnt. Greene, his daughter burnt with others. Phil[a] Company join'd by or aided by Cooke, Cooper, Simpson, J. H. Payne, Mrs Darley Dwyer & others, but season not productive (1811-12) Mrs John Duff first appear'd & with success rarely equal'd in any city (says Mr Wood). see p: 427 M[irror] of Taste [Vol. IV, December, 1811] for distruction of Richmond Theatre. Mr Calbraith see M of T. 3d Vol. p: 114.

1812 Mr Whitlock return'd from England & play'd in Phil[a]. The old Theatre in Baltimore was taken down & a splendid new building erected at a cost of 66,000$.

1813 Mr Whitlock return'd to England & is still living in London (1832). Mr & Miss Holman play'd in y[e] Chesnut St[t] Theatre successfully. Holman embark'd in an opposition scheme in Walnut St[t] Th: and fail'd and he went to Charleston S. C. and after a season as Manager there, he closed the house & went to England, on his return brought the Lady he afterward married—after his death??? Wood says sail for N. Y. he died soon after. Mrs Holman married Clawson, was divorced from him & married Sandford. The New Theatre Baltimore ope[d] in the face of the British blockading squadron (says Wood) 10th May.

1815 Fennell appear'd for the last time on the Phil[a] Stage, and played K Lear (says Wood) his powers, memory all were gone & he died soon after. See Polyanthos Vol: 1, for life of Fennell.

Corwain. Sully promises information. He died of consumption—fine taste. Went to London & placed his funds with a merchant who fail'd & he lost all. *Sargeant.* 6 or 7 years in London: not a close student. Told S. that he could not distinguish dark blue from purple or [blank] from black.

Kean mention'd by Kelly as in Decr 1791 being ye Cupid in Cymon. In 1794 Kemble dismisses the boys & among them Kean. In 1814 he made his first appearance 26th Jany as Shylock. (see Reminiscences p: 377) Octavo

Meeting of Penn: Academicians Octr 18th 1824. C. W. Peale in ye Chair on motion of [William] Strickland: A committee for rules in regulation of schools & John Haviland & Rem P. appointed. Resolved to meet once a month. A Council was elected to meet y^{e} *board of Directors.* Gideon Fairman, Rem: P: John Haviland, John Neagle, James B. Longacre, Charles B. Lawrence. Rules & Bye laws were at next meeting adopted, & their proceedings reported to the *board of Directors.* Mr Wm Kneass, engraver of the mint elected a member *subject to approval of the Directors.* Hugh Bridport elected a member. Mr [John] Bell is proposed to lecture on Anatomy & consents. Professor had lectured on ye history of the Arts. A room in the Academy was selected for Professor Bells lectures. [Jacob] Eichholst was a Member, and [Thomas] Doughty. *In March & April no quorum,* & so & so & the next meeting was *April 13th 1829.* by request of Mr [Joseph] Hopkinson president of the Academy to app^{t} Comm^{s} to cooperate with the Directors preparatory to the next Exhibition: A letter was read inviting Artists to Exhibit & offering privileges to Artists in the Institution—approved. They agreed to return to their labours in the support of the Academy as their claims had been satisfactorily adjusted by the Academy. [Thomas] Birch, Eichholst & [Bass] Otis appointed a Com: to join the Directors in hanging pictures and a comm. was appointed to make preparations for Study. Ap^{l} 24th Mr Neagle the Secretary wrote to the president acknowledging his letter "Your letter embraces every point *except one* & this was thought to be an unintentional omission—defining the duties of the keeper (Thackara). They inform H. of their proceedings. They expect *the Ancient to be seperated from the modern Works.* Rooms for study. Admission to the Library without interruption from the keeper & his duties defined. They had wished to close the Academy except to Strangers between the Annual exhibitions.

1816 The 11th of May the City Council of Baltimore passed an ordinance directing the tax of 10 dollars per night on the Theatre to be appropriated to the relief of the families of those Citizens killed at North Point. West (says Wood) brought out his famous troop of Equestrians from Astley's and perform'd 27 nights in the

Walnut Street house (sometimes a Theatre, sometimes Circus) to an average of $807 per night while the average of the Chesnut St^{t} Th: was 550 p^{r} Night.

1817 In Novr Incledon play'd or sung in Phil^{a} at y^{e} Chesnut St^{t} Th: & shortly after Phillips—the latter continued to attract (says Wood) longer than any one except Cooper.

1818 J. Wallack open'd in Baltimore as Macbeth & was very successfull. J. H. P.'s Opera glass (1826) makes frequent mention of him as S. Price's Hero.

1819 Mr & Mrs Bartley (formerly Miss Smith) open'd at Baltimore on the 8th Feby. He was a favourite but the people were dissapointed in her. She offended greatly by acting Hamlet. "Her recitation of Allens' Ode was (says Wood) certainly very near perfection—in fact she always recited when she should have acted."

1820 Miss F[rances] Wright's play of Altorf was play'd in Phil^{a} the 5th of Jany. On Easter Sunday April 2^{d} the Chesnut Street Theatre was consumed by fire (says Wood) by which the loss was immense—every thing except the mere walls. Within a few Weeks the Washington Theatre was burnt, by the carelessness of some conjurer to whom it was let for a night.

1821 On the 8th of August the New Theatre at Washington was open'd by Warren & Wood. Forest commenced the 2^{d} Decr in Phil^{a} in young Norval.

1822 The Orphan Assylum was burnt with 24 children. A Benefit was given for the Charity at the Walnut Street Th: (the other lying in ruins) and produced the great receit of 1742$. On the second of December the present (1832) Chestnut St^{t} Th: was opened.

Mr Taylor produced an effect by a trick that is deserving of notice only to be censured. His Octavian was distinguished from other Octavians not by better playing, but by a beard the natural growth of the players chin, cherished for the purpose. He made his debut at a time when decency required the use of the razor, if his birth had been put off for a few years he must have adopted some other plan of operating upon the spectators of his *entré* for at this time every dandy is equally qualified to play Octavian by a sallow skin, lack-lustre eye like <*Estifania's necklace*> the pearls of Estifania's Necklace, and the chin of a London Old clothsman. But fortunately for Taylor a real beard prov'd as captivating & attractive at that time as a real Elephant has since.

How lamentable is the mistake of the Director of a Theatre or an Actor when he loses sight of the truth, so essential to the Drama that the Stage is <*the mirror which is*> to reflect Natures Image & <*not to*> as in a mirror by imitation and is not raised to exhibit realities. If a painter to give brilliancy to a button lays on gold leaf he is no longer a painter, but a gilder, he sinks the Artist to the mechanic.

Bignel "partner of West & died at Charleston" was one of a Company with Riley (the Itinerant) and Warren at Taunton about year 1787.

Jefferson—his father Manager at Totness.

Bernard in 1813 open'd the New Theatre Albany it being just finish'd (Jany 18th)

The English Theatre is charged by an English writer with disgraceful arrangements in arrangements which would disgrace the most dissolute city on the Continent.—and seem intended to justify the severest denunciations of those who entertain religious scruples on the score of the Drama.

For Matthews see [Michael] Kelly's Remin^{s} p: 319 & 337 for Cooke and Mrs Bartley (then Miss Smith)

For Blanchard see [*Life of Frederick*] Reynolds p: 37 2^{d} Vol: Holman the same & pp: 40: 41. For Merry p: 53. Wood speaks of Merry's punning. He being in company with one of Kings Ministers, the noble Duke said "His Majesty by supporting the constitution has proved himself a good Upholder" "True said Merry but a bad Cabinet maker." But there is real wit in his remark Being in company with a coxcomb he remarked to a friend "I would go barefoot &c to Holyhead & back again to see a fellow, one half as clever as he thinks himself."

1826 Mrs Austin's appearance on the opening of Drury Lane on Septr 23^{d} in Countess Almaviva. Same night Wallack play'd Don Felix—a good attitudinarian & his forte exaggeration.

Mrs Sloman play'd Cora 25th Septr opening Night at Covent Garden. Blanchard at Cov^{t} Garden. Sir Phillip Modelove. (Arrah now Teddy my jewel & have they hoisted you from the stage into the pit?) In this year (1826) The Park, Chatham, La Fayette & Bowery Theatres were all playing. (see Bills in O. G. p: 62) Sandford had the Albany Th: at this time. The principal men McCready, Booth, G Barrett—Women Mrs Hilson, Entwistle, Sandford, G Barrett. Barretts mother then playing. At Baltimore Forrest was then playing. Holland who play'd at ye Bowery when Miss Rock was there is mention'd O. G. p: 69. Mrs Alsop a daughter of Mrs Jordans is likewise mention'd & particularly on occasion of Talma's visit to the Theatre London. She poisoned herself in New York.

Mrs Gordon & her daughter Miss White at the Grove Theatre. She was the illegitimate daughter of Walton White who was a Major in ye U. S. Army of the revolution. She played at the Park Theatre. Married a Mr Limbert & being left a widow was teaching a school at Savannah in 1820.

1832 Memoranda Th: Mrs Hamblin of the Bowery Th: is Blanchards daughter & made her London appearance at the Haymarket —in 1826 she play[ed] at Boston. Stanley the Boston Hero at that time, Pelby likewise there. 2 Theatres or rather 1 & a Circus-Theatre (see Op: Glass, p. 61)

Friday Octr 12th Miss F. Kemble made her first appearance before a Phil[a] Audience in y[e] Tr. of Fazio. On Monday Doctor Birds Tr: with Forest is to be played in Arch St[t] and Kemble & Daughter play in Chesnut St[t].

Mr Wheatley tells me that left England with his father in the *Geo Barclay* for Phil[a] in 1793 (Aug[t]) and arrived at Glostor Point 1st of Oct[r]. The greater part of Wignels company were on board the ship. Fennel had arrived before them & came on board at the Point. Green had a Wife with him & Miss Wilelms his future wife was on board. Mrs Rowson & Mrs Shaw were part of the Company & among other Musicians *Dangel*. Green became intemperate as did his second Wife & after being discharged from the Th: of Richmond took laudanum & thereby died. Has a son living. Green kill'd himself in 1822.

Mrs. Ellis. Miss Ellis her daughter a pretty girl tall, genteel, modest, play'd little parts at the Park Theatre about 1810 or 11. She afterward went as a part of Bernard's company to Canada & being now an Actress play'd a good Line. Goldsmid a son of the Banker then in the Army & at Quebec saw her in Morgiana being enamour'd of her married her & carried her home where she has proved worthy of the fortune she shares with him.

Mrs Hatton is perhaps still alive—she was lame when here—became afterward enormously fat, and in England publish'd novels &c under the appellation of Ann of Swansey the place of her residence.

Wheatley tells me that when young he made part of a Company at a private Theatre in Berkeley Street Soho, of which Hilson and his father were members

Messrs Hill. McGaven says the daughters play'd likewise.

Mrs Young died ab[t] 2 years ago. e i in 1830

Rider, Trott & Canter three painters together at Charleston at one time.

Seeley the name of Krimmels teacher at home. His excellence—dismissed by Duke of Wirtemberg—Bonaparte employs him. Rider's adventuring with the French Army.

DIARY OF WILLIAM DUNLAP

June 26, 1833—December 31, 1834

New York City

(Manuscript volume lettered *Memoirs 30* owned by The New York Historical Society)

MEMOIRS 30

Memoirs or Daily Occurances Wm Dunlap

1833

Continued in this book to Decr 31st 1834 inclusive

New York Wednesday June 26th, 1833 My last notes are in a book with marbled cover. We have another rain. It will be seen by the last vol: that I was very busy in Phil^{a} that I was not at ease as to health, that I saw many persons to collect materials for my history of ye Fine Arts in America, yet I left much undone. This day June 26th 1833 I sit down again in New York to continue my labours & enjoy the blessings conferred upon me, and be thankful! Receive a letter & twelve dollars from R. H. Waller of Rutland Vt. Write acknowledging the receit. Read in Review. Clear in afternoon. Ev^{g} again rain. Irritation continues.

Thursday June 27th 1833. Clear. Th: 64. Read in American Review. Write on Hist^{y} of Arts. Irritation continues when I walk. Feverish in the night. 3 OClock. Dr McLean says it is altogether a disease of the bladder. He prescribes Balsam of Copeiba, 15 drops night & morning with sugar & water. Write. Read review of life of [Sir Humphry] Davy. Begun wth ye Balsam.

Friday [June] *28th* Clear. Th: 66. Irritation continues. Write on Hist^{y} &c. Write to James Robertson Esqr Cashier of the Branch Bank of ye U. S. at Richmond requesting information from Mrs Edwards the half sister of Henry Bembridge Esqr the painter respecting him. Read Prince Pückler Muskau's England with pleasure & profit.

Saturday June 29th 1833. Clear Th: 67. Write on Hist[y] of Arts. Irritation continues tho' I have avoided walking out. I do not go out to day. Doctor Frances calls & promises me the remaining Vols of Collier [164] & [Nathan] Drake's Shakespeare. Read the German prince and the Weekly Mirror. Use the partial tepid bath.

Sunday June 30th Clear. Th: 70. Less irritation this morning. Read as yesterday & write on Hist[y] of Arts & Artists; afternoon some irritation. I take the balsam morning & night 15 drops & drink more tea than usual. Keep the house.

Monday July 1st 1833. Clear. Th: 72 at 5 A M in the afternoon 80. Write on Hist: Ride to the library. Receive communication from Verplank. See Morse & his defence of my friend J. Fennimore Cooper against Gould & I am grieved to say Charles King. Call at E[vening] P[ost] office & Mirror. Less irritation. Receive a very pleasing letter from Allston & promise of continuation. Read Edin: Review & German prince.

Tuesday July 2d Th: 76. Clouds. Write. Clears. Th: 80. Mr [A.] Bradish a young Artist brings me letters from Sam[l] Hotchins jr. of Geneva N. Y. & Neagle of Phila. Read [James Sheridan] Knowles's play of the Wife. It very dramatic, very extravagant & very hard to read, yet I presume plays well. I am free from irritation 4 OClock P. M. Having dined after 4 & drank tea. Thus my hopes from the warm weather and continued perspiration are disapointed. Evening & night rain.

Wed[y] July 3d 1833. Clouds. Th: 78. Feverish & head ach. Write. Hard rain. By the last arrival from Eng[d] we hear of [Edmund] Keans death. Yesterday W[ashington] Irving was thrown from a Gig & injured. At 2 OClock Th: 74. Rain continues. Read in German prince. This an extraordinary book.

[164] John Payne Collier's *History of English Dramatic Poetry and Annals of the Stage to the Restoration,* 3 vol., 1831.

Thursday July 4th 1833. Another fourth of July, clear & pleasant. Bells & drums & guns & crackers are sounding. My disease prevents my looking at the thousands of well dressed people who throng the streets or the thousands of proud youths who march under their proud standards and feel willing to emulate their forefathers. Afternoon, Th: 70. Notwithstanding my above supposition (I will not call it determination) I rode down to the park & cross'd to Clinton Hall for a bundle of books sent to my Wife by her sister Mrs Dwight, they are the works of her husband Dr Dwight, 4 vols travels 2 poems. With my bundle I was stop'd by the press in Br^{d} Way on my return & after long standing was obliged to walk home, all the stages numerous as they are being throng'd. Read in German prince & write on Hist^{y} of Arts. Evening walk on Broad Way as far as Niblo's Garden but do not go in.

Friday July 5th 1833. Clear. Th: 70. Walk to the Br^{d} Way to learn the am^{t} of mischief done by the falling of a temporary erection in Niblo Garden. A man & two women much injured & many others hurt. My disease appears to be nearly gone, No irritation. Write on the hist^{y} of ye Arts. Read. Go to Library, Mirror Office, [William] Hamiltons painting room, [Thomas S.] Cummings d^{o} & rode home.

Sat^{y} July 6th Clear. Th: 70. Mr Reuben R Thrall of Verm^{t} call'd for the miniatures of R. H. Waller & I gave them to him yesterday. Walk in the Square. Write from 7 to 2 incessantly. Read. Walk to the Bowery. I have no irritation from walking. Rain in Night.

Sunday [July] *7th* Clear. Th: 73. Write on Hist^{y} of Arts. Read German prince. Walk moderately.

Monday [July] *8th* Clear Th: 75. Write as above. Walk down town. Call on Cummings & Morse. Go to Clinton Hall. They are distributing the pictures. The

Exh^{n} receits are about $1400. Go to Library. Take Frankenstein. Ride home. Frankenstein by the Auther of the *Last Man, Perkin Warbeck,* Mary Shelly the widow of y^{e} poet, the daughter of Wm Godwin & Mary Wolstonecraft. I gallop'd over these 2 Vols: The ideas are too outré for any sympathy with the characters.

Tuesday [July] *9th* Last ev^{g} Showers. This morning clouds. Th: 80. Walk. Write on Hist: Arts: Haydons picture of the Entrance into Jerusalem was <*painted*> commenced about 1816, finished *after* 1818. Was taken by execution with several other pictures upon Mr Haydon's insolvency, and sold at Auction, it was said these pictures were sacrificed for little more than the cost of their frames. The "Entrance &c" belongs now (in whole or part) to Mr James McMurtrie & is on Exhibition in y^{e} west of this state. The judgement of Solomon was a few years since offerred to an American gentleman for 500 guineas. A sum in Mr Allston's opinion far below its value. Before Haydon had finished his "Entrance &c" he was offered 2000 G^{s} for it. Gave check for $18 in full to Doctor V[alentine] Mott. In Bank $129.35. Th: 75.

Wed^{y} July 10th 1833. Th: 72. Clear. Walk down town. See Durand & engage him to Engrave my portrait for the Hist^{y} of the Arts. Library. Read Mr [Nicholas] Biddle's oration lay^{g} the corner stone of the Girard College for the liberal education of White (poor, male) orphans children. Who is the Architect? It is to be 160 feet front, 217 in flank. Columns 6 feet Dia: 53 feet high. Grecian Corinthian. It is 1¼ miles from Phila (See Amer^{n} July 9th & same paper for Kemble & daughter at Albany. Took Quart^{y} Review. Call at the Harpers. John Inman has married Clara Fishers Sister [Caroline]. Harper thinks he has injured himself by Theat^{l} connection. See [Stephen H.] Gimber, Mezzotinto engraving &c. Durand tells me Vanderlyn is more disposed to aid in giving me notices of himself than I thought he would be. He is poor.

Harper puts in my hands a book by Parson Fidler [165] which is almost amusing from its excessive ignorance & stupidity. Why should such a book be republished here? My manuscript of Zeb Spiff is in John Inman's hands.

Thursday July 11th 1833. Clear. Th: 70 A square containing 1000 acres is one mile & a quarter long. A parrellologram of 1¼ miles long & ¼ broad contains 200 acres. Write on Hist^y of ye Arts. Go to Library, Mirror office, Clinton Hall, Cummings's, Ingham's. The latter shows me a lovely miniature of his painting the finish exquisite; the colouring very fine, the hair superb. The hand too small or it would have been perfection. Ev^g Walk. Night a thunder shower. Th: 76.

Friday [July] *12th* Clear Th: 74. Write on Hist^y Go to the plaster-mans, dissapointed in a figure. Paint on Richard and Kenneth.[166]. Read. Write again. Afternoon read Quarterly Review, Memoirs of Dr Burney by Madam D'Arblay, severe but from the extracts not too much so. The proof that she was 25 instead of 17 when Evelina was published is very curious. I am gratefull to her for former pleasure, I am sorry that her age is so weak as to write in such a style or endeavour to perpetuate a deception.

Sat [July] *13th 1833* Light clouds, Th: 74. Write & paint. Read. Th: 78. Walk.

Sunday July 14th Clear. Th: 76. Write. At 10 P. M. the Th: in the usual place 80. In the entry below & exposed to a current of air 84. At 12 OClock in this usual place (upper entry or passage) 82, Lower entry doors open as before 85. At 2 OClock in ye usual place. 84. Afternoon Thunder & Rain. Th: 80.

[165] Rev. Isaac Fidler, *Observations on Professions, Literature, Manners, and Emigration in the United States and Canada, made during a Residence there in 1832*. London, 1833; N. Y., 1833.

[166] This picture, illustrating a scene from Sir Walter Scott's *The Talisman,* was painted for Charles P. Clinch. It was exhibited at the tenth annual exhibition of the National Academy of Design, in 1835, no. 19 in the *Catalogue*.

Monday [July] 15th Clear. Th: 74. Read. Write on hist^y of arts. Write to Robt Gilmore. Go to Hamilton's painting room, he is preparing to go to Scotland intending to be back in 3 mo: Go to Library & bring home Croker's Boswell. I hope I shall recall the pleasure I experienced when read^g Boswell's John[son] with Smith & Brown. Receive another delightful letter from Allston. Begin a letter to him. Write on Hist^y of Arts. Read Croker. Ev^g Walk.

Tuesday July 16th 1833. Clear. Th: 71. Walk. Wind so cool at ½ past 5 that I button my cloth coat for comfort. This reminds me of July 1816. Write on Hist: Arts. Paint on Richard & Kenneth. Walk out of town between 1 & 2. Write on Hist^y Read Croker.

Wed^y [July] *17th.* Light clouds. Th: 72. Write on Hist Arts. Send off letter to Allston. Write. Paint. Read in Croker & Sully's scrap book.

Thursday [July] *18th.* Clear. Th: 72. Walk. Write. Walk to Durand's, Harper's & get my MSS of Zeb Spiff. He said he did not remember what he had agreed to on the subject. I repeated & he assented. I said I would take it home & correct & whenever he could "slide it in" (his expression) it should be ready. "You will call in & remind us." To Library. Read Architecture by Danl Wadsworth in Silliman's [American] journal [of Science] for July 1833. Verplank reminds me of the Rubens pictures belonging to Mr [George] Calvert, Bladensburg. We go to Columbia College & see a Smibert & a copy of Copely's Dr. [Myles] Cooper. My reading to day is principally news papers & New York Mirror to which I contributed remarks on Fidler.

Friday [July] *19th* Walk. Th: 71. Morning Clear. Afternoon Clouds. Paint on Richard & Kenneth. Receive letter from Robt Gilmor of Baltimore with list of his pictures &c. Ev^g sultry. Walk to Ingham's to meet the Council of y[e] Nat[l] Academy. I had at last meet[g] of y[e] Academy proposed giving a dinner to Leslie on his arrival, it was refer[d] to y[e] Council. We now appoint a Comm. to attend to it. Thunder & rain in the night.

Sat[y] July 20th 1833. Clouds. Th: 73. Write. Read. Paint on R & K. Ev[g] Walk.

Sunday [July] *21st* Light clouds. Th: 72. Write to Wm A. Whitehead: Collectors Office Key West: respecting Amboy in consequence of his request of May last. Read Croker. Walk. Must I refrain from this exercise so delightful to me?

Monday [July] 22d. Clouds. Th: 74. Clears Th: 82 at 2 P M: Write. Paint on R & K. Read Croker. At 5 OClock th: 85. In July 1832 I see but one day marked so high, the Th: hangs in the same place. *That* day was the 3d after it was from 72 to 76 until Aug[t] 14th, 81. This was a cool summer & the cholera raging.

Tuesday [July] *23d* Clear. Th: 79. Cooler night. Read & write for Hist[y] Arts. Read Croker. Th: falls to 76. Walk. Ev[g] Morse brings me his further controversy with Editors in defence of Fennimore Cooper.

Wed [July] *24th* Clear. pleasant. Th: 74. Write to James F. Cooper & Carry letter to the post Office. Leave in Bank $119.35. Call on Cummings, on Morse: he shows me two blackguard insulting letters from Gould (the "Critic" Counting house clerk) to him exulting in having caused distress to Coopers family & sending Morse a No. of a paper in which his critique of the Bravo is approbated, with expressions like this "try again Mr Morse." &c. To Library. Ride home. Th: 83. Thunder. Wind. Rain. Th: 82. Morse showed me how to make a valuable colour by roasting Ivory instead of burning it. The bath is Ivory black, the[n] merely roasting it (even leaving it partly white) gives a beautiful brown, a rich, transparent colour superiour to Vandyke brown, only less deep.

Thursday July 25th 1833 Read Croker & paint on R & K. Clouds Th: 76. Theodore S. Fay sends me a letter from Mr J. S. Sturgeon complaining that the Mirror had asserted that a copy of a picture exhibited by him was exhibited as an original (or rather as a specimen of his painting) and that his pictures are very bad & seems to threaten the author of such truths.

Friday [July] *26th* Th: 72. Clear. Doctor [Samuel] Beaumont calls on us. Doctor Frances brings me 2d & 3d Vol: of Colyer. Paint on R & K. Ride to Town and see Th: S. Fay. Library. [William] Rollinson (who promises notes on Engravers), [Robert W.] Weir (who promises of painters) See letter of Greenough. Rec[d] notice of Gondolfi from Maine, receive letter from Judge Hopkinson, respecting Pine. Read in Mirror.

Saturday July 27th 1833. This vile paper teazes me. Clear. Th: 72. Read. Walk. Paint on R & K. Write on Hist: Arts. Read Croker and Collyer. Th: rises to 78. Walk.

Sunday [July] *28th* Clear. Th: 77. Read Collier annals. Write. Doctor Beaumont with us. Th: 70.

Monday [July] *29th* Clear. Th: 72. Paint on R & K. Write on Hist[y] of Arts. Doctor Beaumont reads to me, & leaves with me MSS of his Cousin Wm. Beaumont surgeon of the U. S. Army respecting the uses of the human Stomach & its powers &c with experiments on a man cured by him whose stomach had been wounded &c.

Tuesday July 30th 1833. Th: 74. Read Croker. Write on Hist. Arts. Begin 2d letter to Wm. Whitehead. I have reason to think that what I have called stricture & supposed to be a return of former disease is stone or gravel in the bladder. Ride down town. Go to Bank: leave 104.35. Call on Washington Irving, out of town. Go to Library & to Merchants Library. Ride home. Read Dr

Beaumonts MSS. Heat encreased to day; & in ye afternoon a gust with hard rain left the evening cool. Take soda & soap, one pill.

Wed^y^ [July] 31st. Clear. Th: 72. By request re-write preface to Dr Wm Beaumonts book on Experiments & observations on the Gastric Juice &c. Read over the MSS. Write a notice of the intended publication. Walk. Read Croker. Walk. Take the Copeiba.

Thursday August 1st. Clear. Th: 72. Take the Copeiba. Paint on R. & K. Doctor Beaumont took his cousins MSS. & returns to Plattsburg to day. Read Croker. Write on Z. Spiff. Walk.

Friday Augt 2d. Clear. Th: 73. Write on Z. S Read Croker. Ride to Leonard St. Call on Verplank: Cummings, Mirror Office, Library. See some pictures at [Eugene] Prudhomme's & at [Joseph] Bonfanti's. Ride home. Ev^g^ Walk.

Sat^y^ Augt 3d 1833. Clear. Th: 72. Paint on R & K. Take the Copeiba. Ride to Wall St. Leave in Bank 94.35. Library. Ride home. Write on Hist: Arts. Read Croker. Take Copeiba.

Sunday Augt 4th Clouds. Th: 74. Take Copeiba. Write on Z. S. and on Hist: Arts. Read Croker. Ev^g^ Hard rain.

Monday [July] *5th* Rain. Clouds. Th: 73. Clears & with my wife ride to Wall St. & then walk to Steamboat, embarking at 10 A. M. for Perth Amboy. Fare for 2, 25 cents. Put up at Arnolds Hotel kept by the son & Widow of Lewis Arnold. Call on our old, sick, friend Mrs Sophia Brown who lingers cheerfully on the brink of the grave with religious patience & hope of another life. Go to Arnold's & take Dinner. We then go to James Parker and are good naturedly scolded for going to a Tavern, engage to dine with them next day & then go to Mr Bell's where we took them by surprize as at Parkers, stay till evening, then visit Mrs Brown again and go Arnolds for the night.

Perth Amboy Tuesday Aug[t] 6th 1833. Up before 5. clouds. Walk to the Hill where I once own[ed] a farm. The hedge of 3 thorn'd Acacias in part remains grown to trees. Return & go to Mrs Bells with my Wife to Breakfast. Miss Caroline Taylor on a visit from Platsburg. Leave my Wife while I visit the church Yard, walk on the shore from thence round the point to the site of Doctor Johnson's lower house, no vestige, but the excavation for cellars. 3 or 4 old apple trees remain of the orchard. Bell owns now both upper & lower Farms. Mr Bell relates anecdotes of Mr [John] Watson the painter & his nephew [Alexander]. Old man bed rid, Nephew roofing the House. Woodpeckers hammering as told by Bunnell the Sheriff & Barrack master. Governor Franklin used to board with Bunnell when he came from Burlington to meet the Legislature which sat by turns at that place & Amboy. Capt[n] John Skinner & his untimely death & the mutilation of the body near Hollyhead. He had been made a post Captain by George 4th on his visit to Ireland in Skinners vessel. His sister Effy married Oliver Barberie & when a widow lived with her brother until death. Watson the painter came to America immediately after the 1715 rebellion as did parson [William] Skinner. Watson lived to be upwards of 80. His nephew, Mrs Browns uncle had been in the English Navy but the uncle making him his heir induced him to leave his profession & come to Amboy where he lived with him and attended upon. The old man had a house adjoining the one with the painted Windows. He had a great many pictures most by himself. They were all lost & destroyed in the war. There is a tablet in the E. Church giving the names &c of the donors of the land belonging to the Church to this day. By will one of them bequeathed the house for a parsonage in which his Wife should die. It is the old parsonage house first occupied by Parson Skinner. Dates on the tablet. Visit with

MRS. WILLIAM DUNLAP (ELIZABETH WOOLSEY) (1768-1848)

By William Dunlap

(In the Theodore Salisbury Woolsey Collection)

my Wife our friend Mrs Brown again & the Misses Parker & Terrell. Then go to James Parker's. Rain commencing and leaving my Wife at Mr Parkers I embark in a furious storm on board steam boat at 3 OClock, arrive a little after 5. Still hard rain. Go throw it to W W Woolsey's & get a great coat & umbrella and leaving a letter from Mrs Haggerty (whose husband is sick at James Parker's) for Doctor John Francis & get home and dried by tea-time.

Wed^y August 7th 1833. Clear. Th: 76. Read Croker. Write on Hist: Arts. See Francis in the ev^g who has been to Amboy & left my Wife still at Mr Parker's.

Thursday [August] *8th.* Th: 76. Cooler out. Read Croker & Collyer. Write on Zeb Spiff. My Wife returns. Read. Walk.

Friday [August] *9th.* Rain. Clears early. Th: 72. Read Croker. Write on Hist^y Arts. Walk down town. See Weir. Cummings. Go to Library. Walk home. Receive Wm. T. McCoun's Bond for $2000.

Saturday [August] *10th* Clear. Ther: 68. Paint on Richard &c. Read Croker. Write on Hist of Arts. Walk.

Sunday [August] *11th* Clear. Th: 70. Walk. Read. Write on Hist. Arts. Read. Ev^g with Charles Rhind see some specimens of Arabic man^t and Persic, a Turkish Almanac, the Ancient book a scroll, it was printed when R was in Constantinople. A beautiful inlaid chest of 18 by 12 inches (about) gold & ivory persian manufacture. He says Constantinople in situation resembles N. Y. Our battery if extended more to the East answers to the <*Golden Horn &*> Seraglio, Brooklyn Heights to Pera & the Storehouses below to Galata, the water of the sound to the Golden Horn. The waters of the Hudson to those of Marmora and the Bay to the Bosphorus. New Jersey stands in place the Asiatic shore & Scutari, but is lower.

Monday August 12th 1833. Clear. Th: 72. I have taken of the soda pills & think they are beneficial as laxatives. I have taken for two days milk as part of my food. My general health is good. Read Croker. I am delighted with this book, not less for having read with great pleasure the first edition of Boswell in my youth & in company with my friends Smith Brown & Johnson. The Gigantic powers of Sam[l] Johnson appear more manifest to me than ever, but the blots on his character blacker than ever! His memory, his wit, his knowledge consequent on applicat[ion] & memory, his powers from these & quick wittedness—all admirable! but as a moralist or a christian he is lamentably deficient. Vain, jealous, irascible, envious, the flatterer of rank & power, the contemnor of liberty of every description, the advocate of duelling habitually indifferent to the feelings of others, the preacher of mans pains & miseries, denying the good and exaggerating the evils of life, calling the grateful acknowledgment of the good we enjoy *cant,* How this man can be called *the* Moralist of England is to me a subject of wonder. He was a combination of Greatness & littleness. He made the powers of mind bow to the paltry distinctions of birth & title, he was subserviant to the great and brutally rude to all merit that dared to question his infallibility. Paint on Richard & Kenneth. Ride down town. To Bank & leave $84.95. To library. To [George W.] Twibill's to see a paint[ing]. see a good small full length of Trumbull very like. Twibill hinted at the difference between his small pictures & his last. He attributed it to his leaving off painting to study Law when he was appointed Commissioner of Claims. He told Twibill that Stuart could not interest Washington in conversation when he sat to him, the president not relishing his manners, whereas with him he was at his ease. Finish reading the first vol: of Croker.

Tuesday Aug[t] 13th 1833. Clear Th: 75. ½ past 6 A. M. Don't take pill this morning. Write on hist: Arts. Doctor Johnson's remark that he fancied there were no Singing

Birds in the Highlands of Scotland reminds me of the remark of Europeans in Am[eric]a of the same kind. He was travelling in Aug[t] & September. Birds sing at the season of incubation. Finish the appendix to 1st Vol: Croker's Boswell. Th: 4 OClock P. M. 82.

Wed[y] Aug[t] 14th 1833 Clear. Th: 74. Read Collier 3d Vol: Take this morning a soda pill. I find this memorandum respecting printing but have forgotten from whom obtain'd.

1000 Copies octavo. 400 pages.

paper about	$300
printing	330
Bind[g] in boards	120
	750

It can be done much lower now. Paper may be purchased on credit of 3 or 6 mo: printing to be paid for on delivery of the work, a disc[t] made of 5 pr ct. Messrs. [Thomas] Illman & [Edward] Pilbro Engravers now possess the plates of Trumbulls Bunker Hill and Montgomery. They are at the corner of Barrow & Greenwich St[s] [A. C. de] Poggi was the publish[r] Weir met with him in Italy. Walk down town & back. Th: 78. Read in North American Review.

Thursday [August] 15th Clear. At 5 A. M. Th: 75 at M. 78. Paint on R & K. Read North Am. Review & Collier. Ev[g] Rain. Note verses of V's M[illegible] Wa[l]ler wishes alteration in the Miniature painted for him. Ev[g] Hard rain & thunder.

Friday [August] 16th Clouds Th: 74 Alter Miniature for Waller. Read Review. Call on Illman & Pillbro'. The latter bo[t] the plates of Trumbull's pictures of Warren & Montgomery in London within a year. He purchased of [blank] who purchased them of a pawn broker who had had them many years. Read Collier. Walk. Ev[g] Hard rain for many hours and thunder.

Sat^y [August] 17th light clouds. Th: 73. Walk. Read. Go down town (walk) Ride home after visiting Library &c. Evening walk. Read Collier.

Sunday Augt 18th 1833. Clear. Th: 70. Cold out of doors. Walk. I yesterday deliver'd at the Franklin house the 2 Miniatures for Waller, to the Barkeeper for Barrett. Read Collier, Cushings Spain. Write on Hist: Arts. Mr Andrew Bell of Amboy with us. He remembers Thomson (Count Rumford) when after being in ye Sec^y of States Office as first Clerk & Under Secretary he came out here to join a regiment of Horse raised for him. He immediately return'd. Mr Adams whose name is connected with roads is nephew of an Auctioneer in this place during the War of Revolution who sent for his nephew to this Country & Bell was at school with him at Hackensac N. J. Mr Bell remembers seeing Arnold ride through the streets of N. Y. attended by British officers, he in his full suit as an American General, before his new coat had been prepared.

Monday Augt 19th Clear. Th: 70. Took Copeiba & this morning soda pill. Rode down town Went Library & to old Coffeehouse slip walking & then home. Mr Bell related the following told him by Mrs Van Rensaeller & her by the subject. Mr Vanbeuren when in England dined several times with the King & Queen *en famille.* At the first dinner he was next the Queen who was attentive to him & he was in doubt whether he should ask her to drink wine with him—he decided not. After dinner the King rose & addressed a complimentary speech to him with wishes for the happiness of America & the friendship of the two Nations. Again V. B. fell in doubt whether he should reply. He decided not to do so. Going from the dinner with Earl Grey, he mentioned his doubts on both points. "You did right to omit both. None but the King drinks with the Queen & no reply is to be made to a compliment from the King." I remarked that Johnson had so decided when G: 3d complimented him. But if an

American had done otherwise it would have been at least excusable. I doubt the rising of King William to speak—this may be added in passing through two editions.

Tuesday Aug[t] *20th 1833.* Clear. Th: 70 1 P. M. Took Copeiba & soda pill. Paint on R & K. Read Croker 2d Vol: The immoralities of Johnson's morality would perhaps be a useful subject for a publication in the Mirror. It does appear to me that when we take into consideration the weight given to his decisions & maxims he is the abettor of more mischievous falshood than any writer I know. Let us consider this assertion "All men will naturally steal" or "There is a strange route about deep play whereas you have many more people ruined by adventurous trade" evidently placing them on a footing if not giving the preference to the Gambler, or "it is better that some should be unhappy, than that none should be happy which would be the case in a general state of equality" This last is a complicated subject because we know that a general state of equality cannot exist among men. But the context makes Johnson's assertion amount to this it is better that the mass of mankind should be poor & oppressed, it is better that these beggars should be wretched & those vagabonds prey on society on their way to the gallows, & all this mass of vice & misery exist, otherwise the great could not be as they are, revelling in super[f]luity, which *makes them happy.* Now all this is false & a most pernicious falshood. This mass of vice & misery, it is true, is caused that the great may revel in riches, but though the beggar is made unhappy the lord is not happy. That state of equality of which man in civilized society is destined to partake & is capable of enjoying, so far from causing that "none should be happy" must cause a greater quantity of happiness in the whole society and by eradicating ignorance & vice, must lessen the number of the unhappy, annihilate beggars, thieves, and other pitiable subjects of crime & punishment, and leave no source of unhappiness than the inevitable ills that flesh is heir to. Not the ills that flesh creates.

The evil consequence of such maxims from a man who is held up as the great moralist, is incalculable. All Johnsons notions of civil Government are pernicious: and his enmity to free enquiry equally so. If Johnson had been consistent he would have confined knowledge to the few and deprecated printing; but he advocated the diffusion of knowledge which is one of the strong arms working out political equality.

One source of Johnson's im[mo]rality was his egotism & vanity. He asserted falshoods to show his dexterity in supporting them. Another & more excusable, was his early poverty which render'd him an adorer of rank, power & riches. He felt his superiority; but could not forget that he owed his bread to the King & his Prime Minister. If there had been no King & Court, he might have labour'd (he felt) for a scanty subsistance. But he felt wrong, in a society where equality prevail'd politically, Johnsons mind would have commanded something better than a pension.

"A curious work" says Croker "might be written on the reputation of painters. Horace Walpole talks somewhere of *"Ramsey & Reynolds!"* And Ha[y]ley who dedicated his Epis[tle] (such as it was) to Romney" (as Cumberland did) "What would a picture of Ramsey or Romney now bring at Auction." (See European Mag: 1788 for Barretti & Mrs. Piozzi.

Wed^y^ Augt 21st 1833. Clear Ch: 70. Take Copeiba & Soda pill. Read Croker. Paint on R & K. Read over Morse & Trumbull 1833. Read Croker. Mr Illman (Engraver) borrows my head of Washington to correct his Mezzotinto plate of a full length.

Thursday Augt 22d 1833. Clouds light. Th: 70. Read Croker. Walk down town. Mirror Office. Willis one editor is in Italy, T. S. Fay another is going to Florence for his health. Fay (whose biography of J H Payne see) tells me that P. has disgusted his friends, that he never sees him. He spoke in strong terms. Go to Library. Look at review of 2d part of Faust, and at notice of Rumford. Can it be true that he solicited a commission in the rebel Army as Trumbull says he did? Call at Parker & Clovers, at Frothinghams, at Arch: Robertson's. He says Trumbull told him that Sir Wm Howe would not sit for his portrait in the Bunker Hill & West painted in the head. "As I saw the same touch through the whole" says he "and I look'd sharp whe[n] he said this, I thought he might have touched more." I told him I thought not, but he persists in the belief that the composition of all Trumbull's early pictures are from West, directly or indirectly. He says that Trumbull told him that it was with difficulty he got his certificate as a member of the Cincinati, it was opposed, by whom he does not recollect. I rode home. Took Copeba & 2 soda pills. From the lips of a man impure in [ch]aracter we receive no injury when he praises priori paulo purganti & declares the book fit for ladies, but when such recommendation comes from the sage, the pious, the morality teacher of England, it is as mischievous as it is false. In many instances Mr Croker points out the contradictions, laxities & improprieties of Boswell & his hero, but not in the greatest point the falshoods utterred against civil liberty, indeed in this Croker confirms the errors of the others. The great wit, wonderful power of memory & other intellectual faculties, profound erudition and many virtues of Johnson only render his errors more fatal, his mischievous maxims more mischievous. Again "that misery is the lot of man" is a gross falshood & although contradicted by the sense of existence & the love of life, is of incalculable mischief in the practical deductions flowing from it. This great preacher of truths visits a place where four old persons are afflicted with the diseases incident to age, and he exclaims "This is life!" Can any thing be more palpably false. He might as well go to the Hospital or the cemetery & make the same comment. We never as individuals draw a free breath without enjoyment, and when we go to the street, the public place or theatre or Church, we see hundreds enjoying the blessings of health. Disease is the exception and for that Death is the remedy. This great moralist gave a public toast "Here's to the next insurrection of the Negroes in the West Indies." This disciple of truth writes in his "Taxation no Tyranny" "How is it that we hear the loudest *yelps* for liberty among the drivers of Negroes?" The loud *yelps* for liberty were among those who had been cursed by negro slavery forced upon them by the *drivers of Negroes,* the Government & people of England. The yelpers for liberty were those who have been striving to abolish negro slavery after having shaken off the chains Johnson would have rivetted on them. When life is represented as a state of misery is it not to represent the giver of life as any thing but the beneficent source of good? Again Johnson says "I found my friend at Stowell very dangerously diseased. Such is life." The great evil of propagating such *stuff* is, that it is recommended by the high character of the propagator. Ev[g] Walk. Read.

Friday August 23d 1833. Clouds. Th: 73. Walk. Took the Copeiba & one soda pill. Read Gibbon's Rome. Read Croker's B. This book is a mine of amusement & instruction. To one whose character is formed it is rich in moral teaching. It presents views of English life of the last century no where else to be found and with a truth of delineation as admirable as it is rare. We are likewise introduced to the company of the Wits, the Literati, the Statesmen, the bookmakers & the booksellers of that time. We see them sick & well, drunk & sober, in the bed chamber & the dining room & the withdrawing room, in their nightgowns & slippers, brown bobs & black stockings or in the pompous display of bagwigs, toupees, powder'd curls, laced ruffles, velvet coats, laced waiscoats, sattin breeches, silk hose & diamond buckled shoes & knees. It is a most precious depositary of useful information, but must not be received as guide in politics or morality. Walk out of town. Write of Hist: Arts. Th: at 4 P. M. 72.

Sat^y^ Augt 24th 1833. Clear. Th: 68. Up before 5. This was to attend my daughter to ye Steam boat for Hyde park. Took Copeiba; no pill. Ride to Barclay Street & see my daughter on board the "Champlain" & with her cousin & Mrs Ed^d^ Pendleton. Though so frequently seen, the crowd of Ladies & gentlemen entering one of these superb vehicles is ever a subject of admiration. Walk home by ½ past 7. Read the fascinating Croker. At 9 A. M. again ride down town. Call on Cummings, Post Office, Bank & leave 64.95, Library, Clinton Hall; [William J.] Bennet, McCouns. Walk home. Write & read.

Sunday [Aug.] *25th* Clear. Th: 68. Up rather late ½ past 6. Walk. Read. The immorality of Johnson's political opinions and his hideous reverence for aristocratical institutions and titled men, can here have no ill effect, unless to encourage those having possession of Wealth to endeavour to ape the aristocracy of Europe. That can be of little consequence, the derision such fools draw on themselves checks such propensities or renders their folly harmless. The pitiable weakness of so powerful a mind as Johnson in respect to flattery as recorded by Boswell tends to lessen the blind submission which many might be inclined to feel towards the maxims of a man so acceptable to the key which "opens the hearts of the selfish. We are all pleased with praise. But when we find that the flattery of a weak or contemptible person delights us we have reason to regard the pleasure as a proof of our imbecility. Write an essay for the Mirror on Crokers work.[167] I find in one of Mrs Thrales letters the phrase "Gentleman-artist" meaning an Amateur painter. Leonardi da Vinci, Rubens, Vandyke, West, Reynolds, Raphael, Lawrence, were not Gentlemen!

Monday Augt 26th 1833. Clear. Th: 72. Paint on R & K. and begin two portraits Read & write. Th: 77.

[167] Printed in the *New-York Mirror,* XI, 82, Sept. 14, 1833.

Tuesday [August] *27th* Clear. Th: 74. Paint. Read. Write. I have taken Copeiba 15 drops at night, sometimes in y[e] morning & sometimes the soda pill: Read Croker. Th: rises to 80. In y[e] [word omitted] slight showers.

Wed[y] [August] 28th Clear & dry. Th: 74 and out cold. Walk. Paint. Walk to Mirror office. Fay goes for Italy next Sunday. I am to write to Greenough. Walk home. Th: at 3 P. M. 72. Read Croker.

Thursday [August] *29th* Occasional Clouds. Th: 72. Hail at noon. Th: 65 in evening. Paint & read. Afternoon. Walk. Take Copeiba.

Friday [August] *30th* Clear. Th: 63. Write to Horatio Greenough by Theodore S. Fay. Paint. Read. Write. Walk. Ev[g] Th: 66. Mr Herring called wishing information respecting Stuart & offerring communication respecting Trumbull.

On the Northern Army being ordered from Ticonderoga to join Washington behind the Delaware Tr: accompanied it, but was sent with Arnold to Rhode Island and while there received his Commission as Deputy Adg[t] Gen[l] but the date not corresponding with the time of enlis[g] the service as such, he sent it back saying he would not accept it with that date after some correspondence his offer of resignation was accepted: He then went home & thence to Boston. Mr. Temple (Sir John) was the person through whom he & his father received assurances of the safety of going to England. (He had not mentioned Thompson Count Rumford to Herring as connected with his arrest.) He carried letters from Franklin to West, who told him to copy a picture, chose the Madona, Stuart painting in West's rooms at the time. When arrested carried to y[e] police office. Speech to the Magistrates, difficulty as to a prison as they had been burnt, objects to Clerkenwell as a place for blackguards & the Tower as too expensive after having a choice of place given him by the Secretary of State. Addington's acct. of y[e] affair to West and Wests interference with the King. When released order'd to leave England. Embarks in y[e] [blank] Frigate, puts back, distress'd &c. Returns to his Father's. Goes to his brother the Commissary & is a storekeeper for him. Returns to England &c When a Commissioner of Claims during an interval of meeting goes to Paris & without passport to Amsterdam & there the French Minister gives him passports. Adventures in Germany—meets in a Genl officer an old acquaintance of his fathers who had been wth Rochambeau. carries the Bunker Hill picture & plate to Paris, cannot get a passport to return to England. Mr. [Charles Cotesworth] Pin[c]kney &c cannot help him. Taleyrand. poker. David goes with him to the Minister of Police & procures a passport. "This is a good republican, an officer who fought at Bunker Hill & here is his picture of the Battle &c Adventure with the Cavalry officer & final bribing the Captain of the Calais packet for 100 G^{s} to sail back immediately to Dover.

Saturday Augt 31st 1833. Clouds. Th: 66. Read Croker's Boswell. The Authors of ye Univ^{l} Hist: Gent: Mag. Dec: 1784. Ride down town. Call on Ja^{s} Herring who gives me a MSS biography of John Trumbull taken down from Trumbulls dictation for publication. Call at Mirror Office, Library & at Durands. Write notice of Ja^{s} Herring & begin copy of MSS. respecting Trumbull. Read Croker.

Sunday Septr 1st Light Clouds, Th: 70, Rises at noon to 74. Write. Walk. Read. Write. Walk & meet David Hadden. Ev^{g} windy clouds.

Monday [Sept.] *2d* Clear. Th: 66. Paint. Read Write. Read in Mirror & finish Croker.

Tuesday [Sept.] *3d* Clear. Th: 67. Write. Ride to Wall St. & walk to Arch^{d} Rogers's to meet my daughter but she & her friends had not return'd from Hyde Park. Walk home, calling on Cummings, met Bryant & promised to see him at his house at Hoboken. he told me that Verplank had return'd & I went to see him: rec^{d} his Discourses from him. He thinks the Dutch picture of De Ruyter in the Thames was complained of by England, advises to write J. Q. Adams respecting West & the Elgin marbles. Says that Col^{l} Burr complains of Trumbull not placing him in the picture of Montgomery at Quebec, observing that as history it ought to be truth, and the last words spoke by Montgomery were addressed to Burr "We shall be in the fort in two minutes." he received the grape shot & fell in his Arms. Here a gallant officer who served throughout the War was a prominent actor in the scene & is altogether omitted. Why? The persons introduced besides the hero are Major [Jacob] Cheesman, Major [John] Macpherson (aids) Col^{l} Donald Campbell, Col^{l} [William] Thompson, an Indian Chief (who probably was not there (I will ask Burr who was there) Major [Return Jonathan] Meigs of Connecticut, Captn [William] Hendricks (Rifleman) Captn [Samuel] Ward, Lieut^{t} [William] Humphries, [Samuel] Cooper, [Matthias] Ogden. The first three the Artist says are real likeness. "The others are intended as mere memorandums of men who were either distinguished or killed or wounded in the action: and of whom no actual Portrait could be obtained." No Col^{l} Campbell lived many years after the revolution. Col^{l} Burr who ought to be where Ogden is (Bye the bye is this Ogden Col^{l} & Governor of New Jersey?) is still alive. The portraits said to be real likenesses (by the Artist) in his Bunker's Hill are Genl Warren, Putnam, Howe, Clinton, Major Pitcairn, Major Small, Lieut^{t} Pitcairn. The others as above, men of whom no actual portrait could be obtained. It may be observed that all the *real likeness* in the Montgomery are dead men and in the Bunker's Hill Warren is dying, and except Putnam all the other real likenesses are English officers. I remember to have heard at the time the picture was painted that Rawdon refused to set for his portrait & Trumbull therefore gave a view of his back. Mr Arch^{d} Robertson says Trumbull told him Howe would not set and that West painted in the head of that hero. Verplank says that John Randolph was at one time partial to Trumbull, but afterwards showed great contempt of him & used to relate some amusing anecdotes. That unhappy Woman, Trumbulls Wife, he says, there is reason to believe was the illegitimate daughter of Lord Thurlow, who had several children of this description, took no special care of them but left them an annuity of 300 a year for life. Rufus King told Verplank the well known story of the marriage, the Lady being handed into church (where T with King & [Christopher] Gore were waiting with ye priest) from a Coach which drove off & that after the immediately performed ceremony (King giving the bride to T.) King asked who is this lady I have given to you & was anser'd "Mrs Trumbull, Sir." The secret has been kept, but Verplank supposes that Rufus King knew who she was. Write to John Quincey Adams. Thos. A. Cooper calls on me relatively to the projected benefits for the fund for his children which he wishes to be raised for their use to be applied through him until their marriage or death, in case of which to fall to him. By the Phil[a] arrangement he thinks he is excluded from participation even after the death or marriage of his children. He has six daughters, four over 14. He thinks of *Priscilla* as an Actress, *a la mode de* Miss Fanny Kemble. I am to see & consult Noah. Write on Hist[y] of Arts & a Communication for Evening Post respect[g] Dr Beaumont.

Wednesday Sept[r] 4th 1833. Clouds. Th: 70. Write on Hist: arts. Walk to post office, to Battery place, A Rogers's, to Library, Mirror Office, Cummings & ride home. Clear & warm. Read in Marshal's Washington. Henry Brevoort accosted me in the street presenting his hand after the manner of old & intimate friendship. I did not expect ever to have met so; but the dismissal of all former feeling and cordial reciprocity of kind greetings were much more pleasant to me than any recollections of a former scene. We talked of J. F. C. and his intended return. He expressed his high estimation of him & of his family, lamented his manner of abording strangers & the errors in respecting his character which it led to. B says he expects to return to Europe shortly: took my address & promised to call on me. Met Graham & spoke of T. A. Cooper and the intended benefit for a fund for his children. Evening Th: 76. Walk.

Thursday [Sept.] *5th* Clear. Th: 76. Write & paint. Th: rises to 80. Warmer out. Finish the Trumbull MSS. Ev[g] brilliant northern lights.

Friday [Sept.] *6th* Clear. Th: 74. Ride to James Herrings. Examine Dr Waterhouses communications respecting Stuart. Notices curious & gross errors in the Encycl^{a} Am^{a} I am agreed to furnish a Biography of Stuart & one of C B Brown. Bring home Waterhouses MSS. & more of Trumbull. Call at Mirror Office, Library. Talk with Verplank respecting Benefit for Coopers Children. See Noah who revives his assurances of sending me his new paper [*Evening Star*] which is now on the eve of publication. Receive letter from Wm Whitehead (Key West) Read in Mirror. Ev^{g} Quarterly Review.

Sat^{y} Septr 7th 1833. Clouds. Th: 74. Write very steadily until 3 OClock P. M. Read Quarterly Review, Gibbon's decline &c. Write again from 4 to 6 P. M. Ev^{g} rain. Read.

Sunday [Sept.] *8th* Storm. Th: 70. Read. Write. Afternoon clears. Walk. Write till 6 P. M.

Monday [Sept.] *9th* Clear. Th: 69. Write to Mr Wetmore (Utica) Write on hist of Arts as yesterday. Call on John Frazee who promises me notes of himself & his progress in Sculpture & his partner Launitz. Read in Quarterly Review. Bo^{t} Dwights Germany at a book stall for 50 cents. Began a Biographical Sketch of G. Stuart for the National Portrait Gallery. R^{d} Review & N. Y. Monthly Mag:

Tuesday [Sept.] *10th* Clouds. Th: 68. Look in H[enry] E Dwights Germany. I read it when first published with pleasure & profit. Since then the young and most amiable author died of consumption, intelligence, learning, eloquence, all extinguished when in their prime & strength! Strasburg. Its Cathedral spire 490 feet, a beautiful Gothic unrivalled with its 100 spires & fairy architecture, from y^{e} highest spire you look down upon the City, the Rhine & the black forest. Walk down to Verplanks. A Robertsons, Library, Post Office & Bank. In Bank left \$36.41. I always find myself poorer on settling my Bank acct. than I had previously supposed. Met a Gentleman who bargained for two portraits of his daughters for \$100.

He is to call on me. Ev^{g} Mr James Herring leaves with me "Scraps" which had been sent on to Dr Waterhouse & returned with some additions by that gentleman respecting G. Stuart.

Wed Septr 11th, 1833. Clear. Th: 66. My general health is good. Write and read. Walk in y^{e} Ev^{g}.

Thursday [Sept.] *12th* Clouds & rain. Th: 65. Finish Biog^{y} of Stuart for Nat^{l} Port^{t} Gallery.

Friday [Sept.] *13th* Clear. Th: 60. Walk down & call on W Irving, not in town. Library, Mirror Office, Harper's, shuffling & ranting. Walk home. Read Annu[l] Reg^{r} 1832.

Sat^{y} [Sept.] *14th* Clear. Th: 58. Paint. Walk. In one of my walks met [James] Kent. "You look very well. I'm well too. how old are you? "Sixty eight" "I'm seventy. I have got the whip hand of you. I'll keep ahead." Read Ann: Reg^{r}

Sunday [Sept.] *15th* Clear. Th: 60. Read. Walk. Write proposals for publishing in 2 vols 8vo of 400 pages my Hist: of rise & progress of ye F. Arts in U. S. In Hist^{l} Soc: lib^{y} are several drawings of buildings by D[avid] Grim. Write on Zeb Spiff. Look in Greek Grammer.

Monday [Sept.] *16th* Clear. Th: 63 to 65. Paint on Rich^{d} & Kenneth. Look in Greek Grammer. Walk. Read. Walk. Read & look in Greek Grammer.

Tuesday [Sept.] *17th* Clear. Th: 62. Walk. Write. Read. Walk down town to Durand's. See his engraving from Vanderlyn's Danae. Young [George W.] Flagg [Washington] Allston's Nephew. Call on Cummings. Go to see [Francis] Danby's "Opening of the 6th seal. Fine effect & colour. Go to Library. Bank, leave $16.41. Back to Library. Call on Morse who had a message from Allston for me, he is preparing another letter, is painting several small pictures. Gabriel & the Heavenly host &c. Morse says I go to him as to the sun to imbibe light. He has a large painting room but from debts & poverty cannot put up his great picture for finish. Call at Durands painting room & see some excellent specimens of his painting in portrait & Landscape. Walk home. Among my visits was one to the Opera House over which I walked.

Wed^{y} 18th Septr 1833. Rain. Th: 69. Write on Hist. Arts. Read in Greek Grammer. T. A. Cooper calls on me wishes me to see McLean, Verplank &c & get a Committee formed for his childrens benefit. Write on Zeb Spiff. Receive a letter from Key West from W Whitehead respecting Amboy, a very pleasing letter with a copy of my reminiscences as by agreement & urging a continuance. Read Greek Grammer.

Thursday [Sept.] *19th* Mist. Th: 70. Write on Zeb Spiff. Go down town on T A C's business. Call on G. C. Verplank, consents cheerfully to aid in the business, on Hugh McLean who lends his name, go to Mirror Office. meet T. A. Cooper at Fairlie's Office, go to P. Hone's, he declines lending his name, will contribute, is engaged in writing strictures on his friend English Hamiltons book. Go to Pauldings who cheerfully joins his name, and Washington Irving not being in town Paulding is to write to him. meet Cooper again by appointment at Noah's Office. He objects to the delay of writing to Irving & I go with him again to Paulding who agrees to use Irving's name. Go to McL's office & Paulding joins us, and suggests other names, and after agreeing on the advertisement go to Walter Bowne's, not in, to James Munroe who cheerfully joins his name, go to Peter Stagg who denies his name but promises assistance. This bring me to near 4 P M & I walk home. Th: 78 and in ye street much higher.

Friday Sept[r] 20th 1833. Write for T. A. C. T A C calls & leaves papers. Ride down town & call on Walter Bowne, he enters into the plan zealously but declines giving his name. On W. T. McCoun who gives his name. On Mr W Ireland who declines giving his name. On the Hosacks, do not see them, on Jos: O. Hoffman who gives his name cheerfully as does R. Riker. Deliver the papers to T A C. Go to Library & make extracts Ride home. Th: 79. Read papers left by C. (I met Vanderlyn in y[e] street & had friendly conversation relative to his memoirs. See Morse. Order frames at Parker & Clover's) The first of C's letters to Charles J. Ingersol states his distress, his wife lay dead surrounded by children, requests a loan of $500 on security of house furniture. date March 1 1833. on y[e] 30th he writes the same, says there is a mortgage on his house for $4,500 wishes to raise more on it, sends a schedule of Articles to pledge for a loan, appeals to him as a friend. On the 16th April he writes the same. "Mr Rockhill spoke to me on the subject of a Benefit in Phil[a]. Ap[l] 20th from N. Y. to the same respecting a Benefit. May 3d to the same, says that to effect a sale of one of his houses (there are a large & smaller on y[e] same lot) he has had repairs &c & has sold furniture at public Auction, thanks him for measures taken relative to a Benefit & suggests certain matters. 3d of May writes that he concurs in the wishes of the Comm: that the money raised be disposed of so as to form a provision for his children and names as trustees, Rockhill, A. D. Bache & Ingersol. June 12th he says "I told you that I should want out of y[e] proceeds of the Benefits not less than 1000$ and proposes Mortgages as security. On the 18th June he refers to Mr Rich[d] Davies as to the security. On the 19th June Mr Ingersol answers that the Committee do not agree to the loan of the money they have rec[d] on trust not deeming the security sufficient. Mr Rockhill absent. June 20th C addresses the Trustees & says that in a conversation with Mr Ingersol May 3d he thought much might be done provided "all the money so collected in Phil[a] and other places should constitute a fund to be vested in trustees, the interest for the use of myself & children, and the principal to be at my disposal in the event of their marriage & my survivorship." That he wrote a letter to that effect to the Comm: and that it was tacitly understood that his necessities were to be relieved by a loan from the fund raised. he states his disapointment from the refusal to loan what he thought was agreed upon. To this Ingersol & Bache reply that I expressly said his acts relative to loaning from the fund must be governed by the Trustees, that they do not consider the second Mortgage sufficient security, that they do not consider themselves authorized to loan the money to him under *any* circumstances, and they offer to advance the Interest on the sum received 102.78 on 1713 and send a receit to be signed by his oldest daughter. To this C replies that he demands as a right the loan. He states the agreement made by him to be in consequences of Ing[ls] assurances. (There is a letter from a Mr Lewis denying the assertions of Ingersol & Bache that Lewis acted as Rockhills representative in positive terms) July 6th Mr Ingersol sends copies of Coopers letters to him. July 7th Mr Rockhill having return'd addresses a letter to him appealing to him for help against the misrepresentations of Ingersol & the "misprision" of Bache. He details all the circumstances & refers to the letters. Aug[t] 24th Rockhill answers "This fund has been placed in our hands in trust for the use & benefit of your children and as *their* is no particular directions given, we are bound to use a sound *discression* and to act according to law" He then proposes that he (Cooper) take measures to be appointed legal Guardian of his Children. "We will then pay the interest of the fund to you" during life the distribution after to be made by the Trustees. He then suggests that for any additions to the fund ,"any future Comm: should give more explicit directions to the Trustees. (The words marked [in italics] are so spelled.) In answer to this C protests that the Benefit was intended for him & through him to his children & rejects. Rockhill replies that if he will not permit his children to receive the interest, nor qualify himself to receive it, it must be an accumulating fund to be divided among the children when the youngest is of age. On the 10th Septr C sends a paper for the trustees to sign saying that they were appointed as trustees of the Cooper fund & that they agree "to dispose of all future bequests or benefits which may accrue to said fund in the way following, to wit, *to invest all such proceeds to the best of their judgments so as to produce the best interest and pay the same to the s^{d} T. A. C. in* [blank] *payments for the said purpose*" (the support & education of his children) "*and in case of the death or marriage of either or all of the said Child^{n} the principal of the said fund pro rata in such case to be at the disposition of s^{d} T. A. C. / hereby fulfilling the intentions,* as we believe of T. A. C. in requesting our services & of our fellow Citizens in appointing Trustees in the premise." This the Trustees declined signing, and after some further correspondence between C & R he advises him Septr 12th that the Trustees "will receive any funds from you *hereafter* on the conditions *set forth in that paper*" to this he pledges himself & Mr Ingersoll, and he further says he considers them as very reasonable. In consequence C draws up a paper to be presented to the N. Y. Comittee saying that I. B & R will receve & apply any monies as above marked & underscored to the mark / T. A. C. call'd & wish'd me to deliver the papers above noticed to Wm M Price. Read in G[reek] Gram-[ma]r

Sat^{y} Septr 21st 1833. After rain in ye night clouds. Th: 75 and decreasing. Read in Greek Grammer & Franklins familiar letters. How lovely! Ride down Town. Call on Cummings. On W M P. & deliver T A C's papers to him. To Mirror office & receive letter from Doctor S Beaumont with some pages of his Cousins book. Call on John Frazee. Model for a monument of Washington. Walk home. Read & write. Th: 72. Finish Franklin's fam: letters. R^{d} Greek Gr.

Sunday Septr 22d 1833. Clear. Th 69. Colder out. Take 2 soda pills. Write to Wm. A Whitehead Key West. Read

Dwights Germany. Unwell, headache, no appetite. Fast until tea time. Ev[g] exercising in Greek under the instruction of my son.

Monday [Sept.] *23d* Clear. Th: 64. Write on Zeb Spiff. Walk. Write for the Mirror on English Travellers. Ev[g] Greek exercise. I have passed thro life without being able to decipher a Greek word or name, I am ashamed of it, when so little exertion would at least have accomplished that much. Even now I learn my alphabet & enjoy the opening of another avenue to knowledge although I may have time to enter but a little way.

Tuesday [Sept.] *24th* Clear. Th: 62. Warmer out. Ride down town. Call at Mirror Office. Have an acct. of the Cooper meeting from Adams & afterward from Morris & R. Riker. Committees & trustees were appointed & they are to meet Monday 30th. Go to Library & extract from Audubon. To post Office. to W W W's. Ride home. T. A. C. call'd during my absence. Walk read. [Isaac] D'Israeli's curiosities [*of Literature*] Greek Grammer.

Wed[y] [Sept.] *25th* Clear. Th: 68. Write on Zeb Spiff. Read D'Israeli & Greek Grammar.

Thursday [Sept.] *26th* Clear. Th: 66. My daughter preparing to visit friends at Amboy. Write to Doctor S. Beaumont. Rode down to French Church walk with my daughter & accompanied her to y[e] Swan Steam boat. Meet there Wash[n] Irving & H. Brevoort. Irving professes himself convinced that Democracy is the only true system & expresses his astonishment after 17 years residence in various parts of Europe to see the superiority in our state of Society. I told him I had always been a Democrat and saw in the system not the bringing down of the few but the exaltation of the many. He said he was convinced of it. That his feelings & political creed was changed. He stated the contrast between the misery of some parts of Europe and the discontents & anxieties of all, with the general animation, cheerful pressing on to something better ahead & enjoyment of the present which appeared every where in this country was amazing to himself & kept him in a fever of excitement & exultation. Afternoon. Th: 74. Read Star & Mirror. Greek Grammar. Walk. Leave in Bank $6.41. Noah's Star commenced yest[y].

Friday [Sept.] 27th 1833. Clear. Th: 69 at sunrise. Write on Zeb Spiff. Paint on Richard & Kenneth. Read D'Israelli & Greek Grammar. Walk. Receive notice signed G. C. Verplank that I am apointed one of the Cooper benefit Comittee to meet Monday ev[g] 30th at Shakespere Hotel. The above belongs to Friday & *Sat[y]*.

Sunday [Sept.] *29th* Clear. Th: 70. Write on Hist[y] of Arts & Zeb Spiff. Read as yesterd[ay] D'Israeli & Greek Grammar.

Monday [Sept.] *30th* Clear. Th. 70. Write on Zeb Spiff. Read D'Israeli. S. F. B. Morse called to consult on the Exh[n] of his picture of the Gallery of y[e] Louvre. Rhind called. R[obert] C. Wetmore called with a child he wishes a portrait of.

Tuesday Oct[r] 1st Light clouds & cool. Th: 68. Write. Go down town on foot. Call on R. C. Wetmore & see his wife. They are to determine the size of the picture. A full length $150 or half 75. Go to Wm T McCoun & receive 60 dollars (half years interest) Leave in Bank $66.43. Call on Morse & assist in arranging his picture. Go to Library. Morris's Office. Price has refused the [Park] Theatre to Cooper untill 18th December. Advise to take the Bowery. Walk home. Find that Cooper has been here & left mem: that he will call tomorrow morning. Write on Zeb Spiff. Ev[r] read D'Israeli and Greek Grammar.

Wed[y] October 2d 1833. Violent rain storm which begun yesterday 2 P. M. Th: 69. R[d] Greek Grammar. Write.

Paint on Richard & Kenneth. Write on Zeb Spiff. Mr Wetmore calls & determines on y^e $75 picture. Afternoon clear & pleasant. Ev^g Greek Grammar.

Thursday [Oct.] *3d* Clear. Th: 66. Write. At 10 first setting of Mr R. C. Wetmore's little boy Frederick. Walk down. See T A Cooper & go with him to Mirror Office. Morris out of Town. Write a note for T A C to take to Henry Ogden respecting taking the Bowery Theatre for ye Benefit. The refusal of the Park thrown on [Edmund] Simpson by Price. Go to Library & Morse's. Ride home.

Frid^y [Oct.] 4th Clear. Th: 60. A person unknown brings me a Tragedy with a well written note from a young lady requesting my opinion "If fit for the Stage." I have foolishly complied. Paint on Mr Wetmore's child. Begin a second Richard & Kenneth on a larger ground. Ride down town and leave in Bank 56.43. Buy brushes at 1.25 ye doz. Walk home. Write on Zeb Spiff, read Greek Grammer. having become familiar with my alphabet I am led on to further study. Receive a very pleasing letter from Edmund A Wetmore of Utica, enclosing Copley's bill of sale for pictures in 1769 and 1770. Read American Quarterly, Greek Grammer.

Sat^y [Oct.] *5th* Clear. Th 58. Write on Hist^y Arts. Paint on Mr Wetmores child & on 2d Rich^d & Kenneth. Read. Walk. Write on Zeb Spiff. Walk. Ev^g read Am^n Quarterly & Greek Grammer.

Sunday Octr 6th 1833. Clear. Th: 62. Write for Ev^g Star a notice of Doctor Wm Beaumonts book. Write. read. Walk. Ev^g read the young lady's tragedy which though not fit for the stage has points of merit.

Monday [Oct.] *7th* Clear. Th 62. Read in Review. Write on Zeb Spiff. Paint on Mr Wetmores child. Walk. Write. Read in Review and in Greek Grammer. Ev^g begins to rain.

Tuesday. Hard rain. Th: 66. Write on Zeb. Paint on the drapery of the childs picture. Read & write. At 2 P. M. it clears. Write on Zeb Spiff. Ev^{g} walk. Read Greek Grammer.

Wed^{y} [Oct.] *9th* Clear. Th: 66. Write for Mirror, Mr [Robert] Merry. Write on Zeb. Paint on ye childs drapery. Walk down town. Buy Coal. Go to Mirror Office. To Morse's room his picture on Exh^{n} to friends. To bank & leave 36.43. To library. Walk home after leaving communication with Ev^{g} Star. Read in [James] Morier's Zohrab. Write. Evening read Greek Grammer & Zohrab.

Thursday [Oct.] *10th* Clear. Th: 64. James F. Cooper has directed Morse to take a house & prepare it for him which he has done (in part) has taken one in Bleecker St^{t} Write notice of Morse's Exhibition. Paint on Mr Wetmore's Child's portrait. Write on Zeb. Ev^{g} read Greek Gr: & Zohrab.

Friday [Oct.] *11th* Clear. Th: 61. Colder out. Write & read. Paint on the childs picture untill eleven A. M. Write. Read Zohrab. My daughter comes home from Amboy. Cummings calls.

Sat^{y} [Oct.] *12th* Clouds. Th: 58. Paint on the Childs portrait untill 1 P. M: Write on Zeb. Read Zohrab. Hard rain came on ab^{t} 2 P M. and continued with violent wind through the night. Ev^{g} Greek Grammer. Finish Zohrab. No[t] satisfied.

Sunday Oct^{r} *13th 1833*. Clouds Th: 62 Look over letters from Charles Brockden Brown, Elihu Hubbard Smith & William Johnson, of dates from 1794 to 1805. Rain. Write on Zeb Spiff. Read Dwights Germany.

Monday [Oct.] *14th* Clear. Th: 60. Paint on Childs portrait & on Richard & Kenneth. Walk. McGaven calls and wishes me to engage in repairing pictures. Write on

Zeb Spiff. Afternoon, Council of ye N[ational] A[cademy of Design] meet at my house & we determine to open the school of the Antique in ye afternoons from 2 to 4 ins^{d} of Evening & make it free to Students. Ev^{g} read Dwights Germany.

Tuesday [Oct.] *15* Clear. Th: 59. Paint on the Childs portrait. Ride down to Read St^{t} call on Cummings who goes wth me to the Star office where he had left my notice of Morse's picture with [Thomas] Gill & it is published as an advertisement. Noah rectified the whimsical blunder which made Morse his own eulogist. Call on Morse, at Library, at McGavens Gallery & agree to repair a picture, at Durand's. Walk home. Read Godwin's Deloraine & Greek Grammar.

Wed^{y} [Oct.] *16th* Clouds. Th: 63. Read Greek Grammer Paint on childs portrait. Write on Zeb Spiff. Read Deloraine. Rain in night.

Thursday [Oct.] *17th* Clear. Th: 66. Write on Zeb Spiff. T. A. Cooper calls on me. The Benefit is to take place next Thursday at ye B[owery] Th. Finish Deloraine. It is full of Genius & knowledge, but prolix, terribly so. Repetitions of ideas in whatever language are tiresome. There are improbabi[li]ties too, which mar the plot. Write on History of the Arts. Read Dwights Germany. Greek Grammer. Rain in night.

Friday [Oct.] *18th* Clear. Th: 66. Read in Greek Grammer. Paint on portrait of the Child. Work on Hist: of Arts. Walk. Ev^{g} read in Greek Grammer & Dwights Germany.

Sat^{y} [Oct.] *19th* Clear. Th: 50. Write on Hist^{y} of Arts. Ride to town with my daughter to Morse's Exh^{n}. At Bank & leave 21.43. at McGavens, at Library, at Mirror Office, Cumming's, at Ingham's. Walk home after calling at Dr Francis's to whom I mentioned for the first time Zeb

MARGARET DUNLAP (1791-1837)

By William Dunlap

(Courtesy of Miss Ethel Carmalt and Miss Geraldine W. Carmalt)

Spiff. & suggested his friend [Samuel] Wards looking at it with a view to forwarding it with the Temperance Societies.

Sunday 20th Octr 1833. Rain. Th: 57. Write on Hist^y Arts. Rain all day. Ev^g read Victor Hugo's Bug jargal as translated. Rain all night.

Monday [Oct.] *21st* Rain continues. Th: 53. Read on St Domingo. It appears to me that a comparative statement of the slave & Negro question in this country & in St. Domingo would be useful. Declaration of '76 all men equal. F. Convention all free citizens have equal rights. The class of free men of colour in St D: holding plantations and slaves, none such here, limmitted or no mixed race of English & Negro, extensive in St. Domingo. Free negroes here not admitted to privileges of whites, of course claiming them when strong enough, policy of ye South not to permit free blacks to remain among them. Necessity for seperating the races. The first rising of ye Negroes in St. Domingo was instigated by ye Royalists and priests, if ever they rise in our country (south) it will be impelled by fanatics either Methodists or others. In St. Domingo their numbers made them formidable, here they must sink instantly, in St. Domingo the Whites forced ye mixed men, men of property & education to join ye slaves & blacks, here there are none such. As England interfered in the affair of St. Domingo, so she might in a contest between black & white here, for experience will never teach, and as there she would here be defeated & disgraced, but here the blacks would be sacrificed, in St. Domingo they triumphed owing to numbers & the education of the mixed breeds. The English invasion of St. Domingo was the effective cause of the liberty of the St. Domingo blacks. Slavery hav^g been abolished in St D there followed the war between the mixed race & ye black, ye 1st under Rigaud the 2d under Toussaint, the black prevailed. They had number & T was a great man. If the English succeed in liberating the slaves of their Colonies they must follow the steps of Toussaint, who they endeavoured to overthrow in St D. Bonaparte treacherously sacrificed Toussaint Louverture, a better if not a greater man than himself and sent his brother in law Le Clerk to enslave the freemen of St. D. They murder'd, tortured, could not subdue. The romance of the slave king or Bug jargal has all the faults of the exaggerated style, it is a monstrous romantic melodrama for the closet. The Historical Sketch by another hand is very valuable. Write on Hist: Arts. Receive another very pleasant letter from W Allston. Rain all day hard.

Tuesday Oct[r] *22d 1833* Rain. It has rained for 48 hours. Th: 53. Write on Hist: of Arts. Rain ceases in the afternoon. Read Greek Grammer.

Wed[y] [Oct.] *23d.* Th: 52. Clear. Walk down town to Cummings'. Charles Lesley has arrived. To Mirror Office. Library. McGavin's. Walk home. Ev[g] Write a Biography of T A C for Mirror.

Thursday [Oct.] *24th* Clear. Th: 57. Walk down town. Deliver Biography of G. Stuart to Mr Herring and that of T A Cooper to Morris. Look for Leslie in vain. And the same of Jarvis. See Frothingham & make notes. Walk home. Fatigued. While speaking with R. Riker in the street an old Gentleman came up enquiring for A. Burr's offic. R accosted him as Gen[l] Pawling & introduced him as a veteran who had fought with Montgomery at Quebec. The old man began to fight his battles oer and finally left us to seek his fellow soldier. I afterwards saw him still enquiring for Col[l] Burr and he took my arm while I led him until I found Burr's office for him 23 Nassau Street. I then left him. he is upwards of 80, erect but superannuated. Write on Hist: Arts.

Friday [Oct.] *25th* Write. Walk down town. Th: 57. Clear. Read Fuseli.

Sat[y] [Oct.] *26th* Clear. Th: 56. Read [Henry] Fuseli's life by [John] Knowles, a poor performance. Write on Hist: Arts. Read Fuseli's lectures. Very good. Read in German Grammer and Greek Grammer. Ev[g] Fuseli: Receive a note from Mathew Carey wishing to see me at the City Hotel. T A C. had told me he was in town.

Sunday Oct[r] 27th 1833. Clear. Th: 54. Walk to the City Hotel: M: Carey had gone. His note ought to have reached me on friday. Write a note to post Master for publication. Read Fuseli's lectures.

Monday [Oct.] *28th* Clouds. Th: 56. Read Fuseli. Charles Clinch to see his picture of Richard & Kenneth. Dr John Francis calls & takes part of Zeb Spiff. Walk to McGavin's, Morris's, Library. Bank and leave $5.43. Go to Waldo & Jewets & take notes. W. promises more. Leave wth Leggett [168] to Post a few lines to y[e] Post Master. Walk home. Read Fuseli. Write on Hist: Arts.

Tuesday [Oct.] *29th* Clear. Th: 54. Read in Greek Grammar. Go to McGavin's and paint. Walk home. Read Fuseli. Ev[g] read Greek Grammar.

Wed[y] [Oct.] *30th* Clouds. Th: 50. Paint on Richard & Kenneth & y[e] Child's portrait. Write on Hist: Arts. Read F. and Greek Grammar.

Thursday [Oct.] *31st* Clear. Th: 46. Ice out of doors. Walk with my Wife to Brooklyn to see C. Woolsey's family. See pictures at McGavins Brooklyn & call returning at his Gallery Chambers street. Call at Morris's. Walk home. Ev[g] read Greek Grammar.

Friday Nov[r] 1st Clear. Th: 44. Walk to McGavin's Gallery but it was not warmd & I did not stay to paint. Gave [James] Van Orden proposals for hist: Arts to print. Go to Library & Mirror Office. Morris says that at y[e] last meeting for y[e] Cooper benefit J[ames] I. Roosevelt, Pell & [blank] made speeches against the letter of

[168] William Leggett, editor of the *N. Y. Evening Post.*

y[r] Committee & moved to have it denied & the assertions respecting Simpson & Price apologized for, but Morris by stating truth defeated them. I wrote a part of Morris's letter to Cooper say that if his daughter was ready & willing and her appearance on y[e] Stage determined, now was the time (for him & her sisters)

Sat[y] [Nov.] *2d* Clouds. Th: 49. Write on Zeb Spiff. Read Blackwood. Walk. Clear.

Sunday [Nov.] *3d* Clear Th: 52. Write on Zeb Spiff. Walk twice an hour each. Read Blackwood. Read Greek Grammar.

Monday [Nov.] *4th* Clear. Th: 50. Read Blackwood. Write on Zeb Spiff. Walk to Cummings, McGavins, library, home. Write. Read [William] Ellis Polynesia. J. H. Paynes man collecting names called on me. Says he has 250, wants 5000. Ev[g] Greek Grammar.

Tuesday Nov[r] 5th 1833. Clear. Th: 47. Walk to Wm T McCoun's & receive $200, which deposit and draw 20 leaving 185.43. M. M. Noah's office to forward Cooper benefit. P. Hone having published a letter disapproving the address of the Committee, they send him 20 dollars he had paid for tickets & request them to be returned. W. Irving is raising money by personal application. John Mason gave him 80 having already paid 20 for Tickets. Call at Lithograph Office [blank] and see young [John] Crawley's work, it is very good. Mirror Office. Van Ordens for proof of my proposals. T. S. Cummings Hear that J. Fennimore Cooper had arrived. Walk home. Go to J F Cooper's house 4 Bleeker St[t] & find some ladies waiting for the family. Receive the following

Quincy 2 Nov[r] 1833

William Dunlap Esq[r]
at 64 Sixth Avenue New York

Sir

Your letter of 3 Sept[r] last was received at my house during my absence upon an excursion for the benefit of my health. A pressure of occupation since my return has hitherto delayed the acknowledgment of its receipt, and now permit me only to add that I will take an early opportunity to answer it more fully.

I am with much respect Sir

Your ob[t] Serv[t]

J. Q. Adams

Ev[g] read Ellis.

Wed[y] Nov[r] 6th Clouds. Rain. Th: 46. Write on Zeb Spiff. Call at J. F. C. and see his wife and daughters. Write. Read Ellis. Ev[g] Morse & Fennimore Cooper call and set with us. I go with them to Cs to see some pictures, Morse's Copy from Rembrant & an original Rembrant. As Cooper says nothing of Bentley I fear my hopes were unfounded.

Thursday [Nov.] *7th* Clear. Th: 48. Receive invitation from the Committee for Cooper benefit to attend to night. The Council of N. A. meet with me this afternoon. Write on Zeb Spiff. Afternoon the Council with me. Ev[g] at Bowery Theatre where by politeness of Col[l] Morris of y[e] Mirror I took a comfortable seat although the house was literally crowded to overflowing. I heard Miss Wheatley sing with pleasure but Mrs Wood (Miss Parton) gave me delight and exhibited powers & skill of a very superior grade. I staid until ½ past 10 & the entertainments were far from over.

Friday 8th Nov[r] 1833 Th: 52. Indian summer weather. Mr Charles Rhind called & left with me sketches by himself of the scenery at & near Constantinople & letters on the subject written when in that part of the world. I walked to Ingham's, out, to Durands & saw him, to Herrings saw his wife, to Mirror office saw Morris, to Library & after reading y[e] threatening paragraph in the E Post went to that Office & talked with [William] Leggett in presence of Bryant on the subject diswading him from further publication. I told him that his assertion that Power & the Wood's only played for Cooper by Simpson's permission & claiming [illegible] for him was *untrue*. He spoke of enmity to Cooper on the part of Price & Simpson arising from Cooper's preference of ye Bowery Theatre on his return from England. This is a story of Simpson, which I told Leggett was false as I understood from Cooper who was ready to prove it so. Met Ogden & Morris & went with them to Bowery Theatre wishing to take Cooper to Leggett, missed of him, return'd to Mirror Office, to Morse's & find J. Fennimore C. with him, he tells me my book has not sold & Bentley of course owes me nothing, he says America is of no value with the English & Bently would not republish De Kay's Sketches on Turkey. Go to Mirror Office & find T. A. Cooper who wishes his conduct brought before the public. Walk home fatigue. [James] Creighton was waiting for me wishing me to entrust my Death on ye pale horse to a friend of his. I offer'd to sell it for 500 dollars. he takes time to consider. Receive letter from Allston which I must answer. He seems anxious to know if I received his last. Ev^{g} read Ellis

Saturday Novr 9th 1833 Misty Th: 59. Write letters: to Allston, Chester Harding & Henry Sargent. T A Cooper calls & wishes me to accompany him to E: Post Office which I do & he satisfys Legget that Simpson had misrepresented him. Call on Leslie, he had left town, go to Mirror Office & thence home. Afternoon rain. Ev^{g} read Ellis. And letter rec^{d} from W Whitehead (Key West) respecting Amboy with copy of mine to him

Sunday [Nov.] *10th* Clear. Th: 60 Look of Charles Rhind's Sketches & letters. Write letters to T[homas] Doughty, A[lvin] Fisher, Alexander & Isaac P. Davis of Boston and to Fred^{k} R. Spencer, G. W. Newcomb & S[tephen] H. Gimber of N. Y. Walk. Read Ellis. Th: 62.

Monday [Nov.] *11th* Clear. Th: 60. W. T. McCoun having requested me to draw up resolutions for thanking the individuals who assisted in getting up the Cooper Benefit, do so. Sold my Death on the pale Horse to Wm. Barnard Ring for 500 dollars, 100 p^{d} down and the remainder as soon as possible, the second hundred certainly within 12 months, as per writing, James Creighton being witness & Guarantee for Rings fulfilment. Write letter to Robt Gilmor. Ride to Post Office & Bank: leave 284.43. Go to library, W. T. McCouns. walk home. Rain. Read Ellis' Re[se]arches to the end of Vol 1st

Tuesday [Nov.] *12th* Clouds. Th: 61. Write to Wm. A. Whitehead, Wm. Strickland, John Neagle, Thos. Sully & Henry Inman. Clear afternoon. Walk. Read Dwights Germ^{y}

Wed^{y} [Nov.] *13th* Clear. Th: 57. Write to Doctor S. Beaumont & Francis J. Oliver, to James McMurtrie & Mathew Carey. Walk R. W. Weir's who gives me MSS biography, to Ingham's, to Durand's, to Cummings', to Morris's, to Arch Robertsons, to Post Office, to Bank leave 275.43 Library, to Hoboken Ferries. home. Evening Mr Stebbins from the Mercantile Association called to engage me to lecture at Clinton Hall for February next. To answer on Friday. Terms $25 a lecture. My Wife called to Mrs Gracie's who is dangerously ill.

Thursday Novr 14th 1833. I omitted this yesterday. Mr [Moses] Swett's introduction to me & his promise to furnish notes on hist^{y} of Lithography in this Country. At his office saw specimen of engraving in line by Mr [Thomas] Kelly. Read Weir's biography. Write to Mr [Abraham] Godwin of Patterson, to N[athaniel] Rogers and A[braham] J[ohn] Mason. Go to Hobocken & meet the Sketch club at Bryants. after a walk on the Banks. Take tea & return. Read Flints patter.

Friday [Nov.] *15th* Rain. Th: 57. Ride to Wall St^{t} & tell Stebbins that I will undertake 3 Lectures, 2 on ye Arts of design & 1 on the Drama. Weather clears. Go to Library. Morris's. Durands. Home. Begin to read Cooper's Headsman. To day Mrs. Gracie[169] died. My Wife has

[169] Esther (Rogers) Gracie, widow of Archibald Gracie. *N. Y. American,* Nov. 16, 1833.

been 2 days with her. Mr Brown called wishing me to certify respecting y[e] merits of lithographic specimens. Refer him to y[e] Council. I to day saw Mr [Nathaniel] Rogers (miniature painter) and Mr [Abraham J.] Mason (Wood Engraver) they engage for assistance in my work respecting themselves &c Ev[g] read Headsman.

Sat[y] [Nov.] *16th* Clear. Th: 50. Read Headsman. Write to the Agates, Geo: Cooke, [Girlando] Marsiglia, Rembrant Peale [Henry C.] Shumway, [John W.] Dodge. Finish 1st vol: of Headsman. The introduction of the characters is skilful & the storm superb. Ev[g] anecdotes of English painters (Walpole & C[o]

Sunday [Nov.] *17th* Cold & Cloudy. Th: 47. Hard frost out doors. Write on Hist[y] of Arts. Write to Messrs the subscribers gained by Mr Mason in Boston. 6 letters. Ev[g] attend funeral of Mrs. Gracie. Read Walpole.

Monday Nov[r] 18th 1833. Rec[d] letter with Biography from Fred[k] R. Spencer. Th: 44. Walk to Durands, Cummings, Morris's (who is to engage all his agents for my Work) Parker & Clovers, Library, Post Office, Bank, leave 255.43, McGavens, Home. Read Headsman & receive letter from Rob[t] Gilmore. Read Headsman

Tuesday [Nov.] *19th* Clear. Th: 44. Finish Headsman. The construction of the plot is a masterpiece of invention. The moral is sublime. The language too artificial. The characters well drawn. The incidents pathetic. The descriptions vivid & poetical altho true. Write on Hist: Arts. Receive letters from Sully & Sargeant. Read Walpole.

Wed[y] [Nov.] *20th* Clear. Th: 44. Write on Hist[y] Arts. Read Mason on Wood Engraving. Write to Mr [Ezra] Ames (Albany) Jos: Hopkinson, J. R. Lambdin, Jacob Eichholtz (Lancaster) Read Walpole. Write to [Edward F.] Petticolas (Richmond) Thos. Williamson & John Crawley (Norfolk) Read.

Thursday [Nov.] *21st* Clouds. Th: 43. Write J. Q. Adams, S. M. Hopkins, L. Cruttenden. Walk to Durands, Cummings, Inghams, Library, Post Office, J. F. Coopers, home. Read Walpole & Mrs [Mary Austin] Holl[e]y's Texas. Ev^{g} Sketch Club with me very thinly attended. Rain.

Friday [Nov.] *22d* Rain. Th: 46. Write to Edm^{d} A Wetmore returning Copley's bill of sale for picture, Geo: Fairman U. S. P. Phil^{a} respecting his father. Write on hist^{y} Arts. Read Mrs Holly's Texas.

Sat^{y} [Nov.] *23d* Clear. Th: 48. Write on Hist Arts. Read Walpole.

Sunday [Nov.] *24th* Clear. Th: 50. Write as yesterday. Afternoon walk. Ev^{g} read. [Robert W.] Weir called & communicated facts respecting himself & [Horatio] Greenough. I have determined that Morris shall print my book & he undertakes to arrange with the publishers.

Monday 25th Novr 1833. Rain & last night and continuation to day. This is the 50th anniversary of the retreat of the invading Armies of Britain & the evacuation of this place. That day was cold & in the evening or night it snowed. Write on Hist. Arts. I rec^{d} on Saturday a letter from Doctor Waterhouse dated Cambridge Novr 10th apologizing for not answering my letter. his letter is a rambling affair with repetitions of what he wrote to Herring. Rain storm all day. Finish 2d Vol: Walpole. Th: 48. Rain in the night.

Tuesday [Nov.] *26th* Clouds. Clears away. Th: 48. Prepare to paint on Mr Wetmores child. Receive letter from Mr Dodge & a call from Mr Shumway on ye subject of their biographies. Write to Ball Hughes, Martin E Thompson, Wm. S. Mount, T. Sully, Alex^{r} Lawson, Doctor Moore U. S. Mint, Wm Kneass, Christian Gobrecht. Walk down town to Post Office. To Bank & leave 235.43, to Cummings & Library. Ride home. Read Walpole.

Wed[y] [Nov.] *27th* Clear. Th: 44. Ice out doors. Write to N[athaniel] Jocenlyn [*sic*] N. H. to J. W. Hill, to Raphael Hayes, Sam[l] Osgood Boston, J[ames] Whitehorn, 215 Fulton, G[eorge] W. Twibill, J. C. Ward, Andrew Richardson, George Miller, W[illiam] M. Oddie, E[dward] D. Marchant, J[ohn] G[adsby] Chapman, Alex[an]dria, D. C.

Thursday [Nov.] *28th* Clear. Th: 46. Walk to Durand's, Morris's, Post Office, Library, Clinton Hall, dine with Arch[d] Rogers. See a beautiful Miniature Group by Miss [Anne] Hall. Write to A[lexander] Rider Phil[a]

Friday [Nov.] *29th* Clear. Th: 44. Write to Bass Otis Receive letter from Eichholtz, gain from Vandervoort [170] notices of Jos: Wright. Write to B. Otis, C. C. Wright, M. Fürst, John Evers. Walk to Mason's, to Durand's, Cummings, Morris's, E[vening] Post office, G. C. Verplank's, Post Office, Am[n] office and home. paid 7.50 J[s] Van Orden leaving Bank 227.93. Write on Hist[y] Arts. Read Walpole. Rain all night.

Sat[y] *Nov*[r] *30th 1833.* Clouds & rain. Th: 45. Write to Rob[t] Mills Washington. H. C. Beach buys my Historick Muse (Head size) for $50. Ride to Parker & Clovers & deliver & receive. Go to [Thomas] Cole's & and with him to Mr [Luman] Reed who has paid him 500 dollars for a Landscape painted this summer & ordered 4 more at that price. The first was painted without any stipulated price. On seeing [it] R aske[d] the price "I should be satisfied with 300 dollars but gratified by receiving five" was the answer. "You shall be gratified" was the rejoinder. Cole's pictures painted this summer are very fine. Go to Bank & leave there 277.93. Rain all day. Read Walpole. Papillon on Wood Engraving.

[170] Probably either William Ledyard Vandervoort or Peter Ledyard Vandervoort, sons of Peter and Sarah (Ledyard) Vandervoort, and brothers-in-law of Joseph Wright, both of whom were then merchants in New York City. *N. Y. Hist. Soc. Collections 1905* (*Abstracts of Wills*, XIV), 138-39; *N. Y. Dutch Church Baptisms,* II; Dunlap's *Arts of Design,* I, 314; *N. Y. City Directories.*

"The Art of Engraving & working off from plates of Copper till 1490. But in 1460 Finiguerra a Goldsmith of Florence by accident which might have given birth to the rolling press without the antecedent discovery of printing did actually light upon the method of taking off stamps from an engraved plate. Casting such a plate into melted brimstone he observed that the exact impression of the engraving was left upon the surface of the brimstone marked by black lines. He repeated the experiment on moistened paper rolling it gently with a roller—it succeeded. He communicated the discovery to Baccio Baldini who pursued the invention with success & engraved plates from drawings. From Italy engraving travelled to Flanders (The first stamp of Finiguera is dated 1452) La Lanze, Du Chesne & W. Young Ottely. (See Walpole 5th Vol: p: 7) In Flanders Martin of Antwerp was followed by Albert Durer. (The invention of etching by aqua fortis is claimed by Parmegiano but disputed by others, it was of great use in facilitating the arts of design as painters etch'd their own designes) Lucas of Leyden succeeded Albert. When Marc Antonio Raimondi the contempo[or]ary & friend of Rafaelle engraving was placed by the side of painting. This art reached England in a rude state in 1483. (Ames, Dibdin) but the first book ornamented with copper cuts in England was published by Thos. Raynalde in 1540 & the first Engraver known was Thomas Geminus 1545. To men who have enjoyed life for the greater part of century two or three hundred years appears as a short period for the perfection to which an Art has arrived. This suggests the comparison between the notions which an infinite & eternal being forms of time & the notions form'd by a finite & short lived creature. The Child thinks a year an immeasurable portion of time, the youth thinks the same of ten or twenty years, the old man sees in hundreds but a transient period, the Eternal truly must think of ages but as moments. It was not until 1610 in ye time of Elizabeth that engraving of portraits had arrived at even a decent perfection, yet how great the improvement in one century after. In 1630-40 Vandyke etched & engravers (his countrymen) were found fit to engrave his portraits & worthy to be painted by him. No engravers English till near 1700. P[rince] Rupert invented Mezzotinto: after he had retired from fighting in England. He conceived the notion of impressing a black surface on paper & scraping the lights from seeing a soldier scraping the rust from his fuzee. He communicated his notion to a painter & they contrived to imitate the roughness produced by the rust by means of a steel rasp & having produced the black surface went on to scraping out the lights. But this invention is claimed by others & the prince is said only to have invented a new tool, since superseded by a better. The art was carried to great perfection in England of which V[alentine] Greens print from B: Wests Agripina & J[ohn] Dixon's from Reynolds' Ugolino are given as prominent examples.

V. Green was West's neighbour in Newman Street & often at his house, when I was in London 1784 to 7. Rain. Correct proof of Stuart for Hering.

Sunday Dec[r] *1st 1833* Thin clouds Th: 49. Write on Hist[y] of Arts. Received yesterday 7 numbers of Herring and Longacre's Portrait Gallery. Rain. Read Walpole.

Monday [Dec.] *2d* Clouds & a little rain. Write on Hist[y] Arts. Afternoon ride to Herrings & to Durands to meet Council of N. A. Ev[g] read Foreign Review.

Tuesday [Dec.] *3d* Clouds. Th: 48. Write to Henry Ward Esq[r] respecting Miss Ann Hall's biography, to Henry Clay, Frances Kearney, Samuel Maverick. Receive letters from W. S. Mount & Henry Winthrop Sargent & write to the last. Write on Hist[y] Art. Ev[g] read Foreign Review.

Wed[y] [Dec.] *4th* Clouds. Th: 48. Write on Hist[y] of Arts. Receive letter & biography from Chester Harding. Write to him & to [William] Rollinson (N. Y.)

Thursday [Dec.] 5th Clouds. Th: 50. Walk to Herrings, to Masons. Meet W[illiam] Page who promises notice of himself. Go to Cummings's, Francis's, Hosack's (who presents his essays), McCouns, McLeans, Morris's, Post Office. See Verplank he has a Mezzotint of Washington to show me. Walk home. Write to Sully & Waterhouse

Friday [Dec.] 6th Clear. Th: 50. Write on Arts and to D[aniel] Dickinson, Rob[t] A. Salmon, Henry C. Pratt, John Clifton, James B. Longacre, John G. Chapman, D[avid] C. Johnston, W[illiam] J[ames] Hubard, J. H. Mifflin, N & F Monachisi, Jos: B. Ord, Hugh Bridport, E. Percival, J[ohn] A. Woodside, Rob[t] Sully, David V Smith, Mrs. Staughton,[171] S[amuel] Scarlet, A[bram] B. Rockey.

[171] Mrs. William Stoughton (Anna Claypoole Peale), daughter of James Peale, afterwards Mrs. William Duncan. See the Bailey and Goodspeed edition of Dunlap's *Arts of Design,* III, 322-23.

Saturday Decr 7th Clear. Th: 48. Ride to Cummings. Walk to Judsons, to Mirror Office, Bank & leave 257.93, Post Office, Library, Miss Demming, home. Write to Wm. A. Wall (New Bedford) Mr Leggett calls & wishes me to see what he is doing for my 2d part of Hist^y Th: article Forest.

Sunday 8th Decr 1833. Rain. Write on Hist^y Arts, and to J[ohn] S[tephans] Cogdell, Thos. Middleton & John B. White, Charleston S. C. Read. Biog^y of Burney, *flashy* the letters of the Editor when young have nature & sprightliness.

Monday [Dec.] *9th* Clear. Th: 47. Send check to C[harles] Judson for $134.19 leaving in Bank $123.74. Write Andrew Bell, pay Clayton & Van Orden $6, leaving in Bank 117.74.

Tuesday [Dec.] *10th* Clear. Th: 48. Write to And^w Bell.

Wed^y 11th Clear. Send for Doctor McLean. Last evening Cole & Cummings with me. Finish D'Arblay's Burney. With the exception of some early letters, it is a wretched vain hyperbolical piece of egotism.

Sat^y Ev^g [Dec.] *14th* In this interval I have had little ease except from laudanum. Th: Yesterday 42. To day appears colder & high wind with threatening of snow. Thursday Ev^g rec^d an invitation to meet Mr [Richard] Westmacott the sculptor at J[ames] G[ore] Kings at Highwood a carriage to be sent for &c for Sunday, of course decline. Friday my daughter returns from Mr Kings. Receive letters from Henry Sargent & M: Carey. To day receive letter from Mr Chapman of Alexandria. Finish 2d Vol: Ellis's Polynesia. I am this evening more at ease than for some days, but under medical influence.

Monday Decr 16th 1833 Clouds. Yesterday a few inches of snow. Read in Dwights Germany. In bed part of the day. I have yet very partial relief. I drink three tumblers of Congress water very early, 3 times a day take a powder of Camphor opium & Nitre. I drink a pint of flaxseed tea. the complaint continues. Draw from Bank $20 leave 97.74. McLean has just order'd Castor oil. Aft[n] Snow.

Thursday [Dec.] *19th* Clear after a long storm of rain & wind. I yesterday lay in bed until evening for ease from pain & read Ellis's Pol[ynesian Researches] Rec[d] a letter from Henry Clay refferring me to H. Clay jr. his son. Letter from Dr. S. Beaumont by Dr. W. Beaumont who presents his book. I rise about 10 to day & write & read with more ease in regard to my complaint than for some days.

Sunday [Dec.] *22d* Still confined to my room with some alleviation of the symptoms. Yesterday in bed until ev[g]. Physician's prescriptions much the same. Read Ellis. Read Rhinds M. S. S. The weather fine & mild. In the afternoon Mr. Rhind sat with me & gave me a verbal detail of his embassy & voyage to Constantinople, with the difficulties he met with then & since.

Mond[y] [Dec.] *23d* Weather the same. I had a bad night partly from the omission of anodynes, principally from the diseased action of digestion & irritation. I am up at 10 OClock but without apparent amendment. Read. Take y[e] anodyne powder.

Tuesday 24th Dec[r] 1833. Mild. Rain. I am better this morning & was so last evening & night. The inflammatory symptoms have abated much, but I cannot yet omit the powder of Camphor, Nitre & opium. My drink is tea of the bark of the slippery elm, 1 oz. boil'd in a quart of water, 1 pint a day. My food bread, Coffee, potatoes. I read Rhinds letters & Gibbon. Write to H. Clay jun[r] Lexington Kentucky. Read in Croley's Salitheal.[172]

[172] *Salathiel, a tale of the past, present and future,* by the Rev. George Croly, American edition, N. Y., 1833, 2 vol.

Wed[y] [Dec.] *25th* Clouds & mist. Continue mending as I hope. Every morning a bottle of Congress water before rising now begins to act as a cathartic, yesterday & to day. Read as yesterday. Receive a letter from James Creighton, Baltimore saying that Mr. Ring had put up y[e] picture of Death &c at Fredericktown, that it is craked & some of the paint pealed off &c & offers me 150 dollars in 6 months or the picture &c I answer, "You saw the picture when last opened. I advised opening it here & letting me repair if wanted. I cannot break the bargain, but if I am presented immediately (in 20 days) with 200 dollars, I will give up the agreement or send a receit in full. Instead of the last I say "The only consideration that could induce me would be money in hand (or with[n] 20 days) & even that must be more than you offer. It must be upon the principal of making a large disc[t] for cash & not that the picture was damaged when you received it.

Rain all day. Read Rhind's M. S. S. and Croley's Saletheal with interest.

Thursday 26th Dec[r] *1833*. Clear. Th: 48. I now go down to my meals but retire to my chamber after. I am mending I hope fast. Read as yesterday & find Rhinds truth more interesting than Croly's flights. I have omitted the andyne powders. Noon obliged to take the choric ether & the powder (one) pass the day comfortably and night. Was visited by Mr. G[eorge] Cooke with his biographical notice of himself. *Bowman* he says was a carpenter (Westward) took up portrait painting, got some work at Washington, went to Phil[a] could not get on, return'd to Washington almost starving, boldly shipt himself for England & persuaded E W Smith to pay his passage. Was assisted by [John Y.] Clarke who married a Neice [172a] of *Girard's* of Phil[a]. Got employment in Lon-

[172a] Henriette Girard, daughter of Jean Girard and niece of Stephen Girard, married first Henri Lallemand, and second, Dr. J. Y. Clarke. J. B. McMaster, *Life and Times of Stephen Girard* (1918), I, 463; II, 338, 415; Stephen Simpson, *Biography of Stephen Girard* (1832), iii; and Stephen Girard's will, *ibid.*, appendix, 6.

don for a time, returned to Am^{a}. (He was in London same time as Harding) at home unemployed went to Canada. In London was taken to the house of a Nobleman but turned off for courting his daughter. Went to Rome, had an affair of Gallantry there & got off, perhaps return'd home from Rome? Mr Stebbins sends to see if I can Lecture now, answer that I must have until Feby at least. Mr Cummings calls.

Friday [Dec.] *27th* Clear. Th: 46. I am better this morning. Read & write. (Madam Planteau, see Cook's letter) Write to Vandervoort, [Henry] Gahn, Wash Irving, Jos Irwin, Charles R Leslie, James K Paulding, James F. Cooper, Honble Wm. Cranch D C Jarvis F. Hanks. Receive letter from John Crawley. Read Lights & Shadows [137] &c.

Sat^{y} [Dec.] *28th* Clear. Th: 43. I have continued mend^{g} & have taken no Anodyne or other Medecine the last day. Write & read in Club book. Receive letters from A. Bell & Wm A Whitehead. Read Rhind's M. S. S.

Sunday Decr 29th 1833 Clear. Th: 43. Mr Mason called with his notes on Wood Engraving. Read Stories. Write to G. G. Howland. My health improves. Walk in Washington Square. Read Rhind.

[Dec.] *30th* Monday. Rain. Th: 44. Write on Hist. Arts. Draw from Bank 20 leave $77.74. Feel no improvement to day until late. Write on Hist: Arts. Read Club Book. Walk in the Square on the *31st* which is a mild day. Th: 47. Receive comm^{n} from G. C. Verplank.

Jany 1st 1834. Clear & mild. Th: 49. The last year commenced in rain but even warmer weather than this & so continued until the 8th. My health was then better: otherwise my condition is now happier than then. Read

[173] The American edition of M. M. Montgomery's *Lights and Shadows of German Life* was published in Philadelphia in 1833.

& write as yesterday. I cannot join in the visitings customary to the day. At 4 P. M. take my Anodyne & my bed.

Thursday [Jan.] 2d Rain. Th: 46. Read Mrs Halls "Buccaneer." [174] Write on Hist: Arts. Receive a polite letter from C. R. Leslie, promising communications for my work & offering his own & brother's (T. J. Leslie's) names as subscribers. Suffered great distress in the evening only aleviated by opiates.

Friday [Jan.] *3d* I am much better this morning, which is clear. Th: 48. Write to John Gregg Esq[r] of Canandaigua. Write on Hist: Arts. Write to James Cochran (Oswego). Receive letter from G[ardiner] G. Howland saying he has written to Mrs Green respecting Copley. One from R. M. Sully promising information as likewise one from Remb[t] Peale. My distress increased again in the evening & I have only relief from Anodynes.

Sat[y] [Jan.] *4th* Clear. Th: 40. Little or no abatement of my disease. Write a little. Read the Buccaneer a powerful tale.

Monday [Jan.] *6th* I was yesterday worse. To day somewhat better. Weath[er] cold. Some snow. Receive letter from T. Sully & a letter from W B Wring. Write to James Creighton that Wring's letter by its style precludes an answer, that if he (C.) wishes the business settled he had better commission some one here to offer me a sum in hand for a receit in full & that probably my necessities & the wish to avoid controversy will induce me to accept it.

Tuesday [Jan.] *7th* Clear. Th: 36. Write on Hist: art: & to Mr [John A.] Woodside Phil[a]. My disease is no better. I have taken to day 3 powders, 1 dose choric

[174] *The Buccaneer,* by Mrs. Samuel Carter Hall (Ann Maria Fielding), London, 1832, was published in Philadelphia in 1833.

ether in 3 tumblers of Congress water & my food arrow root except breakfast of buckwheat cakes & coffee. Ev[g] J. Fennimore Cooper sits with me, he has been to Phil[a] & Washington. Read "Delaware" [175]

Wed[y] [Jan.] *8th* Clear. Not quite so cold. The last days past it has frozen on the N side of the house in all the chambers. Read & write though still in much pain at times & taking medecine as yesterday.

Thursday [Jan.] *9th* Send for McLean as my disease continues. Write to Gilbert Russel, Hugh Reinagle & J. W. Jarvis by James Freeman who goes to New Orleans. Write to Mrs Whitehorne New Port R. I. respecting her brother Malbone.

Sunday 12th Jan[y] 1834. Rain. Th: 42. I have continued much the same in health & sufferring. Read in Walpole's letters, in Delaware a Novel in favour of Aristocracy dedicated to Washington Irving. Write on Hist: Arts.

Monday. Clear. Th: 42. Health much the same. The efficient medecine seems to be the powder of Camphor, Nitre & opium. Read & write on Hist: Arts. Mr [Samuel] Ward called yesterday & left biog[l] sketch of his sister in law Miss Hall. Read Bulwer's England.

Tuesday [Jan.] *14th* Clear. Th: 40. Write to Remb[t] Peale in answer, To Geo. W. Hatch, E[nos] T. Throop respecting Mrs Lupton, A. J. Davis, I. Town, Peter Maverick jr. W. Rollinson, A. Anderson. My health appears somewhat better. Read & write as usual on Hist: Arts, & write to [John W.] Paradise respecting himself & father [John Paradise], to Stebbins respecting Lectures

Wed[y] Jan[y] 15th 1834. Clear. Th: 41. Leave in Bank 57.74 by drawing out 20. Write on Hist. Art. Read Bul-

[175] *Delaware, or the ruined family,* by [George P. R. James]. The American edition was published in Philadelphia, 1833, 2 vol.

wer's Eng[d] My health much the same. Receive letter & biography from Charles Robert Leslie with Sir Martin Archer Shee's address to the Students of y[e] R. Academy. letters from Neagle, John Stephans Cogdell of Charleston S. C. (with biography) Dan[l] Dickinson (with biography). Neagle says that Strickland promises me a communication. Read Walpole & Bulwar.

Thursday [Jan.] *16th* Clear. Th: 39. My health much the same. Write on Hist[y] Art. Receive a very pleasing letter from Judge Cranch (Wm.) Washington D. C. Read Walpole & Bulwer. Write to C. R. Leslie.

Friday [Jan.] *17th* Rain. Th: 42. Receive letter from J. K. Tefft of Savannah requesting Autographs. from C. C. Wright promising information on dye sinking. My pain is more acute than usual & of longer duration. Begin to take an infusion of a herb called (I believe) Bucha sent to me by my physician Dr McLean. Visited by Mr John [V.] Dixey who promises notice of his father [John Dixey] &c.

Saturday [Jan.] *18th* Clear. Th: 48. My desease less painful. Write on Hist: Art. Read Bulwer.

Monday [Jan.] *20th* Yesterday it rain'd & the Th: at 50. G. P. Morris called & we determined that the History of the Arts should be put to press immediately at his office to be work'd off by degrees. A. J. Mason brought me his Hist[y] of Wood Engraving. I suffer much both yesterday & to day. Th: still 50 & clouds. Write on Hist: Arts. Receive a letter from R. Gilmor. Read review by Walpole.

Tuesday [Jan.] *21st* Clear. Th: 44. I have not experienced so much pain as of late as far in the day as noon. Write on Hist. Art. Write Messrs. Augur, Durand & Ingham & Tisdale.

Thursday [Jan.] *23d* Yesterday & day Clear. Th: 40 & 38. No change in my disease. Write to E. T. Throop, John Delaf^{d} & Wm. Leggett & <*A. Anderson*> Visited by two Misses Maverick with specimens of Lithography & by old Mr Rollinson with biog^{l} notices. Receive letter & notices from Henry Cheeves Pratt. Ingham with me Ev^{g}.

Sat^{y} 25th Jany 1834. Clear: Th. 34. Receive letter yesterday from Henry Clay jun^{r} promising further communication & to day receive C. B. Johnsons biography and his scraps. Last ev^{g} Davis with me & is to give notices of Architecture. Write on Hist: Arts. Read Walpole. Roscoe.[176] My health much the same & at times great sufferring. Appetite good. Food simple.

Sunday [Jan.] *26th* A snow storm. Th: 36. Pain not so great to day at any time yet. Read Bulwer. Write on Hist. Art. Weather clears at 12, with little snow on ye earth. We have had in fact none yet. Write on hist: Art & to Morris. Read Roscoe.

Monday [Jan.] *27th* Clear & colder. My disease no better perceptibly. Read my journal at Oxford in 1786. Roscoe. Write. Read Roscoes life & look over his Catalogues as published by himself after his failure of Banker. Receive another very valuable letter from Leslie most of it relative to Mr West.

Tuesday [Jan.] *28th* Clear. Ther: 38. My disease much the same. Write to C. R. Leslie. Read. Roscoe & Review. Write on hist: art.

Wed^{y} [Jan.] *29th* Clear. Th: 40. Some of my symptoms appear better. Write on Hist. Art. Read review. At 11 OClock Doctor Mott performed the operation of sounding by introducing the proper instrument into my blad-

[176] *The life of William Roscoe,* by his son, Henry Roscoe, (London, 1833); Boston, 1833.

der & pronounced my disease stone. I can scarcely realize my situation although I had long thought it probable. I am now 12 OClock tolerably quiet. The remedy for this disease has always appeared to me dreadful, but submission to my duty I hope may bear me through & a few years of comparative health may reward. "Thy will be done." This expression which ever in my heart cannot fail me now

Friday Jany 31st 1834 Clear and mild weather. I passed yesterday without unusual sufferring but took more than usual laudanum. Last night restless. To day no unusual sufferring & no laudanum yet at noon. Receive another letter from Leslie & one from Bridport. I have read to day principally in review. At 2 OClock pain. Laudanum. Pass the Ev^g & night in tolerable ease. Mr. James Herring with me in ye Evening.

Saturday Feby 1st 1834. Cloudy but mild. My disease hopeless is much the same until something decisive is done for a change. Yesterday drew from Wm T. McCoun 200 dollars & deposited in N. Y. Bank, leaving there 257.74. R^d M.S.S. Biography of Dewitt Clinton for Mr Herring: who leaves 2 more Nos. of the National Gallery of Portraits. Write to Dr [Chauncey A.] Goodrich and to Mr [George W.] Flagg (New Haven). Read review.

Sunday [Feb.] *2d* Clear & very mild. I have ease but by laudanum. Read review & works on Architecture. Visit from G. P. Morris & his brother in law Hopkins. Visit from Wm Jewett & biography. A. B. Durand sat with [me] some hours & was joined by R. W. Weir & J. F. Cooper.

Monday [Feb.] *3d* Clear & very mild. My disease the same, but I fear it wears me away. My good physicians McLean & Francis promise to watch & give me warning & I am willing to get on with my work, but final relief can only be in the operation. Write to Charles King at the suggestion of G. P. Morris & to Washington Irving a second letter at that of C. R. Leslie. Write of Hist: Arts. Mr Geo: Cooke called & sat with us part of y[e] Ev[g] & the remainder I have devoted to History & Analyses of Architecture. I am thankful for a comfortable day comparatively & for the attentions of many friends.

Tuesday Feb[y] 4th 1834 Clear Mild weather. Th: 50. I have the same pains & the same comforter. Write on Hist: Art. Read old reviews. Mr Rollinson, Messrs. Hicks & Rhind the same. Pay Judson a quarters rent & leave in Bank $188.

Wed[y] [Feb.] *5th* Clear, warm & spring like. I have to day 10 OClock not yet needed laudanum. Yesterday took 30 drops morning & 30 evening. My disease the same. Write on Hist: Arts. At 12 take laudanum 30 dr. In the afternoon visited by Mess. Weir & Oddy. Read N. A. Review. At night 45 dr: Laudanum.

Thursday [Feb.] *6th* Clear & Warm. Yester[y] Th: 52 to day 54. Write to P. Hone & to Professor [Joseph] Henry, Princeton. Write of Hist: Art. N. Rogers calls & gives notices of himself. [Eliab] Metcalf is dead within a few days. Doctor Hosack calls & sits with me. Receive letters from C. R. Leslie & S. Scarlatt. Evening T. Cole with me.

Friday [Feb.] *7th* Snow. I am apparently rather better. Write on Hist. Art. Read reviews. Snowing ceases leaving an inch on the ground as has been the case this winter several times.

Saturday Feb[y] 8th 1834. Clear. health much the same. Write on Hist: Art. Read reviews & Mirror.

Sunday [Feb.] *9th* Mild rain. Health the same. T. S. Cummings with me. Receive a very friendly note from P. Hone in answer to my request for a Catalogue of his pictures and the Catalogue by himself. Write on Hist: Art. Read reviews.

Monday [Feb.] *10th* Clouds clear in Afternoon. Send letters to John R. Murray, G. P. Morris, W. Allston & C. R. Leslie. Write on Hist. Arts. Read in Henry Dwights Germany & Gibbons. No change in my health perceivable.

Tuesday [Feb.] *11th* Clear. Th: 48. Mild as spring. I suffer more pain to day. Read in Ney's life, Gibbon. Agree with James Perkins to take house 64 Sixth Avenue for next year at 316 dollars rent. Write on hist. Arts. Receive from G. G. Howland Mrs Eliz: Clark Green's answer respecting her father [John Singleton Copley] merely referring me to [Francis] Leiber's Am: Enc: the information there given she says she furnished.

Wed[y] [Feb.] *12th* Clear & somewhat colder. Health the same. Read in Museum of Foreign Lit[re] & Art sent me by Charles King. Write to T. S. Cummings to get the Enc: Amer[a] for me. Write on Hist: Art.

Thursday [Feb.] *13th* Clear. Th: 45. I have not been able to day to take my pen until near 1 OClock & after 50 drops of laudanum. I have suffered acutely. Read as yesterday. Write on Hist. Art.

Friday [Feb.] 14th April-like showers followed by clear warm weather. I am to day more comfortable. Write to Henry Clay jun. and on hist. Art: draw out 20 dollars & leave in Bank $237.74. Write to Charles King, to John Quincy Adams. Read in Museum of Foreign Literature & Early Navigators. Cumming calls.

Saturday Feb[y] *15th 1834*. More pain and less strength. The weather pleasant, a little damp, Th: 50. Look over Cummings sketch of hist[y] of Miniature painting. Write a notice of the forthcoming of Cole's Angel & Shepherds for Mirror. Read as yesterday. Write on Hist: Arts.

Sunday [Feb.] *16th* Clear. Th 55. I have taken 45 drops of laudanum before procuring comparative ease. Read & write on Hist: Arts. but not until near noon. Besides visits from McLean & Francis I have to day seen Cummings, Cole, V[ice] Ch[ancellor] McCoun & his 2 sons, and Davis.

Monday [Feb.] *17th* Clouds. Th: 53. Mr [Nathaniel] Joscelyn of New Haven calls & promises me notes on [Hezekiah] Augur, [Elkanah] Tisdale, [Samuel B.] Munson, A[nson] Dickinson, [Mosely I.] Danforth, M: Brown, Douglas (Savanna) Joscelyn (of N. Carolina) and many others. Receive another very pleasant letter from [Charles Robert] Leslie giv^{g} me at my request notices of his sister [Anne Leslie]. in Ev^{g} Miss Wright the daughter of Joseph Wright & granddaughter [of Patience Wright] called & give some particulars of her father, Grandmother & Aunt Platt.[177]

Tuesday [Feb.] *18th* Clear & warm as spring. My sufferrings have been this morning very acute & continued. At 11 I am at comparative ease with 50 drops of laudanum. Receive letter yesterday from Robt. Mills (Washington D. C.) Write on Hist: Art: Receive news paper from Savannah Georgia merely to let me see that my work is there announced & the subscription paper left with a keeper of a reading room. Receive letter from Francis Alexander now of Boston giving his Autobiography. Ingham with me in the Evening.

Wed^{y} [Feb.] *19th* The mild weather continues. My morning sufferrings not quite so acute as yesterday. My physicians say Mott has no hesitation in saying that notwithstanding the previous disease of former years in ye parts where an operation must be performed for my relief, the prospect of successful result is with him un-

[177] Mrs. Ebenezer Platt (Elizabeth Wright), daughter of Joseph and Patience (Lovell) Wright. H. D. Perrine, *The Wright Family of Oyster Bay* (N. Y., 1923), 90.

doubted. I this day complete my 68th and enter my 69th year, with the prospect of a speedy termination of life, or improved health for a short period. This journal displays my present state of health & my sufferings for months past. Write on Hist^y of Art but not until after 12 OClock. Read miscellaniously. Little ease through the day. Afternoon & night hard rain.

Feby 20th 1834. Clear: warm as spring. I have not suffer so much this morning. Read in Museum of For. literature. Write to Joshua Shaw, A. B. Durand & Robt. Gilmor. Write on Hist. Art. Suffering again at 2 P. M. Th: 56. Read Museum.

Friday [Feb.] *21st* Clear. Th: 56. Very severe pain until I took 40 drops laudanum. Write a note to McLean. Begin an accurate Chronological arrangement of Articles in a book like a Childs copy-book. Receive letter from Washington Allston. W W Woolsey with me. Read Museum.

Saturday [Feb.] *22d* My pain to day not so severe. As I wrote yesterday to McLean saying I should be ready to submit to the operation to day, I am in expectation of Doctor Mott, & I hope relief through sufferring. Receive letter & biog^l notice from Francis Kearny, & Two biographical notices by Mr. J. Hanks of himself & young [G. Washington] Tyler. Doctor McLean calls & shows me a note from Doctor Mott saying he has two operations to perform to day besides other business, he defers ye operation until next week. Write on Hist. Art & read in Museum. Receive letter from Mr [Henry C.] Flagg, the father of the young painter [George W. Flagg].

Sunday 23d Feby 1834. Rain Th: 56 Last evening J. F. Cooper past an hour with me cheerfully as usual. He described Wm Godwin to me. The old man has his residence in a house connected with Westminster & the Office given him which is nearly sinecure, he is 80 &

upright, very short & small. At this time C visited him previously the old man had called on him & introduced himself. I am Wm Godwin, the same had happened in respect to Thos. Campbell, and in Paris, on the staircase of Coopers Hotel, in respect to Walter Scott.

Doctor Mott has been with me; again sounded for the stone; & has appointed 12 OClock next Wed[y] for the operation. To day the instrument encountered the stone immediately at the neck of the bladder. Mason calls & sits with me. Read. Write on Hist: art: W W Woolsey & his son in law W S Johnson with me.

Monday [Feb.] *24th* Clouds. Th: 57. My sufferings are not so great this morning as they sometimes are, but I have had recourse to 40 drops laud[m] Read in Maddens infirmities of Genius. Write to H. C. Flagg Esq[r] Attorney at Law New Haven respecting his son George. Receive letter from Mr James Whitehorne. Write on Hist: Arts.

Tuesday [Feb.] *25th* Clouds. Th: 55. Write & read as yesterday. Rain in y[e] Even[g]

Wed[y] 26th Clear & colder. Up at ½ past 9 & preparing for the operation.

Friday March 14th 1834. Some days back drew $20: leaving in Bank $217.74. This is my first mem: since the operation of 26 Feb[y] which proved terribly protracted & severe. Hosack talked of a minutes operation. McLean said he had seen a quarter of an hour before he extracted the stone. I was under the knife & other instruments of torture more than an hour. I have received many letters not read until within a few days, the most important are from Mr Latrobe respecting his father [Benjamin H. Latrobe], H. Greenough (Florence), Wa. Irving [178] respecting Newton. I have answered Latrobe's, Shaw's,

[178] The letter from Washington Irving, about Gilbert Stuart Newton, dated New York, March 9, 1834, is printed in Dunlap's *Arts of Design,* II, 302-304.

Lambdin's. I am now sitting up in an easy chair for half an hour. My surgeon & my friends McLean & Francis have been all that could be wish'd.

Sat[y] [March] *15th* Last night & this morning y[e] deepest snow we have had. I have yet seen no one but my family & physicians, except my friend Francis J. Oliver of Boston. I am to day sitting a short time in my easy chair. Clears off mild. Write to R[obert] Mills Wash:

Sunday March 16th 1834. Clear & mild. Sit up as yesterday. Write to Wm A Whitehead.

Monday 17th Cloudy but still mild. I am sitting up my hour & reading Walpoles letters. The process of healing seems to proceed. Receive a letter from Paulding excusing himself from giving anecdotes of Jarvis. My friends have been very assiduous in calling, but I have seen no one yet. J. F. Cooper being here this ev[g] I sent him Greenough's letter & he told my family that Morse had rec[d] a drawing from Greenough of the intended Washington which they say is sublime.

Tuesday [March] *18th* Clear & mild. I am sitting up but not at my ease. Read Walpole. See Arch[d] Rogers, & C. C. Ingham for a few minutes. Receive letter from R. Gilmore respecting B. Latrobe & his father's biography. Letter from Sully & send him his Mem: & scrap books.

Wed[y] [March] *19th* Three weeks since y[e] operation. Weather clear & like summer. Read Walpole. See W W. Woolsey. Read Mirror.

Thursday [March] *20th* Clear. Th: 61. Again sitting up for my daily hour or two. Read Mirror. In a late Ev[g] Post is published a letter from Greenough to Morse. I am told by Mr. Al[x] Robertson that the Wife of G. Stuart

Newton has written to her friends in Boston to come or send for her, he being in a mad-house. In the ev[g] Ingham told me that Newton is dead and that Leslie dissatisfied with his situation at West Point would leave it and return to England the tenth of next month. This was announced to Morse by Leslie's brother who had been the cause of his accepting the professorship.

Friday March 21st 1834. Draw 20 from Bank leaving $197.74. Rec[d] yesterday a letter from James B. Longacre & answer it to day. Read Miss Martineau & reviews. I have assurance that the injury done to the prostrate gland by the *stone* has caused a dangerous ulcer & a communication with the rectum. This makes my case critical.

Sat[y] [March] *22.* Clear but cold. I am up for a time, but have no symptoms to encourage me. Read reviews.

Sunday [March] *23d* Clear; not so cold. I have pass'd a comfortable night: but have cholic now in the day. T. Cole with me. It was [Henry] Carey L's brother in law told them (Cole & Morse) of the intended return & the[y] intend seeing Leslie on tuesday. Cummings with me. Read reviews.

Monday [March] *24th* Clear & milder. Read.

Tuesday 25th Rain. Receive memoir of young Flagg from his father. I am up as usual & I hope better, but very feeble. I have not seen Mott for four days, Francis very attentive. Read reviews. Write to Mr Scott for my Manuscript

Wed[y] March 26th 1834. Clear & colder than some time back. Th: 49. It is now 4 weeks since the operation. I sit up to day with more ease. Receive yesterday my M. S. from Mr Scott. May I hope shortly to proceed with my work. Read for amusement.

Thursday [March] *27th* Clear & cool. Receive yesterday a very ingenious sheet of caricatures from D. C. Johnson, Boston. I feel to day very inanimate & weak. My companion in London Thos. Moore Agent for British packets &c, called & I saw him. E Hicks likewise. Read a little. Moore says Newton is not dead.

Friday [March] *28*. Clear & warmer. I do not feel any accession of strength. West in a letter to Lord Elgin in 1811 thus speaks of the Phidian Marbles of the Parthenon "In the last production of my pencil which I now invite your Lordship to see, it has been my ambition though at a very advanced period of life, to introduce those refinements in art, which are so distinguished in your collection. Had I been blessed with seeing & studying these emanations of genius at an earlier period of life, the sentiment of their pre-eminence would have animated all my exertions; and more character and animation and expression and life would have pervaded my humble attempts at historical painting." (To be introduced in life of West.) W W Woolsey, his son Theodore & Wm. S. Johnson with me. Hear my daughter read

Sat[y] March 29th 1834 Clear & mild. Again I am sitting up, languid & weary. I have not seen Mott for 3 days. Read. Th: 58

Sunday 30th Clear & cold. Weir calls & sitts with me. Morse has seen Leslie who certainly goes. The place is to be offer'd to Weir, who if so will accept. The Washington pictures probably stop'd. Leslie's picture of Columbus & Egg very fine

Monday [March] *31st* Clear & cold. Messrs. Cole & Cummings with me yesterday. Cole had been to West Point to see Leslie; who having left his wife's mother in his furnished house in London, a lease unexpired, returns to renew the lease & hastens as to a home. One of the reasons for disapointment is the uncertainty of the continuance of the institution. He has been employed in the school and has made drawings for it. Messrs. Aspinwal & B W Rogers with me yesterday. My feelings continue much the same & I have not yet seen Mott since Wed^{y} last.

Tuesday April 1st. Rain. Mild. Mott came yesterday noon & says the wound is closing well. The internal injuries he does not pronounce upon, but waits the healing of the incision. Charles Woolsey & wife with me yesterday. To day my hours of sitting up are more comfortable. Write to C. C. Wright respecting a packet he was to have sent to Mr Tefts which is not received. Read Miss Martineau. My daughter reads to me as I lie in bed.

Wed^{y} Ap^{l} 2d Rain. Read Mirror &c I am as yesterday apparently. It is now 5 Weeks since the operation & have gained some strength. W. S. Johnson announces to us another son. A. Rogers with me.

Thursday Ap^{l} 3d 1834. Fine clear day. I am up & comfortable. My strength encreases. I do not understand the extent of the injury I have received from the stone & the operation of dissecting it from the bladder & prostrate gland, but I have hopes that nature is operating a remedy. I sincerely beleived it to be my duty & the will of God that I should undergo this operation & to his will I hope in all to resign myself with thanks & gratitude. Read a little & think a little relatively to my Hist^{y} of Art. I have not ceased many days from occasionally thinking of it. T[homas] W. Moore call'd & left with me some English papers after sitting a while.

Friday [April] *4th* Fine clear day. I am up before 9 OClock & comfortable. But the injury done to essential parts appears to me great. Read Eng: papers &c &c

Sat^{y} [April] *5th* Fine clear day. Dr Mott was with me last Monday & not since. McLean yesterday. My strength encreases. Write to C. R. Leslie. Read Miss Martineau.

Sunday [April] *6th* A cold March day. I hope my general health is better. Read Miss Martineau. Cole with me, says pictures are coming in for our exhibition, that Government have made offers to Leslie. The Vice Chancellor [William T. McCoun] & his sons Sidney & Joe, with me.

Monday [April] *7th* Rain. My general feelings as to health are improving. A. Robertson with me, says C. C. Wright has sent the Autographs to Tefts. Dr. Francis presents me with life of Thos. Eddy prefixed to which is a pretty good engraving by [Thomas] Illman from my portrait for the N. Y. Hospital. Read.

Tuesday April 8th 1834. Rain. My strength encreases slowly. Read Eddy's life. Messrs. Cole & Cummings with me

Wed^y [April] *9th* Clearing. Th: 56. Read Eddy &c. Mott appears to have abandon'd me. McLean says he speaks favourably of the internal difficulties of my case. It is now six weeks since the operation which McLean says was fifty times more severe than any operation for the stone he ever witnessed. Write a little for my hist^y of Arts. *Ab^t 1 O'Clock Mott with me.*

Thursday [April] *10th* Rise at ½ past 10 after a night of fever & sweating, feeling feeble & dispirited. It still rains. Read in Reviews. Some years ago I heard [Joseph] Lancaster (whose name has been given to a system of teaching) lecture at Norfolk Va. A few years after I met him at Saratoga Springs & again heard him. I pronounced him a Quack. I find a coinciding opinion in a letter from Sir Walter Scott to Potwhale Kenwan "Lancaster is a mountebank."

Friday [April] *11th* Clear. Th: 56. Up at 9 OClock Read & write a little on hist: Arts. I do not experience returning strength for some days.

Saturday [April] *12th* Clear. Th: 58. Write a little on Hist: Arts: Read. *Sculpture by West. Portfolio 1810.* These two mem: were made in presence of C R Leslie who with Morse paid me a very pleasant visit. He persists in going home & he will answer any queries I make. Leslie appears younger than I anticipated, is frank in his manner & very prepossessing. The sculpture by West was the apotheosis of Nelson of which Morse is to give me more. The portfolio contains a letter from West respecting Sully which perhaps I have already noticed. Mr. Al. Robertson came in. Dr Hosack bro^t some letters & papers.

Sunday April 13th 1834. Clear Th: 62. I feel an encrease of Strength & went down stairs this morning. Read & write. J. F. Cooper with me an hour almost wild with politics. The after part of the day I am not so well again. Th: 66.

Monday [April] *14th* Clear. Th: 66. I know of no change in my health. Yesterday Mason, Cole & Mr Aspinwall sat with me. Cole says the exhibition of his picture [179] yields poorly. Read and write a little. Dr Mott with me, he wishes me to gain more strength before he attempts to rectify my disease further & recommend air & riding.

Tuesday [April] *15th* Is memorable as the first day I have been out since the day before New Year, *when* I had flattered myself that I was getting well & did not yet know my disease, although confined for nearly the whole of December. I ought to be very thankful for the portion of health restored & hope! I am & do. The grass in Washington Square, the early leafing trees, the fresh air was all delightfull for a time.

[179] *Angels appearing to the shepherds.*

THOMAS EDDY (1758-1827)
By William Dunlap, 1827
(Courtesy of The New York Hospital)

Wed^y April 16th 1834. Clear. Th: 68 before 8 OClock A M. Walk in Washing^n Square with my daughter's aid. Write on Hist^y Arts. Read in Blackwood. Seven weeks have passed since the cruel operation. I this day sat up 9 hours.

Thursday [April] *17th* Clear. Ther: 68. Up at 7 A. M. Write on hist: Arts. Walk with my daughter & receive much pleasure. Afternoon Dr Francis with us. *Th: 74.* Arch^d Rogers with us & his fine family who have all been anxiously attentive to me.

Friday [April] *18th* Clear. Th: 64. Up at ½ past 8, feeble. Walk a little way with no pleasure & more fatigue than before. Read.

Sat^y [April] *19th* Rain. No improvement in my health. Receive [Mosely I.] Danforth's beautiful print from Leslie's picture the Widow & Uncle Toby, but from whom I know not or whether as a present or merely to examine. Write Neagle & to Joscelyn. I find written in pencil on the back of the print "presented to Mr Dunlap by Mr Leslie" Write on Hist: Art. Read with pleasure "Sketches of Fashionable life."

Sunday [April] *20th* Clear. Th: 62. Read as yesterday. Walk in ye Square with my Wife. McLean calls. My symptoms much the same, my strength perhaps increasing. Write on Hist. of Art. Messrs. Cole & Cummings with me. T. W. Moore & B. W. Rogers. Leslie by invitation met the Artists of the National Academy & their friends on the ev^g of ye 15th at Clinton Hall

Monday 21st Ap^l 1834. Light clouds Th: 64. Write on Hist. Art. Take a short & painful walk: read in Sparks' Amer: Biography. Night rain & thunder.

Tuesday 22d. Th: 62. Showers. Read as above, feel somewhat better. Write on Hist: of Art.

Wed^y 23d Rain. Th: 56. Eight weeks, I am no better than a week ago, that I can perceive. Write on Hist: Art. [Lewis P.] Clover (Late ye firm of Parker & Clover) called & says the subscription list has encreased. Read Magazines.

Thursday [April] *24th* Clear. Windy. Th: 58. Write on Hist. Art. Mr Al. Robertson with me. Try a little walk but find it too cold. Read parts of Cooper's Pilot. Receive an interesting letter from Professor Goodrich [180] of Yale College respecting the Smybert picture of Dean Berkely & family.

Friday [April] *25th* Th: 55 but out doors snow which melts as it falls. Write on Hist Art. Read Pilot.

Sat^y [April] *26.* Clear. Th: 54. I feel stronger this morning. Write on Hist. Art. Read Pilot. Rain in ye afternoon & night.

Sunday [April] *27th* Clear. Th: 52. Read & write on Hist. Art. Clouds & light snow. Cold high wind all day. Cole & Cummings my only visitors. I have little ease to day.

Monday [April] *28th* Windy. Th: 50. I have not seen Mott since the 9th. Write to Chester Harding & to Henry Greenough care of his father David Greenough Esqr Boston, & to Professor Goodrich New Haven & to Harding of Buffalo. Write on hist: Art. Try a walk but find too much wind. Dr McLean with me. Read in Pres: Dwights travels. Note to write to Robt. Mills Washington resp^g James Hoban.

April 29th 1834. Showers. Th: 54. On settling my bank book find that I have in N. Y. Bank 109.97. Look at my memoranda & see that I have omitted in previous statem^{ts} to credit ye Bank with last rent paid Judson

[180] Chauncey A. Goodrich's letter, dated Yale College, April 20, 1834, is printed in Dunlap's *Arts of Design,* I, 28-30.

68.75 & probably a check for 25. Receive an interesting letter from Mr Lambdin who now resides at Louisville Read Gibbon. Dr Mott has been with me & recommends my present course till we see what Nature will do for me.

Wed^{y} [April] *30th* Clear. Th: 56. Nine weeks since the operation. I have improved in strength the last week. Walk with my Wife to see Mrs. Beach Lawrence. The day has not passed without sufferring a pain at night in my right hip. Read Gibbon & Shakespere.

Thursday May 1st 1834. Clear. Th: 59. Write on hist. Art. Freeman comes to see me. Vandechamp $30,000 & is going home, a good painter & a gentleman, having made his fortune in New Orleans in 3 years. Jarvis has returned to New York. Read in Gibbon & Trevelyan. Walk a little way.

Friday [May] *2d* Clear. Th: 58. Read Trevelyan. Write on hist: Art. Ev^{g} Ingham with me. The Nat. Acad^{y} Exhib^{n} is receiving ab^{t} 30 dollars a day.

Sat^{y} *May 3d 1834.* Clear. Th: 61. I have no certainty of improvem^{t} in my health. Read in Gibbon. Write on Hist. Art. Williamson of Norfolk has been in N. Y. and did not see me. This is strange. He left word & his name at Nat. Acad^{y} but *could not* come to see me. Alex Robertson with me, says that Arch^{d} his brother knew all the circumstances of Raeburn's marriage, that he married the widow of a man who shot himself, & that all Cunninghams story of the young lady, the picture &c &c is romance.

Sunday [May] *4th* Clear. Th: 63. Read Gibbon, & write on hist. Art. J. F. Cooper with me from 10 to 1. McLean with me. Ev^{g} at 5 take a pleasant walk in the Square. Messrs. Ingham & Cummings with me & then the two brothers [Frederick S. and Alfred T.] Agate.

Monday [May] *5th* Clouds. Th: 62. Read Gibbon. Write of Hist. Art. Read Pepys. Rain very hard & all night.

Tuesday [May] *6th* Clear. Th. 62. Read Pepys. Write on hist. Art. Walk to the Square, return & continue to write. Ev[g] Cole and Cummings with me.

Wed[y] [May] *7th* Rain. Th: 62. Ten weeks since the operation & my state (in my opinion) very doubtfull. Read Gibbon & Pepys & write on Hist: Art. Much unwell the afternoon.

Thursday [May] 8th Clear. Th: 62. My feelings are better to day. Read Gibbon & Pepys. Write on Hist: Art. Write to Robert Mills of Washington. McLean with me & speaks encouragingly. Walk a little. Showers & again clear. Read Pepys, a most contemptible coxcomb surrounded by infamy & knavery.

Friday May 9th 1834. Clear. Th: 62. Walk in the Square. Read Gibbon. Write on Hist: Art. Read Pepys.

Sat[y] 10th Clouds & Showers. Th: 62. Read Gibbon. Write on hist. Art. Al[r] Robertson with me. Read in Ritchies "Ghost hunter."

Sunday 11th Clouds. Th: 60. Read & write on Hist: Art: J. F. Cooper with me. Afternoon W. Sidney McCoun, Ingham & Cummings. Rain.

Monday [May] *12th* Clouds. Th: 63. Read Gibbon. Write on hist Art. Arch[d] Robertson with me. He says Cunninghams acct. of [Sir Henry] Raeburn's marriage is all a romance. That he married a widow of the name of Leslie who had children & property, & by this aid visited Rome. Clouds & high wind.

Tuesday [May] *13th* Sun & clouds. Th: 58. Read Gibbon. Write on Hist. Art Read Romances. The cold winds prevent going out.

Wed[y] [May] *14th* Clear. Th: 54. Eleven weeks since the operation, yet very weak & with little perfect ease. Read Gibbon. Write on Hist. Art. Ev[g] Doctor Porter wth me. Begin Miss Edgeworth's Helen.

Thursday [May] *15th* Clear. Th: 54. Out doors last night. Ice. "In all but *truth* there is a principle of decay & dissolution." Miss Edgeworth. Freeman calls on me & is going West. S. L Fairfield Editor of the North American Mag: brings me introductions from Neagle. Write by him to Edm[d] A Wetmore. Write on Hist. Art. Read Miss Edgeworth. Ev[g] Gulian C. Verplank with me. He brought extracts from letters written in 1773 & 1775 from Gulian Verplank his grandfathers brother relative to West & Copley.

Friday 16th May 1834. Th: 54. Clear & cold, ice every night. Read Miss Edgeworth. Write on Hist. Art. Dr. Mott with me, his last visit was the 29th Ap[l]. He says I am better & may expect improvement—it comes slowly. Frazee (John) calls on me says he has written part of the memorandum for [me], is going to Richmond Va. to take a bust of Judge [John] Marshall & will give me his memor. when he comes back & Launitz's. Takes a memorandum & is to see Mrs Edwards, Bembridge's sister & on J. Robertson Esq[re] Cashier of the Branch Bank. Ev[g] Weir & Mr Hoxie call on me. W. goes to West Point tomorrow, is to finish his memoir there for me, presses me to come & stay a week with him by & bye.

Sat[y] [May] *17th* Th: 54. Clouds. Read Miss Edgeworth. Write on hist: Arts. Alex Robertson with me. Receive letter from Robt. M. Sully with memoir & again promise of examining the old Virginia family pictures. Mr Hicks with me.

Sunday [May] *18th* Clear. Th: 60. Walk in the Square for the first time alone since my illness. Write to Robt. M. Sully, A[nthony] L[ewis] De Rose. Read review.

Write on hist. Art. J. A. Mason with me, brings memoir of Wm Mason & takes his book on players Country houses &c. Walk again. Th: 64. Ev^{g} J. F. Cooper with me.

Monday [May] *19th* Clear. Th: 62. Read review. Walk in ye Square. Write on Hist. Art. Th: 66. Walk again Letter from W. A. Whitehead now at Perth Amboy. I rise now about 7 & become tired enough to go to bed from 5 to 7 in ye evening.

Tuesday May 20th 1834. Hazy. Th: 70. Read in Gibbon. Write on hist. Art. Th: 72. Walk too warm, & my feelings adverse to exercise. Afternoon, Walk & find it too cool. Read Gentleman's Mag. 1815.

Wed^{y} [May] *21st* Hazy. Th: 66. Read. Walk but in pain. Meet Nelson in the Square. Write of Hist. Arts. Twelve weeks since the operation. Ab^{t} noon ride in ye Stage with my daughter up the 8th Avenue & back with pleasure. Read Mag.

Thursday [May] *22d* Clear. Th: 70. Read life of A. Hamilton by his son John. Walk in Square. Write on Hist. Art: Dr Francis & afterward McLean with me. Read Pilgrims of the Rhine. A very trifling book. Bulwer says it has given him more pleasure in the writing than his other works—what says the reader? Miss Wright called & brought an english notice of her grandmother in London Mag. of 1775.

Friday [May] *23d* Cloudy, misty. Th: 66. Read Bulwer. Write on Hist. Art. Clear. Not well enough to go out.

Sat^{y} [May] *24th* Clear. Th: 68. Write on Hist. Art. A note to Morse. Ride in omnibus to Fulton Street, call on Clover, Morris (not in) Go to Exh^{n} of Nat: Acad^{y}. Ride home, fatigued & hot. Th: 77 in the usual cool place in my entry & rises to 78. Ev^{g} lightning, rain.

Sunday [May] *25th* Clear. Th: 73. Walk in square, read & write. Endeavour to make correct lists of subscribers to my work. Read in A Hamilton's life by his son John C. Th: 76. Thunder & hard rain. Ev^{g} Cummings with me.

Monday [May] *26th* Clouds. Th: 66. Read in Life of Hamilton. Write on Hist. Arts. Walk twice to day but in pain. Alex Robertson with me in y^{e} Even^{g}.

Tuesday May 27th 1834 Clouds. Th: 68. Draw 20 dolls from Bank leaving $89.97. Write on Hist: Arts. Read in Life Hamilton. Walk with more ease & entirely round Washington Square. Miss Deming calls on us. She has improved in her painting. Clear & pleasant.

Wed^{y} [May] *28th* Clouds. Th: 64. Write on Hist: Art: Read in Moliere in y^{e} original. Cold rain, begins ab^{t} 3 P. M. and continues all night very hard as I am obliged to know as I pass a sleepless night from cholic. Sleep in the morning.

Thursday [May] *29th* Cold rain. Th: 60. Read Moliere. Write on hist. Art. Incessant rain.

Friday [May] *30th* Clouds. Th: 60. Read Moliere. Write on Hist. Art.

Sat^{y} [May] *31st* Clouds but appearance of clear^{g}. Th: 58. Read Moliere. Write on hist Arts. Ride to Read St. & call on Cummings & wife. Cole comes in & I walk with him to see his Angels & shephards part of which is sublime. The Ange[l] a failure & he promises to repaint that corner. He has lost by the exhibition upwards of $90. I see [Robert Ball] Hughes Uncle Toby & Widow which is a poor thing. It has been exhibited to pay a dry-good merch^{t} for a debt of Mrs Hugh's 8 or 900 dollars and now the bills are bro^{t} in & neither Hughes or his Creditor will pay the printer, bill poster &c. Go to [John] Parker's

& to Clover's. Go to Morris's & see him & Scott, the printing is to go on immediately. Go to Nat: Acad^{y} Exhibition & Mercantile Library. Ride home without much fatigue and very hungry. Read after dinner in Moliere's Bourgeois Gentilhomme & Morris Mirror. Take from Morris a Book with subscibers names to complete

Sunday June 1st 1834 Hard rain Th 60. Attend to subscription list. Write on Hist. Art. Read Moliere. Correct 2d proof of 1st sheet Hist. Arts. Mr Scotts Mem.

Composition	254.40
Press	95.40
	349.80
63 reams paper @ $4........	252
Binding	150
As I have chosen paper at $4.75 I must add........	47.25
For 1000 Copies of ea Vol........	$799. 5

Monday [June] *2d* Clouds clear away. Th: 64 Write on Hist. Art. Walk in y^{e} Square. Th: rises to 68; out doors warmer. Aft^{n} high wind. Ride up 8th Avenue to 39th Street. Cole & Cumming with me. Ev^{g} Morse & J. F. Cooper with me. Smith, a painter lives now at Florence who was born in New York or on Long Island about the year 1747 and in 1764 having painted & determined to be a painter went to Italy & has there remained ever since. Morse & Cooper knew the old gentleman personally. He never excelld as an Artist & has probably made picture dealing a business.

Tuesday [June] *3d* Clear. Th: 63. Write in Hist. Arts. Ride to Warren St^{t} Call on Dr McLean & sit with Miss [Ann S.] Glass. Call on W. S. Johnson (not at home) Call on Mrs McCoun & sit with her. To Mirror Office, Morris not in, he is going to Charleston. Give Lawson my name to honor Forest with a dinner $5 express condition that I pay nothing but L to write pd opposite. See John Inman. Ride home. James Kent in y^e^ carriage who seem's unconscious of my long sufferrings. Ev^g^ John Woolsey with us.

*Wed^y^* [June] *4*. Clear. Up & writing on Hist. Arts at 6 OClock. Fourteen weeks since the operation. Ride to Mirror Office & see Morris. Call on Rubens Peale & ascertain that his father never returned to England after his visit from 1771 to 1774. Walk to Durand's former place of abode & found that he has removed to 94 Duane Street. Walk to Ingham's & sat with him. Captn [Philip F.] Voorhees of the Navy came in and renewed acquaintance reminding me of my Wife & self travelling with him from Norfolk. We were much pleased with him then. He now had a Wife with him. Rode to upper part of Broadway & then walk to St. Mark's Place to see J. F. Cooper, he not at home & Mrs. C. not well. Meet Mrs Kent in ye street, & tho' her husband did not yesterday seem to know I had been ill, she did & invited me back to the house: I pursued my walk home, a little too far, but still pleasant. Afternoon walk in the Square. Read Moliere & write on Hist: Art: Call on my neighbour E. Hicks. Ev^g^ the son [181] of S. Conant called to see me & I was glad to send kind remembrances to his grandfather & uncles at Brandon.

Thursday June 5th 1834. Hard rain now & all last night. Write on Hist. Art. Th: 64. Read in Moliere & Cunningham's painters. Rain storm all day.

Friday [June] *6th* Clear. Th: 64. Write on Hist: Art: Walk over to J. F. Cooper, he was out. Walk to Br^d^ Way & take stage to Ann St^t^. See Morris. Go to Mercantile Library & Nat^l^ Acad^y^ Exhibition room. Read in New Engl^d^ Mag. on Engravers. Write. Walk. Evening J. F.

[181] Probably Claudius B. Conant, son of Samuel S. Conant (1797-1830), and grandson of John Conant (1773-1856) of Brandon, Vermont. See F. O. Conant, *History of the Conant Family* (1887), 299, 389.

Cooper with me & advises me to publish my work myself (if I do not sell the edition) giving credit & mak[s] discount according to the numbers taken by the individual Bookseller.

Sat[y] June 7th 1834. Receive corrected proof from Mr Scott & more definite information respecting the cost of printing & binding 2 Vols of 432 pages each.

For 1000 copies of a vol: of 432 pages

Composition	254.40
Press	95.40
63 reams of paper @ 4.75....	299.25
Binding	150.
For making alterations on the proofs (perhaps)	50.
ea: Vol.	$849. 5

Of course the cost of the two vols will be, when bound $1698.10

For 1500 copies of a Vol. of 432 pages

Composition	254.40
Press	143.10
95 reams paper @ 4.75......	451.25
Binding	225.
Alteration on proofs	50.
ea vol	$1123.75

or for the 2 Vols 2247.50

Correct proof. Write of Hist. Art. Walk to St. Marks Place & at 10 partake of breakfast with J. F. Cooper and family. My breakfast was before seven. We walked to Bleeker St[t] & rode to Ann St[t]. I saw Scott at his printing office. Call on Cummings & on Durand & then ride home. Mr Bradish port[t] painter & Mr Dezang of Geneva were waiting for me. Th: 72. Write on Hist. Art. Mr. Davis call'd on me & is to give me a note of the Designs furnished for public buildings by Mr Ithael Town & himself in various parts of y[e] U. S. J. F. Cooper calls & brings

JOHN ADAMS CONANT (1800-1886)
By William Dunlap, 1829
(Courtesy of The Metropolitan Museum of Art, New York)

me a notice of booksellers & publishers making for sale in Aug[t] next, and his letter to his Countrymen

Sunday June 8th 1834. Clear. Th: 69. My health & strength is improving perceptibly. Read in Cooper's letter. Walk round the Square before 8 OClock. In 1831 H. Greenough & Morse came from Italy to Paris & went to Gaglianini's to obtain J. F. C's address. Finish Cooper's letter which has great force & truth. Walk. Dr McLean calls & sits with me. Write at G. P. Morris for the Mirror. Th: 74 to 76. Walk in the ev[g]. J. F. Cooper calls & sits with us.

Monday [June] *9th* Clear. Th: at 6 A. M. 72. Correcting proof. At 10 A. M. Th: 76. Write on Hist. Arts Read in Portfolio 3 P. M. Th 82. It is always to be remembered y[t] my Th: hangs in a cool entry, 2d story or first floor. Pay Charles Judson $68.75 for rent to 1st of May last; leaves in Bank $109.97

68.75

$41.22

Write on hist. Arts. I have in Bank now $21.22.

Tuesday [June] *10th* Clear. Th: at 6 A. M. 76. Write on Hist. Art. I am deprived of y[e] exercise of walking by a lame foot. Try the experiment of omitting my single glass of wine or half tumbler of brandy tody as I had before been obliged to reject porter & ale, and make my dinner to day of Bread & Milk & strawberries. Afternoon ride up the 8th Avenue to 13th St[t] & back. The Th: rose to 80 & has fallen to 76 at 4 P. M. Read Cunninghams Northecoat. I have to think my milk dinner will help me.

Wed[y] June 11th. Rain y[e] night. Clouds Th: 76. Fifteen weeks since the operation. I gain strength but my walks are stopt by my swelled foot. Write on Hist. Art. Receive letter from Anthony Lewis De Rose, with biography & subscription. Continue the Milk diet. Ride for about 50

minutes in the afternoon in y[e] Stage. Read Cunningham. What a sad mean scoundrel he proves Northcote to have been. Repeats [William] Hazlitts stupid attack upon J. F. Cooper. Note Hazlitts grammer "nor wished it to be forgotten by others, that he was the American Walter Scott; the real one" that is the real American Walter Scott—who is he? "never troubled himself about the matter.

Thursday June 12th 1834. Clear. Th: 72. Read in Cunningham. Write on Hist. Art. Ride to Leonard St[t] to see G. C. Verplank. Gone to Phil[a]. Call on Ingham & Herring receive 12th No. National Portrait Gallery. Ride home before eleven & write on Hist. Art. Receive letter from Henry Greenough who is to see Allston & then communicate to me. Read Herring's 12th No. One good plate in it, Col[l] [Aaron] Ogden by [Asher B.] Durand. Afternoon T. S. Cummings & H. Inman with me, the latter renews his promises & tells me that Henry Pratt, proprietor of the admired Garden on the Schuylkill told him that his father was a painter.

Friday June 13th Clear. Ther 70 Write on Hist. Art. Read Cunningham. Write to Henry Pratt of Phil[a] respecting his father.

Sunday 14th [*sic for 15th*] Clear. Th: 66. On Friday I was attacked with Diarrhoea which in the night was violent & required medical advise. Francis came to me. I had in vain attempted to take laudanum, which was rejected with puking, by adding 2 drops of oil of Cinnamon to 30 drops of laudanum the stomach received it, & baths of flannel & Brandy & Vinegar stopt the complaint after two repetitions. I am seated as usual this morning, having taken by order, a dose of [illegible] magnesia. I was at ease during the day, & night sleeping much. Afternoon I have hitherto to day been at my ease. Francis & McLean both with me. Write on Hist: Art. Read Cunningham. Called upon by the younger Agate who says his brother [Frederick S. Agate] is going to Italy in the Autumn. Rain all night.

Monday June 15th [*sic for 16th*] *1834*. Clouds. Th: 68. Recovering I hope from the attack of Diarrhoea. Read Cunningham. Draw from Bank $20, leaving $1.22. Write on Hist Art. Pass a comfortable day

Tuesday [June] *16th* Clouds. Th: 67. Up at 5 OClock & at my writing after quiet sleep without laudanum. I have written several pages to day. Afternoon read Edinburgh Review on Life of Sir John Moore. Rain without & pain within. A stormy night with thunder.

Wed[y] [June] *17th* Clear. Th: 68. Sixteen weeks since the operation. Cholic all night. No laudanum. Write on Hist: Art. Finish my Autobiography bringing it up to 1833. Read Edin: Review. Ride up 8th Avenue. Call on the daughters of Joseph Wright.

Thursday [June] *18th* Clear. Th: 69 at 6 A M. Write on Hist. Art. Pine. Th: 72 at 2 P. M. Rode to Warren Street & arranged with Wm T. McCoun to endorse my note or notes for paper. Walk to Clinton Hall. To my printers, to Mirror Office & then to Town & Davis's & Morse's new room. Receive invitation to attend private Exhibition of 4 Original pictures by Pan[n]ini representing the monuments of Ancient & Modern Rome, this coming at 8 OClock Academy, Barclay Street. Rec[d] from Wm S. Johnson an acct. of the substituting a copy for the original of a portrait by Stuart. Write for some hours on Hist: Art. Walk in Square, & call on Mrs De Rose to acknowledge receit of her husband's letter. Read Edin: Review

Friday June 19th 1834 Clear. Th: 70 at 5 A M. Write on Hist. Art. Ride to Leonard St[t] & call on Verplank—accept his invitation to visit the Lunatic Asylum with him tomorrow. Take a long walk to see old pictures &

found them packt up. Go to Clinton Hall, Mirror Office & ride home. Write on Hist. Art. Read Ed: Review. To day in the street a woman accosted me by name who I immediately recognized as the Madam Jumel Aaron Burr married about a year back. She had been a supernumary at the Theatre before Jumel married her. "You dont know me Mr Dunlap" "Oh, yes, Mrs Burr, How does Col[l] Burr do?" "O, I dont see him any more. He got 13,000 dollars of my property, and spent it all or gave it away & had money to buy him a dinner. I had a new Carriage & pair of horses cost me 1000 dollars he took them & sold them for 500." "Where does Col[l] Burr reside now?" "With a silver Smith in the Bowery of the name of Burr—young Aaron Burr." I turn'd off glad to part from her. What confidence can be placed in the words of such a woman it is hard to say, but Burr's marrying her makes any thing told of him credible. I pass a night of cholic.

Sat[y] June 20th Clear. Th: at 5 A M 70. Write on Hist: Art. At 12 G. C. Verplank & Capt[n] [James] Lovet called with a Coach & we rode out to the Lunatic Assylum: the happy project of Thos. Eddy, whose portrait, the 2d I painted for the Hospital hangs in the Governors' room. I accompanied the Commissioners through the building erected for the most outrageous or noisy patients of the Males, & saw some curious & some pitiable objects. Doctor [James] McDonald the very intelligent physician of the institution accompanied us. There was outrageous maniac, locked in his room, naked & lying in hay, who after answering a question as to his sleeping, burst into horrible outcries, shouts & yells. He would keep no clothes on him, tearing them off, but at times was more quiet & was then permitted to go out with a keeper. There was but one other who had any restraint & that was a leathern belt which passed round his body & arms, leaving his hands at partial liberty. He was very anxious to know when he should let out. The Doctor told him that after the strap or belt could be taken from his arms he might soon be set at liberty, but reminded him that he had misbehaved when his arms were free. Some were silent & one sunk into perfect idiocy, but generally they were lively & talkative. One very bustling young man addressed every body, gave the characters of the inmates & called upon me to see the finest head and face in the world—"he's an Indian" said he "but such a head you never saw" I followed him to a tall swarthy stupid looking figure, whose dark hair he push'd back that I might see his forehead. "There" said he "There's a face, is it not more than human, the countenance of a God rather than a man." This was said of a physiognomy of the most common kind made pitiably stupid by disease. I saw this chatterer shewing a small box to some one filled with pebbles which he said were jewels. Perhaps the most curious object was Andrews, a man convicted of murder, but proved to be insane. He is 50 years of age or more, wears his grey beard long over his breast, & his hair cut short. He was pleased by the salutations of the Commissioners, knew them, and after answering some questions rationally commenced with astonishing volubility on his favourite topics. He was asked if he would be glad to see Governor Marcy. "No. He's my enemy, and you are my enemy." "Would you know him?" "How should I know him when I never saw him?" "Is this gentleman Govr Marcy?" pointing to me. "No. How do you do, Sir" and shaking hands with me. "Do you live in New York." "Yes." "Are you mad?" "not more than most folks." "I shot that man who was killed at [blank]. My orders are obeyed, if I say shoot that man, it is done. They fire when I give the word as a regiment fires at the command of its Colonel. I say it & they are dead. When the powder Mills blew up at [blank] and [blank] and [blank] were killed, I did it! Besides there is the Emperor of China and his sister the Empress." And then he flew off again, but dwelling principally upon his power to destroy. The patients having dined many of them were lounging under a shed, with benches, where they enjoyed the open air. One young gentleman was walking rapidly from one end to the other readin[g] Freneau's poems. "That" said V. "is Doctor

Loring once a prominent young man & well educated." He entered freely into conversation & connectedly, but hurried & in manner, though apparently happy. His mother kept a great boarding hous[e] in N. Y. years ago, & I remember a brother once in the U. S. service. Capt[n] Lovet asked him if he was not coming to town soon. "No" was his reply, "Mrs [blank] and her daughters often enquire after you." "Do they live in [blank] Street yet?" "In the same place. One of the daughters is lately married." "Which?" and I perceive no symptom of insanity but in the eye, & constant smile. A tall young man with great glee invited every one to toss coppers, "head or tail" with him. He wanted some silver, but he would play for a box of segars. The Doctor toss'd a cent with him, he first cried "head" then "tail" as it came down & insisted very pleasantly that he had won the cigars. I was told that he became insane in electioneering, with its attendant drinking & would soon be well.

My strength did not suffice to go through the main building, & I left my companions for rest & a sopha. We dined at an excellent table, Mrs [Ira] Ford, wife of the principal presiding, her husband being absent, and a little after 4 began our return ride loaded with flowers. Every thing about this excellent institution is beautiful & in perfect order. I hope to see the part I most interesting [*sic*] at another visit. The ride appears to have done me service. Ev[g] looking over Dennie's Portfolio 1st Vol.

Sunday June 21st 1834. Th: 70. Light clouds. Write on hist: Art. Have return of Diarroeha, go to bed, apply brandy & take laudanum. Am relieved & in the afternoon, get up & write for some hours. Examine Dennies portfolio & make extracts.

Monday [June] *22d* [*sic* for 23rd] Clear. Th: at 5 A. M. 73. Write on Hist. Art. Th: at 11, 77 at 12, 79. Attack of Diarroeha again & again Laudanum & bed at 4 P. M. Ev[g] look over Dennie's Portfolio.

Tuesday [June] *23d* [*sic for 24th*] After rain, clouds. Th: at 5 A M 74. Write on Hist. Arts. Rain again. Clear. Examine portfolio. Write on Hist. Art. 4 P. M. Th: 80. Evening, rain & Thunder

Wed^y June 24th 1834. Light Clouds. Th: at ½ past 5 A M. 75. This is seventeen weeks since the operation. My strength has diminished by Diarroeha. Write on hist. Art. Suffer from the injurd Bladder. Write on H. A. Ev^g Diarroeha. Laudanum & Brandy application. Look over Portfolio for 1803.

Thursd^y [June] *25th* Cl: Th: 5 A M. 73. Write on H. A. At 8 oclock rain. Write on H. A. & look over portfolio. At 3 P. M. partially clear. Th: 78. Write on H. A Even^g Diarroeha, laudanum & pain through the night

Friday [June] *26th* Clear. Th: at 5 A M. 72. Write on Hist. Art. after a short walk in ye Square continue writing. Read Gibbon. John Woolsey with us. More comfortable to day.

Sat^y [June] *27.* Clouds. Th: 69 at 5 A M. Write on Hist. Art. Receive notice of Mr Wm Rush from his son. Rain. Mr Alex Robertson with me. From him I received Trumbull's acct. of West's behaviour relative to the panarama [of Niagara Falls] & [Robert] Barker. I read distinctly my acct. of the transaction & he confirms it with the addition that I considered W. as uttering a falshood to him when he call'd on him. Write on Hist. Art. Look over portfolio Vol. 4th. Rain in the night.

Sunday [June] *29th* Clouds. Th: 68. Write on H. Art. Rain. Look over portfolio. Francis with me, says F. Kemble married P[ierce] Butler without the consent of her father who has not spoken to her since but has returned home with 50,000 dollars in his pockets. (dates since the 13th are wrong) Write and look over Portfolio. The day is cloudy & occasional rain. I now get no exercise. Ev^g Cholic, as almost every evening. Health comes slow to the aged.

Monday June 30th 1834. Clear. Th: at 5 A M 69. Write on Hist Arts: between 9 & 10 walk in ye Square & return to my writing. Evening Cholic. I cannot take food, except at breakfast, without this effect, sometimes violent.

Tuesday July 1st. Clear. Th: at ½ past 5 A M 70. Walk in square. Write on Hist Art, until 5 P. M. being stronger than usual. Francis sees me. Look over portfolios. Read in John Randolph's letters.

*Wed^y^* [July] *2d* Rain. Th: 74. at 5 A M. Eighteen weeks since the horrid operation. Write on Hist. Art. Clears. Th: 79. Walk. Write on H. A. and to Mrs [Gill] daughter of C[harles] Catton and to Messrs. A[lvin] Fisher & T[homas] Doughty. Evening & night disturbed & painful. Thunder and rain.

Thursday [July] *3d* Clear. Th: at 5 A M 78. Walk with pleasure in the Square. Write letters to T. Sully jun^r^, John C. Hamilton and Ed^rs^ of American. Begin letter to C. R. Leslie. Ride to Cedar Street, Go up to Library & look over port Folios. Go to Morse's, to American Office, Post Office & ride home. Light showers. Finish letter to Leslie, respecting having the Hist. Art. published in London. Evening Cholic and Diarroeha. Read in ye day Randolph.

Friday [July] *4th* Light Clouds. Th: 75. Get up as usual between 4 & 5 but pain & nausea send me back. Get up better at ½ past 6. Read Randolph. Write on Hist. Art. At 10, Diarroeha & in bed the remainder of the day. Ev^g^ J. F. Cooper called me. He gave me the most rational account of Trumbulls mysterious marriage that I have heard. He says that 7 or 8 years ago, he dined in a company of Gentlemen among whom was my former (perhaps my present) friend Wm Johnson & an English Gentleman. The latter when it happen'd that Trumbull & wife were the subjects of conversation, told this story. There was an old gentleman, formerly a military man, Col^l^ or Genl Williams, who had a young Wife, with whom

Trumbull became too intimate. Finally Williams had intimation that the lovers intended to elope, either *that,* or knowledge of the shame inflicted on him, induced him to have an interview with the seducer of his wife for a settlement. He told him that he knew of his situation with Mrs W. & her preference, that he wished to avoid public scandal; and therefore, offerred Trumbull the lady & 800£ per year during her life, if he would take her, & to save appearances, marry her. This was accordingly done. Mr Johnson afterwards said to Cooper, this is a strange story and it reminds me of a circumstance confirmatory. Walking in Company with my Wife Mr & Mrs Trumbull & an English gentleman & lady, the latter preceded him & Mrs. Johnson & Mrs Trumbull. Trumbull was with the English folks, & they were talking of acquaintances in London. Suddenly Trumbull looked back & said "Do you hear that Mrs W.?" and correcting himself added "Mrs Trumbull." It has often been suggested that Trumbull received this woman from her keeper with an annuity. This is something like it & more probable.

Saturday July 5th 1834. Clouds. Th: 74 at ½ past 5 A. M. Write on Hist. Art. Send by my son to Mr Scott my note in favour of Wm. T. McCoun for $299 25/100 dated July [blank] 1834 to be endorsed by Mr McCoun & given for 31½ reams of paper @ 4.75 for 1 vol: Hist. Art. About 10, lie down & sleep an hour: then write again, far from feeling well. Afternoon lie down & sleep ½ an hour. Write again. No cholic at night, but pain & take laudanum. Sleepless until very late.

Sunday July 6th 1834. Cloud & mist. At 5 A. M. Th: 74. Walk in square. Write on Hist. Art. Write to Wm. A. Whitehead finishing my reminiscences of Amboy. Write to Wm. T. McCoun respecting note & money. Dr McLean with me. B. W. Rogers. Ev^{g} J. F. Cooper. Ev^{g} take a prescription of my friend McLean & am better through ev^{g} & night. Th: 80.

Monday [July] *7th* Clear. Th: at 5 A M 77. Walk in the square. Write on Hist. Art. 10 A M. Th: 80. Continue to write. At 3 P. M. Th: 84. Sleep an hour. Write as before Read Gibbon. Ev[g] pain Receive an invitation to see a collection of pictures from Mr Maddox.

Tuesday [July] *8th* Clear Th: a[t] ½ past 4 A M. 82. Walk in square. Write on H. A. Th: at 7, 80 and at 10, 83, at 11, 84. Finish biography of Malbone. Begin Trott. 2 P M. Th: 86. 4 P. M. 88. Suffer from heat & indigestion. The heat is said to be in the shade out of doors Th: 96.

Wed[y] [July] *9th* Clear. Th: a[t] 5 A M. 83. Write on Hist. Art. 19 Weeks since the operation. At half past eleven A M. Th: 87. Write on Hist. Art. At 12. Th: 88. A south wind springs up & at 4 the Th: is 87. Write on Hist. Art.

Thursday [July] *10th* Clouds. Th: at 5 A M 80. Write on Hist. Art, using notes by R. Sully, received yesterday. Call on Miss Wright & receive letters from her grandmother & notes respecting her father. Call on Illman & desire him to send home my Washington. Afternoon hard rain & thunder. Write on Hist. Art. At 4 P. M. Th: 78, and weather clearing. Ev[g] J. F. Cooper and Morse with me.

Friday 11th July 1834. Light clouds Th: at 5 A. M. 76. Drink Saratoga Water. Write on Arts. Walk in Square, quite cool out. Write again on Hist. Art. On the house being open'd the Th: sinks to 73. At eleven lie down and sleep. Read in Magazine sent me from Phil[a] by S. L. Fairfield with my proposals on the cover. (North American.) After din[n]er write on Hist. Arts. At 2 P M. Th: 75. Write on Hist. Art. Correct proof. Leave in Bank this day $81.22. Ev[g] Mr Verplank call'd to invite me to go with him and Mr Heard to the L Assylum again. I hope I may be well enough to accompany them.

Saturd[y] [July] *12th* Clear. Th: 5 A M. 74. Write on Hist Art. Houdon. Th: at 7 A: M: 72. Walk to Broome St. to see Charles Rhind Esq[re] who through his connection with ship captains and Packet Agents undertakes to forward by proof sheets to Frank Ogden at Liverpool from whence packets & parcels go to the parcel office London & and are distributed. Rhind has been, & is, painting a panoramic View of Constantinople taken from a hill on the Asiatic side & including Galata, Scutari, y[e] Bosphorus &c. It is very interesting.

Go at 12 OClock with G. C. Verplank & James Heard to y[e] L Assylum and visit the various parts of the house & the top of it. Dine & reach home at 5 P. M. The arrangements and appartments of this institution are admirable. A reading room with newspapers & Books, in one of the rooms in the mens division. An appartment devoted to female needle work in one division of the female department. The women, some of them genteelly drest, all very cheerful & much disposd to talk. "Mr Dunlap, would I make a good picture?" enquired a pretty little woman. "Certainly. A very good one." "Ah you would make it so at all events." The widow of Brockholst Livingston was here, a little old woman who I remember a beauty, full of health, tall & of proud deportment. A strange & melancholy scene, although most of the inmates appear happy.

Sunday July 13th 1834. Clouds. A cold N. E. wind. Last night broken rest & no sleep after 2 OClock A M. Up at 4. Walk up the avenue before sun rise but find it too cold. Examine proof. Write. Mr Rhind lets me know that Mr [Joseph] Fowler, Agent of the old line of Liverpool packets has undertaken to forward under special care of the Captains my proof sheets as they are ready. Write to T[homas] J. Leslie Esq[re] West Point for his brother's address in London. Very hard rain. Write on hist: Art. Read Rogers Italy. Rain storm ceases at 8 P. M. I pass a comfortable night.

Monday July 14th 1834. Clears Th: 74 at ½ past 4. Write on Hist. Art. Ride with my wife to Ceder Street. Call on Morse & get C. R. Leslie's address, No. 41 Portman Place, Edgeware Road. Walk to W. W. Woolsey's and to Arch[d] Rogers's. Walk to Wall Street and ride home. Th: 78. Write on Hist: Art. Th: 3 P. M. 82. Call on E Hicks. Ev[g] J. F. Cooper & daughter with us. Sleep well until 3 A M. Up & walk in Square before sun rise.

Tuesday [July] *15th* Clear. Th: 76 at 4 A. M. Examine proofs & write on Hist. Art. Make up a pa[c]kage for C. R. Leslie, containing slip from y[e] Mirror, a note to him, and 2 forms of my book. Carry the above to Mr. Rhind's, Broome St[t]. 8 OClock Th: 79. Write on hist. Art. At 12 Th: 83. Mr Lawson, Forrest's friend, called to ask permission to put my name at the head of the complimentary publication, gold medal, and Dinner to be given to the Tragedian. I consented, but it is not expected that I can either pay money or eat or preside at the dinner. Mr N Rogers called & left memoranda of himself as a painter. Says Mrs Metcalf has her husband's prepared for me. Receive a letter from Sully with notices of C. B. King & says a letter has been sent to me relative to Mr Pratt 10 days ago

Wed[y] [July] *16th* Th: 5 A M. 80. Last night rain & thunder. Clouds. Write on Hist. Art. 20 weeks since the operation. I have a symptom, which makes me fear the accumulation of calculus again, or the pain may proceed from the untreated ulcer. The hot weather enfeebles me. Write to Weir & to Allston, and to Noah. Write on Hist. Art. Th: 82. Disturb'd night.

Thursday July 17th 1834. Clear. Th: 80 at 5 A M. Walk round the square. Write on Hist. Art. Miss Wright calls with further documents relative to her Grandmother & father. Write on Hist. Art. At 11 A M. Th: 82. At 2 P. M. 84. Continue to write on hist Art. 3 P. M. rain & thunder. Write on hist. Art. Ev[g] McLean with me, he directs me to drink the soda water, made by the powders as useful in dissolving or prevent[g] calculus. Cooler.

Friday [July] *18th* Thin clouds. Th: a[t] 5 A M. 77, out o' doors much cooler. Walk in square but painfully. Write on Hist. Art. Ride to Wall Street. Enquire for Mrs Shaw's (the daughter of Pratt) letter in vain at the Post Office. Look for Joscelyn at the Mechanics Bank up stairs, out. Go to Noah's office, to Library, to Stoneall's [182] to enquire for Jarvis, he has no painting room. boards at Mrs Child's [183] (his sister) frequents Stoneals is much changed S: says by paralysis. To Mirror Office & then ride home. Write to Sully & Frazee. Write on Hist. Art. Walk. Ev[g] Cholic subdued by 30 drops of Laudanum. I fear the Soda water disturbs me.

Saturday [July] *19th* Clear. Th: at 5 A M. 72. Write on Hist. Art. Rode to Lib[y] Hist: Soc: and by aid of Doctor Francis got in but we could not find Ceracchi's trial. Rode home & went to bed sick. obliged to send for Francis & obtain ease by Laudanum & hot fomentations. Noah publishes a notice of my Work.

Sunday 20th July 1834. Up by 8 A M. Clear. Th: 70. Far from well. Write to E Forrest. Write on Hist. Art. Read Mirrors. Ev[g] J. F. Cooper with us.

Monday [July] *21st.* Clear. Th: at 5 A. M. 72. Write on Hist. Art. J. W. Jarvis calls & gives me dates & memoranda, but he is a mere wreck, paralytic & his memory affected. At 4 P. M. Th: 76. Write on Hist. Art. Although very feeble & constant uneasiness in y[e] abdomen. Ev[g] correct proofs until 9. Disturbed after going to bed by drums & other military musick to a late hour.

[182] James C. Stoneall, of the Shakespeare Hotel, at the corner of Fulton and Nassau Streets. *N. Y. City Directory,* 1834.

[183] Elizabeth Child, widow of Lewis Child, boarding-house, 331 Pearl Street. *N. Y. Directory,* 1834; *N. Y. Commercial Advertiser,* Jan. 13, 1840.

Tuesday [July] *22d* Th: at 5 A. M. 76. Write & correct proofs. Noon Th: 80. Write on hist. Art. 2 P. M. Th: 82 Write on Hist Art. My health is improved to day. Ev^{g} John Frazee called & says that Mr Robertson Cashier of Bank Richmond Va. acknowledged receit of my letter, took ye memorandum Frazee carried respecting Bembridge & said he would write immediately. Correct proofs.

Wed^{y} [July] *23d* Clear. Th: at 5 A. M. 76. 21 Weeks since the operation, no health. Examine proofs. Make an Index for Hist. Arts, leaving the referred to pages to be added. Frazee calls with a carriage & takes me to see his heads of Danl Webster & [Nathaniel] Bowditch. He has done well. Bowditch makes an ancient philosopher. Th: at noon 81. Write on Hist: Art. Ev^{g} Cholic.

Thursday [July] *24th* Sick with diarrhoea. Clear. Th: at 7 A. M. 78. Correct proofs. Write on Hist: Art: Diarroeha contin^{g} take laudanum. Lawson calls ab^{t} the Forest Dinner. Th: 82. Write on Hist Art. Receive an answer from Weir promising biography & pressing me to pass a week with him. I wish I were well enough! Pretty good night.

Friday July 25th 1834. Clear. Th: at ½ past 5 A M. 79. Write to Weir, and to James E. Cooley No. 151 Br^{d} Way respecting sale of book. Write on Hist: Art: Almost constant pain. Th: at 4 P. M. 84. Write on Hist. Art. Ev^{g} correct proof. Sleep by laudanum.

Saturday [July] *26th* Clear. Th: a[t] 5 A M. 82. Write on Hist. Art. At 11 A M. Th: 85. Write on Hist. Art. Write to Vanderlyn claiming his promise & proposing questions. So far to day my health is better than for some days. At one P. M. Th: 86. Still write on Hist. Art. At 2 P. M. Th: 88. Eat a dinner of Mutton soup with a few clams in it: and again write on Hist Art. At 3 P. M. Th: 90. Strong south wind. Frazee brings me his biography in part. At 5 P. M. Th: 90. At 7 still 90. Leave off writing.

Sunday [July] *27th* Clear. Th: at ½ past 5 A M. 84. Write on Hist. Art. At 11 A M. Th: 88. Write as above. Ev^{g} Al^{r} Robertson with me. Read Doct^{r} Dwights Travels.

Monday [July] *28th* Clear. Th: a[t] 5 A M. 79. The night has been comfortable. Write on Hist. Art and to Francis Ogden Liverpool. Th: at noon 82. Afternoon, read proof. I to day tried a bread & milk dinner, the milk boil'd. Read Dr Dwight. There has arrived by y^{e} S. list of to day 7 vessels from Eng & Fr: with 964 Steerage passengers & 122 Cabin d[itt]o. J. F. Cooper with us. Tells me Morse has sold his picture of y^{e} Louvre & his copy from Rembrandt, the last for $200.

Tuesday July 29th 1834. Light clouds & rain. Th: 79 at 5 A M. Write as usual. Correct proofs. Receive from R W Weir continuation of his biography.

Wed^{y} [July] *30th* Clear. Th: 72. Make up packet of printed sheets for C. R. Leslie, Esqre R. A., No. 41 Portman Place Edgeware Road London, under cover to Francis Ogden Esqre Consul for the U. S. of America at Liverpool. Write as usual. 22 weeks since the operation. Walk to C Rhinds to give him the packet for England. At 3 P. M. Th: 72. Write on Hist. Art. Continue my boil'd milk dinner. Receive notice from Thos. Doughty. Receive a discouraging letter from Cooley respecting sale of book. Receive the biography of Matthew Pratt & very curious it is. Receive letter from Sully. Receive letter from Jos. Irwin Fort Monroe. Walk up the Avenue. Read in Dr Dwight.

Thursday [July] *31st* Clear. Th: 70. Last Evening Mr Cummings & Mr Newcombe called on us. Write on Hist. Art. & to Francis B. Winthrop to say that I will with my wife pay him a visit next week. Leave in Bank $51.22. Messrs. Cummings & Cole called on me, the latter left some sheets of biography. Walk. Correct proof. Write on Hist. Art. Continue the boiled milk dinner. Fennimore Cooper & Morse with us. Morse sold his picture for the price he asked, that he did not mention. J. F. Cooper will write me a letter for my book answering queries.

Friday Aug[t] *1st 1834.* Clear. Th: at 5 A M. 72. Write on Hist. Art. 10 OClock. Without any acute pain my feelings are very wretched. I found relief from 20 drops of laudanum & abstinence. At 5 P. M. Th: 76. Read & correct proofs.

Saturday [Aug.] *2d* Clear. Th: at 5 A M. 72. Correct proof & write on Hist. Art. 9 A. M. unwell with cholic: take 15 drops laudanum. I am relieved. Ride to Library & take Coply's life, walk to Scotts & the book of Franklins letters. Call at Mirror Office & get Greenoughs letter to Morse (N. Y. American) Call at Clovers. Sit a long while in Br[d] Way with B. W. Rogers and Elwin before getting a coach to ride home. Receive letter from Neagle. Mr Lambdin called in my absence. Correct proofs.

Sunday [Aug.] *3* Clear. Th: at 5 A. M. 74. Write on Hist. Art. Walk in square. Th: at noon 78. Write on Hist. Art. Read in Dr Dwights travels. Preparing to go tomorrow with my Wife to F. B. Winthrop's at New Haven. Engage a carriage to be with us at 6 to morrow morning. I am not well enough to go from home, but it may be of service to me. Ev[g] J. F. C. with me.

Monday [Aug.] *4th* Clear. Th: at ½ past 4 A. M. 74. Write on Hist Art. Embark (after riding with my Wife to the Wharf) on board Steamb[t] & leave N. Y. at 7. Pay 75 cents for coach. $4 for passages. Pleasant voyage & land between 1 & 2 P. M. Ride to F. B. Winthrops, pay 50 cents. I see that Hillson died at Louisville of apoplexy in July. H Gahn died of same yesterday N. Y. One case of Cholera in N. Y. Mrs Dwight tells me that Earle painted herself & husband in 1777. Pass a restless night almost.

Tuesday [Aug.] *5th* Up before 5 and read in Sparks' [*Writings of George*] Washington.

High esteem in which Govr [Jonathan] T[rumbull] was held by Washington who considered him as a principal pillar of ye cause. he was in 1775, 65 years old. "We have to guard a semicircle of 8 or 9 miles." "Our works & those of the [enemy] are so near that each sees what the other is doing." (July 1775) "The enemy about a mile from us both at Bunker Hill & Roxbury" Augt Mr [Edmund] Randolph taken into the Gen^{ls} family as aide instead of Mr. [Thomas] Mifflin appointed Qr. Mast^{r} Genl. Mifflin who *had been an aid,* is called Major Mifflin, but when Col^{l} Jos: Reed, Wash^{ns} Sec^{ty} left Cambridge in Oct., Robt Hanson Harrison was invited by W. to become one of his aids was announced as such on his arrival & rec^{d} a Col^{ls} commission serv^{g} as secretary. 2d Nov^{r} "I have been hon^{d} wth your favor of the 30th ult. by *Mr Trumbull*" To Govr T. The Comiss^{y} Genl was Joseph Trumbull, son of ye Govr. Edmund Randolph had been an aid previous to November 1775. Brook Watson was a merchant in Montreal in Octr 1775 when Eth Allen failed in his attempt on the place, in a letter to Wm F[ranklin] Govr of N. J. he says Coll Allen & a few despicable wretches" &c Watson went to Eng^{d} in ye vessel with Allen who was (& his companions kept in irons) & Watson abused Allen during ye voyage.

After breakfast walk up to the "Trumbull" Gallery, a neat building, the Gallery is divided into two Apartments in one is Trumbulls small Revolutionary & miniature portraits &c &c, in the other Berkeley picture, Govr Yale & President Styles too bad to be preserved or the painter called an Artist. Two portraits by Stuart, 2 by Morse, several by Joscelyn, 1 by Kneller (Geo 2d) lackadaysical. No catalogue of this apartm^{t} Col Trumbulls Cata: The Berkeley picture is far better than I had remembered it. The Amanuensis is very good as is the Dean & the painter. This building cost $4000 and will pay a good interest. The 1500 a year is by a subscription principally Danl Wadsword & Prof: Silliman contributing largely as relatives to the painter. So that the pictures are a gift to the Colledge from T. & the subscribers. Go to the Athenaeum. For Kean see New Monthly of London May 1834. Go to Joscelyns & see one very fine head [by] him of Garison the abolitionist or Anarchist. Joscelyn has Capital rooms. Young Flagg is painting in New Haven. Wall is here. Return to Mr W.'s & go to the Library to write & read Sparks again.

It is time & high time that we should discriminate between the mercenary & selfish who took up arms to serve themselves & looked only to promotion & the patriotic soldiers of the revolution. By indiscriminatly making heroes of the hundreds who were worthless and mingling them with real heroic & disinterested spirits of the time, we injure the latter & discourage the efforts of the future patriot. There are men who cry revolutionary soldier with laudatory epithets as loudly for a Gates as for Schuyler a Green or a Washington, who would shout as loudly for the man who resigned because not rank'd where he thought he ought to be and the man who said place me where I can serve best, at the head or in the ranks, for a Morgan or a [blank], for a Whitcomb who tho' having a regiment was omitted in new modell^{g} the army & finding that his men w^{d} not re-enlist if he was omitted offer'd to join them in the ranks or a [blank], again for a col^{l} Brewer who gave up his reg^{t} rather than Whitcomb sh^{d} not have his original station or a [blank] meaning by these blanks men who clamoured for rank or pay, or threw up commissions because disappointed of expected rank or pay. I say we ought to record the true patriots as such & the selfish for their worth. Among the men composing the officers of an Army the mass will have no other than mercenary or ambitious motives, they are neither patriots or heroes. Wm. Palfrey was an aid to Genl Charles Lee & after to Genl Wash^{n} with Lt. Col^{l} Commission. On the 20th Novr Washington mentions Mr. Baylor, Mr Harrison & Mr Moylan as of his family. Mr. Custis (Mrs Washington's son) was with her in Va the last of Novr 1775. Washington says "Such a dearth of public spirit, & such a want of virtue, such stock jobbing, and fertility in all the low arts to obtain advantages in this great change of military arrangement, I never saw before & pray God's mercy that I may never witness again." Yet these are men classed by some with the men who sacrificed or risqued all for their country. And again "Such a mercenary spirit pervades the whole that I should not be surprized at any disaster that might happen." He mentions a Mr White whom he sho[u]ld be sorry to take in his family in consequence of any encouragement formerly given, as it is necessary that his aids "should be ready at their pen." Mrs Washington & her son Custis join'd ye Genl at Cambridge the 11th Decr 1775. In Decr Wash^{n} had still hopes that Col^{l} Reed would rejoin him as an aid. The discontent'd officers threw difficulties in the way of recruiting the army! Yet these are all revolutionary heroes. The 23d of Jany 1776 Wash^{n} solicits Col^{l} Reed to return to his family. "Mr Harrison is the only gentleman of my family that can afford me the least assistance in writing." Mr Moylan is occupied as Commissary. "I know of no persons able to supply your places in this part of the world [with] whom I would choose to live in unbounded confidence." Genl Schuyler had a wish to retire from service before the reverse in Canada, he then declared his resolution to continue.

It appears that it was not determined until after Jany 1776 that aids to the Commander in Chief were to rank as Lt. Col's & aids to Major Gen^ls to rank as Major. The *latter* were allowed 2 the former 3 aids.

In Jany 1776 Wash^n thanks Reed for a picture of himself sent to Mrs W. It was painted by a Mr Campbell whom W^n says he never saw, who "made a very formidable figure of the Commander in Chief."

"Gates had been appointed to the command *in Canada*" (after Montgomeries death) but before he reached Albany the army had evacuated that province & come under Genl Schuyler as Commander of the northern department" Gates pretended that the command of the northern department belonged to him. "The instructions of Genl G. were too explicit to raise a doubt in any other mind than his own" and Congress decided against his pretensions, he was however supported by a *New England* party in Congress.

Messrs. Flagg & Josclyn called on me. The latter gave me the following notices.

[Elkanah] *Tisdale.* A man of wit & genius, early in life drew, he designed some plates for an edition of [John Trumbull's] McFingal. In New York painted Miniatures during Trumbulls first visit to America *with his wife.* Painted their miniatures, went to Hartford in 1817 and joined a company for making plates for Banks, he designed the vignettes, designed for Echo.[184] In 1820, painted miniatures in N. Y. Joscelyn had left the Graphic Company but Tisdale continued attached to it until 1825. Engraved one of the plates. This company consisted of Brewster (dye sinker) N. Joscelyn, [Asaph] Willard & [Eleazer] Huntington. Tisdale wrote the "Gerrymander" and made designs for it.

M. I. Danforth was born in Hartford. (has brothers now near N. Y. & Cumings the Broker is acquainted with him) Began to engrave in 1818 as a pupil of the Graphic Company, removed to N. Haven & engraved there 1821. For Hudson, publisher in Hartford he engraved a copy of one of R. Morghen's plates so like the original that Hudson did not publish it, keeping it to appear hereafter as *a Morghen.* Danforth joined the Nat^l Acad^y of Design and drew in the School. Went to London to perfect an engraving from a picture by Morse of Dewitt Clinton, for which a subscription was attempted but the project failed & the picture was not just to D. In London he studied at Somerset house and drew assiduously from the Elgin Marbles, his drawing attracted attention & admiration. He then painted, copying some of the old masters, but in water

[184] *The Echo,* [by Richard Alsop and Theodore Dwight]. See Duyckinck, *Cyclopædia of American Literature,* I, 495-96.

colour with great truth & effect. In 1829 N. Joscelyn & he lived together in London. Leslie, Newton & Sir T. Lawrence were his friends and admirers. He formed himself as an engraver & did not place himself with any master. He engraved Leslie's port[ts] of Scott & Irving and a daughter of L[d] Holland's for an Annual. He is a moral and religious man & of a retiring disposition.

Lucius Munson born in 1796 N. Haven. Attached to painting but had determined to retire as a farmer, but Joscelyn persuaded him to pursue his studies as an Artist. Began to paint portraits in N. Haven in 1815. In 1817 studied drawing in N. York. Painted in S. Carolina in 1820, in 1821 went to Bermuda, painted rapidly to gain money to carry him to Europe. He went to Turks Island & while exerting himself took sick & died, probably 1822.

N. Joscelyn. Born in N. Haven 1796. Commenced painting 1820, went Savannah & painted. Exhibited with Nat[l] Academy 1826, in Lond[on] 1829. (Engraving at Hartford from 1818 to 23.) Long established in N. Haven & connected now 1834 with *Smith Joscelin* his brother. promises memoranda.

Anson Dickinson born in Milton, Litchfield.

Geo: Munger born in Guilford. After arriving at years of maturity had the small pox so bad that for eleven years he could not pursue his studies. In 1816 painted Miniatures of extraordinary merit and died in 1824 at the age of 41.

New Haven Wed[y] Aug[t] 6th 1834. Up at ½ past 4 A M. Write and read Sparks's Washington. The 17th March 1776 y[e] British evacuated Boston. From 10 to 1200 refugees or loyalists went with them. The army was 8906 men. "Aids de Camp are persons in whom entire confidence can be placed." The pay of A. de C's was at first 33 dollars a month; in March 1776 it was raised to 40, rank Lt. Col[l] In May 1776 Gates was promoted to the rank of Major Gen[l]. In June 1776 Wash[n] mentions Col[l] Trumbull (Jos: y[e] Commissary Gen[l]) being disatisfied with the allowance made him & recommends more. *Gates* appointed in June 1776 to command in Canada.

Went with Mr Winthrop to Mr Augur's & had interesting visit. Embark at 12 & arrive at 64 Sixth Avenue at 8 P. M.

New York [Aug.] *7th* Slept without anodyne & find the Th: at 5 A M 80. Clear. Correct proofs. Write on Hist: Art. At Noon Th: 82. Write on Hist. Art. G. C.

Verplank with us in the evening. Mentions a young man of the name of Jamieson who has distinguished himself by cutting cameos in conch-shells, invites me to go with him on Saturday to the Assylum.

Friday Aug[t] 8th 1834. Clear. At 5 A M. Ther: 80. Slept till one without Anodyne but had taken 15 drops laudanum in the day. At 2 took a julep anodyne. Write on Hist. Art. Walk a little way. Take 15 drops laudanum. At eleven A M Th: 82. Write on Hist: Art. Last Monday one case of Cholera was reported, to day we learn that 2 poor people have died in a Shanty in this Avenue & a third is dying with this disease. Write on Hist. Art. At 12 take as yesterday ½ pint boil'd milk with bread. Sleep an hour. Read in Dwights travels. A thunder shower. At 5 P. M. an attack of Cholic & Diarrhoea prostrated me & was only relieved by applications of hot brandy externally & 60 drops of laudanum internally.

Sat[y] [Aug.] *9th* Clear. Th: at 7 A. M. 78. Yesterday evening received communications from Henry Greenough respecting Horatio his brother & from Vanderlyn relative to himself, which I read this morning. To rail against the corporation & praise V. seems to be all that is thought of by the writer. Sleep a while. Dr. Francis calls. Write on Hist. Art. Rec[d] from Wm T. McCoun $100 pay James Perkins a quarter's rent $79. J. F. Cooper with me. Rain in y[e] night.

Sunday [Aug.] *10th* Clouds. Th: 78. Look over proofs. Up at 5 A. M. but not well. Read. Rain again. Write on Hist Art. Th: a[t] 12, 80. Francis calls & I take a rhubarb mixture. No ease. Pass a sick day. Mr McCoun calls. Read in Dr Dwights travels. The Board of Health have announced 17 deaths by Asiatic Cholera up to yesterday noon. Read in Morris's Mirror. Very poor.

Monday August 11th 1834. Clouds. Ther at 6 A. M. 77. Write on Hist. Art. Hard showers. Clears 10 A M.

Receive a letter & M.S.S. plays from Alex[r] Allen. The letter induces me to promise to read them. Take 15 drops laudanum. Write on hist: Art. After dinner write again. Th: 79. Walk a little while in y[e] Square. Read Dr Ds travels. Correct proofs. Cholera report 5 in 24 hours. No rest until 15 drops more of laudanum gives it.

Tuesday [Aug.] *12th* Clear. At 5 A M. Th: 78. Look over proofs, write on hist. Art. After breakfast walk. Write on hist. Art. There are doubts of the report of the board of health respecting cholera & one of our Editors pledges himself for 18 deaths and others dying during y[e] time the board tell us of 5. My friend Dr Francis calls & says that the Editor is right, the board more afraid of the Merchants than of lying, I add. My season of pain arrives about 10 A. M. Th: 80 & rising, but I write on Hist. Art. About 1 P M. sleep a little, take 15 drops of laudanum. Write on hist. Art. At 3 P. M. Th: 85, continue to write after a dinner of 2 Eggs & br[d] & butter. 4 P. M. Th: 86. Look over proofs & write on hist. Art. Receive a letter from Wm Whitehead with copy of my last. He has married Margaret Parker. Rain in night.

Wed[y] [Aug.] *13th* Clear. Th: at ½ past 5 A M. 80. Feelings of debility. Walk a little way. At 1 P. M. Th: 82. Cool & fresh wind. Write on hist. Art. At 2 P. M. Th: 84. Read in Dwights travels. Obliged to take 20 drops laudanum. 24 Weeks since the operation. The continued irritation of the bowels I consider as a consequence & if not remedied I presume must terminate fatally.

Thursday August 14th 1834. Clouds. Th: at 5 A M. 78. Make up a packet for C. R. Leslie Esq[re] R. A. No. 41 Portman Place Edgeware Road London, under cover to Francis B. Ogden Consul for the U. S. of America at Liverpool. I send to Leslie this time forms from 6 to 11 both inclusive & a rough proof of form 12 & I send him *Shee's address.* Write on Hist. Art. Walk to C. Rhind's & deliver packet for Liverpool. Walk to [Abraham J.]

Mason's Canal St. & return Percy Anecdotes. See some beautiful English publications. Ride to City library & look over part of [Matthew] Carey's [American] Museum. Ride home. Receive a letter from Theodore Dwight jun[r] corresp[g] sec[y] of y[e] American Lyceum saying the Executive Committee had appointed me to furnish an Essay on painting to be read at their 5th annual meeting in May next & published with their proceedings. Write on Hist. Art. Read proof. Write to Scott in hopes to send more sheets to Leslie, and to Arch[d] Robertson for documents relative to the Wallace Box. Take 20 drops of Laudanum after going to bed.

Friday [Aug.] *15th* Clear. Th: at 5 A M. 78. Examine proof. Write on Hist. Art. Write T. Dwight jr. accepting. Write on hist: Art. Receive from T. Sully a note respecting Pratt. Ride to Scott office to get it inserted & receive 2 forms more to send to Leslie by tomorrow's packet, which will give him to form 13 inclusive. Form 12 has a misprint, p: 89 *is* for *be* and *be* for *is*. I would willingly reprint the leaf. The other misprint in form 7. Scott will reprint the leaf. Take 15 drops laudanum about 5 P. M. Th: continues 76 to 78 all day. Write to Sully to have Pine's biography copied from Edwards's book.

Saturday Aug[t] 16th 1834. Clear. Th: at ½ past 5 A. M. 72. Write on Hist. Art. I was too late at Rhinds therefore Leslie will only have to form *eleven inclusive.* Walk to Mason's & look over engravings. Walk to Herrings & receive No. 12 & 13 National Portrait Gallery. Agree to write biography of Brown (C. B.) for him. Recommend that Longacre look at Sharplesses Port[t] of Brown before adopting mine. Walk to T. S. Cummings & sit with him. Walk to Scotts & show him the misprint. It appears that it is all the fault of the printing office. Walk to City Library. See Verplank. Examine Scotts Napoleon relative to Ceracchi & find nothing take out Napier. Walk to Wall Street & ride home. Write on Hist: Art. Arch[d] Robertson calls & leaves documents. Look in Napiers Peninsular War.

Sunday [Aug.] *17th* Clear. Th: at ½ past 5 A. M. 71. Write for Hist. Arts. Walk in pain. Take 15 drops laudanum. Afternoon write as above. Some rain. Read in Napier. Doctor Francis with us. Ev^g at my neighbour Hick's. Alex^r Robertson came in & told us that his wife died of Cholera this afternoon taken at 2 A. M.

Monday [Aug.] *18th* Clear. Th: at 6 A. M. 74. After a good night, I am in pain & take laudanum 15 drops before breakfast; after which write on Hist: Art: The day past uneasily and in the night diarroeha.

Tuesday [Aug.] *19th* Clear. Th: at 6 A M. 72. The reported cases & deaths by Cholera have encreased to 17 deaths & 33 new cases yesterday, the day before rather more. Began to print the Hist. Art on the 1st June that is 80 days ago and I have only about 120 pages. Write on Hist. Art. I yesterday received a pleasant letter from Allston relative to M. Brown, Flagg & W. S. Mount. Ride down Town to Library & examine Cary's Museum. Go to Scotts & look over a proof. Scott agrees positively that he will print 12 pages a day from this time which will finish the printing by Novr 1st so that I may publish by the 15th. Take from Library [Thomas] Roscoes Spanish Novelists. Read. Write. Correct proofs. Take 15 drops laudanum.

Wed^y 20th of Augt 1834. Clear. Th: at ½ past 5 A. M. 72. Look over proofs. Write on Hist. Art. Walk in square, meet De Rose who tells me Rembrandt Peale is now painting at New York. Write on Hist. Art. and to Washing^n Irving respecting Wm. E West. 4 P. M. a day of pain. It is now 26 weeks since the operation. Read in Quevedo: Receive from Sully the extract from Edwards relative to R. E. Pine. Write on Hist. Art. Pass a good night without laudanum.

Thursday [Aug.] *21st* Clear. Th: at 6 A. M. 71. Write in Hist. Art. Obliged to take Laudanum. Write to H.

Clay Jr Maplewood near Lexington Ky and to Jno H. B. Latrobe, Baltimore. Walk. Write on hist Art. Read in Roscoe's Spanish Novelists. It appears to me time mispent to translate these authors at this time of day, the wit is extravagant caricature and love novels stale from repetition.

Friday Augt 22d 1834. Clear. Th: at 5 A. M. 73. Look over proof. Write on Hist. Art. Walk. Obliged to take 15 drops laudanum & sleep. Write on hist. Art & correct proof. No sign of Mr Scott's 12 pages a day yet. Ev^{g} Walk in square. Th: rose to 76. Francis reminds me of Delano[y].

Sat^{y} [Aug.] *23d* Clear Th: at 6 A. M. 74. Examine proof. Write to Allston. Write on hist. Art. Doctor Francis called by appointment & took me in his gig to Beekmans and [blank] Beekman's to see pictures of the family at the first house some very poor & others poor by Abraham Delanoy jun^{r}, remember'd by me in 1780, at the second two pictures by L. Kilbrunn the heads very clever & some by Delanoy. This house was the country residence of the English Commanders during the revolutionary war. Return^{g} we call'd in Green Street & saw a head cleverly painted marked "portrait of Benjamin West the celebrated Limner of Philadelphia painted by his friend Abraham Delanoy jr. limner. Then went to Scotts printing office & look'd over a proof & rode home fatigued. Sleep a little. Take 15 drops laudanum. Read Mirror. Write for Hist. Art. Diarroeha as I presume in consequence of too much exercise for my reduced strength. Francis kindly calls to see how I bore the ride & found me in bed. After 1 OClock obtained ease & sleep by more laudanum. My situation is critical.

<*Will this paper continue so bad? Is there no remedy?*>

Sunday Augt 24th 1834. Clear. Th: at 6 A. M. 74. Correct proofs. My breakfast 1 cup of coffee. Write on hist

Art. Francis calls. Lie down for an hour. Dine with some appetite on breast of Duck, a little rice & a little potatoe. Drink weak brandy & water. Th: at 2 P. M. 81. Write on hist. Art. T. S. Cummings with me. Night Diarroeha.

Monday [Aug] *25th* Clear. Th: 6 A M. 76 in the house, much lower out. Cummings bro^{t} me this note of Twibill. Born in West Chester County Pennsylvania." Take 20 drops of laudanum before rising. Examine proofs. Ride to Scotts printing Office. Walk thence to Library & take [George] Ord's [*Life of Alexander*] Wilson. Ride home. Write on hist. Art.

Tuesday [Aug.] *26th* Clear. Diarroeha & great part of day in bed. Read life of Wilson. Take 15 drops Laudanum. After a dinner of a little hash'd lamb, very little rice & a custard, read proofs. Write on hist. Art. Morse with me & the Council of the N. A. were to come but did not. Ev^{g} correct proofs.

Wed^{y} [Aug.] *27th* Clear Th: 70 at 6 A M. Examine proofs. Write on Hist. Art. The young Dramatist Allan called & I returned his Manuscripts advising him to think of some other employment. Leslie painted Dr Francis in spring 1816. It is 27 weeks since the operation I think of too often, but for which I thank God & yet hope from it a little health. Correct proofs. Write on Hist. Art. Ev^{g} 15 drops Laud^{m}.

Thursday Augt 28th 1834 Clear. Th: at 6 A. M. 68 Look over proof. Write on hist. Art. Diarroeha. Francis calls accidentally. Write on hist: Art. Afternoon in pain. The oldest Agate calls. He sails for Italy next month to stay 2 years. Draw $20 & leave $31.22. Even^{g} take 20 drops laudanum. Sleep pretty well through y^{e} night.

Friday [Aug.] *29th* Clear. Th: at 6 A M. 67. Write to T. Cole requesting some further particulars. Write on Hist Art. Doctor Francis with me. Write on Hist. Art.

MRS. JOHN ADAMS CONANT (CAROLINE D. HOLTON)
BY WILLIAM DUNLAP, 1829
(Courtesy of The Metropolitan Museum of Art, New York)

Ev[g] correct proofs until 10 P. M. Take 10 drops laudanum.

Sat[y] [Aug.] *30th* Clear. Th: at 6 A. M. 68. Write and correct proofs. Make up a packet for C. R. Leslie Esq[re] R. A. No. 41 Portman Place, Edgeware Road London. Enclosed to Francis B. Ogden Esq[re] Consul for the United States of America at Liverpool. This packet contains forms from 8 to 18 both inclusive. Write on Hist. Art. and now and then read Blackwood. Take 20 drops laudanum. Write on hist Art. Correct proof.

Sunday [Aug.] *31st* Clear. Th: at ½ past 6 A. M. 68. Write to Rubens Peale for date of birth of his fathers children. Write on hist: Art. Doctor Francis with me, is to examine if [Mark] Catesby drew his birds. Audubon kept a shop in Br[d] Way & failed. Th: at noon 68. Write on Hist. Art. Take laudanum twice, morning and evening. I take quenine also.

Monday Sept[r] *1st* Rain. Th: 70. Write on hist: Art: Read in Blackwood. Sleep. Receive letter from Neagle, the Artists of Phil[a] are formed and forming into a Society or School of Arts. Write on Hist: Art: Glad to sit by a fire. Ev[g] correct proof.

Tuesday Sept[r] *2d 1834* Clouds. Th: at 7 A. M. 70. Correct proofs. Write of hist. Art. Take 15 drops laudanum. Write on hist. art. Washington Irving with [us] all the evening. Correct proofs until late.

Wed[y] [Sept.] *3d* Clouds Th: at 7 A M. 72. This is the 28th week since the operation. My strength has not increased for some time. Nay I fear it has diminished. Th: rises to 80. Severe cholicky pain, take laudanum. Receive letter from Jn H. B. Latrobe who says he waits for information from an uncle in England previous to fulfilling his promise respecting his father. Read in foreign Quarterly. Rain all night.

Thursday [Sept.] *4th* Rain. Th: at 7 A. M. 78. At 4 A. M. severe Diarroeha, take 30 drops of Laudanum. Write to Neagle for information respecting Peale (Rembrandt) and to S. L. Waldo respecting himself, and on Hist. Art. At 3 P. M. Th: 75. Rain. Correct proofs. Receive a letter from Neagle & answer it. Dr. [Perlee] Pine calls.

Saturday [Sept] *6th* Clear. Write on Hist Art & Correct proofs. T. S. Cummings brings me treatise on painting in Miniature. Receive specimens of binding at 20 cents a vol. Scotts estimate originally 15 cents, a good binding may be had @ 12½. Read proofs. Take laudanum at 10 P M.

Sunday [Sept.] *7th* Clear. Th: a[t] ½ past 6 A. M. 74. Take 1 gr: quenine. Walk in the square without pain. Read proofs. Write on Hist. Art. Take 15 drops laudanum. Afternoon rain. Write on Hist. Art: I took a second gr: quenine before my dinner, 2 Eggs & 2 spoonfulls of boiled rice. Thunder. Ev^{g} take 15 drops laudanum. Read Sands.

Monday Septr 8th 1834. Th: at 1 P. M. 72. After a night of cholic & laudanum, & diarroeha this morning which relieved me *without* laudanum McLean calls to see me, & I am to try opium pills 3 gr: each inserted in the rectum every evening for 3 or four days. Read Sands & Foreign Quarterly. Saml L. Waldo calls & leaves a biograp^{l} sketch. Write on hist. Art. Correct proofs. Afternoon apply the opium pill which causes much irritation. Ev^{g} correct proofs.

Tuesday [Sept.] *9th* Clear after a hard shower. Th: a[t] 6 A M. 74. The opium pill has so far operated successfully that I have slept well. Re examine proofs. Write on Hist. Art. 9 A M. Hard rain. Pain. take 15 drops laudanum. Take boil'd milk & bread for my dinner. Write on Hist. Art. Correct proofs. Write on hist. Art. Apply the opium pill which appears to help me. Ev^{g} correct proofs.

Wed^{y} [Sept.] *10th* Thin clouds. Th: at 6 A M. 70. This is the 29th week since the operation. I passed a comfortable night the last. Correct proofs. No appetite for breakfast, take some & my stomach rejects it. Lie down & sleep an hour. Th: at noon 71. Write on Hist. Art. Eat a little dinner. Apply the opium pill in the evening, after examining proofs.

Thursday [Sept.] *11th* Clear. Th: 68 a[t] 7 A M. Write on Hist. Arts. Walk to Miss Wrights. Write on Hist. Arts. Doct^{r} McLean with me. Obliged to take 15 drops laudanum at 12 OClock. Write on Hist: Art: Walk between 4 & 5 OClock but find it too cold & symptoms of cholic immediately applied the opium pill. Slept ½ an hour. Evening correct proof. Write to Wm Bennett respecting Wall. Write to A. J. Davis respecting himself, I Town & Architecture generally.

Friday Septr 12th 1834 Clear. Th: at 8 A M. 64 & continues so through the day. As on the 10th my stomach rejects food & I attribute it to the application of the opium pill. Correct a proof in bed. Dine with appetitie & write on hist: Art. Sleep. Cummings & Newcomb with me. Ev^{g} correct proofs. The Widow of C. B. Brown is dead. Much Cholic. 15 drops laudanum and no ease. Ease & sleep well.

Sat^{y} [Sept.] *13th* Clear. Th: 64. Look over proofs at ½ past 6 A. M. Write on hist. Art. About 11 obliged to take 15 drops laudanum. at 1 P. M. correct proofs. Walk in the square with my cloak on. Write on Hist. Art. Ev^{g} correct proof. Ob[l]iged to take 15 drops laudanum more. Sleep pretty well

Sunday [Sept.] *14th* Clear. At 7 A. M. Th: 64. take 1 gr: quenine. Correct proofs and arrange materials for 1st

Vol: Hist. Art. ½ past 10 in pain. Read Mirror & Foreign Review. Fanny Kemble see Mirror of Sept[r] 13th 1834. Took a 2 gr: quenine before my dinner but pain obliges me to take 20 drops laudanum at ½ past 4 P. M. Read Foreign quarterly. Francis calls.

Monday [Sept.] *15th* Clear. At ½ past 6 Th: 64. Write to Wa: Irving some queries respecting artists. Write on Hist: Art. My morning more ease than usual but pain at noon obliges me to take 15 drops of laudanum. I had previously taken a walk with some pleasure. Read Foreign review. Write on hist. Art. Remb[t] Peale calls & leave[s] notice of himself. Correct proofs. Pack up forms from 19 to 42 (each inclusive) for C. R. Leslie Esq[re] R. A. No. 41 Portman Place Edgeware Road London to be sent to morrow to Francis B. Ogden Consul at Liverpool. Correct proofs.

Tuesday Sept[r] 16th 1834. Clear. Th: at ½ past 6 A. M. 64. Correct proofs. Write on Hist. Art. Write to Frazee Pain & 15 drops of laudanum. Write on Hist. Art. Francis calls on me: he & McLean have had another consultation on my situation & another prescription is ordered. Continue the quenine pills. Write on hist. Art. Walk. Write on hist. Art. Correct proofs. Take more quenine; dine & write on hist. Art. My daughter carried my packet for Liverpool to Charles Rhind early this morning. Gave my note for $300 to George P. Scott & Co. dated this day & due in 90 days. Ev[g] correct proofs. Much pain & more Laudanum (15 drops)

Wed[y] [Sept.] *17th* Clear. Th: at 6 A M. 66. I had a better night than usual. Take quenine. This is the 30th week since the horrid operation. Write on hist. Art. Correct proofs. Rain. Write on hist. Art. Read Quart[er]ly foreign. Ev[g] much pain, take 15 drops laudanum.

Thursday [Sept.] *18th* Clouds. Th: 70. Correct proofs. Write on hist. Art. Walk a little way but soon tire. Write on hist. Art. Receive a note from Scott wishing instead of the note for $300 in his favour one in favour of Wm. T. McCoun which I send him. Correct proof. Write on hist. Art. In pain: which is removed by lying down. Write on hist. Art. Ev[g] correct proofs. pain. 25 drops of Laudanum. Broken sleep in the night & restlessness.

Friday Sept[r] 19th 1834. Clouds. Th: at 6 A. M. 72. Draw from Bank $30. leave $1.22. Continue to take quenine. Write on Hist. Art. Pain. Dr Francis with me. Take a mixture, tea spoon full first time. Correct proofs. Write on Hist. Art. Pain & 20 drops of laudanum. J. F. Cooper and Morse with me. Correct proofs.

Sat[y] [Sept.] *20th* Clear. Th: at 7 A M. 72. Receive a letter from Edm[d] A. Wetmore enquiring if Freemen (James) is competent to paint a portrait & worthy of employment. Write answer in y[e] affirmative. Walk over to J. F. Cooper's & breakfast with him & Morse. C's family at Coopertown at present. Walk home. take quenine before breakfast & the mixture since. Write on hist. Art. Write on Hist: Art: Correct proofs. F. Cooper & Morse with me. A. J. Davis with me. Correct proofs.

Sunday [Sept] *21st* Clear. Th: at 6 A M. 70. Write on hist. Art. Walk. Write on hist. Art. Much pain, take y[e] mixture. Cummings and Cole with me. Write on hist. Art. Dr. Francis with me take quenine. dine. write on hist. Art. Walk. Even[g] Dr. Francis brings me a letter on Wilson &c. A Robertson with me. *Take no laudanum to day.*

Monday [Sept.] *22d* Clear. Th: at 6 A M. 70. Write on hist. Art. Walk. Write on hist: Art. Correct proof. Walk. Write on hist. Art. Waldo call'd on me & paid me $20 for 4 copies of my work for himself & Jewett. I read to him the biographical Sketch of himself. Write on hist. Art. Durand calls on me & I make some memoranda from him. Morse calls. We determine to open the Acad[y] at night & ordered accordingly. Francis calls in the ev^{g}. Write on Hist. Art. Correct proofs. I have pass'd two days without taking laudanum. I take ye quenine and the caminative mixture. There appears to be improvement in my health generally.

Tuesday Septr 23d 1834. Clouds. Th: at 6 A M. 70. Examine proof. Write on hist. Art. Remb^{t} Peale calls on me & leaves his Italy & further Memoranda. Write on hist. Art. Walk without pleasure. Ev^{g} correct proofs. Obliged to take 15 drops laudanum after going to bed. Slept well. Hard shower.

Wed^{y} [Sept.] *24th* Clear. Th: at 6 A M. 70. This is 31 weeks since the operation. Let me be thankful to God for the health & strength allowed to me! I am thankfull! Write to James F. Cooper to Coopers town. To S. F. B. Morse respecting New Haven. On hist. Art. Walk with more strength than yesterday. Look over Peale's Italy. Receive letter from Nathl Jocelyn of New Haven & answer it. Correct proofs. Write on hist. Art. Cummings with me. In pain take 15 drops of laudanum. Ev^{g} correct proofs until eleven P. M. Sleep pretty well.

Thursday [Sept.] *25th* Clear. Th: at 6 A M. 67. Correct proofs. Write on hist. Art. Write to Andrew Jackson P^{t}, Robt. Gilmor and Francis J. Oliver. I wrote yesterday to T. Sully. Write to M: Van Buren and John Neagle. Write on hist. Art. Much pain. John Vanderlyn calls on me & leaves further notices of himself and 2 pamphlets. Pain. Took laudanum twice 15 and 20 drops. Ev^{g} correct proofs.

Friday [Sept.] *26th* Clear Th: at 6 A M. 66. Correct proofs. Write on hist. Art. Dr Francis calls. Walk but returned tired & in pain. Sleep. Write on hist. Art. Ev^{g} correct proofs.

Sat^{y} [Sept..] *27th* Clouds. Th: at 6 A M. 68. Correct proofs. Write on hist. Art. Walk. Write to T. Williamson,

Charles Fraser, J. S. Cogdell, Robt. W. Weir & Gregg of Canandaigua. Evening writing on Hist Art & correcting proofs.

Sunday Sept[r] 28th 1834. Clouds. Th: at 9 A M. 66. Correct proofs. Write to Allston, Henry Clay jr. Jno H. B. Latrobe, on Hist. Art. After[n] much pain. Francis with me. Pass a good night. Rain.

Monday [Sept.] *29th* Clear. Th: a[t] ½ past 6 A. M. 64. Write to S. Wescott P. M. Hudson, G. P. Morris. Dr Francis with me, very much engaged in forwarding my work. Write on hist. Art. Make up package for Leslie: and write a letter to him. Write on hist. Art. Walk. Write to L[everett] Cruttenden, S[amuel] M. Hopkins, Oliver G. Steele Buffalo, A. C. Mulliner P. M. Newburgh.

Tuesday [Sept.] *30th* Clear. Th: at 7 A M. 58. Correct proofs. Walk to C. Rhind & deliver package for Leslie to be put by Mr [William B.] Taylor of the post office in the Consuls bag according to directions rec[d] from Francis B. Ogden in a letter from Liverpool yesterday. Write to E. V. Stoddard New London, Henry Adams Litchfield, W. D. Starr Middletown, F. J. Huntington Hartf[d], E. B. Kelley Poughkee[p]sie, Z Clark Troy, C & M. Morse Rochester, B. W. Wheeler, Providence, Gen[l] Godwin Patterson. Write on hist. Art. Correct proofs. Walk. Write on hist. art.

Wed[y] Oct[r] 1st 1834. Clear. Th: at ½ past 6 A M. 60. Warmer out of doors. This is the 32d week since the operation. For some days my strength has improved & I have experienced less pain. This is the third day that I have not taken laudanum, nay it is the fourth, thank God!

Yesterday evening Morse & Durand with me on Council business relative to the schools of the Academy. Correct proofs & sleep well last night. This morning writing on Hist. Art: At 9 A M. Th: 62. light clouds. Write on hist. Art. & a note to Morse. Francis brings up proofs & I look them over. Write on hist. Art. Receive letter from J. F. Cooper. Write to Jacob Eichholtz Lancaster, Danl Small York, S. Ritter, Reading, Col^{l} Gardiner Post Office Washington, J Peacock Harrisb^{g}. Write on hist. Art. Ev^{g} Correct proofs. Rain in the night. Sleep well. No laudanum.

Thursd [Oct.] *2d* Clear. Th: at 6 A M. 68. Look over proofs. Write on hist. Art. Walk. Call from Dr Pine. Th: at 2 P M. 72. Write on Hist. Art. Read in [Thomas] Campbell's [*Life of Mrs.*] Siddons. Nathl Rogers called & bro^{t} me Metcalfs biog^{y} and some fine grapes. Walk. Call on E. Hicks.

Frid^{y} [Oct.] *3d* Clear. Th: a[t] 5 A M 70. Look over proofs. Write on hist. Art. Ride with Dr Francis, Dr Downs, Mayr. Correct proofs at office. Get Dr B's book of Leibenau. Ride home. Read Campbells Siddons, merely eulogium. Write on Hist. Art. Walk. Correct proof and make a list to be called on for subscription, or rather I begin it. My daughter is copying in a proper blank book the list of those who have already subscribed.

Saturday Octr 4th 1834. Clouds. Th: at 6 A M. 69. I continue improving & have taken no laudanum for many days. Thank my Creator & Preserver! Amen! Look over proof. Continue making List of names. Write to Robt E Launitz 33 Macdougal St^{t}. Ev^{g} correcting proofs.

Sunday [Oct.] *5th* Clear. Th: at 6 A. M. 67. Out of doors cold. Correct proofs. Continue the list (321 at 10 Clock) At 12 Walk. Th: 65, in ye house. Ev^{g} A. B. Durand with me & Gulian C. Verplank.

Monday [Oct.] *6th* Clear Th: 62. Write on Hist. Art. Durand gave me in Trumbulls handwriting an inscription which is engraved on a brass sword by Durand at

T's request. Go to printing office & to Clinton Hall. Ride thither & back. Write on List. Ev[g] Morse with me until 10. Correct proofs till 11.

Tuesday [Oct.] *7th* Clear. Ther: 62. Correct proofs. Write on Hist. Art. Ride down town. Correct proofs & ride back again. Call on the Mayor [Cornelius W. Lawrence] and take his subscription. Francis calls. Write on hist. Art. Receive letter from Jno H. B. Latrobe promising me his fathers biography on the 18th inst. Receive letter from Weir with notice of Oddie & [William] Maine. Evening more unwell, but still no laudanum.

Wed[y] [Oct.] *8th* Hazy. Th: at 8 A M 62. Rise with head ach. Write on hist. Art. This is the 33d week since the operation. Write on hist. Art. Ride to printing Office & correct proofs. Ride home. Write in hist. Art. Cummings calls on me. Ev[g] write on hist. Art.

Thursday Oct[r] 9th 1834. Th: at 6 A M. 66. Thin clouds. Write on hist. Art. Ride down to Chamber St[t] walk to Meigs' office & take his signature. Go to Arch[d] Robertsons, to Clover's & to Page's, who has made a Mezzotinto of Forest very clever from a painting of his own. to Scotts office & correct proofs. See Herring, Durand. Ride home very much fatigued & sleep ½ an hour. Receive note from Frazee who has now 7 Busts to do for y[e] Boston Atheneum, promises me y[e] remainder of his biog[y]. Letter from Neagle with 2 subscribers. J. R. Smith has already been turn'd out by the artists. Letter from Francis J. Oliver with his subscription & notice that O[liver] C. Greenleaf his friend will receive & distribute the copies of my work to Boston subscribers at 5 per cent & pay the money to Mr. Oliver. Letter from S. M. Hopkins (Bradish a subscriber) books to be sent to Mr Bogert Bookseller Geneva. Mr. W. G. Wood, son of Jos: Wood Miniature painter of former days called & subscribed, his errand was to know what I had said of his father. Write to Neagle. Ev[g] wrote on Hist. Art.

Friday [Oct.] *10th* Clear. Th: a[t] ½ past 6 A M. 64. Write on hist Art. Ride to Recorder's Office [Richard Riker] take his signature. Walk to Scott's Office & thence Wm. G. Wood's at Record Office, thence to Vice Chancellor's [William T. McCoun] and back to Scotts. Correct proof & ride home: find a letter from Allston. Write on hist. Art. Ev^{g} Diarroeha take 15 drops Laudanum. sleepless night. Diarroeha continues until morning.

Saturday [Oct.] *11th* Clear. Th: at 8 A M. 59. Write Scott for proofs on revises Receive a letter from Wm. Page respect^{g} himself. Write on hist. Art. Obliged to take 20 drops laudanum. Continue writing. Receive letter from John Greg of Canandaigue subscribing for 2 Copies of my work for himself and Alex^{r} Duncan & remitting an order for $10 on Prime, Ward & King. He informs me that Mr Morse of the firm of Morse and Harvey of Can^{a} bookseller will call on me & by him I am to send the 2 copies. Ev^{g} severe Diarroeha. Laudanum &c & again in the night.

Sunday Octr 12th 1834. Lie in bed till noon. Correct proofs in bed. Francis with me. I am in part relieved. Clear day Th: at noon 60. Mem: Trumbull gave to Arch^{d} Robertson the maiden name of his wife as Hope, the daughter of Wm Hope of Perthshire. She was born 1st of Augt 1774 near London: died 12th April 1824. Her bust was made by Cardelli & with her husbands ornaments the American Academy. Write on hist. of Art. Ev^{g} making out list. Francis with us & gives anecdotes of Kean.

Monday [Oct.] *13th* Clear. Th: 62. Write on Hist Art. Walk. Write on hist. Art. Ev^{g} correct proofs.

Tuesday [Oct.] *14th* Clear. Th: at 8 A M. 58. Receive letter & biog^{y} from Wm. G. Wall. Write on hist. Art. all day. Ev^{g} correct proofs.

Wed^{y} [Oct.] *15th* Clear. Th: at 8 A M. 54. Correct proofs. Write on hist. Art. This is the 34th week since the operation. My danger appears to be from diarroeha of which the attack on Sat^{y} last was severe but yielded to laudanum immediately & I have taken none since & am as well as before it. Rec^{ve} letter from Williamson, no subscribers at Norfolk for my book, his boys doing well. Receive letter from Neagle with several names & an acc^{t} of their new Academy: which they call the Artists fund Academy. Ride to printing office & correct proofs & ride back. Receive package from Neagle. Prepare package for Leslie, from form 3 to 30 both inclusive directed to him No. 41 Portman Place Edgeware Road Lond. & inclosed to Francis B Ogden Consul of the U. S. States of America at Liverpool (these forms of the 2d Vol:) Ev^{g} correct proofs.

Thursday Octr 16th 1834 Clear. Th: at 6 A. M. 50. Write to Neagle. Write on hist: Art: Ride to printing Office & correct proofs. See G. P. Morris. Ride home. Write on hist. Art. Receive letter with biography of Thomas U. Walter from Neagle, & letter from A Bradish with payment for copy of hist. Art to be sent to Geneva to Mr Wynkoop. Write on hist Art. Mr Morse with me in the ev^{g}. The [illegible] of the National Acad^{y} *opened* last ev^{g} Morse bro^{t} me some steel pens but they are hard to use.

Friday [Oct.] *17th* Another package was sent off yesterday to Leslie. Strange that I do not hear from him. Cloudy morning. Th: at ½ past 6 A M. 54. Write on Hist. Art. Ride to printing Office & Correct proofs. Day Warm. Write on hist Art. Francis brings me a very beautiful picture of Mrs (Doctor) Jay & infant by Miss Hall. Ev^{g} make out list. Read in Review & Mirror.

Saturday [Oct.] *18th* Clear. Th: at ½ past 6 A M. 61. Write on hist Art. Noon go to Scotts & correct proofs. Go to Lewis Clover's & he agrees to take my work for

Subscribers & for sale. Ride home. Th: 66 out of doors much warmer. Receive letter from Jno H B Latrobe & a packett which I return'd to Po[s]t Office as the postage was $6. Ev^{g} correct proofs. Read in Quarterly Review.

Sunday Octr 19th 1834. Rain. Th: at 7 A M. 66. Write on Hist. Art. Write to Jno H. B. Latrobe. Read in Review & Mirror. Cummings calls to see me. Write on hist. Art. Weir passes the evening with me. Write on hist. Art. Cholic, but avoid laudanum.

Monday [Oct.] *20th* Clear. Th: at ½ past 6 A M. 59. Write on hist. Art. I have in Bank $91. Read Q: Review. I have met with nothing for many years that I think so fine as the extracts from *Phillip van Artwelde.* Write on hist. Receive letter from Leslie. Bently declines publishing. Letter from R. Gilmor the Booksellers at Baltimore decline buying. Poor encouragement. Leslie's letter is dated 20th Augt from Pine apple Place instead of Portman Place & he makes no mention of receiving any of the sheets of the hist: Art: so that I suppose they have all failed. Ev^{g} correct proofs. Take laudanum.

Tuesday [Oct.] *21st* Clear. Th: at 7 A M 56. No amendment in my health. Write to Leslie. Write on hist: Art. Ride to Herring, not in. Walk to Ingham, not in, to Durands & set a while, to Scotts & Morris, to Paff's & he shows me two very fine pictures & others curious. Ride home. Read in Review. Lawson (formerly of the Mercantile Advertiser) called & brought me a memoir of C. C. Wright. Ev^{g} in pain but do not take laudanum.

Wed^{y} [Oct.] *22d* Clear. Th: at ½ past 6 A M. 55. Write on Hist. Art. Ride to Wall St^{t}, visit Library. Walk to Scotts, to Herrings & ride home. Write of hist. Art. Read in Campbells Siddons which has hung heavily on my hands. Ev^{g} correct proofs. Dr Francis with us. The wretched ends of Alex^{r} & Wm. Hosack, Alex^{rs} sons. Wm was in ye lowest state of poverty & Bush the Irish Anatomist wished to seize the body.

Thursday Octr 23d 1834. Clear. Windy. Th: at 7 A M. 54. Write on Hist. Art. Go to Morris's & Scott's and return ½ past 1. Write on hist. Art & Index. Ev^g correct proof. Look into Mrs Sherwood's Nun.

Friday Octr 24th Clear. Th: at ½ past 6 A M 54. Begin a Biographical sketch of Charles Broc[k]den Brown for Herring & Longacre. Ride to Park & walk to Mirror office. See Morris. Go to Scotts & correct proofs. Ride home. Receive letter from C. R. Leslie dated Petworth (Lord Egremont's seat) Seat Septr 17th 1834. By this he acknowledges the receit of two parcels of my printed sheets. Gives some critisms & wished for alterations, expresses his pleasure at seeing what he has seen & promises to renew his efforts with the Booksellers on his return to London. Even^g correcting proofs.

Saturday [Oct.] *25th* Clear. My Th: stands at 63 but it is in consequence of putting up one of *Notts* stoves yesterday in the entry below. Correct proofs. Write to Leslie, Pine Apple Place, Edgeware Road London. Write on hist. Art. Ride to Post Office & put in the letter for Leslie, go to Library, to Morris's who is now active in promoting my subscription list, to Scotts & correct proofs, ride home. Ev^g correct proofs. Read.

Sunday [Oct.] *26th* Rain. Look over proofs. Write to Theodore Woolsey, N. Haven. Write on Hist. Art. Read Q^y Review.

Monday [Oct.] *27th* Clear & mild. Write on hist: Art. Ride to Warren St^t Call on Wm T. McCoun, Dr H McClean, Mirror Office, Post Office (the packet of Latrobe having been sent to Washington is to be returned) Library, Scotts printing office, Mirror Office again & find letter from Latrobe authorizing me to use the memoir as I wish. One of ye house of Morse & Harvey Canandagua calls on me & undertakes the delivery of any copies for that place or Geneva if left with Collins & Hanna No.

230 Pearl St[t] before 15th Nov[r]. Write on Hist. Art. Evening correct proofs. Read. My health has appeared to be improving, my strength has increased, and my appetitie is perhaps too good.

Tuesday Oct[r] 28th 1834. Clear & mild. Write on Hist. Art. Go with my Wife to see Mrs Francis, did not see her. Ride to Mirror office. Morris going in with the plan for subscriptions. Go to Scotts & correct proofs. Receive Mr Latrobes memoir which had not gone on to Washington. Reading it. Ev[g] correct proofs. Read Latrobe.

Wed[y] [Oct.] *29th* Clear & mild. This is the 36th week since the operation. My health and strength are improving. Am I thankfull enough for my many blessings? No. Write on Hist. Art. Ride to Scotts Office & Correct proofs. Ride home, find a letter from B. H. Latrobe. wishing no abstract of his brother's memoir but submitting to his arrangements: which gives me full latitude. Write on hist. Art

Thursday [Oct.] *30th* Clear & mild: but I feel the cold too sensibly. Write on Hist. Art. Go to Scotts & correct proofs. Morris going on wth subscribers. *Mem:* pd. 6 dollars for 8 oz. of M.S.S. Write on Hist. Art. Write to Benj[a] H. Latrobe. Read Review.

Friday [Oct.] *31st* Cloudy & colder. Looking over & correcting Index for History of Art. Some one sent me from Phil[a] No. 1 of Green Room Companion. It treats John Howard Payne severely. Ride to Scotts & correct proofs. Ride Home. Read The Deformed [185] a Novel. Ev[g] make up package with sheets from form 31 to 48 inclusive of Hist. Art for C. R. Leslie No. 12 Pine Apple place Edgeware Road Lond[n] Receive a packet from H. Augur of N. H. with his biography.

[185] *The Deformed; and the Admiral's Daughter.* [By Mrs. Anne Marsh-Caldwell] London, 1834, 2 vol.

Sat^y Novr 1st 1834. Cloudy. Reading Augur & second part of Frazee. Write on hist. Art. Ride to Scotts correct proofs. See Morris. Ride home. Afternoon & Ev^g hard rain. Read the Admirals daughter, And continuation of John Frazees.

Sunday Novr 2d 1834. The tops of the houses & the grass plots & flower shrubs are cover'd with snow. The latter partially like lace work. The pavements are dry. Read Frazee & write on hist: Art. Correct proofs. 10 A M. Clear & mild. J. F. Cooper comes & sits the morning with me. Finish the Admiral's daughter. A good Novel. Inman & Cummings with me.

Monday [Nov.] *3d* Clear. Hard frost. Write on Index. Receive letter from Neagle. Callaghan is the man who is to deliver to subscribers in Phil^a & the books are to be deposited with Neagle. Ride to Scotts office & correct proofs. Ride home. finish Index.

Tuesday [Nov.] *4th* Clear. Took a fruitless walk in search of Robert Robertson who engaged to try for subscribers. Fenimore Cooper called & we rode to Scott's office. See Morris. Ride home. Read Hannah Mores biography

Wed^y [Nov.] *5th* Warm rain. The 37th Week. My health improving. Send the last portion of the hist: Art to Scott with Index. Yesterday received from Weir an Extract from a book published in London 1825 by Elmes [186] being the character of Trumbull & his pictures. Read H. More. Read Mirror. Rain ceases at noon. Go to the poll & vote. Ev^g Correct proofs

Thursday [Nov.] *6th* Clear & mild. Write to G. Chapman Alexandria D. C. Ride to Scotts & correct proofs. See Morris. call on H. Inman & on Cummings. Morse informs me that Wyatt has sent us a beautiful cast of a

[186] James Elmes, *School of the Fine Arts,* 1825, 3 vol.

Nymph entering a bath from Rome. The charges upon these presents ruin the Academy. Ride Home. I am not so well—an irritation that puts me in mind of calculus in the bladder torments & alarms me. Ev[g] write on Hist. Art.

Friday Nov[r] 7th 1834. Clear & mild. Write to H. Augur New Haven. Read in "Mary of Burgundy" [By G. P. R. James]. Inman told me of an instance of Trumbull's characteristic cunning and meaness yester[day]. He brought a large Miniature to him belonging to y[e] King family which some ignorant person had half wiped out by way of cleaning it & required Inman to repaint it. It was a beautiful copy of [Gilbert Stuart's] Washington from [James] Heath's engraving & he worked it over; placing the print before him. He returned it & charged 25 dollars. Which Trumbull said he would get for him. Inman was going to Albany & Utica & offer'd Trumbull to take some of his prints of the "Declaration" & try to sell them for him. The polite offer was accepted with thanks, 2 copies put up, the price 20 dollars but to Agents an allowance of 5. It happen'd that in displaying the prints at Albany one was torn on the margin & as no purchaser appeared Inman concluded to charge himself with one & return the uninjured one. The damaged one he presented to a friend & on returning the other to Trumbull told him all the circumstances. With all the usual *courtesy* the great man replyed "I have received the money for your work & now we are even." Thus swindling the youth out of 10 dollars who if he had sold it was only to be charge[d] 15. Inman was too much astounded to make reply or remonstrance, but the transaction is not forgotten. Rode to Library. Call on Morse—we go to N. Acad[y] to see Wyatts Nymph, very beautiful, to Scotts & correct. Walk [to] Dr Francis's. Ride home. Read in "Outre-Mer"

Saturday Nov[r] 8th 1834. Clear & mild. Read. Ride to Wall St[t] put letter in P. O. for And[w] Bell Esq[r]. E post

Office. Library, Mirror Office, Scotts & correct proofs. Ride home. Receive letter from N. Jocelyn with apologies. He says he & Professor Woolsey are "doing what we can for the subscription here." New Haven. Read Mary of Burgundy.

Sunday [Nov.] *9th* Clear & mild. Th: at ½ past 6 A M. 38 out o' doors. Read Mary of Burgundy. (Th: in ye house, in the entry of the second story, the Nott stove being in the entry of the first, or ground floor, 64) Correct proof of form 58 vol. 2d. One hundred dollars is due from Creighton the 11th inst. Walk up the Avenue. Read again.

Monday [Nov.] *10th* Clouds. Th: at ½ past 6 A. M. 40; & in the house as above 64. Read Mary of Burgundy, finish reading it. Ride to Ann St^t^ go to Mirror Office & to Scotts—correct proofs. Ride home.

Tuesday [Nov.] *11th* Rain all night mist & clouds & wet this morning. Th: in my entry 64 out of doors at 7 A M. 46. Read. Hard rain. Write on Hist. Art. Weather clear. Ride to Cedar Street. Go to Morses: not in. Go to Wyley's he wishes to be publisher to my book & demand 10 per cent. Go to Library & then to Mirror Office & Scotts where after correcting proofs ride home. See J. F. Cooper & Weir. Evening Morse & N. Jocelyn with us. Jocelyn encourages me to hope that New Haven may give me several subscribers. Correct proofs until midnight.

Wed^y^ Novr 12th 1834. Clear. Th: at 7 A. M. in the house 68, out of doors 40. Draw from Bank $20 leaving $71. Read in Hannah More after correcting proofs. *The 38th Week.* Write to Neagle respecting Callaghan & subscribers. Ride to Wall Street & Post Office, to Morse & receive his subscription money. See there Dr Dekay. Go to library, meet Verplank in y^e^ street & break off from him on seeing James Creighton pass as if he wished to avoid me. I reminded him that 100 dolls were due on the purchase of Death on the Pale Horse he talked evasively but would call before he embarked for New Orleans. I told him the money must be paid, he is rich from the exhibition of Adam & Eve. See Clover who says Creighton has been here these 10 days. In his letters he has promised to call but has pass'd through N. Y. & avoided me. Go to Mirror Office & to Scotts & correct proofs. Ride home.

Thursday [Nov.] *13th* Clear & mild. Th: in house at 7 A M. 67: out o' doors 44. Put papers relative to Creighton in my son's hands. Correct proofs. In the North Am[n] Rev[w] for October it is asserted that "Under cover of the popularity acquired by his Wieland Ormond & Arthur Mervyn, C. B. B. in 1794 tried a monthly Magazine & American Review in Philadelphia. But it would not do." And again that after "Edgar Huntly, Clara Howard & Jane Talbot" on the strength of the reputation which these won for him, set up, in 1803, the Literary Magazine & American Register; and in 1806 an Annual Register; the gravest periodical enterprize, this latter, which the country had yet witnessed. He carried it through 5 vol's & the former work through 8, conducting the two together besides occasional contributions to the Port folio & other works &c. "The last Vol: of the Register was issued but a few weeks before his death." William H. Prescott "our coadjutor" is the author of y[e] biog[y] of C. B. B. in Sparks's collection. Ride to Verplanck's, see some of Weir's best pictures, go with V to Stewart Watsons painting room & see him, his pictures & more of Weir's. To Mirror office & to Scotts & correct proofs. Ride home. Read in N. A[n] Review. Ev[g] correct Index.

Friday Nov[r] 14th 1834. Cloudy & Hazy. Th: in house 64 out of doors at ½ past 6 A M. 48. I presume that this day will finish the printing of my 2d Vol: *Geo: Sutton* 181 Front Street ships goods sent to him for Charleston S. C. free of commission (see E. Post Nov[r] 13) Write to

J. R. Lambdin Louisville. Read Review. Ride to Morris's & Scotts & back. find Cole & Cummings wait[g] for me. Correct proof.

Sat [Nov.] *15th* Clear. Th: in house 67 out of doors 30. Correct proof. 7 A. M. Wrote to C. R. Leslie No 12 Pine apple Place Edgeware Road London. Read in N. Am[n] Review. Receive in pamp[h]let form an address from Chas Fraser delivered by him on the 19th Sept[r] last to the Euphradian Society in Charleston S. C. Walk to 520 Broom Street & see Mr Cole's new pictures 2 small jewells & 2 larger paintings being the first two of the sett of 5 for Luman Reed Esq[re]. All these are in fine style & will encrease the reputation of the painter. Cole reminds me that I have left unnoticed a painter of Boston now in Paris John Mason, he was in Europe 10 years ago & returned home. Walk to Mirror Office & Scotts & see the last sheets of my Work & send off the whole to Leslie e. i. the remainder completing that already sent, & both Vols in another bundle giving thus duplicates. Ride home (or rather part of the way) & dine after 4 OClock. Th: out of doors 28. Read in Review.

Sunday Nov[r] 16th 1834. Snow on the earth & still falling. Th: in y[e] house 58. Out of doors 24, at 7 A M. At noon 36 and in the house 62. Write on Biography of C. B. Brown for the Nat[l] Port[t] Gallery. Read in Hannah More, a dull dull book with occasional sparkles.

Monday [Nov.] *17th* Clouds. Th: in house 54 and out doors 31. Read in Mirror. Willis's panorama of Stamboul agrees well with Charles Rhind's. Read in H Moore. Write to Robt M. Sully. Rain & sleet. Write on Biography of C. B. Brown. Hard rain. Read in Miss Edgeworths tales for children & give up Hannah More.

Tuesday [Nov.] *18th* Rain. Th: in y[e] house 60 out of doors 44 at 7 A M Read Miss Edgeworth. Settled with Geo P. Scott & Co and took their receit for two notes am[t]

857.58. One of these notes for 300 is payable Dec[r] 19th the other for 557.58, Feb[y] 20th 1835. This am[t] for printing includes for alterations $50, for prospectuses $10, for copyright $1, & book for subscriptions $1. The whole exceeding the estimate made for 432 p: p: the vol: by $157, the work having extended to 925 pages instead of 864. $72 being deducted from 857.58 leaves for printing $785.58. The 2000 volumes when bound will cost me

printing &c	857.58
Binding	250.
Exclusive of paper	$1107.58
Paper probably	650.42
Postage, advert[g] &c &c......	242.
	$2000.

or 2 dolls the sett.

Even[g] read[g] Miss Edgeworth.

New York. Nov. 18, 1834

Rec[d] from W[m] Dunlap two notes amounting to Eight hundred & fifty seven 58/100 dollars, which when paid will be in full of all demands for printing

$857.58 [Signed:] Geo: P. Scott & Co

Wed[y] Nov[r] 19th 1834. Clear. Th: in y[e] house 64 and out o' doors at 7 A M. 40. This is the 39th week since the operation. My health & strength improving. Ride to Wall St[t] call at American Office. Call at Star Office, Library, Mirror Office, Cummings, Inghams, ride home. Frazee calls on me & says he has obtained some subscribers for me in Boston & wishes to try Brunswick & Rahway. Finish Biography of C. B. B. Reading Walsh's review.

What can in contrast show more opposite
Than harmony and foul chaotic discord.
As God is love so God is harmony:
And all confusion is his opposite.
Chaos and darkness uproar and contending

Elements, are all abhorrent, hateful
To the mind of man in innocence array'd as
    fashioned by his God.
Man's heaven is love & love is harmony!
When the Eternal by his high decree
Compell'd the mass chaotic to subside
Into that order which the Universe
Obeys in all its myriad Suns and Worlds
Revolving; into that wondrous ceaseless
Moving, living, life infusing, whole,
Whose end shall be perfection. Harmony
Was by the great Creator introduced
To still contending atoms, to oppose
The ills inherent in primeval matter.
Matter resists and evil must abide
Until the final triumph of the law
Of love, when all obedient to his will
Shall in perfection sing his praise; and love
Eternal through his Universe abound
In never ceasing endless harmony:
Then shall his kingdom come, his will be done!
Wed[y] Nov[r] 19th 1834

Thursday Nov[r] 20th 1834 Clouds Th: in y[e] house 58 out-doors at 7 A M. 42. Read in Review. Walk to Coopers, he is finishing a Tale to be published in London. Ride part of the way to Mirror Office, walk thither to Scotts, see the book binder (Griffiths) [187] respecting some handsome binding for presents. Ride home or nearly so. Read Review. Walk at Sun set. Ev[g] Read review

Friday [Nov.] *21st* Clear. Th: at 7 A M. 64 in y[e] house, out o' doors 34. Read review. Write an article in praise of Coles recent pictures. Ride to Library. Walk to Mirror office & Scotts. Ride home, find y[e] card of Jno. G. Chapman of Alex[a]. Read in review. Read in H. More

[187] Herman Griffin, of H. & H. Griffin, bookbinders, Ann Street. *N. Y. City Directory,* 1834-35.

Sat^{y} [Nov.] *22d* Clouds. Th: in ye house 62 out o doors 34. Read in review. Ride to Library. Walk to Beaver St^{t} to see J. G. Chapman who has come to reside here, out, see his Wife. Walk to Library, to Mirror Office. Ride home. Read [Walter] Wilson's Defoe. Rain.

Sunday [Nov.] *23d* Clear. Th: in house 62 at 7 A M. Out o' doors 38. Read Wilson's De Foe. "The word *Tory* is Irish and was first made use of in Queen Eliz^{ths} Wars in Ireland." A robber & murderer belonging to neither army preyed upon all indiscriminately. In the Irish Massacre 1641 they were baneful instruments. In England in 1680 the word was applied to the adherents of Charles 2d & ye Duke of York, passive obedience men, persecutors of dissenters, advocates of popery and kingly tyranny, & it became so common that the party owned the appellation. *Whig* is scotch & applied first to the Cameronians who looks for conscience sake. The word first signified the refuse or what was called the Whig of the milk—sour milk, and the enemies of the pres[by]terians applied it to them saying "A scotch presb[yt]erian was still more sour." In America in 1776 Whig meant ye opposers of the pretensions of the English parliament & Tory the friends of the Ministry, now Tory is applied to the Jacksonmen or supporters of the pretensions of the president & Whig to their opponents, the same men (the rich and the commercial) who were ultra federalists & advocates of England against France.

Walk up the Avenue. On returning read Wilson's De Foe again. Afternoon Cole and Cumming with me. Ev^{g} read W's De Foe.

Monday 24th Novr 1834. Clear, windy. Th: at 7 A. M. in ye house 62: out o' doors 36. Read Wilson's De Foe. Women introduced on ye Stage after ye Restoration & obscenity to please Charles. Coke says "the more obscene pleased the King the better." Yet Charles issued edicts against Vice & profaneness. Jeremy Collier 1698. Ride to

Library, call on Clover, Morris, Scott, Griffin the book binder, ride home. Ev[g] read Wilson's De Foe.

Tuesday [Nov.] *25th* Clear. Th: in house 59 out of doors 31. Examining lists of subscribers. Write to Th: Woolsey, Edmond A. Wetmore, & Dr S Beaumont. Walk in the Square & see the finest display of uniformed Militia, in respect to men, dress & accoutrements that I ever saw, but the cold north wind drove me home without seeing them reviewed. This anniversary of the retreat of the English from our city & shores called out all the uniformed troops. It is fifty one years since I witnessed that event and the triumphal but modest entry of Washington. Read in Miss Edgeworth. Begin a Tale for Mirror.

Wed[y] Nov[r] 26th 1834. Clear, remarkably so. Th: at 7 A M in house 58, out o' doors 30. Write on Tale. Ride to Wall St[t] walk to State St[t] & then to Arch Rogers & then to Library & then to Mirror Office. Ride home. Draw $20 & leave in B: $51. Read Wilson's De Foe 2d Vol. This is the 40th week since the operation. It is long since I have been obliged to take laudanum & for some days past I have not taken quenine or the carminative mixture, my appetite continuing good and my strength slowly encreasing. I return thanks to my creator.

Thursday [Nov.] *27th* Clouds. Th: at 7 A. M. in y[e] house 55. out of doors 34. Write on Tale. Clear. Ride to Mirror Office & call at printing office. Binding will not be done until Sat[y] 100, Monday 200 more, & Wed[y] 300 more. So that I cannot publish until Wed[y] 3d Dec[r]. Receive letter from Leslie who cannot get the work publish'd in London his letter Oct[r] 6th. A letter from Cogdell with 5 subscribers. This makes my list to this date 550. Evening Wilson's De Foe. Carolina so called from Charles 9th of France, abandoned, claimed by Charles 2d of Engl[d]. Granted in 1663 to 8 noblemen & gentlemen. Colonized by independants or Dissenters. Locke's constitution 1669 confirmed 1689. In 1704 a tory party prevailed & deprived the Dissenters of their rights & Episcopalians rule them, censured by ye House of Lords, and redress obtained e. i. toleration or freedom of religion. 1705 the name Kit-Kat used. Garth called Chaplain to Kit-Kat. I had supposed the phrase first used by Johnson's & Co. Kit-Kat club.

Friday Novr 28th 1834. Clear. Th: at 7 A. M. in y^e^ house 58 out o' doors 32. Finish "The Ghost murderer" a Tale for y^r^ Mirror. James Creighton pays me $100 on acct. which I deposit have^g^ in Bank $151. Ride to Warren St^t^ call at McCoun's & W. S. Johnson's. Walk to Mirror office and to Scotts & then to Collins & Hannay who send no more goods West this season. Walk to Library & Bank and ride home. Read in Wilson's De Foe, a great part of which is at this day unreadable, but there are gleanings.

*Sat^y^* [Nov.] *29th* Clouds. Th: at 7 A M in ye house 60 out 44. Read in Wilson's De Foe. Receive a letter from Robt M. Sully who has taken it in dudgeon that his name is not among the Artist[s] mentioned on my prospectus. Write an answer acknowledging my belief in his merits & requesting not to trouble himself *to assist* my work as he says he will. His letter lowers him in my opinion much. Rain all day. Read Wilsons DeF. & finish the 3d vol:

Sunday [Nov.] *30th* Clear. Th: in ye house 64 out 39. This is the day of the Eclipse: & the sun rises as bright as on a summers morn. Hosack and Francis call. Walk, it become colder. Before the Eclipse Th: 45 sinks during it to 44. Morris calls. Read in Gibbon.

Monday Decr 1st 1834. Clear Th: in house 62 & out 30 at 7 A M. Morris called on me yesterday & wished me to give notice of my works being for publication on Saturday next & subscriptions taken by me at the Mirror Office until then. Write notes to Charles King & to Theodore Dwight. Ride to Warren St^t^ receive from Wm T.

McCoun $65 which being deposited makes my credit $216. Met Verplank at Morris's & put down names to call on for subscriptions. Go to the bookbinders. Go with Morris to American Office & Custom house. C. King takes down names to apply to as does Henry Ogden. Call on Mr [Isaac R.] St. John No 20 Wall Street, who will discount my draft on J K Tefts. Go to Library, find the time of sailing of vessels for Key West, Savannah & Charleston. Walk to Mirror Office again & ride home at 3 OClock. Call'd at the office of the Daily Advertiser & receive from Th: Dwight his History of the Hartford convention. Call on Legett at the office of Ev[g] Post among my calls to day. Evening gave James Perkins my check for $79 which leaves in Bank $137. Began to read De Foe's Col[l] Jack. Prepare a further list of names (by desire of Morris, Verplank and King) to be sent to for subscriptions. See T. A. Cooper to day.

Tuesday Dec[r] 2d 1834. As yesterday became warm, so to day we have rain. Th: in house 64 out 44. Receive letters from Edmond A Wetmore & James E. Freeman from Utica. I may send on 6 copies of the work Freeman is employed to paint 2 pictures for the corporation, & has offers of loans to send him to Italy. Wetmore is as ever very friendly. Rain continues. Read Col. Jack.

Wed[y] Dec[r] 3d 7 OClock A M. Light clouds. Th: in y[e] house 62 out 38. This is the 41st Week since the operation & my health is improving. I am not enough thankfull. Write to Wm Leggett & to J. K. Teft. Walk to Leggetts 4th St[t], to J. F. Cooper's St Marks place, ride to Beekman Street. Walk to bookbinders Ann St[t] to Mirror office, to 52 Pine St[t] to E Post Office & to American Office, Wall St[t], to Morse's room, to Knickerbocker Office, to Swords's [188] Br[d] Way, to L. P. Clovers Fulton, to Mirror Office, to Clovers' & pack books, ride home, all this without much fatigue. Read in Dwights history of the Hart-

[188] Thomas Swords, of Swords, Stanford & Co., booksellers, 152 Broadway. *Longworth's N. Y. City Directory,* 1834-35.

ford Convention. Ev^{g} finish Col^{l} Jack which does not in the conclusion answer the commencement—indeed it is poor.

Thursday [Dec.] *4th* Clear. Th: in the house 60: out o' doors 28 at 7 A M. Read in Dwight's history of H. C. Ride to Ann Street, go to book binders and Mirror Office & to Office of Starr, to Clovers & pack books, again to Mirror Office & ride home. Write to J K Teft, J. S. Cogdell, W A Whitehead & Jno Neagle in answer to letter received to day.

Friday Decr 5th 1834. Clear Th: in ye house 60 out 7 A M. 30. Write advertisements of the publication of my book: to be had at the Mirror Office, at L. P. Clovers & at 64 Sixth Avenue. Ride to Ann St walk to Mirror Office to Bookbinders & order 134 copies to Clovers, 100 to Mirror Office & 800 to 64 Sixth Avenue. Walk to Clovers & pack 2 setts for Norfolk, to Williamson & Irwin. Write to Williamson. Walk to Knickerbacker Office & take a number, then to Wall Street & receive 54 for draft on J. K. Tefts, Savannah for 55. To Bank & deposit 75 leaving $212. To the Offices of American, Daily Advertiser, Journal of Commerce, Courier and Star. To Morses's rooms, not yet returned. Ride home. Write to James H. Caldwell N. O. L Cruttenden Albany, Edmond A. Wetmore, Utica, John Neagl Phil: Rain all night.

Sat^{y} [Dec.] *6th* Violent storm of rain & wind. Th: 7 A M in house 60 out 51. Read: Knickerbocker. Write to O. C. Greenleaf & Francis J Oliver, Boston. Rain ceases at 10 OClock. Dr Francis calls. Ride to Ann St^{t} walk to Mirror Office and to Book binders. Receive notes from Lawson & Wm Leggett. Write to Leggett and to Weir. Walk to Clovers back to Mirror Office, again to Clovers, ride home. Read in Knickerbacker, North Am^{n} Mag: has as well as that noticed my work.

Sunday Decr 7th 1834. Clear. At 7 A M. Th: in house 62 out 36. Fosdick calls. Walk up avenue to 21st Street.

ROBERT SNOW

By William Dunlap

(Courtesy of the Museum of the Brooklyn Institute of Arts and Sciences)

Read Dwights Hartf[d] Convention. Cooper calls, thinks the French Chambers will not pay the money promised & that a war must ensue. Walk through the square with him. He has just finished a romance called Monnikins, speculates in cotton likewise. I sent him off to see Cole's pictures. Afternoon walk again the weather being remarkably fine. I cannot go through Dwights book. It is ultra English.

Monday [Dec.] *8th* Rain. Th: in 64, out 48. Clears about 10. Windy. Ride to Ann St[t]. Walk to Mirror Office, to Book binders, to Clovers, to Mirror Office. Wall St[t] & deposit $115 leaving $327, to Office of E. Post, to Library, to Mirror Office & then ride to Hudson Street & walk home. Receive letter from Robt. M. Sully apoligizing & begging to be my Agent in Richmon[d] and Petersburg. letter from Lambdin (Louisville) he is going to Mobile. Write to R M Sully appointing him my agent.

Tuesday [Dec.] *9th* Clear. Th: 7 A M in the house 62 out 28. Write a few lines for M M Noah. Ride to Ann Street, walk to Mirror Office, to Clovers, to Library, to Offices of Starr & E. Post, to Morse's, leave a copy of my work with T[heodore] Dwight at Daily adv[r] office, deposit at Bank 168 making there 495$. Walk to Morris', or Mirror Office & leave with him $100. Ride home; receive 2 letters from Leslie of Oct[r] & Nov[r]. He seems anxious that his anecdotes &c written from West Point should not appear in my work: but all his letters on the subject came too late. Read Quar[ly] Review.

Wed[y] Dec[r] 10th 1834. Clear. Th: at 7 A M in y[e] house 62 out 27. This is the 42 week since the operation, there is no change of late. Read in Review. Ride to Ann St[t], walk to Mirror Office, Book Binders, Clovers, back to Mirror Office, again to Clovers, ride home. Read Review.

Thursday [Dec.] *11th* Clear. Th: at 7 A M. in y[e] house 60 out 27. Read in Review. Send out copies of my work to subscribers. Receive letter from Neagle acknowle[d]ging rec^{t} of first box sent wth 26 copies, all delivered to subscribers & more wanted. Callaghan wants 30 more &c. Francis calls & shows me a letter Trumbull has given King for publication respecting my book, principally detailing a volunteer military service performed by him in 1778. I sent word to King that I had no objection to the publication.[189] Afternoon with Leggett respecting Memoir of Forrest who is now in Paris, goes to Italy & thence to England purposing to be home in ab^{t} a year. Ev^{g} read review.

Friday [Dec.] *12th* Clouds. Th: at ½ past 7 A M. 60 & out o doors 36. Rode to St Pauls, walk to Clovers direct a box for 30 copies for Neagle, to Mirror Office, to Book binders, to Mirror Office, to Post Office, Library & Morse's room, to Mirror Office see Verplank, to Vice Chancellors see Wash^{n} Irving & R[obert] Bogardus, the latter is aggrieved by a passage in ye biography of Cogdel & if he proves his assertions Cogdel is a scamp. Introduced to Sheridan Knowles, not prepossessing. Ride home after walking to White Street.

Sat^{y} [Dec.] *13th 1834* Light clouds. Th: at 7 A M. 54 in ye house, the fire in ye stove going out, out o doors 35. Rode to St Pauls, walk to Clovers, to Mirror Office, to Cummings, to Inghams, ride home. Ride with Verplank to Lunatic Assylum, walk through the building with a committee of ye Corporation who are to erect an Assylum for pauper Lunatics on Blackwells Island. Dine & ride home. Find a complimentary note from Wash^{n} Irving. Read in Defoe's plague.

Sunday [Dec.] *14th* Clear & floating clouds Th: at 7 A. M. in house 63 out 38. Read in Defoe. At 8 OClock a squall with a little rain & then a clear sky with high

[189] John Trumbull's letter was published in the *New-York American* (of which Charles King was editor), on December 13, 1834, with a long review of Dunlap's *Arts of Design*.

N. Wind Th: 30: at 10 A. M. At ½ past 12 the Th: on being put out fell from 60 to 21: so that the temperature out of doors has fallen since 7 A. M. 17 degrees: the sky clear & wind high. After dinner went to Mr Fosdick's to meet Henry Inman but he was detained at home by Ashtma [*sic*] his potent enemy. Fosdick related the attempt of Jarvis to carry off a child from his wife who had seperated from him. Fosdick & two others pursud J & his assistand & rescued the child restoring it to its distracted mother, he know likewise of his previous unacknowle[d]ged Wife's poison[g] herself. I saw a miniature said to be Oliver Cromwell by Cooper, & Leslie's fine copy of Hogarth's Gale of Calais, bought with another picture at auction both for 5/6. At 5 P. M. the Th: on being put out sunk to 9. Read Defoe.

Monday [Dec.] *15th* Clear. Th: at 7 A M in y[e] house 50 out 8. Read Defoe. It becomes cloudy. Ride to St Pauls & walk to Clovers & thence to Mirror Office. Write a letter to C King in answer to one published by Trumbul dated 9th & write to Neagle with rec[t] for box. Walk to Ingham's and thence home. Look over lists of Subscribers & read Gibbon.

Tuesday Dec[r] 16th 1834. Light clouds Th: at 7 in house 44 out 28. Read Gibbon. Look over lists. Ride to St Pauls: walk to Clovers, to office of Mirror, to Clovers, to Library, to Mirror Office & thence to [Moses] Swetts to see his Copy of Stuarts *General* Washington, back to Mirror Office & write for it. Receive letter after riding home from O C Greenleaf acknowledging rec[t] of 30 copies. Write to him stating that $4 a sett is the price to booksellers & quote Mr Olivers letter wherein he say G. will deliver &c for 5 pr Ct. (this I say shall be indepen[den]t of charges. Read in Register.

Wed[y] [Dec.] *17th* Clear. Th: in doors 53, out 14. This is the 43d week & my health is established. I am thankful! Ride to St Pauls', walk to Clovers & correct lists of

Subs: to Mirror Office, to Wall St[t] to Morse's who is business in repelling popery, to Wily & Long's [190] by invitation & take lunch & coffee, take up note for 300 dollars & leave 195$, to Mirror and then walk home. Receive letter from James Kent & from Rev[d] Charles Henry Alden of Phil[a]

Thursday [Dec.] *18th* Snowing. Th: at ½ past 7 A. M. 54 in & 28 out o' doors. Read in Annual Register. Write to Mr. Alden. Read in Annual Register for 1833 where see the Funeral of Kean. But little snow falls & the day passes in mist & fine rain.

Friday [Dec.] *19th* Light clouds. Th: at 8 A. M. in 54 out 34. Ride to Wall St., go to Post Office, to Library, to Clover's, to Mirror Office, ride home. Read V. Hugo's Lucrece Borgia.

Sat[y] [Dec.] *20th* Light clouds. Th: at 8 A M. in 57 out 33. Finish Lucrece B. Post Office, Walk to Clovers, to Library, to Mirror Office, ride home. Read Foreign Review. There is in Victor Hugo great force & great extravagance. The Foreign review cuts up [James E.] Dekay's [*Sketches of*] Turkey.

Sunday Dec[r] 21st 1834. Clear. Th: in 60 out 32. Read foreign review. Walk. J. F. Cooper calls & stays till 2 OClock full of politics anticipations of evil. Make out bills for books delivered. Read review

Monday [Dec.] *22d* Clouds. Th: in 60 & out 36 at noon. Make out bills. Receive letter from Neagle, he had rec[d] y[e] 3d box. Read in review.

Tuesday [Dec.] *23d* A sprinkling of snow on the earth. Clear. Th: in 62 out 34. Ride to St Pauls. Walk to Clover's, to Mirror Office. Wiley & Long offer me $3.50

[190] Wiley & Long, (John Wiley and George Long), booksellers, 161 Broadway. *N. Y. Directory,* 1835.

for the remainder of my first edition. Receive Waldimar from the Author, John J: Bailey. Walk to Duane St^{t} to Durand's (he has orders for 160 of his prints of Ariadne from London), again to Clover's, ride home. For Spanish painters see Vol: 13 Foreign Review in N. Y. City Library. Same place German Artists at Rome. Pd 45.65 dollars for a Nott Stove & pipe &c reduces my bank credit to $149.35.

Wed^{y} [Dec.] *24th* Threatening snow. Th: at 7 A M in 62 out 32. Walk to Dr [John] Torrey and leave 3 setts of my work for Mr Shaw & thence to Durands, Clovers, Mirror Of., Library, Morse's, again to Mirror Office, to Gould & Banks', to Clovers again, to Long & Wiley's & find that I misunderstood Wiley's offer which is to take the books & distribute & sell at their risque, being accountable for not returned to me at $3.50 the sett. Ride home. Read in Mirror & write an article for Daily Advertiser in recommendation. Write to Neagle & send it by Revd S. Jocelyn Engraver who calls with note from Augur requesting his M.S.S. biography. This is the 44th week. Hard rain.

Thursday [Dec.] *25th* Snow, the ground slightly covered. Th: at 8 A M. in 60 out 32. Write "It might have been better, it might have been worse." Read in Foreign Review. Clear weather at noon.

Friday Decr 26th 1834. Clouds. Th: at 8 A M 52 in 20 out. Not so well this 2 days. Francis calls. Read Gibbon. Receive a letter from S. Dewitt Bloodgood offering information of pictures & artists. Write accepting. Read Gibbon.

Sat^{y} [Dec.] *27th* Clear. Th: in 56 out 22. The earth very slightly coverd with snow, which dissolves before noon. Ride to Post Office, walk to E Post Office, to Library, to Mirror Office, District Clerks office, M[ichael] Paff's & Clovers, ride home. Receive letter from J. K. Teft. Read in [James] Halls tales of ye West.

Sunday [Dec.] *28th* Clear. Th: in 56 out 19. Read as above. Write to J. R. Lambdin. Read Hall.

Monday [Dec.] *29th* Snow storm. Th: in 56 out 29. Read Gibbon.

Tuesday [Dec.] *30th* Clear. Th: in 56 out at noon 38. A deep snow. Ride to Mirror Office, walk to Bookbinders, Long & Wiley's, Clover's, Wm T McCouns & home. As Long & Wiley will not guarantee the sale of any portion of my work I have made no arrangement with them.

Wed[y] [Dec.] *31st* Morning pleasant, clouds at noon Th: in 56 out 32. Read in Gibbon & [Henry] Hallam. Walk to St Marks Pl: & set with J. F. Cooper. This is the 45th week since the operation and my general health continues to improve. This is a contrast to my situation on the last day of the year 1833 which ought to make me thankful & improve my good feelings in every respect. I receive from Rembrandt Peale his book on drawing entitled "Peales Graphics" & his circular with an addition in his handwriting thanking me "for the very handsome manner" in which I have answered this little book, he likewise sent the "Ev[g] Star" cont[g] his letter to me on my hist[y] of Art. I will send to the *Star* for publication a letter of thanks for his books and his criticism.

My next diary is in a book similar to those which immediately preceeded this.

Copies of Hist: Arts: to be sent

11 To Savannah for J. K. Teft with a draft at sight on him for $55 either to be sent to him or presented for discount to Messrs J[oseph] D. Beers & I[saac] R. St John, New York

25 To Philadelphia to J. Neagle

5 To Albany to Mr Steele, care of L. Cruttenden who will collect and remit the money.

30 To Boston, to O. C. Greenleaf care of Francis J. Oliver who will collect & remit.
6 Key West for Wm A Whitehead to be sent freight paid to Messrs J. & C. Lawton Charleston S. C. who will forward them to Key West.
Washington City
6 New Haven
4 Utica <*6*> copies if I can forward them
10 New Orleans, Lewis Adams
3 Perth Amboy to Andrew Bell: by the Napoleon in charge of Mr Hagar
4 Charleston S. C. to Chas Fraser
5 D[itt]o Mr. S Cogdell
3 to Bleeker, Vanschaik & Steele to O[liver] Steele's Book Store Albany.
5 to L[everett] Cruttenden for S[tephen] Van Ransaeller
48 more Phil[a]

165
8 Boston Frazee
6

173
2 Norfolk

175
3 are to be sent to Plattsburg
2 Geneva
2 Canandaigua
9 Bacon

191

INDEX

INDEX

Pages 1-360 are in Volume I; pages 361-587 are in Volume II; pages 589-851 are in Volume III.

(A figure in parenthesis following the page number indicates how many times the entry appears on the page.)

DATE DUE
